Dear Harry . . .

OTHER BOOKS BY D. M. GIANGRECO

Roosevelt, de Gaulle and the Posts: Franco-American War Relations Viewed Through their Effects on the French Postal System, 1942–1944

Stealth Fighter Pilot

Airbridge to Berlin: The Berlin Crisis of 1948, Its Origins and Aftermath
(with Robert E. Griffin)

War in Korea, 1950–1953

Delta: America's Elite Counterterrorist Force
(with Terry Griswold)

Dear Harry . . .

Truman's Mailroom, 1945–1953

The Truman Administration Through Correspondence with "Everyday Americans"

D. M. GIANGRECO

and

KATHRYN MOORE

STACKPOLE BOOKS

Copyright © 1999 by D. M. Giangreco

Published by
STACKPOLE BOOKS
5067 Ritter Road
Mechanicsburg, PA 17055
www.stackpolebooks.com

Printed in the United States of America

10 9 8 7 6 5 4 3 2 1

FIRST EDITION

Library of Congress Cataloging-in-Publication Data
Dear Harry : The Truman Administration Through Correspondence with
 "Everyday Americans" / [edited by] D.M. Giangreco and Kathryn Moore.
 — 1st ed.
   p.   cm.
 Includes bibliographical references (p.   ) and index.
 ISBN 0-8117-0482-3
  1. Truman, Harry S., 1884–1972—Correspondence.   2. Presidents—
United States—Correspondence.   3. United States—Politics and
government—1945–1953—Sources.   I. Giangreco, D. M., 1952–   .
II. Moore, Kathryn.
E813.T713D4   1999
973.918′092—dc21   98-53789
                                                          CIP

"Work hard, keep your mouth shut, and answer your mail."

—Advice given to Harry S. Truman by political boss Tom Pendergast
when the newly elected senator left for Washington in 1933

CONTENTS

Foreword by George M. Elsey, *ix*

Preface, xi

A Few Words on the Editing, xv

CHAPTER 1
Truman, his staff, and "everyday Americans"
1

CHAPTER 2
Civil rights and 1948 presidential election
32

CHAPTER 3
World War II, Potsdam Conference, demobilization of the armed forces,
cessation of hostilities, occupation of Germany, continued rationing,
unemployed veterans, Easter Egg rolling at the White House,
the Truman Balcony, the Marshall Plan, Sacred Cow,
and death of Mother
80

CHAPTER 4
Aid to Greece and Turkey, Palestine and the birth of Israel, Churchill
correspondence, the Marshall Plan, the Berlin airlift,
1948 presidential election
130

CHAPTER 5
Personal questions, suggestions, look-alikes, and "nut mail"
174

CHAPTER 6
The MacArthur firing
231

CHAPTER 7
The atom bomb
279

CHAPTER 8
Korea
327

CHAPTER 9
*Joe McCarthy, Marine Corps' "propaganda machine,"
assassination attempt, and the Hume affair*
360

CHAPTER 10
Threats, friends, atom bomb, and leaving office
426

Notes, 483
Correspondence Index, 490
Index, 501

FOREWORD

BY GEORGE M. ELSEY

Calvin Coolidge, as befitted a man raised on a Vermont farm, was such an early riser that he often reached the White House office before his staff arrived. Curious, he would walk downstairs to the mailroom, look through the first morning delivery, and open and read the letters addressed to him.

Harry Truman also was raised on a farm. He, too, rose early, but preferred a brisk morning walk through the streets of Washington to poking around the mailroom. He could not have read all his letters even if he wanted to, and by his time the volume was too great for any one person to read. The American people had begun deluging the White House with mail during the great depression of Herbert Hoover's era. Hoover received letters by the thousands —some angry, some sad, many desperate pleas for help. The torrents of mail increased during Franklin Roosevelt's New Deal, and there was no let-up during the grim days of World War II nor in the Cold War that followed.

Although he could not see all his mail, Harry Truman insisted on reading a broad sample because he wanted to know what the man and the woman on the street were thinking. Mail, he thought, gave a better sense of the public mood than did the highly touted polls, which he had no more respect for than he had for political pundits of the press and the air. On the eve of the 1948 election, when a national news magazine published the unaminous opinion of fifty political analysts that Governor Dewey would trounce him, Truman snorted to his aide, "I know every one of those fellows, and not one of them has enough sense to pound sand into a rathole."

Although he was interested in public opinion as reflected in the mail, Harry Truman never let it influence his decisions. He felt it his duty to shape opinion, not to follow it. Indeed, in many areas there simply was no public opinion until the president spoke. This was especially true in foreign affairs. The United States in the early days of the Cold War was in uncharted waters. Truman had to lead the country, through speeches and messages to Congress, to understand and accept the Truman Doctrine, the Marshall Plan, NATO, the Berlin Airlift, and other unprecedented initiatives.

D. M. Giangreco and Kathryn Moore with prodigious effort have plowed through countless files of letters to Harry Truman during his White House years. In *Dear Harry*, we are treated to a fascinating selection. A goodly percentage is critical, for it is a truism in political life that naysayers write more letters than well wishers. This bothered Truman not a whit. His aphorism, "If you can't stand the heat, get out of the kitchen," summed up a lesson he had learned in a quarter-century of rough-and-tumble politics. No event in his presidency brought such a torrent of criticism as his firing of Douglas MacArthur. When he relieved MacArthur of his command in the Far East for publicly disavowing the government's foreign policy, Truman knew that he would "catch Hell." He was unperturbed, knowing that he was standing on the fundamental principle of civilian control of the military as laid down in the Constitution.

Occasionally a burst of critical mail was prompted by one of Truman's own letters. His well-known penchant for shooting from the hip was evident in an angry letter to a music critic who found fault with daughter Margaret's singing. And he was less than thoughtful when he wrote to a member of Congress about the Marine Corps' "propaganda machine." In *Dear Harry*, we can feel the public's blood pressure rising along with Truman's as the mail poured in.

The letters are broadly grouped by subject. Well-written essays and notes provide the historical context of each topic. Collectively they present a first-rate account of many of the problems that confronted Truman and his responses to them. We are treated to a sympathetic but not adulatory portrait of an "everyday American" thrust into a position of extraordinary responsibility and the judgment of his fellow "everyday Americans" on his performance.

Not all the letters are from the public. Scattered throughout are some replies. Those that Harry Truman dictated himself or wrote hastily in longhand are brief to the point of terseness. This was, after all, his normal speech pattern. Replies prepared by staff members for the president's signature tended to be long-winded efforts to explain administration policy. As the anonymous author of some of these responses, I frankly admit a half-century after the fact that the incoming letters are far more interesting than the letters we drafted for our boss to sign. Enjoy *Dear Harry*!

PREFACE

Americans are not particularly shy about letting politicians know what's on their minds, and in Harry Truman, they believed that they had a president they could level with. When a small business owner from Atlanta or a housewife from Decatur wrote to Truman, it was they who chose specifically what issues they wanted to discuss. They chose the words and manner in which their thoughts would be conveyed, and even the timing of the letter—no waiting to cast a ballot with limited, unsatisfactory choices, and no politician or political party to "not get it quite right."

The letters, telegrams, and postcards used in this book come almost exclusively from the files of the Harry S. Truman Library in Independence, Missouri. The material makes for fascinating reading, and although only a small percentage received replies, it was immediately apparent that the White House staff had actually read all the letters they were receiving and that Truman had read many as well. There is no exact count of letters on hand, but Truman Library archivists venture that it is in the "low hundred thousands," perhaps reaching as high as a half-million, with the majority of the material running from one to four paragraphs in length.

Correspondence is divided into numerous large groupings with the material in *Dear Harry* coming mostly from the President's Personal File (PPF) and the White House Official File (WHOF). It is further broken down into a large number of categories, such as labor relations, desegregation, the Cold War, McCarthy, the atom bomb, Korea, and foreign policy. Truman's small White House staff further divided this material by year and into "pros" and "cons," with carbons of the president's occasional responses attached. In raw volume, the file on the MacArthur dismissal in 1951 is by far the largest, containing more than 90,000 letters and telegrams, with most arriving within the space of just one month.

Dear Harry includes the more interesting items from this mass. The material runs the gamut from impassioned letters from parents whose sons had died in Korea to questions from schoolchildren about Truman's reading habits. The physical form of the letters ranges from the child's poorly written scrawl to formal ones, perfect in every way. Truman's responses almost invariably are three brief paragraphs. While the majority of the letters in *Dear Harry* are from private citizens, a sprinkling also come from the occasional bombastic senator, and a few come from world figures such as Winston Churchill (who liked to offer advice) and Chaim Weizmann. The names of some correspondents—J. Robert Oppenheimer, Upton Sinclair, Gene Tunney—would have been familiar to many of their fellow Americans, while others as diverse as Morrie Amsterdam and Barry Goldwater would be better known to future generations.

The great variety of correspondence on subjects such as World War II and its aftermath, desegregation, and the establishment of Israel are presented, including the "fringe" letters. Portions of some chapters are distinctly light in tone and contain the mini-controversies that dogged Truman throughout his presidency, such as the furor over his addition of a balcony to the White House, and the time he threatened Paul Hume, a music critic who gave Truman's daughter Margaret a bad review (Truman said that after he got a hold of him, he'd "need a new nose . . . and a supporter below"). There is also a chapter containing a portion of the nearly inexhaustible amount of material that Truman referred to as "nut mail." This frequently included all sorts of oddball trivia from individuals who wished to share their thoughts, postcards, cartoons, or birthday greetings. Meanwhile, other writers took their best shots at trying to get the president to endorse/see/try/come to/give away something, and the White House constantly received photos of the Pope, mothers, or neighbors—in each case someone that a breathless writer found to have an amazing resemblance to the president. A good deal of "nut mail" came from people who claimed to have known Truman when he was younger, taught him in school, or even had saved his life during World War I.

When we originally conceived of *Dear Harry,* we thought the subjects would fall into two general categories, domestic and international. And so they did. But one of the most fascinating things about working with the letters was seeing how peoples' concerns in the international sphere were intertwined with concern for what was happening in their own backyards. From the perspective of those writing letters, it was all local and had a direct effect on politics at home.

The content of *Dear Harry* is driven nearly as much by what people didn't write as the letters actually in the files. For example, pivotal events such as the establishment of the Marshall Plan, aid to Greece and Turkey, and the Berlin Airlift all failed to generate as much mail as the Hume affair. The files on the atom bomb were also a surprise, for while there was more than enough varied material spread from World War II through Korea to create a strong chapter showing how public attitudes toward nuclear weapons evolved over time, the volume of letters was actually lower than we anticipated. On the other hand, the chapter on the developing Cold War contains some extraordinary material from Winston Churchill that we had not expected to find.

Nearly all communications between Truman and heads of state were written "by committee" in a stilted diplomatese and, in any event, are beyond the scope of *Dear Harry*. However, Churchill was, as the British say, "out of government" at the time. Moreover, the two men admired and respected each other, and their letters are, for the most part, personable and quite familiar. Churchill was destined to become prime minister once again, and his letters have the ring of his "former naval person" correspondence between himself and Roosevelt. We trust that readers won't feel that we're moving too far afield of *Dear Harry*'s format by publishing a selection of their correspondence from shortly before Churchill's "Iron Curtain" speech through the opening shots of the Korean War.

In a work of this sort, where a given letter may touch on items as diverse as the assassination attempt by Puerto Rican nationals, a razor-tongued comment by Truman, or even a half-dozen more subject areas, there obviously is much potential for overlap. One thing that helped keep this problem manageable was the sheer quantity of material available to us. The wide-ranging nature of many letters, in which individuals drew links or parallels to other current events, actually worked to our advantage by allowing subsidiary material to be folded into primary subject areas so that the "big picture" isn't lost. For example, you can't read a chapter on desegregation without gaining an understanding of election-year politics in 1948—a subject more deeply covered later in the book. Another example is the atom bomb material, which includes letters from the beginning to the end of the Truman administration within the context of a wide range of foreign and domestic events. Throughout *Dear Harry*, we have tried to ensure that a reader won't be able to move through the chapter on the Korean War, for example, without getting a taste of the MacArthur controversy. Conversely, the chapter on MacArthur touches on nearly all the key events in the Korean War.

We would like to thank the many individuals who lent their assistance to the production of *Dear Harry*, particularly Jack and Barbara Moore; Colonel Phillip W. Childress, U.S. Army, Retired; JoAnne Knight; John Reichley; Belva K. Wilson; Donald L. Gilmore; Congressman Ike Skelton; Margaret M. Blue; Rick Montgomery; Major Terry Griswold, U.S. Army, Retired; Vaughn Neeld; and James W. Leyerzapf of the Dwight D. Eisenhower Library. Robert H. Ferrell spent a considerable amount of time providing a valuable review of the manuscript, as did George M. Elsey, who also offered many useful insights into the internal operations of the Truman White House. The staff of the Harry S. Truman Library, including Pauline Tester-man, Ray Geselbracht, and Randy Soell, was helpful in every way, with Dennis Bilger and Liz Safly locating even the most obscure items from the often incomplete information we supplied them. Former Marine Lieutenant Gale C. Buuck was also gracious enough to supply the only letter in *Dear Harry* that did not come from the archives of the Truman Library.

A FEW WORDS
ON THE EDITING

The informal—and hastily written—nature of most letters to President Truman often resulted in dropped articles and prepositions. Although less common, this can be found in the letters from Truman and his staff as well. In all cases they have been added silently. Likewise, minor misspellings occurred frequently because of dropped or transposed letters; these also have been corrected silently. Where large numbers of misspellings are characteristic of a letter, we have retained them without note and generally have tried to avoid jarring additions to letters by adding bracketed words or [sic]. Interesting misspellings such as "thot" for thought and "indoctrinization" for indoctrination have been left as they appeared in the original text. Misspellings of proper names, however, such as McArthur for MacArthur, are noted, as are occasions when the meaning is ambiguous as to whether the author was being clever or simply making a Freudian slip, as in the sentence, "How about getting down to brass tax [sic]."

The original punctuation has been retained as much as possible, but we found that commas often were needed for sentences to read clearly. An effort was made not to overcapitalize terms like "first family" and "foreign relations committee" in the text and notes, yet such capitalization in letters is retained. Writers handled ship, newspaper, and magazine titles in a variety of ways, but we have uniformly run them in italics.

Telegrams to President Truman are reproduced as they originally appeared, completely capitalized. Items produced in this form, however, become extremely difficult to read if they contain more than about a dozen lines, so lengthy examples, such as Sen. Joseph R. McCarthy's warning of communist infiltration of the State Department, have been converted to upper and lower case for clarity. On several occasions newspaper clippings sent in by the public have been reproduced. For these reprinted items a sans serif, or block, type style was used so that they could be easily differentiated from letters.

As many as two dozen assistants worked under Correspondence Secretary William D. Hassett. Since one of their jobs was to underline the subject of a letter, key ideas of correspondents, or portions of letters that might be of interest to the administration, they were commonly referred to in the White House as "markers." Not all letters contained underlines from these assistants, but we have included them whenever they were found. This treatment has necessitated that portions of text underlined by the letter writers themselves be run in italics for emphasis. Penned additions to typed letters also are run in italics and are clearly indicated by the bracketed word "longhand."

CHAPTER ONE

TRUMAN • HIS STAFF • "EVERYDAY AMERICANS"

The sun had already dipped well behind the tall poplars as the elderly man in a white fedora and crisp, gray, double-breasted suit strode across the avenue. Approaching the curb, he quickened his pace to clear the way for an ambulance rushing its charge to a hospital on New York Avenue, the white cane in his left hand barely touching the pavement every fourth step. From the corner it was just a few feet to his destination, and he pivoted on his right wingtip to reach for a briefcase carried by one of the three large gentlemen accompanying him.

The evening commute from his office across the street had been closely watched by a policeman. The officer smiled and waved as the pedestrian strode hurriedly past his station in one of two white guard booths flanking a four-story, brick residence. The old man acknowledged with a nod, and another policeman at the steps leading to the front door said, "Good evening, Mr. President."

"Good evening, son. A fine night, isn't it?"

The president moved purposefully up the steps to 1651 Pennsylvania Avenue, swinging his cane up under his right arm, which was pulled tight to his side by the weight of the overloaded briefcase. He reached for the screen door of Blair House, but head usher J. B. West beat him to it. Cheerful, informal greetings were exchanged with West and butler Alonzo Fields, who, upon taking the heavy case, frowned and noted out loud that the president should try to relax more. The president, however, just offered a wide grin, and the twinkle from behind his wire-rimmed glasses let Fields know that far from being angry at the butler's impertinence, the former Missouri dirt farmer appreciated the concern.

Contained in the briefcase was a large assortment of documents from a thick, tabbed file the president kept on the left-hand side of his desk: agency reports, diplomatic mail, personnel recommendations, background papers, proposals for speeches and public appearances, messages from cabinet members, copies of pending legislation, and notes on ideas that needed further study. It also contained a sizable batch of letters forwarded to him by his trusted correspondence secretary, William D. Hassett, a quiet, scholarly Catholic and former newspaperman who had been dubbed "the Bishop" by his first presidential boss, Franklin D. Roosevelt.

Twice every day, usually after the morning staff meeting and then upon President Truman's punctual return to the Oval Office at 3:00 P.M. from lunch and a nap, executive clerk Maurice Latta or his assistant, William J. Hopkins, would present Bill Hassett's "gleanings" in what was referred to as the reading folder, while items requiring immediate attention, such as executive orders, treaties, nominations, bills, and other such documents on which decisions had already been made were contained in a signature folder. Truman, who often stated that he had to sign his name more than 600 times a day, customarily attended to the signature folder's contents on the spot and immediately turned it back over to Latta or Hopkins.

While this may seem a simple way to do business today, it was a far cry from the often helter-skelter manner in which documents had traditionally been handled by previous chief executives. The president's work habits enabled his staff to easily keep track of important papers, decreased duplication of effort, and allowed the various departments and agencies to receive almost immediate answers to their queries. Once the signature folder was out of the way, Truman would quickly scan Hassett's folder, taking note of the more important or interesting items flagged by the correspondence secretary before he put it aside, returning to it whenever there were a few free moments in his busy daily schedule. Nearly always, these letters followed the president "home" to the Truman family's private quarters on the upper floors of the White House or to Blair House, where the family lived during the first weeks of his administration and again during the extensive renovation of the historic Executive Mansion between the West Wing and recently constructed East Wing.

The president's wife, Bess, would rather have had him leave the letters and paperwork behind at the office. She was painfully aware of her husband's propensity for overwork and had been against his joining the Democratic ticket as FDR's running mate in 1944. Even before the presidential campaign, it was clear to many in Washington that Roosevelt's health was deteriorating rapidly and that he was not likely to live to see the end of a fourth term in office. The Trumans' daughter, Margaret, later wrote of her mother's fears: "Everyone was talking about the toll the presidency had taken on FDR. She envisioned an equally deadly impact on Harry Truman. . . . If he pushed himself to the brink of a breakdown as a senator, what would he do as a president?"[1]

Harry S. Truman was sworn in as the thirty-third President of the United States at 7:09 P.M. on April 12, 1945, before his family and a key group of governmental officials hastily summoned to the White House Cabinet Room. Almost an hour and a half earlier, Hassett had solemnly announced to stunned press pool reporters in Warm Springs, Georgia, that Roosevelt had died of a massive cerebral hemorrhage, as Mrs. Roosevelt, in Washington, told the vice president why he'd been called in secret to the White House. Even though Truman knew about FDR's grim condition, he had been momentarily speechless at hearing the news but then asked Mrs. Roosevelt if there was anything he could do for her. He recorded in his diary only that she replied, "What can we do for *you*?" and told Margaret that she continued on to say, "for *you* are the one in trouble now."[2]

With the full weight of the U.S. government and all the questions of war and peace now squarely on his shoulders, Harry Truman buckled down to the enormous task ahead of him. He had apparently intended to try to pace himself (and keep Bess happy) by confining work to the office as soon as the initial crush had abated. It was not to be. Throughout his first week in office, he still entertained the idea that he might soon be able to just go home after the workday was done, but by Thursday, April 19, he finally had to face facts: "At the end of appointments for the day I turned to the accumulated papers that demanded my attention. There were many documents to sign, a bill to veto, reports and messages and diplomatic cables to read. When I was ready to make my way across Pennsylvania Avenue to Blair House, I again found it necessary—as I did from then on—to take with me another accumulation of papers."[3]

Although he soon developed his simple system for efficiently handling this material, imposing a high degree of order to the chief executive's office, the actual volume of reading faced by the president each evening remained, by Truman's own choosing, essentially undiminished, for two reasons. First, as a voracious reader since childhood, his natural instinct was to go over virtually everything that came his way. For example, when the U.S. ambassador to the Soviet Union, Averell Harriman, returned from Moscow on April 20 to brief the new president on the provisions of the Yalta Treaty, he later confessed to being rather surprised at their meeting: "I found that President Truman had already read the Yalta Agreements and all the post-Yalta telegrams. He was fully familiar with the details of our difficulties and with Stalin's failure to carry out his agreements. This was my first experience in understanding just how avid a reader President Truman was." Harriman also noted that on another occasion, he "had only read the summary and conclusions" of a report he wanted to discuss with the president but was embarrassed to find that Truman had read the entire report. "I never made that mistake again!" said Harriman.[4]

President Truman had made a valiant effort to suppress this urge to read everything and granted an early concession to the sheer volume of material passing over his desk by simply signing "routine" paperwork. Unfortunately for his eyesight, however, he soon found this modest delegation of authority less than satisfactory and returned to examining virtually every document. In a June 1 diary entry, he wrote: "Have been going through some very hectic days. Eyes troubling somewhat. Too much reading 'fine print.' Nearly every memorandum has a catch in it and it has been necessary to read at least a thousand of 'em and as many reports. Most of it at night." A delegation of authority was absolutely essential if a job as "tremendous" as the presidency was to be tackled, and he later noted that he "succeeded in surrounding [him]self with assistants and associates who would not overstep the bounds of that delegated authority. They were," he said, "people I could trust."[5] But though this eventually served to lessen his nocturnal reading, it by no means put an end to it.

The new president also found himself signing off on documents that had ostensibly been approved by Roosevelt without actually reading them closely. On one well-publicized occasion, this attempt to carry on FDR's policies backfired with embarrassing consequences. After the May 8 cabinet meeting, the foreign economic administrator, Leo Crowley, and acting secretary of state, Joseph C. Grew, brought to Truman's attention "an important order in connection with Lend-Lease which President Roosevelt had approved but not signed," which directed that the volume of aid sent to the Allies end once Germany had been defeated. "I reached for my pen," Truman recalled, "and, without reading the document, I signed it. The storm broke almost at once."[6] Instead of a gradual lessening of aid, the two gentlemen ordered a literal interpretation of the order, and virtually all Lend-Lease operations were completely shut down, with ships at sea even being ordered to turn about in midocean. The president immediately rescinded the order, but the damage was already done. Said Truman: "Stalin at Potsdam would bring it up every chance he had, that we cut off Lend-Lease while he was still getting ready to go to war with Japan. . . . I think Crowley and Grew put it over on me that morning. That taught me a lesson early in the game—that I should always know what was in those documents myself, personally, and I had to read all night some nights to do that."[7]

The second reason that Truman worked so late into the night was that, according to Margaret, her father "was always a demon letter writer."[8] Intensely interested in what "everyday Americans" were thinking and feeling, he often commented that a president must "listen to what people are saying." Said biographer David McCullough: "As President, he felt more than ever a need to see and make contact with what he called the everyday American. And he always felt better for it."[9] Many Americans felt this way toward "Harry" as well and believed that in him they had a president they could level with. Consequently, the volume of mail that had risen more than tenfold during the Roosevelt Administration to an average of roughly 6,500 letters per day didn't drop back off, but continued to climb steadily and would run into the tens of thousands when a subject like the firing of General Douglas MacArthur was running hot.

Throughout the young American nation's first century, the volume of mail to its presidents had never been so much that the man himself could not maintain it with the normal secretarial help. Thomas Jefferson was pleased that citizens in the republic knew they could write him—something that a man or woman of common birth would certainly never dream of doing toward a European monarch. He found, however, that though this new thing called democracy had freed their hands to write, it left them in a quandary as to exactly how to address their president, whom they frequently called "your Excellency" in these letters. Jefferson read virtually all the letters that came across his desks at his home in Monticello and "the President's House" in Washington City, answering a good many of them himself.

By the end of the nineteenth century, the rapid growth of the country (and especially its politically conscious middle class) contributed to a steady increase in the amount of mail addressed to the president, until roughly 500 to 600 letters were arriving at the White House daily. A full time mail clerk, Ira Smith, was hired to relieve the pressure on President William McKinley's secretary by scanning the incoming mail and, depending on the nature of the request or comment, directing it to one of the various departments, such as Treasury or Agriculture, or to the president himself.

For thirty-six years, Smith and his small filing and messenger staff toiled in a first-floor room at the rear of the West Wing, their job remaining essentially unchanged through eight administrations. Meanwhile, upstairs in the Executive Mansion, the handling of the mail was performed in whatever manner its current occupant saw fit. In most cases, a president would dictate his own replies or they would be written by a secretary authorized to sign the chief executive's name, and it was not unusual for presidents to author personal replies. Woodrow Wilson, in particular, was well known for spending many trying hours before a typewriter composing his own letters. Over the years, the work habits of the chief executives had little effect on Smith, but profound changes in the country and the election of FDR in 1932 soon changed the clerk's staid routine for good.

The stock market crash of 1929 and Great Depression were national calamities that cast millions of people out of work and into poverty. Businesses failed by the thousands, savings of a lifetime were wiped out overnight, and the federal government seemed to have little interest in alleviating the suffering, believing, according to Secretary of the Treasury Andrew W. Mellon, that the slump would eventually "liquidate itself." The Great Depression was arguably less severe on Americans than the one of 1893–96, but a family threatened with the loss of its home received little comfort from the calm assertion of Mellon that once things bottomed out, "enterprising people will pick up the wrecks from less competent people," or the news from John D. Rockefeller that he and his son were "accumulating shares" sold at rock-bottom prices because "fundamental conditions of the country are sound."[10]

The downward slide seemed without end, and with a generally more literate public than existed in the nineteenth century, coupled with the advent of radio, the suffering was brought into virtually every household. Herbert Hoover made a genuine effort to end the depression but seemed out of ideas and, in any event, was constrained by his own political philosophy, which viewed calls for increased government intervention—and the powerful executive branch such actions would ultimately lead to—as potentially more dangerous than the plummeting economy. Consequently, the few tentative forays that were made to counter the depression seemed cruelly misguided to the average American. Said Will Rogers, "The money was all appropriated for the top in the hopes it would trickle down to the needy."[11]

Roosevelt, then governor of New York, had a different view of how government should operate. Skillfully using radio to his advantage, FDR electrified an increasingly frustrated and angry electorate, who saw in him perhaps the last chance to save America's faltering institutions. Calling for a "New Deal" for "the forgotten man at the bottom of the economic pyramid,"[12] FDR was viewed with distaste even by many at the top of his own Democratic Party, who feared he was a demogogue. As unemployment climbed toward 25 percent of the workforce, though, a record turnout on election day handily swept the Republican candidate, Hoover, out of the White House. The Democrats landed both a president and a solid majority in both houses of Congress (and the next off-year elections would find a freshman senator from

Missouri named Truman joining their ranks on Capitol Hill). "The little fellow," said Will Rogers, "felt that he never had a chance and he didn't till November the Eighth. And did he grab it!"[13]

Even before the new president took the oath of office on Saturday, March 4, 1933, it was apparent to the bespectacled mail clerk that there was a new spirit alive in the land. Where Ira Smith and his small staff had previously dealt with hundreds of letters per week, they were suddenly having to cope with a flood of mail. Moreover, instead of trailing off after a postelection surge, the daily volume leveled out at approximately 6,500, which meant that what had been roughly two weeks' worth of mail was now arriving every day. Presidential Secretary Louis McHenry Howe was as amazed as anyone at the "appalling number" of letters arriving, and taking pen to paper, he computed that if half a minute was allowed for each item, "a trained eye might skim 2,880 in a twenty-four-hour period, without time for anything else."[14] Once it became clear that the storm would not soon abate, monies were appropriated to permanently increase the size of the mailroom staff to twenty-five men employed full-time at sorting, digesting, and distributing the mass of correspondence under the direction of Smith, who now had the exalted title of chief mail clerk.

Not all letters, of course, went to the president. As before, much could be shuffled off to appropriate departments and agencies, and indeed, fully three-quarters of the mail was handled in this manner. And although the daily average was already remarkably high when measured by previous standards, the volume could suddenly balloon to nearly unmanageable proportions—especially after one of FDR's "fireside" radio addresses. For example, when he spoke of the effort to stave off foreclosures of private homes through the use of Home Loan banks, more than 70,000 letters arrived almost immediately appealing for help.

Many correspondents wrote seeking employment; others offered a pat on the back for a job well done or criticized some aspect of FDR's New Deal policies. Almost every letter routed to the president's office received some form of acknowledgment. For subjects of wide public interest, a form response was usually made available. A note might also be sent from Howe or one of his assistant secretaries, Stephen T. Early or Marvin H. McIntyre, stating that a letter had been forwarded to a certain agency. An answer might even come from FDR, who always liked to look at a cross section of the incoming mail. These presidential responses were signed by the president himself but, after 1935, were authored almost exclusively by Bill Hassett, whose witty, ghostwritten replies seemed totally out of place coming from a man of such solemn demeanor but fit perfectly with Roosevelt's public image. Hassett would dictate anywhere from sixty to a hundred brief letters per day, six days a week, for nearly ten years and was ultimately responsible for producing approximately a quarter million letters under his own name or FDR's.

When Harry Truman assumed the presidency, he initially asked Roosevelt's staff and cabinet to stay on, yet ended up having to replace nearly all of them with his own people within six months. Bill Hassett, however, was not only kept on board but elevated to a senior staff position after the president personally prevailed upon him not to retire. The title correspondence secretary was created for Hassett, and his West Wing office was considered to be "the nicest one in the White House, next to the President's,"[15] which brought Hassett much gentle ribbing from the other senior staffers.

To junior members of the president's staff and outside observers interested in exactly who exercised what degree of influence over the president's time, the other presidential secretaries were certainly of more obvious importance than the unassuming Bill Hassett. It was "the Bishop" that Harry Truman called "indispensable,"[16] however, much to the befuddlement of later historians, who had a great deal of trouble understanding why Hassett's duties rated a newly created, top-level post for a job that ostensibly could have been handled by a good administrative assistant. Somewhat condescendingly, one young special assistant later summed up Hassett's job in these terms: "Unquestionably, these correspondence duties were vital to presidential operations. They had to be done and done well. But it was largely by accidents of history and personalities that throughout the Truman administration, these duties rated one of the top five White House staff posts. . . . [The job] was of a considerably less critical nature than the work performed by [John R.] Steelman, [Charles S.] Murphy, and the other two secretaries."[17]

If Harry Truman had heard this, he would have screwed up his face and uttered his own succinct view of such comments: "Hogwash!" or, perhaps, one of the more colorful phrases that so often got him into trouble. Truman, as noted earlier, had an unquenchable thirst for what his "everyday Americans" were thinking yet greatly distrusted both poll results and poll takers. For him, the daily stack of troubles and dreams that he pored over late at night—from places like Skull Bone, Kentucky; New York City; Boise, Idaho; and Conway, Florida—was the next best poll to the one made by Americans in the voting booth, and it was to Hassett that he entrusted the job of overseeing what correspondence reached his eyes.

The former Vermont newspaperman, who toward the end of Roosevelt's life found himself becoming a combination secretary, aide, and de facto press secretary, had never actually chosen which letters were seen by FDR but did not disappoint his new boss. Hassett also scoured newspapers from across the country, kept Truman abreast of public opinion, and would funnel select clippings of items he thought the president should see, sometimes marching a news story into the Oval Office if he believed that it shouldn't wait for the reading folder. Hassett served as correspondence secretary until the final days of Truman's second term, when he was succeeded by Beth Campbell Short, an experienced newspaperwoman and wife of Truman's last press secretary.

Virtually every night, the president would go over the letters from across the nation and mounds of other accumulated paperwork. "At nine o'clock," recalled Chief Usher J. B. West, "Mr. Truman picked up his briefcase, took Mrs. Truman by the arm, went into his study, and closed the door. They worked together to eleven o'clock almost every night, editing his speeches, discussing his policies."[18] On those evenings when the workload was heaviest, Harry would keep at it long after Bess retired. If Bess was on one of her extended stays back home in Independence, Missouri, and there were no visitors, poker game, or state function demanding his attention, the president would get to work immediately after the 7:00 dinner hour, pausing now and then to check in on Margaret and her girlfriends, who, West noted approvingly, tended to make whatever portion of the residence they appropriated "look like a college dormitory, with record players, bridge games, pincurls, corsages," and other sundry items scattered about.[19]

The president's nocturnal routine rarely varied, even when he was out of Washington, and Truman's diary and memoirs are replete with references like this one from the Potsdam Conference in Germany: "I worked late that evening on a big batch of mail that had arrived from Washington."[20] During his whistle-stop campaign across America during the 1948 elections, a daily mail pouch would be waiting when his train pulled in for one of the trackside rallies, and the mail followed him down to Key West, too, when he vacationed at the Little White House. Even a cruise on the presidential yacht couldn't keep Truman from wading into his self-imposed "daily press of paper work. . . . If I went out on the *Williamsburg*, for instance, a [sea]plane would bring mail and newspapers every morning, usually around nine or nine-thirty."[21]

The president's stamina was a marvel to everyone who knew him. Still, he was not a young man, his health was not perfect, and the frequent eighteen-hour days sometimes caught up with him. "He had a tendency," said Margaret, "to ignore his illnesses until they either went away or they floored him."[22] General Omar Bradley noted that "he was President at practically all hours . . . Saturdays, Sundays, weekdays, and I almost always found him at a desk with a bunch of papers in front of him." The general remembered one instance, though, when he was pleased to see that Truman was apparently taking a little relaxation. "I did find him one time not behind a desk. This was about eleven o'clock at night when I took a message over to get clearance on it. I found him in his dressing room, reading a book. Before I left, I commented that I was glad to find him not working but reading a book. And he held up the book for me to see. The subject of it was the economics of government. So I still didn't catch him dead-beating it."[23]

The president would rise at 5:30 each morning, except some Sundays, and be out the door for his 120-pace-per-minute walk by 6:00. An exercise regimen followed at the pool and gym in the connecting link between the Executive Mansion and West Wing, where he would hit the exercise machines, do twenty-five sit-ups, and swim with his thick glasses on, using an odd, choppy sidestroke to keep his head above water. At 8:00, Harry sat down with Bess and Margaret to a hearty, low-calorie, high-protein breakfast, and by 8:30 he was at work with his private secretary, Rose Conway, dictating responses to the previous night's readings. The president's replies were generally brief, commonly three paragraphs of one or two sentences each. Every once in a while, a letter from a perfect stranger would hit a nerve, and a lengthy answer would flow out, like this one to the publisher of a small newspaper in Childress, Texas, who offered his support at a time when Truman's popularity was plummeting and every day brought new attacks in the press.

> *My dear Mr. Higley:*
> I read your note of the fourteenth with considerable interest, as I did your telegram of the twenty-first of November 1946.
> People never know all the facts in connection with decisions that have to be made here. They have a perfect right, however, to go up or down on their feelings and appreciation as they choose. The man who sits in the President's chair has no time for consideration of impulsive feelings. The American people are almost as volatile as our Spanish friends are to the South.
> You no doubt have been to a ball game when the short stop would make a home run in an early inning and fail to catch one out in the field later. He is a hero the first time and they throw pop bottles at him the second time. He needs sympathy in both cases but seldom gets it, so I never pay any attention to bricks that are thrown my way. Neither of them means anything in the final analysis when

a job is to be done. All the President can do is get the best alignment of facts that he can and make the best decision of which he is capable in the public interest and let the river take its course and that is what I do.

People think apparently that the President is made out of cast iron and that he can work eighteen hours a day for three hundred and sixty-six days a year. If he decides to get away from it for a few days rest, then there is a chance to throw more bricks. That makes no difference either to me.

Sincerely yours,
HARRY S. TRUMAN

Margaret Truman recalled that "among the minor pleasures of Dad's off hours was reading letters from crackpots—what we all called nut mail" and remembered how he once commented that "there is an immense number of nuts in the USA."[24] Correspondence petitioning for Truman's attention on countless matters often surpassed the nut mail's ability to put a smile on the president's face, and there was undoubtedly a certain amount of overlap between the two. In one whimsical letter to his cousin Nellie Noland in August 1951, the president wrote: "Bill Hassett and myself have decided to start a new religious sect when we're done saving the country. . . . [Bill] furnishes me with acceptances to resignations, handles religious and sectarian correspondence, writes 100-year-old congratulations to old ladies and old gentlemen whose relatives think the President of the United States should take notice of such contributions to the public welfare. He also takes notice of the annual meetings of the D.A.R.'s, Colonial Dames, U.D.C., Sons of the Revolution, Knights of Columbus, Elks, Eagles, Shriners, B'nai B'rith, Jewish Welfare Society, etc. etc. ad lib. We always discuss whether we'll pull out all the stops, ring the bells and give 'em the full treatment or whether we'll just be coldly formal. It's quite a game. We also have to decide on the days and weeks to celebrate—such as Foot Happiness Week."[25]

With Hassett now spending a considerable amount of his day monitoring and managing the incoming mail, he obviously had less time to personally write responses. The very considerable amount of correspondence never seen by the president but worthy of acknowledgment was jobbed out to the other senior secretaries and presidential assistants, who in turn shuffled much of it to their own assistants but answered a remarkable number of letters themselves. None of them, however, could match the dogged fortitude of Truman's energetic personal physician, a young army surgeon at Walter Reed

Hospital named Wallace Graham, who had recently been promoted to the rank of brigadier general. The good doctor earnestly tried to answer *every* letter inquiring about the president's health, such as this one addressed to the secretary of the president from a concerned "private citizen" who lived but a short distance from the White House.

> *Sir:*   *23 July 49*
>
> Has the President a psychiatrist to keep a watch over his mental health as he has a physician to keep him in overall physical condition?
>
> Without in the least intending to imply any physical or mental health trouble in the President, nor to underestimate the ability of his physician, it appears only good sense, in the light of present medical knowledge, for the Chief Executive to have the most complete medical attention, and if he does not have adequate or definite attention given his mental health, the addition of a psychiatrist to his present staff seems eminently worthy of serious consideration.
>
> > *Respectfully,*
> > *Everett B. Anderson*
> > *(private citizen)*

> *Dear Mr. Anderson,*   *July 26, 1949*
>
> Thank you for your letter of July twenty-third. You may be assured that your interest in the President's welfare is greatly appreciated.
>
> I am happy to inform you that the President has available to him the services of all types of specialists, to keep him in the best of condition, physically and mentally. We are ever aware of the strenuous demands of his position, and his well-being is our constant concern, not only for his own good but for the good of the people of this country.
>
> With appreciation for your thoughtfulness and all good wishes.
>
> > *Sincerely yours,*
> > *WALLACE H. GRAHAM*
> > *Brigadier General*
> > *Personal Physician to the President*

The doctor was regularly kidded by other members of the White House staff for answering "nut mail" and took the ribbing in good humor. The president himself even got into the act with the young Dr. Graham, who happened to be the son of the physician taking care of his mother, Martha Ellen

Truman, back in Independence. In a letter to his mother in the summer of 1946, Truman related that during a weekend cruise on the *Williamsburg*, "I asked him to let me see some of [the letters]. He brought me about two dozen and I gave them one tear across the middle and threw them in the ocean. He almost wept because he thought I'd lose some prospective votes by not answering these letters."[26] A few years later the chief executive apparently repeated the stunt when he noticed Graham on the yacht's fantail dictating replies to a lapful of letters into a recording machine. Picking up the papers from the startled doctor, Truman laughed and flung them over the side, saying, "You constantly tell me to relax. Now you relax."[27]

As for Hassett, in spite of having to devote more time to screening letters, he was always able to write plenty of what FDR had called "Hassett Valentines." Margaret said that Hassett's "delightful sense of humor and an unlimited vocabulary, as well as a fund of good jokes and stories" allowed him to "write the friendliest letter with the most words saying absolutely nothing [while] turning down a request or soothing an irate voter."[28] A typical Hassett Valentine was sent to an Ohio eye doctor who made an unabashed effort to meet the president. (Underlined type represents portions of the text highlighted by one of Hassett's two dozen or so assistants who did the initial marking of key ideas and assigning of correspondence.)

My Dear Mr. President: *August 30, 1945*

In a recent news item by the Scripps-Howard columnist, Earl Wilson, I learned that nearsightedness interferes with your swimming activities to such an extent that you are compelled to wear ordinary spectacles during the time you are in the White House pool.

There is a perfect answer for this problem, and it is the wearing of invisible, unbreakable plastic <u>contact lenses</u>. As you probably know, more than 50,000 persons in the United States are already wearing these lenses, and many others at the rate of more than 5,000 a year are being fitted for them.

They are easy to apply and to remove. In your case you would have the added advantage of being able to see normally and to open your eyes under water, because the plastic lens acts as a protection to the cornea and moves right with the eyeball. It would be a matter of a minute or two each time you go into the pool to insert your contact lenses, enjoy your swim with clear vision, and then remove them immediately afterward if you so desire.

In the hope that I may be of some service to you, and through you to the country, and for the more general promotion of the use of this type of lens among Americans of all ages who can use them to good advantage, I take this opportunity <u>of offering to go to Washington and stay as long as necessary in order to fit you with contact lenses</u> so that you may be able to enjoy your swimming more than you have in the past.

I shall be glad to do this at my own expense, including the furnishing of the contact lenses.

I am, Mr. President,
Yours faithfully,
Stanley H. Golden, O.D.

That this letter was included in the reading folder probably had more to do with the fact that it was interesting or informational rather than Hassett actually thinking that the president would want to fly the man out to Washington. It went back to Hassett via Maurice Latta, who received a handwritten note from Rose Conway "to tell party he appreciates the interest but he can't do it," and adding "Letter not for President's signature." The Hassett Valentine followed on September 12.

My dear Mr. Golden,
Thank you in the President's behalf for your letter of August thirtieth. While he cannot avail himself of your kind offer, I do want to assure you of his sincere appreciation of your friendly thought in writing to him.

Very sincerely yours,
WILLIAM D. HASSETT
Secretary to the President

Obviously, many letters were asking for something, and most writers' attempts to meet the president were more thinly veiled than Golden's. But to Hassett and his staff, who handled dozens, perhaps hundreds, of similar requests daily, such attempts were much more apparent than their authors realized. Often there was little that could be done in response except to send another Valentine, like this one posted from the U.S. Naval Station at Key West, Florida, when Hassett accompanied Truman on one of his working vacations.

My dear Mr. President: *11 February 1952*

We here in Corvallis [Oregon] for the past few years have been seriously in <u>need of a larger hospital</u>. By several sustained drives we are aproaching our goal.

Our firm is enlisting your support in this community project.

We are sponsoring a mince-meat pie baking contest which closes on 11 March 52 which is open to all persons, male or female, in this community. At the end of the contest the pies will be judged and a public auction will be held. All funds received from this auction will be donated to the Good Samaritan Hospital.

To stimulate interest in the contest, and also in the bidding at the <u>auction</u>, we are <u>enclosing a pledge which we hope you will see fit to use</u>. We will <u>bid in a pie for you at your pledge price</u> and will send the pastry to you Air Mail Special Delivery.

Mr. President, with your valued assistance we are positive we can make this <u>Mince Pie Baking Contest</u> a huge success.

> *Sincerely,*
> *Rex E. Smith*
> *Star Trading Center*
> <u>*(Enclosure of contest ad*</u>)

My dear Mr. Smith,

Your recent letter to the President, with enclosures, has been received and I am indeed sorry we are unable to grant your request. So many similar ones are received daily that it is not possible to comply with them.

I am sure you will understand that failure to meet your wishes does not indicate any lack of interest on the part of the President in the many worthwhile undertakings which are brought to his attention.

> *Very sincerely yours,*
> *WILLIAM D. HASSETT*
> *Secretary to the President*

Letters not making any requests, but simply supporting Truman and his policies, were often answered by someone on his staff, but an individual with a degree of stature or political influence, such as a county judge or city alderman, was much more likely to receive a brief personal message from the president than an average citizen writing on the same subject. Letters critical of Truman and his policies were almost invariably unanswered. Unlike FDR, who sometimes had Hassett try to change the minds of letter writers who disagreed with him, Truman viewed such efforts as a waste of time—time infinitely better spent on swaying the uncommitted or bucking up his supporters. On the rare occasions when Truman did respond, his answers were usually short and tart, as in this letter to an Oklahoma City doctor who protested the president's health-care proposals:

> Dear Dr. Moorman,
> I read your letter of July seventh with some surprise.
> It is perfectly apparent that you are not familiar with the Public Health Program advocated by this Administration.
> I am sorry you haven't taken the trouble to enlighten yourself on the subject.
>
> Sincerely yours,
> HARRY S. TRUMAN

Truman was also rather unappreciative of the efforts of organized pressure groups who tried to influence his actions by sending him mounds of preprinted cards or letters on some bill or project they opposed. Less apparent were formula-type letters that, at first glance, appeared to be regular correspondence but were still easy to spot because of the similarity of wording. As early as his Senate days in 1935, he had been known to ceremoniously burn such offerings. The preferred method for handling this material, however, was developed early in the Roosevelt Administration. FDR's secretary, Howe, wrote that "they are virtually the only letters coming to the White House which are not really read. If we are really interested in the matter they discuss, we pile them up and estimate, from the size of the stacks, the extent of the sentiment for or against."[29] Only on very rare occasions would Hassett include such an item in the night's reading folder—usually as a joke—and he also had his staff or the mailroom staff count them. All would be tossed out when the pile reached an inconvenient size, and the total number received would be written on a single representative sample retained for the archives.

During or immediately after the president's morning dictation, he transferred the balance of the reading folder's material to his thick desk file tabbed with the names of the dozen or so people attending the daily staff meeting—an affair that originally convened at 9:00 but was soon moved back to 9:30, and eventually to 10:00, in an effort to give everyone ample time to prepare.

"There was always time for some humor in these meetings," remembered Charles Murphy, who served as special counsel to the president. "And notwithstanding the fact that we all felt that we were living in the eye of a hurricane, these staff meetings were usually relaxed. In fact, as I look back, I think they may have been the most relaxed periods that most of us enjoyed during the day."[30] Truman's executive clerk, William Hopkins, said that "the material in the President's reading folder customarily reappeared" at this time, "and . . . he would pass out to them documents in their area of responsibility, or on which he wished their advice or recommendations."[31]

Often Bill Hassett had already routed items from the previous day's mail to some of these same staffers, but now, along with memoranda on various queries or matters the president wanted raised with a certain agency or department, would come additional correspondence he wanted answered. He also expected letters to be answered promptly, and each person would sign his or her own name since, according to Beth Short, "Mr. Truman did not permit the use of an auto-pen," which would allow facsimile signatures of the president.[32] "When you saw a document leaving the White House signed Harry S. Truman," stated Hopkins, "it was the president's act, not the act of some staff member using his name."[33] Truman frequently asked that a response be prepared for him, and the routine would start a new cycle with a finished letter appearing within a day or two in the signature file or as a draft in the reading file.

Unless it was an item following a strict formula, such as a "thank you" note, Truman made it a point to quickly read everything he was to sign, and on occasion, the president found that he had to kick a draft response back to its author. The following letter is from a soldier at Fort Campbell, Kentucky, and the proposed answer was written by Major General Harry H. Vaughan. The general was a long-time friend of Truman who was now serving as one of his military aides, and like another old friend, Press Secretary Charlie Ross, Vaughan had a knack for writing in Trumanesque style when the situation called for it.

Dear Mr. Truman,
Our camp newspaper had the enclosed clipping about your desire to make a parachute jump.

We of the 11th Airborne Division Quartermaster Parachute Maintenance Company feel a tinge of pride in our work; as we have yet to have a man fall out of a parachute harness we adjust. If you wish to fulfill your ambition to make a jump, please accept our offer to fit you to a parachute.

As a qualified "rigger" here in charge of adjusting harnesses on all our parachutes, I also have 154 jumps to my credit. The enclosed extract speaks more eloquently as to my qualifications than I could.

. . . We are quite sure that you must have a parachute for emergency purposes in your private plane, "The Independence."

I am at your disposal to go to Washington for a special fitting.

Respectfully,
Willie F. Brown

Dear Sgt. Brown,

I read with interest your letter of recent date as well as the commendation of 19 September 1945.

Permit me to congratulate you on your very excellent record and the good work you are still doing.

I have had a desire for many years to make a jump but I doubt the Secret Service, my Aides and other people who boss me around will ever permit it. Also it is just possible that I have waited too long to make my first jump and am not supple [enough] to land gracefully.

Sincerely yours,
[Unsigned]

Truman, however, realized the inherent problems of such a response and returned the draft with a line crossed through it and a handwritten note at the bottom.

Harry: I doubt the advisability of this. There will be 40 or more divisions before we are through and this would set a precedent for numerous stunts. I don't think the President should be a stunt man. We can plead press of business which is absolutely true.

HST

As appointments secretary, Matthew J. Connelly was on the receiving end of the multitude of requests for Truman to appear at various functions, inquiries for personal audiences, and innumerable off-the-wall requests. Connelly routinely responded in the most courteous manner possible, in letters that were often composed by his assistant, Joseph Feeney, but some requests inevitably slipped through the cracks and went unanswered.

My dear Mr. President: *March 4, 1946*

On January 24, 1946, I wrote a letter requesting you to send me a suit of clothes for the purpose of using in my wax display entitled "Truman in Wax," along with all the Presidents which was on display at Woodward & Lothrop, in their F Street windows, in your city.

I regret I could not have one of your suits to adorn the Truman figure, and not having a reply from you, I used a suit which was not so effective, where you were concerned.

While in Washington, many of your friends and acquaintances who viewed the display, and the notices concerning the same, expressed regret, that a suit which you had worn could not also be displayed.

One person inquired as to why it could not be arranged for a suit of your clothes to be used in this display, in view of the fact a suit of clothes had been given by you to Madam Tussaud's Wax Museum of London.

In response to this inquiry, I exhibited a copy of my letter to you, together with the registered return receipt card. This person claimed he knew one of the writers on one of the Republican papers, wanted to take me to this writer saying that this paper would give a very unfavorable story and this of course I would not adhere to.

Another person suggested that if I would display the wax figure in a suit of under clothes, shirt, collar and tie, socks and shoes, less the suit of clothes with a sign reading "Waiting for a suit of clothes from the President," to which I did not fully subscribe.

As far as the suit of clothes is concerned, I am dismissing it from my mind entirely but I do feel hurt to know that I have not had any acknowledgment or any interest manifested.

> *Very respectfully,*
> *Haywood B. Maxey*

My dear Mr. Maxey: *March 8, 1946*

Your letter of March fourth has been received. I am glad to assure you that your request of January twenty-fourth to the President received most careful consideration, and I regret exceedingly to learn that through inadvertence no word in acknowledgment of that letter was sent to you.

Recently the President has received so many requests of a personal nature that in fairness to all it has been necessary to adopt a policy of declining them. I am sure that, upon reflection, you will understand why the President cannot do the many things which, as a private citizen, he would be glad to do.

Very sincerely yours,
MATTHEW J. CONNELLY
Secretary to the President

Rebuffs, like the following to a Cliffside Park, New Jersey, pharmacist, were always made in the gentlest possible manner, with attention paid to making it clear that the sender's letter had indeed been read. It was written by the executive clerk, Hopkins, for Connelly's signature.

My Dear Mr. President: *Sept. 4th 51*
Thru the years of public contact, I <u>realize</u> more forcefully than ever a crying <u>need for medical control</u>. The <u>white collar worker is so mistreated</u> almost to the point of charlatanism. If you <u>can spare me a few minutes interview I have a sure fire health plan that can answer the middle income workers health problem.</u>

Thanking you to give this very important matter your considered opinion.

Sincerely
Arthur P. Grosman
Grosman's Prescription Pharmacy

My dear Mr. Grosman: *September 11, 1951*
Your letter of September fourth to the President has been received and I want to assure you that the spirit of helpfulness which prompted your request is appreciated. Unfortunately, it is impossible to arrange an interview with you just now, as there is no immediate prospect of a relaxation of the official duties facing the President now that he has returned from his trip to San Francisco where he opened the Treaty Sessions.

Should you wish to send a memorandum to the President, in my care, concerning the plan you have in mind, I assure you it will be given careful attention.

Very sincerely yours,
MATTHEW J. CONNELLY
Secretary to the President

Mr. Grosman never did send a memorandum outlining his plan—and no one probably expected him to. If he had, it actually would have been channeled to someone in the administration with expertise in that subject, because Truman and his senior staffers believed that the kernel of a good idea could well come from a completely unexpected source. But unlike the New Jersey pharmacist, who decided not to pursue the matter even after receiving a degree of official encouragement, other correspondents, such as a doctor from Brookline, Massachusetts, identifying himself as the president of the American Institute of Master Sciences, Inc., in Miami, Florida, wouldn't take no for an answer.

> *Dear Sir:*   *May 7, 1945*
> Can you tell me the hour of day your birth occurred [on] May 8, 1884?
> In Scientific Appreciation, I thank You—
> > *Sincerely,*
> > *Dr. Adrian M. Ziegler*

This letter arrived during the momentous period at the beginning of Truman's presidency, one of the busiest—and certainly the most hectic—of his time in office. At least a full month passed between the time Dr. Ziegler posted his letter in Massachusetts and his receipt of an initial White House response. It was written on June 4 but mailed to the printed return address on the doctor's envelope, his business address in Florida.

> *My dear Dr. Ziegler:*
> In the absence of Mrs. Truman who is now in Missouri, I am writing to acknowledge the receipt of your letter of June 1st.
> I am bringing your inquiry about the President to the attention of the Executive Office.
> > *Very sincerely yours,*
> > *REATHEL ODUM*
> > *Secretary to Mrs. Truman*

Eventually the query ended up in Bill Hassett's hands, and a Valentine (not one of his more soothing efforts) was sent to the doctor's home address on June 13.

My dear Mr. Ziegler:

Your letter of May seventh has been received and, in reply, I am exceedingly sorry that just now, when it is so very important to conserve the President's time for urgent official duties, it is impossible to bring queries of this nature to his attention. You will understand, I feel sure.

Very sincerely yours,
WILLIAM D. HASSETT
Secretary to the President

The good doctor, however, did *not* understand and wrote Hassett on June 15. (The ellipses are the writer's own, and do not indicate excised portions of his letter.)

Dear Sir:

I have your letter of 6/13 in the mails today and I thank you for writing me.

At the risk of seeming to be a nuisance, which I do not intend and hope you will pardon, I am again writing . . . this time . . . with the suggestion that you ask either the President's wonderful mother . . . or his gracious wife . . . about the hour of Day our President actually "arrived" on this sadly Disrupted Earth (as of today).

This is purely in the interests of science regardless of what our personal opinions may be and I will be deeply grateful if you can find 5 minutes to clear this point for us . . . in a busy day of your own. No need to bother the President. I had hoped you would get in touch with either his mother or wife as one would be likely to know the time, and of course, his mother should know best.

I do not want to create any adverse reactions on your part . . . and hope I haven't . . . and again may I reiterate . . . 5 minutes . . . personally . . . to check this point for us . . . because of its very real importance . . . and for your part I still add my thanks and gratitude. I am absolutely sincere in my scientific researches along these lines.

Sincerely, and with every best wish to
yourself and the Truman family
Dr. Adrian Ziegler, Phd, PsD, etc.

No further letters were sent from the White House, but if Dr. Ziegler's letter had arrived even a few months later, when Truman's staff was better organized and the crush of events had begun to subside, this same question would probably have been answered to his satisfaction within only a week or two. Questions from members of the press were always answered promptly, however, no matter how trivial.

> *Dear Mr. President:*　　　　　*June 7, 1945*
>
> I am writing a series of short articles for the *Saturday Evening Post* on the favorite foods of the favorite sons of all the states.
>
> You are, of course, Missouri's favorite son. I've read that you especially like ham. I don't blame you, for the Missouri way of curing ham is excellent.
>
> If your favorite food is ham, will you please tell me the foods you especially like to eat with it to make up the perfect dinner, such as vegetables, kind of bread and dessert?
>
> I shall sincerely appreciate it if you will be the favorite Missouri son in this caravan of illustrious Americans.
>
> *Most respectfully yours,*
> *Martha Ellyn Slayback*

Forwarded to the press office, it was immediately sent over to Mrs. Henrietta Nesbitt, the head housekeeper the new president had inherited from the Roosevelts, by Assistant Press Secretary Eben A. Ayers. Even this effort, though, was spoiled by the fact that Harry Truman's staff was not yet truly *his* staff. Ayers's boss, Press Secretary Charlie Ross, was a longtime chum from the president's boyhood and would have been able to field the question with accuracy and good humor, but he was extremely busy. Moreover, with Margaret out of school during the summer break, both she and her mother had headed home to Independence, Missouri, and were also unavailable. This left Nesbitt, who made up the White House menus, the next logical person to ask.

Unfortunately, the new first family did not measure up to Mrs. Nesbitt's high standards, and she had never deemed it necessary to find out exactly what the president preferred for his meals. This and other similar household matters naturally led to a certain amount of tension between the Truman women and the housekeeper, whom they found openly condescending. For example, even though she had been told repeatedly that Truman hated brussels sprouts, Nesbitt insisted on having them served up several nights in a row. At one point Bess began to issue detailed instructions to the housekeeper, who, according to Margaret, then grandly declared: "Mrs. Roosevelt never did things that way." When Ayers's request arrived, the most Nesbitt could (or was willing to) do was go back into her records and see what else was served the last time ham was the main course.

> MEMO FOR MR. AYERS: June 11, 1945
> I don't know that ham is the favorite food of the President but he does like it.
> This menu was used several weeks ago and he seemed to enjoy it.
>
> Clear Soup
> Baked Ham, Pineapple Garnish, Spinach Dinar,
> Harvard Beets, Mashed Potatoes, Hot Bread
> Cherry Pie
> Coffee
>
> /s/ Henrietta Nesbitt

While not terribly satisfactory, it was probably the most that Ayers was going to get to work with, and he composed a brief letter for the press secretary's signature.

> Dear Miss Slayback: June 11, 1945
> This replies to your letter of June 7 addressed to the President.
> I am not sure that I can give you the exact information you want as to the President's choice for a "perfect" dinner. His diet, like that of all good Americans, is subject to the restrictions of rationing but when these restrictions—and the supply of ration points—permit, his favorite food is steak or ham.
> So far as a complete meal is concerned, the menu of a recent White House dinner which he enjoyed may be helpful. I am enclosing a copy for your information, and I trust this will meet your needs.
>
> Sincerely yours,
> CHARLIE G. ROSS
> Secretary to the President

As for Nesbitt, her days at the White House were clearly numbered. Shortly after Bess got back from Independence, she had a little talk with Harry about the housekeeper, who was soon encouraged to retire from government service.

There seemed to be no end to Americans' interest in their president, and while many a citizen asked much the same questions as his neighbors across the country, such as what the "S" in Harry S. Truman stood for, where Truman was born, and what his favorite song was, to which various stock answers could be given, Ayers frequently had to go hunting for information from Truman's private secretary, Rose Conway, who had worked for him since his early days in the Senate. Over the years, Conway learned much about the Truman family's history, and she knew enough about her boss to be able to respond to Ayers's requests without having to bother the president or Bess very often, as in the following.

Dear President,　　　　　　*Oct 25 1945*
I would like to know what your official title was in World War I and was it the 3rd baseman of the Giants that saved your life? He himself was killed. I am asking this favor of you because I have been sick 6 1/2 years and am going to try for a prize.
Hoping a reply.\ Yours Respt
C W Thomsen, St. Joseph, Mo

Ayers—
The President's official title in World War I was "Captain"—"D" Battery, 129th Field Artillery. The President's life was never saved by anyone.
Rose A. C.

Dear Mr. Thomsen:
This will reply to your letter of October twenty-fifth, addressed to the President.
In answer to your inquiry, the President's official Army rank in World War I was "Captain." He commanded Battery "D" of the 129th Field Artillery. The other portion of your inquiry as to someone having saved the President's life apparently is based on misinformation, as his life was not saved by any individual during his service in France.
Sincerely yours,
CHARLIE G. ROSS
Secretary to the President

On some occasions, what people wanted to know was so obscure that even Conway had to solicit an answer from the president.

My dear Mr. President: *October 25, 1945*
I am a senior at <u>Waycross Senior High School</u>, Waycross, Georgia, and am preparing a talk on "<u>Favorite Books</u>" for an assembly program during book week, November 11–17.
I would like very much to know what was your favorite book during your school days. Why did the book <u>appeal to you</u>? Has the book influenced you in any way? Is there anything in particular that you still <u>remember about</u> the book?
I shall greatly appreciate an answer.

> *Most respectfully yours,*
> *(Miss) Jackie Anderson*

Mr Ayers—
The President said New Testament or Dictionary.

> *[unsigned by Conway]*

Dear Miss Anderson: *November 9, 1945*
Your letter of October twenty-fifth, addressed to the President, has come to me for acknowledgment.
During the President's boyhood there were two books which he found particularly helpful to him, the New Testament and the Dictionary. I am sure you understand why both of these appeal to him, and it is hardly necessary for me to tell you that the New Testament he found always an influence for good in his life.

> *Sincerely yours,*
> *EBEN A. AYERS*
> *Assistant to CHARLES G. ROSS*
> *Secretary to the President*

A few inquiries would also go directly to Ross or other members of the president's staff. In a similar vein to the above letter was this one from a newspaper reporter and would-be author in Kansas City, who received an almost immediate reply.

Dear Charlie Ross: *May 6, 1946*

I am writing to you for the answer to a question you perhaps are in a better position to answer than anybody except the President himself. Perhaps you will have to go to him for the answer. Here's the question:

What books did the President read from the Independence public library when you and he were high school students together?

What were Harry's favorite books, which he remembers now as impressive to a kid?

And, incidently, what was the quality and range of the Independence public library in the years around 1901? You ought to be able to answer that one as well as anybody.

You remember me, I fancy, I am the chap who popped up at the White House last September 1 in a dirty white suit, with a rather messily gotten-up biography of Harry, which he and you were good to read, and he to correct. Oddly enough, no publisher yet has had wit enough to accept it.

I should like to see the President when he is in Kansas City May 18. Will you ask Mr. Connelly whether he can work me in?

With all good wishes, I am sincerely:
Edward Schauffler

Dear Schauffler: *May 9, 1946*

I will answer your questions as well as I can.

1. The President read practically all the books in the Independence Public Library.

2. History was a favorite subject. He early formed a liking for Mark Twain, who still is his favorite humorist. He has read the Bible several times. As a boy, of course, he read all the Henty books. Among the earlier poets, as I discovered the other day, Dryden is a favorite. I recall that in Miss Tillie Brown's high school class we read and discussed George Eliot's "Silas Marner." He liked this book and recalled the high school study of it.

3. My memory of the Independence High School Library in the years around 1901 is rather vague. Of course this was the only library I knew at that time and I had no standard of comparison. It seemed to me then pretty fabulous. As I look back on it now, it seems to me that it must have been somewhat meager and yet I think it was prob-

ably as good or better than most school libraries. I well remember the
librarian, Miss Carrie Wallace.* She was a real lover of books and
guided us in our reading. Also we had the great advantage of having a
really inspired teacher of English in Miss Tillie Brown.

To sum it up, the President has read widely and remembers a great
deal of what he's read. I think his memory is really extraordinary.

Sincerely yours,
CHARLES G. ROSS
Secretary to the President

Ross neatly ignored the writer's request for a private audience with the
president but otherwise supplied a fairly comprehensive answer. Schauffler's
biography eventually was published under the title *Harry Truman—Son of
the Soil,* but at the time he may have been looked upon as just another of the
countless harmless eccentrics to write to the chief executive. On rare occasions, the correspondence of such an individual would also circulate among
some of Truman's staff, as when an acquaintance of White House special
assistant Philleo Nash wrote the president to support his dismissal of Gen.
Douglas MacArthur in Korea. Renzo Sereno of Peru, Illinois, sent one letter
to Truman on April 13, 1951, and a carbon copy with cover letter to Nash
the next day.

Dear Mr. President:

Thank you for upholding, under circumstances of great political
strain, the duties and the rights of the President of the United States
and for maintaining the constitutional authority of your office along
the principles established by the Law and rooted in tradition by our
greatest military commander, General Washington.

May I have the liberty of bringing back to your mind the utter-
ance of Edmund Burke upon the pitiless parliamentary attack which
ended with the ousting of Lord Bute: "What was the distemper of
the Kings in the last century has become in this the distemper of
Parliaments." Almost two centuries have elapsed since Burke's utter-
ance and never were his words truer than they are today.

---

*The Independence Public Library and Independence High School Library were one
and the same, a two-room facility adjacent to the school containing approximately
2,000 volumes. Carrie Wallace was a cousin of "Bessie" Wallace, the future Bess Truman.

Thank you, Mr. President. Popular temper may condemn you and politicoes may fight you to the bitter end. In upholding the rights of your high office against an aroused public opinion and against the brazen fury of your political adversaries you have well deserved the gratitude and admiration of your country and of all men, the free and those who yearn for freedom. Your steadfastness and your courage have kept our Republic free and have kept it the world's best hope.

> *Respectfully yours,*
> *Renzo Sereno*

Dear Philleo,

Please find herein enclosed copy of a letter to the President on the present situation. I am sending a copy to you because I imagine that you and your office are busy tabulating correspondence. I believe that the letter should count for five, because Emily, Laura and Dante agree with it and, schizoid as I am I find that both my selves are in agreement on this issue.

MacArthur, I believe has some traits in common with Julius Caesar, namely his coiffure and his willingness to cross the Rubicon and double cross the Republic. There the common traits end, because Caesar won his own battles and wrote his own Commentarri. The slogan by which he is known in these regions is: First in war, first in peace, last in Nebraska and Wisconsin. Enough however of the secular arm of the Hearst papers.

Life keeps on as usual and my labors are seeing, in a dim far away vista, a plausible end. As it was to be expected, now that the book is almost finished, I have the desperate wish of re-writing it, which I may well do, so that I can license to the presses, as people said in other days, a finished product. When the book will be out, I'll find myself without friends because I feel that any person who'll go to the trouble of reading it, will have no reason of keeping in terms of friendship with the author.

Give our best to Edith and the girls. I trust Goliath grows up to be a responsible dog, able to make his own decisions and to distinguish between human limbs and fireplugs.

> *as ever*
> *Renzo*

In keeping with the policy of answering most letters of support, a form Valentine was duly dispatched on May 1.

My dear Mr. Sereno: *April 13, 1951*
The President was deeply gratified by the expressions of approval which your letter conveys to him. This note brings you an assurance of his appreciation of your thoughtfulness in writing.
                         Very sincerely yours,
                         WILLIAM D. HASSETT
                         Secretary to the President

By the time this left the White House, much of the staff had ended up seeing the letters, thanks to Nash's having routed it to many of the second-tier workers such as the president's administrative assistants, David Bell and David Lloyd; Connelly's assistant, Feeney; and Murphy's special assistant, Dick Neustadt. When the unusual pair of letters made their way back to Nash, he found their routing slip filled with initials and comments. "Phil— who is this character?" queried Bell, and Ken Hechler, who worked under administrative assistant George Elsey, wrote, "I think the Pres. would have enjoyed the schizoid half of the letter that went to you." Nash must have agreed with Hechler, because he apparently had Hopkins slip it into the daily reading folder. Truman found the letters amusing yet insightful and signed off on a brief note to Sereno.

Dear Mr. Sereno: *May 7, 1951*
Many thanks for your interesting and helpful note. There are many lessons in history for those who take the trouble to learn them.
I appreciate your warm words of support and your concern about the constitution. It has been reassuring to know how many Americans feel strongly about preserving constitutional processes and have written the President to say so.
                         Very sincerely yours,
                         HARRY S. TRUMAN

Dear Sir: *Feb. 22, 1947*

Are you able to tell me whether there will be held the annual egg rolling at Easter on the White House lawn? Also what are the requirements for admission? I hope to bring some high school seniors to Washington about this time and they wish to attend, as they have never done so before, as spectators, of course.

What time does it start and when does it close? Thanks.

Yours truly,
Mrs. Carol Brinkley
Lexington, N.C.

My dear Mrs. Brinkley: *March 20, 1947*

In response to the query you make in your letter of February twenty-second, I regret to advise that there will be no egg rolling ceremony at the White House this year.

However, if you will present this note at the East Executive entrance when you come to Washington, arrangements will be made for you and the students you mention to see such portions of the White House as are open for sightseeing purposes. Visiting hours are from 10:00 A.M. to 12:00 noon, except Sundays, Mondays and holidays.

With best wishes for a most enjoyable trip to Washington.

Very sincerely yours,
MATTHEW J. CONNELLY
Secretary to the President

CHAPTER TWO

CIVIL RIGHTS • 1948 PRESIDENTIAL ELECTION

"You, Mr. President, will never have to live in a Negro neighborhood."
—woman in San Jose, California

The odd messages from Dr. Sereno's two "selves" were a welcome break from the kinds of letters that usually crossed Philleo Nash's desk from citizens wishing to share their views with the president on what was then called race relations or minority rights. Nash and his boss, David K. Niles, "divided up the field," with Niles acting as the president's liaison to Jewish organizations and the labor-liberal coalition, while Nash kept in constant touch with "the black cabinet," a discreet committee made up mostly of black Americans serving in the administration's many departments and independent agencies. This committee never met as a group and had no visible structure so that it would not become an easy target for those wishing to thwart equal rights. "One of the reasons why there had never been a permanent race relations agency in government was that none had ever survived long," said Nash, and all involved were "acutely aware that we were operating in a highly controversial area." Thus a behind-the-scenes approach was deemed essential if their work was to continue relatively unimpeded.

The "black cabinet" received no instructions from Nash, whose job was to keep the president informed through Niles, and he was strictly limited to being "of help to them by advancing their programs and bringing additional resources into play"[1] without "interfering with cabinet duties and responsibilities [or] crosscutting other White House staff responsibilities. It would have been very easy to get everything into a terrific bind by overreacting—thinking that this pervasive, sensitive, and controversial problem should be the basis for interfering with every single decision." This had to be guarded against with the utmost diligence, since the lack of specific agencies dealing with this issue meant that "the area of race relations was everybody's business

32

and yet nobody's business." Moreover, "the term 'civil rights' didn't exist as such until President Truman's commission."[2]

As Nash later explained: "The whole theory and philosophy, in the minorities operation, was that the big problem of civil rights could be handled by dealing with the small problems before they got to be big ones and before they got to be presidential responsibilities." "It was," said Nash, "an area that was of obvious importance and yet so difficult and so touchy, so threatening to national unity. If you did something, it was liable to be wrong, and if you did nothing, it was most certainly to be wrong."[3]

An indication of just how touchy the question was came early in the administration, when a storm arose over Bess Truman's attendance at a Daughters of the American Revolution function immediately after the organization had refused permission for a musician to perform at the organization's Constitution Hall in Washington because of her race. The first lady, a long-time member of the DAR, had already accepted an invitation to a tea party to be held in her honor, an event that was publicly announced through the normal media channels in Washington and the East Coast. One of those who took note of the upcoming tea was Adam Clayton Powell, a U.S. congressman and pastor of the Abyssinian Baptist Church in New York's Harlem district.

In a series of events that Bess and family believed was calculated to advance the prestige and political aspirations of the congressman, Powell's wife, pianist Hazel Scott, attempted to arrange a performance at the private hall, knowing that she would be refused. The refusal was then publicly denounced by the congressman, who also sent a telegram to Bess (with additional copies made available to the press) the day before the October 12 event. In it, he warned that "no good will be accomplished by attending and much harm will be done," adding, "if you believe in 100 percent Americanism, you will publicly denounce the DAR's action."[4]

Bess knew that her husband was already formulating plans for one of the great breakthroughs against discrimination, the integration of the armed services, and he was already in a fight over his proposal to make FDR's Fair Employment Practices Committee into a permanent body instead of just another temporary wartime agency, but as daughter Margaret put it, "she was not going to let a congressman tell her where she could have a cup of tea." Powell was attempting to manufacture a replay of an ugly incident in 1939, when noted black singer Marian Anderson had been barred from Constitution Hall and Eleanor Roosevelt had resigned from the DAR in protest. Bess, however, was not cut from the same cloth. Margaret wrote that while her mother "was not a segregationist," she was also "not a crusader."[5]

The first lady fired back a telegram of her own, noting what Powell was already well aware of: "The invitation . . . was extended prior to the unfortunate controversy which has arisen." Even though she "deplores any action which denies artistic talent an opportunity to express itself because of prejudice because of race origin," she pointedly stated that "the acceptance of the hospitality is not related to the merits of the issue."

Characteristically, Harry immediately wired a message in support of his wife, and as would happen so often during his presidency, shooting from the hip created more problems than it solved. Truman informed Powell that "he despised such a philosophy [as the DAR's], but in a free society neither he nor Mrs Truman had the power to force a private organization to change its policy."[6] Powell, of course, released the president's telegram to the press and, in a public statement, referred to Bess as "the Last Lady."

As expected, the American public was not silent on the subject either.

Honored Sir: *October 13, 1945*
Thanks for your stand <u>on the DAR and the Negro matter</u>.
The negroes in the South are impudent enough now without the backing of them in high places in the Government and it is with great relief that we realize that the FIRST lady in the land is not following in the footsteps of Eleanor.
                              Respectfully,
                              R. T. Arnold, Jacksonville, Florida

My dear Mr. President: *October 21, 1945*
As one of the voters who helped to elect you to Vice-Presidency and hence to Presidency of the United States, I feel a right to express myself on the question of <u>Hazel Scott</u> and its much broader implications.
My imagination has never been able to grasp the amazing contradiction existing in the situation of having a Jim Crow city as the Capital of this supposedly greatest democracy in the world. That in itself is an outrage to any really honest citizen of democracy. But, to have the government itself, the body which rules us all, sanction and encourage this kind of discrimination by allowing tax exemption to a body which practices discrimination in its crudest and stupidest form, is truly a sad commentary on the state of our nation.
I was shocked to hear that Mrs. Truman did atend the D.A.R. tea, even after this incident. I can only hope that she is remaining in

the D.A.R. with the hope that she can do more to reform it by remaining than by withdrawing. Anything less would be unbefitting the First Lady of our country. I shall hope to read of her real activity in this direction.

I shall certainly express to hear too, of stronger action on your part than has thus far been taken.

Sincerely,
Esther Eisen, Bronx, New York

My Dear Mr. President: *October 15, 1945*

The attached carbon copy is sent to you so that you may know what I have written to the member of House of Representatives from New York.

So that you may also know that many real Americans become indignant, aroused, infuriated, but say nothing.

Congress or any other politicians, regarding what Mrs. Truman does or where she goes to tea, or trying to stop her because of some unrelated incident, is infringing the personal liberty of the women in these United States.

I consider the comments and newspaper columns, as well as radio comments, which I heard and read last Friday, Saturday and Sunday, very disgusting and uncalled for.

Particularly so at this time when veterans returning from battle fronts and overseas services, are delayed docking in New York because of strikes, strikes, strikes, strikes.

My husband gave his life in this war; my father was in [the] Spanish American War, both my grandfathers were in the Civil War, but I have to be downtrodden and governed in New York City by persons holding political jobs who are not even able to speak the English language. Pardon my poor typing.

I am not a crank either as I am usually level headed and reserved but there is always "a straw which breaks the camel's back" and an uncle of mine used to say "beware the fury of a patient man." I write because I am furious!

Americans who never concerned themselves too much about home affairs are becoming intensely aroused and they are waiting until the boys get home for them to do something.

I wonder!

Respectfully but sincerely,
Mary J. Butler

A substantial number of letters criticizing the president's lack of firm action against the DAR were received from labor unions, traditionally strong supporters of the Democratic Party and organizations whose active support would be needed if the president was going to get legislation pushed through Congress.

>*Dear Mr. President:*   *October 17, 1945*
>
>The recent controversy over the refusal of the Daughters of the American Revolution to permit Hazel Scott to exhibit her artisitic talents reminds our Union of the fundamentals of our Democracy, and of the obligation of our Union.
>
>Every member who joins our organization must take a solemn obligation, from which we quote a part thereof:
>
>"I promise never to discriminate against a fellow worker on account of creed, color or nationality, nor will I knowingly wrong a brother or see him wronged if in my power to prevent it."
>
>When you read our obligation in light of the fundamental and underlying principles of Democracy, you will arrive at the conclusion that the Daughters of the American Revolution are not following the underlying principles of Democracy as expressed in our Constitution and as expressed in our Obligation.
>
>Our Union has unanimously gone on record protesting against the acts of the Daughters of the American Revolution in discriminating against Hazel Scott. One is reminded of the similar action of the DAR in discriminating against Marian Anderson, who sang to thousands of people under the sheltering cover of the Lincoln Memorial. We insist that such action be taken that is consonant with the principles of Democracy in legislating, if necessary, against the discrimination of people on the ground of race, color or creed. We request you to use your best offices in accomplishing this result, and in seeing that Hazel Scott secures a place in America which will be free of discrimination.
>
>We await your response.
>
>> *Yours very truly,*
>> *Glenn R. Blake, Secretary*
>> *Building Service Employees Union, Local No. 49*
>> *Portland, Oregon*

Many Americans, especially in the South, were pleased that Mrs. Truman had not "buckled under" to pressure but were less than happy with her husband's condemnation of the DAR's racial policy. The following letter from a drugstore owner in Boston, Georgia, was typical of many that displayed a condescending attitude toward blacks and suggested that the South should be left alone to handle its own problems.

> *Dear Mr. President:*   *Oct. 14th. 1945*
>
> This is a great and glorious country. The Four Freedoms, being paramount, enhances this greatness and glory for here you can give expression, orally or in print, of our approval or disapproval of public acts without fear of the firing squad or concentration camp.
>
> If I remember correctly, I wrote to you about two years ago, when you were a Senator and Chairman of the Truman committee investigating the waste of public funds on screwball projects. In this letter I assured you of my warm approval of your excellent work. I still have the letter of acknowledgement and thanks.
>
> This time, however, I regret to say, Mr. President, I find myself not in accord with you.
>
> I was just reading in the papers your <u>denunciation of the D.A.R.</u> for their refusal of this building to a negro woman for a concert. I am extremely surprised and pained over this action on your part, for it seems to me that the D.A.R. of whom my wife is a member, have a perfect right, supposedly guaranteed by our constitution, to say who may and who may not appear on their premises without outside criticism, especially our Chief Executive.
>
> It is claimed that the negress is an artist in her profession. Does this give her extraterritorial rights? Mr. President we have a case in our town that is analogous, since she is a negress and also an artist in her profession.
>
> She is our cook and I can truthfully say without fear of contradiction, that she can cook the best corn muffins, corn dumplings, hoecakes and chocolate pie that any mortal ever tasted. She is no novice when it comes to fried chicken, Southern style, and as for chicken pie she is without peer. She can take the toughest O.P.A. [Office of Price Administration] roast imaginable and coax it to tenderness and, with a wee bit of garlic, decoy you a city block.
>
> Mr. President I shall desist from further eulogy of this artist's talents for I can almost visualize your mouth watering as I enumerate her many delectable dishes. Her prowess with a skillet is beyond compare. She is a real artist and far more sought than a piano player.

I have to keep my eye on my neighbors—doggone 'em—for fear they will sneak her out the back kitchen door.

Now, Mr. President, should Annabelle—that's her name—insist on displaying her culinary art in the ladies club-room in my little town and they graciously refused her request, do you think in the crisis that it would be your prerogative, as Chief Executive, to step in and slap the ladies' wrists for their faux-pas? Mr. President, do you think the D.A.R. ladies committed a grave offense, warranting your interference, in exercising their God given rights?

Your act has given the newspapers great headlines and the woman's husband refers to your wife as the "last lady." Thank God for that compliment for Mrs. Truman. More power to her. We have had enough of a "first lady" who recently vacated. This woman has stirred up more racial hatred and dissension than all others from the time of Harriet Beecher Stowe to the present time.

Your act of condemnation only aggravates the situation for we people of the South, both white and black, can handle and solve our problem, but only without the interference of the *Chicago Tribune* and other outside agencies. It must and will be done from within. Let those who want the piano player hire a hall, but as for me, please let me keep Annabelle.

Mr. President, I thank you for your time and forbearance.

With kindest regards to you and the "last lady." I remain,

Very sincerely,
Rodden W. Adams

One of the more thoughtful letters from a DAR member came from a woman in Laconia, New Hampshire.

Dear Sir: *October 17, 1945*

As a member of long standing of Liberty Chapter D.A.R., of Tilton, N.H. I am writing to protest against your attitude toward this organization.

I know it has become fashionable in the last few years to belittle the patriotism of the descendants of the men who fought and died to make this nation the greatest on earth, but I did not think that after the splendid way in which you have carried on since the death of the late president Roosevelt that you were too big in your outlook to allow yourself to become involved in a racial controversy, whatever the provocation, especially in these troubled times.

After all Constitution Hall is a PRIVATE concern for it was paid for by the individual chapters as a meeting place for its officers and members and to house its very valuable collection of colonial records. If the members who have charge of the rental, for some reason best known to themselves, deem it advisable to withhold rental to any business or organization, whose business is it but these same members who helped to raise the money to help pay for it?

There must be several PUBLIC halls in such a city as Washington. Might it not be interesting to know how many times THEY have, or have NOT, been rented to negroes? If some of us who have been to Washington didn't know that the "grapevine" regarding negroes is as strong in that city as in many southern states this furor would be ludicrous, but this is the second attack within a few years and it has gotten past the stage of being funny.

From my long association with the D.A.R. I know that its members resent discrimination against any person of color or creed and it does seem just too bad that because we take a just pride in our ancestry we must be vilified as Nazis. I do not think that I have to tell you that there are people who would give all they possess to be able to say that the blood of our pioneers flows in their veins. I ask you! Is it not something to be proud of?

May I say in closing that we are grateful to Mrs. Truman for the stand she took on the matter.

Our national officers have not seen fit, as yet, to reply to this controversy, but when and if their explanation is forthcoming, I hope as much publicity will be given to it as has been given to the start of this thing and that said explanation will be more graciously received than it was last time. I suppose it is permissible for anyone as busy as you to make errors in judgement, which we hope this will turn out to be. Though still resentful that so much unpleasant publicity has been given to something that is dear to my heart, I wish you continued success in the office to which you have fallen heir and done so splendidly in. By the way, I am a Republican but my sentiments do not color this letter as I have several times voted Democratic.

Yery truly yours,
(Miss) Christine M. Bruce

As for Adam Clayton Powell, Truman issued orders that the congressman was not to set foot in the White House as long as he was president. Truman steadfastly avoided discussing the unsavory affair with biographers and made no mention of it in his two-volume memoirs. As far as Harry was concerned, he closed the book on the matter at the end of a lengthy letter to his mother and sister back in Independence, Missouri: "Glad you sold the car. Will have the title of the coupe put in my name and then you can drive it. It may as well be in good use and it is in good condition. Keep 35 pounds of air in the tires and have it greased once in a while and have the oil changed every thousand miles. . . . A high-brow preacher from N.Y. has been annoying us. He's a Congressman, a smart aleck and a rabble rouser. He got nowhere. Hope you are both well and happy. . . . Harry."[7]

"This was a time for testing the new president," said Philleo Nash. The drive to improve industrial production during World War II had allowed Franklin D. Roosevelt to assist black workers through the establishment of the Fair Employment Practices Committee (FEPC) with a minimal amount of political risk to both him and his party. Now, with Roosevelt gone, conservatives of all types saw a chance to start rolling back his New Deal policies, and certain members of Congress picked the FEPC as a good place to start by threatening to hold up virtually all war appropriations with a filibuster over the committee's continued existence. "Some liberals had dared to support the FEPC as long as they could ride FDR's coattails," stated Nash, "but now they were fading rapidly. Its all history today. Truman did stand up; he refused to be intimidated by the filibuster or panic in the face of a war financed by continued resolution. FEPC was saved, though with a shortened life."[8]

A compromise was reached on the FEPC question with an agreement to fund the agency for an additional six months instead of a year. This and other early compromises encouraged many in Congress to believe that they could return the country to "normalcy" now that the New Deal "Roosevelt nonsense" was as dead as the man. But if the forces aligned against equal rights thought the former dirt farmer from Missouri would be happy just to declare victory on the FEPC extension and settle back for a while, they were mistaken. Four days after his V-J Day proclamation, on September 6, 1945, Truman sent his twenty-one point "Fair Deal" to the Hill. The domestic legislation he proposed clearly aimed to lock in Roosevelt's policies as the country faced the difficult transition out of its wartime economy. Said Truman:

> One of the key items of the program was the recommendation for a national reassertion of the right to work for every American citizen able and willing to work. It was a declaration of the ultimate duty of government to use all its resources if supply-and-demand methods should fail to prevent prolonged unemployment. I felt that

in normal times we had to look first to private enterprise to provide jobs and that the government should do all it could to inspire enterprise with confidence. But that confidence, I emphasized in the message, would have to come mainly from deeds, not words. . . .

I was convinced that along with full employment there had to be equal opportunity for all races, religions, and colors. This fundamental of our political philosophy should also be an integral part of our economy. The Fair Employment Practices Committee, which had operated during the war, was continuing through the transition period. I had already requested legislation placing this committee on a permanent basis, and I repeated that recommendation in the twenty-one-point message.[9]

In 1946, after many innocent lives were taken during repeated outrages against minorities, Truman appointed a Civil Rights Committee to "get the facts behind these incidents" and report on what needed to be done "to offer adequate protection and fair treatment" to all citizens.[10] To the utter disgust of many southerners, in 1947 he became the first president to address the annual convention of the National Association for the Advancement of Colored People. Later that year, he signed the report of his Civil Rights Committee, "To Secure These Rights," which laid out in clear terms the need for federal legislation in the face of local and state authorities either abridging or failing to uphold constitutional guarantees. In February 1948, he asked Congress to enact specific legislation to abolish segregation and discrimination, and in July, he announced executive orders to end discrimination in the armed forces and civil service. When southern Democrats walked out of their party's convention that election year over his insistence on retaining a strong civil-rights plank in the party platform, a reporter pointed out to the leader of the revolt, South Carolina governor Strom Thurmond, that "President Truman is only following the platform that Roosevelt advocated" at every convention since 1932. "I agree," replied Thurmond, "but Truman really *means* it."[11]

Truman himself freely admitted that he "was raised amidst violently prejudiced Southerners,"[12] and warned White House usher J. B. West that when his mother, Martha Ellen, visited "she definitely will not sleep in the Lincoln bed."[13] As a brash, bigoted young man, he had written many letters to Bess during their courtship that included comments like "negroes ought to be in Africa" and that one man was as good as another "so long as he's honest and decent and not a nigger or a Chinaman." Although Truman, as president, would still tell jokes in private that featured various racial stereotypes and would on rare occasions blurt out comments such as "that damn nigger preacher" when informed of Adam Clayton Powell's attacks on his wife, the views of the man in the White House had little in common with those of his youth, and prophetically, he had also written Bess in 1911 how he had come to firmly believe that "experience teaches sympathy."[14]

It was Truman's experience in "the Great War" that broke the chains of the past and started him on the long road to becoming the president who would openly propose, in 1948, the landmark civil-rights legislation that would finally pass Congress in 1964. Cast into a national, American army, the Baptist farmer soon found that his best friends in the world were a Jewish supply sergeant and a Catholic chaplain. Shortly after his arrival in France, Captain Truman was put in charge of the city-bred Irish Catholics making up the 129th Field Artillery's "Dizzy D" battery, a rough and ready bunch who had handily discarded several commanding officers but fell into line with the country boy who led them effectively during the bloody fighting in the Argonne Forest.

Immediately after the war, Truman went into the haberdashery business in Kansas City with his new Jewish buddy, Eddie Jacobson, and kept many of the Catholics he'd fought with as lifelong friends. One of them, young Jim Pendergast, introduced him to his father, Mike, who, along with his uncle Tom, or T. J., controlled much of the area's politics. The business of Truman & Jacobson did well for a time during the postwar boom but was not sufficiently capitalized to outlast the bust portion of the cycle in 1921–22. A propitious offer by Mike Pendergast to place Truman's name in nomination for the judgeship of Jackson County's rural eastern district allowed him to jettison his failing business. Most of his Battery D friends enthusiastically endorsed the idea, but a few argued against it, fearing that their former captain was simply too honest—and perhaps a little too naive—to do well in politics. One of them, Edgar Hinde, told him flat out that he "just wasn't the politician type," to which Truman offered the candid response, "Well, I've got to eat."[15]

Hinde later described his friend's first campaign speech, given to war veterans at a small auditorium in rural Lee's Summit, as "the most painful thirty minutes in my life. I just couldn't wait for him to finish," but noted that in time he "learned how to make a speech."[16] The worst that opponents could dredge up on Truman was that he had backed a Republican veteran of the 129th for county marshal two years earlier. Truman won by an exceedingly slim margin. As one of the county's two district judges serving under a presiding judge (administrative posts generally equivalent to those of a county commissioner), he was part of the triumvirate that directly controlled the county purse strings through the hiring and firing of employees and the awarding of contracts for such lucrative activities as road maintenance and repair.

By virtually all accounts, he was a sound manager of the county's money, cutting its million-dollar deficit in half in just two years, and was responsible for a vast improvement in the rural roads through his aggressive policies. Tangles with his political mentors, the Pendergasts, were few. He understood and helped fulfill their patronage needs but refused to hire people who he did not believe would get the work done and insisted on honest contracts resulting in first-rate construction. Though the ethics of the new eastern judge were sometimes annoying to the Pendergasts, it was clear that they needed him just as much as he needed them. As General Vaughan later explained: "Old Tom Pendergast wanted to have some window-dressing . . . [and] he could say, 'Well, there's my boy Truman. Nobody can ever say anything about Truman. Everybody thinks he's okay.'"[17]

Running for a second two-year term in 1924, Truman discovered that quality performance and the Pendergast machine were not enough. The Ku Klux Klan, which had remained nervously on the sidelines during the first election, found him to be "less than 100 percent American" because of his obvious willingness to both hire and work with Catholics and Jews. While the *Kansas City Star* endorsed him, stating that everyone who believed in good government should vote for Judge Harry Truman, reputed local Klan chief, Todd George, announced that his organization, the Independent Democrats of Jackson County, was "unalterably opposed" to Truman.[18]

The Klan was then riding a wave of popularity that was strong enough nationally to dash the presidential hopes of the Democratic governor of New York, a Catholic named Al Smith. Within a few years, the Klan would be understood for what it truly was, but at this point, the organization was unfamiliar to many Americans, who thought of it as little more than a group of self-proclaimed superpatriots. During the 1922 election, Harry Truman himself went to meet a Klan organizer at the urging of Hinde, a Klan member, who argued that belonging to the secretive, racist body was "good politics."[19] The meeting ended abruptly when demands were made that, if elected, he guarantee to limit his hiring only to those whom the Klan deemed to be "true Americans," and a subsequent Klan effort to whip up feelings against Truman was abandoned only when Hinde and other local Klan members who supported Truman threatened a revolt.

By 1924, however, the Klan was at the peak of its power in Jackson County, Missouri, with cross burnings becoming a regular entertainment at

Crandall's Pasture near Lee's Summit and death threats arriving at Truman's door. In a move that fits nearly everyone's image of the scrappy, headstrong campaigner, Truman made a spur-of-the-moment decision to confront the Klan in person. To the horror of some friends, he jumped into his old Dodge roadster and drove down to a daytime outdoor meeting in Lee's Summit of the "Independent Democrats" minus their sheets.

Nearly a thousand people were there as he made his way up to the stage and saw that he "knew every durned one of them."[20] The wiry, little man glared at the astonished crowd for a moment from behind his thick spectacles, then proceeded to harangue "the damn cowards" at length about how they were "a bunch of cheap, un-American fakers."[21] Truman told them that "anybody that had to work behind a sheet was off the beam," and aware that most of those attending knew he had been in business with a man whose name was distinctly non-Gentile, he cast the cruelest stone possible at his tormenters: "My partner in the haberdashery business, Eddie Jacobson, had told me that the fellow that was organizing the Ku Klux had to be a Jew because nobody but a Jew could sell a ninety-five-cent nightgown for sixteen dollars"—the amount charged for their white robes.[22]

Truman finished speaking his piece, descended from the platform, strode to his Dodge as the crowd parted like the Red Sea, and headed north toward Independence in time to stop two carloads of his shotgun- and baseball bat-armed supporters hurrying to make a rescue that would have resulted in a considerably less elegant ending than his smooth exit. "You don't need guns," he told them. "Those guys are scared when they don't have their sheets on."[23] But whether or not the Klansmen were scared, Truman's brave act was political suicide in 1924. He lost the election and did not return until a wiser electorate brought him back by a landslide two years later as the presiding judge, a countywide judgeship that included Kansas City, Missouri, and brought him into contact with the needs of a large black electorate.

At the end of his first four-year term in 1930, Harry Truman's integrity and hard work earned him another lopsided victory. In 1934, he squeaked by in a tight primary race to win the Democratic primary for U.S. Senate, then handily galloped past his Republican opposition to represent his state in Washington. From this position, he became even more aware of the inequities facing blacks in America and of his party's careful noting that they were a politically cohesive group that could be of decisive importance in certain elections. Two years later, Truman helped write the Democratic platform supporting Roosevelt's try for a second term, a platform that carried a strong plank on race relations. Unlike some politicians, who saw such things as little more than the studied creation of lofty principles or vague proposals that they wouldn't have to worry about following through on, he often stated that "party platforms are contracts with the people . . . agreements that had to be carried out" and consistently supported legislation to abolish the poll tax and end the practice of lynching.[24]

Truman's senatorial reelection campaign in 1940 was, arguably, even more of an uphill fight than the one he faced in 1948. The indictment of Tom Pendergast on tax evasion charges and subsequent collapse of his political machine left Truman open to a flurry of criticism, even though it was apparent that he had never been a party to anything illegal or even unethical by the standards of the day. In addition, his staunch voting record for laws to promote increased opportunities for blacks left him vulnerable to lingering bigotry in Missouri's rural counties. Like most issues he felt deeply about, Truman chose to attack this one head on and picked the Missouri State Fair at Sedalia, in the heart of Klan country, to fire the opening salvo of his reelection campaign. Speaking to a sea of white faces, he presented a statement on civil rights that left no room for equivocation:

> I believe in the brotherhood of man, not merely the brotherhood of white men but the brotherhood of all men before the law. I believe in the Constitution and the Declaration of Independence. In giving Negroes the rights which are theirs we are only acting in accord with our own ideals of a true democracy.

Referring to the systematic denial of rights and violence organized against Jews in Germany—which was well publicized by the press in the United States and even the Nazis themselves—he issued a warning:

> If any class or race can be permanently set apart from, or pushed down below the rest in political or civil rights, so may any other class or race when it shall incur the displeasure of its more powerful associates, and we may say farewell to the principles on which we count our safety.
>
> In the years past, lynching and mob violence, lack of schools, and countless unfair conditions hastened the progress of the Negro from the country to the city. In these centers the Negroes never had much chance in regard to work or anything else. By and large they went to work mainly as unskilled laborers and domestic servants. They have been forced to live in segregated slums, neglected by the authorities.

Negroes have been preyed upon by all types of exploiters from the installment salesmen of clothing, pianoes, and furniture to the vendors of vice.

The majority of our Negro people find cold comfort in shanties and tenements. Surely, as free men, they are entitled to something bettter than this. . . . It is our duty to see that Negroes in our locality have increased opportunity to exercise their privilege as freemen. . . .[25]

Years later, when recalling how southern delegates to the 1948 convention seethed over his "self destructive" devotion to racial equality, Truman commented that "what they didn't understand was that I'd been for things like that all the time I was in politics. I believe in the Constitution, and if you do that, then everybody's got to have their rights, and that means *everybody*. . . . The minute you start making exceptions, you might as well not have a Constitution. . . . If a lot of folks were surprised to find out where I stood on the colored question, well, that's because they didn't know me."[26]

But if many Americans weren't sure just how firmly the president believed in the things he said, they were more than willing to share their thoughts with him. The letters coming across the desk of Philleo Nash ranged from quick notes fired off in anger over some aspect of Truman's racial policy to lengthy diatribes using discomfort over his efforts to end segregation as a starting point for criticisms covering a bewildering array of topics. In the great majority of cases, the letter writers believed either that Truman was moving too fast in his push for equal rights or that he was simply dead wrong on the subject, and Nash later recalled how "Bill Hassett, with his marvelous sense of humor, used to send over memos to us addressed to the 'Department of National Headaches.'"[27]

Dear Mr. President: *October 30, 1947*
I imagine your friend Henry Wallace* got a tremendous kick out of reading your comment on the report of your Civil Rights Committee. When you come up for re-election next year it would not surprise me to find him running on the same ticket with you as Vice-President. Your recent stand on the Negro question will no

---

*An effective secretary of agriculture and later vice president under FDR, Wallace was Truman's secretary of commerce until September 1946, when his pacifistic, pro-Soviet stance finally became too much for Truman. He ran for president in 1948 on the Progressive Party ticket. In private, Truman referred to him as "a dreamer" and a representative of the "American Crackpots Association." (See chapter 4.)

doubt cause many thousands of Negroes to vote for you, but this stand of yours will cost you hundreds of thousands of white votes.

I shall take great pleasure in voting against you in 1948.

> *Yours very truly,*
> Chas. H. Doggett

Truman's winning the election did nothing to silence criticism of his stance on equal rights, and one Georgia Democrat was most unwilling to extend a "honeymoon" period to his reelected chief.

Dear Sir: *January 25, 1949*

Having just returned from Washington, where I was a member of the Georgia delegation attending your inauguration, I feel it necessary to write you regarding the proposed Anti-Segregation and F.E.P.C. portions of the "so-called" Civil Rights bill.

The writer was born in Ohio; served six years in the United States Marine Corps; lived and was in business in New York City for twenty years, therefore, I think I have a fairly good conception of the issues involved.

In 1925 I moved my family from Ohio to Georgia, so that it was not necessary that my daughters go to school with Negroes. I could have moved to Missouri and obtained the same results, and could do so today, as I understand that segregation in the Public Schools of Missouri is still practiced. Missouri, being the home state of the President, it seems peculiar to me that segregation has not been abolished there.

My family have lived peacefully in Georgia for twenty-five years, and without any racial troubles of any kind. We have Negroes working with us and we get along fine, but I can assure you that if the Congress of the United States should pass any legislation forcing the people of Georgia and other States to eliminate segregation of the races, or to put into effect F.E.P.C., the country will be faced with a Civil War, and I will participate to the fullest of my ability and strength.

Leave the South alone—leave the Southern Negro alone—allow Wallace and his ilk to mix and mingle as much as they please, but permit us to handle our own affairs and the Negro will be much better off.

> *Respectfully,*
> C. L. Foster
> Columbus, Georgia

A frequently expressed fear in letters attacking Truman's civil-rights initiatives was that they would lead to miscegenation or, more specifically, that virtuous white women would become prey for the wanton sexual desires of aggressive black males. A good many letters focused solely on this subject.

> *Dear Mr. Truman*   *July 22, 1948*
> Although you are advocating <u>Civil Rights</u>, we cannot believe that even you would condone the attitude <u>of the negro men and boys toward our daughters</u>. . . . They seem to think that they are privileged to make improper advances to them on the streets and elsewhere. Girls in the South are not safe either at home or on the streets any more. The situation is appalling, and we are appealing to you in the name of American <u>womanhood to please</u> explain to <u>the negroes</u> the <u>meaning</u> of <u>"Civil Rights."</u>
> Mr. Truman, you are a busy man, but are you too busy to look into the safety of the daughters of America? I have three daughters and am voicing the appeal of every mother in the South.
>
> > *Respectfully yours,*
> > *Mrs. M. V. Page*
> > *Anderson, S.C.*

Copies sent to Senators Burnet Maybank and Olin D. Johnson of South Carolina.

> *Dear Honorable Sir,*   *March 2, 1949*
> In regards to your F.E.P.C. Bill, and Civil Rights vs. States Rights that you are trying so hard to put over on the American People.
> I have just one, particular, question that I would like to ask you and your honorable political advisors, which I would like to have you take into consideration.
> The question is this. Would any of you gentlemen be willing to sleep with a negro?
> Pretty strong, eh? Well, think that one over, before you go too far.
>
> > *Yours for better Government,*
> > *Wm. B. Findlater*
> > *Grand Rapids, Mich.*

It wasn't unusual for writers taking this tack to attempt to bring the gravity of Truman's actions home to him by pulling his own daughter into the picture, as did this woman who lived near Edgemere, Idaho, in an undated letter received on October 20, 1948. She also, like many Americans, assumed that Truman would not be returned to office after the elections to be held a few scant weeks away.

> *Dear Sir:*
>
> Mr. President, I'm only a farmers wife, co-owner of the A. Y. Ranch here in Northern Idaho. I usually keep quiet and let the men do the talking, but on the question of your <u>CIVIL RIGHTS bill</u> I must have my say/.
>
> Are you completely out of your mind? DO you really want to start another Civil War?. Have you no respect or LOYALTY to the AMERICAN WHITE PEOPLES?. What was it your own MOTHER said about the yankie [*sic*] president who freed the negroes in the SOUTH?. WHAT would she do if she knew what you were trying to force upon the people of the COUNTRY SHE LOVED SO DEARLY?. Read your BIBLE man. It will tell you not to mix the colored races with the white races; GOD promises destruction to the peoples who do mix with the colored races; Do you want to be responsible for the destruction of our Beloved America?.
>
> Mr. President, you are on your way out of the White-House and if you want to go back to Missouri to your old home, what do you think your neighbors will have to say to a man who is a traitor to the Southern peoples and their way of life? And not only the Southern people but the Northern peoples as well don't approve of your Dictator-Ship ways.
>
> What was it the Jap servant said to his Lord in California the year the war broke out? ((YOU WAIT UNTIL WE ARE IN POWER, THEN YOU WILL HAVE TO WORK FOR ME)) No Mr. Truman, the AMERICAN PEOPLE WILL NOT STAND FOR THAT SORT OF THING/. And you, a well educated man ought to know they wont/.
>
> Do you want Margret [*sic*] pestered to death by the colored men trying to court her?. That is what will happen if your bill is passed. And if Margret is like all other WHITE GIRLS she will grow up to hate the man responsible for the law/. Even out here in the North, the white women aren't safe on the streets after dark, police or no police/.
>
> I dont say kill the colored race off, SEND them back where they came from or put them on a reservation like the Indian.

I'm <u>sorry I ever voted to put you in office; since you have become</u> the <u>nuisance you are/</u>.

Sincerely Yours,
Mrs. C. L. Porter

A lengthy letter written by a woman in San Jose, California, managed to touch on virtually every theme commonly heard in segregationist circles. To differentiate text underlined by Hassett's assistants, called markers, from that underlined by the letter writer, all words highlighted by the author are printed here in italics.

Dear President Truman: *March 8, 1949*

As one of your constituents, I am taking the liberty of <u>criticizing your program on two major subjects, viz., military preparedness and racial legislation,</u> particularly as the latter affects our veterans; but first I wish to commend you for your splendid effort to win the election and your program to help the laboring class and the underprivileged generally.

We, like other nations, have demonstrated that preparedness does not guarantee victory, nor does lack of same assure defeat. The feverish way we are preparing for that final war of extinction is nothing short of suicidal. The constant talk of it over the radio and the printed word tend to create a hopeless attitude among the people; and, if continued, will eventually cause all women to refuse to bear children to be fed into the war machine as soon as they reach high school age. It seems that all the fathers of the world can think of to settle their differences is to kill off their sons that become more and more ruthless each time. Those who survived the last war, however, still have some faith in their future, and this brings me to your proposed non-racial-discriminating housing measure.

To me it seems a cruelty to penalize our young veterans by forcing them to live among Negroes in order to take advantage of the Government's aid. No other class of citizens and no other individual citizens are required to live among Negroes in order to obtain a loan for a home. You, Mr. President, will never have to live in a Negro neighborhood; nor will the Congressmen who vote for your bill; nor will wealthy citizens; yet you would force poor GIs to do so in order to get a home.

In, Los Angeles, where I lived for about 30 years, I have seen whole districts of small homes sacrificed to Negroes, who, through an agent, bought houses therein, thus depreciating the value of such homes in the neighborhood, as no white people would buy them when they found out about the Negroes; so they had to sacrifice them to other Negroes in order to get out of the neighborhood. Some people were very angry and some were very sad. However, I believe that all of these White people would have been glad to see the Negroes well-housed in nice districts but away from the White districts. You may think this race-discrimination, but, believe me, it would be better than forcing them to live side by side with revolt and loathing in their hearts. We have more consideration for our animals.

From friends in Los Angeles, I have heard that the Negroes were taking over down-town L.A. as an estimated ten thousand had moved in to do war work. I could not believe some of the stories. But in 1946 I had an opportunity to spend six months there and was very much surprised at the change. Big husky Negroes, who looked as if they could lift hundreds of pounds, elbowed their way into street cars and grabbed seats away from White women who were compelled to stand; some of them up in years like myself. Women would bump into white women and scatter their packages all over the sidewalk then turn and laugh at them picking them up. Some of them, of course, are better mannered, but there is a reason which I will name presently.

Whatever progress the Negroes in America have made today, or whatever privileges they enjoy, they owe to the White race. My own family suffered several casualties as a result of the Civil War to free the slaves, but one of my Uncles, while home on sick leave, told his Mother that when the slaves were set free, they would swarm all over the north demanding their *rights*. This prophecy is being fulfilled today—50 to 80 years later. It is not inconceivable that in the future, Negroes would take away all the rights and privileges of the White race in their present locations by making conditions intolerable for them; causing the White race to withdraw to locales where restrictions could be enforced by co-operative means, if no other, leaving the otherwise helpless poor to lose faith.

I have lived in the South and know that White people, who are compelled by poverty to live in Negro districts, are known as "poor

White trash," for the reason that being so associated, such people become like the Negroes and seem to forget their ancestral heritage. So I feel that those in a position to do so should try to restore the White race there to equality with their own race and make it possible for the Negroes to advance among their own people but separate from Whites. Should your measure be passed, I fear the GIs will not buy the Government financed homes and the Negroes will take over, which might turn out to be a very good type of segregation, which would not help the better class of White GIs nor please the Negroes either.

Until recently, we had a law here in California prohibiting intermarriage between Negroes and Whites. A test case in Los Angeles caused a judge to rule the law unconstitutional and the White woman in the case married a Negro, thus sacrificing her claim to her race—an almost incredible thing for a White woman to do. If many White people in the lowest social brackets followed this lead, there would be, in a few generations, an in-between race out to make trouble by disrupting our institutions and the home life of the descendants of the founders of America and other White immigrants who helped the early settlers to build up the country, trouble which might even lead to another civil war. I do not expect to be here to see this, but my descendants might.

If you refer to the Negroes' "Who's Who," and study the physiognomy of the men and women listed therein, I think you will find it apparent that most of them are half-breed. Half-breeds are increasing rapidly, due to evil-minded, unscrupulous, though *educated,* White men, who not only betray the Negro women (probably servants or students) with whom they consort without marriage, but their country as well. This is the only way to account for such Negroes' desire for education which they undoubtedly inherited from their White progenitor. If this is not true, then we are witnessing the *greatest phenomenon* of all time, vis. a Negro slave race from darkest Africa passing by members of the White race who have had a background of centuries of European culture, and in a fraction of a century's time. Most of us have never seen our names in any Who's Who, even though our ancestors in America date back to the 1620s.

After having pioneered this country and laid the foundation for the greatest civilization the world has ever seen, are we going to hand

<u>over all the prerogatives of the White race to the Negroes?</u> We have already permitted them to sit in judgment of White-race offenders in the lower courts. Shall we appoint them to the higher courts and to the Supreme Court? Shall we elect them governors of states or even president (should some of them qualify) displacing White applicants for these offices? Shall we permit them to marry into the White race in every state of the union and thereby cause the White race to become a mongrel race, never quite sure whether their off-spring shall be black or white? Just where are we going to draw the line? And, wherever we draw it, will we not be acccused of race prej-udice, intolerance, etc. as at present?

In one of the letters to the editor of *Look* magazine, Dec. 21, '48, Mrs. Timothy C. Hal writes ". . . one tenth of the nation has some Negro blood. This one tenth did not get that way from legal inter-marriage." Mrs. Roosevelt, in her column in *Ladies Home Journal* for December '46 writes: "At the present time I think that intermarriage between Negroes and Whites may bring to both of the people involved great unhappiness, because of the social pattern in which we happen to live, etc." This reply is predicated upon the assump-tion that the present social pattern is wrong and that time will change it so as to make intermarriage right and proper socially and morally. Those persons and organizations who favor equality seem not at all disturbed at the prospect of intermarriage, even though they must know that the White race could be swallowed up by the dark races of the earth in some future age.

There are many verses in the Bible which indicate that God dif-ferentiated between peoples. Moses is quoted as saying: ". . . the Lord has chosen you to be a peculiar people unto Himself, above all the nations that are above the earth." Deut. 14:2. I do not think that Moses meant that God despised all other peoples on the earth, but He differentiated to the extent that He wanted the people addressed to be separate that they might not lose the progress they had made by consorting with the black races. Otherwise, there would be no purpose in creating or evolving the different races, which, somehow, have survived to the present age when there is a growing tendency to mix them together. Carried to the ultimate, this could result in the complete absorption of the overwhelming black races of the earth in some future age. You will see by this that I am one who believes in reincarnation. I believe your program to bring more immigrants into the United States will contribute to unemployment and more racial difficulties.

As to the Jews, they are backing this agitation for race equality for reasons of their own—not that a Jew would touch a Negro with the tips of his fingers racially. They are the most race-conscious people on earth, and I have always admired the way they keep their racial strain practically pure. I believe they think they can promote their interests by this subtle means and prevent any uprising against the Jews in America, such as developed in Germany.

The people of the earth need a new spiritual awakening, which would cause all people to recognize the fatherhood of God and the Brotherhood of man without, however, breaking God's laws or trying to change the pattern. That the difference between races is here is proof that God intended them to be so until such time as *He* changes the pattern.

If you have read this far, Mr. President, I thank you for your consideration.

Respectfully,
Mrs. I. Hughes

Unlike Mrs. Hughes, some writers felt no need or inclination to reach for high moral ground when writing their president and put their names to letters that set standards for crudity, such as this one from a former soldier living in East Syracuse, New York.

Dear sir;   *9-18-48*

During the war I was stationed at several places in the South. It was quite nauseating in hot weather to have to mingle with stinking Negroes on the streets and in the stores. I was *very thankful* that I did *not* have to inhale Negro aroma while eating in restaurants and sitting at the movies.

Down there, there are so many more Negroes than up here. Quite a few times large Negroes coughed in [my] face and stepped on my toes. They do lots of things (annoying things) without realizing they are doing such, or maybe it is just plain orneriness. I know several ex-GIs here in Syracuse who feel just as I do.

I think (we think) it would add to the unity of the nation if we let the southern states handle their own internal affairs.

The Whites and the Blacks in the South get along with each other remarkably well. Much better than most people in the North seem to think.

Very Respectfully,
Howard M. Boyd

Almost as if responding to the above letter, a black man in Memphis, Tennessee, penned a letter to Congress but changed his mind and sent it to the president. Niles promptly wrote him back, emphasizing that it was Truman who was behind the bill (and not Congress, where it was meeting the expected stiff opposition).

~~Dear Congress:~~ Mr. Pres.   April 22, 1949
Let me tell you why I would like to see the civil rights bill pass. I think it would stop people from pushing others off the sidewalk & making [a] remark saying, "get over Negger & when you see me coming, get off the sidewalk." Or when you get on a street car & hand over your transfer to the conductor & he snatch it from you, & when he give you a transfer he stick it in the palm of your hand & push it away. They dont want you to get on the street car first &, quiet natural,* you have to pass by them to get to the rear of the car, but they dont want you to touch them.

Sometimes you be talking to them & they dont understand & you repeat it and they still dont understand. Then, you know, you are compell[ed] to raise your voice & then they say you are trying to be smart & one told me to watch out, he would get me kill[ed]. So that is some of the reasons I would like to see it pass.

Yours Truly
Dave Dandridge, Negro of U.S.A.

Dear Mr. Dandridge: May 10, 1949
I have your letter of April 22nd, address to the President, in which you tell him how you feel about his civil rights program.

The President feels very strongly about all kinds of unfair discrimination, and it is to help prevent such things that he has put forth his civil rights program.

---

*"Quiet natural" means quietly and calmly so as not to provoke a reaction.

Legislation, however, can only be a means to an end. Some of the things you have experienced will be corrected only when there is a real change in the minds and the hearts of men toward one another.

> *Cordially,*
> *DAVID K. NILES*
> *Administrative Assistant to the President*

Opponents of civil rights frequently quoted the Bible or provided lists of passages that they interpreted as proof of Divine support for segregation.

> *Dear Mr. President:*   *Jan.29th 49*
> I know that you, no doubt, will not see this letter, personally—but I would like to take this opportunity, regardless, of referring you to the Holy Bible, the Book of Genesis, the ~~sixth~~ ninth chapter and the 22nd, 25th & 26th verses. This, in my opinion, is an answer to <u>your Civil Rights problem</u>.
> You believe the Holy Bible? Do you not? I'm sure you do, being a Mason, and taking all your oaths upon this book of books. Do you believe that we should change God's laws, made so many thousand years ago? Yes, I know later on it says "all men are created equal." They were created equal, but because of the sin of Ham, the descendants of Ham lost that equality.
>
> *Fraternally,*
> *Mrs. W. G. Helen Harrison*
> *Collingwood Chapter O.E.S.*
> *[Order of the Eastern Star]*
> *Toledo, Ohio*

One man from Chicago was well ahead of his time, offering a suggestion that would be taken up by millions of Americans—black and white—within a generation.

> *Dear Sir:*
> I am very interested in the Civil Rights Bill. And as I understand, according to law, in order for my people to be equal they must have a flag to represent them, in order for them to be recognized in all parts of the world.

Therefore you would have to give them their proper name from the country their ancestors were brought from, which would be the true name of our race "African Americans." I understand very well how the name "(Negro)" came about, but I don't believe from the will of God that any race of people should carry the stain of any other name given by another race of people there[by] keeping them ignorant. You see we have stood by you in every effort in defending your country, so it would only be right for you to give my people their proper name. And it would be more appropriate by the will of God that you practice Christianity as you teach it. The time has come for every individual to know his own native land.

Therefore you have the responsibility to take the Civil Rights Bill before congress again.

Sincerely yours,
Henry L. Anthony

The "Dixiecrats" who walked out of the Democratic Convention soon fielded Strom Thurmond as their own candidate in the hopes that they could deny the election to Truman, Wallace, or Republican Thomas E. Dewey and thus throw the election into the largely segregationist House of Representatives. While hardly fond of Truman's racial policies, many ardent southern Democrats were horrified at the prospect that such a tactic could well propel a Republican back into the White House and tried to keep fellow Dixiecrats in the fold by claiming that Truman was merely playing election-year politics.

Truman moved quickly to disabuse southern party officials of such ideas but rightly feared that if he beat that drum any more than necessary, he would almost certainly alienate even more southern voters before the election. In the end, many segregationists tended to believe what they wanted to believe. Even his sister, Mary Jane, would confidently asssert that "Harry is no more for Nigger equality than any of us,"[28] in spite of his strenuous efforts to speak plainly and compassionately to his family on this sore subject at the time his mother was dying: "Mamma won't like what I have to say [to the NAACP] because I wind up by quoting Old Abe. But I believe what I say and I'm hopeful we may implement it."[29]

Many please-say-it-ain't-so letters came to the president from anguished Democrats like this housewife who lived on a country road outside little Sanford, Florida.

Dear Pres. Truman: *Sept. 10, 1948*

Please give one minute of your valuable time to the reading of this letter, the contents of which is of greatest importance to a vast number of *Southern Democrats*.

I am a Southerner. A Kentuckian. Have lived in Florida the past twelve years. My husband and I have solicited votes for outstanding candidates in a number of elections in Orlando, Winter Park, and Sanford. Of the many I will mention only two, Senator [Claude] Pepper, and the late Franklin D. Roosevelt. We would like to see you elected and have the opportunity of soliciting for you and Sen. Barkley, if we thoroughly understand your program, and agree with you on same.

There is much bitter comment and a great majority is against "Civil Rights." Would you kindly explain just what your Civil Rights program incorporates? I have read up on the subject, but wish you to state plainly what is expected.

I think it only right that the Negro should have the right to vote, and should be protected by law as other citizens. . . . The Negro has not, and never will reach the state of intelligence (even with reasonable education) to be allowed certain privileges. He lacks true common sense which the Lord failed to give him. Most Southerners are laboring under the impression that you expect us to meet and accept the Negro socially. Personally, I think there is a vast difference in "Civil Rights" and "Social Rights." This is the main point I wish explained.

I lived in Chicago three years during the last war, and the social contacts, the inter-marrying of whites and negroes, was the most disgusting thing I have ever experienced. I would not want a son or daughter in service that had to share camp with the Negroes. I would let a child go uneducated before I would permit them to attend school with a Negro. Would you wish your daughter to mingle with them socially? Would you like a Negro for a son-in-law? . . .

If you had not incorporated this into your program at this time, as the Southerner is laboring under the impression you have, you could have been assured of re-election. It's going to take some rather deep thinking and clever maneuvering to convince the Southern people that this is no time to change horses in the middle stream, and that it is better to retain a democratic president than to take a chance with a republican. Even though it has been years, we haven't forgotten the hard times we experienced during their administration.

I heard on the radio that some Negroes had already applied for admission to an Orlando white school. This coming at this early stage of the game, only adds flame to fury. The Negro schools throughout the South are good, well-equipped schools, so why should they be allowed to attend with the whites? Is it because Mr. Negro wants to show his authority, and if given any further privileges, they will try to take possession here as they are doing in the North.

The average Southern Negro is well satisfied with things as they are. So why change? They are treated kindly. The Bible says, "Everything after its own kind." If God had wanted the Negro to be one of us, he would have made him white and not black.

I wish to apologize for this lengthy letter, and do hope that there is going to be some way and means of re-electing you. You have chosen a most desirable running-mate. We have had many demonstrations of his concrete judgment on important questions in the past. Personally, I think and hope, there has been some misunderstanding throughout the South in regard to your program. May I have an explanation?

With <u>best wishes for</u> your <u>success in the</u> coming <u>November election</u>, I am,

> *A much interested citizen,*
> *Mrs. Harry Voss Boyles*

As has been previously noted, Truman and his staff did not generally answer correspondents criticizing administration policy. When Harry received a letter from an old friend from his Battery D days in the First World War, however, he felt compelled to give a response that was both comprehensive and completely off the record. The somewhat abridged letter below was written by Ernest W. Roberts, who had served as a corporal in the 129th Field Artillery's C Battery and was then associated with the Faultless Starch Company of Kansas City.

Dear friend Harry: *Saturday Nite*

Please pardon me, in my TYPING, and aproaching you as I am but I am close to you as I know you in my humble way.

Harry, in this letter, I could say many things to you and maybe correct you, as I think. I will not do that but allow me to pass this on to you. . . . We should *appease* our thoughts and let the South be the South. . . . Oh Harry, you are a fine man but a poor salesman so listen to me—You can win the South with*out* the "Equal Rights Bill" but you cannot win the South *with* it. Just Why? Well, You, Bess and Margaret, and shall I say, myself, are all Southerners and we have been raised with the Negroes and we know the term "Equal Rights." Harry, let us let the South take care of the Niggers, which they have done, and if the Niggers do not like the Southern treatment, let them come to Mrs. Roosevelt.

Harry, you are a Southerner and a D—— good one so listen to me. I can see you don't talk domestic problems over with Bess. ????? You put equal rights in Independence and Bess will not live with you, will you Bess.

Well Harry, I have said my piece and I am only a boy who travels, helping you, but you are making it hard on me. . . .

Most Sincerely
Ernest W. Roberts

Dear Ernie,   *August 18, 1948*

I appreciate your letter of last Saturday night from the Hotel Temple Square in the Mormon Capital.

I am going to send you a copy of the report of my Commission on Civil Rights and then if you still have that antebellum proslavery outlook, I'll be throughly disappointed in you.

The main difficulty with the South is that they are living eighty years behind the times and the sooner they come out of it the better it will be for the country and themselves. I am not asking for social equality, because no such thing exists, but I am asking for equality of opportunity for all human beings and, as long as I stay here, I am going to continue that fight. When the mob gangs can take four people out and shoot them in the back, and everybody in the country is acquainted with who did the shooting and nothing is done about it, that country is in a pretty bad fix from a law enforcement standpoint.

When a Mayor and a City Marshal can take a Negro sergeant off a bus in South Carolina, beat him up and put out one of his eyes, and nothing is done about it by the State authorities, something is radically wrong with the system.

On the Louisiana and Arkansas Railway when coal burning locomotives were used, the Negro firemen were the thing because it was a back-breaking job and a dirty one. As soon as they turned to oil as a fuel, it became custom for people to take shots at the Negro firemen and a number were murdered because it was thought that this was now a white-collar job and should go to a white man. I can't approve of such goings on and I shall never approve it, as long as I am here, as I told you before. I am going to try to remedy it and if that ends up in my failure to be reelected, that failure will be in a good cause.

I know you haven't thought this thing through and that you do not know the facts. I am happy, however, that you wrote me because it gives me a chance to tell you what the facts are.

> Sincerely yours,
> HARRY S. TRUMAN

[Longhand] *This is a personal & confidential communication and I hope you'll regard it that way—at least until I've made a public statement on the subject—as I expect to do in the South.*

Sure enough, when Truman's campaign train rolled into Texas a month later, he made it a point to shake hands with a black woman, to the accompaniment of boos from the crowd, when he found a Confederate flag being waved at a rally in Waco. At Rebel Stadium in Dallas, however, arrangements had been made ahead of time to quietly drop segregation for a day. The first integrated rally in Texas history went off without a hitch as the Missourian ripped into his Republican opponent. Dire predictions that race riots would erupt in Dallas and that large numbers of voters still leaning toward the president would cast their votes to the Dixecrats proved to be unfounded. Said Truman, "That rally was just as peaceful as any of the others. If you just give people a chance to be decent, they will be."[30]

Years after he had returned to private life in Independence, he reminisced at length with biographer Merle Miller about the intolerance and bigotry that had so often inflamed Americans, touching upon the Alien and Sedition Laws; McCarthyism; attacks against Masons like Andrew Jackson; the burning of Catholic churches; the Ku Klux Klan; J. Mitchell Palmer and the Red Scare after World War I; the relocation of Japanese-Americans into what he had no qualms about calling "concentration camps"; and the Mormons who were evicted from one location after another, including Truman's hometown, where "they even called the militia to help chase them out."

"People in Independence haven't changed a bit," he said. "The old people hate [Mormons] just as much now as they did then. It's a violent prejudice. I don't feel that way, and a great many of the people of Independence do not, but you take the old-timers, the old Independence families, they won't have anything to do with Mormons." When asked why, Truman, who was already hot, proceeded to get hotter. "Well, why does a South Carolinian hate to eat at a table with a nigger? It's the same feeling exactly. It's a prejudice, and it doesn't make any sense, but it's there. And some people in public life take advantage of those prejudices."[31]

Truman believed that if Americans, like this woman from St. Petersburg, Florida, were provided with "a little leadership," they would come down on the right side of the civil-rights question.[32] Like so many people from both the North and the South, she found it extremely hard to know exactly what should be done.

> *Dear Sir:*   *July 20, 1948*
> I deeply apologize for writing for I know that the form and expression of this letter is not worthy to be sent to you. I am an elderly woman, for years a <u>teacher and school executive</u>, now retired.
> I have been <u>deeply interested</u> in your plans for a <u>complete civil</u> rights program for the negro race. Theoretically you are perfectly right. The condition of the negroes is a disgrace to our country. If they are ignorant, if they have to struggle against every obstacle to obtain the merest justice, if they have been compelled to live in hovels, to work for small wages, to lack honor and respect, it is indeed the fault of the Nation and of the individuals who have kept them so.
> In spite of this there has been a gradual change for the better. We have seen schools and colleges established, better housing, more liberty, and many of the Negro race advancing to positions of dignity as doctors, lawyers, ministers, teachers, farmers, technicians, etc. etc.
> The only difficulty in your plan in such a State as Georgia is that it requires a sudden <u>change from the plan</u> that is slowly but surely working for the final total full release of the Negro. I believe you could get the Southern Democrats to join <u>with you in full</u> accord if you <u>drew up a plan which</u> would not demand <u>everything at once</u>. But would offer Federal <u>aid for better schools</u>, better housing, better pay, recognition of talent and ability; but restricting political power until the average Negro is better able to use it.
> If suddenly all restraints were released vicious men would use the ignorant Negro vote for their own uses, honorable white men would be pushed aside. We have had the same problem in New York City

when ignorant immigrants were used to defeat decent government by city bosses.

This is what the decent citizens of Southern States fear. You are totally right in the final aim; but the practical working out of this ideal must be done in close cooperation with those who have to live daily with the problem.

We must first teach the Négro, give him better personal conditions, more opportunities. This must be done. The Negroes in Florida can go in any store, try on dresses and shoes, but they cannot go to a white church, or to a white theatre, they do not seem to have a decent bathing beach even in this terribly hot weather. Yet the <u>Negro wash women</u> are getting <u>Five dollars a day</u> for house work. Everything is so inconsistent. I admire their ability to adapt themselves to such conditions. But I greatly fear, if I were so treated, I would have murder in my heart most of the time.

I have known and admired many Negroes, some of them servants in our Northern home, some farmers, some doctors, some ministers, some companions in college, or in welfare work. To me the difference is never in color, but in personal advancement, point of view, and character.

Have you read some of the many recent books which clearly present the Negro problem? I am glad to say that these novels may be educational to white men who read them. One is "A Star Points North," another "Bitter Fruit."

I will be hoping that you can find several wise and tolerant Southern men who will, with you, solve this problem. Perhaps make it a five or ten year plan which will finally bring to pass what you desire.

With every wish for your success,

I am faithfully yours,
H. Grace Parsons

As Cold War tensions mounted, the question of equal rights could not be separated from the wider realities of international politics, and Truman pointedly noted to Democrats who wanted to go slow on his civil-rights initiatives that such a course "would be inconsistent with international commitments and obligations. We could not endorse a color line at home and still expect to influence the immense masses that make up the Asian and African peoples" and that it was vital that Americans "practice what we preached."[33]

The Communist Party in the United States, which had previously demonstrated little interest in racial matters, now came to the conclusion that black Americans would provide fertile ground for expansion in this country and added a strongly worded civil-rights plank to their campaign platform in 1948. In spite of the strenuous efforts of black communists, most notably actor-singer Paul Robeson, few inroads were made by the Communist Party, as the vast majority of blacks easily recognized a come-on when they saw one, and the highly influential ministers in their community churches would not abide an alliance with "godless communists" even for the sake of civil rights. At their 1950 national convention, long before McCarthyism became a household word, NAACP delegates vowed to purge known communists from their membership. Anticommunists were overjoyed at how things were turning out, while Communist Party members and their sympathizers felt cheated.

> *Dear Mr. Truman:*   *January 7, 1950*
>
> On January 15 thru January 17 a <u>National Emergency Civil Rights Mobilization</u> is to descend upon Washington. I am sure that you will give it your earnest support. It is doing two jobs. Giving to the people of the Negro race their rights and education beside taking faith away from communists with whom the Negro people have looked to.
>
> > *Thank you.*
> > *Richard Schneider*

> *President Harry S. Truman:*   *May 28, 1952*
>
> The leaders of the Communist Party have been jailed and others are today being tried under a law which was passed one hundred years ago. This law was enacted for one purpose, namely, to deny the Negro people their rights as citizens of these United States. The Negro people refused to accept this law, but the government refused to remove it from the statute books; hence, at a later date they could again use it. This law, the <u>Fugitive Slave</u> Law, was upheld by the Supreme Court <u>in the infamous</u> Dred <u>Scott decision</u> of 1850. It stated that the <u>Negro has no rights</u> which a white man is bound to respect.
>
> Because the Communist Party in 1948 included in its platform that it was on record as being against this inequitable and unequal treatment of Americans, the leaders of the party are today charged with conspiring to advocate the overthrow of the United States government by force and violence.

There is only one way that a government can be overthrown. When the people of a country become dissatisfied with the form of government under which they are living, they will seek ways to change that system. However, as things stand today, when people through a political party try to educate and agitate for issues like equal rights, they are accused of subversive activities. Evidently anybody who speaks out against the grafting crooks in the Democratic and Republican parties is a subversive.

Let us look at the facts: The <u>Communist Party</u> has been on the ballot for many <u>years in many</u> states, running candidates for President, Congress, Senate, etc. until 1948. When the <u>party in 1948</u> came out for <u>civil rights for Negroes</u> (and meant it), nothing was said about it. But when Mr. Truman, in order to gain the Negro vote, also demogically came out for civil rights, he got re-elected to office. Since that time Mr. Truman's government as well as the Congress and the Courts have taken many steps to keep the Negroes from enjoying civil rights. The <u>Democratic Party</u> (as well as its loyal <u>opposition, the Republicans</u>) knows that if Negroes in the South could vote that the Senators and Congressmen coming from the Southern states who enact the reactionary laws would not be there today. Laws such <u>as F.E.P.C.</u>, anti-poll tax, anti-lynch bill, decent housing, price and rent controls, etc., would be enacted if the Southern Dixiecrat coalition were broken, according to Mr. Truman's own admission. Yet the party which fights for the Negro franchises to break this coalition is today hounded and is trying by <u>Truman's F.B.I. and crooked "Justice" department to be destroyed</u>.

Bear this in mind: It is not the Communist Party or the Communist leaders who are on trial. It is the Negro people and the Bill of Rights. The sooner the American People awaken to this, the sooner will we put an end to this terrible political persecution for the crime of thinking.

Yours very truly,
Hezekiah C. Climons

Few correspondents had their wishes so quickly and throughly fulfilled as this black woman from Walton, Kentucky, who had served in the military (probably the Army) during the war. She pointed out that as commander in chief, Truman needed no special legislative authority to bar segregation and discriminatory practices in the armed forces as well as the federal civil service. Within a few months, the president did just that by executive order.

> Dear Mr. President   March 12, 1948
>
> I am not dictating to you. I am merely stating facts. If you want to be in the White House four more years, be the man we think you are. You <u>can win the re-election if you end racial segregation in the armed forces, discrimination in all Federal departments and Jim Crowism</u> in all the United States. <u>You have the power to do that without new legislation</u>. Be presumptuous. We negro people will back you up. You can prevail, now is your probability. Send out your proclamation without any procrastination. You could start there in the White House, half of your body guards could be black. I served in World War II. I will die gladly before I will serve in World War III under the present conditions. This is the way we all feel.
>
> Very truly yours.
> Mrs. Amelia A. Dixon

The announcement that executive orders had been issued to end discrimination in the armed forces and guarantee colorblind employment practices in the federal civil service came at a time of considerable political turmoil in the United States. Just two days after the Democratic Party nominated Truman for president at 12:42 A.M. on July 15, 1948, Dixiecrats in Birmingham, Alabama, nominated Strom Thurmond as a states' rights candidate who would ensure that government policies would not "reduce us to the status of a mongrel, inferior race." On July 27, Henry Wallace was nominated as the candidate of the Progressive Citizens of America and pointedly refused to repudiate the support of the Communist Party and its sympathizers.

Retaining the support of as many traditionally Democratic voters as possible was of critical importance after these defections. The labor-liberal coalition, whose home turf consisted of the largest northern industrial areas, was particularly vulnerable to the seductive call of what Truman called the "pie in the sky" Progressives, yet the president could move only so far in courting them without either going against his own firm beliefs or undercutting his effort to delicately wean southern voters away from the Dixiecrats after their initial surge of popularity.

That the staunch Democrats of the South had actually bolted from the party had come as a shock to Truman and his advisors. Clark Clifford in particular was caught flat-footed by the Dixiecrat defection. A successful trial lawyer before the war who had joined Truman's staff as a naval aide and risen to become special counsel to the president, he had signed off on a confidential report earlier in the year titled "The Politics of 1948," which had smugly asserted, "As always the South can be considered safely Democratic. And in formulating national policy it can be safely ignored."[34]

Now Niles, Clifford, Elsey, and others in the Truman team were scrambling to balance the demands of the labor-liberal coalition with political realities in the South. As expected, Truman's gutsy moves on equal opportunity in the military and civil service were seen by black Americans as a clear—and substantive—gain on the civil-rights front, but they were not enough for the liberal intelligensia, who always demanded more, irrespective of the wider political ramifications for the party. Despite the obvious need to retain their support, Truman decided that, during the run-up to the election, it would not be wise to beat the South over the head with the fact that he was steadily dragging it toward desegregation.

It also came as no surprise when Adolf Berle's Liberal Party of New York pressed for more and increasingly specific statements on civil rights. Truman later stated that Berle had repeatedly said he was "100 percent for me," but as far as Truman was concerned, Berle and others like him weren't "for anybody but themselves and their own special interests."[35] Truman would not be pushed into making statements he feared would be damaging to the campaign, but neither could he afford to alienate Berle, who had a relatively strong influence on the very same liberal-left voters that Wallace was targeting in New York, a state that was believed to be vital to a Democratic victory in November.

Under normal circumstances, Niles would have been the one who handled the matter, usually with a phone call or personal meeting in New York City. Circumstances dictated, however, that a bigger gun be employed to keep Berle and his followers in line. Clifford was a rising star in the Truman administration, and by now it was relatively well known within certain circles that he was a close confidant to the president on both domestic matters and foreign affairs. He was deemed to be the best choice of who on the White House staff should sign a letter addressing the concerns of Berle and his party.

Dear President Truman: *August 9th, 1948*

At the request of the Committee Against Jimcrow in Military Service and Training, The Liberal Party of New York State wishes to join with that Committee in asking you, Mr. President, to issue a statement that will be the policy of the United States Government to work for the elimination of segregation in the Armed Forces of our country. We believe such a statement by you, following the excellent Executive Order abolishing discrimination in the Armed Services, would have an inspiring effect both at home and abroad, and would strengthen American democracy immeasurably.

May we also ask that you set forth in definite terms, the authority and responsibility of the special committee for the elimination of discrimination in the Armed Forces, just as was done in connection with the elimination of discrimination in the civil service of our federal government.

Your executive orders meant much to all who treasure democracy. We believe that affirmative action on our suggestions will increase confidence in our democracy and strengthen our national defense, both morally and physically.

> *Respectfully yours,*
> *ADOLF A. BERLE, Jr*
> *State Chairman*
> *BEN DAVIDSON*
> *Executive Director*
> *MARX LEWIS*
> *National Legislative*
> *BENJAMIN F. McLAURIN*
> *State Executive Committee*

Dear Mr. Berle: *August 18, 1949*

Your letter of August 9 to the President asking that a statement be issued with reference to the policy of the United States Government regarding the elimination of segregation in the Armed Forces has been referred to the writer for attention. The President appreciates your interest in this important subject.

The President's position has already been made clear and it is felt that a formal statement is not needed. I should like to call your attention to paragraph 1 in the President's Executive Order of July 26, 1948, which contains the following declaration of policy by the President:

"It is hereby declared to be the policy of the President that there shall be equality of treatment and opportunity for all persons in the armed services without regard to race, color, religion or national origin. This policy shall be put into effect as rapidly as possible, having due regard to the time required to effectuate any necessary changes without impairing efficiency or morale."

Your attention is also directed to a public statement made by the President at a weekly press conference on July 29, 1948. At that time, the President, in answer to a question, stated in effect that his advocacy of equality of treatment and opportunity in the Armed Forces envisioned eventually the end of segregation in such forces.

I join with the President in expressing best personal wishes.

Very sincerely yours,
CLARK M. CLIFFORD
Special Counsel to the President

Truman ultimately lost New York State to Dewey when Wallace, as feared, pulled enough votes from his ticket to give the Republican the edge he needed. The "Solid South," however, was broken by Truman's persistent call for a return to the Democratic fold, with Thurmond winning only four states. The Dixiecrat defections, together with an unexpectedly strong Democratic showing in the western states, was enough to give Truman the election. Although the Liberal Party would later try to climb aboard the victory bandwagon, any support it may have given the president was half-hearted at best, and Berle's name was absent from their congratulatory letter to Truman.

Black voters had answered the president's call in record numbers, and large turnouts by blacks in Ohio and Illinois were undoubtedly a major factor in the Democrat victory there. Yet even though Truman's famous executive order garnered considerable attention in the press, it was inevitable that even voters deeply interested in the controversy would somehow miss the news that momentous events were taking place, as did this woman from Detroit. Uncharacteristically, Hassett's staff was behind the curve on this one, and instead of bringing the writer up to date by sending an informational reply pointing out the recent presidential initiatives, a standard Valentine was sent. This may have been due to the fact that the former newspaperman was absent from the White House for weeks at a time during the critical summer of 1948 because of an alcohol problem that had been worsening over the previous year and was finally reaching critical proportions. During Hassett's absences, the office's work was managed by his secretary, Alice Winegar. Within a month, he would be sent to Walter Reed Hospital for "health reasons." Although this letter's response went out under his name, Hassett may well have had absolutely nothing to do with it.

Hon. President of the United States, Aug. 4, 1948

I would like to protest against segregation in the draft law. It seems that any citizen who is asked to give the supreme sacrifice for his country, should be treated with every courtesy and respect.

The greatness of our nation has been achieved mainly by the breaking down of barriers—barriers between religious groups, classes, and various nationalities.

Separation is a contradiction of our constitution "All men are created equal."

Sincerely,
Verna Wacker

My dear Miss Wacker: *August 14, 1948*

This is to acknowledge the receipt of your letter to the President. You may be sure that your interest in writing and submitting an expression of your views is appreciated.

Very sincerely yours,
WILLIAM D. HASSETT
Secretary to the President

Resistance to integration was stiff from some quarters in the military—particularly the Navy—but Truman forced the issue anyway, and in the end, it was found that there were few difficulties. Harkening back to a time thirty years earlier, when he found that the Catholic troops he led in battle were men with fears, desires, and abilities little different from his own, Truman was convinced that the human bonds forged in war would last a lifetime and spread throughout society. "Experience on the front," he maintained, referring to Korea, "has proved that the morale of troops is strengthened where Jim Crow practices are not imposed."[36] And the Korean War itself had hastened the process. Said Nash: "There were large numbers of blacks in the garrison troops in Japan who had to be thrown into Korea very fast. Circumstances and fate had a lot to do with what happened thereafter. Units and individuals had to be put into combat so fast that it was impossible to unscramble them."[37]

Yet even with the urgency of war and the commander in chief of armed forces ordering changes in racial policies, black Americans entering the service of their country were only too well aware that Truman's command had no more than moral authority once a serviceman left base.

Dear Mr. Truman;   *January 2, 1951*

My entry into military service for the second time is drawing near. During my enlistment in the last war, I encountered a great deal of segregation, both on military bases and on liberty. It is my understanding that segregation in the armed forces has been abolished, but nothing has been done to assure service men that they will not be segregated while on leave.

Perhaps the men (including yourself) who run this government do not realize the significance of the present conflict in Korea. It is not a mere communistic effort to combat democracy, but it is a racial war to push the whites out of Asia. The problem of racial conflict probably does not enter your mind, except at such time when you are immediately presented with a civil rights situation. But it does enter my mind, not only in brief moments, but twenty-four hours a day. You see Mr. Truman, I am a Negro.

I have been living in this capital of democracy for three and a half years while attending Howard University. In June I am scheduled to graduate and to seek my professional ambitions. But my ambitions will have to be cut short because of your mobilization plans. Yes, I am one of the thousands of Negroes who constitute part of your reserve forces.

While dwelling in this capital of democracy, I have been confronted with every type of segregation that it is possible to conceive of. Your democracy has failed and has done so in the shadows of its own essence. It is not my desire to serve in the armed forces, giving my life if necessary, and to be subjected to the most depriving segregational policies existing in any capital in the world.

As a veteran, as a citizen, as a Negro, and as an American I urge you to use your resources to abolish segregation of any type against any member of the armed forces in the United States and in foreign continents as well.

Sincerely,
Stewart A. Street

As Truman's second term neared its end, it was clear that the man most likely to succeed him was decidedly more cool than the president on the civil-rights question. This voter in Austin, Texas, was less than happy about the situation.

Dear President Truman: *June 11, 1952*

General Eisenhower's stand on civil rights—that he would leave it up to the individual states—is a capitulation to the Southern Dixiecrats who still are "slavery-minded." If this policy had been followed consistently from 1850 to the present, the Negroes in Southern States would still be slaves, working 10 to 16 hours a day for board and room and whatever extra crumbs their Dixiecrat masters might want to toss to them. It seems to me that the Federal Government should guarantee the basic civil rights of all its citizens.

Governor Byrnes'* threat to abolish the public schools in South Carolina if Negro children are allowed to attend the same schools as white children is an extremely un-American threat, and I cannot imagine American citizens standing for such action. I was raised in Illinois and I went to schools where Negro and white children studied together in the same classrooms—a demonstration of Democracy in Action. Why do southerners allow Negroes to nurse their children, take care of their homes, and cook their food, but will not allow them to sit in the same classrooms with white students? When American citizens in the South casually try non-segregation, they will find that it is very beneficial to both Negroes and white persons. It would be a lesson in Democracy for the Dixiecrats.

I believe that Senator [Hubert] Humphrey is the best choice for the next president. We can count on him to put up a real battle for civil rights, extended social security, compulsory health insurance, military forces strong enough to whip the Soviet Union, if necessary, fair labor policies, fair agricultural policies, good foreign relations and many other progressive policies. I believe that Federal Security Administrator, Ewing,† would be an ideal vice-president.

Many newspapers have endorsed Taft or Eisenhower for president. However I believe that the *people want and need* <u>Senator Humphrey for President and Mr. Ewing for Vice-President</u>.

Very truly yours,
Dwight L. Hubbart

---

*James F. "Jimmy" Byrnes had served as Truman's secretary of state until 1946, when the president felt it was time for Byrnes to return to South Carolina politics.
†Oscar Ross Ewing of the Federal Security Agency, which administered public health, social security, education, and other services.

If Hassett passed this letter along to the president (and we have no way of knowing, since such items did not receive any special markings), it is certainly the kind of letter that would have gotten a rise out of his boss—something the playful Hassett enjoyed doing. Humphrey had publicly advocated that the Democratic Party draft Eisenhower for president at its 1948 convention and was a principal member of the Americans for Democratic Action (ADA), a group of noncommunist New Deal Democrats working to keep party liberals from swinging over to Wallace.

The antics of the ADA had amazed and appalled Truman, not only because he had faithfully and stubbornly carried the banner of Roosevelt's policies, but also because the ADA was advocating that Eisenhower head the Democratic ticket even though neither they nor anyone else knew anything about his views on civil rights, Social Security, taxes or, for that matter, Soviet expansion. And to make matters worse, the ADA and Humphrey, who made a rousing keynote speech at the convention, were pressuring the president in much the same way as Adolf Berle to take actions that would jeopardize the election. It was Truman's considered opinion that Humphrey and his followers were nothing but a bunch of "crackpots" who, in their quest for political purity, actually *wanted* the South to bolt.[38]

Subsequent events during the Eisenhower administration involving civil rights and other matters did little to enhance Truman's opinion of Eisenhower either. In May 1954, the Supreme Court struck down the principle of separate but equal schools, and ugly incidents soon followed, such as state authorities calling out the Arkansas National Guard to bar black students from attending white schools. "If the fella that succeeded me had just given people a little leadership, there wouldn't have been all that difficulty over desegregating the schools, but he didn't do it. He didn't use the powers of the office of the President to uphold a ruling of the Supreme Court of the United States and I never did understand that. If he'd got out front and told people that they had to uphold the law of the land, it's my opinion that they'd have done it."[39]

Perhaps the most touching letters on segregation were those written by children, particularly by those who could not understand why they were treated differently from white girls and boys. Few, if any, of such messages reached the president, but all were kept with the note "child's letter" penned at the upper left by one of Hassett's markers.

Dear President Truman   *received March 9, 1951*
Today we were driving home. And we got on a subject. I don't know how this happend. But Mom said that colerd people can't

even go in to a drugstore. And get something to eat. After all colerd people are made by one person. And that's God. And I'm sure he dosen't like what's happing.

What every one wants I'm sure. Is freedom. And freedom [is] what there going to have.

Olie Westheimer

Dear President T.

On the other letter I sent you I forgot to give my add. So I'm writing you again. My add. is [————] Waterman St. Louis 5 Mo. I am 9 years old.

Olie Westheimer

Judging by the penmanship and phraseology, the following letter from an eleven-year-old boy in Washington, D.C., was probably dictated to his mother, who cleaned it up for him and put it into proper form.

Dear Mr. President,   *June 20, 1949*

I live about three yards from a white playground, yet it is a public school playground. I am a colored boy and not allowed to go on it. All the white boys enjoy playing with me. But I am put off by the adult managers. I am writing you for a consideration because my playground is 4 or 5 blocks away. My parents are afraid of me being hit by cars. I am eleven years old. Please answer.

Sincerely,
Andrew S. Evans

Older children were able to express more complex thoughts and, like this young lady from Greensboro, North Carolina, frequently tried to get themselves a presidential pen pal.

Dear Mr. President;   *Jan. 24, 1951*

How are you today? Fine I hope. I know that you are wondering who is writing you. Well, <u>I am a 15 year old Negro 10th Grade school girl</u>. I am speaking for my History class since we are interested in the News and World Affairs.

Mr. Truman since I am supposed to be a free person I feel that I have rights to communicate with you personally.

Every time war starts members of the opposite race start talking about freedom. I am living in a town where we have no freedom. Here in *Our Times* they have listed some personal rights as follow:

1. Worship as we please.
2. Enjoy freedom of speech, including radio, television, and movies.
3. Enjoy freedom of the press.
4. Move about the country freely.

We cannot do these. One of my friends was skating in the Caucasian settlement on her way home. The white children called the Police who forced her home. That's why we can't move about freely. We cannot organize and support the political party of our choice. We cannot vote as we please, we cannot run for public office, we cannot choose our own public officials, yet Americans tell people of foreign countries that everyone in America is free.

I am not writing this letter for publicity but to give you my personal opinion of the world today.

The majority of us never think about praying until war starts, but we should pray for these things not to happen. We can never have complete peace and democracy afar unless we get it in America first. We should get the beam out of our own eye before we can take it out of someone else's eye.

I know that you have a lot of things said about you and you have a lot to think about so don't let this perplex you, because I think you are a very good President. Mr. President some children told me not to write you, but I feel that you could understand just as well as anyone else. I know that I am only one person but I am speaking for a whole class who is interested in you and your cabinet.

Mr. President if you are not too busy, I would like to correspond with you and get your opinion on the things that I have fore said. We also saw you speak on television, at school of about 1,000 children.

Sincerely yours,
Arlene Williamson

With Truman's return to Independence, Missouri, only days away, a letter arrived from Roy Wilkins of the NAACP. Although Truman and Wilkins would later have a parting of the ways over the civil-rights movement's increased use of direct-action tactics such as sit-ins, which Truman felt openly flouted the law, Wilkins wanted him to know that the accomplishments during his administration were recognized and appreciated by black Americans.

Dear Mr. President: *January 12, 1953*

You must be receiving many letters and your hours in these last days of office must be filled with many duties, but I felt that I could not see you leave Washington <u>without telling you how</u> I feel about <u>one phase of your administration</u>.

I want to <u>thank you</u> and to convey <u>to you my admiration</u> for <u>your efforts in the civil rights field</u>, for your pronouncements and definitions of policy on <u>racial and religious discrimination</u> and seg-regation.

You have many accomplishments on record during your tenure of the White House (many more by far than is admitted publicly by the Republicans or the majority of our nation's press) but none more valuable to our nation and its ideals than your outspoken champi-oning of equality of opportunity for all Americans without regard to race, color or national origin.

Mr. President, no Chief Executive in our history has spoken so plainly on this matter as yourself, or acted so forthrightly. We have had in the White house great men—great diplomats, great politi-cians, great scholars, great humanitarians, great administrators. Some of these have recognized inequality as undesirable, as being at variance with the democratic principles of our country; but none has had the courage, either personal or political, to speak out or act in the Truman manner.

You spoke, Sir, when you knew that many powerful influences in your own party (and in the party of the opposition) would not heed you. You reiterated your beliefs and restated your demands for legis-lation when political expedience dictated a compromise course. This is sheer personal courage, so foreign to the usual conduct in political office—high or low—as to be unique in the annals of our govern-ment. But it was worthy of the Presidency of the United States of America. No little man, no mere politician would have sensed the fitness of such conduct in the nation's leader.

Your <u>great desire was to achieve peace</u>. Your sincere efforts toward this goal have saved us from a Third World War thus far and have laid a foundation on which others, if equally devoted, can bring peace to the world.

In urging that America erase inequality between its citizens, as citizens, you were outlining a component of the complex mosaic for peace in the world: the hope, dignity and freedom that democracies offer mankind in contrast to the offerings of totalitarianism. Your sure realization of the truism that preachment without practice would be powerless as a force for peace is a measure of the quiet greatness you brought to high office.

As you leave the White House you carry with you the gratitude and affectionate regard of millions of your Negro fellow citizens who in less than a decade of your leadership, inspiration and determination, have seen the old order change right before their eyes:

Their sons are serving their country's armed forces in pride and honor, instead of humiliation and despair.

A whole new world of opportunity in education is opening to their children and young people.

The barriers to employment and promotion on the basis of merit have been breached and will be destroyed.

Some of the obstacles in the way of enjoyment of decent housing have been removed and others are under attack.

Restrictions upon the precious citizenship right of casting a ballot have been reduced and soon this right will be unfettered.

Some of the cruel humiliations and discriminations in travel and accommodation in public places have been eliminated and others are on the way out.

But in addition to these specifics, Mr. President, you have been responsible through the pronouncements from your high office, for a new climate of opinion in this broad area of civil rights. By stating a government policy, by relating that policy to the cherished ideals of our nation, you have recalled for the American people that strength of the spirit, that devotion to human welfare and human liberties, that made our country man's best hope for the things all men hold dear.

In their prayers for your health and long life, Negro Americans are joined, I am sure, by hosts of other citizens who have had their spirits renewed and their convictions strengthened by your espousal of the verities of our way of life.

You have said often that the people will act when they have understanding. The people who have had their faith fanned fresh by you will not fail to press toward the goals you have indicated. No change of personnel or party labels will stay them.

May God's <u>blessing and guidance be with</u> you in your new endeavors.

Respectfully yours,
Roy Wilkins
Administrator, National Association
for the Advancement of Colored People
New York, New York

Dear Mr. Wilkins: *January 14, 1953*

It was good of you to write as you did. The progress in equal rights that has been made in the past seven years is a source of pride and satisfaction to me and I am very glad to have your confirmation of what I feel is a substantial change. It is most gratifying to me to have you say that there is a new climate of opinion on civil rights. Respect for human rights is fundamentally a thing of the mind and heart. As a government we must take the steps that improve human rights; as a people we must feel deeply about them.

Your prayers and good wishes for me and for my family are deeply appreciated.

Very sincerely yours,
HARRY S. TRUMAN

NEW YORK, NY   MAR 11 1947
PLEASE INFORM BY WIRE COLLECT WHETHER TRADITIONAL
EGG ROLLING CEREMONY ON WHITE HOUSE LAWN THIS EASTER
WILL BE HELD. THANKS.
PACKARD
THE NEW YORKER

MR. PACKARD: MARCH 12, 1947
RETEL, EGG ROLLING CEREMONY WILL NOT BE HELD THIS
YEAR.
EBEN A. AYERS
ASSISTANT PRESS SECRETARY

CHAPTER THREE

WORLD WAR II • POTSDAM CONFERENCE • DEMOBILIZATION OF
THE ARMED FORCES • CESSATION OF HOSTILITIES • OCCUPATION
OF GERMANY • CONTINUED RATIONING • UNEMPLOYED VETERANS •
EASTER EGG ROLLING AT THE WHITE HOUSE • THE TRUMAN BALCONY
• THE MARSHALL PLAN • SACRED COW • DEATH OF MOTHER

Despite the imminent end of the Nazi regime in Germany, the Second World War was far from over when Truman took the oath of office, and many Americans were quick to share their ideas for the postwar world with the new president.

Dear Mrs. [sic] President;-   *May 22, 1945*
The Threat in Europe and Pacific Strategy
Whether those in other sections are so concerned or not, I have no evidence, but I do know that we in this community are fearfully concerned in two particulars and I wish to so advise you. I have no selfish interest because my tall, dark son was killed on Leyte last January and I have no other son involved;
1. We recognize a terrible threat in Europe. I need not review that situation—you are wholly aware of it. As our troops are returned and the remainder are reduced to a certain strength— Stalin, or his generals, may create an incident and then—developments will come rapidly and we will be at war again. This is a real threat—it just cannot be discounted, and our boys should be brought home immediately and removed from any further participation in war in Europe.
2. As soon as the Philippines are subdued, and the few necessary islands taken and developed to protect that area, as soon as the industries of Japan are destroyed or rendered ineffectual, our boys should be withdrawn from that theater.
A. The British and the Dutch should clear their own islands.
B. We should furnish the necessary equipment to China and let the Chinese fight the China battle.

As it seems to be now indicated, we propose to use our boys until the last Jap is killed or captured—that guarantees the killing of tens of thousands of eager lads, and it is a bootless sacrifice. Public opinion here will not support it; "Will public opinion, generally support it later?"

Respectfully, but with all the energy created by a broken heart, I cry out to plan an end to this terrible slaughter of American boys.

> *Very respectfully,*
> R. A. Robinson
> *Fremont, Neb.*

Truman found the good advice of another attorney so amusing that he made time to dictate a brief response on the eve of his departure to the Potsdam Conference.

Dear Mr. President: *June 29, 1945*

A perhaps foolish suggestion:

1. That the Japs be told in leaflets, by loud speakers and so forth that if they surrender, when we receive the surrender of Japan, we will make it a condition that they will be allowed to return without punishment of any kind; and if this is not accorded by the Japanese government that they will be settled on a beautiful island and their wives sent for and brides provided for the unmarried. Of course, we could pick out one of the Dutch East Indies like the Celebes.

2. That the rice fields of Japan be bombed with oil and fire bombs.

3. That you obtain definite proof that lend lease weapons and munitions were used by the French in shooting and bombardiering the natives in Syria and Algiers. This will give you a great talking point when you meet de Gaulle.

4. Also, for de Gaulle—that 3,500,000 acres in France are devoted to growing wine so that Frenchmen can drink a quart and a half a day. 1,000,000 acres will provide handsomely for the fine wines which the French export and part of the remainder at least should be devoted to growing food such as wheat, barley, soybeans and so forth.

We have stopped the manufacture of Bourbon Whiskey because of a shortage of corn. The annual export of wines from Algiers runs into the billions of francs. Algiers was once part of the granary of the Roman Empire

Congratulations to you on your magnificent record up to date.

Yours very sincerely,
James W. Gerard
Attorney and Counselor at Law
New York, NY

Dear Mr. Gerard: *July 3, 1945*
Appreciated very much your letter of June twenty-ninth and the suggestions which you made. I am glad to have them.

Your suggestion about the French wine is an especially good one.

Sincerely yours,
HARRY S. TRUMAN

Most people, however, were more concerned with matters closer to home.

Mr. President:
I am an American.
A free American.
I want to remain a free American.

Therefore as a free sovereign American citizen (I insist with all earnestness that *all* emergency war measures and agencies) be *entirely* terminated not later than three months after the war is over.

Yours respectfully,
Roy T. Otman
Los Angeles, Calif.

The apparent success of the Potsdam Conference at establishing transitional Allied military control over Germany and a framework for postwar cooperation in Europe (the provision that the Soviet Union would enter the war against Japan was still secret) prompted a spate of congratulatory letters to Truman. All acknowledgments were signed by the president and were frequently worded in such a way that the sender could be reasonably certain that someone had actually read the letter.

My dear Mr. President: *August 8, 1945*

Just a line to say "Welcome Home" and congratulations to you and your staff for a fine job well done at Potsdam.

> *Cordially,*
> *Joel L. Schlesinger*
> *Newark, NJ*

Dear Mr. Schlesinger: *August 11, 1945*

You don't know how much I appreciated your note of the eighth. It was kind and generous of you to send it.

I hope I will always deserve your good opinion.

> *Sincerely yours,*
> *HARRY S. TRUMAN*

PRESIDENT HARRY S TRUMAN   AUGUST 8, 1945

THE RESULTS OF YOUR POTSDAM CONFERENCE ARE HEARTILY APPROVED BY OUR ASSOCIATES BY ALL APPARENTLY EXCEPT HARD BOILED REACTIONARIES. YOU HAVE SETTLED ALL DOUBTS AS TO WHERE YOU STAND ON THE COMMON MAN'S PRAYERS. YOU ARE NOW SECURELY ON YOUR OWN.

C. H. BRYSON, CHAIRMAN REPUBLICANS FOR ROOSEVELT LEAGUE COLUMBUS, OHIO

Dear Mr. Bryson: *August 11, 1945*

I certainly did appreciate the telegram which you sent me.

It was kind and generous of you and I hope I will always deserve your good opinion.

> *Sincerely yours,*
> *HARRY S. TRUMAN*

Dear Harry: *August 6, 1945*

From all I can hear and learn, I believe you did a grand job at the Potsdam conference. I have only a small conception of the problems confronting you, but I have absolute confidence in the fine results you are achieving for our country.

> *Yours sincerely,*
> *Clyde*
> *J. C. Nichols Company*
> *Kansas City, Mo.*

Dear Clyde: *August 11, 1945*

Thanks a lot for your note of August sixth. It was kind and generous of you to send it to me.

Sincerely yours,
HARRY S. TRUMAN

The sudden—and completely unexpected—surrender of Japan in August 1945 accelerated Americans' desire to see the boys brought home as speedily as possible. Truman's explanations that soldiers were already being processed out at a rate of 650 men per hour, and that the rate would climb to roughly 25,000 per day by January 1946, only seemed to feed the public's impatience. Organized labor also got into the act. Anxious to see their ranks swelled with returning veterans, unions mass-produced cards like the one below and urged people to sign their names and send the cards to the president and members of Congress.

Tens of thousands of such items arrived at the White House, but campaigns of this sort were given little credence by Truman and his staff. Consequently, after the initial batch of cards arrived, they were no longer even forwarded to Hassett's markers but were simply counted and either placed in the "permanent Out File" or forwarded to an appropriate government agency when they began to take up too much table space. A representative sample would be retained from each successive stack for the archives.

Mr. I. R. T. Smith   *December 14, 1945*
File Room.

78,295 of the attached card were today sent to the War Department.

Mr. [Thomas R.] Padgett
Mailroom

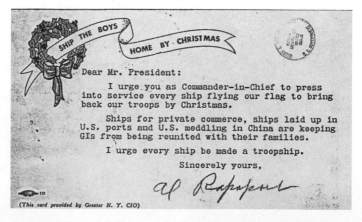

Demands that the return of servicemen be radically increased were genuine, however—and *loud*. The Army had originally believed that an orderly demobilization would release over 5 million men by July 1946. Political pressure forced an almost helter-skelter acceleration, and by April, nearly 7 million discharges had been processed by the Army, together with almost 3 million more by the Navy and the Marines. These numbers, though impressively huge, meant little to those still in uniform and wating for their tickets home. Their enlistments called for them to serve for "the duration" of the national emergency, and with the war now over, they were understandably impatient.

> *Dear Harry,*   *March 15, 1946*
> Please hurry and sign [the] duration so that we—the draftees—can get back to civilian life.
>
> > *Yours truly,*
> > *Nicholas George   James R. Burch*
> > *M. Debbandt   Kelly R. Smith*
> > *R. Debbandt*
> > *Camp Beale, California*

Not all servicemen wanted to leave the military, and an exasperated mother from Lincoln, Nebraska, wrote the president requesting that her son be allowed to stay home after he chose to reenlist.

> *Dear Sir:*   *March 29, 1946*
> I am writing you personally but with the hope that other mothers like myself would like to have you stop this experiment of the atomic bombing [Bikini Island tests]. My son John is scheduled to go, and I can't help worrying for him and these other boys. He's a member of the regular Navy and serving his second enlistment and has been in this war from the very beginning.
>
> He was an original member of the U.S.S. *Bristol.* He did convoy work the first part of the war, later serving as communications on the U.S.S. *Denebola.* He had been recommended for school on his return last November from six months on the Marshall Islands. I have had four sons in the service; one receiving the Purple Heart, two Bronze stars and clusters, and one receiving the Soldier's Medal in China. One served with Patton's army.
>
> [Johnny is] still in the service. He has a wife and six-month-old baby girl in Portland, Maine. He will be twenty-three years old in

June. I'm enclosing some clippings and hope today they will help to make my objective clear. I think they have more than done their duty, and please let Johnny and these other boys stay home.

God bless you and help you.

> *Sincerely,*
> *Mrs. R. L. Hutton, Sr.*
> *Lincoln, Neb.*

My dear Mrs. Hutton: *Arpil 2, 1946*

Your letter of March twenty-ninth to the President has been received. May I assure you that your interest in writing and submitting your views is appreciated.

I am returning the enclosures to the letter inasmuch as it is felt you would wish to keep them.

> *Very sincerely yours,*
> *WILLIAM D. HASSETT*

Truman, the first president in many decades to have served in uniform, let alone combat, was greatly admired by servicemen, who appreciated his dogged rear-guard action to minimize the impact of defense cuts. Three seamen aboard the seaplane tender U.S.S. *Albemarle* could tell that his praise for their efforts was more than political hot air.

Dear Mr. President:

We felt very proud indeed to receive your letter of thanks for our service toward a great cause.

Your thoughtfulness of us who returned, and of those who died on the field of battle is greatly appreciated.

We served during the war to the best of our ability, and now we remain to serve, for any emergency which may arise.

Thanking you again, we remain

> *Sincerely yours,*
> *William F. Shadlowsky*
> *Samuel Montoya*
> *Gilbert C. Barela*

People, civilian and military alike, were anxious to put the war behind them, and numerous proposals were put forward on how to appropriately signal and celebrate the end of hostilities.

Dear Sir: *October 25, 1945*

Would it be possible on the day that <u>you or Congress</u> declare the <u>war at an end</u>, to have <u>our entire nation</u>, at home and abroad, stand at a given time to be announced by you over a nationwide <u>radio hook-up and shortwave to our armed forces</u>, and sing the first verse of our National Anthem, with a <u>government band playing from the White House or such designated point</u>. May we also remain standing for a minute of silent prayer for those who made the supreme sacrifice.

I would also like to suggest that you call the nation to rise by <u>three raps of the gavel, and close with one rap, on our American Legion bell,</u> which I would be very happy to bring to the White House. We use this American Legion bell in calling our New Haven Railroad American Legion Post #119 to order twice a month. Being a legionnaire, I know that you will appreciate just what this would mean to our Post and myself.

> *Yours respectfully,*
> *Elwood H. Stewart*
> *Past Commander, The American Legion*
> *New Haven, Conn.*

Re: Armistice Day: *October 11, 1945*
Most Honored Sir;

Last evening at a meeting of our local American Legion Post here in Southampton, N.Y., we had a discussion concerning our Annual Armistice Jamboree, and the question arose just what could be done about the annual celebration of V-E Day, V-J Day, and also the day you officially declare the end of the war.

As <u>Armistice Day</u> is fast approaching, it occurred to me that there might be a possibility of your declaring the end of the war to take effect at 11 a.m., November 11th, 1945, so that veterans of both War No. 1 and No. 2 could celebrate together, and so that another holiday would not be added to our already holiday-laden calendar.

I trust that you do not feel I am presumptuous in making this suggestion. Permit me to congratulate you on your many successes to date as our Commander-In-Chief, and for being a 100% American. Keep up the good work.

> *Faithfully yours,*
> *Wm. I. La Fon, Jr., Past Commander*
> *Malcolm Ross White Post #433*
> *American Legion*

From a distance of many decades, the answer to the simple question of whether the Second World War was over seems equally simple. At the time, with rationing still partially in effect, the absence of signed peace treaties with America's two principal antagonists, and indeed, American soldiers forcibly occupying both countries, matters were not as clear as they appear today. The legal ramifications of this question plagued business-labor relations for years, and even as late as the Berlin Airlift in 1948, Truman continued to receive inquiries like the following from frustrated parties struggling to get a straight answer from the highest authority.

My dear President Truman: *June 11, 1948*
It is of considerable importance in a dispute with the Ohio Bell Telephone Company <u>as to whether or not the war is over</u>. We have an arbitration award which is to remain in effect quote, "for the duration of the war in which the United States is now engaged."
The Union is of the opinion that the war is over.
Will you kindly answer as soon as possible the question; Is the War over?
I believe your position in this matter may have considerable bearing in the settlement of this dispute.

> *Sincerely yours,*
> *Charles C. Gabriel, President*
> *The Ohio Federation of*
> *Telephone Workers, Inc.*
> *Cleveland, Ohio*

My dear Mr. Gabriel: *June 15, 1948*
I have your letter of June eleventh and in response to your inquiry wish to inform you that the President proclaimed the cessation of hostilities of World War II, effective twelve o'clock noon, December 31, 1946. However the President at that time and again on July 25, 1947, emphasized that the emergencies declared by the President on September 8, 1939, and May 27, 1941, and the state of war continue to exist. In this connection, I am sending you the attached copy of press releases for your convenient reference.

> *Very sincerely yours,*
> *WILLIAM D. HASSETT*

Questions persisted into the last days of the Truman Administration.

Dear Mr. President:　　　　　*January 5, 1952[3]*

I <u>have tried, without success, to find out</u> whether or not <u>"the Duration,"</u> as applied to the Second World War <u>has been terminated.</u>

<u>If "the Duration" has been terminated, would you be kind enough to send me the date of such action.</u>

Respectfully yours,
Robert B. Pender
Utica, N.Y.

My dear Mr. Pender:　　　　　*January 10, 1953*

Your letter of January fifth addressed to the President has been received. With reference to your inquiry, I wish to advise you that the President proclaimed on April 28, 1952, that the national emergencies declared to exist by the proclamations of September 8, 1939 and May 27, 1941, be terminated.

Very sincerely yours,
MRS. JOSEPH SHORT
Secretary to the President

Until the fighting spread to the Pacific in 1941, with the entry of Japan and the United States into the, until then, largely European war, the configuration of 1914–18 was called "The Great War." The truly worldwide character of the conflict after Pearl Harbor prompted increased use of the terms World War I and First World War in place of the original name in order to clearly define the situation and magnitude of the fighting ahead. Identifying the conflicts simply by number lacked poetry, and after the defeat of the Axis nations, there was some discussion in Congress and the press on whether a more appropriate name could be found than the popularly used—and by now semiofficial—World War II. A man in Houston, apparently fed up with what appeared to be a never-ending stream of American resources being sent overseas, from lend-lease to the huge shipments of food and medicine to Europe and Asia, offered his own suggestion.

Mr. President:　　　　　*Nov. 8, 1946*

<u>I understand that the U.S. Government wants a name for the present war.</u>

I herewith suggest a name that should suit every class of Americans. One class would consider a tribute to their God while the more intelligent class would realize its true meaning.

Here it is: "The War of F.D.R."*
*FREE DELIVERED RESOURCES

> *Yours truly,*
> *A. C. Jessen*
> *Houston, Texas*

The nagging possibility that defeated Germany's dictator was still loose in the world added to the ambiguity of the times. Unlike most correspondents, who wanted some form of presidential assistance or were very generous with their free advice, an attorney in Buffalo, New York, was so sure that his idea for running down the Nazi leader would work that he literally "put his money where his mouth is."

My dear President Truman: October 23, 1945

Newspaper comments from time to time seem to indicate the possibility that Adolf Hitler is still alive.

His name is now historically synonymous with evil. Hitlerism has soiled the pages of history causing the death of millions of innocent persons, the destruction of property, and what is even worse, has caused a perversion of the soul of millions more. It would be tragic if the trail of blood, oppression and foulness that he has left could again be followed by activation and further growth of Hitlerism upon his return from hiding.

Since Hitler and his followers had been proven devoid of ideals and were, and still are, motivated by selfishness, greed and avarice, I feel that his own followers would be tempted to, and would turn Mr. Hitler over to the Allied Authorities provided the price is sufficiently large.

I herewith tender the enclosed check in the sum of $5000.00 which I hope will form a nucleus for further sums to be contributed by public-spirited Americans for a fund to be offered as a reward to the person or persons causing the capture, apprehension and trial by the Allied Commission of Adolf Hitler.

It would seem that the sum of one-half million dollars would be a sufficient attraction for the most ardent adherent of Mr. Hitler.

The award to the person or persons producing this result shall be left entirely in your discretion.

> *Sincerely and respectfully yours,*
> *William J. Brock*
> *Buffalo, N.Y.*

Dear Mr. Brock: *October 29, 1945*

The President has asked me to acknowledge your letter of October twenty-third and to thank you for bringing such a generous proposal to his attention. Commendable as is your motive, such a generous donation to serve as the nucleus for further sums to be contributed by public spirited Americans for a fund to be offered as a reward for the apprehension of Hitler, the President does not feel that he can assume the responsibility which acceptance of your donation would entail.

Accordingly, I am returning herewith your check in the sum of five thousand dollars. I am sure you understand the President's position.

Very sincerely yours,
WILLIAM D. HASSETT

Despite the horrors of the Nazi regime, many Americans were sympathetic to the common people of Germany, who were faced not only with rebuilding a nation whose infrastructure had been largely destroyed during the war, but also with great privation—and, some maintained, starvation—during the coming winter. A U.S. senator from New Jersey, whose own son had died in the war, was anxious that the mails be reopened so that relief parcels could be sent to destitute Germans.

Dear Mr. President: *December 14, 1945*

I know you have established a War Relief Control Board, of which the Executive Director is Mr. James Brunot.

Thousands of your best American people have reached the conclusion that we are not serving humanity in the proper way unless and until we give food, clothing and shelter, so far as lies within our power, to all afflicted people in the European countries. This is particularly true with reference to the millions of Germans and Italians who were not responsible in any way for Hitler.

I rather feel that it will be a blot on our historical escutcheon if future generations find that we sat by and delivered food, clothing, shelter and heat to certain groups of people in Continental Europe while at the same time we stood idly by and watched millions starve and freeze to death.

Certainly little babies and innocent children and helpless old men and women in Germany and Italy should not be neglected because they happen to live in countries whose dictators and rulers tried to destroy the better things in the world.

I feel very strongly on this subject, and knowing you as I do, and believing that you would like to be a follower of the life of Christ, I hope you may find it within your power to take the necessary steps to give whatever relief we can afford to all innocent peoples without discrimination.

Thousands of Americans of German descent are banded together in the hope that this Government will open up the mails to Germany and Italy and will allow not only mail but relief parcels to be sent to private citizens in those two countries by their loved ones in this country. The timing in everything is the most important thing in life, and it will do no good to open up the mails and grant citizens in this country the right to send help after the people in Europe are starved, diseased or dead.

Many citizens in this country are willing even to charter ships, if necessary, and pay for them, providing our Government will grant that privilege to them.

Mrs. Hawkes and I lost our son in this war but his loss does not create vengeance and bitterness in our hearts so that we are willing to idly sit by and see millions of innocent people in Germany and Italy, or even in Japan, starve to death when there is ability in this country to send relief.

In connection with the $1,350,000,000 additional funds for UNRRA, I shall not vote for it unless this discrimination is clearly and completely removed from the Bill when it comes to a final vote.

I know you are very busy but we have professed great humanitarian principles and nothing is more important than to see that we carry though with credit to ourselves insofar as lies within our power.

I take this opportunity to wish you, Mrs. Truman, your daughter and your Mother as pleasant a day on Christmas Day as you can possibly have in view of the load you are carrying as head of the Nation.

With affectionate regards, I remain

> *Sincerely yours,*
> *J. W. Hawkes*
> *Senator, New Jersey*

Truman was not impressed with Hawkes's plea and felt that the U.N. Relief and Rehabilitation Administration was handling the situation as well as could be expected, considering the magnitude of the problem. He decided that the best person to craft a carefully worded reply was Samuel Rosenman, who had left his position as a justice of the New York Supreme Court to become one of Roosevelt's principal advisors and was now Truman's special counsel. Truman scrawled a message to Rosenman across the top of Senator Hawkes's letter, and signed off on the response.

[Longhand] *Judge: Fix him up an answer calling attention to the slowness of Congress to act on important measures and take him up on his attitude to UNRRA. HST*

Dear Senator Hawkes: *December 21, 1945*

Thank you for your letter of December fourteenth.

I am sure you understand that the postal system and the communication and transportation systems of Germany are in the state of total collapse. It has so far been impossible to set up any general integrated postal system for the whole of Germany.

While the situation in this respect in the American zone is better than in other zones, there is as yet no possibility of making deliveries of individual packages in Germany.

Our efforts have been directed particularly toward taking care of those who fought with us rather than against us—Norwegians, Belgians, the Dutch, the Greeks, the Poles, the French. Eventually the enemy countries will be given some attention.

While we have no desire to be unduly cruel to Germany, I cannot feel any great sympathy for those who caused the death of so many human beings by starvation, disease and outright murder, in addition to all the regular destruction and death of war. Perhaps eventually a decent government can be established in Germany so that Germany can again take its place in the family of nations. I think that in the meantime no one should be called upon to pay for Germany's misfortunes except Germany itself.

Until the misfortunes of those whom Germany oppressed and tortured and obliviated, it does not seem right to divert our efforts to Germany itself. I admit that there are, of course, many innocent people in Germany who had little to do with Nazi terror. However, the administrative burden of trying to locate those people and treat them differently from the rest is one which is almost insuperable.

Very sincerely,
HARRY S. TRUMAN

The senator was less than happy with Truman's response and immediately released his letter to the press in an effort to bring additional pressure to bear on the "mean spirited" Missourian. Hawkes's effort was generally ignored, and what feedback Truman did receive was laudatory.

Dear Sir;   *February 8, 1946*

The Society for the Prevention of World War III* extends its <u>congratulations to you on your letter of December 21st to Senator Hawkes of New Jersey</u>. You have decisively refuted the argument of pro-German elements who are promoting the crusade of "Food and Mail to Germany."

The policies you have outlined in the above letter will most certainly go a long way in dispelling the hopes of the pro-Germans that the United States will afford "special treatment" to those who have murdered so many of our boys. It was a telling blow against the propaganda machine of the pro-Germans which has been working assiduously for the perversion of American ideals of humanity. That propaganda is a camouflage for their aim to revive a strong and aggressive Germany.

With one hand this propaganda attempts to whip up sympathy for the Germans and with the other endeavors to open the mails so that the "Fatherland" can be deluged with anti-American, anti-Semitic and anti-UNO [United Nations Organization] propaganda. Your letter serves notice to the pro-German cabals that the United States Government does not intend to become the victim in this dangerous game.

The Society for the Prevention of World War III is gratified to note your wise and courageous stand on this question and we assure you that you have the full support of a great majority of the American people.

---

*The Society for the Prevention of World War III was briefly active after the Second World War. Its membership included an extremely long list of individuals involved in the arts, academia, and religion, including Frederick W. Foerster, historian Allan Nevins, film producer Darryl F. Zanuck, novelist Mary Ellen Chase, William Shirer, and fellow war correspondent Quentin Reynolds (who several years later would win what was then a massive award, $176,000, in a libel suit against Truman's Hearst Newspapers antagonist, Westbrook Pegler). Rex Stout, best known as the author of the Nero Wolfe detective series, was the organization's president.

Thank you for your interest in our common cause.

> *Respectfully yours,*
> *The Society for the Prevention of World War III*
> *Miriam Stuart*
> *Executive Secretary*
> *New York, New York*

Dear Miss Stuart: *February 13, 1946*

Please accept the President's thanks for your letter of February eighth. He is very glad to have your approval of the position he outlined in the letter to Senator Hawkes of New Jersey which you cite.

> *Very sincerely yours,*
> WILLIAM D. HASSETT

As the situation stabilized in Germany, the U.S. military government steadily released former German soldiers back into the population after determining that they were not guilty of any war crimes. The youngest soldiers, in their mid and even early teens, were some of the first to be paroled. Most had been hastily drafted in the final days of the war and were not the fanatical members of the Hitler Youth organizations that the Nazi propaganda machine had so effectively publicized. It was believed that they posed no threat to the U.S. occupation forces—who were responsible for feeding them while they were prisoners of war, so they were set free and subjected only to the same restrictions as the rest of the population. Two doctors in New York thought this and the subsequent release of even more POWs was a terrible idea and fired off a telegram to Truman. Hassett decided that it should be forwarded to the U.S. military governor in Germany, Lt. Gen. Lucius B. Clay, whose address was obtained and written at the bottom of a carbon copy.

THE PRESIDENT:

WE ARE EXTREMELY DISTURBED BY CLAY'S LATEST STUPIDITY IN GRANTING AMNESTY TO MILLION YOUNG NAZIS. DARE WE BECOME SOFT TOWARDS THESE GERMANS WHO MADE POSSIBLE BELSEN AND BUCHENWALD. CLAY'S PRESENT ACTION AND PAST RECORD FORCE US TO URGE HIS IMMEDIATE REMOVAL.

ALFRED A. BOLOMEY AND

HENRY D. LAUSON, M.D.

NEW YORK, NEW YORK

German recovery was severely complicated by many factors, including the country's division into four occupation zones, which were administered by the French, British, Soviet, and U.S. militaries, and the destruction wrought on its cities and industries during the last year of the war. Money was practically worthless in the immediate postwar economy, and it was increasingly difficult to get industry back on its feet as Soviet authorities flooded their zone with paper currency of an almost identical design to that being issued in the U.S. and British zones. German citizens resorted to a barter system to acquire nearly all basic goods and luxury items, and even the U.S. military government found itself in the embarrassing position of having to officially sanction and take part in the system. Many soldiers took advantage of the chaos, actively engaging in the flourishing black market of stolen and misappropriated goods, and some reaped huge financial gains.

> *My dear Mr. President:*   *February 18, 1947*
>   If the stories being told by the men returning from the <u>occupation zone in Germany</u> are true, it is enough to make decent minded citizens of America hang their heads in shame. What is wrong with the administration of our overseas forces? Surely you can do something to check those individuals who, because of circumstances, make a profit out of human misery.
> *Sincerely yours,*
> *A. V. Borkey, Director*
> *Fort Dix Young Men's Christian Association*
> *Wrightstown, New Jersey*

Within the United States, the transition from an economy geared to support a massive war effort to one of peace was accomplished with comparative ease, although to Americans chafing from half a decade of rationing and price stabilization, the changes seemed either jarring or agonizingly slow. By the end of 1946, price controls had been lifted from thousands of items, and rationing was almost completely gone.

One woman, not knowing what she should do with her leftover books of ration coupons, placed them into an envelope addressed simply "Washington D.C. Attention Mr. Truman (President)," with a return address at the Fairoaks Hospital in Pasadena, California. Her name was Mary Staley Soon, and she had been issued them for her then infant son, Richard—a strapping twenty-eight-inch, twenty-pounder at nine months—in 1943 or early 1944. The envelope and its contents were shuffled over to Matt Connelly's office, which was apparently having some clerical problems at that time, and her last name was left off both the letter for his signature and the address on the return mail.

My dear Mrs. Staley: *February 4, 1948*
    In as much as there was no letter of explanation accompanying the books which you forwarded to the President, I am returning them to you herewith.

Very sincerely yours,
MATTHEW J. CONNELLY

The post office was unable to deliver Connelly's letter and the ration books, which were returned to the White House about two weeks later. When the contents were rechecked, it was noticed that the young woman's last name had been omitted. The contents were repackaged and mailed again on February 20, this time not to the return address, but to the five-year-old address on one of the books. Moreover, the last name of Soon, which was clearly written in several places on the original materials, became "Loon" on the new address label and internal White House memoranda. It was returned a second time and placed in the files.

A man from Ashland, Ohio, felt so overwhelmed with guilt over having used gasoline ration tickets that weren't issued to him—an activity that could result in the censure of patriotic citizens, a stiff fine, and even jail time—that he probably would have returned them, too, if they hadn't been used up long before. Instead, he unburdened himself to Truman.

Dear Mr. President: *February 10, 1947*
    This letter may seem like a trivial thing to you, but to a man with a guilty conscience, and to one who is endeavoring to live for, and to serve God the following is not a trivial matter.
    First I wish to state that I am writing this confession to you because of your high office, and because you represent the people of the United States of America against whom I have sinned. I firmly believe in the old doctrine of confession and restitution so hear me patiently.
    During the last war I was engaged in full time Christian work as a missionary of a well-known Sunday school organization. My task was to open Sunday schools where there was no other means of religious education. Wherever I organized a Sunday school, I then assumed the duties of a pastor in that neglected community. This

work included preaching services, conducting Sunday schools, business meetings, home visitations, etc.

This work naturally required a good many miles a month of traveling. The local board would only allow me four hundred and fifty miles a month. This was only about a third of what I actually needed. I appealed to the district board in Detroit, and they upheld the decision of the local board. I then appealed to the regional board, and they upheld the decision of the district board but also stated that the local board could reconsider the case and grant the gasoline if they saw fit. The local board refused to act.

At that time the local rationing board was in an upheaval. The district board had installed a new head clerk and a few other employees. This created two factions in the board, and the situation was never cleared up to my knowledge. I found myself right in the midst of the whole thing. At the time I was working for the price control board checking prices in outlying stores and meat markets in the county. In my regular work I passed through many of the small towns in the county, and it would only be a matter of minutes to stop in a store and check prices. Working for the price control board placed me on one of the warring factions on the local board. I soon resigned.

One of the clerks in the ration board told me that she knew definitely that I was being discriminated against because I was assisting the price control panel; therefore, I couldn't get more gas. Be that as it may.

Not being able to get more gas, I began receiving offers of both gas and tickets from friends, so I took them. I never bought tickets, but they were given to me. One man would buy the gas for me and turn in his tickets. Another was a farmer who told me to pull up to his pump and he would fill my tank. I never paid for the gas I received nor did I give him any tickets. On other occasions, folks gave me tickets and I purchased gas with them.

The entire time I was doing this I knew I was doing wrong, but I kept telling myself that it was all right because the board had discriminated against me. I couldn't quiet the voice of conscience then and I can't now; therefore, I am writing to you. Two years have gone by, and I still hear that small voice. I am asking you to forgive me for the thing I had done against the United States. I not only seek this from you as the representative of a great people, but I am also seeking God's forgiveness. I am a Christian, and I don't want this thing bothering me any longer. In order to be right with God, we must be right with our fellow men. A clear conscience is of great value. I want mine cleared.

Yours truly,
T. Elmer Johnson

More of the wartime emergency controls and war powers were lifted after Truman signed Decontrol Acts in March and July 1947. But despite his efforts to handle the changeover in a careful and systematic manner, commodity speculation and pent-up demand for goods long in short supply pushed prices higher and higher. Whether an American thought this was good or bad depended on his or her own situation.

Dear President Truman:

May I add my insistence to the many others received by you to please return rationing. I cannot feed my family much more than slop with prices the way they are now. Even if it means a Black Market, I see very little difference between Black Market operators and the Republican racketeers who, by their incredible greed have brought people like me to such a desperate situation.

Sincerely,
Mrs. Edward Calven
Hollywood, Calif.

Dear Mr. President: *January 13, 1948*

As a housewife who waited in long lines for hours, and then perhaps obtained a few oxtails, I am bitterly opposed to rationing, and black markets that just naturally go with it. If that is the only way the Administration can think of to bring prices down, it is a poor one to my way of thinking. Our country got along fine through all of its history without such methods, why is that the only way all of a sudden? I do not like to believe the things that Mr. Daniels [sic] of Texas says about Mr. Anderson,* but it is difficult sometimes to disbelieve. PLEASE NO RETURN TO RATIONING.

Cordially yours,
E. F. Bouton
Brooklyn, New York

---

*Clinton P. Anderson was then the secretary of agriculture and would be elected a senator from New Mexico later that year. His antagonist was Price Marion Daniel, a newspaper publisher in Texas and the state's attorney general, who would eventually follow Anderson into the Senate.

For some, the continuing squabble over price decontrol was of great importance. But as this telegram from a woman in "N. Y., City" indicates, the war's lingering effects involved more than the price of hamburger for others. The message was turned over to the War Department.

> HONORABLE HARRY S TRUMAN   MARCH 25, 1947
> AM INFORMED THAT <u>US ARMY AIR FORCES</u> AND GROUNDSMEN ARE MOVING BACK INTO <u>NEW GUINEA</u> THIS WEEK TO MAKE DETAILED MAPS FOR THE WAR DEPARTMENT OF CERTAIN SECTIONS. I WOULD PERSONALLY LIKE TO MAKE AN APPEAL THAT THE REGION KNOWN AS <u>HOLLANDIA</u> LEADING INTO <u>SHANGRILA VALLEY</u> BE INCLUDED IN THIS SURVEY AS MY HUSBAND <u>SGT. STEPHEN FRANKS</u> 33739544 WAS ONE OF AT LEAST 100 MEN AND TEN SHIPS REPORTED <u>MISSING</u> OVER THAT AREA FROM WHOM NOTHING HAS EVER BEEN HEARD NOR ANY DEFINITE INFORMATION RECEIVED. IT IS THE BELIEF OF MANY PERSONS THAT OUR BOYS MAY BE ALIVE IN THAT AREA AND FOR THIS REASON THIS PERSONAL APPEAL IS BEING MADE TO YOU PERSONALLY BY MANY OF THE PEOPLE CONCERNED.
> ANNA FRANKS.

Another letter suggested some form of recognition for an Illinois family that suffered three sons killed in the war. It was returned to Sen. Scott W. Lucas, who had originally forwarded his constituent's letter to the White House, when it was discovered that the family was only one of more than 7,000 to have lost two or more sons in the fighting. Matt Connelly had received the letter from Lucas and passed it on to Hassett for his opinion. Hassett then sent it to Lt. Col. R. B. Marlin in the War Department and received verification that the three sons of Mr. and Mrs. Raymond Sherman—Homer, Robert, and Donald—had indeed been killed in action.

The language in Marlin's memo gave Hassett the impression that the estimate of 7,000 included all the armed services. Such wording is commonly used, however, when referring to Army personnel alone. The War Department records available to Marlin at the time included only the Army and Army Air Force, and not the Navy, Marines, Coast Guard, and Merchant Marine. Consequently, the total figure actually is larger than what Hassett had before him.

July 26, 1946
MEMORANDUM FOR SECRETARY CONNELLY

Dear Matt:

I am afraid that Senator Scott Lucas took the easiest course by forwarding to you the request from Martin R. O'Brien, Aurora, Illinois, for a message of condolence to Mr. and Mrs. Raymond Sherman who lost three sons in the war.

Of course it is tragic that this worthy couple suffered so great a bereavement. I submit herewith draft of a proposed letter for the President's signature. However, I recommend that the letter should not be sent.

Colonel Marlin, in his memorandum to me, points out that although exact figures are unobtainable it is estimated that more than seven thousand families have lost two or more sons in the war.

In the circumstances I do not think we should single out one family for special recognition by the President. Such action would only cause the other families to feel that the President was unsympathetic toward them.

W. D. H.

Dear Senator: *July 30, 1946*

The President has received your letter with respect to a message to <u>Mr. and Mrs. Raymond Sherman</u> and the loss they have suffered during the war.

I know you will understand that there have been so many instances of this nature that it would be impossible for the President to single out one family for recognition of such losses. I regret, therefore, that it will not be possible to comply with the suggestion made to you by your good friend, <u>Mr. Martin R. O'Brien</u>.

With best wishes,
Sincerely yours,
MATTHEW J. CONNELLY
Secretary to the President

[Longhand] *Ret O'Brien's letter to Lucas*

For a former serviceman trying to restart his life after the war, the search for a job—any job—was the first order of business. Millions of others were in the same boat, however, and citizens across the country did what they could to help connect veterans with work. The enterprising chairman of a Jobs for Veterans Campaign in St. Louis thought that getting Truman to endorse their efforts was worth a try.

Dear Mr. President: *December 17, 1946*

As the No. 1 Missourian, our Committee would like to make a request of you, which we believe would enhance the chances of making our "Jobs for Veterans" Drive a real success here in St. Louis.

The pamphlet enclosed with this letter will outline the ideals and purpose of this drive, and you, as an ex-Army Veteran can appreciate the meritorious aims involved.

We would like to have a statement endorsing this Drive for Veterans from you as President and as a Missourian and would like to respectfully request that it be arranged that suitable publicity be given it.

May I take this opportunity of thanking you on behalf of all the veterans of St. Louis and surrounding areas who are in need of employment and being placed in the proper jobs for the gracious cooperation that we know you will extend to us in this endeavor.

Sincerely yours,
Henry W. Simpson
Jobs for Veterans Campaign
St. Louis, Mo.

Dear Mr. Simpson: *December 27, 1946*

This is in acknowledgement of your letter of December seventeenth addressed to the President requesting him to make a statement endorsing the local St. Louis campaign to obtain "Jobs for Veterans."

I need hardly tell you that the President has a warm spot in his heart for every enterprise looking to the welfare of Missouri or Missourians. May I explain to you, however, that these drives for jobs for veterans are happily being carried out in every part of the country. The President has heartily and with enthusiasm endorsed the campaign on a national basis.

It would not, however, be consistent for him to single out one local or community campaign for special recognition. Since he has not in a single instance written such a message as that which you request, I am sure you will appreciate the difficulty of making an exception.

> *Very sincerely yours,*
> *WILLIAM D. HASSETT*

A man in Brooklyn was outraged that Congress seemed so ungrateful for the sacrifices of those who had fought in the war and warned the president that he should expect to keep seeing letters from him until Truman did something about the situation.

> *Mr. President;*   *July 17, 1947*
> *Dear Friend:*
> I am writing to you because you entered office as the president at a crucial time. The greatest president of this century, Franklin D. Roosevelt passed away, leaving you, his successor, the presidency at a very crucial moment. Franklin D. Roosevelt was whole heartedly for our country's fighting forces, now the American veteran.
>
> The veteran is my main reason for writing now. The Congress of today has passed a bill for a 15 percent increase of rent. The veteran has had enough fighting, how about making an effort to help today's vets?
>
> I am not a veteran, just the president of the Junior and Senior Airclub, known as the J. & S. A —J S A. I want the returned veteran to have a fair deal. Mr. President, how about getting down to brass tax [*sic*]. Get a move on and stop this Congress from doing the rottenest thing ever.
>
> Please see what you can do. I shall keep writing until you do something for the vets.
>
> > *Yours truly,*
> > *Mr. Isadore Don*
> > *Pres. of J. & S. A.*
> > *Brooklyn, New York*

Requests for the president's help on disputed benefits claims were forwarded to the Veterans Administration in Washington. From there, they were invariably sent to the very office that was being complained about in the first place. This so outraged one former soldier from Chicago that he wrote an angry letter to Truman on the back of a form letter that read: "This will acknowledge receipt of your communication dated September 27, 1947, which was addressed to the President of the United States. Your communication has been referred for consideration and reply to the office having jurisdiction, the Veterans Administration, Regional Office, 366 West Adams Street, Chicago 6, Illinois. Fl8-55, May 1946 replaces Form 680 which may be used. Dir., Veterans Claims Service." The envelope was addressed to "HARRY S. TRUMAN (Personal)" by the disgusted vet.

> Mr. President: Oct. 15, 1947
>
> Why direct these communications to the Veterans Administration which is bound in red tape and functioning under obsolete laws. It is your duty to recommend to the Congress new laws or advise so that justice can be done to Veterans of both World Wars No. 1 and No. 2.
>
> The people are getting fed up on political hypocrisy and political buck-passing. It would be better for the United States if you gave your time and attention to the business of the people who elected you. You have definitely no business in Europe and should keep out of their damnable politics. Let the whole damn bunch of them stew in their own juice and they won't be so damned ready to start another war. You were elected by the people of the U.S. Give your time and attention to their business—that is what you were elected for.
>
>   Walter Mathiesen
>   Chicago, Ill

Offers to help veterans poured into the White House in the years immediately after World War II and increased again during the Korean War. But the White House had neither the staff nor the time to act as anything more than a conduit to route individuals' letters to agencies that might or might not be able to help, and it had no real ability to match up requests with offers. In September 1951, Clarence A. Runte, president of the Badger State Dental Laboratory in Milwaukee, Wisconsin, offered to furnish ten sets of dentures a month to the Army at no charge. Hassett thanked him for his generous offer and passed it on to the Defense Department. Several months earlier, a letter had arrived from Mrs. William B. Ward of Tampa, who asked Truman's help getting dental work for her husband. Hassett, writing from the presidential retreat at the Key West Naval Base, assured her that the request was being forwarded to the Veterans Administration. In another instance, a woman seeking assistance for her husband wrote in her native

Hungarian, and Hassett's staff had to send it to the State Department's Division of Language Services.

> TRANSLATOR'S SUMMARY OF COMMUNICATION
> Language: Hungarian
> Date of communication: No date. [April 1948]
> Addressed to: The President
> Name and address of writer: Mrs. C. M. Harris
> > Sail River Camp
> > Port Angeles, Washington
>
> Substance of writer's statement:
>
> The writer was born in the United States, but brought up in Hungary. She is married to a young timber cutter and lives with him in a cabin on the shore of Puget Sound. They are too poor to afford even a coal range such as most of their neighbors possess. During the 3½ years her husband spent in the Army, his heart and kidneys became affected, so that he has been ordered to change to a less strenuous occupation. His greatest desire is to own a fishing boat, but he is unable to buy one.
>
> Since the President earns "millions and billions of dollars" and has many wealthy friends, he ought to welcome the opportunity for a good deed. He should send the writer's husband a twin-engined fishing boat with housekeeping facilities. As the nearest store is ten miles distant, the writer also asks the President to send her an automobile.

Whereas ongoing food shortages were a very real concern, they also offered Truman an opportunity to do away with a Washington tradition that had grown way out of hand, the annual rolling of Easter eggs down the White House lawn. Periodic Easter egg hunts had been held on the grounds, beginning with Dolley Madison in the early nineteenth century, but it was Lucy, wife of Rutherford B. Hayes, who initiated the first presidential egg rolling in 1878. The event grew steadily over the years, until as Eleanor Roosevelt recalled, it eventually drew more than 53,000 children, parents, and onlookers to the south lawn. The result: "180 children were lost and found; two people were sent to the emergency hospital; six people fainted and twenty had to be treated for small abrasions."[1]

The last event had been held in 1941, after which it was canceled for security reasons during the war years. The prospect that the grounds might soon be overrun again was not a pleasant one for the White House staff, which had to organize, supervise, and clean up behind the event, and head usher Howell Crim officially recommended that it be dropped. Although the Interior Department confirmed that the whole affair had gotten to be quite a mess, they were more than willing to get together with Crim and forge ahead if the president so desired. Truman, however, pulled the plug, yet tried to do so in a way that would reinforce one of the administration's current themes:

IMMEDIATE RELEASE   *April 10, 1946*

The Easter Monday egg rolling in the White House grounds, in abeyance during the war years, will not be resumed this year.

This decision is in line with suggestions received from many thoughtful persons who have urged the necessity for food conservation at this time. Food continues to be Europe's most critical need. The food crisis is acute also in Asia—in fact in most of the countries of the world.

The President has made repeated appeals for the conservation of food—through personal sacrifice where necessary—in order that starving millions all over the face of the earth may be given a diet that will sustain life.

In the circumstances it is felt that the waste of so valuable a food product as eggs would not be consistent with the effort to feed starving millions and that the Nation's capital should set the rest of the country a good example in food conservation.

Eggs were indeed a scarce commodity at that time, and Truman may have genuinely thought that the event was a useless waste of time. The statement, however, had the look and feel of what a later generation of Americans would call "spin control." Many believed that they could see right through it.

Dear Mr. Truman: *April 10, 1946*

I've just heard over the radio that you do not intend to have the old tradition of egg rolling on the White House lawn this year. I was really disappointed when I heard this. You said that Europe must be fed and this would not be proper. Wasn't there just as much starving people (as the newspapers claim) during the war as there is now? I would think there would be less now. I am not against helping the people of Europe, but so far as I know, there has been plenty of eggs; in fact, more than there was during the war. I don't think the eggs will be wasted, for many children look forward each year just to this event.

So please don't break the tradition of egg rolling.

Sincerely yours,
Evelyn Wash
Fords, New Jersey

P.S. I don't think those eggs that would be used for egg rolling will make Europeans starve. Do you?

The seemingly plausible story that Harry's wife, Bess, was behind the cancellation also began to circulate.

Mrs. Truman:

Was indeed surprised when I read that you as the first lady of the land, called off the Easter egg hunt which our *American* children have enjoyed.

I, being an American born and raised in the USA, when I see what the president spends for the European people, especially at present, it may lead to another war with his meddling.

Your excuse is there are too many poor people hungry, but you surely do not mean us *Americans,* when your dear husband just destroyed so many carloads of potatoes here in Florida; these potatoes could well have been given to the poor. You speak of saving a few dollars for eggs, which our *American* children may enjoy on Easter, when our president is squandering millions on foreigners.

Yours truly,
Mrs. Josephine Powell
Hollywood, Florida

The main reason Appointments Secretary Matthew Connelly gave Acting Secretary of the Interior Oscar Chapman for discontinuing the Easter tradition was the "torn-up condition of the grounds" (which actually affected only a very small area) during some badly needed maintenance on the White House. The dilapidated central structure, the Executive Mansion, had started receiving piecemeal repairs soon after Truman was sworn in, but virtually anything done to it attracted attention—and criticism. When one looks at the letters that were coming in over the relatively minor upgrades, which immediately preceded the Easter egg flap, it is easy to see why Truman's staff thought the egg-shortage story would fly.

Dear Sir: *Jan. 12, 1946*

The morning paper announced plans for extensive repair and improvement to the White House, which no one would be anything but glad to have done ordinarily. However, when materials and labor are so scarce, is it setting a good precedent for the country to approve unnecessary use of scarce items when thousands desperately need adequate housing?

Furthermore, it seems only fair that all public or business construction, new or remodeling—banks, hospitals, schools—should be held up to give precedence to home building. By making materials available strictly for new housing or enlargement of old housing to accommodate other persons, would not today's desperate need for living space be more quickly met?

I wish to urge continuance of O.P.A. [Office of Price Administration] in price control and especially as to rents. Living costs are about to swamp a great many of us as it is; without O.P.A. protection we couldn't afford a single room apartment!

Sincerely,
(Mrs.) Mildred Spears
Lookout Mountain, Tenn.

Dear Mr. President: *Jan. 14, 1946*

For the past year and a half, I have been trying to build a house so I may have room for my son, returning from service in May. With all of the government "red tape," material shortages, high labor costs, etc., I have had quite a struggle. Now I must pay my income tax, and from that tax money, $1,650,000.00 is to be spent enlarging the White House!

As a taxpayer, I protest this move at this time! It is taking an unfair advantage of position.

Sincerely,
Clara M. Locke
Memphis, Tenn.

Dear Mr. President: *Jan. 29, 1946*

It is a little difficult to understand why you, a very temporary resident of the White House, should feel that you have the right to make changes in a building in no way belonging to you, but that *does* belong to the American people.

The House of Washington, Jefferson, Lincoln, and all our *real* statesmen, is beloved by all native Americans, and they are enraged at the suggestion even, of adding a cafeteria, radio station, amusement hall, or even offices, built with the taxpayers' money and without asking their consent.

Even the excavation for this outrage was put over without the country knowing of it.

Must you make yourself more unpopular week by week by doing stupid things of this kind?

> *Yours truly,*
> *Caroline Fox*
> *New York, New York*

The haughty members of the Georgetown Garden Club took a somewhat different tack, professing concern that Truman might "mar the structure." However, claims that the group was motivated to write because of fears that the work would "detract from the value of the White House as a home and a symbol of democracy" had the ring of busybodies fearful that their new neighbor from Missouri was a vulgar little man who would make their own property values sink.

Dear Mr. Pesident: *January 21, 1946*

The Georgetown Garden Club has instructed me, on the behalf of the Executive Commitee, to communicate to you the opinion <u>of that organization regarding the proposed additions to the White House</u>.

While we recognize the increased demands on the executive branch of the government, <u>we feel that any changes in the White House to provide more space can only be regarded as a serious violation of the character of that building</u>, as the residence of the head of a great democratic country. The White House, beautiful as it is architecturally, is much more than a building. In its simplicity it epitomizes in the minds of most of the citizens of this country the friendliness of the Chief Executive for the people whom he represents. It now has a gracious quality befitting this relationship. To mar the structure with additions, however desirable for convenience, would in our estimation detract from the value of the White House as a home and as a symbol of democracy.

In this respect, we feel that its unpretentious quality is in most favorable contrast with the grandeur of the palaces of other chiefs of state.

We urgently request that the plans for additions be abandoned and that a solution of the problem of office space be found through some other means.

This request is most respectfully submitted.

> Respectfully yours,
> Mrs. Carroll Greenough, President
> Georgetown Garden Club

But if the good ladies of Georgetown had to suffer through the president's obvious disregard of their enlightened opinion, they were about to get another shock. Every summer for nearly a 120 years, the south side of the Executive Mansion had sprung awnings to shade its rooms from the blistering sun. Truman did not like awnings and was particularly repulsed by the seven large ones, which, "attached about half way up the beautiful columns looked always as if they'd caught all the grime and dirt in town."[2] Eventually he hit upon an idea that would both get rid of the eyesore and also provide the family with a place to relax outdoors "without 20,000 people staring at them."[3] Borrowing from Thomas Jefferson's use of galleries behind the columned buildings at the University of Virginia, Truman proposed that a balcony be built out from the second-floor Oval Study, to shade the Blue Room below.

> *My dear Mr. President:*   *November 26, 1947*
> Last summer, at the invitation of the Chief Usher, certain members of the Commission of Fine Arts visited the White House to review proposed plans for a second floor porch on the south portico. At that meeting it was suggested by the representatives of the Commission that before anything is done it would be desirable to have the recommendation of one of the country's outstanding architects, one thoroughly familiar with the White House. Several names were suggested and William Adams Delano, Esq.* of New York, who some years ago developed plans for the addition of a fourth floor in the White House and who had served on the Commission of Fine Arts and later on the National Capital Park and Planning Commission, was invited to report upon the matter. The Commission were

---

*William Adams Delano, a cousin of Franklin Delano Roosevelt and member of the National Commission of Fine Arts, was one of the most highly respected architects in America. His designs included enlargements to the U.S. and Virginia military academies and the Japanese Embassy and Carnegie Institute buildings in Washington, as well as La Guardia Airport and numerous other prestigious construction projects in New York City.

astonished when informed that Mr. Delano gave his endorsement to the proposed project and indicated that, in his judgment, the porch would not in any way detract from the dignity of the south portico. Frankly, the Commission rather expected that Mr. Delano would recommend against the proposed change.

Subsequently, at a meeting in Washington on August 28, 1947, the Commission gave careful consideration to the question of erecting a porch on the south portico of the White House and the Chairman was directed to address a letter to the Chief Usher, from whom the request for advice was received, opposing the project. The last paragraph of this communication stated in part that "the Commission of Fine Arts have given this matter most careful and thoughtful consideration and they are hopeful that the President will not make a formal request to change the exterior of the White House."

The Commission still feel that a porch would seriously mar not only the south portico but as well the entire south facade. A window would have to be cut down to provide a door to the porch, which in itself would materially change the design of this, the most notable of American historic monuments. If these proposed alterations are made they will be the first substantial ones in the exterior of the central element of the White House in 118 years or since the addition of the north portico in 1829 which, we have every reason to believe, was a part of James Hoban's original design.

In the circumstances the Commission are confident that the stand they have taken in this matter is thoroughly sound and consequently they hope that, in the interest of preserving the integrity of the original design of the White House, the President will abandon the project.

> *Most sincerely and respectfully,*
> *For the Commission of Fine Arts*
> *Gilmore D. Clarke, Chairman*
> *Washington, D.C.*

My dear Mr. Clarke: *December 2, 1947*

I read your letter of November twenty-sixth with a great deal of interest and some surprise.

My understanding was when the matter was discussed with you with regard to the arrangement on the south portico that when Mr. Delano made up his mind, the situation would be satisfactory to you. Now you confess that you hoped he would make up his mind in a manner that you approved of and that you didn't enter into the matter at all with an open mind—that is a great statement for the Chairman of The Commission of Fine Arts to send to the President.

I can't understand your viewpoint when those dirty awnings are a perfect eyesore with regard to that south portico. I have had them painted; have had them washed and they have been renewed every year and they still look like hell when they are on the porch.

Of course, I wouldn't expect you to take into consideration the comfort and convenience of the Presidential family in this arrangement. The President is not to be considered but the outside appearance of the White House it seems to me is your principal reason for existence, and I can't see how anybody could come to a conclusion that those dirty awnings are better looking than an arrangement which is approved by the White House architect and by Mr. Delano.

I certainly would like to have your reasons for preferring the dirty awnings to the good looking convenient portico and then maybe I'll come to a conclusion on the subject. I don't make my mind up in advance. However, I'll have to be convinced.

Sincerely yours,
HARRY S. TRUMAN

Truman found it bordering on the bizarre that the Fine Arts Commission—or anyone—could prefer the use of the unsightly awnings, which put "the beautiful columns out of proportion."[4] And besides, the awnings were no more a part of James Hoban's original design than the proposed balcony. Truman decided to proceed with the addition, on the strength of Delano's hearty approval. But though the endorsement from the highly respected Delano prompted the commission to refrain from *public* expressions of criticism, some members made sure to voice their opinions to the movers and shakers in Washington. Said daughter Margaret, "You would have thought he had just announced he was going to replace the White House with a lean-to or a split-level bungalow, to hear the howls from Congress and the press."[5] Truman understood that anything could be jumped on during an election year, but he was genuinely surprised at the volume of the furor.

Dear President: January 8, 1948
I would like to know if it is Necessary to have the New Porch put onto the WHITE HOUSE. Why not put some of that fifteen thou-

sand dollars into some homes for the men that fought in the war and are now homeless.

Did it ever come to your mind that this November is election and after that I am quite sure that you will have no use for the Porch. Maybe the New President would like a porch there. So why don't you wait and let the new President decide for himself whether he wants a porch. Some of us fellows have worked hard, and that takes a lot of our income tax to build a porch like that. So why don't you postpone the work until after election.

> *Yours truly,*
> *A Former Democrat*
> *Fred Tunningley*
> *Linden, Mich.*

Honorable President Truman: Jan. 14, 1948

Instead of spending fifteen thousand dollars to construct a porch to the White House, don't you believe it would show more consideration and appreciation to our Veteran boys who have no place to live, and whom the construction men are selling flimsy constructed houses to for about double their cost to spend this amount of money to find out just how these boys are being robbed?

It's really a shame to take advantage of these young innocent boys in the manner in which many dealers have.

If our boys had not given their lives and time, these swindlers that stayed home in safety would now be under a government where they would have found out what it means to have a country of freedom and plenty for all. The money did not pay the price or save our country; it was the boys who faced the battle and now should be treated so that they may now be able to enjoy a home and rest in peace instead of a few money hogs getting it all.

> *Very sincerely,*
> *Leonard F. Dawson*
> *Denver, Colo.*

Another letter criticizing the president quickly evolved into a discussion of the economy centering on tax policy and the European Recovery Program (ERP) or Marshall Plan.

Dear Sir: *January 25, 1948*

I write to <u>protest against the structural change in the White House south portico</u>—this belongs to the American people and you are only a *very* temporary tenant and you have not—as yet—*ever* been elected *President.* As architects are against this change, you should abandon your plans. I say you are temporarily a tenant because I think your poorly advised vetos of a tax revision in our terrific war time taxes (income tax and others) will lose for you the election come Nov. 6, 1948. Your proposed $40 a person tax cut is unsatisfactory. We want a genuine 30% tax slash together with the *community* property tax plans—but of course you are against any relief for the American— only a huge *"dole"* for Europe—E.R.P. I hope and pray our intelligent Congress will prune the spendthrift Marshall Plan by 40% and your 1948 superduper budget by a good $5 billion. Some thrift in Washington would quickly *deflate* this "Truman Inflation" we are enjoying as well as strict curb on labor demands. *No more strikes or increased wages for a year.*

But Mr. President, please don't veto any more tax bills; it's cruel and unnecessary. You will have more tax income with lower taxes through more business.

Respectfully yours,
Ronald C. Campbell
North Plainfield, New Jersey

By far, the vast majority of letters came from women, specifically, housewives who had supported both Presidents Roosevelt and Truman through all the wartime rationing and shortages. Before that they had scrimped during the depression. Now they were fighting their new enemy—inflation. Consequently, news of the balcony struck a raw nerve. Here they were living in cramped quarters with their growing families and husbands whose salaries were barely meeting the cost of living. These housewives were not going to sit quietly by while this porch addition became a reality.

Mr. H. Truman,   *Jan. 16, 1948*

No doubt you will never see this letter but could not resist to tell you what I and hundreds of other citizens of this country think of you and your <u>wild-hair idea</u> of adding to the White House, especially at this time. Every day you scream yourself hoarse about saving food, help to save the peace, and then you go and spend unnecessarily on a new addition to satisfy your own whims, which no other President has found need of. Food is too damn expensive for most of us to waste and no doubt myself and my husband could live as good as we do on what waste goes into the White House garbage can every day. The matter of installing a bathtub and electricity is an entirely different matter.

If the material used in the porch could have been used to build a veteran's home, I know for a fact it would have brought you many more votes, after all they are the ones who fought to keep the White House as it was.

As far as we are concerned, the sooner you go back to the Missouri cornfields the better, that is about your speed of judgment. Why don't you practice what you preach?

Erma J. Thomas
San Diego, Calif.

Dear Mr. Truman   *Jan. 20, 1948*

I feel that it is my duty as an American citizen and taxpayer to tell you how disappointed I am in your choice of building a porch on the White House at this particular time.

You have asked the public to buy only necessities to order to help curb inflation.

Do you consider your porch a necessity this year? Don't you think a few years hence your same plans would be less expensive?

I sympathize with the fact that the President of the United States has a great burden and needs home-like relaxations. I believe that all of the other obstacles confronting you including architectural disputes can be overcome. You men with tired minds deserve a porch. But <u>NOT NOW</u>!!!

I am an average American citizen, twenty-six years old, wife of a former veteran that is a postal employee letter carrier, and the mother of four children under five years old.

I know I can adequately match your needs for a porch. I believe sincerely in my heart that I need a porch much more than you do. The estimate for my porch is $500 in comparison to your $18,000 estimate.

My husband's weekly salary is $53.00. We are just barely able to meet our current expenses. We find ourselves unable to give our children a good many necessities.

We would be contributing to inflationary forces by having a porch put on our little house. Now, because we certainly would not be able to meet the payments on it in the future.

My two youngest children have not been out in the winter because I have no place to put a carriage and have it sheltered from all of the snow that is on the ground. I am trying to raise strong healthy Americans.

Mr. Truman, I resent greatly as a taxpayer, paying for a porch for you that you do not need nearly as much as millions of others.

Millions of more unfortunate taxpayers, I am sure, would be grateful if you would put that $18,000 toward their housing fund. I am sure they need homes more than you need a porch.

Yes, Mr. Truman, I am afraid that all of your smooth talk and supposed honesty in speeches that won me over has been erased. Why don't you "practice what you preach?" to quote a phrase.

Your porch has lost my vote for you.

> *Sincerely,*
> *Grace B. Miller*
> *Hartford, Conn.*

Dear Mr. President: *Jan. 23, 1948*

This morning reading the *Cleveland Plain Dealer* newspaper, I came across a picture of an artist's version of the future appearance of the White House with the balcony added. As the opinion of one person of our great United States, I would like to say that people are sure making a very to ado about the addition. I for one would like to say that this will sure be an improvement to the White House and for future use for years to come.

Now really Mr. President, if people would be more interested in world affairs concerning prices on food and etc., rather than carrying on about your affairs. Our loaf of bread probably wouldn't cost 20 cents today at least 5 cents more than it should be.

The working man and his family certainly can't live and provide the necessary things for his children with prices like this.

Let's do something about lowering prices and not trying to give the worker a raise. With a raise the prices will only go *higher* and *higher.*

> *Yours truly,*
> *Mrs. Carl E. Miller*
> *Lorain, Ohio*

Dear Mr. President: *Jan. 16, 1948*

I read in the paper a few weeks ago that the White House is to have a new porch at a cost of $15,000. I believe that the White House should be kept in perfect condition, but how in the world can we afford to do any building at this time?

We have a family of four lovely growing children. My husband is earning a salary in keeping with the times, but we just cannot seem to save any money to buy a house or build one. Homes that cost $10,000 or less to build 30 or 40 years ago are selling for twice the original cost with large down payments.

We are being evicted on May 1st, and like thousands of other Americans we *have no place to go.* I do not believe this condition is right or necessary in this great and prosperous land of ours, and I would like to know when something will be done about it. Adequate housing for all at prices we can afford to pay seems to me to be the most urgent problem that Uncle Sam must solve—*now.*

      Respectfully yours,
      Helen C. Bisley
      Oak Park, Ill.

Dear Sir: *Feb. 11, 1948*

I want to voice a protest against the use of lumber and labor to build a balcony on the White House.

Why should you use the lumber and labor for something as unnecessary as a balcony when lumber has been so scarce and high priced that for eight years I have climbed a ladder to the second floor.

We know people who are trying to make a home in a chicken coop because of the housing shortage. The lumber and labor that goes into building that balcony would build a home for some deserving G.I.

You wouldn't have a home in the White House if it weren't for our boys who left their homes to fight and protect this country. Everywhere we go the people are talking about how wasteful it is to build a balcony when housing is so scarce in this country.

Parents and children are being separated because they can't find homes. Even in this zero weather families are being evicted, a case near here with six children.

We are glad you don't have to live with your conscience.

Yours sincerely,
Mrs. W. G. Faustine
Mrs. J. H. Gehrfein
Erie, Pa.

Sir: *Jan. 8, 1948*

It is my earnest wish that you reconsider your plan to build a balcony on the White House. The people of the United States have a special feeling for this historic mansion, and any addition to the structure will ruin its appearance. Of course, the American people also do not like a "fait accompli"; they feel it is a betrayal of their confidence.

There are many ways in which this $15,000 could be used, not abroad but right in this United States of America, in helping those who are ill and will die because nothing can be done for them due to lack of funds.

Most respectfully yours,
(Miss) Helen Meyer
Spencer, N.Y.

My dear Mr. President: *Jan. 11, 1948*

I feel very strongly opposed to the change you are contemplating making in the structure of the White House by adding a second floor balcony.

That House belongs to the *nation,* not to you personally. The part of the year that it could be of any use to you to sit out on is just about four months. The White House is air-conditioned so that it is not uncomfortable for you even in the very warm months, and you can go into the mountains at the camp ex-President Hoover gave to the government if you want to be out in the open at night in the summer.

I think is is a very presumptuous and unwarranted step for you to take. I think it would spoil the appearance of the structure. I hope you will decide not to have it done.

Very truly yours,
(Miss) E. Matthews
Washington, D.C.

Numerous organizations, societies, and commercial architects also wrote to express their displeasure.

> *Mr. President:*   *Jan. 23, 1948*
> The Board of Managers of the <u>Colonial Dames of America</u>, which is a Society founded many years ago and dedicated among other things, to the preservation of mementoes of our historic past, has learned from the press with grave concern, of a proposed addition of a balcony to the south front of the White House.
> While the convenience of such a balcony may be conceded, the Board of Managers with all respect, Mr. President, regard such an addition to the White House as a defacement of an historic shrine. Such action, Mr. President, again with all respect, the Board of Managers regards as tantamount to vandalism, and it desires to file a vigorous protest against such action.
>
> > *Very respectfully,*
> > *Caroine Trevor*
> > *Corresponding Secretary*
> > *The Colonial Dames of America*
> > *New York, N.Y.*

> *Dear Mr. President:*   *Jan. 17, 1948*
> May I respectfully ask you to reconsider your decision in the matter of the Balcony, for the second floor of the White House, and to accept the ruling of the Fine Arts Commission.
> As an architect who has studied the Colonial Style and practiced it for twenty-five years, I am convinced that the balcony, as proposed will mar one of the finest public buildings which our country possesses.
>
> > *Very sincerely yours,*
> > *Otto Langmann*
> > *Architect*
> > *New York, N.Y.*

A Jefferson scholar at the Philadelphia Museum of Art couldn't have disagreed more, however, and sent one of the very few letters praising Truman's addition. It arrived when the President and various senior staff were vacationing at the Little White House in Florida, and Hassett immediately handed it over to his boss.

Dear Mr. President: *February 26, 1948*

May I take the liberty of writing you that I am one of those who view the new balcony at the White House with approval.

As you doubtless know, the south portico of the White House was an addition proposed by Jefferson. It happens that I have written a volume dealing with Jefferson as an architect. It was Jefferson who, in America, popularized the type of the tall portico. In designing the University of Virginia he faced exactly the problem you now face at the White House, namely, to gain privacy for the family, sitting out of doors, when the main floor of the porticos was overrun by the public. He solved this at the University by adopting a hanging balcony under the portico. I am sure he would have approved your balcony at the White House, so admirably carried out by Mr. Delano.

> *Yours sincerely,*
> *Fiske Kimball*
> *Director, Philadelphia Museum of Art*

Dear Mr. Kimball: *February 29, 1948*

I can't tell you how very much I appreciate your thoughtfulness in taking time out to write me about the balcony in the White House. I am very happy that you approve it.

I think it will add to the architectural symmetry of the White House, and that is the only reason in the world that I wanted to have it built. The awnings on those columns absolutely distorted their proportions.

I was not thinking of my own comfort when the program was inaugurated.

> *Sincerely yours,*
> *HARRY S. TRUMAN*
> *Submarine Base, Key West, Florida*

Truman later maintained that he had known all along that there would be an outcry over the addition. "It didn't surprise me a bit," he said. "That was an election year if you recall. And anyway people get in an uproar whenever any change is suggested in the White House. My goodness, when Mrs. Fillmore wanted to put in bathtubs, the way people screamed and carried on you'd have thought it was the end of the world, but, of course, eventually everybody calmed down."[6] Truman told both his staff and family that once the balcony was completed, people would like how it "broke the skinny perpendicular lines"[7] of the portico columns, and it wasn't long before he was proved right, as the much-maligned project began to receive grudging approval from the public and press.

> *Dear Mr. President:*   *April 28, 1948*
>
> I have just compared pictures of the White House, <u>before the balcony</u> was added and <u>after</u>. I have read for weeks criticism directed against your person because of this balcony. I am only one of millions of plain citizens who also have read of and heard this criticism.
>
> May I be so bold to say that I think that <u>you have done a nice piece of work</u>, which truly has brought about a <u>decided improvement in the looks of the White House</u>. I have deeply resented and do deeply deplore this foolish criticism and I want you to know that at least one man feels it's way past time we got behind our President to work hard for our country in every constructive way possible, instead of throwing destructive crititism at him for every minor action.
>
> I am nominally a Republican, but I am beginning to find myself pulling for you for four more years in the better appearing White House.
>
>   *Respectfully,*
>   *Roy A. Barton*
>   *Caribou, Maine*
>
> May God Bless and Guide You!

> *My dear Mr. Barton:*   *May 3, 1948*
>
> Your friendly letter of April twenty-eighth has been received. Please be assured that the confidence in the President's leadership which your words imply is deeply appreciated.
>
>   *Very sincerely yours,*
>   *WILLIAM D. HASSETT*
>   *Secretary to the President*

> *Dear Mr. President:*   *March 28, 1948*
>
> The <u>news that</u> your balcony on the south porch of the White House <u>is completed is welcome, indeed</u>. May you and your family enjoy it to the fullest extent and forget that any citizens were so lacking in understanding as to voice opposition to the project.

It is a pity that some one years ago did not think of adding to the residence such a necessary haven of relaxation for our Presidents.

I admire your good judgment in conceiving the plan and your calm dignity in seeing that it was accomplished.

Sincerely and respectfully yours,
Anna G. Kummel
Trenton, N.J.

Dear Mrs. Kummel: *March 28, 1948*

Thank you for your kind letter of March twenty-eighth, addressed to the President, which has come for me for acknowledgement.

It was good of you to write and, I assure you, the President is gratified to receive such sympathetic expression of your views.

Sincerely yours,
CHARLES G. ROSS

While the storm over the "Truman balcony" came and went, other, seemingly inconsequential, matters over which the president had no control would simmer for years. Near the end of the Roosevelt administration, the Army Air Force made a shining, new C-54 aircraft available for occasions when the president needed quick transport. The plane required meticulous care, and ground personnel, mindful that Hindus venerate cattle, began calling it a "sacred cow," as in the dictionary definition "a thing regarded as sacrosanct and immune from violation." Reporters almost immediately picked up on this and used the term as a way to add a bit more color to their stories. Within a very short time, virtually everyone, including the White House staff and Truman's own daughter, Margaret, was calling it "The Sacred Cow." This had gone on for many months with nary a word of protest before the first critical letters appeared.

Dear Mr. President: *December 28, 1945*

I enclose a clipping from this morning's *New York Times* in which the presidential airplane is referred to as the "Sacred Cow." Also I have heard this name used several times on the radio recently when speaking of the president's airplane. This seems to me to be discourteous to the President of the United States on the part of the press and radio as well as ridicule of a religious belief of millions of people in India—the Hindus. Needless to say, these same press and radio people would *never dare* to refer to the President's official airplane as the "Holy Ghost." Yet they freely make fun of Hindu religious belief. I believe those smart alecks of the press and the radio have a well deserved trip to the woodshed coming to them. I hope that they soon get it and from the decent members of the press and radio. It surprised me to see the *New York Times* printing this kind of corny humor. This shows how well the smart alecks of the press and radio have been able to spread around their gag in ridicule of a very ancient religious belief.

I have made twenty-five trips around the world for my employer —a travel firm directing world cruises. Of the several thousands of American world travelers who have accompanied me, I have never seen more than a half dozen in all who ever were deliberately disrespectful of sacred places and sacred things in foreign lands. Maybe when the boys of the press and radio get around a little more they will be less inclined to indulge in that kind of humor.

Respectfully yours,
Robert A. Grimsel
New York, N.Y.

Dear Mr. Grimsel: *January 9, 1946*
Your letter of December twenty-eighth, addressed to the President, has come to me for reply.

The concern you express over the name that has been applied to the airplane used by the President is understandable, and I assure you the interest which prompted you to write is appreciated. You are entirely correct, of course, in your assumption that the name "Sacred Cow" is entirely unauthorized and unsanctioned.

This plane is a C-54 that has been used for some time, not only by the President, but for various government officials and employees on official missions and trips. It has had no official name other than the technical designation of its type—C-54, and the origin of the appellation to which you refer in your letter is not known here.

Sincerely yours,
CHARLES G. ROSS

Honorable Sir: *May 29, 1946*
I believe it will encourage you to know that thousands of Americans are praying and fighting to retain our glorious heritage, and that God protect us from error. It must be admitted that too many

have too much money to think about praying or America and do nothing.

Please <u>permit me to protest the name of Sacred Cow for your plane</u>. One would think you were an Indian (not American Indian either). This causes offense to God and man, a Cow or a plane cannot be sacred. We cannot expect God to bless us when we willfully violate the very first commandment.

<u>May we urge that the policy of raising prices</u> for all groups if it continues can only bring us chaos. What we need to arrive at is a living standard at a REASONABLE LEVEL.

Justice must be placed back on the pedestal. People must be able to respect the sound judgment of courts and the heads of our nation. If it is proper for me to satisfy my differences with a fellow American through the medium of the courts then labor and other similar groups must also do so. <u>When we fail to settle human affairs through courts and resort to strikes</u> we are tearing down the three fundamental and proper divisions of government under which we have operated successfully these many years. A strike is a form of warfare, as are any other threats, and when we say this we realize that employers must be fair. Justice, after all, originates in the hearts of people. It must be accepted to succeed, when it is forced, it fails. Today people are thinking in terms of force, this is contrary to the principles given to us by JESUS CHRIST HIMSELF, win by love, win by education, win by sacrifice, force leads to strife, strife leads to bloodshed, bloodshed leads to death.

> *Yours very respectfully,*
> *A. W. Ponath*
> *Attorney At Law*
> *Appleton, Wis.*

Dear Mr. Ponath: *June 5, 1946*

This is in acknowledgement of your letter of May twenty-ninth, addressed to the President.

The White House, I can assure you, always welcomes an expression of the views of those who, like yourself, are concerned about the important problems of the day. Your interest in writing is appreciated.

With reference to the name of the airplane used by the President, I should tell you that this is a C-54 model and has no other official name. Newspaper writers have used the term "Sacred Cow" but this usage is entirely unofficial and I am sure with no thought or intention of offending anyone.

Sincerely yours,
CHARLES G. ROSS

Numerous letter writers tried to be helpful by suggesting other names for the aircraft.

Dear President Truman: *March 3, 1946*
The name of the plane used by the President of the United States seems to be the "Sacred Cow."

That name sounds like untutored India, but we are Americans and proud of it.

Cows are sacred to the Hindus, but we are of Pilgrim origin. No other nation in the world was ever founded as was America, and we believe that her present position among nations is due to that fact.

The name may only be a joke, but Americans have not been wont to joke about "sacred" things, and we feel that our fine Christian President Truman deserves a better association.

The "Sacred Cow" can easily be painted out and a respectful, respectable name substituted. Lest I be critical without being constructive, let me suggest "Envoy," "The Friendly," "Never Alone," "The Lincoln," "New Day," "Let's Go," "Service," "The America," "The Missouri," "Faith," or some far better American name for our presidential plane.

Assuring you of hearty interest and sympathetic appreciation for your every effort toward the best of America. I remain,

Respectfully yours,
May Bel Thompson
New York, N.Y.

Dear Mr. President: *May 22, 1946*
Until you change the name of the great aeroplane from the "Sacred Cow" to the "Eagle," the machinery of the nation will not go. The eagle is the symbol of our land given to it by God in the Covenant. The cow is the emblem of pagan India and all of us have seen pictures of it blocking the path of vehicles as well as passersby. We were given the plans for the aeroplane, first to the Wrights, and

then greater ones, until it was our vast production that made clouds of them over the enemy. Won't you, for the sake of those brave young eagles who gave their lives for this great land, change the name to the "Eagle"? The Old Eagle, Bald Eagle, but an eagle of some type. Try it President Truman and let's see if God won't help us if we ask Him to get the wheels started again for only He can do it.

> *Sincerely,*
> *Mrs. M. K. Duncan*
> *Dayton, Ohio*

Little could be done, however, except replace the aircraft, which could then be given its own name. But Truman thought this alternative absurd, and his staff patiently answered every constructive letter of this sort as they waited in vain for the subject to die away.

> *Dear President and Mrs. Truman: January 1, 1946*
> I wish to suggest changing the name of the President's private plane to the "Hawthorne," Missouri's official floral emblem.
>
> > *Sincerely,*
> > *Ex. Lieut. C. Stewart Peterson*
> > *Baltimore, Md.*

> *Dear Mr. Peterson: January 4, 1946*
> Your letter to the President relative to changing the name of his C-54 plane, has been referred to me.
> The name associated in the public mind with this plane, that is the "Sacred Cow," is one that grew up during Mr. Roosevelt's administration. Just who is responsible for it, I am unable to discover. However, I doubt very much if a term of that nature which has become associated in the public mind would be affected greatly even if the President gave an official name to his plane. I doubt very much if the press would cease using the term even though the President named his plane as you suggest.
>
> > *Sincerely,*
> > *HARRY H. VAUGHAN*

Virtually everything Truman did during this period seemed to generate intense criticism, but tragedy in the family brought many letters of profound sympathy. Soon after signing the Second Decontrol Act, Truman received word that his bedridden mother, Martha Ellen, had contracted pneumonia. The president's staff immediately ordered the Sacred Cow made ready, and Truman took off to be at her bedside. While he was en route, the ninety-four-year-old Mama Truman passed away. The grief-stricken president had been extremely close to his mother, and of all the cards and letters of condolence he received, including many from powerful heads of state and the pope, it was the ones from everyday Americans, and especially those from people who knew his mother, that meant the most. A woman from Poplar Bluff, Missouri, also thanked him for securing help for her mother-in-law.

Dear Friend,   *July 28, 1947*

Greetings to you. I write to you to try to <u>comfort you</u> in your <u>loss of your mother</u>. I and everyone are grieved. We kept close in news of her illness and how devoted you were to her in her last illness. Your loss is great, yet these things must come to pass. I know of your belief of another life in Heaven, and there is no use to tell you that. I know how proud she must have been of you. Go on from here being like she wanted which is as you are. Sir, you are grieved, but you would not call her back. I wish I could say the right things to comfort you, but I'm sure you know what I am trying to say. I know that <u>you will meet her on that great day</u>. I believe that because I do believe in you. I know you to be a just man. I loved Roosevelt. I love you as much. I believe you will guide your people through the years to come.

<u>I am the one who wrote to you</u> three weeks ago for my poor <u>mother-in-law, Mrs. A. Moyer</u>, whose son is in the Army, and she received only $37 a month. She has already received a back paycheck for $583 and will <u>now receive $90 a month</u>. Mr. Truman, she <u>cried over that from happiness</u>, and a letter of her thanks will follow. Now it's things like that which you did that goes deep into the hearts of people, the little guys like us. We all believe in you. She told me that your letter to her would always be treasured. Now I am as proud of that letter as her.

Be comforted Mr. Truman, you and your family. I wish you all well. Good luck and God bless you always.

Your true friend,
Mrs. Shirley V. Owens
Poplar Bluff, Mo.

My dear Mrs. Owens: *July 31, 1947*
The President has received your letter of July twenty-eighth and appreciates the interest which prompted you to write. He wishes me to tell you how very grateful he is for your expressions of sympathy.
Very sincerely yours,
MATTHEW J. CONNELLY

Dear Mr. President: *Jan. 7, 1948*

With eggs so urgently needed by Europe's children, we are wondering whether the White House would graciously accept from us eggs, made of plastic, appropriately colored, so that Washington children need not be deprived of the time honored and eagerly awaited Easter Egg Roll on the White House grounds.

As consolation prize, BARTON'S BONBONNIERE would be happy to present a chocolate Easter egg to every child who so worthily rolled a synthetic one to help feed Europe's children.

Very truly yours,
BARTON'S BONBONNIER, INC.
Herbert Tenzer
Chairman of the Board

Dear Mr. Tenzer: *January 13, 1948*

This is in reply to your letter of January seventh, addressed to the President.

Your offer to send a quantity of plastic and chocolate eggs for the Easter Egg rolling is appreciated. As you perhaps know, however, the egg rolling on the White House grounds was discontinued through the war, and because of the food situation and other conditions since, has not been resumed. No plans have been made to hold it this year and it is unlikely that it will be attempted.

Sincerely yours,
CHARLES G. ROSS
Secretary to the President

CHAPTER FOUR

AID TO GREECE AND TURKEY • PALESTINE AND
THE BIRTH OF ISRAEL • CHURCHILL CORRESPONDENCE •
THE MARSHALL PLAN • THE BERLIN AIRLIFT •
1948 PRESIDENTIAL ELECTION

Historians have argued long and hard over what started the Cold War between the United States and Soviet Union. Some cite Churchill's Iron Curtain speech at Fulton, Missouri, in March 1946. Others believe it was Truman's decision to offer Greece and Turkey assistance in their efforts to combat communist guerrillas and Soviet pressure for territorial concessions. Still others state that it was the recognition by U.S. policy officials that the communists' goals had not changed since 1918—only their tactics. Regardless of exactly how and when the Cold War "began," in 1947 the U.S. policy changed from cooperation, or at least, attempting to get along with Soviet communism, to one of "containment."

Charles E. Bohlen, who served as advisor-interpreter at Teheran, Yalta, and Potsdam and later as U.S. ambassador to the Soviet Union, had rare insight into Soviet-American relations. He believed that though a number of decisions were reached at Potsdam, "some of which lasted, many of which did not," the conference itself "cannot be regarded as vital." Said Bohlen: "Most of the policy lines on both sides had been laid down before the meeting. After Potsdam, there was little that could be done to induce the Soviet Union to become a reasonable and cooperative member of the world community. Discrepancies between the systems were too great, the hostility of the Soviet Union toward capitalist countries too great."[1]

Bohlen traced some of the first U.S. misgivings concerning Soviet postwar goals to Yalta and the Soviet handling of the Polish question, followed by the failure of the Soviets to live up to the Declaration of Liberated Europe when they systematically installed communist regimes in the Eastern European countries. This was followed by the failure of the Soviets to pull their troops out of Iran in 1945. In 1941, the British and the Soviets had jointly occupied the strategically located nation to prevent possible German occupation. The agreement with the Iranian government provided for withdrawal of these troops within six months after hostilities ended. The British withdrew as provided, but the Soviets continued to occupy the northern third of the country, Azerbaijan, well into 1946 and only yielded after the United States brought the issue before the U.N. Security Council.

These events were followed by communist attempts, supported by the Soviet Union, to take over Greece and Soviet pressure on Turkey to allow it military access to Turkish territory. Great Britain, which had been heavily supporting both governments, came to the United States in February 1947 and stated it could no longer afford the drain on its fragile postwar economy. This came as a shock to U.S. foreign policy makers, who, until then, had not realized the extent of Britain's decline as a Great Power. Truman, supported by a bipartisan Congress, took up the challenge. Bohlen maintains that "it was in the face of such realization that the United States, in the person of President Truman, made probably the biggest decision for the future of American policy."[2]

The Truman Doctrine, as it later came to be known, directly involved the United States in the never-ending tumult of European power politics.

> *Dear President Truman*   *received 3/28/47*
> The Declaration that United States security is involved in the maintenance of Greek-Turkish integrity is a history shaping utterance without parallel.
> You have my vote and some.
>
> > *A Republican,*
> > *E. Schmiat*

Letters like the above were somewhat scarce, however. That the president's action set the country on a course far different from that of George Washington's and Thomas Jefferson's was not well understood at the time, and Americans critical of the policy focused almost solely on the perceived faults of the "despotic" nations we were supporting.

> *Dear Mr. President,*   *April 13, 1947*
> I just heard over the radio that Mr. Wallace had declared in England that you agreed the U.S. had embarked on an imperialistic program.
> What sadistic irony it is for the cradle of liberty, a people who first got rid of the institution of king and divine rule, shown now to

be backing miserable petty tyrants like George and <u>Paul of Greece</u>. And in the name of "aiding *free* peoples" anywhere.

I'm <u>sick of double-talk. It is funny from a comedian, but not from my president</u>. The Greek people aren't free, except to starve and pay taxes, neither are the Turks. And every report I've read, even Stewart Alsop's, admits the vile corruption of the Greek government.

I want my son to grow up in a peaceful world. I want him to grow up in a free and democratic America. Peace is indivisible. The course we are following leads to war, to our being globally detested, and to the end of freedom here.

I also heard that the Republicans intend to present you with an omnibus bill incorporating their infamous demolition of the Wagner <u>Labor Relations</u> Act so that you must accept or veto it—and lose the modifications you had asked for.

Veto that bill, Mr. President, in the name of Franklin D. Roosevelt! Remember your pledge two years ago.

> *Earnestly yours,*
> *(Mrs) Marcella Schubert*
> *New York, N.Y.*

The skill and perseverence of King Paul of Greece confounded his critics, however. The brutal civil war was eventually won, with the help of the United States and its military advisors operating under Lieutenant General James A. VanFleet, but not before thousands of Greek children were carried off by the guerrillas to perform forced labor in the mountains and neighboring communist countries. While the fighting still raged, a young girl in Georgia sent the president a brief essay that a friend of hers had written as a school assignment. Both the letter and the school assignment were written on lined tablet paper.

> *Dear Mr. Truman:*   *June 13, 1947*
> I consider it an honor to be writing you. I have no special reason for sending you this essay, but I am, Mr. Truman. One of my classmates wrote the essay about two months ago, and you have made things come out just as the essay begged. I am glad you signed the Greek-Turkish Aid Bill. I saw you sign it at the movies.
> Annette Chalker (the girl who wrote the essay) won first place over all the schools in our county with this essay. She's fifteen years

old. I think she doesn't know I'm sending it to you; please don't let her know. All I ask is write her a letter if you have time and tell her how you liked it. I am,

Cordially yours,
Bonnie Adams
Kennesaw, Ga.

AID FOR OUR FRIENDS—THE GREEKS

The Greeks have long been among our most steadfast friends, and today, more than ever, we should help them in the time of their destruction. If we help them, they can probably retain their independence; if we fail them they may be forced to join the Balkans' bloc of the sovietized countries. Greece is the only Balkan nation still outside of the Soviet Union. The Soviet Union covets Greece and wishes to absorb her into the Soviet sphere. So long as the bulk of her people live as poorly as they do now, Greece will be vulnerable to Soviet propaganda. To remain free she must improve the standard of her living. There is only one country in the world to help her—the United States.

. . . When history's most terrible war was over, blood and tears were to flow no more, but they flow anew in tortured Greece.

While the people of Greece shiver in roofless houses and walk through the streets without shoes or overcoats, fortunes are amassed in Athens. Greece is probably the only country of postwar Europe that has not applied a modicum of economic controls. . . .

This crisis is acute. Greece is a poor country and always has been. The aim of communism now is dictatorship and delivery of Greece to Russia. There they are trying to bring down the sructure of the Greek government. If Greece loses the sources of her only strength, she will either crawl in behind the iron curtain or starve.

It will cost a lot to put Greece back on her feet. The area of the Mediterranean—Dardenelles is of strategic importance and great value. Therefore, money spent in that area would [not be] misdirected. There is only one country financially fitted to aid Greece—the United States.

The British in Greece know that the Greeks are in a spot. It is obvious that the British government cannot prevent a communistic uprising between and throughout Greece. By the time this happens the British hope Uncle Sam will have put a sturdy finger into the hole in the dam separating Greece from Soviet Russia.

By helping Greece, the Americans shall have a unique opportunity to prove the real value of American friendship.

> *By—*
> *Annette Chalker*
> *Kennesaw, Ga.*

My dear Bonnie: *June 30, 1947*

The President has received your friendly letter of June thirteenth. He wants you to know that he appreciates your thought in letting him see that essay written by Annette Chalker and he asks me to extend best wishes to both of you.

> *Very sincerely yours,*
> *WILLIAM D. HASSETT*

Just across the eastern Mediterranean from Greece and Turkey was another hot spot where the British were having considerable trouble—Palestine. Most of Europe's Jewish population in areas under Nazi control had been rounded up and systematically murdered or worked to death in concentration camps during the final years of World War II. After the defeat of the Nazis, thousands of displaced survivors, particularly from Germany and countries now under communist control, were anxious to go to the ancient Jewish homeland in Palestine. Britain had earlier promised to facilitate immigration to the area, which they governed under a mandate going back to the First World War, but because of complaints from Arabs there and in neighboring states, they now greatly limited the number of Jews who could enter. Immigration could hardly be stopped, however, and many thousands succeeded in entering the country illegally, as civil strife within Palestine threatened to break out into open warfare between Jews and Arabs.

Dear Mr. President: *October 10, 1945*

I venture to call your attention to this letter from me recently published in the *New York Times*. The danger of an explosion in the Near East seems to me very real and very serious.

With warm admiration of your accomplishment in your infinitely difficult task and with all good wishes, I am

> *Sincerely yours,*
> *Virginia C. Gildersleeve*

Gildersleeve's letter was published in the October 9, 1945, edition under the headline "Havens for Homeless Jews: All United Nations Held Responsible for Proportionate Share." She had been the dean of Barnard College (Columbia University) since 1911 and had been involved in what she later called "many a good crusade" in the international sphere.

To the Editor of the New York Times:

The situation in the Near East is apparently approaching a crisis; very soon violence and bloodshed may result. For this I fear our country is partly responsible.

I believe sincerely in the peaceful settlement of disputes, a policy to which the United States is now committed, and I am deeply interested in the Near East through connections with American colleges and universities in that area. I am therefore greatly distressed by the policies now being urged on our Government, policies which threaten violence and upheaval in that critical region of the world.

Sooner or later Arabs and Jews must sit down together and reach an agreement regarding life in Palestine. Why should they not now gather about a conference table to arrive at some adjustment and avoid violence?

Surely it will be no kindness to the Jews to secure by force their admittance in very large numbers to a section of the world where they will have as neighbors many millions of enemies.

Are not some Americans urging the plan of forcing Britain to force the Arabs to admit the homeless Jews in order to escape our own responsibility toward these unfortunate persons? The conscience of the world should recognize the obligation of us all to help the homeless Jews whose persecution by Hitler we have so bitterly denounced. Each of the United Nations should accept its proportionate share of those Jews who seek new homes. The Arab nations have already offered to accept their share.

What will be the number the United States should admit? Perhaps 200,000? Then let Congress admit these over and above the usual immigration quotas. And let U.S. stop evading our responsibility by urging that our Government force Britain to force Palestine to take in far more than its share. Thus we may avoid setting the Near East aflame.

Virginia C. Gildersleeve

Hassett sent the letter and clipping to Maurice Latta, Truman's executive clerk, with a reminder to Latta that Gildersleeve had served on the U.S. delegation to the United Nations Conference on International Organization in San Francisco, where the U.N.'s charter was finalized and ratified.

> *My dear Miss Gildersleeve:*   *October 15, 1945*
> I appreciated very highly your note of the tenth enclosing me a clipping from the *New York Times* of October ninth. Your letter in the Times was most interesting and I was certainly glad to have an opportunity to read it.
> The Jewish and Arab situation in the Near East is a most difficult one and has caused us more difficulty than most any other problem in the European Theater. I am hopeful that we will get it worked out on a satisfactory basis.
> I have been in touch with the Prime Minister of Great Britain and eventually I think we will arrive at a solution.
> *Sincerely yours,*
> *HARRY S. TRUMAN*

As the situation in Palestine continued to deteriorate, the British government no longer had the resources or the will to keep the peace. The British submitted the problem to the U.N., which proposed that the country be divided into separate Arab and Jewish states that would cooperate with each other economically. As for the holy city of Jerusalem, it would form part of an international zone under the direct control of neither side. On November 29, 1947, the U.N. General Assembly voted in favor of the partition, and Arab nations immediately walked out of the meeting, declaring that they would not abide by the decision. British forces, which were scheduled to be completely withdrawn from the disputed area on May 15 of the following year, pulled back steadily to the ports and airfields and turned over administrative functions in a haphazard manner to both Arab and Jewish authorities. Two days before the last troops were to depart, the Arab League, made up of surrounding nations, declared that its own forces would enter Palestine on the heels of the British and "administer" it pending the establishment of an Arab state throughout the whole country.

Truman had long taken a great interest in the plight of Europe's Jews and their desire for a homeland. Against the advice of what he described as the "striped pants boys" in the State Department, who he believed undercut his

initiatives in their effort to support the British position, Truman had steadfastly backed calls for a separate Jewish state. He was then facing the very real
possibility that war might break out between the United States and the
Soviet Union and wisely rebuffed requests to send troops to Palestine, but it
was U.S. recognition, not soldiers, that backers of the new Jewish state most
wanted. On the day that the Arab League stated its intention to take over the
British Mandate, the elder statesman of Jewish independence, Chaim Weizmann, wrote to Truman from his hotel in New York.

Dear Mr. President: *May 13, 1948*

The unhappy events of the last few months will not, I hope,
obscure the very great contributions that you, Mr. President, have
made toward a definitive and just settlement of the long and troublesome Palestine question. The leadership which the American government took under your inspriation made possible the establishment of
a Jewish State, which I am convinced will contribute markedly
toward a solution of world Jewish problems, and which, I am equally
convinced is a necessary preliminary to the development of lasting
peace among the peoples of the Near East.

So far as practical conditions in Palestine would permit, the Jewish people there have proceeded along the lines laid down in the
United Nations Resolution of November 29, 1947. Tomorrow midnight, May 15th, the British Mandate will be terminated, and the
Provisional Government of the Jewish State, embodying the best
endeavors of the Jewish people and arising from the Resolution of
the United Nations, will assume full responsibility for preserving law
and order within the boundaries of the Jewish State; for defending
that area against external aggression; and for discharging the obligations of the Jewish State to the other nations of the world in accor-
dance with international law.

Considering all the difficulties, the chance for an equitable adjustment of Arab and Jewish relationships are not unfavorable. What is
required now is an end to the seeking of new solutions which invariably have retarded rather than encouraged a final settlement.

It is for these reasons that I deeply hope that the United States,
which under your leadership has done so much to find a just solution, will promptly recognize the Provisional Government of the
new Jewish State. The world, I think, would regard it as especially

appropriate that the greatest living democracy should be the first to
welcome the newest state into the family of nations.

Respectfully yours,
Chaim Weizmann

Dear Doctor Weizmann: *May 15, 1948*
I appreciated very much your letter of May thirteenth and I sincerely hope that the Palestine situation will eventually work out on
an equitable and peaceful basis.

Sincerely yours,
HARRY S. TRUMAN

Weizmann, who had moved from London to New York in order to
work more closely with the large network of supporters pressing for U.S.
assistance, had secretly met with Truman on at least two occasions. The
reply from the president on May 15 was courteous and seemingly vague, but
his real answer had come in spectacular form the previous day when, within
moments of the scheduled midnight announcement that the Jewish state
was now a reality (6:00 P.M. in Washington), the White House announced
the United States' de facto recognition of the new country that called itself
Israel. Wild celebrations broke out in New York, but at multiple locations
along the disputed frontier, the regular armies of Egypt, Iraq, Transjordan,
Syria, and Lebanon entered Jewish territory and attacked its fortified farm-
ing communities.

Before the Arab offensive lost steam and the first of several U.N. cease-
fires was declared, significant portions of the land allotted to Israel were
overrun, particularly by the Transjordan Army, which was British supplied
and led. Israeli forces eventually regained many key areas, particularly the
Negev desert region from the Egyptians and virtually all of Galilee in the
north. In the meantime, Chaim Weizmann had been elected president of
the new provisional government council. On the occasion of Harry Truman's stunning victory in the 1948 elections, Weizmann again wrote the
president, both to congratulate him and to press for more favorable treatment of the fledgling nation while Truman was, presumably, in high spirits
and a mood to be generous.

Dear Mr. President: *5th November, 1948*
Permit me to extend to you most hearty congratulations and good
wishes on your re-election. We in this country have been watching

the progress of the Presidential contest with bated breath and I am sure that I am speaking the mind of the bulk of my people when I say that we feel deeply thankful that the people of the United States have given you the opportunity of shaping the policies of your country and the affairs of humanity at large during the next critical four years. We interpret their vote as an emphatic endorsement of the policy of peace, security and ordered progress in world affairs for which you have stood since you assumed your high office and for the continued prosecution of which men and women in every part of the globe pray with all their hearts. May you be granted health and strength to carry out your noble purpose.

We have special cause to be gratified at your re-election because we are mindful of the enlightened help which you gave to your cause in these years of our struggle. We particularly remember your unflinching advocacy of the admission of Jewish refugees to Palestine, your determined stand against the attempts to deflect you from your course, your staunch support of our admission to statehood at Lake Success* and your recognition of the fact of its establishment within an hour of our proclamation of independence. We pray that your assistance and guidance may be extended to us also in the coming years. We have succeeded in the past twelve months in defending our independence against enemies from every quarter—north, south and east, as in Biblical times—and in setting up the framework of our State. Enemy armies are still on the borders of our country, maintained there, I regret to say, by the vacillating attitude of the United Nations which have imposed a truce that is becoming ever more, not a forerunner of peace, but an instrument of war. Our essential aim is peace and reconstruction. While the eyes of the world have been turned on to the battlefields in the south and north, we have succeeded in liquidating one refugee camp after another in Europe and bringing the chance of a new life to thousands of ruined men and women whom the world has all but forgotten. We have brought over 62,000 since we attained independence. To develop this great effort at human rehabilitation we need, above all, three things: first peace; second recognition; and third financial and economic support for the execution of those large projects of agricultural and industrial devel-

---

*Lake Success, near Mineola on New York's Long Island, was the U.N.'s temporary headquarters while its permanent home was being built in New York City.

opment which are essential for the absorption of newcomers and economic progress of the country.

The most important requirement at this moment is that this unreal and untenable truce be brought to an end and be supplanted by a speedy and enduring peace. Over two months ago we asked the Mediator to call both sides to the conference table, but the other side rejected our offer. We have no aggressive designs against anyone and we are at any moment ready to negotiate a peace settlement. Our enemies have failed in their efforts to beat us by brute force although they outnumbered us by 20 to 1. They are now endeavouring through the medium of the Security Council to undermine the decision taken by the General Assembly last November and to deprive us of the undeveloped areas of the Negev which offer space for new homes for many thousands of our uprooted people, and which will remain a desert land if they are annexed by the neighboring Arab States, as is evidently intended. This is the real purpose behind the Security Council's Resolution introduced by Great Britain which to my deep regret was supported by the American Delegation. We have no choice but to oppose this design which would destroy last November's decision of the General Assembly and would reduce us to a state of permanent insecurity and vulnerablity.

I pray with all my heart that you, Mr. President, may use your high authority to put an end to these hostile maneuvres. We have successfully withstood the onslaught of the Arab States, who were sent against us by the British, almost like a pack of hired assassins. I am saying this with deep pain because I have throughout my life been deeply attached to Great Britain and have suffered for that attachment. But the evidence unfortunately all points in this direction, and even as I write we are receiving constant reports of Great Britain rearming the Arabs to enable them to re-start hostilities against us. Having failed in her efforts to wipe out our young commonwealth, she now appears bent on detaching the Negev from our State. I feel emboldened to ask for your intervention in this matter, remembering the deep sympathy and understanding which you displayed when I had the privilege of stating to you our case on the Negev and displaying to you maps showing its potentialities for settlement. It was with a deep feeling of elation that I left you on that day to prevent this part of the country, which was allotted to us last November, from being detached from our State. Sheer necessity compels us to cling to the Negev. Our pioneers have done yeoman work in opening up this semi-arid country; they have built pipe lines through the desert, set up agricultural settlements, planted gardens and orchards in what was for many centuries a barren land. They will not give up this land unless they are bodily removed from it.

I venture to hope that clear and firm instructions be issued on this vital matter to the American Delegation in Paris which has of late, apparently, not received directives corresponding to the views, which, I know, you hold on the subject. I would further plead that you may find it possible to direct the competent authorities to enable us to secure the long-term financial assistance which is urgently needed for the execution of the great scheme of reconstruction which I had the privilege of submitting to you in the Summer.

With every good wish,

Sincerely yours,
CH WEIZMANN

Truman asked his liaison to Jewish organizations, David K. Niles, to craft a response. The results, however, were anything but routine. Niles, a loyal and particularly valuable presidential assistant, was also a fervent supporter of the besieged nation who, at one point, had become so frustrated over the problems confronting the Jews that he actually threatened to quit if Truman didn't state his support of their cause more emphatically. By this point in the administration, Truman's early problem of staffers' slipping things by him for his signature was a thing of the past, and Niles, apparently believing he knew the president's mind on this subject but fearing that others on the staff would tone down the response, played a sleight of hand with the letter. It is also possible that this was done at the request of Truman, who personally believed that the Negev area should go to Israel. Assistant Press Secretary Eben A. Ayers described the episode in his diary entry for January 29, 1949:

> One of the things that came up, brought up by Bill Hassett and Charlie Ross, was an exchange of letters between the president and Chaim Weizmann, head of the new State of Israel. It came up in two ways. Some day ago the president handed Bill Hassett a letter from Weizmann with the suggestion he get together with David Niles, admininstrative assistant, and prepare a reply. Later Bill reported that the letter was a very tricky one, involving about all of the issues of the Palestine situation.

Then a day or so ago Charlie Ross received a query from Merriman Smith of the United Press about a letter supposedly written by the president to Weizmann. Smith said something about it had come out and particularly a report that such a letter had been sent in the regular mail, under a five-cent postage stamp.

Yesterday Bill and Charlie got together and set out to clear up the matter. With Bill Hopkins, executive clerk, they found that the president had written a letter or signed a letter written to Weizmann late in November. According to Hopkins' recollection he had never seen the text of the letter, but it had been presented to the president by Niles who seemingly had written it, and that after getting it signed he had taken it with him and told Hopkins that he was keeping the file.

Charlie and Bill then sent for the file and obtained it from Niles' office. It showed that the president had signed a rather lengthy letter of about two pages which not only acknowledged congratulations upon the president's election from Weizmann but went on to compare the background of the two men, in the president's own words, and then went further into the issues involving Israel, and particularly boundaries, which have been one of the most delicate of these issues. The letter virtually placed the president in the position of endorsing all of Israel's claims.

The president said that he had received a letter of congratulations from Weizmann and had turned it over to Niles for the preparation of an acknowledgment. He said Niles brought it to him, and he signed it but did not think he [had] read it. Neither he nor anyone else could explain the sending of the letter in regular mail with a five-cent stamp, but everyone agreed that it probably was never seen by anyone in the department of state and that Secretary of State Acheson probably knew nothing of it.

The text has not become public, but should it come out it could prove embarrassing and add to the difficulties in dealing with the Palestine-Israel problem.

This all led Bill Hassett to comment that during the Roosevelt administration it had been found that on occasion several letters would be sent to one person because of failure to handle things through one person in the White House; as a result, it was determined that everything should go through the late Maurice Latta, whom Hopkins succeeded. As Bill Hassett said, the more people who see these things the less likely of something improper going out. It was also agreed that any communica-

*tion between the president and the head of another state should go
through the department of state.*

*The president said there apparently was nothing that could be done
about this case, but he indicated his intention of saying something to
Niles about his handling of the correspondence.*

Westbrook Pegler, a newspaper columnist despised by Truman, had written only a few days earlier that the president was in the pocket of the Jewish
lobby and that Niles was the man delivering the marching orders. Ayers
noted in his diary that "the idea, of course, was ridiculous," but the letter to
Weizmann, who had since been elected to the presidency of Israel, was
indeed far beyond official policy at that time and was the kind of thing that
critics of Niles were talking about.

Dear Mr. President: *November 29, 1948*

Today—the first anniversary of the Partition Resolution—is a
most appropriate time for me to answer your last letter, dated
November 5th.

As I read your letter, I was struck by the common experience you
and I have recently shared. We had both been abandoned by the so-
called realistic experts to our supposedly forlorn lost causes. Yet we
both kept pressing for what we were sure was right—and we were
both proven to be right. My feeling of elation on the morning of
November 3rd must have approximated your own feelings one year
ago today, and on May 14th, and on several occasions since then.

However, it does not take long for bitter and resourceful opponents to regroup their forces after they have been shattered. You in
Israel have already been confronted with that situation; and I expect
to be all too soon. So I understand very well your concern to prevent
the undermining of your well-earned victories.

I remember well our conversation about the Negev, to which you
referred in your letter. I agree fully with your estimate of the importance of that area to Israel, and I deplore any attempt to take it away
from Israel. I had thought that my position would have been clear to
all the world, particularly in the light of the specific wording of the
Democratic Party Platform. But there were those who did not take
this seriously, regarding it as "just another campaign promise" to be
forgotten after the election. I believe they have recently realized their

error. I have interpreted my re-election as a mandate from the American people to carry out the Democratic Platform—including, of course, the plank on Israel. I intend to do so.

Since your letter was written, we have announced in the General Assembly our firm intention to oppose any territorial changes in the November 29th Resolution which are not acceptable to the State of Israel. I am confident that the General Assembly will support us in this basic position.

We have already expressed our willingness to help develop the new State through financial and economic measures. As you know, the Export-Import Bank is actively considering a substantial long-term loan to Israel on a project basis. I understand that your Government is now in process of preparing the details of such projects for submission to the Bank. Personally, I would like to go even further, by expanding such financial and economic assistance on a large scale to the entire Middle East, contingent upon effective mutual cooperation.

Thank you so much for your warm congratulations and good wishes on my re-election. I was pleased to learn that the first Israeli elections have been scheduled for January 25th. That enables us to set a definite target date for extending de jure recognition.

In closing, I want to tell you how happy and impressed I have been at the remarkable progress made by the new State of Israel. What you have received at the hands of the world has been far less than was your due. But you have more than made the most of what you have received, and I admire you for it. I trust that the present uncertainty, with its terribly burdensome consequences, will soon be eliminated. We will do all we can to help by encouraging direct negotiations between the parties looking toward a prompt peace settlement.

Very sincerely yours,
HARRY S. TRUMAN

Truman couldn't very well retract the letter, and it is not at all clear whether Niles, who emerged unscathed from the incident, had acted beyond the president's intent in bypassing the White House staff. Truman, in fact, had the complete text of the offending letter reproduced in his *Memoirs.* One can only guess how much of a factor the letter might have been in encouraging Israeli intransigence in later negotiations with the Arabs. The fact that

U.S. arms remained embargoed to both Israel and its enemies in an effort to promote negotiations made it clear that Truman's policy was one of mediation and compromise among all parties, yet it did little to diminish his stature with supporters of Israel.

> *Dear Sir:*   *February 3, 1948*
>
> The gratitude of the 700 members of the Yonkers Chapter of Hadassah goes to you for your part in granting de jure recognition to the State of Israel.
>
> We are proud of our government's part in extending this recognition which we hope will be an effective medium, we feel, in achieving an amicable settlement of Israeli-Arab differences.
>
> > *Sincerely yours,*
> > *Yonkers Chapter of Hadassa*
> > *Sadelle S. Ellman*
> > *Yonkers, N.Y.*

> *Dear Mr. President:*   *May 12, 1949*
>
> In the past I have written to you letters of criticism for which I ask to be excused. But this time I am writing to you a letter of appreciation.
>
> I want to express to you my deep appreciation for the part that you have <u>played in Israel's establishment</u> as a nation and the support that you have given in bringing Israel in, as a member of the United Nations. Your interest in Israel was an act of justice and fair play that only an American can understand.
>
> History shows that Israel's enemies go down in shame, and that Israel's friends are crowned with glory. You, Mr. President, have shown with your deeds that you are a friend of Israel, and therefore, your name too Mr. President, will be glorified in history.
>
> > *Yours, with highest respect,*
> > *Dr. Abraham Lebow, Optometrist*
> > *Jersey City, N.J.*

THE PRESIDENT, THE WHITE HOUSE   FEB. 16, 1949

TO MILLIONS OF PEOPLE THROUGHOUT THE WORLD YOU MORE THAN ANY HEAD OF A NATION HAVE BROUGHT TO REALITY THE LIVING STATE OF ISRAEL, AND IN A VERY REAL SENSE YOU

HAVE MADE BIBLICAL PROPHECY COME TRUE. BUT WHAT IS EVEN
MORE IMPORTANT RESIDES IN THE FACT THAT YOUR ACTION IS
ALSO IN THE INTEREST OF THE WORLD PEACE. GOD BLESS YOU.
    A. N. SPANEL
    PRESIDENT INTERNATIONAL LATEX CORP.
    NEW YORK, N.Y.

Dear Mr. Spanel: *February 15, 1949*
Many thanks for your kind words about the recognition of Israel.
    I cannot say too many times that I would rather have lasting
peace than be President.
    Recognition of the State of Israel seems to me an act of simple
justice to a people who suffered untold miseries before, during and
after the Second World War.

                         Very sincerely yours,
                         HARRY S. TRUMAN

Not everyone was pleased with the state of affairs. As the Israelis consoli-
dated their hold over territory under their control and negotiated with a host
of neighbors who only months before had been trying their best to destroy
them, complaints—with varying degrees of legitimacy—made their way into
the press and generated more letters to Truman.

Your Excellency: *June 22, 1949*
As a man who believes in tolerance towards a neighbor's creed or
race, I was glad to see the Jewish people finally saved from further
persecution in Europe. I am astounded, however, by the reports
coming out of Palestine of the intolerance which these same people
are showing towards Christians and Arabs alike.
    I know that you certainly would not deliberately foster intoler-
ance in any land and I hope that you will find occasion to express
yourself against the intolerance that is being practiced today in The
Holy Land.

                         Very truly yours,
                         Joseph J. Trainer
                         Newtown, Pa.

Particularly galling to some was that Jeruselem was not going to be the
"international city" that the U.N. had proposed. Although the idea held

great attraction to many Americans, it was completely unworkable in the city itself. Moreover, Arab nations in general—and Transjordan in particular—were unalterably opposed to such an arrangement, and major portions of the city were under the control of Arab troops. In March 1949, Transjordan signed an agreement with Israel under which the "New City" of Jerusalem would remain a part of Israel, while the "Old City," as well as most of the land allotted to the Palestinians, would fall under Transjordan's control. Curiously, correspondents demanding that Israel comply with the earlier U.N. resolution detailed no criticism of Transjordan and failed to take into account that Israel could not turn over land it didn't possess.

Honorable President Truman: June 22, 1949

We wish to inform you that we believe *Jerusalem and its environs must be internationalized*. It is imperative that the Holy Places be safeguarded, not only for the present but for the future as well. We believe that the decision of the United Nations commission, following its consideration of the <u>Palestine question</u> after February, 1947 should be respected. Israel should not be admitted into the UN if she does not fulfill its orders and fails to stick to her own former stand on the question. We think there can be no compromise.

Yours truly,
Rosemary Yager
Clara E. Yager
Frances C. Yager

It was also clear that the temporary end to the fighting would not last and that the area would be a source of trouble far into the future.

Dear Mr. Truman: December 16, 1949

In 1944 we were privileged to be admitted into the White House and greet you personally, along with 30 other missionaries and former missionaries of the Northern and Southern Baptist Convention. One year ago this past November the final factor in influencing our vote was a statement earlier on election day by a newspaper correspondent in connection with some decision you had just made to the effect that "thus did President Truman follow his Bible-trained conscience."

Here is what lies so heavily on my heart that I can no longer refrain from making some effort to approach you with it: namely,

THE NEW STATE OF ISRAEL. I lived there nearly six years—
from 1936 to 1941. I read and speak their language as can be verified through at least one of our federal government agencies. I feel
like I know the mentality and inclination of the body politic of that
new state.

Palestinian Hebrews, without intending to be so, are Eastern
Europeans primarily. Their customs, politics, outlook, and other
characteristics bear the spirit and imprint of Eastern Europe.

IN A CRISIS BETWEEN RUSSIA AND THE UNITED
STATES THERE IS LITTLE, IF ANY, DOUBT WHICH DIREC-
TION THEIR NATURAL SYMPATHIES WOULD FALL. The
five and one-fourth million American Jews, because of blood ties
with these people, enhanced by a small measure of religion and sentiment, have clamored for our statements in every instance to side with
Israel as over against the Arabs. Little do they realize that in the forthcoming crisis when the American public awakens to the fact that this
small minority caused our government to go out on a limb for the
State of Israel at the expense of alienating the Arab countries, they
will doubtless loathe the position they took and their own kinsmen
who caused them to take it.

Nothing has punctured the reservoir of good will for America
among the Arab countries so completely as our pro-Israel policy. In a
crisis between Russia and America we shall need Arab sympathy. Has
not the time come, therefore, to modify our policy in the Near East?

Over 700,000 Arab refugees are living in worse conditions than
the Jews coming out of the camps of Europe. Letters to us from the
Near East indicate that this situation is burning deeply into the naturally vengeful Arab heart a permanent hatred not only for Jews but
for America.

Only yesterday Israel again defied the United Nations concerning
Jerusalem. Their hand certainly needs to be called once and for all.

IF THERE IS ONE THING I FEEL CERTAIN ABOUT IT IS
THAT THE POLITICAL AMBITIONS OF OUR HEBREW
FRIENDS IN THE NEAR EAST ENVISION MORE LARGE
AREAS OF ARAB TERRITORY UNDER THEIR DOMINION
AND THAT THERE IS SO MUCH FOOLHARDINESS AND
FANATICISM GROWING OUT OF THEIR COMBINATION
OF NATIONALISM, RACIALISM, AND RELIGION (such as

Shintoism and Nazism) THAT THIS WILL BE A MAJOR SOURCE OF GRIEF AND BLOODSHED FOR DECADES TO COME.

We expect to be again in Washington soon and would like so much to discuss this matter with you, but shall refrain from asking for the privilege unless at some time you, yourself, should want it to be so.

With deepest appreciation for your leadership, I remain,

> *Sincerely yours,*
> *Dr. H. Leo Eddleman*
> *Parkland Baptist Church*
> *Louisville, Ky.*

Your pastor, Dr. Pruden [Dr. Edward Purden, pastor of First Baptist Church in the capital], and I have appeared on Convention programs together.

My Dear Mr. President: *February 19, 1948*

The Wallace victory in New York City possibly proved slightly shocking to you. I pray that you will not let it cause you to stoop to cheap politics in an effort to offset it. Rather, may you continue the statesmanlike course you have been treading.

It has grieved me a bit recently to hear—and I don't believe it—that your Palestine policy is a bid for the Jewish vote of New York City. The charge also has been made that your Civil Rights Campaign is intended to garner the Negro vote in Harlem. Nor do I believe that. Never mind the cynics. They can never hurt you.

At the same time though, Mr. President, I would urge you to reconsider our policy in Palestine. If the Jews are truly interested in establishing a homeland, there are many other spots in the world much more adaptable to their needs which could be negotiated without the threat of bloodshed. Portugal probably would gladly sell them some of her African possessions.

Besides, the land of Palestine could support only a comparatively small portion of the world's Jews.

The historical claim of the Jews to Palestine goes back over three thousand years. Reliable ethnologists inform us that none of the Jews today are descendants of the original tribes that inhabited Palestine.

I fear, Mr. President, that time will remove the mask from the Zionist movement to reveal it as a Communist Front. A preponderance of the Jews now finding their way to Palestine come from Middle and Eastern Europe. The question of whether they are all really Jews could seem worthy of investigation.

Then, too, we should consider the fact that the Palestine issue is the only one of major importance in which Russia and the United States have voted on the same side in the United Nations. Could the Russians be using the Zionist Organization as a front eventually to gain the rich mineral resources of the Dead Sea, dominance of the Suez Canal and thereby control of the Near East, Asia, The Dardanelles, etc.? If they're not using it, certainly they could quickly subdue it.

Until our Palestine policy was enunciated, we rightfully claimed the friendship of the Moslem World. Could the United States afford to be at war with one eighth of the world's population which roams in bands from Dakar, West Africa to the Philippines? Our modern arms would be of little avail against such a people. We would have to resort to the tactics of the Indian Wars. Rest assured, fight us the Moslems will if we resort to force to drive them from a homeland to which they are entitled by all ethical considerations.

It was especially nice of you to acknowledge receipt of the suggestion for dealing with protests over Myron Taylor's continued presence at the Vatican. Thanks a lot.

> *Respectfully yours,*
> *James S. Alderman*
> *City of Dallas, Texas*

As one might expect, Truman was in great demand by Jewish organizations, and the Hassett Valentines flowed.

Dear Mr. President,   May 25, 1950

We are a group of young American men and women who served as volunteers with the armed forces of Israel during the Israel-Arab conflict. <u>May we please have an expression from you that we could read at our convention on June 24 in New York</u> as to how we may best serve in helping maintain good relations between our country and the <u>State of Israel</u>.

We seek a direction by which we might turn our experience to aid in the cause of peace and good will.

Please reply directly to my home address as per below.

Sincerely,
Samuel Z. Klausner
American Veterans of Israel
New York Chapter

Dear Mr. Klausner: *June 5, 1950*

This is in acknowledgement of your letter of May twenty-fifth to the President that I regret very much to advise you that it will not be possible for him to send the message you request for the forthcoming convention of the American Veterans of Israel.

It has become necessary for the President greatly to curtail his personal correspondence in order to devote all of his energy to those official duties which he alone can perform and which he cannot delegate to others. In the circumstances, it is impossible for him to comply with all of the requests he receives for special messages. I am sure, upon reflection, you will understand why the President cannot do many things which in different circumstances he would be glad to do.

Very sincerely yours,
WILLIAM D. HASSETT

Truman was frequently unhappy with the tactics of Israel's supporters in the United States, but he never regretted his efforts to establish a Jewish state. Niles later recalled that when Isaac Halevi Herzog, the chief rabbi of Jerusalem, came to the White House, "Rabbi Herzog told Truman, 'God put you in your mother's womb so you would be the instrument to bring about the rebirth of Israel after two thousand years.' I thought he was overdoing things, but when I looked over at the President, tears were running down his cheeks."[3]

Most American Jews felt similarly, and Truman received letters like the following one long after he returned home to Independence, Missouri.

Dear Mr. Truman: *29 April 1952*

On the eve <u>of the Fourth Anniversary of Israel</u>, permit me to write you how <u>happy you have made me and countless others in your unparalleled help and assistance for the emancipation of Palestine</u>.

In my humble opinion and no doubt in the mind of every good law-abiding Jew, Israel <u>Independence Day should be synonymous with Harry S. Truman</u> Day.

May the good Lord spare you for many, many years to come, enjoy good health and happiness with your family.

Again THANK YOU.

Sincerely,
Elizabeth Lee Siegel
NYC

Although problems in the Middle East generated a great deal of press coverage and letters to the White House, they seemed more like a distracting sideshow compared with the threatening situation in Europe. Long before the formulation of the Marshall Plan, the United States made loans to numerous European nations in an effort to help them stabilize the chaotic situations they found themselves in after the war. To many Americans, sending money to "foreigners" was tantamount to pouring it down a rat hole, and protests were made against sending any money at all, or against sending it to specific countries that had incurred the correspondents' disfavor.

Dear Mr. President: *January 17, 1947*

Last week I saw in the paper where the Italian Premier departed for home with a Fifty Million Dollar payment by the United States Treasury in his pocket. This is not a loan—but a payment!

Italy not only stabbed France in the back and raped Ethiopia but Italy was also OUR enemy in this war. Italy fought us, killed our soldiers, but after long and costly fighting we licked Italy. What has Italy got on us that her Premier can come over here and collect FIFTY MILLION DOLLARS?

I know the wife of a G.I. who works hard to make twenty-five dollars per week. Our government takes seventy cents each week out of her pay for income taxes. This G.I. and his wife have very little to get along on, yet the government takes SEVENTY CENTS each week out of her pay. Then our government pays Italy FIFTY MILLION DOLLARS. It will take many, many weeks at seventy cents per week from the pay envelopes of hundreds of thousands of G.I.'s and their wives to make up fifty million dollars.

I am very badly upset about this payment of fifty million dollars.

What I want to know is: How was this job done? I want the names of every person connected with it. I believe you can find it out. I may decide to start a big investigation about this fifty million dollar payment. The taxes we pay sometimes come pretty hard and yet some great big baboon in Washington has paid Italy fifty million dollars. I repeat that I want the names of every government official in any way connected with the approval of this payment. I am pretty well burned up and I want the intimate details of how this monstrous piece of business was ever accomplished.

I await your early reply with keen anticipation.

> *Yours very truly,*
> *Harold W. Connolly*
> *Attorney At Law*
> *New Bedford, Mass.*

Americans sent Truman advice on almost every facet of foreign policy, and one didn't have to be a U.S. citizen to offer him the benefit of one's opinion. It might actually be read by the president, especially if it came from someone like, say, a former prime minister of Great Britain.

[Longhand] *Private.*

My dear Harry,   *29 June 1949*

I feel I ought to send you the enclosed memorandum which has been written by a very able young member of our Party in the House of Commons, Mr. Alec Spearman, as the result of his visit to Greece. I should be grateful to you if you could, among your preoccupations, find time to read it. I cannot vouch personally for the facts, but you have no doubt full information. In view of the very great responsibility I undertook in 1944–45 to save Athens from falling a prey to the Communists, as it would have done, and in view of the adoption of this policy at great expense by the United States, I venture upon the following comment:-

Intervention by a great State in the internal affairs of a small one is always questionable and entails much complicated argument. If the great State thinks it right to intervene surely they should make their intervention effective by using the overwhelming power they have at their disposal. Not to do this is only to prolong the agony at immense expense and possibly to final disastrous conclusion. I hope you will consider this as it affects the future in many ways.

I was deeply impressed by your statement about no fear to use the atomic bomb if the need arose. I am sure this will do more than anything else to ward off the catastrophe of a third world war. I have felt it right to speak, as you may have seen, in terms of reassurance for the immediate future, but of course I remain under the impression of the fearful dangers which impend upon us. Complete unity, superior force and the undoubted readiness to use it, give us the only hopes of escape. Without you nothing can be done.

Yours sincerely,
Winston S. Churchill

Truman sent the letter to his new secretary of state, Dean Acheson, for comment and received a prompt reply.

MEMORANDUM FOR THE PRESIDENT

Subject: Mr. Churchill's Note Regarding a Visit to Greece

It is recommended that acknowledgment along the lines indicated in the attached draft be made to Mr. Churchill of the "Note on a Visit to Greece," which he recently forwarded to you. The note in question was actually prepared by Mr. A. C. M. Spearman, a Conservative Member of Parliament, who visited Greece for ten days in May. It reflects the well-known views of high British officials in Athens.

Dean Acheson

DRAFT

Thank you for sending along the notes on Greece which I have called to the attention of Secretary Acheson, Ambassador [Henry F.] Grady, and General Van Fleet.

While I appreciate the danger of over-optimism in the Greek situation, our own reports from Greece do reflect an increasingly hopeful situation. General Van Fleet is confident, in fact, that the present Greek forces, with the help of some additional American and British equipment now being provided, will be able to reestablish security up to the frontier areas this year. Communist pressure from Albania and Bulgaria will perhaps continue to cause trouble, but this should present less of a problem with Yugoslavia out of the picture. In these circumstances and especially in view of the over-all requirements of the proposed United States foreign military assistance program, it would not be feasible to increase the scale of American military aid to Greece at the present time.

I am confident that American officials in Greece will continue to work with their British colleagues in estimating Greek military requirements and in their other activities in that country. The effectiveness of Anglo-American cooperation in Greece has indeed been most gratifying. While complete integration of the British and American military missions in Greece, as suggested in the note you sent me, is an attractive proposal, I am not persuaded that it is essential and I believe that it might involve certain administrative and even political difficulties. For example, top command of the Greek forces is now effectively unified and vested in the person of General Papagos, whose relations with both the American and British Missions are, I believe, satisfactory. Integration of these Missions might, therefore, suggest the contrary and would certainly be interpreted by Soviet propaganda as a tightening of Anglo-American "imperialist control" over Greece.

Acheson's draft displayed the standard written-by-committee feel that was commonly signed off on by Truman in communications with heads of state and other notables, but this was certainly not how he addressed Churchill. Truman replied in the same conversational tone he used in all letters to people he considered his friends, and he ignored Acheson's unspoken suggestion that he not respond to Churchill's comment about the atom bomb—a very sensitive subject in the court of world opinion. The secretary of state, who undoubtedly was given a copy of Truman's letter, would at least have been relieved to see that the president did not *directly* refer to the weapon.

> *Dear Winston:*   *July 2, 1949*
>
> I appreciated your good letter of the 29th most highly, and read the enclosed note on a visit to Greece by Mr. Alec Spearman with a great deal of interest.
>
> I am in agreement with you that Greece must be kept from the hands of the Communists, and we expect to do everything possible to fulfill that objective.
>
> I am not quite so pessimistic as you are about the prospects for a third world war. I rather think that eventually we are going to forget

that idea, and get a real world peace. I don't believe even the Russians can stand it to face complete destruction, which certainly would happen to them in the event of another war.

I hope you are in good health and that everything is going well with you. It is always a pleasure to hear from you.

Sincerely yours,
HARRY S. TRUMAN

Actually, Truman had been carrying on a lively, if sporadic, correspondence with Churchill ever since the statesman was booted out of 10 Downing Street by the British electorate in the midst of the Potsdam Conference.

My dear Mr. President,			*January 29, 1946*
I avail myself of the fact that your personal pilot is going from here to-morrow to Washington to send you these few lines.

It is very kind of you to place a powerful plane at my disposal and I am going to Cuba in it on Friday for a week. I have abandoned my plan of going to Trinidad as it is too long a hop for pleasure-time, but I am examining the possibilities of going to Veracruz, which is on the sea level and where I hear the scenery is very fine for painting. I shall be back here on February 10.

I am very glad to know you are coming along this coast. I will certainly come out and see you on your ship if you would wish it. I need a talk with you a good while before our Fulton date. I have a Message to deliver to your country and to the world, and I think it very likely that we shall be in full agreement about it. Under your auspices anything I say will command some attention and there is an opportunity for doing some good to this bewildered, baffled and breathless world.

I have just received a telegram from Harry Hopkins' wife saying that he is failing rapidly. I have a great regard for that man, who always went to the root of the matter and scanned our great affairs with piercing eye.

Let me congratulate you in what seems to be an improvement in the strike situation. My feeling, as an outsider, has been that there is so much good work and good wages going about at this time that the common interest of the State and the workers is enormous and will prevail, after the inevitable, convulsive movements of post-war readjustments have had their hour.

With kind regards and all respects,

> *Yours sincerely,*
> *Winston S. Churchill*
> *Miami Beach, Florida*

My dear Mr. Churchill: *February 2, 1946*

It was a pleasure to furnish you with a pilot and I hope you had the use of him as long as you needed him.

I shall probably be in Florida on the eleventh of February and will immediately get in touch with you. I hope you find it convenient to visit me on the yacht. I know you have a real message to deliver at Fulton and, of course, I shall be most happy to talk with you about it.

It certainly was too bad about Mr. Harry Hopkins, but I had been expecting it for almost a week. He is a great loss to the country and especially to me, because he was familiar with all the meetings which Mr. Roosevelt attended during the war.

I sincerely hope you are having a good rest and enjoying your visit in Florida. Veracruz is a lovely city at this time of year and has some very beautiful scenery. One of the most beautiful mountains in the world is just a short distance from Veracruz—seeming to rise right out of the Gulf of Mexico when you are coming into the harbor, to a height of over 18,000 feet. That mountain, Mount Rainier in the State of Washington and Popocatepetl at Mexico City, I think, are our most beautiful peaks, principally because they stand alone and are not surrounded by other mountains.

I am looking forward to a pleasant visit with you.

> *Sincerely yours,*
> *HARRY S. TRUMAN*

The message to deliver at Fulton referred to Churchill's upcoming "Iron Curtain" speech at Westminster College in Fulton, Missouri, in which he called for Western nations to unite in opposition to the Soviet Union's desire for "indefinite expansion of their power and doctrine." Truman enthusiastically approved the speech, drafts of which his chief of staff, Adm. William Leahy, and secretary of state, Jimmy Byrnes, had proudly been shown by Churchill even as it was being written. Churchill traveled to Fulton with Truman on the president's private train, where White House personnel eagerly ran off mimeographed copies for the press. Truman himself gave the introductory remarks before the speech. But although the address was one of the defining moments of the emerging Cold War and is among Churchill's finest orations, it was Harry who "caught hell" for it at the time from the press and from Americans who thought he was pushing the country toward World War III. Though Truman could clearly see that the United States and the Soviet Union were on a colision course, the term Cold War had not even come into existence yet, and Truman was operating far out in front of public opinion. He pulled back from an outright public endorsement of the speech and even claimed that he'd never read it beforehand.

Niles, who had also worked for FDR, once observed, "Roosevelt did not believe in getting out too far in front of the people. He had far greater patience than Truman and planned long-range educational programs to win popular support before he acted. When Truman saw a problem, he wanted it settled on the spot."[4] But as the emerging threat from the Soviet Union became more clear to him, Truman did his best to increase public awareness of Soviet expansionism. On February 9, 1946, less than a month before Churchill's speech, Stalin announced that peaceful coexistence was "impossible under the present capitalist development of the world economy" and stated that production of consumer goods "must wait on rearmament," as the Soviets embarked on an immense five-year program of industrial and armament expansion "to guarantee our country against any eventuality." This was followed, two weeks later, in the midst of escalating tensions between Western and Soviet occupation authorities in Germany, by a lengthy memorandum from the U.S. chargé d'affaires in Moscow, George Kennan. In it, Kennan clearly articulated and reinforced the warnings on Soviet intentions that Truman had already received from senior members of his administration like Averell Harriman and James Forrestal, as well as Leahy, Marshall, and Acheson. Truman stated privately to Harriman and others that the failure of the Soviets to pull their troops out of Iran might lead to war. To reporters, however, he would only answer, "I have nothing to say about it." He would let his staff do the talking and let the eloquent words of Churchill stand on their own.

Churchill, as a humble servant of the king and the British people, also took every opportunity to promote Britain's interests, albeit in a global or European context. When North Korean troops invaded South Korea in June 1950, with the support of the Soviet Union and Chinese communists, a widely held fear in London, shared by Truman, was that the thrust may have been only the opening move in a coordinated communist effort to embroil U.S. forces in the Far East and thus leave Western Europe open to a Soviet invasion. When it became apparent that the United States was going to send a substantial portion of its greatly reduced armed forces to the Western Pacific, the former—and future—prime minister typed a letter discussing European security issues with no mention at all of the desperate fighting in Korea.

[Longhand] *Private*
My dear Harry,   *13 August 1950*

I dare say and certainly hope that you read my speech at the Strasbourg Assembly and I trust you will have an account presented to you of the deeply interesting debate which led up to the great majority by which the Resolution for a European Army was carried. This is of course to me the fruition of what I have laboured for ever since my speech at Zurich four years ago. I enclose a marked copy of what I said at that time.

The ending of the quarrel between France and Germany by what is really a sublime act on the part of the French leaders, and a fine manifestation of the confidence which Western Germany have in our and your good faith and goodwill, is I feel an immense step forward towards the kind of world for which you and I are striving. It is also the best hope of avoiding a third World War.

The only alternative to a European Army with a front against Russian aggression in Europe is, of course, a kind of neutrality arrangement by Germany, France and the smaller countries with the Soviets. This is what the Communists are striving for, and it could only mean the speedy absorption of the neutral European countries by the methods which have subjugated Czechoslovakia, as they would be in a sort of no-man's-land between Britain, with its American air-bombing base, and the Soviet armies. They and their cities and junctions might all become involved, especially if these countries were used for the rocket bombardment of Britain.

Although none of us can tell what the Soviet intentions are, I have no doubts that we ought, at this stage, to reject the strategy of holding the Channel and the Pyrenees and strive for the larger hope.

The point however on which I wish particularly to address you is, what will happen to the Germans if they send a substantial contingent—say five or six divisions—to the European Army, in which Britain and, I trust, Americans will be strongly represented, and the Soviets retaliate by invading Western Germany? Would the United States treat a major aggression of this kind into Western Germany in the same way as it would treat a Soviet attack on France, the Benelux or Britain, or should we let these German people, whom we have disarmed and for whose safety we have accepted responsibility, be attacked without the shield of the atomic deterrent? I should indeed be grateful if I could have your views on this.

You will note that I said at Strasbourg that if the Germans threw in their lot with us, we should hold their safety and freedom as sacred as our own. Of course I have no official right to speak for anyone, yet after the firm stand you have successfully made about Berlin, I think that the deterrent should be made to apply to all countries represented in the European Army. I do not see how this would risk or cost any more than what is now morally guaranteed by the United States.

Perhaps you will consider whether you can give any indication of your views. A public indication would be of the utmost value and is, in my opinion, indispensable to the conception of a European front against Communism. Perhaps it may be the case that Mr. Acheson, or your representative in Germany, has already given an assurance in this respect.

You may perhaps have noted the unexpected and fortunate fact that the view of the German Delegation, who represent all parties in the German Government, is that Germany should send a contingent to the European Army (say of five or six divisions), but should not have a National Army of her own. I had feared they might take the opposite view, namely, 'let us have a National Army with its own munitions, supplies, and the right to re-arm, and we will then give a contingent to the European Army.' I need not say what an enormous difference this has made to the French view. They and we can get it both ways.

With kind regards.

> *Yours sincerely,*
> *Winston S. Churchill*
> *Chartwell, Westerham, Kent.*

Dear Winston: *August 18, 1950*

I certainly appreciate your good letter of August thirteenth. I read with deep interest as I had already read your Strasbourg speech and the copy of the speech which you had made four years ago.

We are living in a tumultuous and uncertain age and I am sincerely hoping that the right decisions may be made by our Government to create a condition that will lead to general world peace.

I hope that everything is going well with you and that sometime
in the not too far distant future it will be possible for us to see each
other again.

Please remember me to Mrs. Churchill.

Sincerely yours,

HARRY S. TRUMAN

Churchill certainly excused Truman the brief reply, knowing that the president had a rather full plate at the moment. He had made his effort to ensure that the danger to Western Europe was not overshadowed by events in the Pacific, and both he and Truman knew that, even as their letters crisscrossed the Atlantic, the first British troops of what was eventually to become a sizable contingent were being rushed up to Korea from Hong Kong. When Truman declared a state of emergency, increased the size of the U.S. armed forces, and recalled four National Guard divisions into service, the majority of the new troops actually went to bolster the defense of Europe. Moreover, the United States was, by now, fully enmeshed in a huge aid program that aimed at nothing short of the complete revitalization of Europe's war-ravaged economy.

In hindsight, passage of the European Recovery Program of 1948, or the Marshall Plan, seems almost a miraculous event. It was launched by the administration of an unelected, "lame duck" president whose loss of the upcoming election appeared to be such a virtual certainty that both press and politicians openly talked about his administration being "scheduled" to leave office in 1949. Indeed, Truman's personal popularity was perceived to be so low by his own party that he was actually pressed *not* to assist in the congressional campaign of 1946.

A program of continental dimensions, the Marshall Plan expended more than $12.5 billion (equivalent to roughly $65 billion today) at a time when a worried Pentagon, virtually disarmed by postwar budget cuts, was making a solid case for increasing funding; numerous domestic agencies were, with heavy congressional support, clamoring for enlarged welfare programs; the U.S. Treasury Department was intent on building upon the existing budget surpluses; and the Democratic Party did not hold a majority in either house of Congress.

That the Marshall Plan became a reality was due to the energetic efforts of many individuals: the Republican chairman of the Senate Foreign Relations Committee, Arthur H. Vandenberg; eminent Republicans Henry L. Stimson and Robert Patterson, who had both become secretaries of war under Roosevelt; Truman himself; and of course, Secretary of State George C. Marshall, a man venerated by Truman as "the greatest living American" and "the great one of the age."[5] Curiously, Joseph Stalin was also a key figure behind the passage of the Marshall Plan, and Truman once remarked that without his "crazy" moves, "we never would have had our foriegn policy . . . we never could have got a thing from Congress."

The Soviets made a tactical blunder in their outright rejection of the Marshall Plan, because the U.S. Congress almost certainly would have balked at economically supporting communist countries if the Soviet Union and its satellites had agreed to participate. When Czechoslovakia appeared ready to accept, Stalin called key members of the Czech government to Moscow and threatened them with severe consequences. Under this pressure, the Czechs backed off, but their show of independence in accepting the invitation was evidently too much for Stalin. In February 1948, a Soviet-backed coup eliminated the last vestiges of an independent Czechoslovakia, and a communist government was installed.

Continuing efforts to reach a Four-Power agreement on Germany also went nowhere, and it became obvious that the Soviet Union had no intention of permitting unification of Germany. The United States and Great Britain decided to go forward with plans for the creation of a West German state. Before this should become a reality, they decided, among other things, to implement the long-planned currency reform in order to bring stability to the monetary system in the Western occupation zones, which were flooded with "occupation currency" produced in the Soviet zone. It was realized that both of these plans would be opposed by the Soviet Union and would most likely result in a confrontation. The most likely spot for that confrontation was the exposed outpost of Berlin, which was located deep within the Soviet occupation zone.

Starting in March 1948, the Soviets began to interfere intermittently with surface transportation from the British and American zones to the Western occupation sectors of Berlin in an effort to intimidate both the German populace and Western forces by displaying just how vulnerable the city was to a blockade. Americans immediately rallied around their president and the embattled U.S. military governor in Berlin, Gen. Lucius Clay.

President Harry Truman   *April 2, 1948*
Herein is a copy of a cable, dated April 1, 1948, sent by us to Gen. Lucius Clay, Commander of U. S. Military Government, in Berlin, Germany:

WE EARNESTLY URGE YOU TO KEEP OUR SUPPLY
TRAINS MOVING.
    WE CANNOT BACK DOWN NOW.

Middletown Citizens Committee
Middletown, Ohio

With the implementation in the Western zones of the long-expected currency reform on June 18, 1948, the Soviets decreed that the Potsdam Declaration had been violated. When the Western powers in Berlin refused to cede power to the Soviet Occupation Authority, the Soviet blockade of Berlin began in earnest.

Instead of attempting to break the blockade by conventional means, such as sending through heavily armed and combat-ready convoys of supplies—a dangerous and extremely risky proposition at best—a more creative and less provocative solution was decided upon. The city and its 2 million inhabitants would be supplied by a virtual conveyor belt of aircraft. Even among Truman's detractors, there was great support for this tactic, and from its ad hoc beginnings, the airlift steadily grew into a massive operation, stunning in its scope and complexity. Some, however, thought it ridiculous that the United States had gotten into this situation in the first place and were convinced they knew who had gotten it there.

Dear Sir: *September 12, 1948*

The so-called "Berlin Crisis" is entirely an outgrowth of your own incredible stupidity.

When you attended the Potsdam Conference to arrange final details for the occupation of Germany, it was your duty to look out for American interests and insist upon the establishment of a corridor to the American Zone for ingress and egress to the city. This you failed to do. Possibly this was because you believed Joe Stalin to be a "good old chap," as you expressed it some time ago. But I am inclined to think that you were just too dumb to know that such a corridor was necessary.

In the meantime, you seem to be willing and even eager to force this country into a war with Russia merely for the purpose of "saving face." If you do this, the blame for such a war will rest upon your own shoulders, and the blood of American boys butchered in this war will be on your head.

Read the enclosed article from the *Los Angeles Times* of September 12, and then perhaps even your <u>feeble mind will grasp the fact that the Berlin Crisis can be solved without dragging the United States into war</u>.

> *Yours truly,*
> *Philip Johnston*
> *Los Angeles, Calif.*

As the blockade and airlift dragged on, more and more correspondents offered their suggestions on how to end the crisis.

Dear President Truman: *December 4, 1948*

Like every American, I have been watching the Berlin situation with great concern. A thought occurs to me in connection with it, which I am passing on to you in all humility. You have hundreds of experts on the job far more capable than I, who may have had the same thought and discarded it for excellent reasons. Yet, on the off chance that it has not been considered I am prompted to make this suggestion.

Might it not be possible to reconcile the Berlin situation by having the United Nations take both Russia and the United States out of this highly controversial area, and bring in several of the smaller nations to govern it?

I do not want to seem presumptuous in making this suggestion but because it seems to me to have a germ of possibility I feel that I must pass it along.

> *Sincerely,*
> *Arthur B. Baer*
> *Stix, Baer and Fuller*
> *St. Louis, Mo.*

Dear Mr. Baer: *December 17, 1948*

Please accept the President's thanks for your letter of December fourth. He greatly appreciates having this thoughtful expression of your views regarding foreign relations.

> *Very sincerely yours,*
> *WILLIAM D. HASSETT*

My dear President Truman: *November 10, 1948*

The writer like many other citizens of the United States would like to have definite action in matters that pertain to Berlin. There is no question in my mind but that you know more about it than any other man in America. However, you probably would like to know about the feelings and thoughts of others. Therefore, I am suggesting that you, as President of the United States, <u>delegate General Douglas MacArthur as our representative to handle the affairs in the Reich</u>.

Our great General has demonstrated his ability to handle Joe Stalin in Japan. He has an excellent staff there to carry out his program. Why not let him set up a program similar to this in the Reich to handle the situation.

I wish to congratulate you on your recent campaign and your successful conclusion of that job.

Sincerely yours,
Joseph C. Lewis
Associated Engineers, Inc.
Fort Wayne, Ind.

My dear Mr. Lewis: *November 18, 1948*

Permit me to acknowledge your letter of November tenth, which has been received in the absence of the President. You may be assured that it will be brought to his attention at the first opportunity. Meanwhile, I want to thank you, in the President's behalf, for your kind congratulations.

Very sincerely yours,
WILLIAM D. HASSETT

Suggestions on how to handle both the situation in Germany and the four-way presidential "catfight" between Truman, Republican Thomas Dewey, Progressive Party candidate Henry Wallace, and "Dixiecrat" Strom Thurmond came from yet another contender, the former Presbyterian minister and perennial Socialist Party candidate, Norman Thomas, whose primary focus was on his closest ideological bedfellow, Wallace.

Dear President Truman: *Spetember 11, 1948*

This letter is not being written for publicity and will not be released at any time. I am writing because I want to tell you that I appreciated the firmness and patience with which the governments of the United States and the other Western nations have been conducting the negotiations about Berlin, and because I want to bring to your attention some remarks I shall deliver tonight at a dinner honoring <u>Luigi Antonini</u>, Vice-President of the <u>International Ladies' Garment Workers Union</u>.

In my talk I shall propose that the American government put before the Paris United Nations General Assembly the actions, in Berlin and elsewhere, by which the Soviet dictatorship menaces the peace of the world. I believe the Kremlin's actions fall within the provisions of paragraph 2 of Article II concerning the functions of the General Assembly.

I shall also suggest that the State Department confer with all presidential candidates about referring the Berlin crisis to the United Nations so that—as far as possible—our critical relations with the Soviet Union may be taken out of the realm of campaign politics.

Such a conference would put <u>Henry Wallace</u> on the spot. If he did not go along, he would be even more isolated, and less harmful to the United States, than he is now. If he goes along, it will make things more difficult for Stalin.

In either case, it would demonstrate the essential unity of all American non-Communist opinion against Soviet aggression and would strengthen the chances of maintaining world peace.

I should appreciate hearing from you on your opinion concerning this proposal.

> *Sincerely yours,*
> *Norman Thomas*
> *Socialist Party Campaign Headquarters*
> *New York, N.Y.*

Truman needed all the help he could get in the crucial state of New York (only one candidate in the previous eighteen elections had won without carrying the state), and he was more than willing to send the generally well-liked Thomas a gracious acknowledgment if it would keep him and his loyal core of followers from swinging to Wallace.

My dear Mr. Thomas: *September 14, 1948*
I read your letter of September eleventh with a great deal of interest and I appreciate very much your writing me about the situation in Berlin.

Every step possible to maintain peace will be taken in regard to the settlement of this matter. I am still hopeful that a peaceful settlement can be reached.

I certainly appreciate your interest in the matter and thank you for writing me about it.

Sincerely yours,
HARRY S. TRUMAN

For many ardent New Dealers, however, there was almost nothing Truman could do right, and Wallace was accepted as the rightful heir to FDR's throne. Weeks before Truman even announced his bid for reelection, one liberal in New Orleans came to the conclusion that Truman's candidacy was already dead and that the choice of Sen. Howard McGrath as the new Democratic Party chairman had done him in. McGrath, a comparatively conservative Democrat, had only recently taken over the chairmanship from long-time party operative Bob Hannegan, an individual who was himself less a New Deal Democrat than a skilled politician. (Hannegan, for example, had urged Truman not to veto the Taft-Hartly Act, which severely curtailed the power of labor unions.)

Dear President Truman: *February 20, 1948*

Chairman McGrath has just about ruined any chance for reelection you might have had. He is ably abetting the Republicans.

Like myself, 10 percent or more of American voters believe in Henry Wallace. Of this 10 percent, not over 2 percent are communists. We regard ourselves as liberals. But when we express mildly liberal views, we are called communists by reactionaries. Now McGrath has joined this group. He implies that the recent New York election was won by the votes, not of liberals, but of communists. By implication, he attacks Wallace, thus nearly equaling the New Orleans or McCormick press.

The thing to make clear is this. When McGrath attacks Wallace, he is by implication, attacking every liberal who believes in Wallace; but who, as the lesser evil, will vote the Democratic ticket.

Your re-election, or a Democratic victory, depends on this liberal vote. McGrath is antagonizing it.

If the reaction of most liberals is like my own; they are convinced that your recent utterances were not sincere. Of course they could be wrong, but actions speak much louder than words.

You kept the ineffable [Edwin] Pauley and fired [Harold] Ickes. You ousted Wallace, Landis, [Marriner] Eccles, and every other liberal and replaced them with reactionaries or worse. You give no support to the world's main hope, the U.N. You refer to price controls as police state methods. You propose drafting strikers into the army. You insist on universal military training, i.e., the State of the Military Police. You rush headlong toward war, apparently with no idea of where you are going. You keep Snyder, Forrestal, Harriman in the cabinet.

Then you seem to feel that a few words about reactionaries will convince liberals that you are liberal.

The liberal vote will be split. Many, like myself, intend not to vote. Many will vote for Wallace, feeling that the Republicans can be no worse than the present administration, and that four years in power will discredit them. Some will vote for Stassen, under the impression that he is more liberal than Truman, if they have the chance.

My feeling is that labor was too quick to repudiate Wallace. Had they held off a few months, they might have forced more concessions from a reactionary government, but now they are committed.

Most liberals do not regard you as responsible. They feel, that like Harding, you have been betrayed by your "friends."

> *Sincerely,*
> *Richard Ashman*
> *New Orleans, La.*

Although fewer in number, Truman also received letters of support that displayed a firm grasp of what he called "the facts."

Dear friend Harry: *March 20, 1948*

I am not addressing you, as you will note, in your official capacity, but personally.

I just finished reading Maurice Milligen's article in the *Kansas City Times* relative to his book which will appear for sale on the market in the near future entitled *Missouri Waltz.* Should it not be *Missouri Mule?*

It is said that this book is a factual one covering his experience in connection with the investigation and prosecution of Mr. Pendergast many years ago. To me, as a lawyer, it is a lot of "bunk"—Pendergast entered his plea of guilty, received a minimum term, served it, and died, and that's all there is to the story.

Of course, we all know what's in the back of this fellow Milligen's head. First, he did not receive the appointment as U.S. District Attorney in 1945, and all "ham and eggers" have agreed to fight the Champion. U.S. Senator Jim Reed, who was a personal friend of mine, spent the last 25 years of his life along those lines with little, if any, success, other than publicity, of course.

Your recent talk was well received in this state by all of the fair-minded thinking people, and, in addition thereto, we think your denouncement of Wallace and his gang was the best possible move you could have made at this time. Perhaps that will hold him for a time.

I met you at the Democratic "Pow-Wow" in Topeka, Kansas, a few years ago when you addressed the Democratic gathering of Kansas.

I'm an uncle of James R. Sullivan, an attorney, of Kansas City, Missouri; also, I'm closely associated with D. H. Hill, Democratic State Chairman of this State.

Wishing you well, I am,

> *Sincerely yours,*
> *Jerry E. Driscoll*
> *Russell, Kansas*

Dear Mr. Driscoll: *March 29, 1948*

I can't tell you how very much I appreciated your good letter of the twentieth and how highly I appreciated your comment on Maurice Milligen's proposed book.

His idea, of course, is to add to the "smear campaign" which is going on about the present occupant of The White House and if that will give him any pleasure or buy him any cereal I suppose it is all right.

You were very kind to write me as you did.

> *Sincerely yours,*
> *HARRY S. TRUMAN*

As the Democratic Convention neared, a correspondent in Philadelphia —writing on Independence Day—was convinced that the candidate's worst enemy was the candidate himself. His method of addressing the president suggests that he wasn't one of Truman's greatest admirers.

> MR. TRUMAN—THE WHITE HOUSE   JULY 4, 1948
> DEAR SIR—
> I THINK IT IS BETTER FOR YOU TO LEAVE THE CONVENTION TO ITSELF, AND STAY IN WASHINGTON. I THINK SUCH A COURSE MAY SAVE YOUR ELECTION.
> WE WANT YOU WITH YOUR HAND RIGHT ON THE HELM AT WASHINGTON.
> RESPECTFULLY,
> L. E. MORRIS
> PHILADELPHIA, PENN.

Another Philadelphian, finding the convention to be a droning, lackluster affair, urged Truman to fire it up.

> THE PRESIDENT, THE WHITE HOUSE   JULY 13, 1948
> I AM DISGUSTED WITH THE DEFEATED ATTITUDE OF THE DELEGATES TO THIS CONVENTION. I HOPE YOUR NOMINATING SPEAKER WILL BE AFFIRMATIVE AND AGGRESSIVE. I AM PROUD OF THE RECORD OF YOUR ADMINISTRATION. THE COUNTRY WAS NEVER MORE PROSPEROUS. NO APOLOGIES NECESSARY. GIVE THEM HELL AND GOOD LUCK.
> PATRICK H. O'BRIEN

Truman had wanted to personally thank the gentleman who sent this telegram, but his staff was unable to obtain an address. The man certainly got what he wanted, however. Truman, his appearance delayed till almost 2:00 A.M., electrified the previously moribund delegates with a highly charged extemporaneous speech that called the Republican's bluff. Throughout the campaign, the Republicans championed numerous proposals that were usually areas of Democratic concern and which they had, in fact, blocked Truman from carrying out. Many Democrats rightly claimed that Republican promises were purely a cynical effort to entice as many voters away from their party as possible—promises that they would conveniently forget once they had regained the White House. But their protests, following on the heels of Republican initiatives, were ineffective and had a crybaby ring.

Truman had a better idea. The night before his address, Ayers outlined the president's campaign strategy in his diary: "If he can keep the swear words out of it, [he will] tell them just what he thinks. He said he was going to wind up by calling Congress back for a special session" immediately after the convention ended. Truman explained to Ayers that "if he called the [Republican-controlled] Congress back he could then put up the Republican platform promises to the members and call on them to live up to their promises. If they pass the legislation he could show they were forced into it; if they did not it would show them up." Truman told the assembled delegates that it was time for the Republicans to either put up or shut up, and as historian Robert Ferrell later noted, he "turned the sleepy, hot convention (there was no air conditioning and the hall was a steam bath) into a shouting frenzied mob."[6] Delegates went back to their home districts completely reinvigorated and ready for the tough campaign ahead. Truman's opponents were not amused.

THE PRESIDENT, THE WHITE HOUSE   JULY 15, 1948
YOUR MUD SLINGING SPEECH ASSURES YOU OF YOUR DEFEAT IN THE SOUTH. I AM GLAD YOU WERE NOMINATED FOR AN EASY VICTORY FOR DEWEY.
WILLIAM A. HEUSINGER
SAN ANTONIO, TEXAS

As expected, the sullen members of the recalled House and Senate accomplished almost nothing, and Truman beat up the "Do-Nothing Congress" for the rest of the campaign. Despite confident predictions that he would, at best, come out a narrow loser, he emerged the winner on November 2, 1948—and without New York State.

Truman boarded the train in Independence for his victory ride back to Washington. When it stopped in St. Louis, he was handed a newspaper, which he gleefully held aloft for the throng of well-wishers to see: a copy of the *Chicago Daily Tribune*, which proclaimed, somewhat prematurely, "DEWEY DEFEATS TRUMAN" in a banner headline. He also received a telegram from the *Washington Post*.

President Harry S. Truman, Independence, Mo.
You are hereby invited to attend a "Crow Banquet" to which this newspaper proposes to invite newspaper editorial writers, political reporters and editors, including our own along with pollsters, radio

commentators and columnists for the purpose of providing a repast appropriate to the appetite created by the late elections.

The main course will consist of Breast of Tough Old Crow En Glace. (You will eat turkey.)

The Democratic National Committee has agreed to furnish the toothpicks to be used by the guests who (it is feared) will require months to get the last of the crow out of their teeth.

We hope you will consent to deliver the address of the evening. As the Dean of American Election Forecasters (and the only accurate one), it is much desired that you share with your colleagues the secret of your analytical success.

Dress for Guest of Honor, white tie; for others—sack cloth.

The *Washington Post* will be happy to arrange this dinner for any date that suits your convenience and pleasure.

                              THE WASHINGTON POST

The Washington Post   *November 6, 1948*

I received on the train your very handsome invitation to me to attend a "crow banquet." I know that we could all have a good time together, but I feel I must decline. As I said en route to Washington, I have no desire to crow over anybody or to see anybody eating crow, figuratively or otherwise. We should all get together now and make a country in which everybody can eat turkey whenever he pleases.

Incidentally, I want to say that despite your editorial opposition to the Democratic ticket, your news coverage of my campaign was fair and comprehensive.

Again, many thanks and regards.

                              Sincerely yours,
                              HARRY S. TRUMAN

Dear Sir: *March 8, 1949*

As recreational director of the city of Marseilles, Illinois, I am interested in holding an Easter egg rolling contest and I would appreciate any information you could give me on this.

I would like to know the age group, length of roll, rules governing the actual roll, and any other information concerning the contest.

Sincerely yours,
Robert B. Hart
Marseilles, Ill.

Dear Mr. Hart: *17 March 1949*

This will acknowledge your letter of March eighth.

There is not a great deal of information I can give you in answer to your inquiries about the traditional Easter Egg rolling on the White House grounds.

The egg rolling was not literally a contest. The South Grounds of the White House were opened on Easter Monday to children and adults accompanied by children. The youngsters brought baskets of colored Easter Eggs which they rolled on the sloping lawn. This custom goes as far back as the time of President Johnson and similar affairs were held at one time on the Capitol grounds and on the grounds of the Zoological Park.

The Easter Egg Rolling on the South Grounds of the White House was discontinued at the beginning of the war and has never been held since. It is not expected that it will be held this year either.

Sincerely yours,
Eben A. Ayers
Assistant Press Secretary

CHAPTER FIVE

PERSONAL QUESTIONS • SUGGESTIONS •
LOOK-ALIKES • "NUT MAIL"

Truman received thousands of letters every day. Many pertained to the "big questions"—war, the economy, foreign affairs. Yet interspersed with these were letters congratulating the president on a good job, complimenting him on his clothing, and inquiring about job opportunities at the White House—in short, everyday Americans writing to their president about everyday matters. One of the most frequent inquiries arriving at the White House regarded the *S* in Harry S. Truman.

Mr. President,   *August 11, 1945*

I am a <u>girl thirteen years</u> of age and my home is in Columbus, Ga. I go to East Highland School and will be in the 7th grade.

My brother Raymond and I had an argument about your name. He said the "S" stood for a name, and I said it was just an initial. Please let us know which is right.

We listen to the news and hope the war will be over soon.

Thank you,
Pearl Shepperd

My dear Pearl: *August 18, 1945*

This is in answer to the inquiry contained in your letter of August eleventh. The "S" in the President's name is an initial only. It seems that one of his grandfathers bore the name of Shippe and the other the name of Solomon; but he was not given either name.

Very sincerely yours,
WILLIAM D. HASSETT
Secretary to the President

Other Americans wanted to know more about the origins of their new president.

Sirs: *April 26, 1945*
Will you be kind enough to inform [me of] the exact date of the birth of President Truman. I should also like to know where he was born.

> *Very truly yours,*
> *A. P. Rogers*
> *New York, N.Y.*

My dear Mr. Rogers: *July 7, 1945*
Your postal card has been received and, in reply, I wish to advise you that the President was born on May 8, 1884, at Lamar, Missouri.

> *Very sincerely yours,*
> *WILLIAM D. HASSETT*
> *Secretary to the President*

Truman also received frequent questions regarding his favorite books, hobbies, animals, hymns, and other personal preferences. A favorite query involved his musical tastes.

Dear Mr. Pres,   *January 16, 1949*
We go to Sacred Heart School in Norfolk, Neb. and are in the eighth grade at 13. We and our parents are Democrats and how. We are sure the only way the Republicans will see the White House is by television. We play in the band at Sacred Heart School. Delores plays first violin and I play first clarinet. Our whole band is Democrats and so is our teacher. We would like to know what your favorite song is, so we could learn to play it. Would you please write and tell us?

> *Sincerely yours,*
> *Delores Peschel*
> *Emily Truedell*

P.S. Don't forget and write. We know you don't have much time but can't you answer two girls' plea?

The response by Charles Ross was that Truman had no favorite song but that he was "especially fond" of various pieces of music, including World War I songs. A similar query came from a woman in Birmingham, Alabama.

Dear Mr. President:

The Woodlawn Music Study Club has its first 1945–1946 meeting soon. Our club thinks it is remarkable our president is a musician.

For our first meeting, would we be asking too much when we ask you to send us the names of your favorite compositions. Any information about your musical career will be truly appreciated.

> *Sincerely,*
> *Mrs. George Allgood, Courtesy Chairman*
> *Woodlawn Music Study Club*
> *Birmingham, Ala.*

P. S. My only child, a son, is on his way home after three years service in the Pacific. We think you are a great president.

My dear Mrs. Allgood: *August 20, 1945*

Your letter to the President has been received. Regarding your inquiry, I have pleasure in stating that the favorite songs of the President include those two so popular in World War I, "Over There" and "Pack Up Your Troubles in Your Old Kit Bag." He also likes the "Toreador" from Carmen; the Sextettes from Lucia and Floradora, and Mendelssohn's "Song Without Words."

May I assure you that the President deeply appreciates your kind words of commendation. He can also well understand the feeling of pride with which you refer to your son.

> *Very sincerely yours,*
> *WILLIAM D. HASSETT*
> *Secretary to the President*

Another music query came from a young girl who apparently had just begun her own music lessons.

Dear President Truman:

I have always wanted to know what a president does through his term of office. Could you tell me? And I would also like to know how old you were when you started taking music lessons, or did you play by ear or note? I am taking piano lessons now and that is why I wanted to know because if I know how you played, I would try much harder. I should love to hear you play on the radio for instance "The Missouri Waltz." Also I believe that it is a fine thing for a man like you to play the piano as a hobby don't you?

> *Love; A Loyal American Girl*
> *Betty Hascall, Age 10*
> *Independence, Ohio*

Dear Betty: *December 3, 1947*

The President is now in Florida and will be away from the White House for several days. I am, therefore, writing in reply to your recent letter.

You asked what the President does through his term of office. He has so many things to do that, even were he here, I am afraid he would not be able to answer your letter himself and I doubt that I can attempt to tell you all of his duties. They are numerous and varied and depend to some extent on what is happening throughout the country and the world.

You also wanted to know how old the President was when he started to take music lessons. He was eight or nine years of age and he has played the piano whenever he has had an opportunity since then.

The President, I am sure, would want me to thank you for your Christmas card and for the fine and loyal spirit which you showed in writing your letter.

> *Sincerely yours,*
> *EBEN A. AYERS*
> *Assistant Press Secretary*

Music was a favorite topic in letters to Truman. A 1950 article in *Look* magazine quoted longtime Washington bandleader Barnee Breeskin as saying, "When he sits down at the keyboard, the President shows that he's boss. His memory is very exact. I have never heard him strike a wrong note." Breeskin was most impressed by Truman's artistry playing Paderewski's *Minuet*: "Usually Truman's pedal work on crescendos isn't awfully good. He doesn't use the loud pedal enough to get any real power. But in the *Minuet*—when the President goes to work on it—that crescendo in the second movement is terrific. You can't play suspended chords like that without training and discipline. Nobody could. A man who can play like that shouldn't even bother picking around at something like the *Missouri Waltz*."[1]

Some of his constituents believed the president's musical ability was too good not to be shared with the American people.

Dear President Truman: *August 9, 1945*

Music is the universal language which speaks to American, Englishman, Russian or Chinese. It transcends all boundaries of race, creed and politics.

Never in the past has a United States Chief Executive possessed such a marked talent for communicating with his fellow men through the medium of music. You have given of this gift freely to your friends and neighbors and of late to Premier Stalin and former Prime Minister Churchill.

I, like millions of other Americans, am proud of this great gift of yours. However, it obviously is impossible for myself and my fellow Americans to personally hear you play.

Hence, may I respectfully suggest that the nation would welcome the opportunity to hear you perform at the piano either through the medium of radio or the phonograph record, or both. No fear that commercialism would touch such a performance need deter you, as any proceeds from sale of such records could be given if you so desire to any war or charitable fund which you may designate.

What could be more fitting than that present and future generations of Americans have opportunity to hear the National Anthem or perhaps American folk songs or the classics played by the President who led the nation to ultimate victory in the greatest war the world has ever known?

Assuming that President Washington or President Lincoln had been musicians, would it not have thrilled you as a Missouri farm boy to have heard a recording of their music? Let me assure you that American boys of the future would be just as thrilled upon hearing such a recording by you.

As Chairman of the Board of Directors of the American Pioneer Guild, let me assure you that the Guild would be only too happy to aid in making arrangements for, or in sponsoring such a radio broadcast or making of phonographic recordings by you. Already the Guild has made recordings of many notable men, including the voices of numerous men now living or who have died only recently who personally knew Abraham Lincoln. The first recording arranged by the Guild was that of the voice of the late Governor Joseph Fifer of Illinois, which record was placed in the Illinois Archives Building by the late Secretary of State Edward J. Hughes.

> *Yours respectfully,*
> *Herbert Wells Fay, Custodian of Lincoln's Tomb*
> *and Chairman of the Board, American Pioneer Guild*
> *Springfield, Ill.*

Dear Mr. Fay: *August 18, 1945*

This will acknowledge your letter of August ninth, addressed to the President.

It was good of you to express your interest, and that of other Americans, in the President's piano playing, and the thought which prompted you to offer your suggestion is appreciated.

I fear that, for the present at least, it will not be possible for him to play for the radio or for a recording. I am sure you will understand how terribly busy he is these days with the multiplicity of tasks that confront him in carrying out the affairs of his office.

It was thoughtful of you to offer the assistance of your Guild in making arrangements for a radio broadcast or in making the recording, and I assure you should the occasion arise we shall be glad to take advantage of your generosity.

> *Sincerely yours,*
> *CHARLES G. ROSS*
> *Secretary to the President*

My dear Mr. President: *August 24, 1945*

The attached clipping from the *Baltimore Evening Sun*, prompted me to write this letter. I do hope that you will forgive me for being so forward . . . but I would like to second the motion! I think that a phonograph record made by you, as suggested in the item, would be a fine thing. If properly handled it could bring much happiness to many people and in many ways.

What I mean is that instead of just making a record of your piano playing for posterity's sake as suggested by Mr. Fay, I suggest you make a record or series of records for public sale, commercially, with the entire proceeds going to some veterans' fund or the fund of some organization that takes care of the survivors of veterans. I fully realize that this would be somewhat unethical, but at the same time it is a very humane and noble deed. Please note that I make this suggestion with the best of intentions.

Perhaps you would like to have the proceeds of such an arrangement go to the rehabilitation of foreign countries ravaged by war, and this, too, may be considered a worthy cause.

In any event, I hope that your efforts as a pianist will be available to the general public, as I would like very much to have a recording made by you, the President of the United States. I'm sure there are others who feel the same as I do.

Being somewhat of an amateur cartoonist, I am taking this opportunity of enclosing a small postcard drawing on the subject, and I hope that you won't take offense at my sense of humor. I have a habit of sending drawings to anyone on any subject and rarely have they been rejected as bad taste. I hope you will like my card, and I also hope that you will forgive me for sending it. I just couldn't resist the temptation. A lot of cards have cards drawn by me, so why not the President? After all, most of us plain citizens consider you a real "square shooter," and I include myself in that category of admirers.

Thanking you for your interest, and here's hoping we'll all be able to hear your piano playing in the near future, thank you!

Sincerely yours,
G. Carroll Utermahlen
Fullerton, Md.

On back of card: "With apologies to the President, of course!"

Busy as he was, Truman still found time to enjoy listening to the music of others. In 1950, he corresponded with a concert pianist whom he had heard on various occasions.

Dear President Truman: *June 22, 1950*

In the Magazine section of last Sunday's *New York Times,* I read a very interesting article regarding your music study, and I was very much surprised and, needless to say, delighted to find my name among the pianists you had heard. I deeply appreciated the fact that your remembrance of my playing should have remained during these many years and should have caused you to place my name among the great pianists whose playing made so lasting an impression.

I have not played in public in over twenty-five years. Certain conditions at that time and since then made it unfavorable that I continue concerting, but I practice sufficiently to play for my friends occasionally.

In 1912 I gave a recital for President Taft and his cabinet in the lovely East Room. It was quite a formal affair. And now, if some day in your over-busy life, you would care to spend a relaxed half-hour listening to some music, I should deeply appreciate, and it would give me *great* pleasure, to play for you and Mrs. Truman, quite *informally.*

In closing, may I add that my husband and I are your staunch admirers. We think you have had the heaviest load of any President and you have carried it with a *smile.*

> *With sincere appreciation,*
> *Augusta Cottlow*

Dear Miss Cottlow: *June 28, 1950*

I can't tell you very much I appreciated your good letter of the twenty-second.

I remember very distinctly your appearance in Kansas City. I went to hear you play every time you came there. If I remember correctly you appeared there about three times.

The White House at the present time is completely wrecked. The wonderful grand piano, I think the best one I've ever put my fingers on, is in storage in New York and we have no other pianos here except the old worn out one that Margaret took her lessons on, on which a concert could be played. Sometime after the White House is finished I'd certainly be most happy to have you come down and play for the family as you suggest.

I am highly pleased that you are still keeping up with your music. In my opinion, your mastery of the piano was most complete.

Sincerely yours,
HARRY S. TRUMAN

Truman held strong opinions about music and occasionally wrote far different letters than the laudatory one to Cottlow. He twice responded angrily to the music reviews of *Washington Post* music critic Paul Hume, receiving no small amount of abuse in the mail and the press for his trouble when one of the letters was published in a daily newspaper (see page 416). Of course, Truman himself was no stranger to criticism, some of which fell into his "nut mail" category. One Massachusetts man worried that his interest in flying rather than traveling by trains would prove to be very unsafe.

Dear Mr. Ross: *October 29, 1946*
In the Sunday *New York Herald Tribune,* I read with interest the acceptance by the government of the Presidential pullman.

Will you be good enough to convey to the President my wish that he make more use of this form of transportation? It has just a [word unintelligible] advantage in restful travel over air travel. In addition to the danger of air travel, there is no time to relax between obligations. I think the President is working too hard and pullman travel would help slow down the rushing around.

Wishing the best of health to the President and to you also. I am

Sincerely yours,
F. H. O'Donnell
Holyoke, Mass.

Dear Mr. O'Donnell: *October 31, 1946*
In the absence of Mr. Ross who is now out of the city with the President, I am replying to your letter of October twenty-ninth.

The concern for the President's health and welfare which prompted you to write is, I assure you, deeply appreciated. It was indeed thoughtful of you to write. As you perhaps have noticed in newspaper reports, the President is now on his way home to vote. He is traveling by train and plans to return the same way.

Sincerely yours,
EBEN A. AYERS
Assistant to Mr. Ross

This writer was still so upset that he wrote to Ross again six months later.

Dear Mr. Ross: *February 10, 1947*

In a recent press conference the President is quoted, regarding the danger of flying "when your number is up, it doesn't matter where you are."

As you probably will recall, I have written to you as Secretary to the President and his close friend, to ask you to use your influence to deter the President from flying. It is the concern of myself and many others not only for the safety of Mr. Truman as a man but the symbol he represents as President. You must have him reconsider his desire to fly for he must as so many others consider first the country and the utter confusion that would follow in the wake of any disaster.

Hoping you and your associates will continue to safeguard the President, and you will earn the deep gratitude of your fellow countrymen.

Sincerely yours,
Frank H. O'Donnell
Holyoke, Mass.

The quote referred to by the previous writer was enough to incur the wrath of an apparent expert on Missourians and Presbyterians.

Dear Mr. President: *2/21/47*

I was quite shocked to read a press dispatch in which you are quoted as saying in speaking of airplane crashes that "It just does not matter what you do, if your time is up, it's up and it will get you some time anyway."

I have often been proud of the fact that my own native state of Missouri has finally landed a man in the White House as President of the United States even though by accident.

However I have long known that a Missourian is noted for his primitive horse sense since he has to be shown and also that Missouri has long ago been famous for leading every state in the Union in the production of horses—horses with long ears. So I <u>feel much humiliated that our chief executive has made a remark that relegates him to the intellectual level</u> of an ignorant Presbyterian. Did you ever realize, Mr. President, that any old fool with a cigarette in his mouth near a gas tank and alcohol in his brain can make a whole group of passengers and crew realize that "their time is up" by an explosion or a crash into a mountain side when a lot of stern discipline from headquarters preventing smoking or drinking would prevent such horrors? Is human life so cheap in your estimation that you are virtually selling the life of the nation to the diabolical liquor and tobacco trust?

Did you ever stop to think that as a possible candidate for President in 1948, you will do well to put more value on human life and homes, and less faith in that monstrosity which has turned the White House into a snake-house as well as a smokehouse and threatens the very existence of democracy and also of our grand forests by forest fires? Millions of Americans would like to know what you intend to do about this matter, for due to your high position, you can do a whole lot to save human life.

> *Yours truly,*
> *Darrin Dudeek*
> *Eugene, Ore.*

P.S. I hope that you will get to see this letter personally. D. D.

In the post–World War II era, there was also much interest in flying saucers and aliens, the most famous "incident" being at Roswell, New Mexico. One journalism graduate student at UCLA decided to inquire about the president's thoughts on this matter.

Dear Mr. Ross,   *April 5, 1950*

I am currently engaged in research for a graduate dissertation which will attempt to analyze the sociological and psychological implications of the flying saucer phenomenon.

In the light of the forceful radio commentary by Henry J. Taylor and the article which appeared in the *United States News and World Report* both of which declared or implied the saucers are aircraft of unusual design developed in the United States, I was interested to learn the reactions of Mr. Truman to the reports.

I understand that the Navy and the Air Force have issued qualified denials to the reports. Does the White House feel such reports are baseless?

I wish to thank you in advance for your interest and help. You may be assured that I will appreciate any information you may be able to give me.

> *Sincerely yours,*
> *DeWayne B. Johnson*
> *Graduate Department of Journalism, UCLA*

Dear Mr. Johnson: *April 11, 1950*

I have your letter of April fifth, inquiring about the reactions of the President to the stories about the flying saucers which have been reported in the press and the radio.

The President has expressed no opinions concerning these reports other than he has no information of any kind about flying saucers.

> *Sincerely yours,*
> *CHARLES G. ROSS*
> *Secretary to the President*

Interestingly, though the public would later pay increasing attention to America's "space race" with the Soviet Union, the fascination with whether there really were flying saucers and visits by alien creatures would almost die out for a while before resurfacing several decades later with charges of cover-up and conspiracy by the government. The age of "The X-Files" had begun, and Truman even fielded questions of a similar nature during a press conference. "Mr. President, have you seen any flying saucers?" Truman: "Only in the newspapers." (Laughter) "Any explanations of them from over here?" Truman: "Only the explanations I have seen in the newspapers. Did you ever hear of the moon hoax?"[2] *

---

*In 1835, the *New York Sun* ran a series of articles which it claimed were authored by an eminent British astronomer and reprinted from the prestigious—and, it turned out, nonexistent—*Edinburgh Journal of Science.* The articles contained sensational details of life on the moon as observed through a giant telescope in Capetown, South Africa, and included descriptions of winged men who populated its surface. Before the "Moon Hoax" was exposed, the circulation of the *Sun* had grown to become the largest in the world and numerous other newspapers had jumped on the story as well.

Most of Truman's correspondence dealt with more down-to-earth matters, however. Some people tried to help the president when they felt he needed assistance in certain areas. A New York tailor attempted to persuade Truman to lengthen his suit coat.

Honorable Mr. President: *October 17, 1945*

Of course I have every reason to believe that this letter is first being read by one of your secretaries. I sincerely hope it comes to your attention.

I am writing merely from the point of view that <u>I believe our President should be the best dressed man in all the world, plainly well dressed with the most becoming type of clothes</u>.

I hope you will pardon my observation, but I can't help but notice how short and unbecoming is the length of your sack coat. I have many times noted this fault, in other figures, as well as the one here enclosed . . . by comparison you will note the length of the coats on the other gentlemen.

Please be assured this letter is far from commercial but simply in the interest of seeing you wear more becoming and better fitting clothes.

I trust you will not feel this too forward, but <u>our representative goes to Washington once every month and if you would grant me the privilege and favor of calling on you, I would appreciate the opportunity of showing you how much more becoming you could be dressed</u>.

Respectfully yours,
Richard Ford
Rogers Peel Company/
Men's and Boy's Outfitters
New York, N.Y.

Truman felt his current style of dress was appropriate, however, and another writer's attempt to help also fell on deaf ears.

My dear Mr. President: *November 19, 1945*

As the dean of all American speech teachers, I feel that it is my distinct privilege and duty to bring to your notice a most important matter which plays a tremendous part in your high office as the nation's Chief Executive—*your speaking voice.*

Remember, Mr. President, that *how* a man says a thing is equally as important as *what* he says, and that no matter how effective the text of a man's speech, if he has not the voice to put it over, the message is lost on the public.

The magic of the speaking voice of your distinguished predecessor—its intimate quality combined with perfect diction and light and shade and color, and its unusual impressiveness and *appeal* won him millions of voters and stamped him as one of the greatest orators ever to sit in the White House.

Contrarily, the monotonous voices of Hoover, Landon, the late Wendell Wilkie [*sic*] and others very largely contributed to their political defeat. In all these cases and countless others, speech played the prime controlling role of victory or defeat.

Speech and nothing else has been my sole business for forty years.

I have carefully—*very, very*—carefully analyzed your speaking voice. May I truthfully inform you of my expert findings? It is definitely and unmistakably a monotonous voice, practically devoid of color, light and shade, carrying little force, appeal or impressiveness. Yet you have an excellent natural middle register quality which happily can *positively* be developed into a speaking voice fraught with all the splendid vocal elements belonging to a fine and expressive speaker. It is a voice whose possibilities of development are almost limitless.

Mr. President, you are doing a tremendous job—bravely and courageously. The eyes of the world are on you. Your tenure of office should be—and can be—a long one. Do not belittle the part which a fine speaking voice could take in such progress.

In a matter of such great and vital importance, I deem it my duty as a loyal American citizen to submerge my own personal interests and place myself unreservedly at your service. With this in view I would be willing to arrange my business affairs to permit me to go to Washington and give you *all* the necessary time until my mission is accomplished—that of making a splendid orator and speaker of our President. This can be done quietly and unostentatiously and confidentially.

Please send any reply to the address below and *nowhere else*. It is my home. I am a widower and live alone.

Believe me, Mr. President, I am,

Sincerely yours,
Paul Gerson
Hollywood Institute of Speech
Hollywood, Calif.

Apparently Truman saw nothing wrong with his "monotonous voice," nor did Gerson's attack of midwesterners and their speech probably do much to endear him to his president. Still, there were others who thought someone needed to coach him on his speech.

My dear Mr. President,   *January 21, 1947*
You will not, I hope, take it amiss that I address you, especially when half of my note expresses an adverse criticism. Your attitudes and performances, in a difficult situation (succeeding Mr. Roosevelt) have been most admirable. In your most recent problems, the turnover of Congress, you have demonstrated Tennyson's idea:
"Self-knowledge, self-reverence, self-control. These three alone lead life to sovereign power; And, because Right is Right, to follow right is Wisdom."
But there is a thin spot in your armor, <u>your voice</u> and your delivery—just the mechanics of these are faulty and both can be improved. I believe ten hours or possibly less would do it. I have seen remarkable results when the man (whose circulars I enclose without his knowing of my act) has worked with classes of teachers who sought promotion to supervisory work. A good preacher could show you emphasis and voice.
I hope you'll continue as President after 1948.
Respectfully yours,
Bridget C. Peixotto, Principal
Public School No. 108, Queens, N.Y.

Truman's office did not respond to letters of this nature. Other inquiries were not personally directed at the president but did ask him to do a variety of things.

Dear Mr. Truman,
Every Thanksgiving at St. Timothy's there is a <u>basketball game</u> between the BROWNIES and the Spiders. We are <u>Brownies and wondered whether you could send us a telegram to be read at lunch before the game</u>. We try to see which of the teams gets the most telegrams.
Do you think that you could possibly send one that would get here by lunchtime on Thanksgiving Day? We are both on the team (for the first time) and are *very* scared.

All you would have to say would be "Good luck to the BROWN-IES" or something like that. We know you are a very busy man, but we want to win so badly, and it would be a lot of fun. It would mean a lot to us. Could you send it to:

The Misses Kerry Hart and Lisa Howe
St. Timothy's School, Catonsville, Baltimore, Maryland.
Thank you so much.

Love,
Kerry and Lisa

P.S. If we can ever do anything for you, please let us know.

My dear Miss Hart: *December 1, 1947*
The letter which you and Miss Howe recently sent to the President has been received and I regret that it is not possible to do as you ask. So many requests of a nature similar to the one you make are constantly coming to this office and the President is unable to comply with them. I am indeed sorry but feel sure that you will understand and will accept the President's best wishes.

Very sincerely yours,
MATTHEW J. CONNELLY
Secretary to the President

Dear Mr. President: *December 1, 1947*
This is my fourth season of presenting Scholastic Basketball in the New York Armories. This year my program will be presented at the 12th Regiment Armory, 62nd Street and Columbus Avenue, New York City.

I am planning to present three trophies this year to be awarded to the winning high school competitors:

The President's Trophy
The Governor's Trophy
The Mayor's Trophy

My committee will purchase the trophies, but I would greatly appreciate your moral support of this fine youth program.

Sincerely,
Joseph F. Kenny, Director of Basketball

HARRY S TRUMAN   APRIL 30, 1952
MR. PRESIDENT. WE ARE JUST THREE AMERICAN JOURNALISTS
ATTENDING THE INTERNATIONAL FILM FESTIVAL. WE VOLUN-
TEERED TO RAISE 1 MILLION FRANCS FOR THE DEVASTATED LITTLE
TOWN OF MENTON CLOSE BY. WE MADE A PLEA ON BOARD THE USS
RONIDE AND USS TARAWA CREW GAVE 200,000 FRANCS. WILL YOU
HELP US TOP OUR GOAL. FUNDS TO GO TO FRANCE. ROCHE, MAU-
RICE, BESSY OR RAYMOND RODEL, CINEMONDE CARLTON HOTEL.
URGENT RESPECTFULLY YOURS.
M/SGT JOHN EDENFIELD (USAFE) VIOLA ILMA ANNE MICHAELS.
CANNES, FRANCE.

Dear Sir: *Nov. 2, 1950*
Our Women's Club is having an auction to buy some light-
weight wheelchairs for the Riverside Zurbrugg Hospital. We would
appreciate it so very much if you would send us a gift or memento. It
will be auctioned off as a surprise package in your name. No one
will know what they are bidding on except your name.
We all thank God you escaped injury in the recent attempt on
your life.
Thank you for your consideration in this worthy hospital project.
Please send to:

> *Mrs. Douglass Bott*
> *Riverside, N.J.*

My dear Mrs. Bott: *November 8, 1950*
I wish it were possible to do as you ask, but your letter is only one
of many similar requests which come to the President daily. Unhappily, he cannot comply in each instance and in order to be strictly
impartial he has no alternative but to decline solicitations of this
nature.

> *Very sincerely yours,*
> *WILLIAM D. HASSETT*
> *Secretary to the President*

THE PRESIDENT   JUNE 2, 1947
LARGE 44 PASSENGER AIRPLANE UNDER OUR CHARTER BEARING
THIRTY-EIGHT GREEK FIANCEES AMERICAN GI'S ARRIVING NEWARK

AIRPORT THIS AFTERNOON. GIRLS TO BE MARRIED TO GI'S AND
BECOME US CITIZENS. WE WILL BE GLAD TO GIVE YOUR WELCOME
GREETINGS IF YOU WISH TO SEND SAME. RESPECTFULLY
   FREIGHT CARGO AGENCY, NEW YORK CITY

Dear Mr. President: *February 5, 1952*
   The Candler Estate in DeKalb County, Georgia is now in the
process of being transferred to the State to be used as an alcoholic
hospital.
   This property is located in Druid Hills, a section adjacent to both
Atlanta and Decatur. The population of this section is approximately nine thousand and is totally without a slum area. The people
of Druid Hills are ministers, lawyers, doctors and teachers, people of
culture who lay more stress on education and refinement than the
acquiring of money and things material.
   This segment of Georgia's population deserves more consideration than it is receiving. With an alcoholic hospital in this location,
the people of this section will be harassed by the mentally depraved
alcoholic, a person capable of committing any crime, murder and
rape included.
   And this, Mr. President, is what our Governor, who is a little less
than a "penny ante" politician, would subject nine thousand people
to for no other reason than that they are not his supporters. Fear and
humiliation: the two emotions that destroy "Human Dignity."
   I know that you can, Mr. President, but will you spare five minutes to save this very small segment of the American population
from the ravages of Huey Long II?
   We fully realize that time is critical; that you bear a heavy burden;
but we appeal to you as our last hope.
                        Respectfully,
                        Lawton Kirkland, M.D.
                        Atlanta, Ga.

   One peculiar request came from a German woman. It was sent to the
State Department for translation.

TRANSLATOR'S SUMMARY OF COMMUNICATION
Language: German
Date of Communication: August 10, 1951

Addressed to: Mr. Adam [*sic*] Truman
Name and address of writer: Mrs. Elisabeth Hugel
                                             Heidelburg, Germany
Substance of writer's statement:

The writer, who addresses the President as "Dear Brother" and claims to have heard through Miss Margaret Truman that Mr. Truman has to undergo an operation, requests money for her passage to America.

In view of the fact that the President has to be operated on, she intends to bring her twin sons to America, as one of them is a physician.

No reply went to this German "sister" of Truman (calling him by the wrong first name probably didn't help her case), nor was one sent to the boy who decided to go to the top man for help.

> *Dear Sir,*
> I heard on the radio that you have 6 tv setes [*sic*]. I am 7 and my Brothers are 10 and 12 and we like tv and can't get one because we need a new roof. Could you lend us one til we get one?
> > *Thank you*
> > *John Stephens*
> > *Scotia, N.Y.*

Of course, there were some matters Truman absolutely had to get personally involved in, such as when he found out that the battleship named after his home state did not contain certain items that, by naval tradition, should have been handed down to it.

> *Dear Mr. President:*   *February 15, 1947*
> Dick Nacy [Richard R. Nacy, a long-time Democratic Party operative in Missouri and executive vice chairman of the Democratic National Committee] and I turned the capitol building at Jefferson City wrong side out yesterday and failed to find any trace of a silver set of any kind. There is no record of any as far as anyone at the capitol can find. Later in the day he and I went to see Governor [Phil M.] Donnelly and suggested to the Governor that such a set should be presented by the state to the new battleship *Missouri*. We told him of the report that a silver service set had been given by the

state to the old battleship *Missouri* and returned to the state when the old vessel went out of service and told him that if such a set was in existence it would be peculiarly appropriate for the state to give it to the new battleship *Missouri*. We then told him of our efforts to locate the old set in the capitol building and of our failure to do so. He called the Mansion and asked the housekeeper, who has been there for many years, whether she knew of any such set or parts of such a set being at the Mansion. She told the Governor that she did not.

The Governor said there was no way for the state to buy a new set without an appropriation by the Legislature and that he would consider the question of him asking the Legislature for such an appropriation. I told the Governor that I was confident that you would be glad to cooperate with him in any appropriate manner to accomplish the objective we were discussing but that I doubted the appropriateness of you making any request to the Legislature for their action. Dick said that he would remind the Governor of our conversation with him and Dick expressed the opinion that the Governor would make the request to the Legislature.

Buck Taylor was not in Jefferson City yesterday but I had talked to him about it on the phone before that. He said that he would be glad to do anything that he could to bring it about.

I am writing Jim Foskett [naval aide to Truman] today asking Jim to have the navy records checked with the hope that we may thereby get definite information concerning the old set.

Kindest regards and best wishes and don't work too hard.

> *Sincerely,*
> "*Caskie*"
> *Jim Caskie Collet, District Judge—*
> *U.S. District Court/Kansas City*

MEMORANDUM FOR: THE PRESIDENT February 17, 1947

I have inquired through the Navy Department and find that the silver service of the old *Missouri* is in storage at the Naval Operating Depot, San Diego. It had been removed from the U.S.S. *West Virginia* at the outbreak of war and has been in storage there ever since.

The Navy Department now is taking steps to have this silver shipped to the U.S.S. *Missouri*. Evidently it consists solely of a solid silver punch bowl and 20 silver drinking cups.

Do you think that it is necessary for me to notify the Governor of Missouri?

> *Very respectfully,*
> *JAMES H. FOSKETT*

Dear Caskie: *February 18, 1947*

I am enclosing your copy of a memorandum which I received from Admiral Foskett.

It looks as if the joke is on us but I would have bet all the tea in China that a long time ago I saw that silver service in the Capitol building in Missouri.

> *Sincerely yours,*
> *Harry*

Occasionally letters harkened back to Truman's childhood. A Missouri native wrote asking if as a child he had attended political picnics in a small Missouri town (and site of a Civil War battle), as she had read. Her query prompted a longer-than-usual response from the White House.

Dear Mr. President: *January 7, 1952*

My parents, Missouri Democrats of about your age, used to attend the Sixteenth of August picnics held at Lone Jack, Missouri. I have read that you, too, attended, and sometimes spoke at, Lone Jack picnics; and I am wondering whether those summer picnics you enjoyed, oratory and all, were the same happy Sixteenth of August affairs?

That information is something I would greatly appreciate since I, who have written several pieces on my native Missouri, am now working on the history of the Sixteenth of August picnics. If you did attend them, I would also like to know, in a general way, in which years.

My interest in Missouri and its history is quite natural; I am, through my father, a second cousin of Missouri's Jim Reed, whom you probably know.

With best wishes for a Happy 1952, I am

> *Very truly yours,*
> *Lenna Gordon Lichy*
> *Fallbrook, Calif.*

ARE YOU SERIOUS ABOUT DRAMATICALLY INCREASING YOUR QUALITY OF LIFE?

GAINING PERSONAL FREEDOM FROM JOBS?

DOES $10,000 F/T, $2,000 P/T
FR IGHTEN YOU

LET ME FR IGHTEN YOU SOME MORE

$100,000 F/T, $20,000 P/T

WHEN YOU ARE SERIOUS AND ARE READY TO DRAMATICALL
INCREASE YOUR QUALITY OF LIFE .
CALL
1 (888) 3 0 2 - 9 7 3 7

WHEN YOU ARE 75% COMMITED
CALL 1 (5 1 0) 5 2 3 - 2 2 3 5

Dear Mrs. Lichy: *January 14, 1952*

The President has asked me to advise you that he attended approximately ten of the Sixteenth of August picnics at Lone Jack, Missouri, between 1892 and 1904. Your letter provoked some very pleasant memories for the President.

He recalled that on the picnic days his father, his brother Vivian, and he would hitch two big mules to a spring wagon and the whole family would set out before dawn for a five mile drive to Lone Jack. The spring wagon had three seats capable of holding three persons each. In addition to the President, his mother and father, Vivian and his sister Mary Jane, they frequently had with them Grandfather and Grandmother Truman.

In addition to the load of people, the wagon also was weighted down with fried chicken, cakes, pies, and many other items of food. At noon, or sometimes before that, the thousands attending the picnic would spread the food upon tablecloths laid on the ground. At around 2.00 p.m., especially in election years, the speaking would start. The President recalled speeches by Senator Francis Marion Cockerell, Senator George Graham Best (famous for a dog story), Congressman William H. Coward and a Colonel Crisp, who ran for Congress several times but never was elected.

One of the stories, told at Lone Jack, which sticks in the President's mind, came from Congressman Coward. The Congressman was illustrating his attitude toward a tariff bill then pending in Congress. Mr. Coward said he could reluctantly swallow some of the provisions of the bill, but there were other provisions he could not stomach. He was reminded, he said, of a farmer on his first visit to New York, having his first experience in a fancy hotel dining room. The farmer was served celery, which he ate, and a bowl of consomme, which he drank. Then the waiter laid before him a lobster. The farmer looked up indignantly and said: "I ate your bouquet. I drank your dishwater. But I'll be darned if I'll eat your bug."

The President feels that a contribution was made to his early political education at Lone Jack. Although he did not pick up the old school oratory which he heard so many times there, he caught the excitement of politics, something he never has ceased to relish.

I hope this has been helpful to you. The President enjoyed the interlude in his busy, wearying life of today, to think back on the time when he was a youngster in Jackson County.

> *Sincerely yours,*
> *JOSEPH SHORT*
> *Secretary to the President*

The president's past—real or imagined—sometimes surfaced as writers asked, "Aren't you the one who . . . ?"

> *My dear President Truman,*   *August 23, 1946*
> We are on our vacation at camp. Our camp is located in Sugar Grove, Penn.
> Every Tuesday we have a hike day. This is the hike day at camp, it is a very nice day for hiking. We hoped it would be the nicest hike day of all and it was.
> We went on until we came to a little cabin. Soon we discovered that it was the same home you were born in. We hope you don't mind that we took a piece of wood.
>
> *Sincerely yours,*
> *Heather Marcus, Patricia Hess,*
> *and Linda Swartzman*
> *Camp Deer Run, Sugar Grove, Penn.*

Unfortunately for those young ladies, the president had not been born in that cabin but in a rather modest house in Lamar, Missouri.

> *Dear President Truman—*   *September 8, 1945*
> Please excuse my audacity in writing you and asking you such an impertinent question.
> <u>Did you in your young days ever work at Mudlavia, hired at the hotel as a bell boy?</u> Why I ask you, a boy by the name of Harry Truman was there, and he came from the south, I think it was Missouri. I believe it was around 1902. We all liked him very much. The housekeeper (Mrs. McArthur) said he will make his mark in the world some day. <u>My name at that time was Mazie Miner. I had charge of the dining room and I think Mr. Sluirpeon was manager, and if not, it was Boss Krauer.</u> It was a health resort five miles from Attica, Indiana.

Wishing to congratulate you on your success and also what I think is great management so far. You certainly had a great deal thrown into your lap.

> *Sincerely,*
> *Mrs. Mazie Rogers*
> *Chicago, Ill.*

Dear Mrs. Rogers: *September 29, 1945*

This acknowledges your letter of September eighth, addressed to the President.

In reply to your inquiry as to whether or not the President ever worked in a hotel in Indiana, the answer is "no."

> *Sincerely yours,*
> *CHARLES G. ROSS*
> *Secretary to the President*

This terse response is more typical of most White House regimes but is rather atypical of the Truman administration, wherein Hassett believed in treating the public with grace and respect. In fact, his "Valentines" influenced the tone of the responses prepared by the rest of the staff.

Dear Mr. Truman: *July 30, 1948*

I am writing to ask if you were at the <u>Eclipse</u> at the <u>horseshoe court on Sunday, July 25, between 9 and 10 o'clock</u> in the morning and pitched a few horseshoes. My daddy was over their [*sic*] <u>pitching horseshoes</u> alone and a gentleman asked if he could pitch a few back to him and he did. My daddy said that it looked so much like you and I wanted to write and ask you if daddy had the honor of pitching a few with you. I am hoping to get a reply from you.

> *A Central High pupil,*
> *Helen Woodley*
> *Washington, D.C.*

My dear Miss Woodley: *August 3, 1948*

Your letter of July thirtieth to the President has been received and the friendliness which prompted it is appreciated.

With regard to your query, the President was on the U.S.S. *Williamsburg* on Sunday, July twenty-fifth.

With best wishes to you,

Very sincerely yours,
MATTHEW J. CONNELLY
Secretary to the President

On a surprisingly large number of occasions, a letter would catch the eye of Truman, who would draft his own response in his own tone.

Dear Mr. President: *July 7, 1950*

Did you take part in the war games that were played in 1912 between Overland Park and Leavenworth and were you a Lieutenant at that time?

I was a student at the University of Missouri and transferred from the Fourth to the Second [Battalion] to take part in those maneuvers.

I would still like to know if you were the squirt Second Lieutenant who made us police every morning before daylight in mud, rain or what have you.

Very truly yours,
John Lynch
Muskogee, Okla.

Dear Mr. Lynch: *July 12, 1950*

I am afraid I can't play guilty to having been the Second Lieutenant who got you up every morning in the mud and the rain. In 1912 I was out on the farm, although still a Sergeant in Battery "B". I did not go on the trip to which you refer—I was trying to harvest a wheat crop in that mud and rain and not having much luck at it.

Sincerely yours,
HARRY S. TRUMAN

[Longhand] *One rank I've never had is that of 2nd Lt.!*

Perhaps one of the most embarrassing "recollections" was by Miss Emma Bouldin of Pryor, Oklahoma, who granted an interview to the local newspaper in 1949. In it she was credited as being one who had "a hand in Harry Truman's education, and it's highly possible that she cultivated the interests that helped him attain the presidency." She said, "'I remember him vividly. He was a small, serious boy who wore glasses and sat in the front row so that he might see the blackboard better.'" She also discussed his difficult time with math: "'I liked that boy and he was a wonderful student—but—I never could teach him long division. I've worried about it for years.'" She said she had taught him one year when his family lived in Harrisonville, Missouri. Unfortunately, Miss Bouldin was not remembered by the president, who insisted he had never been taught by her. Responding to the *Pryor Times-Democrat* publisher required a bit of finesse by Charlie Ross, who obviously did not want this well-intentioned lady hurt by the truth.

> PERSONAL   *August 27, 1949*
> *Dear Mr. Bailey:*
> I have just received a copy of the *Pryor Times-Democrat* for Monday, August twenty-second, containing a story by Ken Jackson to the effect that President Truman in his early youth went to school to Miss Emma Bouldin of Pryor.
> The President, as you know, is an extremely kind-hearted man and he doesn't want to do anything that would hurt the feelings of Miss Bouldin, who is evidently a very nice person. The fact is, however, that Miss Bouldin was not one of the President's teachers. If she had taught him while the Truman family lived in Cass County, Missouri, the President would have been only about two years old.
> The President did not attend school at all in Harrisonville, Missouri, but all his schooling was obtained in Independence, Missouri, to which town the Truman family moved in 1890 when the President was six years old. Apparently Miss Bouldin has got the President mixed up with somebody else.
> It seems to me quite evident that Miss Bouldin told her story in good faith and that Mr. Jackson reported it in good faith. I am writing you the facts in order to forestall any repetition of the error.
> *Sincerely yours,*
> *CHARLES G. ROSS*
> *Secretary to the President*

On other occasions, people mistook Truman for someone else or told him of the doubles found seemingly everywhere. Many sent pictures to prove their point.

Dear Mr. Truman: *August 9, 1952*

Please permit me to write you a line: I wish to write you that you look just like my mother when she was alive. You have the same persona as my mother. The same face and every part of it is the same. You have the same voice, act and walk and talk the same. She had close relatives including one brother in this country.

I include my mother's picture so you can see how it looks. She was 84 years old when this picture was made.

Sincerely yours,
Mrs. Angela Knez
Vallejo, Calif.

My dear Mrs. Knez: *August 9, 1952*

It was friendly of you to send the President that note of August ninth and he asks me to thank you for your kindness in letting him see your mother's picture. No doubt you prize it very highly and for this reason we are returning it to you. Your thoughtfulness in writing is appreciated.

Very sincerely yours,
MATTHEW J. CONNELLY
Secretary to the President

Dear President Truman: *January 27, 1951*

I've heard of people having <u>doubles</u> but I never thought I would ever see the double of our President. Enclosed is a photograph of your double and an item about him which was in my hometown newspaper, the *Detroit Free Press.*

If you appreciate this picture of your double, will you please let me know. I am thirteen years old.

Patricia Ann Cooney
Detroit, Mich.

Dear Mr. President: *May 12, 1949*

Please find enclosed a recent photograph of <u>Thomas A. Thompson of Augusta, Maine</u> and an employee of this company.

This picture has been shown to many people and in almost every instance their reaction has been manifested with such statements which follow: "Why, I didn't know the President has been in Augusta!" or "Doesn't he resemble our President."

Realizing you are a very busy man but also that you are blessed with a great sense of humor, it is therefore my sincere wish that either you or Mr. Thompson should grow a mustache. <u>On a recent trip which Mr. Thompson made to Boston, your Secret Service operators were so vigilant that he had no privacy</u>. He absolutely refuses <u>to grow a mustache, Mr. President</u>, so I guess it's up to you.

Trusting you will give this matter some serious thought and attention, I wish to remain

> *Yours very truly,*
> *Fred K. McFarland, President*
> *McFARLAND SALES COMPANY*
> *Augusta, Maine*

Dear Mr. McFarland: May 18, 1949

This is to acknowledge your letter of May twelfth, addressed to the President, and to thank you for the photograph of Mr. Thomas A. Thompson which you enclosed.

It is an interesting picture and it was thoughtful of you to send it. I don't know what you are going to do about the mustache unless you succeed in getting Mr. Thompson to change his mind.

> *Sincerely yours,*
> *CHARLES G. ROSS*
> *Secretary to the President*

Dear Mr. Truman,   April 20, 1948

Enclosed in this envelope you will find a copy of a <u>photograph of my uncle</u>. Almost everyone who saw this said immediately, ". . . that looks like President Truman. . . ." What do you think?

I am a photographer for my school newspaper, ass't photo editor in fact of The ADMIRAL of Christopher Columbus High School and have taken pictures of many celebrities. In addition to this, I was a major in the BLUE-STAR BRIGADE for the 4, 5, 6, 7, and 8 war loans, 1 victory loan, and I am still selling now during this present campaign. During all of these loans, I sold roughly about $15,000 or more.

Waiting to hear from you and wishing you the best of luck in November,

I remain sincerely,
Allen E. Greller
Bronx, New York

My dear Mr. Greller: *April 23, 1948*

The President has received your letter of recent date with the enclosed snapshot and he asks me to thank you for your friendly thought in writing to him. He has noted your letter with much interest, and he extends his best wishes to you.

Very sincerely yours,
WILLIAM D. HASSETT
Secretary to the President

Dear Mr. President,   *Feb. 2, 1950*

In the Sunday issue (Jan. 29, 1950) were <u>printed look alikes of Your Excellency</u>. The clipping I am enclosing was the only <u>woman look alike</u>. And to say her happiness is complete now is more than true. <u>Our Bertie Moon Chapter, American War Mothers was named in her honor</u>. President Coolidge signed the Congressional Charter of the American Northern National Chapter on Feb. 24, 1925. Our beloved Bertie Moon is a World War I mother, a charter member and a past chapter president of a local chapter. She is also a Lady of the Grand Army of the Republic. <u>She is seventy-seven years young</u> and loved by all. You see she is "Our Bertie."

She visited with me yesterday and confided "how she would love to send this clipping to our beloved President—he is such a wise man" but that she was afraid because she didn't know what to say. So I said I would do it. Mr. President, would you please send her a little note? That will make the sunset for her the most glorious in all the world.

Kindest regards to you from Bertie Moon and myself.

Sincerely,
Mrs. Marie J. Mills
American War Mothers
Minneapolis, Minn.

Dear Mr. President: *June, 2, 1947*

Enclosed is a clipping taken from the "Universe," an English Catholic newspaper—the issue of March 7, 1947.

The clipping is a photograph (profile) of Pope Pius XII. The picture I thought resembled you so much I thought I would send it on.

Sincerely yours,
Francis B. Grady
Scranton, Penn.

A man in Chicago decided not to take his chances by writing directly to the White House but instead wrote to his congressman.

Mr. Langer,   *3/12/47*
Dear Sir and Senator,

I am taking the pleasure to write to you and [am] asking you for a friendly favor. My name is John A. Neustaedter from Fargo, N. D. and formerly from Valley City, N. D. You remember me at the party you met at Jones Manole's Restaurant at Valley City. You asked me how you would run at the time before election, and I told you it would be close but you would win. Well that's [word unintelligible] and I am sure you remember. I done better with Judge

Inglert in guessing his political run. Just ask him some time when you meet him.

Now I will get down to business. I live here in San Diego, Calif. sinse May 1, 1942. . . . The poeple call me Mr. Truman. I have several pictures taken and I would like to send them to you to present them to Mr. Trueman and let him look at them and for him and yourself and some of the senators to look at them and se if I really do look like Mr. Truman, and if the Presedent and you think I do resemble him verry mutch. I would be willing to let him keep the one he wants and one for you to. Send back the [word unintelligible] one or all if I don't meet with success. If I am accepted as resembling the Presedent. I wish to have him send me a few lines to show the poeple. My picture was in the *San Diego Tribune* the day after Xmas with a picture of the Presedent and I will enclose it in the letter, but I would prefer to have the Presnt see the better pictures of me. Mabe I don't look so mutch like him as the poeple say. I am 184 lbs., age 66 and 5'10" tall. I am left-handed. I know you are a nice man and gentleman who likes the comon man and I hird you talk a number of times. I do hope you can find time to do me this favor. So please let me hear from [you] as soon as you can by return mail. Wishing you the best of health and success. I will remain

Yours truly
John A. Neustaedter
San Diego, Calif.

Dear Senator: *April 28, 1947*

This is in acknowledgment of your letter of April twenty-fifth, in behalf of Mr. J. A. Neustaedter of San Diego, California, concerning Mr. Neustaedter's physical resemblance to the President.

I regret exceedingly that the reply must be disappointing. For some strange reason, we receive a great many letters from persons asking for personal letters from the President because of their physical resemblance to him. As we have had to decline all other similar requests, it would be difficult to make an exception in this instance.

I am sure that both you and Mr. Neustaedter will understand.

> *Very sincerely yours,*
> CHARLES G. ROSS
> *Secretary to the President*

An enterprising gentleman in Chicago decided that looking like the president could have its advantages, including employment opportunities.

My dear Mr. President—   *July 13, 1950*

In your wise decision and purpose to uphold the rights of all free and liberty-loving peoples, you deserve the true support of every true American.

I am too old to fight <u>at 60</u> but have been told time and again that <u>I look just like Pres. Truman</u>. It is true that I resemble your Honor in proportion, posture, and profile.

Hence I do herewith make application for the position of acting as your double if there is need of a double.

Kindly inform me thru the proper channels how to go about this application and have sent to my home the proper blanks to fill out.

Black Redism must be defeated. I sincerely believe in the righteousness of our cause—the right must win. You have appointed the best man to make that possible, Gen. MacArthur.

> *Yours for victory,*
> *Otto F. Hinz*
> *Chicago, Ill.*

Dear Mr. Hinz: *July 21, 1950*

This will acknowledge your letter of July thirteenth, addressed to the President. The President does not, and never has, employed a double. Your offer to act in that capacity is appreciated but there is no prospect that it will be possible to use your services in the foreseeable future.

> *Sincerely yours,*
> CHARLES G. ROSS
> *Secretary to the President*

Wanting to work for the president was an ambition conveyed in many letters. Some wanted to go to work at the White House, while others inquired about performing tasks for the president, such as shoe repair.

Dear Mr. Truman,   *Sept. 22, 1949*

Perhaps I am writing this letter in vain, as I've heard you only receive the very important mail which comes in. Now I'll get to my point:

My husband is a veteran, and also a shoe repairman in business with his two brothers. I have been married to him three years and I can truthfully say I think his greatest desire is to fix a pair of your shoes. He doesn't want the shoes for publicity, it's only to have the self-satisfaction of repairing your shoes. Believe me he is plenty good, too, as he has won the National Blue Ribbon in his field of work.

If you have a good memory you may remember seeing my husband when you came through Waco coming out to Baylor. He was standing in his place of business on 5th Street in that real "Texas Dress."

Whether you do or don't remember my husband, I still want a pair of your shoes to present to him. If you will send them to me C.O.D., I'll have anything you want done to the shoes and have them back to you as soon as possible. We do any kind of shoe repairing, you name it and we'll do it.

Thank you kindly,

Mrs. C. E. Piazza
Waco, Texas

"We mend the rips, and patch the holes
Build up your heels and save your sole,
We have polishes and also laces,
And we're always glad to see new faces."

My dear Mrs. Piazza: *September 28, 1949*

I regret that it is necessary to send you a disappointing reply to your letter to the President of September twenty-second, but we cannot do as you ask. Permit me to assure you, however, that the friendliness which prompted you to write is nonetheless appreciated.

Very sincerely yours,
WILLIAM D. HASSETT
Secretary to the President

Knowledge of the president's love of music and piano playing prompted some requests.

Dear Harry: *August 19, 1952*

I will be disappointed if you say you have never heard of my ability to tune pianos. I would like the <u>distinction of tuning your piano</u>. It will, of course, be without cost to you.

I am of the other party called the GOP faith. But <u>I slipped the line last time and voted for you as I admire your courage</u> to do the thing you think is right, no matter what it costs you in votes. <u>I wish you were running again</u>.

> *Sincerely yours,*
> *Harold Arman*
> *Hastings Piano Company, Inc.*
> *Hastings, Mich.*

Dear Mr. Arman: *August 30, 1952*

The President has asked me to thank you for your kind letter of August nineteenth for your generous offer to tune his piano. Since he will be moving shortly after the first of the year, there does not seem to be any opportunity for him to avail himself of your proposal. However, he is deeply touched by your sentiments.

> *Sincerely yours,*
> *JOSEPH SHORT*
> *Secretary to the President*

Returning veterans looking for work were frequently the ones writing about White House positions. The next applicant might have done better if he had correctly spelled the president's name.

Dear Mr. Truman,   *Oct. 21, 1949*

My name is Don Roberts, and I am a sophomore at Gardner-Webb College. Mr. Truman, I do hope you will take me serious in this letter because I am not just fooling. I was in the <u>Navy for 19 months and 20 days</u>. I was stationed on the U.S.S. *Philadelphia* which escorted you to Antwerp, Beligium [*sic*].

Mr. Turman, what I wrote you about was that I would like a job working for you as your <u>handy man</u>. I would not care to shine your shoes and do all kind of little jobs for you. Mr. Turman I know that you have the right to hire someone like that and Mr. Turman I would work hard just to get to work around the president of the United States.

Mr. Turman, please do let me hear from you. And I am not interested in the pay. All I want to do is work around the president of
United States. And I know you need someone to lay your clothes
out every morning and things like that, and I would like to do all
your running for you around the White House.

I am of 21 years of age. I don't drink and I am [a] Christian boy.
Hoping to hear from you soon.

> *Sincerely yours,*
> *Don R. Roberts*
> *Boiling Springs, N.C.*

P.S. I would like any kind of job around the White House.

My dear Mr. Roberts: *October 31, 1947*

Your letter of October twenty-first to the President has been
received and you may be sure that your friendly interest in writing is
appreciated. I am indeed sorry to send this disappointing response
but we have no vacancy of the kind you mention.

> *Very sincerely yours,*
> *WILLIAM D. HASSETT*
> *Secretary to the President*

Mr. President: *January 27, 1951*

I am writing to you because I have no other way of getting in
touch with you. I am a veteran of World War II. I served in the following battles:

Midway, Wake Island, Raid on Tokyo, the Battle of Santa Cruz
and Guadalcanal. I am a survivor of the U.S.S. *Hornet* for which I
served from the commission to October 26, 1942. I am also a witness for the sinking of the U.S.S. *Wasp* and U.S.S. *Yorktown.*

I am thankful to God that after going through the above I am
able to try to seek for something which I have wanted for a long
period of time.

I served as stewart [*sic*] mate from 1941 to 1942. Later I received
the rank of officer stewart first class. I served from an ensign to a
vice-admiral. I hope with the above experience, I am in position to
ask for an interview to be considered as one to serve you as a valet.

I will be thankful for any consideration given, and will be glad to
submit recommendations to support what I have said. These recom-

mendations have been signed by chaplains and admirals. I also have photographs that I will gladly present, as well as my service autograph book.

I will appreciate a reply as to an interview at your earliest convenience.

Most sincerely,
Charles W. Brooks
Washington, D.C.

My dear Mr. Brooks: *January 31, 1951*

I am indeed sorry to have to send you a disappointing reply to your letter of January twenty-seventh. However, inasmuch as the President already has a valet, he does not care to avail himself of your kind offer. He wants you to know, nevertheless, that he is deeply appreciative of the thoughtfulness which prompted you to write.

Very sincerely yours,
WILLIAM D. HASSETT
Secretary to the President

Other mail represented various requests for information from Truman.

Dear Sir: *Nov. 27 '45*

As a hobby, I collect materials on animals; dogs, cats and most zoo animals by way of correspondence, pamphlets, news items, pictures, cartoons, and magazine covers.

I would like to know whether you like animals; whether you think the people of our country should treat animals kindly, and whether you think the many paws of your country are doing much for man. Do you own a pet?

You are such a friendly humble man I can imagine you would shake hands with a hero dog as well as with a hero human.

Since I have collected over 15,000 items, my conclusion is that animals are pretty well tied in with the affections and lives of humans and that they do a pretty good job of living in spite of handicaps, physically, and that man on the whole do[es] a pretty good job of caring for them, while editors and reporters do a wonderful job of recording this!

The smile in this picture of me was due to the cordial reception of these two Washingtonians, [a] wild horse and deer of your own City Zoo.

With every good wish for your health, happiness and good luck.

Hazel W. Frese
Collector of Animals
Baltimore, Md.

Dear Mrs. Frese: *December 6, 1945*

Your recent request of the President for information as to his interest in animals has come to me for reply.

As I am sure you will understand, the President is extremely busy these days with the many pressing duties of his office and has almost no opportunity to give thought to matters such as this. He appreciates the interest which prompts the inquiries but he is receiving so many of this nature that it would be impossible for him to take the time to answer them without neglecting his official work.

For my own part, I can tell you that the President does like animals. He had much to do with them in his boyhood days on the farm and he has always retained his liking for them and, of course, his belief that people should treat them kindly.

Sincerely yours,
CHARLES G. ROSS
Secretary to the President

The next inquiry brought a very short negative response from the White House.

Dear Mister President,

This is probably a very strange request, but I collect a very *strange thing, fingerprints.* If it's not too much trouble, may I have yours? If so, will you please take the prints of your <u>two thumbs</u>. Left one on the left side of enclosed card and right one on the right side.

Thank you, and I hope you win the next presidency.

Yours ever faithful,
Russell Hudson Wigglesworth
Durango, Colo.

My dear Mr. Wigglesworth: *February 26, 1948*

In the absence of the President, I am acknowledging your recent letter. I regret to disappoint you but it is not possible to comply with requests of the kind you make.

> *Very sincerely yours,*
> *CHARLES G. ROSS*
> *Secretary to the President*

Other queries necessitated a zero-frills response, since elaboration of any kind could be easily misconstrued or taken out of context. For example, it was well known that Truman had once owned a business with his old friend Eddie Jacobson, who was Jewish, and the name of Truman's grandfather, Solomon Young, sounded of Hebrew origin to some people (who were under the mistaken impression that Solomon was a last name). Long before Truman publicly supported the formation of an independent Jewish state in Palestine, a whisper campaign was well under way that he was secretly a Jew and was hiding his ancestry. In reality, Grandpa Young was a Baptist who, like grandfather Anderson Shipp Truman, moved to Missouri from Shelby County, Kentucky, in the 1840s. The woman who wrote the following letter, possibly tasked to write it by an employer who didn't want his name attached, was from a somewhat exclusive neck of the woods where the Vanderbilt home, Biltmore Estate, is located.

Dear Sir: *October 13, 1945*

It is circulated all through the South and discussed as to President Truman's race—whether he is of Jewish blood or of the Gentile Race. Since he is the President of the United States, we Americans feel we have the right to know. Will you kindly inform me regarding this question.

Awaiting your reply, I am,

> *Respectfully yours,*
> *Mrs. M. Rutledge Wootton*
> *Bank of Ashville Bldg.*
> *Asheville, N.C.*

Dear Mrs. Wootton: *October 13, 1945*

The President is not of Jewish blood. He is of the Gentile race.

> *Sincerely yours,*
> *CHARLES G. ROSS*
> *Secretary to the President*

For others, Truman's brief membership in the Klan in 1920 (see pages 43–44) was the heart-stopper, as this interoffice memo graphically describes.

MR. CONNELLY: *December 21, 1945*
Mr. James E. Dunne called me in a frantic state from LaSalle Hotel, Chicago, saying he had just heard the President was a member of the Ku Klux Klan. He says he wants a confirmation or denial from the President. I checked Files on this and the President wrote him personally May 3rd.

rlk [Roma L. Klar]

A copy of the letter Truman sent to Mr. Dunne could not be located by the Truman Library staff.

Truman's image as one of the common folk asserted itself at different occasions. Horseshoe pitchers learned of his interest in the game and thought he might enjoy pitching a few.

Dear Sir: *Jan. 12, 1947*
I heard over the radio that you and one of your members was <u>pitching horseshoes</u>. I am very fond of horseshoes myself, and also one of my sister's boys. If it could be arranged we would like to come and pitch some with you. You get one of your members to pitch with you then we would have a pair. I am 21 years old and a farm boy. My sister's boy is 22 years old. Please write back and let us know.

Yours truly,
Earl Dunlap
Robbins, N.C.

Dear Mr. President: *Sept. 18, 1946*
Knowing of your interest in our favorite sport, horseshoe pitching, and my interest in all horseshoe pitchers, in that the <u>Ohio pitchers</u> have just selected me to direct the State Association activities for the next four years, I thought perhaps it proper and fitting as one President to another, that if it can be arranged without too much trouble, I would appreciate a <u>friendly game with you at your convenience</u> on my visit to Washington on one day of the <u>10th, 11th and 12th of Oct.</u>, when I am to be at Baltimore at our Insurance Company celebration.

My ringer average is not very high, around 50% and my age 51, so you need to have no fears from those angles.

I will be glad to have your reactions on all of the above and if it can be so arranged I will contact your secretary from Baltimore for the best time suitable for us both.

I am certain that a few moments on the court will help relax you from the many other perplexing matters such as Wallace-ism and many other isms.

Trusting that I may hear from you favorably and that I may have the pleasure of meeting you, and if possible tossing a game or two, awaiting your reply.

> *I am, yours very truly,*
> *Claude A. Benedict, President*
> *Buckeye State Horseshoe Pitchers Ass'n*
> *Johnstown, Ohio*

A more upscale request arrived from a horseshoe club in the Pacific Northwest.

> *Dear Sir:*   *July 19, 1952*
> We are located in the heart of the Columbia Basin, in the state of Washington. As you know by being a Horseshoe Pitching fan yourself, the game is becoming fast a national sport. We here in the Columbia basin would like to be able to hold some good tournaments, but can't get the city or county to build modern courts for us.
>
> I thought we would like something to remember you by as <u>you are the only President who was a Horseshoe fan. We thought if you could see some way to build our Club some modern courts we would name them after you. We would like very much for you to be pitching the first shoes under the lights</u>.
>
> Please answer this letter and let us know about it.
>
> > *Yours very truly,*
> > *Tri-City Horseshoe Pitching Club*
> > *W. T. Branstetter*
> > *Pasco, Wash.*

Truman was also a bowler, so as well as the Truman balcony addition to the White House, the president apparently decided to add something more personal—his own alley. News of this reached his fellow Americans, including one with an automatic pin setter.

> *Dear Mr. President,*   *April 28, 1947*
>
> Reading about your interest in Bowling, and my attention was called to this, due to the fact that I represent the inventor who has invented the <u>Automatic Pin Setter</u> for candle pins and I will be very much interested in installing a set of these machines in the White House for your amusement.
>
> We have several of these machines here in Massachusetts in operation and due to the shortage conditions . . . production has been held up, and we expect at any time to start a major production and have these installed throughout the United States for it eliminates all pin boys and helps the bowling industry to a large extent where pin boys have been always scarce.
>
> I expect to be in Washington around the 10th of May [and] that weekend will be very happy to call at the White House and discuss our machines and their advantages. I personally will be too happy to offer two of these machines and install the same upon your approval in your recreation center.
>
> May I have the opportunity in discussing our invention on bowling, and I am awaiting further to hear from you.
>
> > *Very truly yours,*
> > *William C. Karalekas*
> > *Newton Highlands, Mass.*

Bowling at the White House was apparently a priority, and this letter was given further consideration by Harry Vaughan.

> *Dear Mr. Karalekas:*   *1 May 1947*
>
> I was reponsible for the installation of the bowling alleys at the White House and made the arrangements to have all the work done by the Brunswick, Balke, Collander Company. The alleys have now been completed but inasmuch as this Company did not install an automatic pin setter, I would be interested in talking to you when you are in town.
>
> > *Sincerely,*
> > *HARRY H. VAUGHAN*
> > *Major General, U. S. Army*
> > *Military Aide to the President*

Apparently there was a meeting, but several months later General Vaughan declined the offer. During the intervening time, the writer changed his name, apparently in an effort to Americanize it.

> *Dear Mr. Karal:*   *5 January 1948*
>
> I have no doubt that the Automatic Pin Setter is a great improvement and when you have one perfected for king pins, we may possibly be in the market. As it is, we bowl only with king pins and have neither the candle or duck pin variety.
>
>   *Sincerely,*
>   *HARRY H. VAUGHAN*
>   *Major General, U. S. Army (Res)*
>   *Military Aide to the President*

Sometimes people wrote not so much to ask something as to share a thought with their president. The following letter apparently tickled his heart.

> *Dear Mr. Truman:*   *5 January 1948*
>
> Please pardon my presumption in writing you, but my <u>husband failed to remember me on Valentine Day this year</u>. His excuse being that he was too busy with his work to think about it, and also that he would not have had time had he remembered the day. My theory is that most men are pretty busy and I asked him what he would do if he were president of the United States. I said, "Do you think Mr. Truman was too busy to remember his wife?" My husband says he thinks you were. Now, <u>I would like to know whether or not, with all your problems and worries, you found time to remember Mrs. Truman on Valentine Day</u>.
>
> We have been married twenty years and have a seventeen year-old daughter.
>
> With sincere best wishes, I am
>
>   *Yours very truly,*
>   *Mrs. Edwin C. Hirschfield*
>   *Louisville, Ky.*

> *Dear Mrs. Hirschfield:*   *February 23, 1951*
>
> Your letter brought a moment of relaxation to the President when it was called to his attention. He laughed and said, perhaps to spare

the feelings of his recalcitrant staff members, that he'd make no comment!

Sincerely yours,
ROGER TUBBY
Assistant Press Secretary

One unusual letter was messengered to the White House from the widow of Confederate general James "Pete" Longstreet, a man much vilified in the South because of his mild criticism of Gen. Robert E. Lee's military strategy and his joining of the Republican Party even as it imposed the postwar Reconstruction on the defeated states. Helen Dortch had married Longstreet when she was thirty-four and he was seventy-six. They married in 1897, apparently to the disgust of his children and "Southern war historians [who] found ways to blame Longstreet with everything that went wrong for the South in the war."[3] She spent her nearly sixty years of widowhood defending his memory. In 1952, she was a guest at the White House.

My dear Mr. President: *April 7, 1952*

Permit me to say that I am here attending the Convention of the National League of American Pen Women.

At the White House Tea with which Mrs. Truman honored us Saturday, one of the ushers told me that pictures of General Lee and of my late husband, General Longstreet, hung in the West Side of the White House. I should be very grateful if you would arrange for me to see these pictures tomorrow (Tuesday) as I leave early Wednesday morning.

I shall feel that I have lived to see "The Glory of the Coming of the Lord" in finding the pictures of these two great Confederate leaders on the walls of the White House.

A message to the Statler Hotel will reach me.

I am happy to tell you that I am ardently supporting your Civil Rights program as a matter of common justice to our Negro Americans.

With great regard,

Yours very faithfully,
Helen Dortch Longstreet

The records do not reveal whether Mrs. Longstreet received a response, but it may be assumed she did by telephone because of the limited amount of time available before her departure. The following letter received no response, as it seemingly used the excuse of analyzing the president's handwriting as a means of critiquing his personality.

Dear Mr. President: *May 21, 1952*
I saw your daily prayer which was shown in the *Milwaukee Journal* on Sunday, April 27, 1952, and <u>decided to send you a brief analysis of your handwriting</u>.

You are quick to respond sympathetically. You have deep and lasting emotions. There is a strong indication of suppressed emotions. You have very keen mental penetration. You are an exploratory thinker—you like to dig into facts and see what makes them tick. You are very investigative. Your willpower is very strong which ties in with your purpose in life. You have sufficient skill in creating things to count on this as a strong asset. You are sarcastic and this becomes a genuine liability because, at the present time, your sarcasm is tied in with a resentful and suspicious attitude. The suspicion comes from the resentfulness combined with the analytical ability you possess. You analyze in a negative way and expect to resent.

You have a strong sense of the artistic. Your philosophical outlook on life is well developed. You are only mildly sensitive and you are exceedingly practical. Your materialistic attitude goes back and supports your practicality. You have lots of pride and personal dignity. You are very direct or you come right to the point. You are loyal to what you think is right. You are very empathetic on your decisions. You hold onto your inclinations or desires. You are very determined. Once you start a given job you complete it. You are very persistent and you persist in your habits as you do in everything else. You also have a very strong psychic sense. You feel and sense the invisible. You not only love music, but you have the feel of it as well. You comprehend music as only a master musician understands it. You are very aggressive.

Yours very truly,
James E. Treichel
Certified Grapho-Analytical Psychologist

In some cases, people wrote with their opinions of how he should conduct the nation's business, including whether he should accept the gift of an elephant.

Dear President Truman,   *April 5, 1951*

Our class read the article in the *Junior Scholastic* about the Cambodian King offering you a white elephant. We think you should accept it. You could remove one of the other elephants from the Washington Zoo and put it there.

Our class doesn't like the idea of your asking for a tiger instead. I think it was very nice of the king to offer you an elephant. We hope you will change your mind and accept it after all.

                              Yours truly,
                              Pupils of the Seventh Grade
                              Bryant School
                              Sherman, Texas

Unfortunately for the students and the elephant (nicknamed Harry), it died en route to Washington, D.C., but some photographs were taken, so the president got a glimpse of his gift.

Several months later, the general manager of the Harlem Globetrotters, a World War II veteran who knew of Truman's earlier service in the Ardennes, took the time to send Truman a small token as they traveled across France.

Dear Sir: *12 June 1951*

My conscience would have bothered me, had I not stopped the Globetrotter bus to pick a few bright red poppies—they dot the many fields of blue clover between here and Strasbourg—sent some to parents of lads who will not return. . . .

Also brings to mind the poem—"In Flanders fields, the poppies grow, etc." . . .

Hope you and your family are in the best of health and spirits. We need your firm guidance.

                              With all sincerity,
                              Dave Zinkhoff
                              Philadelphia, Penn.

An acrostic poem by an acquaintance of General Vaughan's was in honor of Truman's birthday.

ON THE PRESIDENT'S 66TH BIRTHDAY

Hear people's plea for peace, prepare your plan
And stay with it to hearten Common Man.

Rare opportunity is yours at hand,
Ring out the message clear, throughout the land—
Your leadership is at their own command.

Strike straight to mark and leave none in the dark.

The highest in the governmental scale,
Refuse to hear no poor man's plaint and tale
Use gifts that God in bounty gave to you.
Make freedom, independence, be as true
As where the Thirteen formed United States
Not for the few, for all in freedom's gates.

E. B. Goodman/May 8, 1950

Dear Mrs. Goodman: *May 18, 1950*
Thanks for the acrostic poem on my birthday. I appreciate it most highly. It certainly was kind and thoughtful of you to remember me this way. Mrs. Vaughan handed it to me at the luncheon.

Sincerely yours,
HARRY S. TRUMAN

One letter that intrigued Truman gave some background on the presidential theme, "Hail to the Chief."

Dear Mr. President: *September 12, 1949*
A friend sent me this from Perth, Scotland. It appeared in the *People's Journal,* August 6, 1949.
I thought it might interest you though you may already know the facts it recounts.

Cordially yours,
Ward Canady
Willis-Overland Motors, Inc.
Toledo, Ohio

"Hail to the chief who in triumph advances" sing the men of Clan Alpine as they row their chief down Loch Katrine, a scene portrayed in this week's episode of our picture story, 'The Lady of the Lake.'
"Now, through some strange twist of history, [this] song is sung for a vastly greater chief than Roderick Dhu—no less a personage than the President of the U.S.A. . . .

"A strange thing is that no one in the United States is sure how it
became the Presidential theme song.* Nearest anyone can get to it is
that it was adopted in the early days of the Republic because of its
title. In America it is practically a song without words, as these have
been almost forgotten.

"The tune itself is said to have come from an old Gaelic melody. . . ."

> First stanza: (Actually there are four)
> "Hail to the Chief who in triumph advances!
> Honoured and blessed be the evergreen pine!
> Long may the tree in his banner that glances
> Flourish, the shelter and grace of our line!
> Heaven send it happy dew,
> Earth lend it sap anew;
> Gaily to burgeon and broadly to grow,
> While every Highland glen
> Sends our shout back agen,
> 'Roderigh Vich Alpine dhu, ho! ieroe!'"

Truman apparently found this quite interesting and followed this up with
a letter to the publisher of the *People's Journal* asking for more information.

Dear Sir: *September 19, 1949*

A friend of mine, the Honorable Ward Canady, has just sent me a
clipping from your good paper of August sixth about the Scottish
song, "Hail to the Chief."

I certainly am happy to have this information, as I did not know
the origin of the song. Knowing its origin makes me all the happier
to stand at attention when it is played on my official arrival at various cities of the United States.

If you can furnish me with any information other than that contained in your paper of the sixth, I shall be most happy to have it.

Sincerely yours,
HARRY S. TRUMAN

---

*The playing of "Hail to the Chief" traditionally dates back to the presidency of
James K. Polk. He was so slight in stature that his entrance usually went unnoticed,
much to his wife's dismay. Sarah Polk then arranged with the Marine Band to play
this as the president walked into a room so that all would stop and note his arrival.

Numerous writers sent information on the Truman family and its British connection, including the following.

Dear President:

Owing to my great admiration for you and also the fact that my name is similar to yours I would dearly like to know if there is any relationship between us.

My father "Job Truman" had two brothers who migrated to U.S.A. (Pittsburgh) many years ago. Their names were Richard and Robert Truman but I have no idea what occupation they followed. The only information I have is that they were christened at Gloucester (England), that Richard was married in U. S. A. and later sent for Robert who followed with his family.

Hoping for a reply and wishing you a long and happy life.

Yours faithfully,
(Miss) E. Truman
Rogerstone Mon., Eng.

Dear Mr. Ross: *June 11, 1946*

The *World Almanac* has received a newspaper clipping from a reader giving what is purported to be a sketch of the ancestry of President Truman. The dispatch, under date of Glendale, Calif., and is credited to the Associated Press, follows:

"Tremayne, Tremaine, Tremaen, Treman, Troeman, and Trewman—all were English ancestors of President Harry S. Truman, his second cousin, Dr. Archibald W. Truman, reports.

"Dr. Truman, medical director and chief surgeon of the Glendale Sanitarium and Hospital, said a genealogical study by his son, Rolland Truman, an attorney in nearby Long Beach, shows:

"The family motto was 'Honor et Honestas' or honor and honesty.

"The family is of Norman origin, the first ancestor in England having arrived from France with William the Conqueror about 1066.

"The English family's coat of arms bears three hands. The family's first immigrant to America was Joseph Truman, who settled in New London, Conn., in 1666 and became the town constable.

"Dr. Truman, Kansas-born, said his grandfather and the President's were brothers.

"Dr. Truman headed Washington Sanitarium in the National Capital for 12 years."

Can you inform the *World Almanac* if the above is true, in part or in whole, or give a few words [as] to the ancestry of the President? The Almanac has the ancestry of all the [presidential] families with the exception of the Truman.

Your cooperation in gaining this information for the 1947 edition of the *World Almanac* will be appreciated.

Sincerely yours,
E. Eastman Irvine
Editor, World Almanac

The president enclosed these two pieces of correspondence in a letter to his cousin Ethel Noland.

Dear Ethel: *June 13, 1946*

I am enclosing a letter from a lady in England who is interested in the family connections.

I received some interesting information the other day. One of our friends in London sent me an oilcloth facsimile of a sign on the back of a London streetcar. It said—

"If It's Truman's It's Best"

This sign referred to Truman's beer which has been famous in England, so I am told, since 1666, when the brewery was founded by Benjaman Truman, about the same time Johnny Walker distillery was founded.

If you will remember, our records indicated that a certain Ben Truman came to this country about 1666—I wonder if this Ben Truman might not have been a son of the famous British brewer— maybe that is the reason that I don't like beer.

I am enclosing another letter from a gentleman who signs himself as Editor of *The World Almanac.* Now I don't think there is anything to all that fancy spelling that he has in there. It is my opinion that our people came from the English "Beer Baron."

Sincerely yours,
HARRY TRUMAN

Although information about Truman's ancestry was lacking, personal records closer to the president emerged. Some workers in the Missouri office of the Health Department felt it was a shame that the president lacked a birth certificate and decided to rectify the situation.

My dear President Truman: *July 26, 1946*

Enclosed herewith find the photostatic certified copy of the record of your birth as it now is on file with the Bureau of Vital Statistics, <u>Missouri State Board of Health</u>, Jefferson City, Missouri.

Since you are not only the star citizen of Missouri, but the nation as well, I felt you should have a <u>birth certificate</u>. However, I would have found it impossible to obtain this record for you had it not been that your mother and sister were very kind in giving me their assistance.

I have been an employee of the State Board of Health for the past five years and in the capacity of Certified Copy Clerk have handled several thousand of these birth applications, and feel it a great honor to have been able to prepare your records.

Like most gifts, there are strings attached, and this one is no exception—I think I might like a position overseas and am uncertain about the procedure of getting one.

In closing, may I personally wish you much happiness. Missouri is very proud of you!

> *Sincerely yours,*
> *(Miss) Marione J. Foerster*
> *Bureau of Vital Statistics,*
> *State Board of Health*
> *Jefferson City, Mo.*

No reply was forthcoming, much to the distress of the people in the Missouri Bureau of Vital Statistics. One of her coworkers, apparently feeling that two years was long enough to wait, decided to try to get a response through the backdoor—via Margaret.

Dear Miss Truman:

Soon, after your father became President, one of the girls in our office kept saying that it was too bad our <u>Mo. Pres. was not registered in our Vital Statistics Bureau</u> of the Dept. of Health.

Finally she paid the $3.00 registration fee, filled out the necessary forms and sent them to his mother and sister with $1.00 for notary fees. They made their affidavits and returned them immediately. Thereupon a <u>Birth Certificate</u> #284637 was filed on July 25, 1946 and a copy sent to the President.

Nothing was ever heard from it, so I imagine it was overlooked by someone.

You may use your judgment in calling attention to this: The name of the girl is Marione Foerster and her name is stamped down in the corner of his certificate.

The Division of Health is under the Mint System and we have a large number of Republicans working here. I just thot that perhaps at this time it might be well to acknowledge this oversight.

I enjoy your singing on the radio over which I heard your very first concert. Congratulations on your success!

My husband was an ardent Democrat, a long-time friend of our deceased Hon. W. L. Nelson of Mo. Dr. Layne is also dead but I have 4 boys (all were in service), all good Democrats.

Best wishes for a sucessful election!

> *Mrs. B. A. Layne*
> *Eldon, Mo.*

Dear Miss Foerster: *July 13, 1948*

I regret to discover that through an inadvertence you may not have received an acknowledgment of the photostatic certified copy of the record of the President's birth. Your thoughtful courtesy in sending the photostatic copy is greatly appreciated, and I desire to assure you of the President's gratitude.

> *Very sincerely yours,*
> *WILLIAM D. HASSETT*
> *Secretary to the President*

Do Americans need better teeth? Fewer commercials? If something needs fixing in the country, one might as well go to the top man to do the job.

Dear Mr. Truman:

This is to call your attention to the fact that the provision of <u>fluorine</u> in the waters of this country will produce sound teeth for the people of this country, a principle discovered by us in 1916.

While so far we have gotten around to demonstrating this to <u>dentists</u>, is that not rather taking the long way 'round to find the short way home? <u>Dentists have no intention of letting a lucrative system</u>

of graft, at the cost of the suffering of all others, slip away from them.

Why not rather take the issue squarely to the people? I am sure, when they find out what it is all about, they will vote for the man who wishes them sound teeth. Local applications, as per dentistry, are not the same as lifelong provision in the water, and besides, cost far greatly more. So why not break up this ghastly "racket"—at the cost of a few votes you can win millions.

Sincerely,
Linus Hogenmiller
Farmington, Mo.

Mr. President   *May 2, 1948*

I just want to thank you for the beautiful Certificate of Bravery for my son. He died the same day as our beloved friend F.D.R.—April 12, 1945 at Okinawa aboard the U.S.S. *Tennessee* (a Marine).

Mr. President, could you or we do something about eliminating all commercials on the radio on Sunday? Personally I think if you asked the companies to give us a break at least once a week, they would cooperate. The good book says Jesus made the world in six days and rested on the 7th. This is only a suggestion. I hope you read it and think it over.

I thank you Mr. President.

Respectfully yours,
Alex MacNicoll
San Francisco, Calif.

Religion and the president's membership in the Baptist Church led to two very different types of correspondence.

My dear Mr. President: *May 8, 1945*

This is a note to thank you for attending Church on Sundays. No person could have had more responsibility than you had last Sunday but you went to Church and thousands were grateful that you did.

You can do more for the Spiritual Life of America than any other man by attending Church Worship Services on Sunday.

We know that you have tremendous responsibilities and every

Sunday morning millions are praying for you. And it is a great spiritual help to know that our President is in Church praying for us.

Please continue to pray for us.

Your friend,
Harry Denman
General Board of Evangelism,
The Methodist Church
Nashville, Tenn.

Dear Dr. Denman: *May 14, 1945*

The President has asked me to thank you for your commendatory letter of May eighth. The President's church membership is very dear to him and his faithful attendance at public worship reflects the reliance which he places on Divine Guidance.

Very sincerely yours,
WILLIAM D. HASSETT
Secretary to the President

My dear Mr. President:

I thought you and Shey [Sherman Minton] might get along better if he is made a Baptist too. I enclose an honorary membership card which I thought you might like to give him when he is sworn in as a member of the Supreme Court. You had better do this privately, however, because it might not be too expedient for you or Shey to do it publicly.

Shey and I have been friends for years and I know that he will get a kick out of this jester.

Respectfully,
Morris H. Coers
Minister, Immanuel Baptist Church
Covington, Ky.

Truman didn't mind being party to a joke and jumped right in.

Dear Mr. Coers: *October 20, 1949*

I certainly appreciated your letter, enclosing me the honorary membership in the Immanuel Baptist Church of Covington, Kentucky, for Sherman Minton.

I have sent it along to him with the information I believe this honorary membership in the Baptist Church will make a better Justice out of him.

As soon as I hear from him, I will send you a copy of his reply.

Sincerely yours,
HARRY S. TRUMAN

Dear Shey—or should I say   *October 20, 1949*
Dear Mr. Justice?:

There is a gentleman in Covington, Kentucky, who has the right slant on things religious. I am enclosing you his letter together with a copy of my reply and the card which makes you an honorary Baptist in the Baptist Church in Covington, Kentucky. This gentleman has a wonderful viewpoint, and I am for him one hundred percent.

I rather think this honorary membership in the Baptist Church will make a better justice out of you—and I don't want any smart remarks on that subject either.

I am hoping to see you before very long.

Sincerely yours,
HARRY S. TRUMAN

Feeling close to Truman led some people to complain about the criticism they felt was unfairly leveled against him throughout his tenure.

Att—Sec. to the President   *March 5, 1948*
Dear Sir:

The picture of President Truman with General Eisenhower and General Bradley which I saw recently at a telenews theater gave me a considerable shock.

Flanked, far too closely, by two tall men, the President appeared at a disadvantage. Both Generals were obviously aware of his discomfiture and smirked.

It was in <u>bad taste and was not fair</u>.

I, myself, am short and feel uneasy if too close to a bigger person. It is only natural.

Perhaps the camera need not be placed as close to him next time.

Yours truly,
(Miss) Marion Johnson
Chicago, Ill.

Dear Mr. President: *January 5, 1947*

Today we returned to school from our Christmas and New Years holidays. I am a senior in high school, and I am in history class. It was told in our history class that you had served time in a penitentiary. A very haughty discussion and argument followed the statement. I sincerely hope the statement is false, but we, my history class, wanted to make sure and find out the definite truth about the matter.

I understand fully that at the present time that there are many more important matters confronting you than ours but won't you try to write me an answer soon? I remain

Very respectfully yours,
Frank Robert Wayland
Colchester, Ill.

Truman also heard from numerous individuals who gave him a pat on the back while taking journalists to task. Interestingly, such letters are almost timeless: Americans writing their president complaining about the unfair press coverage of someone trying to do his job. One can probably find examples of similar letters to Abraham Lincoln.

Mr. President—   *May 10, 1946*

<u>Recently I read an unfair article about you that I could not forget</u>.

The servicemen follow all politics very close because they realize what they left behind when they came over.

I have been overseas constantly since you took over the duties of President. A very large <u>percentage of men over here realize your gigantic task and are backing you up. You have few complaints from this end</u>.

Maybe I'm taking in a lot of men but these are my feelings and I am sure they are omnipresent among the troops.

All people are paid to do a job. Some are paid to do harm. Journalists are one type. Little do they care what they write as long as it suits the paying person.

I would ask a small favor from you. If the task seems insurmountable at times, please stop and <u>remember us who have unlimited faith in your ability as President of the United States of America</u>.

Thank You,
K. A. Whittier, SM 3/6
Fokosuka, Japan

My dear Mr. Whittier: *May 24, 1946*

The President wants you to know that he is deeply appreciative of all the kind things you say about him in your letter of May tenth and asks me to thank you very warmly for your confidence in his leadership. You know, of course, the President is most grateful for the fine service that is being rendered by the members of the armed forces.

I have pleasure in extending the President's very best wishes to you and to the servicemen you mention.

Very sincerely yours,
WILLIAM D. HASSETT
Secretary to the President

Dear Mr. Short: *February 20, 1951*
I wonder if you could let me know, at your convenience, whether egg rolling on the White House lawn on Easter Monday will be reinstated this year. One of the editors has asked me to check with you.

> *Very truly yours,*
> *Louis Forster, Jr.*
> *Assistant to the Editor*
> The New Yorker

Dear Mr. Forster: *February 22, 1951*
Egg rolling on the White House lawn will not be revived this year because the grounds still are torn up as a result of the reconstruction work.

> *Sincerely yours,*
> *JOSEPH SHORT*
> *Secretary to the President*

CHAPTER SIX

THE MACARTHUR FIRING

"How stupid can you get?"
　　　　　　　—Arizona businessman Barry Goldwater

"Mr. Prima Donna, Brass Hat, Five Star MacArthur. He's worse than the Cabots and the Lodges*—they at least talked with one another before they told God what to do. Mac tells God right off. It is a very great pity we have to have stuffed Shirts like that in key positions. I don't see why in Hell Roosevelt didn't order Wainwright home and let MacArthur be a martyr. . . . We'd have had a real General and a fighting man if we had Wainwright and not a play actor and bunco man such as we have now. Don't see how a country can produce men as Robert E. Lee, John J. Pershing, Eisenhower and Bradley and at the same time produce Custers, Pattons, and MacArthurs." Truman wrote these words in his diary on June 17, 1945, barely two months into his presidency and over five long years before the fateful clash between himself and his willful subordinate.

During his long service in the National Guard, Truman had closely followed the career of Douglas MacArthur, and as a full colonel and commander of various artillery regiments, he was privy to virtually all nuances of the assignments-promotions soap opera taking place in the diminutive, between-wars Army of the 1930s. Truman knew that the revered John J. Pershing, who led the American Expeditionary Force in France during World War I, had personally requested that MacArthur approve George Marshall's promotion to

---

*Two elite and long-established Boston families known for their power, influence, and money. Their union produced Henry Cabot Lodge, who, as a Republican senator from Massachusetts, vigorously opposed President Woodrow Wilson's idealistic post–World War I policies. Because of his determined opposition, the Senate failed to ratify either the Treaty of Versailles or League of Nations Covenant.

brigadier general in command of troops, but MacArthur instead banished the future chief of staff and secretary of state to an instructor's job at the Illinois National Guard. It is also highly likely that the straight-arrow Truman was aware that MacArthur had kept a mistress at a Washington apartment in the early 1930s and found hard to swallow MacArthur's claim that actual veterans probably didn't amount to "one man in ten" among the "insurrectionist"[1] Bonus Marchers he evicted from the capital (the Veterans Administration recorded that 94 percent had indeed been servicemen, with fully 20 percent carrying war disabilities). New Deal Democrats like Truman found MacArthur a "bellicose swashbuckler," and it mattered little that he had gone to the mat with Congress and President Roosevelt to fight cuts in the Army's budget; as Army chief of staff from 1930 to 1934, that was his job.

On top of all this was the small matter of what had happened in the Philippines. When it became apparent that the islands would fall to the invading Japanese, Roosevelt had ordered MacArthur to escape and thus deny Japan the propaganda victory of capturing America's most senior military officer. Though this made sense both politically and militarily, it was nonetheless galling for Truman to see Jonathan Wainwright, his old friend from training exercises at Fort Riley, put into the position of surrendering the Philippines to the Japanese.

After the outbreak of hostilities, Wainwright had advocated the immediate implementation of War Plan Orange, which called for the withdrawal of all U.S. and Philippine forces into the Bataan Peninsula, where, with a formidable concentration of U.S. coastal defense forts to their rear, they could both prevent the Japanese from using Manila Bay and hold out for as much as a year while waiting for the U.S. Navy to fight its way across the Pacific to their relief. MacArthur, however, shunned the idea of fighting a prolonged defensive campaign and ordered his army dispersed to cover possible invasion sites, where he hoped to force an early, decisive battle. By the time he realized that his plan would not work, it was too late to move the needed supplies, especially food, into Bataan. If not for a series of brilliantly executed rear-guard actions by Wainwright, the troops would not have made it into Bataan, where Wainwright further confounded Japan's efforts. His "soldier's reward" was to be left holding the bag for a commander who visited his troops only once during his remaining months in the Philippines, an action—or inaction—that earned MacArthur the derisive nickname of "Dugout Doug" to soldiers and Truman alike.

MacArthur was an extremely popular figure in the United States, however, where he was viewed by many as a genuine American hero. In the

Pacific, he maintained his soldiers' respect but was never a popular commander with the men in the sense that Omar Bradley and Eisenhower were. A propensity to avoid visiting units—except on certain, well-publicized occasions—and unfounded rumors that the general lived in sumptuous, hilltop accommodations left a resentment among many soldiers that occasionally boiled over into angry letters that would reach the White House, such as the one forwarded by the mayor of Chicago. Written by Sgt. Leon Zelvis of the 108th Combat Engineer Battalion in the Philippines (a unit with a heavy complement of Illinois residents), it was part of a larger letter requesting that soldiers be sent home from the Pacific and was signed by seventy-one soldiers.

Your Honor; Mayor Edward J. Kelley of Chicago: 6 September 1945
Listen to these words of the fighting Illinois residents of Company "C," the 108th Engineer Combat Bn; for they are not meant to go down in history, but as we so desire, to be considered with understanding, clarity of thought, and acted upon. NOW.

The war is certainly over. We, the great Americans and her Allies have won. We were forced into war to save Democracy, and to prevent the enslavement of the many by the few. Having won we placed our trust of a world of righteousnous, a peacefull and Democratic life, with a World Charter and our trust in God.

Our history in the Pacific should be well known, but we shall here repeat, hoping that the Army's methods of indoctrinatization of thought and action in one track by repetition might apply in your case.

We have had a leader here in the Pacific, General of the Army Douglas MacArthur. Having fought under him we have listened to him. HE has been triumphant in the Pacific War. Yes, we have listened and the more he spoke, the more our admiration for him decreased. For, all he referred to is "I," "I," "I," It was "I shall return," on candy and soap wrappers, and over the air waves to the Philippinos; "I have returned," behind thousands of doughboys ahead of him, and, when referring to getting the President of the Philippines back to his home island, he said, "I shall put you there on the point of my bayonet if necessary." We ask you, "what bayonet"? About all that General MacArthur can do by himself is to park his body in Manila, after the American fighting man won back his home.

Having heard all this, we have passed judgement in our hearts that the General's immediate thoughts are only for himself. . . . The Soldier despairs, diseases, or dies; the civilians prosper; the maggots grow fatter; the jungles grow greener; and General MacArthur is home [Manila]. . . . After four hitches in Hell, we feel eligible for Heaven. For us it is the good old U.S.A. that we once knew.

> *With all due respect, we remain,*
> *Sergeant Leon Zelvis*
> *Staff Sergeant Stanley Cijanowski*
> *Corporal Louis Jones*
> *Corporal Paul Litanicz*
> *[and others]*

The soldiers recognized the fact that for MacArthur (who had not been farther east than Brisbane, Australia, since 1936 and would not set foot in the United States for nearly six more years), "home" was not necessarily his native Arkansas. Truman invited MacArthur back because he felt that the Far East commander "was entitled to the same honors that had been given to General Eisenhower." MacArthur, however, twice refused presidential requests in the fall of 1945 to visit the United States and "receive the plaudits of a grateful nation." He gave "the delicate and difficult situation" in the Far East and his desire to avoid "appearances before Congressional committees on any extraneous issues such as postwar organization . . . involving [him] in controversial issues" as his reasons for refusing to return.[2] As for Wainwright, he became one of MacArthur's staunchest supporters and delivered the speech at the 1948 Republican Convention nominating him as the party's candidate for president. Truman discussed MacArthur's slim chance at receiving the nomination with his aides the following day and, according to Eben Ayers, "commented that it was well that Wainwright did not know what MacArthur had said about him," but stopped short of repeating MacArthur's comments or saying how he had learned of them.

Politics is politics, however, and when Truman was asked by Richard W. O'Neill to sign a commemorative scroll to be given to the general on his sixty-ninth birthday in January 1949, it was clear that no matter how much the president would have liked to have had Hassett handle the matter with one of his eloquent "Valentines," O'Neill was too well connected to be dismissed so easily. O'Neill, who had served with MacArthur in World War I, was the chairman and Wainwright the honorary chairman of the committee circulating the document, a committee that managed to garner an extremely large number of high-ranking military officers and prominent Americans such as former Postmaster General James A. Farley through the time-honored method of snowballing its membership: "Generals ——— and ——— are already on the committee, won't you lend your name as well."

> *Dear Mr. President:*
>
> The enclosed is a photostat of a commemorative scroll to be presented to General of the Army Douglas MacArthur at a patriotic, non-political and non-profit dinner on his 69th birthday, January 26, 1949.
>
> Though it was originally planned by a group of men and women, including myself, who admire and respect the General as a soldier and statesman, to merely send this scroll to him with a covering letter, instead we have just recently decided to stage this anniversary dinner. The number one invitation is extended to you, Mr. President, not only because of your exalted position as President of the United States and Commander-In-Chief of the Armed Forces, but also because of your former status as a combat soldier in World War I.
>
> This committee fully appreciates the stupendous executive task confronting you at this time, and the terrific time schedule to which you must adhere. However, we know too the high esteem in which you hold General MacArthur. Therefore, our committee—your time permitting—would consider it a signal honor to have you personally sign the scroll. If this meets with your approval, a committee of three will be appointed by the Chairman to call upon you at your convenience.
>
> Our committee would like to extend their congratulations on your forthcoming inauguration. We sincerely hope your administration will enjoy peace, prosperity and success in dealing with and solving the domestic and international problems confronting our country. May God bless, inspire and guide you.
>
> *Very respectfully,*
> *Richard W. O'Neill, Chairman*

Truman placed his name at the top of the list in a place reserved for him ahead of the other signatures, but a year later, the general's admirers were back with yet another request, which Charlie Ross outlined in the memo below:

Memorandum for Brigadier General Louis H. Renfrow,
Office of the Secretary of Defense
Dear Lou:

Sometime ago the President signed an ornate and floridly worded commemorative scroll dedicated to General Douglas MacArthur. Now the promoters of this enterprise are back, asking for a letter from the President, to be placed in a special album of letters by the signers of the scroll. The request is contained in the attached wordy letter of Richard W. O'Neill.

I should like your opinion as to whether or not this request should be kissed off. It seems to me that the President went pretty far when he signed the scroll.

If you do think that the [President] should participate again in honoring General MacArthur, I should be glad if you would furnish me with a brief proposed statement for his signature. Thanks and regards.

CHARLES G. ROSS

Renfrow replied immediately and included a possible response from the president.

My dear Charlie:

My first reaction was to recommend "no letter" then I reviewed the whole project and in view of the fact that the President signed the Scroll, it seemed necessary to include a letter from the President to slam that door shut once and for all.

I trust the draft is acceptable as it seems short enough and refers in no way to the wording of the Scroll, but simply to the General's leadership and those who served with him.

Merry Christmas and Happy New Year to you and your fine family and may your years ahead be healthful and happy.

Sincerely,
Louis H. Renfrow

DRAFT
Dear Mr. O'Neill:

In signing the Commemorative Scroll to General Douglas MacArthur I, like all other Americans, am deeply appreciative of the military achievement attained by him and those he led in the Pacific during World War II.

Sincerely,

HST

Truman thought that even this brief statement was too much, and scratched out most of it on the draft version. The only words he didn't change were "Commemorative Scroll to General Douglas MacArthur."

Dear Mr. O'Neill:

I have been happy to sign the Commemorative Scroll to General Douglas MacArthur and thereby express my admiration of his distinguished services to the Nation.

Very sincerely yours,

HARRY S. TRUMAN

The president's letter and others were presented to the general in a set of lavish albums on his seventieth birthday. Both men were at the peak of their careers: Truman had won an upset victory in the previous election, and MacArthur had successfully implemented a comprehensive policy of social, economic, and political reforms in Japan that was the envy of even some New Deal Democrats. Within six months, however, the outbreak of war on the Korean Peninsula on June 25, 1950, would lead to a series of events that would ultimately force each of them from public service.

The United States immediately entered the war with the support of the United Nations, and MacArthur was named the U.N. commander, yet within days, the South Korean capital of Seoul was captured. Undermanned and poorly equipped U.S. and South Korean forces retreated in the face of North Korea's assault as an effective defensive perimeter was hurriedly formed around the vital port city of Pusan, across from Japan. Intense communist attacks against the Pusan Perimeter continued almost without letup into the middle of September, but an aggressive defense led by U.S. Eighth Army commander Walton H. Walker kept the communists off balance and away from the city. As the seige dragged on, the North Koreans were clearly reaching the end of their rope. They had expended most of their Soviet-built tanks during the initial invasion, and their troops were beginning to starve as U.S., British, and Australian aircraft savaged their supply lines.

With communist troops concentrated far from their supply bases in North Korea, the road and rail net emanating from Seoul became increasingly important to maintaining the communists' offensive. These veins could be cut by a U.N. counterstroke at any of several west-coast locations, such as Kunsan, Inch'on or the beaches near Osan. A landing at the northernmost site, Inch'on, entailed the greatest risks because of its dangerously narrow channel and extreme tides. What it offered, according to MacArthur, was the prospect of winning an important psychological victory through the quick, decisive recapture of the traditional Korean capital of Seoul. Moreover, it was such a bad landing site that it was only lightly defended, and with the bulk of the North Korean Army concentrated well away from the area, a U.N. invasion there would not be endangered by strong counterattacks.

MacArthur's intention to invade at Inch'on generated such deep concern among the Joint Chiefs of Staff (JCS) that two members, Gen. Lawton J. Collins and Adm. Forrest P. Sherman, flew to his Tokyo headquarters on July 23 to, as Secretary of Defense Louis A. Johnson related, "try to argue General MacArthur out of it."[3] Johnson, however, fully backed the Far East commander's plan, as did Collins's deputy chief of staff, Lt. Gen. Matthew B. Ridgway. Less than a week before the September 15 landings, the JCS grudgingly approved Inch'on as the invasion site.

The daring amphibious landing was executed almost exactly as planned. Seoul was recaptured by the end of the month, and the 100,000-man North Korean Army besieging Pusan crumbled. In early October, the U.N. General Assembly voted to change the mission of its forces from simply repelling North Korean aggression to achieving a complete military victory and political unification of the peninsula. MacArthur was now free to attack the North, and the U.N. offensive began on October 9 against scattered resistance.

During this period, the Red Chinese made several specific warnings against the use of U.S. troops above the 38th Parallel. U.S. leaders interpreted these statements as little more than a bluff to help stave off the defeat of their communist neighbor, and U.N. forces were allowed to move as far north as a "restraining line" running across the peninsula's narrow neck roughly 100 miles from Korea's northwest border with China. The JCS believed that keeping U.N. troops well away from the frontier would be enough to ensure that the Chinese Army would not enter the war. Only South Korean soldiers would be permitted into the provinces along Chinese Manchuria.

At an October 15 meeting with Truman on Wake Island in the Pacific, General MacArthur remarked that the Chinese would "face the greatest slaughter"[4] if they intervened in Korea. This view was shared by the JCS, and shortly after his return to Tokyo, MacArthur moved the restraining line as close as fifty miles from the Yalu River, which separated Manchuria from North Korea. A week later, all restrictions on the maneuver of U.N. forces were lifted, but the Chinese communists did not sit idly by as U.N. troops neared Manchuria. Even as the Far East commander and President Truman discussed the upcoming victory in Korea, the first of more than 300,000 Chinese moved south across the Yalu.

Heavy fighting erupted with the Chinese just two weeks after the Wake Island meeting and continued into November when, as suddenly as they had appeared, the Chinese infantry melted away to the north. MacArthur was certain that the Chinese would not commit major elements of their army to Korea, and their apparent withdrawal after less than two weeks of fighting seemed to confirm that they were primarily interested in protecting the important power plants supplying Manchuria with electricity from the North Korean side of the Yalu. The communists' fear of the U.N.'s overwhelming air superiority, MacArthur believed, would be enough to keep the Chinese at bay, and their limited forces below the Yalu could be easily dealt with.

Early on the morning of Saturday, November 25, the Chinese struck again, destroying or soundly defeating numerous South Korean, American, and U.N. units. MacArthur's forces were able to withdraw to the south only with the greatest difficulty, and within days of the Chinese onslaught, it was obvious that the Chinese were in Korea not to form a buffer along their border, but to annihilate the U.N. army. MacArthur reported that his men were up against an "overwhelming force" and that "consequently, we face an entirely new war."[5]

During this period, MacArthur pressed vigorously—and publicly—for an expansion of the war into China, arguing that it was virtually impossible to win against an army operating from behind an inviolate frontier. He predicted that if the communists could not be attacked in their "sanctuaries," U.N. forces would face a "savage slaughter" and that "unless some positive and immediate action is taken . . . steady attrition leading to final destruction can reasonably be contemplated."[6]

But as the communists operated from the sanctuary of Manchuria, so, too, did the U.N. from Japan. The JCS believed that if the war spilled beyond Korea's shores, the United States would be hard-pressed to defend the island nation against combined Chinese-Soviet air attacks and keep it supplied in the face of a determined blockade by the 100-strong Soviet submarine fleet based in nearby Vladivostok and, now, the Chinese city of Port Arthur as well. MacArthur's useless assurances that the Soviet Union would stay out of a general war between the United Nations and Red China were ignored.

Both the JCS and the British government counseled President Truman to avoid being sucked deeper into a widening conflict in the Far East. In 1950, no one knew if Korea represented the opening shots in a third world war and perhaps the aim of the Chinese communists to tie down U.S. forces in Asia while the Soviets struck in Europe.

Truman decided to abandon the objective of unifying the Korean peninsula, and the U.N. consented to a resumption of its original aim, preserving the Republic of Korea. In mid-January, JCS members Collins and Hoyt S. Vandenberg flew to Tokyo and handed MacArthur a personal letter from the president in which he outlined "our basic national and international purposes" in Korea.[7] General Collins also wanted to take a firsthand look at the situation on the ground and see how the Eighth Army was faring, now that it was under the command of his former deputy.

Ridgway assumed command of U.N. ground forces on December 26, 1950. Three days earlier, Ridgway's predecessor, General Walker, had been killed when his jeep collided with a South Korean truck on an icy road. The new commander arrived to find both his army and his boss in Tokyo severely shaken by the events of the previous month, and a fatigued MacArthur told him, "The Eighth Army is yours, Matt. Do what you think best."[8] Ridgway immediately moved to instill a winning spirit in his demoralized troops. As soon as the momentum of the communists' offensive slowed in mid-January, he ordered that all units probe north.

General Collins had arrived from the United States in time to witness Ridgway's first effort, a well-coordinated reconnaissance in force code-named Wolfhound, and left with the conviction that the Eighth Army could take care of itself. This was quite a revelation, and after his reports to Truman and the JCS, they "were no longer pessimistic about being driven out of Korea." Moreover, the Army chief of staff made it clear that "General Ridgway was responsible for the dramatic change" in the Eighth Army's fortunes.[9] Collins's visit marked the end of MacArthur's influence on U.S. policy making. The gallant old general was pressing hard to obtain four more Army divisions from the United States, stating unequivocally that he needed that many soldiers just to stabilize the front. Ridgway, however, clearly had the situation well in hand without the additional troops and was confident that the 365,000 men under his command could not only hold their own, but push the half million or so Chinese and North Korean troops back across the parallel. The JCS began to deal directly with Ridgway, bypassing his commander in Tokyo. Characteristically, MacArthur did not take the situation lying down.

Harry Truman's military career did not end with his captaincy in World War I. Here Truman poses with his future military aide, Harry H. Vaughan (left) and future treasury secretary, John W. Snyder, at a summer training exercise in the 1930s. All would attain the rank of colonel in the Reserve Officer Corps and command artillery regiments in the period before World War II.

Truman motoring back from the presidential retreat at near Thurmont, Maryland, with his correspondence secretary, William D. Hassett. COURTESY ASSOCIATED PRESS.

The presidential party during a March 1951 visit to the "Little White House" at the Key West Florida naval base. Front row: Richard E. Neustadt, Col. Cornelius J. Mara, Joseph Feeney, Philleo Nash, Irving Permeter. Center row: John Steelman, Admiral William D. Leahy, President Truman, Averell Harriman, Charles Murphy. Standing: Gen. Robert B. Landry, Adm. Robert L. Dennison, Stanley Woodward, Matthew J. Connelly, William D. Hassett, Joseph Short, Gen. Harry H. Vaughan, and Gen. Wallace H. Graham.

Philleo Nash strums a tune for the President. COURTESY HARRY S. TRUMAN LIBRARY.

White House Press Secretary Charles G. Ross (upper right) and Assistant Press Secretary Eben Ayers (cigarette in hand) pass out copies of Truman's statement on the
national railroad strike of 1948 as Winston Churchill glowers down from a photo on
the wall. COURTESY UNITED PRESS INTERNATIONAL (UPI).

Ayers reads some of the fifteen hundred letters and telegrams received by the end of June 1950 on the outbreak of the Korean War. Nearly all of the early mail congratulated Truman for his efforts to blunt the communist invasion. COURTESY UPI.

A well-placed pillow provides Truman's personal secretary, Rose Conway, with some much-needed back support as she works on the campaign train during the run-up to the 1948 elections.

The presidential party at the 1948 Washington Senators season opener. Front row: Gen. Harry H. Vaughan, Margaret Truman, Mrs. John Snyder, Bess Truman, Harry Truman, Sen. Alfred H. Vendenberg. Second row: Col. Robert B. Landry, Capt. Robert L. Dennison supplying a light to Charles G. Ross, William D. Hassett, and Matthew J. Connelly. Although Harry seems to be enjoying the game considerably more than Bess, she was in fact a big baseball fan and may have been focusing intently on the game.

Truman, in cap and gown, and naval aide Clark M. Clifford laugh heartily at the understated irony of one of Winston Churchill's points. Contrary to his later statements, Truman was fully aware of the contents of Churchill's "Iron Curtain" speech before it was given at Westminster College in Fulton, Missouri.

The President and several of his staff on the train taking him and Churchill to Fulton, Missouri. From left: General Harry Vaughan, Capt. Clark Clifford, Charles Ross behind Truman, and Gen. Wallace Graham. COURTESY HARRY S. TRUMAN LIBRARY.

Truman and his principal advisers after the Wake Island meeting with Gen. Douglas MacArthur. Left to right: Averel Harriman, George C. Marshall, Truman, Dean Acheson, John Snyder, Philip C. Jessup (behind Acheson and Snyder), Frank Pace, and Gen. Omar N. Bradley. COURTESY HARRY S. TRUMAN LIBRARY.

The President takes Gen. Douglas MacArthur by the arm and has a brief word with him before the leaders depart Wake Island. With them is MacArthur's aide-de-camp, Gen. Courtney Whitney. COURTESY HARRY S. TRUMAN LIBRARY.

Truman holding a press conference in the old State Department building. Flanking him left to right are Charles Murphy, Donald Dawson, Bill Hassett, and Eben Ayers.

The President and his staff at a morning meeting in 1951. Left to right: George M. Elsey, Matthew Connelly, William Hopkins, Truman, John Steelman, Gen. Harry Vaughan, Adm. Robert Dennison, William Hassett, Gen. Robert Landry, and Robert Tubby. Hassett and Landry sit flanking the newest addition to the Oval Office, a television cabinet. The gentleman to Truman's right, obscured by Connelly, is probably Charles Murphy, who commonly sat in the chair between Elsey and Truman. The knee at the extreme left belongs to Donald Dawson. COURTESY FPG INTERNATIONAL.

An atomic bomb explodes among target ships during a 1946 test at Bikini Atoll. The uncertain future brought about by the development of nuclear weapons prompted many Americans to write to Truman. OFFICIAL U.S. AIR FORCE PHOTOGRAPH.

After the MacArthur controversy subsided, well-placed concern for American prisoners in Korea was the central theme of most letters on the Korean War. At a military hospital in Japan, Bob Hope clowns with young soldiers who escaped from the communists and were safeguarded by North Korean civilians until the area was overrun by the U.S. Army. COURTESY ARMY NEWS FEATURES.

Murdered American prisoners discovered by U.S. forces. The cigarette pack, discarded matches, and crushed stubs seem to indicate that the men were held in this hallway for a while before being shot. A photograph of a wife or girlfriend lies at the lower left. U.S. ARMY PHOTOGRAPH.

Harry and Bess wave to the press and well wishers as they prepare to board the "Sacred Cow." Americans could and would write to their President about anything, and some were certain that the aircraft's unofficial nickname would be offensive to Hindus.

MacArthur stated emphatically to the Navy's official historian, Rear Adm. Samuel Eliot Morison, that "a theater commander should be allowed to act independently, with no orders from the President, United Nations, or anyone," and repeated it for the stunned admiral.[10] The general's views were not entirely a surprise to Truman and his advisors. As far back as World War II, MacArthur had forcefully advocated that the United States, in effect, shelve its agreements with Great Britain and the Soviet Union to give the war with Germany top priority, and instead spare no effort to allow him to defeat the Japanese first. What was new was MacArthur's repeated and remarkably overt efforts at trying to force the president to conform national policy to his will. Almost from the beginning of the new war in Korea, MacArthur had made public criticisms of Truman's policy—and gotten away with it. He echoed the administration's political opponents when he railed against "those who invariably in the past have propagandized a policy of appeasement in the Pacific"[11] and then put himself publicly at odds with Truman's carefully constructed position on the Nationalist Chinese island of Formosa in a letter to be read at an upcoming Veterans of Foreign Wars convention. Coming only weeks away from the U.N.'s counterattack at Inch'on, Truman refrained from relieving MacArthur on the spot and ordered only that he withdraw his statement.

Disagreements between the two were papered over in the following months, but MacArthur's battlefield reverses near the Chinese border prompted a new round of public pronouncements from his Tokyo headquarters that the war should be widened. Orders from Washington that he must have all future speeches, press releases, and other statements cleared by either the State or Defense Department was adhered to only briefly, and MacArthur's waning influence both in Washington and on the battlefield appeared almost to impel the general to force his will on the unfolding events.

MacArthur's defiance of his commander in chief finally cost him his job. A series of public statements by the general undercut Truman's new peace initiative and made it plain that he was in complete disagreement with the handling of the war. With the full agreement of the Joint Chiefs of Staff, the president decided to strip him of all commands and send him home. The following afternoon, April 10, 1951, General Omar Bradley, accompanied by George Marshall, Dean Acheson, and Averell Harriman, brought the orders recalling the Far East chief. Truman quickly read them over, borrowed a pen from Hassett, and did the deed. He later explained: "General MacArthur was ready to risk general war. I was not." Army Secretary Frank Pace was in Korea when the decision was made to relieve MacArthur. After breaking the news to

Ridgway that he was to take over as chief of the Far East and U.N. commands, Pace asked: "Now do we congratulate each other or shoot ourselves?"[12]

Truman knew there would be trouble, but the firestorm that erupted was far beyond anything he anticipated. A hastily called national address helped keep his support from further eroding but was of little other immediate benefit. Congressmen and senators, including Richard Nixon and Joe McCarthy, demanded MacArthur's immediate reinstatement, and other prominent Republicans, Joe Martin (who had been in direct contact with MacArthur), William Jenner, and Robert Taft, spoke openly of initiating impeachment proceedings against the president. Across the country, flags were flown at half staff or upside down, and angry citizens flooded Congress with nearly 45,000 letters and telegrams condeming Truman. This, however, was only a fraction of the more than 100,000 messages sent to the White House. Truman didn't need to be told that the initial burst of telegrams was running roughly twenty to one against him. When he walked into a staff meeting a few hours after the news broke, his new assistant press secretary, Roger Tubby, scooped up a handful of the pink and blue Western Union messages and held them aloft without saying a word. The feisty president glared at the offending messages and said, "See that fireplace over there, Roger? Go put them in there and set a match to them."[13] Within the next few days, another 13,000 letters and telegrams would arrive at the White House, the majority of them strongly condemning Truman's action.

Dear Mr. President: *April 13, 51*
The most foolish move you ever made in your life firing General Douglas MacArther [*sic*] the most brilliant General we ever had in the history of the U.S.A.

You better put on your hat and coat Harry, and head for home and let the Vice President take over the rest of your term of office for the balance of your term.

The whole country is disgusted with your administration and your appeasement policy.

Your [*sic*] the man that sent Mac. into Korea with a handful of men to be slaughtered and he never has had the support he should have had.

I have been a life long demacrat, but I am not voting for anyone that don't back up MacArthur. You have satisfied the British, who seem to be able to tell you what to do and the U.N. which everybody knows is a joke.

The only way you can redeem your self is to reinstate General MacArthur to his former position. I sincerely hope you do this.

Respectfully,
C. H. Brown
Derby, Conn.

Dear Pres. Truman: *April 27, 1951*
In as much as you have lost the faith and confidence of the American people. It is suggested that you resign, and thus make way for General MacArthur to take your place.

Sincerely,
Russell J. Fonmalt
New York, New York

One of the first telegrams to arrive at the White House was dispatched by a Phoenix, Arizona, department store owner and future Senator at 10:34 on the morning that news of the dismissal broke. Simple and eloquent, it summed up what many Americans were thinking:

THE PRESIDENT
THE WHITE HOUSE
HOW STUPID CAN YOU GET?
BARRY GOLDWATER

Many letter writers attempted to haunt Truman by reminding him of a complimentary remark he'd made about Joseph Stalin over five years earlier in the afterglow of the Potsdam conference.

Sir: *April 14, 1951*
It was a sad commentary on statesmanship when you said "I like old Joe" and a sadder one when you proved it by your action on General MacArthur.

Yours truly,
Lloyd E. Budd
New York, NY

Another resident of New York was so inspired by MacArthur's triumphant tickertape parade through Manhattan that he went home and immediately poured out all his anguish over the state of the nation and the world to the president.

> *New York City's MacArthur Day*
> *Dear Mr. President:*   *20 April 1951*

After listening to you on Wednesday, April 11th I was disappointed, and after hearing General MacArthur's address on Thursday, April 19th I was surprised. I feel that were I to sit idly by, I would be guilty of laxity in my obligations as an American citizen.

To me, an ex-GI same as yourself, it seems so very strange that an agent of the administration, assigned to specific duties in one sphere, could say volumes in matters of importance not only in that sphere but in all-around domestic and international scope, and that, unaided by a staff of high priced advisers. Whereas our President said nothing that the American public did not already know. The staff of so-called domestic and international masterminds failed to make the President's address impressive, nor did they succeed in justifying the general's removal.

Reverting all the way back to the forming of the United Nations Constitution and progressively reviewing all major issues of domestic and international significance, the Administration and its advisers were found wanting in impressing the world, of the aims for good of the greatest world power, and were found wanting in assuring to its countrymen the American way of life, to which the countrymen were entitled by virtue of their know-how and indeed, performance.

Being the world's greatest power, the United States had no need to resort to the veto clause, yet it acquiesced to its incorporation in the by-laws of the U.N., to its own disadvantage.

The Administration with little if any effort permitted political coups in Poland and Czecho-Slovakia thereby more strongly forging the chain of appeasement.

In China, a major power of the U.N. and our ally, a war was permitted between the nationals and the same communist aggressors, by our haphazard policy and assistance, and that was in the early stages of the present Korean counterpart. Then the Administration at long last took the stand that aggression in Korea must be opposed (but just partially) to keep Asia free. But can the freedom of an appendage insure freedom for the bulk of Asia long since over run by Communists? Had the Administration taken a stand in China (its ally), there would not have been a Korean War or 60,000 American casualties. And where does the Administration get the gumption to tell the American people and the world that it strives to keep freedom alive, and then restricts the nationals of China, legal representatives, from protecting their freedom? Is it not more correct that appeasement is not being practiced as heretofore? Only now we seem to be appeasing all our allies (?) and therefore in turn our Soviet enemy. For is it not true that Socialist Britain wants, to extend recognition to China's communists at peace negotiations in Korea, and to turn over Formosa to the communists?. . . Mr. President, I can appreciate quite well, the position one finds himself in, in the execution of the high office of the President of the United States. With all the God given mental abilities no individual can possess the knowledge to be self sufficient unto himself in the execution of said office. Therefore this letter is not written for the sole purpose of criticism. For not one of us is infallible. However, the great among us, upon realizing or upon being convinced of error in judgement, will make an earnest effort to correct some wrong. In my own small way, being concerned over the welfare of my country, I am making this bid, by calling your attention to what my relatives, friends, acquaintances are also concerned about, and would like to see corrected for the common good of all of us Americans. And party affiliations should not stand in the way of said goal.

If all of the aforementioned conditions were the result of the Administration arriving at decisions by doing their duty as God gave them the light to see that duty, then we will charge it to experience and try to profit from its lesson. However, if said conditions were as a result of decisions arrived at through disloyalty or divided loyalty, or for the benefit of some financial interests or for ulterior motives, then the responsible parties should be prosecuted to the full extent of the law, for an example to future aspirants. And if no such laws exist, they should be enacted immediately. . . .

In closing Mr. President, though I subscribe to the subordination of the military to the people's representatives, I do not subscribe to removal of great military minds to appease even supposedly friendly nations.

LONG LIVE AMERICA and not the British cartels, who soak us

for raw materials so we could help them out with finished products via lend lease or Marshall plan.

Walter J. Klejna
Bronx 57, N.Y.C.

Great Britain's opposition to an expanded U.S. commitment in the Far East was seen by many correspondents as one of the main reasons why Truman would not prosecute the war in Korea more vigorously, but it was Secretary of State Dean Acheson who was accused of being the sinister figure behind MacArthur's dismissal. Acheson's stout defense of his former subordinate Alger Hiss against spy charges; his part in formulating a "soft" policy toward the Soviet Union; and his perceived culpability in the U.S. "loss" of mainland China to the communists (as if China were ours to lose) were viewed by many Americans as part of a dangerous pattern of appeasement. With the firing of MacArthur, the anger and frustration finally exploded with perhaps as many as a quarter of all the letter writers who criticized the decision pointing the finger squarely at the secretary of state.

Dear Harry: *April 11, 1951*
As President you should abandon your false pride and misplaced loyalty to Russian and English sponsored interests and start listening to Congress and the American people. If your State Department had its way the Compromising, Appeasing Cowardly English policy would prevail in this country and the Yellow Jack would be flying over the White House. You should have stuck to selling men's shirts instead of American lives. The only thing that seems to arouse you is criticism of your Daughter's voice and Not the frozen limbs of American Soldiers who you sent to war and then sold out for the benefit of your English advisors. Long, sweet words of perfect diction by Dean Acheson mean absolutely nothing. What the hell do you think they are shooting over there in Korea—Tea Biscuits or Baked Apples? MacArthur is reprimanded for having as his dream the conquest of Communism. Can you think of a better dream Harry? I can't.

Here's one vote you can count on losing. My policy is specific and definite and that's more than I can say about you.

Hoping you are Impeached Immediately,
John J. Armstrong
New York City, NY

My Dear Mr. President;   *April 12, 1951*

You should have fired Secretary of State Atcheson [*sic*] and resigned yourself instead of firing General MacArthur. MacArthur may be an egotist but he is also a one hundred percent patriot and an able soldier.

Atcheson should go to England. His pro-British attitude would be more thoroughly appreciated there than it is in the United States. Such an action by him would provide "good riddance of bad rubbish" as far as this country is concerned.

I pray to God that he will save us from the little man who plays at being President and the Secretary who apparently is the real president and who is awaiting the opportunity to play the role of Judas Iscariot and deliver us, as much as possible, into the hands of the Communist powers.

> *Very truly yours,*
> *Frank A. Boland*
> *Columbus, Ohio*

My dear Mr. President:

At 8:00 A.M. the morning of April 11, 1951, I heard a news commentator make the announcement that you had removed General Douglas MacArthur as Commander-in-Chief of our forces in the far east. I am utterly stunned and I believe millions of other Americans experienced the same feeling.

I feel sure that your decision in removing General MacArthur was motivated initially by your personal ego and your inability to gracefully accept opposition to your plans, regardless of the wisdom voiced in such opposition. I do believe, however, that the real cause behind this action has been the constant and relentless boring from within your advisors namely, Secretary of State Dean Acheson. Mr. Acheson professes his hatred of communism orally but I am afraid the roster of aims and accomplishments of the State Department belie his spoken opinions. I believe that now is the time for America to have a man of sufficient stature and experience shaping our foreign policy and not a puppet who dances to the tune played by 10 Downing Street.

We should at this time be marshaling our every weapon to fight the advance of world communism and I believe that the man the Russians fear the most is General Douglas MacArthur. We had the advantage over Russia with the atomic bomb for a time, [but] we no longer have that advantage. We still had the advantage over Russia and that advantage was MacArthur, they fear him. They could develop an atomic bomb but they could not develop a MacArthur. You have divested us of that advantage and have struck a blow for the enemy.

Mr. Acheson claims that General MacArthur was invading the realm of international politics by demanding that the Communist forces in Korea surrender and that he would do better to leave such matters to the State Department. It seems to me a ridiculous situation when a General can not endeavor to end a war which he is fighting through no fault of his own without being hamstrung by a group of political tinhorns.

International pressure on the part of our allies was, no doubt, also a big factor leading to his dismissal. MacArthur was for fighting the war anywhere, anyhow, using any methods possible in order to bring it to an end quickly. This did not suit our allies, though, because they had their international trade to think of. It strikes me that if our allies were as abundant with troops and materiel as they were with their criticism, or to use the parlance of a poker player, which I'm sure you will understand, "If they put their money where their mouths were the game would have been over long since." To quote the General on this situation, "The situation would be ludicrous if it were not for the fact that men's lives were at stake."

In conclusion, let me say that it is my opinion that you have just performed a great disservice to our country and you are running true to form.

> *Respectfully yours,*
> *Miss Connie DiJusta*

Mr. President: *April 26, 1951*
I'M AN AMERICAN!
General Douglas MacArthur, the man you fired has proven he's an American and places his Country and his countries youth and welfare above high pressure politics.

Let's see you do the same as a honest God fearing man!!
FIRE DEAN ACHESON
(A for AMERICA, H, like for HELL!!)
I'm a Democrat, but you'll never get my vote.

> *Sincerely,*
> *Robert W. Knopoik*
> *Benton, Ill.*

Mr. President: *April 14, 1951*

Yesterday I read in the public press that in the last two days we lost five super forts—presumably from enemy air action in Korea, and that each of these planes carried a crew of eleven or twelve men.

Does it occur to you that it is likely that you are directly and personally responsible for the death of many of the members of the crew of these lost planes, to say nothing of the loss of several millions of dollars worth of equipment in this single case?

Does it occur to you that we are fighting a war in Korea, and that if you had permitted General MacArthur to allow our planes to pursue the Chinese? Planes which have been killing our men and destroying our equipment back to their bases and to destroy those enemy bases, that it is likely that this war could have been ended several months ago?

You talk about holding back and making peace overtures to Communist China.

During the past ten months I have read of at least a dozen peace overtures being made to China. With what result? They were all either ignored or contemptuously turned down!

The communist leaders are realists. They are also masters of double-talk and the broken word. Do you think they will pay the slightest attention to anything but force—and diplomacy of the Theodore Roosevelt type?

I wonder if you realize what you have done to the prestige of the United States in Asia in casting MacArthur out as you did?

I wonder if you have the slightest idea of what General MacArthur has actually accomplished for our country in Japan? Or are you piqued primarily because MacArthur refused to accept Mr. Acheson some five years ago as his advisor? Or because among other things General MacArthur some five years ago refused to permit the entry of two Russian divisions in Japan?

What groups have been continuously disrupting and preventing the peace efforts of the United Nations since the birth of that organization? And yet you now say "Let us make another peace offer."

The communists are laughing at you Mr. President, and you are building up a tremendous force in their sanctuary. MacArthur would have prevented this—but you have cast MacArthur out!

Mr. President do you know what death is or maiming? The families of some seventy or eighty thousand American boys do!

Are you going to do what England did at Munich? Are you going to do what England did when Japan invaded Manchuria? Are you going to do what England did when Mussilini [*sic*] invaded Ethiopia? I am afraid that you and Mr. Acheson are going to do just that!

Do you realize that if Mr. Acheson and you had not pulled the American Garrison out of South Korea two years ago the seventy to eighty thousand American boys would likely still be in good health?

Now Mr. President, I realize that your training has been along the line of so-called "practical politics"—the Pendergast way, i.e., "stay in line and reward the boys". I was in the California Legislature for some six years and I understand—but I do not understand double talk, or the science of promise without performance, so I long ago gave up any dreams of aspiration to high office.

However, Mr. President, the time has come for you to grow up! I realize that between meetings with your friends and Mr. Acheson's parties and poker it may be difficult for you to give "personal" study to our national and international problems. I understand your difficulties in this respect. But you must start thinking, Mr. President!

May I take the liberty of suggesting that you commence your education by reading Washington's Farewell Address. After you have read this then read the "Memoirs of Theodore Roosevelt". When you finish these treatises I will be glad to recommend some others—but we must hurry, Mr. President, because in the meantime I am afraid more super forts are going to be shot down and more of our boys are going to be killed, wounded and tortured by the Chinese "who are not at war with us"—so we must indeed hurry and learn—otherwise we may continue to believe things which may not be true.

> *Respectfully,*
> *Charles W. Fisher, Attorney*
> *Oakland, Calif.*

A woman from Buffalo, New York, thought better of her salutation "Dear President Truman," crossed it out on her typed letter, and penned a stiffly formal greeting in an effort to reinforce her displeasure with his decision.

~~Dear President Truman:~~ Sir   *April 16, 1951*
Fifty years ago, I was brought up to respect the president, a man of dignity, greatness, honor and farsightedness. You have none of these qualities. Instead, you surround yourself with crooks, like

Owen Lattimore, Phillip Jessup, Dean Atcheson [*sic*], and Alger Hiss.
I was also taught, we were known by the company we kept.

And then—you discharge a man like Gen. McArthur [*sic*], without even telling him, before you tell the world. A man who has done
a real job, with both hands tied. The American people are fed up
with your blundering and spending. Why don't you smarten up and
resign. You are not smart, or big enough for the job.

Listen to Fulton Lewis, a real American who is fearless and tells
the truth. You might gain some truth and intelligence.

Neva Wellington Kline
Buffalo, NY

P.S. The Wellingtons came to this country in 1670 and they
stand for freedom, liberty, honesty and economy.

Writing from an Army post near MacArthur's birthplace, a young private
obtained official stationery and complained directly to his commander in
chief.

Mr. Prsident,　　　　　　　　*April 11, 1951*
In the past few years I have read of and witnessed many disgusting "sell outs" of our country by the Washington parlor pinks; the
most recent has been the most atrocious. I am revolted and horrified
by the firing of General MacArthur. I'm not surprised though since
I have gradually become accustomed to corruption and disloyalty in
Washington.

However, I hereby raise my insignificant but indignant voice to
demand the impeachment of Acheson, the disloyal dilettante. There
is no room for divided allegiance in the present crisis. I add also, Mr.
President that you would greatly improve world conditions by
removing yourself entirely and permanently from my responsible
position.

Most Earnestly,
Pvt. George Allen
Camp Chaffee, Ark.

Acheson's predecessor and former chairman of the Joint Chiefs of Staff,
George Marshall, was currently serving as Truman's secretary of defense.
Although he was one of the most respected figures on the American political

scene, his failure to side with his brother officer stoked the frustration of some MacArthur supporters and added weight to Republican accusations of a "Truman-Acheson-Marshall triumvirate" leading the nation into "a super-Munich in Asia."

Dear President Truman: *April 13, 1951*

After a great amount of consideration, I would advise you to put politics aside and make a return to being an American. Both parties should first be dedicated to that principal [*sic*].

Your first step must be a removal of Dean Acheson, the Secretary of State; and General George Marshall. Their lives have been dedicated to the appeasement of Communists. THEY MUST GO PERIOD. Perhaps then with the assistance of able leaders you will be able to save American principals for which we fought in the last World War. It is not too late. You have a chance, if you take it.

Appease the Communists, recognize Red China, take our boys out of Korea, let them leash out death to our boys from behind the Yalu, AND YOU ARE BRINGING WAR AND DESTRUCTION TO OUR SOIL. They are not honorable and you know it.

So if you have any honor (a questionable point to this time) listen to the person you called one of the greatest military leaders of all times. MacArthur knows more than you do about this anyway.

> *With all respect,*
> *Francis E. Butz*
> *Fond du Lac, Wis.*

Mr. President.   *April 15, 1951*

You couldn't sell enough neck-ties, socks, shirts, etc. to make a living but you certainly know how to sell out the American people.

For the good of the country America (I mean) why don't you, Acheson and Marshall resign.

I think your daughter would make a much better President than you, at least she knows how to act when criticized and you don't.

You surely know how to make Stalin and Acheson happy by performing such acts as removing Gen. MacArthur from his command in the Far East.

I have lived under three democratic administrations. They have had two world wars and now we have Truman's war or police action in Korea, and a practically bankrupt nation, you and the democrats should be proud of that record.

> *Yours Respct.*
> *William R. Fohne*
> *Los Angeles, Calif.*

The recent public flap over a letter from Truman to *Washington Post* music critic Paul Hume, in which Truman threatened to break his nose because of a critical review he wrote of Margaret's singing, inspired numerous people to goad the president to take them on as well. As with the letters that arrived at the White House after the original event, the written threats of violence were nearly always seen as purely rhetorical, and the Secret Service seldom became involved.

Dear Mr. President.   *April 16, 1951*

No doubt when Mr. [Sam] Rayburn and General Marshall made their recent scare statement that our nation was in grave danger, they knew what they were talking about; because, apparently they had advance information that General MacArthur would be relieved of his command.

Perhaps your administration wishes to continue the undeclared Korean war as more people all the time are believing the present administration wishes to fight a war in order to keep our economy at a high level of prosperity as this is a good vote getter.

Mr. Truman, you would feel differently about this if you had a son fighting in Korea rather than a daughter trying to sing grand opera.

Now, do I get my nose punched, too?

> *Very sincerely,*
> *Donald R. Ferguson*
> *LaGrange, Ind.*

Mr. President: *April 11, 1951*

Your firing of Gen. MacArthur was your most stupid move since you entered public life. You displayed all the requirements expected of an idiot. You proved your disregard and disrepect for the American soldiers and the United States by your "infamous act." Now you have your wish—a lengthening of the Korean War.

Why don't you resign now before Communism takes over the world.

> *Sincerely,*
> *Charles Alsup*
> *St. Louis, Mo.*

P.S. I've already started practicing with boxing gloves so I'll be ready for you when you get around to punching my nose.

To some letter writers, Vice President Alben Barkley appeared as an innocent bystander among the unpatriotic, duplicitous scoundrels dragging the country into ruin.

Dear Mr. President: *April 12, 1951*

I listened with care to your talk last night after I had written you about your infamous treatment of General McArthur [*sic*]. I am glad to learn that you have finally learned that the Communists are our enemies. At least you are not going in today for Red Herrings and Good Old Joe. But apparently you still have not learned how to handle the Reds.

This is part of lesson No. 2 for you. Reds respect strength, not wishy washy policy like that you and Acheson have applied with the help of the British Socialists. The one man they know they cannot fool is General McArthur. I realize that our policy should be unified and that the people should work as a team, but you have fired the wrong one. You should have fired Acheson. He, Lattimore, Jessup, Hiss, etc are the ones that have messed up the Far East. And now you listen to England and France and Belgium. They are taking goods furnished with the American taxpayers money and trading with our enemy. France has a draft law that does not permit her armies to fight OUTSIDE of France. The Socialist regime of Britain would have fallen long ago if we had not been sending them economic aid disguised as military aid. They are already socialistic. That is the first step toward Communism. They have about 13,000 troops in Korea. We have over 250,000. Our boys are dying and being maimed. Our money is being spent. Nationalist China is a member of United Nations. They have a perfect right to fight in Korea. Why should we send troops to Europe to be mowed down by Russian armies, when we can use money to better advantage on large

air planes and the atomic bombs? You have muzzled General Eisenhower. He could not say what he really thought. Acheson has his
pink boys with a finger in every pie. We cannot get together and lick
the Russians, which we are going to have to do sooner or later, when
you and Acheson and that George Marshall, too, play politics with
even the very lives of our sons and husbands.

You and Senator [Tom] Connally and many others say we are a
civilian ruled nation and therefore you had the right to recall General McArthur. That is true. But where is the civilian rule? If Marshall is a civilian I am a cross-eyed turtle crawling up the depths of
the ocean to protest the robbery of the ocean bed from the States by
you and your packed court.

God knows you have bungled many times, but you are playing
with the lives of our loved ones when you kick out the one man who
knows the Orient and has surrounded himself with officers who
know the East.

I ask you to resign. Perhaps Vice President Barkley can bring
some sort of unity out of this tragedy. If you have any love for your
country, you will step down and leave one glorious page in history in
your name to outshine the infamous ones.

Yours very truly,
Mrs. Billie Farrour
Dallas, Texas

Although General Dwight D. Eisenhower had numerous disagreements
with the administration's policies, Truman's dismissal of MacArthur was not
one of them. Unlike his counterpart in the Far East, the commander of all
North Atlantic Treaty Organization forces in Europe studiously avoided any
thing that might have even the appearance of impropriety, and he kept a particularly low profile in the weeks immediately following his colleague's
removal. As the following letter demonstrates, Eisenhower's refusal to take
part in the Capitol Hill catfight was seen by some as being directed by the
president instead of Ike's own sense of propriety—and self-preservation.

My dear Mr. Truman: *April 11, 1951*
. . . If the Russians spent years planning a full scale sabotage plot
against us, they couldn't have done a better job than the job done
Wednesday the eleventh of April. It seems to me that the dismissal

was accomplished in a very sneaky manner, allowing Mme. Pandit [Indian ambassador to the U.S.] to learn before the American people, and most outrageous of all having General MacArthur the last man to know of such a move. I ardently hope and pray that General Eisenhauer [*sic*] will not be brought into a political fracas by ambitious politicians.

 With a great deal of anxiety for the future of America, I remain

Caroline Lee Allan
Philadelphia, Penn.

 Although it was not readily apparent at the time, Eisenhower emerged as the biggest winner from the MacArthur dismissal, and the sentiment expressed in the following letter would only grow in the coming year as much of the bombastic MacArthur's prestige migrated to the general in Europe, who exuded calm, competent determination in his demeanor and endeavors.

Dear Mr. President: *April 11, 1951*

 I am only one of the little people, therefore do not know all the whys and wherefores of what you do, but to me, a grave error has been made in your removing Gen. MacArthur from his command. He, of all the people in authority, has held to his course unswervingly, he is unquestionably an authority on the section that he was in command of, and he has laboured unceasingly against Communism, at all times. I cannot see how England, France, etc., can sway enough opinion in their favor, to make us lose the talents of this great man, in more ways than one. Political questions would seem to fade into the background, when consideration is given to his success, to his plans, and to his carrying out these plans. Suppose he is hard to control? If he has made a mistake yet, it has yet to come to light, he has been right every time, and that is more than can be said for any other public figure, including yourself, except Eisenhower.

 This will probably be lost in the shuffle, but I have gotten it off my chest, and I certainly wish something or someone would persuade you to reconsider this ill-advised move. Nothing but trouble can come of it.

Sincerely,
W. K. Amacker
Shreveport, La.

Nearly all of the mail supporting MacArthur was harshly critical of the president. Letters like the following were few and far between.

> *Dear Mr. Truman,*
> This is the fifth letter I have written and sent to you. So far I am sure the American people (most of them) still feel General MacArthur has the correct plan for our country, this country divided is not good for us. I beg you to call the General and have him come to the White House to see you; talk over this mess and only good will come of it. If you could only see how much good this would do for you and for America you would have already done it. Please show the people of America the way you showed them at our last election. You are busy in Washington and your aides are busy with their important jobs—they do not know how the average American feels and don't let them tell you they do. This will go on and on forever—the papers will never let it die out. Please call the General and show the world.
> *Very truly yours,*
> *Alfred J. Kohner*
> *Brooklyn, NY*

God bless you and help you in your work.

Many of those who wrote Truman were anguished wives and parents of soldiers and draft-age young men. For these writers, the possible political ramifications for the country and the lives of their loved ones were sharpened by MacArthur's dismissal, and they wanted to make sure that Truman knew they had a highly personal stake in the decision he made.

> *Dear Mr. President:*   *April 12, 1951*
> I hope that you will reconsider your removal of General Mac-Arthur. I feel certain that you have made a grave mistake, not only in regard to Korea but also for the disastrous effect it will undoubtably have in Japan.
> My husband is missing in action in Korea. He had nothing but the deepest of faith and trust in the General. He told me how the men worship MacArthur and of the wonderful job he did in Korea against overwhelming odds. Ramond volunteered to fight in this war. He didn't have to, he is a veteran of World War II. He volunteered

because he believed in freedom and because he wanted a free world for the children we planned to have to grow up in.

I can't believe that you know the situation in Korea. Do you think that because we are winning now that that is all there is to it. That we can stop now and pat ourselves on the back and arrange a nice safe peace treaty and forget all the lives that were lost—for what! You said last night that you wanted to stop the war in Korea. Do you really believe you can? Ramond fought in this war and [you] didn't. I have his letters and I know. He believed that Korea was only the beginning, the starting place of the Communist plan to rule the world. He and his buddies believed that the Communists would never consent to a peace treaty. He believed that even if we defeated the Communists in Korea, we would then have to fight "non-existent Russians," just as we are now fighting Chinese "volunteers." He wrote me in one of his letters "My God Rose, why don't people stop talking about preventing a Third World War, this is it now; why don't we get in and fight it!"

You don't feel that General MacArthur can give "His whole-hearted support to American and United Nations' policies," What are these policies? What kind of Country and what kind of president sends its boys out to war with an enemy that retires behind a private little wall, safe from attack, to build up its strength and go back and kill our boys? If that is American and United Nations' policies, then I want no part of them!

General MacArthur isn't starting a Third World War. He tried to fight a war the United States sent him on and to give our boys an even break. The policies he set forth are not wrong, yours are, they will lead only to a standstill in the war and the loss of thousands of good American lives. The Communists don't want peace; they want Asia.

The knowledge that England and India and the other European countries support your decision, is in my opinion nothing to be proud of. In the same breath England supported you, she declared that Communist China should sit in on peace talks with Japan, and that we should cede Formosa, the only free part of China to the Communists! These people know nothing of Korea and Japan and the Far East, how could they? They don't live and work and fight there. The people who do, support MacArthur. What further proof do you need?

I am sending a copy of this letter to my Congressman, my Governor, my newspapers, and any place else it will carry influence. I ask you, not only as a president, but as a man, who will have a conscience to face, reinstate General MacArthur.

> *Sincerely yours,*
> *Rose Foley*
> *Mrs. Ramond P. Foley*

Sir: *April 11, 1951*

As an American citizen and taxpayer, I vigorously protest the removal of General Douglas MacArthur. I am a World War #1 Veteran and have a son twenty years old in College subject to the draft and certainly wish to be heard in this matter.

In my opinion, America should stop taking orders from Britain and Acheson of the State Department, who is either pro-communist or pro-Britain.

> *Respectfully yours,*
> *Harold A. Bowie*
> *Brooklyn, NY*

General marshall [sic], Harry Stupid Truman,   *May 10, 1951*
The Communist Sounding Board, U.N.

Achenson [sic], and Harriman, You are the Traitors to America, American Mother's and Father's, but TRECHEROUS [sic] TRAITORS TO OUR SONS who have died, are dying, and will die in YOUR STALEMATE IN KOREA. It is a BLOODY STALEMATE, and that BLOOD IS ON YOUR HAND'S.

I only wish all of you were on the FRONT LINES IN THE THICKEST OF THE BATTLE, istead [sic] of in AMERICA, BEHIND A DESK IN THE PENTAGON BUILDING during the day, and buying BLUE MINK COATS BY NIGHT, FLUSHED OUT WITH PINK CHAMPEIGN [sic]. . . .

Having gone to the trouble to see how many SONS each of you have, I have been able to find but one who was able to produce a son. That son, no doubt is in college—(bought) under the Truman Law, to exempt certain students who make a certain average. My Son is in Trumans Slaughter House (Army) [and] if he is hurt in any way, shape, or form, all of you "Raw Dealer's are going to pay if I have to take you to the HIGHEST COURT IN THE LAND. (He is my ONLY SON.) . . .

Why isn't HER HIGHNESS, Margaret in the Armed Forces? It does not require any training to carry bed pans, to our son's who carry the Marks of the RAW DEAL SCARS on their bodies.

Mildred C. Fick
Pomona, Calif.

Mrs. Fick typed this letter but wrote down additional notes before mailing it.

There have been 3 unusual Presidents in the History of Our Country—

1. Washington could not tell a lie
2. Roosevelt could not tell the truth
3. Truman never knew the difference.

Knowing you to be a vindictive man, and you are planning to punch our noses—Just come on—I'm ready for you, and may the best man win—If it is a fair punch and you do not TIE MY HANDS behind my back and have a few of your Federal Prison Friends on the side to do your punching. After having read *Look* May 22, 1951 I am wondering how Mrs. Truman can live with her self, knowing the type of Person you really are! Money, means a lot to her no doubt.

Some people appealed to Truman to reach back into his Christian heritage and find the wisdom to reverse his decision to fire MacArthur. A Methodist minister who broadcast an hour-long religious program on several Colorado radio station sent the following.

Dear Honorable President: *April 13, 1951*
Thousands of good American Citizens were completely shocked by the ouster of General Douglas MacArthur. We fear that your attitude is one of appeasement. This is one that does not make for ultimate peace. Also we notice that those who laud your action in this matter are Socialist Britian [*sic*], Communist Party in both Japan and China, Socialist Party Head in United States and Russia Herself.

It appears that you by this grave mistake, have played right into the hands of our enemies. Hundreds of Thousands in this Rocky Mountain Region are behind Gen. MacArthur, believing that his past experience with war, and communism tactics would have greatly helped in this crisis.

Honorable President, remember you are just a man. Humanity is so prone to mistake and error. A Christian Man would be willing to acknowledge this tragic mistake, and right it.

> *Most Sincerely,*
> *Rev. Irving Ball*
> *Longmont, Col.*

While the bulk of such appeals were of an earnest, heartfelt, and constructive nature, more than a few crossed the line into the "nut mail" category. A hand-printed letter from an individual in Winter Haven, Florida, also enclosed a clipping of a letter that the author had succeeded in getting published in an unnamed newspaper. It asked the question "How long, oh Lord, how long will the American people sleep the slumber of ignorance and let the anti-Christ Communists take over and destroy the liberty of God-fearing people, aided by the Truman administration."

> *Dear President Truman—*   *April 16, 1951*
> America is going down—O God—Save the American people and our constitutional government—From good old Uncle Joe.
> We pray in the name of thou son Jesus Christ our Saviour— AMEN—
>
> > *From a God-fearing man and*
> > *A Constitutional American—*
> > *W—B—Botner*
> > *Winter Haven—Fla.*

High school students and even young children held firm opinions on the MacArthur dismissal, and the word from these future voters at Beall High School in Frostburg, Maryland, was that Truman was wrong.

> *Mr. President:*   *April 12, 1951*
> I think you made a very great mistake. It won't prevent war now for we will have war anyway. I think General MacArthur was one of our best generals and always shall be remembered as such. In my

opinion, I think you should be impeached. If you try to run again you will lose anyway. Your best bet is to resign. My grandfather was born in Missouri which I greatly regret.

> *Signed,*
> *Schuler Briggs, George Beall, Billy Preston*
> *Earl Clark, Thomas J. James, Connie Herring*

Mr. Truman: *April 12, 1951*

Do you realize what you have done?

You have Handed the commies new hope. General McCarther [*sic*] was the only man they feared. You have ruined Japan's dream of an empire. You don't realize how they worshipped him. You don't realize what a fool thing you have done? Please take this seriously to heart. It is no joke.

> *Indignantly yours,*
> *Sandra Kay Bridges*
> *Tulsa, Okla.*

P.S. I am eleven years old and will be twelve in May.

Another youngster from Tulsa added his parents' phone number to the return address in case the president desired to discuss matters with him personally.

Dear Harry S. Truman,   *April 22, 1951*

As a personal matter I think you were a pretty big dope to fire MacArthur.

I think you [are] a three letter word for donkey. Quite a few kids that I no do not like you and I don't blame them. Also me myself and I don't like you eather.

MacArthur may have not been following instruction but he was doing his duty to his country.

We have already lost the war!

You are just a big @!!%X=X# and every dumb thing I can think of. He was a five star general, boob.

> *Not yours truly,*
> *Dutch Fitzgerald*

P.S. I am only 12 1/2 years old but I mean it!

Of course, not all young adults were critical of Truman's decision, and whatever their stance, they were likely to be expressing opinions held by their parents. The high-school girl who authored the following letter came from a decidedly partisan household. Susan Pauley's father was a longtime Democratic Party fund-raiser and treasurer who had been instrumental in Truman's being picked over Henry Wallace as Roosevelt's vice-presidential running mate in 1944. Edward Pauley had been a key figure in the establishment of an international shipping pool during World War II, was the senior American member of the Allied reparations commission for Germany, and held a similar position in the Far East when Japan was defeated. Truman was unsuccessful in his effort to have Congress accept his nomination of Pauley as undersecretary of the Navy in 1946.

Dear Mr. President,   *April 29, 1951*

My father, Ed Pauley, does not know that I am writing this, for he is in Texas, but my mother told me that I could write you and tell you how I really feel.

I go to a school called Marlborough, where the Democrats are definitely in the minority. We were allowed to listen to General MacArthur's speech during study period, and when everyone else was crying at the end of it, I couldn't help but think that it was very corny. Maybe this was because of what Daddy had already told me about General MacArthur when he knew him in Japan, and Mr. President, I really felt that you were right.

The first week no one would listen to me when I said that you had a side to present, too, but finally, the second week we had a discussion in class, and our Social Science teacher let me present our side.

I was the only Democrat in the class, but I said what I believe; that it took more courage on your part than MacArthur will ever have for you to dismiss him, knowing what the Republicans would make of it; that you did it for the good of the country and history would prove it so. I tried to explain to them that there were two policies, not just MacArthur's, and that they had a right to make a choice just as you were letting MacArthur make his, but you as Commander in Chief, and as President of the United States of America were fighting for a policy which would keep us out of war.

Mr. President, they really listened, and I am only waiting for the press to print the truth of your side so that I can go back "triumphant," as MacArthur would say, and say, "I told you so."

Mr. President, he may be a great general, but you are a great president whom I know is doing everything possible for peace.

Yours sincerely and respectfully,
Susan Pauley
Beverly Hills, Calif.

Dear Susan: May 5, 1951

I can't tell you how very much I appreciated your lovely letter of April twenty-ninth. I am glad your mother was willing that you should send it to me. Mrs. Truman read it and thought it was a wonderful letter.

We receive so many letters that are not pleasant that when one such as yours is received it helps to make the day brighter.

I am glad you told your high school class what the facts are. I am enclosing three speeches which cover the situation completely and thoroughly and if you will read them you will know just about as much of the Foreign Policy of the United States as the President does.

Sincerely yours,
HARRY S. TRUMAN

Enclosures:

1. "Preventing a New World War" - April 11, 1951 - by the President.

2. "Our Far Eastern Policy" - April 18, 1951 - by the Sec./State.

3. Address at Jeff-Jackson Dinner - April 14, 1951 - by the President.

A Gallup Poll taken shortly after the firing found that nearly seven out of every ten respondents backed MacArthur over the president, but his supporters tried hard to make their own voices heard as well. Truman's long-established policy of sending acknowledgments only to individuals supporting his actions, especially if those people commanded some degree of standing or influence, was strictly adhered to in spite of the crush of events.

My Dear President Truman: April 13, 1951

You are absolutely right, and in the end the people will realize it. Don't lose your sleep!

Sincerely,
Upton Sinclair
Monrovia, Calif.

Dear Mr. Sinclair: *April 19, 1951*

Your letter of April thirteenth means a lot to me. I am most appreciative of the approval which you express in connection with the Far Eastern situation. It helps tremendously to know that you think our course of action is right, and that, in the long run, it will be generally understood that we had no alternative in the interest of world peace.

> *Very sincerely yours,*
> HARRY S. TRUMAN

Dear Mr. President: *April 12, 1951*

May I add my word of sincere appreciation of your courage in meeting the crisis which had been forced upon you by General MacArthur by taking an action which, difficult in itself, made clear to all the world that our American democracy was still functioning along its historic lines.

With high regard,

> *Respectfully,*
> *Dr. James T. Shotwell*
> *Carnegie Endowment for International Peace*
> *New York, New York*

Dear Dr. Shotwell: *April 17, 1951*

It was thoughtful of you to assure me of your approval of the decision which I felt compelled to make regarding the Far Eastern situation. Replacing General MacArthur, one of our great military commanders, means no change whatever in the policy of the United States. In justice to my own responsibilities, and in behalf of world peace, I had no alternative, and I am glad that you agree with the wisdom of this conclusion.

> *Very sincerely yours,*
> HARRY S. TRUMAN

THE PRESIDENT   APRIL 11, 1951

ALL WOMEN RISE UP TODAY TO CALL YOU BLESSED, HAVE TALKED TO HUNDREDS RECENTLY, REPUBLICANS DEMOCRATS ALIKE, MOTHERS OF DRAFT AGE YOUTHS, NON MOTHERS, RICH AND POOR, ALL SUPPORT YOU, WILL SWEEP YOU TO VICTORY IN 52 IF YOU WISH, OUR DREAMS LIE EASIER WITH YOU IN KOREAN COMMAND AGAIN.

BETTY GRAM SWING
VICE PRESIDENT NATIONAL WOMEN'S PARTY
NEW YORK, NY

Dear Mrs. Swing: *April 4, 1951*

It was very thoughtful of you to send me that message of approval on behalf of your associates. I believe that the course we are following is the best course, and it helps tremendously to know that you, and those in whose behalf you speak, support me in the action of replacing General MacArthur. In making this decision I did so with real regret, as he is one of our greatest military commanders. Thank you very much for wiring me.

Very sincerely yours,
HARRY S. TRUMAN

Dear Mr. Truman: *May 7, 1951*

Thank you very much for your letter which pleased me no end. My children will cherish it for the signature always. All three of them support you most enthusiastically in your present debacle. They think you have guts such as few US presidents have had. Please pardon the word but it is a family favorite. We're like that.

When I wired you I was of course speaking as an individual and not for the organization of which I am an officer. We exist, and the members include many of your close friends such as Perle Mesta and Emma Guffey Miller* and hundreds more of all kinds of political thought, but for one purpose and that is for the raising of the status of women throughout the world. We are making great headway at the UN without which we would indeed have cause to despair.

I hope to see Perle in a few days when she speaks at a banquet we are having in Washington. I had a delightful Xmas card from her, and would like to take this opportunity of thanking you for the appointment of so charming and able a diplomat.

---

*These individuals were both prominent in the women's movement. Guffey Miller was a member of the Democratic National Committee from Pennsylvania and numerous women's organizations such as the National Women's Party and National Women's Council. Perle Mesta, Washington's "hostess with the mostest," was a long-time Democratic Party fund-raiser and had recently been appointed U.S. Minister to Luxembourg by Truman.

We wish you well, Mr. President, and are confident that you will come out on top in this most troublesome situation.

Yours most sincerely,
Betty Gram Swing
New York, NY

Eleanor Roosevelt had been serving on the U.N.'s Human Rights Commission, based in Geneva, Switzerland, and periodically sent Truman feedback from her contacts in Europe and anything else she thought might be of value. In this case, she enclosed a summary of an extended conversation she had with a prominent Briton because of his long service in India, along with a letter he had written for publication. Both documents dealt with the situation in the Far East in general, and China in particular.

Dear Mr. President:　　　　　*April 24, 1951*
. . . Colonel Arthur Murray, who is now Lord Elibank, is an old friend of my husband's. He has had a long experience in military and diplomatic life. I also enclose a copy of a letter which he wrote to the *London Times.* If these have no interest, just destroy them but I thought it might be a slant on British thinking that might be helpful.

There is a unanimous feeling over here that your action on General MacArthur has brought new hope into the international situation. If only we can keep China from an all-out offensive which will mean more casualties in Korea, and perhaps set-backs which will tend to make it necessary to carry out the plans which the General has advocated and which we all pray we will not have to carry out. That is the only reason that I thought this conversation might have some value.

We move slowly on the Human Rights Commission but I hope by next week the votes will have been taken and the discussion ended on some of the toughest questions. Ratification by the Senate of whatever is agreed upon is a distant hope, I fear, but one never knows what may happen.

We are taking pretty big gambles these days in so much that we do in different parts of the world that I think it is wonderful that any of the people who carry the responsibility can sleep at night. What a headache the Near East has become!

I saw Ambassador Jessup for a few minutes in Paris where I was last Saturday doing a television program on film with Mr. Schumann and Mr. Monnet which will be flown back to the United

States. They certainly are far behind us in television equipment and of all of the silly things, they have two different television companies and put out two different television sets, and you can not get the programs of the rival companies on the same set! I think it will take some time to develop television in France.

With my very best wishes to you, I am

Very cordially yours,
Eleanor Roosevelt

Dear Mrs. Roosevelt:　　　　*May 1, 1951*

It is always good to hear from you and I am especially grateful for your thoughtful letter of April twenty-fourth. It is particularly gratifying to have your assurance that my action in the MacArthur case has brought new hope into the international situation.

Mine was a stern and unpleasant duty to perform but it was and is my settled conviction that there was no alternative action in the interest of peace and security.

I have been going over with great interest your memorandum of the conversation with Colonel Arthur Murray (Lord Elibank) as well as the text of his letter to the TIMES of London. He surely writes out of a long and rich experience in Chinese and Far Eastern affairs generally and I am glad to have the benefit of his opinions.

Take good care of yourself and guard your health always. I appreciate fully that the task you are engaged in is a hard one.

Always sincerely,
HARRY S. TRUMAN

Old friends of Harry's had seen him weather innumerable controversies, but the unprecedented intensity of emotion in the current storm prompted many to move quickly with words of support and encouragement.

The President:　　　　*April 12, 1951*

Your Lexington friends support you fully in relieving MacArthur. Those making political capital out of this incident will get nowhere. That you should have relieved MacArthur before now is the general opinion here.

Ike Skelton
Lexington, Mo.

Dear Ike: *April 14, 1951*

My sincere thanks for your message. Your assurances that I was right in my difficult decision to make a change of commands in the Far East mean much to me.

All good wishes!

Very sincerely yours,
HARRY S. TRUMAN

Truman's military aide, Harry Vaughan, penned "A good letter Mr. President" across a lengthy letter from a retired colonel who served with MacArthur and passed it on to his boss.

Dear General Vaughan,   *April 13, 1951*

I served under General MacArthur when he was a Brigadier, when he was Chief of Staff of the Army and when he commanded in the Southwest Pacific. My admiration of him is great, my thought of him that he has been one of the greatest if not the greatest all around soldier that this country has produced. Many a time I have stoutly defended him against criticisms addressed against both his military abilities and certain of his marked personal characteristics. At the time of his advance on the Yalu, I fully approved his judgment in spite of the arguments of many of my friends here; although his preparations for applying timely and strict controls to secure an orderly retreat in case of a reverse were inadequate.

Yet his actions in the past few months have gone far beyond the liberties that a soldier enjoys in attempting to secure a modification of the opinions of his superiors. The members of his commands, throughout his service, have obeyed his orders not because they were his but because they thought that, through him, they were carrying out the will of their government. No one has been more insistent than he in requiring that his subordinates refrain from actions that would embarrass him in the carrying out of his mission through the offering of their ideas outside the chain of command. And yet he now considers himself free from those obligations that he has so definitely and severely, yet rightly, required from others.

Nothing can be clearer than that the life and stability of our government depend upon the supremacy of the civil power over the military and that no American soldier, whatever his stature or achievements, can successfully threaten that conception without the direct results of our national life and well being. Our country has no plans for the man on horseback, superior to the rules that govern others, and General MacArthur with his almost matchless mental equipment is fully aware of this. He must also be fully aware of what the end result of military action against the Chinese homeland will be and especially so if we again back Chiang Kai Chek. Assuming the unlikely, even if there were no Russian intervention and we were able to conquer the Chinese Communists and turn it over to Chiang Kai Chek where would we be? Chiang as a friend would be more of a millstone around our necks internationally than the Chinese Communists. If the latter find the ruling of China impossible, and I do not doubt that over a period of time this will prove to be so, then the dissatisfactions and uprisings must be in our favor but if Chiang fails again with our support we also fail most miserably and irretrievably. Whatever may be said by any now, the American people will not support such a war. Even General MacArthur's present most vocal adherents would be even more violently vocal against the continuance of such action when the taxes begin to mount and the casualty lists pour in.

One should never try to adjudge intentions, I suppose, but it does seem to me that with the time short in which to apply the capstone to the MacArthur legend, he has lost perspective. If only he could have let a glorious record alone!

And this impeachment business gives me a pain! Have Senator Wherry [Republican senator Kenneth Spencer Wherry of Nebraska, one of Senator Joseph McCarthy's most vocal supporters] and his pack no duties except the harassing and embarrassing of the President? Why don't they propose something that they could and would back and carry through with if they were in power? And why don't some of the Democrats in Congress stand up and fight like men?

I hope that you won't think that I have become too heated over this matter. The fact is I am more, far more, heated than this letter implies at the way President Truman is being treated by his own party let alone the Republicans who with a few notable exceptions are simply abominable. If these continual crises were over principles, who could complain? But while the pressing interests of the country demand none but honest disagreements, and outside them only the wisest collaboration and cooperation, we are not reaching in all this wrangling the respectability of a mongrel dog fight.

To end upon a somewhat calmer note, am working a good deal at Civil Defense both as a local Director and as County Chairman. It reminds me of the early days of the Organized Reserve and often the results are not at all encouraging but someone has to do these things and I do not approve of letting George do everything.

Please give the President my highest regards, to put it very mildly. I don't see how he stands up under it so calmly and steadfastly! He has it on old Davy Crockett who got so disgusted in Washington that he left with the remark, "You can all go to Hell and I'll go to Texas!" I am not entirely positive that his destination was of the best but it would serve to separate him from the others.

With most sincere wishes for happier days ahead, I remain,

Sincerely yours,
Leslie M. Skerry
Bedford, New Hampshire

The president liked the letter so much that he responded personally and let the former colonel in on something that was not, at that time, well known beyond Truman's top advisors.

Dear Leslie: *April 18, 1951*

Harry Vaughan showed me your letter of the thirteenth. I can't tell you how very much I appreciate it—it is one of the best I've received on the subject.

I can't understand the attitude of the General in this affair— he seems to have lost all sense of proportion. In 1946 I invited him to come back home and receive the Medal of Honor that Eisenhower, Nimitz, Montgomery* and all the rest of the Field Commanders had received but he refused the invitation. Conditions came to such a state as regards to the foreign policy of the United States that I had to relieve him and it is too bad but I have always said Heroes know when to quit. Someday I'll elaborate on that for you.

---

*British field marshal Sir Bernard Law Montgomery did not, in fact, receive a Medal of Honor but was awarded the highest military decoration available to a foreign national, the Distinguished Service Medal.

I hope everything is going well with you.

> *Sincerely yours,*
> HARRY S. TRUMAN

An oft repeated contention by MacArthur supporters in Congress was that veterans (and by implication, their friends and family as well) were solidly behind the general. This, of course, wasn't at all true, and many correspondents made sure that the president knew it.

Dear President Truman: *April 14, 1951*

I wish to offer my felicitations to you on your courageous action of relieving General MacArthur from his commands. As a voter, I admit that your act took a great deal of intestinal fortitude. As a veteran of World War II, I believe that you showed a great deal of tolerance for the General's insubordination.

> *Sincerely yours,*
> *Robert C. Alleyne*
> *Brooklyn, N.Y.*

Dear Sir: *April 11, 1951*

May God bless you for the decision you made to relieve Gen. MacArthur of his command. It has given us new hope that World War III might yet be prevented. At least we know that steps are being taken to prevent it. May you always be guided by the wisdom you have shown today. I am proud of you, as the President of the U.S., in taking this decisive step.

> *Very truly yours,*
> *Mrs. Rose Adler,*
> *wife of World War II veteran*
> *Brooklyn, N.Y.*

Many of the people writing in support of the president believed it was MacArthur's own statements that undercut both his own credibility and that of the United States.

Dear Mr. Truman: *April 15, 1951*

I wish to add my congratulations to those of other thinking people for your courage in taking the action you deemed necessary in connection with General Douglas MacArthur, although you must have known in advance the emotional furor it would create among his fanatical admirers.

For some months, I have been incredulous and chagrined at reading news accounts of his obvious disregard for any authority other than his own. His repeated contradictions of his government, his president, his chiefs of staff and the U.N. seemed brazen and disrespectul, not fitting for a man of his position.

How could the American people have failed to be annoyed at his repeatedly mistaken pronouncements that the soldiers would be home by Christmas, the Chinese Reds would never enter the war, etc.? When our armies under his direction fell time and again into obvious enemy traps, at the price of many casualties, and when his ignoring U.N. policy led to disaster at the Yalu, it became increasingly difficult to have confidence in his ability. Certainly he has been wrong so many times thus far in the Korean War, it would hardly seem a safe policy to assume that his predictions of the correct action to take in the future would have any more validity than his past predictions.

I am one American citizen who feels safer now that he has been removed from command, and approve your action in dismissing him for the above reasons, over and above the fact that he was insubordinate.

> *Mrs. Marjorie L. Arnett*
> *Detroit, Mi.*

Dear Sir: *April 16, 1951*

Your recent action in relieving General MacArthur of his command is one which was long overdue. It was the only thing to be done to insure harmony with our allies, and to prevent the propagandists of unfriendly powers from eternally picking up talking points from the warlike statements which issued from Tokyo.

I hope that this letter will show, in a small way, that not everyone in the United States is interested in making political hay over this event, and that there are individuals who feel that the President did the proper and expedient thing.

Incidentally, I do not make it a practice of writing letters of this kind, neither do I endorse all the actions which are taken by your office. In this case, however, I feel it important that some recognition is shown of the adverse publicity which has been attendant upon the matter, and that individuals should do what they are able to do to mitigate the effects of such publicity.

> *Yours sincerely,*
> *James A. Hayashi*
> *Biochemistry Department*
> *University of Wisconsin*
> *Madison, Wi.*

Truman was happy to acknowledge any words of support but took almost four weeks to send a response to a favorable telegram from Cornelia Pinchot. The former suffragette and member of Theodore Roosevelt's Progressive Party had officially joined the Republicans before her husband's successful bid to become governor of Pennsylvania in 1923 and had remained in that party throughout her extensive efforts to support organized labor in the 1920s and 1930s. Pinchot was a strong proponent of international disarmament and, in 1947, was elected to the board of Americans for Democratic Action, which formed a non-Communist liberal counter to the Progressives of Henry Wallace.

THE PRESIDENT   APRIL 13, 1951
HERE IS ONE REPUBLICAN WHO HEARTILY ENDORSES YOUR ACTION. IT WAS A HARD DECISION TO MAKE AND ONE REQUIRING COURAGE AND INTEGRITY. MY CONGRATULATIONS.
CORNELIA BRYCE PINCHOT

Dear Mrs. Pinchot: *May 8, 1951*
I highly appreciate the fine spirit you have shown in wiring me your approval of my action in relieving General MacArthur of his commands in the Far East. You know, of course, this was a most distressing decision because of the distinguished service he has rendered his country in posts of great responsibility, but I had no alternative. My thanks too for your gracious words of commendation.

> *Very sincerely yours,*
> *HARRY S. TRUMAN*

Although there were far more letters castigating Truman than there were supporting him, the raw quantity of mail, over 100,000 letters by

June, meant that only a comparatively few people who agreed with the president received a Hassett Valentine, and there were no form letters on this subject being sent out from the White House. In the opening days of the crisis, mail was running two to one against the president. Around the third week of the crisis, a surge of letters supporting his actions brought the number of pro and con responses almost into balance.

My dear Mr. President: *April 23, 1951*

Though I wrote you once congratulating you upon your wise removal of General MacArthur, I feel, in view of the hysteria which has swept the country in the last few days of hero worship, that I should tell you again, as one of your devoted friends, that I have perfect confidence in you and that I am sure within the next few weeks your popularity will grow by leaps and bounds and the people will have more confidence in you than ever before. Your thoughtful fellow citizens know full well that you acted with complete honor, wisdom, and courage.

I think that, instead of closing his talk before the Joint Session of Congress with the maudlin statement: "An old soldier never dies— he just fades away," General MacArthur would have done much better and would have expressed the real idealism of the Armed Services if he had said: "A good soldier always obeys his orders; if he doesn't, he is kicked out."

I sincerely hope that all the strain you have been under has in no way impaired your health and I pray that God may continue to give you strength to guide our country with the same devotion and ability that you have manifested throughout your career.

My dear wife joins me in affectionate greetings to you and your dear ones.

> *Sincerely,*
> *Samuel S. Mayerberg, D.D.*
> *Kansas City, Mo.*

Dear Rabbi Mayerberg: *April 28, 1951*

I am indeed grateful for the reassurances of confidence which your very thoughtful letter of April twenty-third brings to me. The decision which I had to make regarding the Far Eastern commands certainly was difficult, but I do have the satisfaction of knowing that

I did my duty as I saw it in justice to the responsibilities placed upon me by the Constitution and the United Nations.

Your solicitous expressions and prayerful wishes are more than appreciated. Many thanks to you and Mrs. Mayerberg for your personal greetings to us.

Very sincerely yours,
HARRY S. TRUMAN

The mail soon returned to its initial percentage of roughly two to one against the president, but the total numbers were smaller and the controversy was clearly winding down. Truman had originally predicted that there would be "hell to pay" for six or seven weeks, and indeed, MacArthur's support, which a Gallup organization had recorded at 69 percent when the crisis broke, plummeted to just 30 percent by the end of May. This was due in no small part to seven weeks of highly publicized hearings of the Senate's Foreign Relations and Armed Services committees, during which nearly all of America's most senior military leaders testified. One by one, the military men stated their great admiration for the former Supreme Commander in the Pacific, and one by one, they dismantled his earlier testimony by exposing the limitations of his strategic view. This came at precisely the same time that news from the front offered its own testimony that the U.N. forces under General Ridgway could handle the Chinese. In a series of battles beginning on April 21, 1951, the communists left more than 200,000 dead on the field, and the collapse of their largest and most costly offensive to date precipitated a general U.N. advance. By the end of May, Ridgway's forces had recovered essentially all the ground lost since April and had done so at relatively little cost.

General MacArthur, however, never conceded that he was anything but right in his views. MacArthur, who had closed his address before a joint session of Congress with the words "Old soldiers never die, they just fade away," did anything but fade as he launched into a busy nationwide speaking tour and made a bid for the 1952 Republican nomination for president. Although the general still had his ardent supporters, Americans now had the measure of the man, and his bid for Truman's job went nowhere.

Dear Mr. President: *March 6, 1951*
For all practical purposes this gesture may be a bit absurd but according to my standards of conduct it is mandatory.

Some months past you received a wire from me among the many protests of your conduct in recalling Gen. MacArthur. I wired a supercilious message of condemnation for what I thought an unwise and unjustified action on your part. At the time I was inflamed by the mass reaction of those around me and came to my judgement with shamefully little knowledge of the situation. I have today been more thoroughly informed of the issues involved and, in consequence, feel obligated to apologize to you even with the certainty that neither the original wire nor the apology will be brought to your attention. One must be set right with oneself and I trust that my withdrawal of the statement in that wire will win my own forgiveness for such impulsive and unfair conduct.

Respectfully yours,
Carol Stone
Sebring, Fla.

Dear Sir: *Feb. 16, 1951*

In March our reading classes will read and study about the various Easter customs observed throughout the world. We would like to know if the Egg Rolling Festivity will be held this year on the grounds of the White House?

May we have a picture of the remodeled White House for our bulletin board? We intend to depict the Egg Rolling Festivity at the White house on our Easter bulletin board.

We sincerely hope that your will be able to grant us our request.

> *Respectfully yours,*
> *Gussie Elzy for 7-7, 7-6, 7-8 classes*
> *J. D. Robinson Junior High School*
> *Toledo, Ohio*

My dear Miss Elzy: *February 20, 1951*

This is in acknowledgment of your letter of February sixteenth to the President with the accompanying signatures of a group of students of the J. D. Robinson Junior High School.

With reference to your inquiry, the Easter Egg rolling on the White House grounds was discontinued during World War II and has not been held since. I regret also that we have no pictures of the White House such as you desire for use on your bulletin board.

I am sorry that we cannot be more helpful to you and your associates in connection with your special Easter project.

> *Very sincerely yours,*
> *WILLIAM D. HASSETT*
> *Secretary to the President*

CHAPTER SEVEN

THE ATOM BOMB

"The world in its present state of moral advancement compared with its technical development, would be eventually at the mercy of such a weapon. In other words, modern civilization might be completely destroyed."
—Secretary of War Henry Stimson

Long before the United States entered World War II, the likelihood that it would eventually be dragged into the conflict prompted a mammoth effort to build up its military and defense infrastructure. Truman was certain that such an undertaking, taken in great haste, would inevitably entail great waste in both time and resources as the greedy and the incompetent attempted to cash in on the boom. He well remembered the First World War and later remarked, "There'd been a hundred and sixteen investigating committees *after* the fact, and I felt that one committee *before* the fact would prevent a lot of waste and maybe even save some lives."[1] The Senate Special Committee to Investigate the National Defense Program, popularly known as the Truman Committee, opened its hearings in April 1941, with the senator from Missouri serving as its chairman and driving force until he was nominated for vice president four years later. Truman, in fact, had even spent much of January 1941 driving incognito from defense project to defense project in his old Dodge to get his own firsthand look at the situation, covering states from Florida to Missouri to Michigan in the process.

The senator quickly gained a reputation for fairness—and tenacity. Although his committee did not get involved in military strategy and personnel, or the size of the defense effort, it frequently moved beyond its purely "watchdog" role, making positive contributions to the improvement of military equipment such as the B-26 bomber and landing craft for discharging men and materiel directly onto invasion beaches. The public also got into the act, as patriotic citizens sent in letters reporting on waste and mismanagement or made suggestions for improving the effectiveness of the war effort.

279

In most cases, the ideas were impractical or were already being looked into or implemented in some form or another; others clearly fell into Truman's "nut mail" category. One such letter he vividly remembered was from a man "who had an idea for building an airplane for every soldier in the Army and filling each plane with a few yards of dirt. His idea was that at a given signal thousands of individually manned planes would fly over enemy capitals and completely cover them with United States soil, thus ending the war without further ado."[2] Nearly all of these writers were sincere in their effort to be of service to their country.

The flood of information coming into his committee necessitated that many avenues of investigation be delayed while others of seemingly more importance took precedence. Initially, references to a project identified only by the code name "Manhattan" were not pursued, but the project's unexplained expenditures began to grow at an alarming rate, prompting Truman to phone Secretary of War Henry Stimson on June 17, 1943. The secretary was regarded as a man of high moral principle who had known or served under every president for the past forty-five years. Stimson's transcript of the conversation recounts how he told the senator that the Manhattan Project was an "important secret development" that only he and a select "group of two or three men in the whole world . . . know about." Truman immediately began to back off: "You assure that this is for a specific purpose and you think it's all right. That's all I need to know." Stimson hastened to add: "Not only for a specific purpose, but a *unique* purpose."[3]

Truman's connections apparently allowed him to find out much more. Nearly a month later, in response to an inquiry by a former Washington senator concerned about enormous land aquisitions around an isolated railroad town called Hanford, Truman wrote that he knew "something about that tremendous land deal." Truman told Lewis Schwellenbach, his future labor secretary, that it was "for the construction of a plant to make a terrific explosi[ve] for a secret weapon that will be a wonder" and added, "I hope it works."

Truman knew that the Manhattan Project was working to construct what he understood to be extremely powerful bombs. But Truman, who had once boasted that a single salvo from his battery's seventy-five-millimeter guns was equivalent to the rifle fire of 862 soldiers, thought of the new weapon as simply a quantum leap in chemical-based explosives technology, not something as unimaginable as the harnessing of the atom to create a blast powerful enough to destroy an entire city. Persistent allegations of waste and inefficiency within the Manhattan Project prompted the senator to break his word to Stimson that he would not pursue the matter. Truman was effectively stonewalled, however, by what appeared to him and his staff to be a high-level cover-up. Stimson considered the senator's persistent and threatening inquiries to be a "nuisance" and Truman "a pretty untrustworthy man" who "talks smoothly but acts meanly."

The death of Roosevelt on April 12, 1945, thrust by-now Vice President Truman into the role of commander in chief. Unfortunately, he had never been let in on the atomic secret by Roosevelt or any of his staff. Immediately after Truman's first Cabinet meeting, Stimson approached his new boss. "He asked to speak to me about a most urgent matter," said Truman. "Stimson told me that he wanted me to know about an immense project that was under way—a project looking to the development of a new explosive of almost unbelievable destructive power. That was all he felt free to say at the time, and his statement left me puzzled."[4]

Truman received somewhat more information the next day from his old friend Jimmy Byrnes, who until recently had been Roosevelt's director of war mobilization and would soon take over as secretary of state, as well as a highly detailed briefing on April 25 by the head of the Manhattan Project, General Leslie R. Groves, and Stimson. The secretary of war described the as yet to be produced atomic bomb as "the most terrible weapon ever known in human history" and stated that the special techniques used in its manufacture would not remain a secret forever. Moreover, he was deeply worried over what this might portend for mankind itself. "The world in its present state of moral advancement, compared with its technical development, would be eventually at the mercy of such a weapon. In other words, modern civilization might be completely destroyed."[5]

The temptation for nations to build the weapon were so enormous, Stimson believed, that "no system of control heretofore considered would be adequate to control this menace. Both inside any particular country and between the nations of the world, the control of this weapon will undoubtedly be a matter of the greatest difficulty and would involve such thoroughgoing rights of inspection and internal controls as we have never heretofore contemplated. . . . The question of sharing [this weapon] with other nations and, if so, shared, upon what terms, becomes a primary question of our foreign relations. Also our leadership in the war and in the development of this weapon has placed a certain moral responsibility upon us which we cannot shirk without very serious responsibility for any disaster to civilization which it would further. On the other hand, if the problem of the proper use of this weapon can be solved, we would have the opportunity to bring the world into a pattern in which the peace of the world and our civilization can be saved."[6]

Stimson informed the president that "steps are under way [to establish] a select committee of particular qualifications for recommending action to the executive and legislative branches of our government when secrecy is no longer in full effect. The committee would also recommend the actions to be taken by the War Department prior to that time in anticipation of the post-war problems. All recommendations would of course be first submitted to the President."[7]

The committee referred to by Stimson had a completely civilian makeup and included, along with Stimson as chairman, Byrnes, acting as Truman's personal representative; George L. Harrison, the president of New York Life and Stimson's special assistant on matters related to "S-1" (a code name for the atom bomb); Ralph Bard, undersecretary of the Navy; William Clayton, assistant secretary of state; Dr. Vannevar Bush, director of the Office of Scientific Research and Development and president of the Carnegie Institution of Washington; Dr. Karl T. Compton, chief of the Office of Scientific Research and Development and president of the Massachusetts Institute of Technology; and Dr. James B. Conant, chairman of the National Defense Research Committtee and president of Harvard University. Known as the Interim Committee on S-1, the body also contained a scientific panel made up of four Manhattan Project physicists: Enrico Fermi, Ernest O. Lawrence, Arthur H. Compton, and J. Robert Oppenheimer.

On May 9, Stimson opened the Interim Committee's first meeting with the words "Gentlemen, it is our responsibility to recommend action that may turn the course of civilization" and covered, according to Stimson, "the whole field of atomic energy, in its political, military, and scientific aspects." In the midst of its deliberations, Stimson received a long letter from a Manhattan Project engineer whose concerns and analysis of the situation largely paralleled deliberations within the committee and the secretary's own views. Oswald C. Brewster, known as "Owl" within the project, sent copies of his letter to Truman, the secretary of state, and Secretary of War Stimson through channels established to handle the passage of classified materials. Under this system, the message to the president did not, in fact, go directly to the White House but was routed to the War Department for examination. Once there, use of the word "atom" and reference to the code names of numerous project sites resulted in the letter's being stamped "secret," and its transit was halted until a decision could be made on what to do with the highly sensitive document.

Needless to say, there were exceedingly few people who could render a decision, and the ultimate authority happened to be one of Brewster's intended recipients. All three of Brewster's copies landed on Secretary

Stimson's desk, and even though the project engineer had technically committed a breach of security, it was partially mitigated by the fact that he had attempted to send his documents through what he believed to be the most secure channels available to him. Upon close scrutiny of the text, Stimson came to the conclusion that Brewster was an honest man and was so awed by his "remarkable document" that he immediately sent one of the copies to the Army chief of staff, General Marshall, to share "the impress of its logic." Stimson further stated that he would "take the President's copy to him personally" or send it through Byrnes.[8]

My dear Mr. President: *May 24, 1945*

Presented herewith is a matter which I believe to be one of the gravest, if not the gravest, questions now confronting the United States and the entire world. It has to do with the policy to be adopted as to the future handling of the Clinton Engineer Works (near Knoxville, Tennessee) and associated projects. This communication is being directed to you through the special channels provided by the Army for material on this subject, but this fact should in no way be construed as Army endorsement of any of the ideas presented but is merely in recognition of my right as a citizen to bring those ideas before you, and on my part it is so done in recognition by me of the continued urgent necessity for the security of this undertaking and my compulsion to avoid any act that would jeopardize that security. Copies of this communication have also been directed to the Secretaries of State and of War through the same channels in the belief that it is proper to bring the matter before them at the same time that it is presented to the President.

This matter is presented with the full knowledge on my part that it is undoubtedly being given very serious attention already by far better minds than mine, and yet I know myself to hold the unpopular and minority view on the question, and therefore feel it my duty as a loyal citizen to attempt to place before you these ideas on the chance that they have not been presented to you before and on the further chance that, while I can lay no claim to any knowledge of statesmanship or world politics, some of these ideas may turn out to be correct and of importance to world peace. The question is of such appalling urgency that I would be derelict in my duty in not bringing it to your attention in the absence of definite information that it was being fully considered from all points of view. . . .

Brewster followed this introduction with an excellent, if spotty, synopsis of the Manhattan Project's history and current status in two pages of single-spaced type before continuing his thoughts on the atom bomb.

. . . The destructive possibilities of the material as I have described it are obvious. With aviation what it is today, it should be possible, with planes based in any country on the globe, to destroy at one fell swoop almost any great city in the world and wipe out the manufacturing, the fleets, and the supply bases of any other country without warning, thereby rendering it helpless almost before it realized it had an enemy.

The country producing such a weapon during the course of a war would gain such an enormous advantage over its enemy that victory would be almost assured regardless of its condition just prior to putting it to use. I do not know whether this weapon could be applied in sufficiently homeopathic doses to make it efficient against combat troops, but certainly against massed supplies, manufacturing centers, nations' capitals, and great cities the effectiveness is apparent. . . .

. . . From my first association with this project I have been convinced, and have been appalled by the conviction, that the successful production of this material by any nation meant the inevitable destruction of our present day civilization. This is not an original thought with me but is shared by many of my associates. One of the most earnest hopes of many of us was that it might be conclusively proved that the thing was impossible. Obviously, however, so long as there was any chance that Germany might succeed at this task there was only one course to follow and that was to do everything in our power to get this thing first and destroy Germany before she has a chance to destroy us. We must forget about the destruction of civilization or at least we must agree that, if civilization is to be destroyed, we should do it one way and prevent Germany from doing it the Nazi way. Thus this project became the most important thing of its kind before the country and still it remained, by what seems another miracle, one of the best kept secrets of our time.

The idea of the destruction of civilization is not melodramatic hysteria or crack-pot raving. It is a very real and, I submit, almost inevitable result. It cannot, of course, be proven until it occurs—and then it would be too late.

The possession of this weapon by any one nation, no matter how benign its intentions, could not be tolerated by other great powers. Those who could not produce the weapon themselves would watch our every move. Our elections, our foreign policy, everything we did would be viewed with suspicion and distrust. If we urged our views on the world on any subject we would be charged with threatening to use this weapon as a club. We would be toadied to and discriminated against, all the world would do lip service as our friends and conspire and intrigue us behind our backs. We would be the most hated and feared nation on earth.

Meantime others would not sit by idly but would also build plants for production of this material. Our best friends could not permit us to be the only possessor of this thing. How could they know where our friendship might be five, ten, or twenty years hence? Others, not our best friends, would be still more anxious for their own legitimate self protection to prepare themselves. I submit that we, the United States, could not rest complacently if, say, Mexico, or France, or Russia, or even Britain were the sole possessor of this means of sudden destruction.

As I say, our intentions toward the world may be most benign, but competition would start—other countries would get it—every country would eye every other country askance, and sooner or later the spark would be struck that would send the whole world up in one flaming inferno of a third world war which would dwarf the horror of the present one.

This thing must not be permitted to exist on this earth. We must not be the most hated and feared people on earth however our good intent may be. So long as the threat of Germany existed we had to proceed with all speed to accomplish this end. With the threat of Germany removed, we must stop this project. Peace is possible, and we and we alone today have it in our power to bring peace to this earth for the first time and this very weapon which we have today almost in our grasp is the means whereby we can help to bring this about.

If this world has learned nothing from this war then we had best give up and revert to the Dark Ages. The world has learned at last that war must not happen again. But it will happen if this weapon, permitting a war to be fought and won possibly in a matter of days, if not even hours, is found upon this earth.

I know nothing of statesmanship or diplomacy or power politics, but I believe we today can go before the world and say something like this:

"We now possess this weapon. We will show it to you and demonstrate what it can do. We will soon have it in quantity and can before any one can stop us being in a position to control and enslave the world.

"We do not want to do this. We do not care to rule the world. We want peace on earth, and we realize there can be no peace if this weapon exists.

"We therefore say to you that we will give up this weapon if you, the rest of the world, will so organize with us that no country on earth shall ever produce this material in a form which can be used for destructive purposes.

"We propose that every power on earth, great and small, shall agree that it shall not produce this material.

"We know that agreements are only made to be broken, so we further propose that this agreement be implemented somewhat as follows:

"1. A group of international observers shall watch the industry of every country. The production of this weapon is such a gigantic undertaking that no country under these conditions could attempt to build the necessary plant in secret.

"2. If any country starts this work the rest of the world shall as one take it over by force and prevent this thing from happening. The time necessary to build the plant would give time to do this.

"3. All known sources of supply of the raw material shall be supervised by an international commission and every pound of the raw material be accounted for. (The sources of raw material in quantity are few—Canada, Czechoslovakia, the Belgian Congo, and probably the Urals. The material is widely distributed in low grade deposits but the difficulty of recovery would be great and could be observed.)

"4. Research (perhaps under international sponsorship) should continue as to the properties of the material and as to methods of production. Particular emphasis should be placed on a search for any easy and simple method, if it exists, as it well may, would greatly increase the hazard and make necessary more rigid control.

"5. The use of this material for power may be permitted if it can be conclusively proven that when in form useable for power it cannot be used for destruction and cannot be used as the first and perhaps most difficult stage of manufacture for destructive purposes.

"We are showing you our good faith in this by having stopped our plant almost on the point of success. We are prepared to proceed with this plant and will proceed and finish it if world agreement is not reached. We will in self defense proceed against any nation which we believe is building a similar plant."

I believe something like that, in substance, would get the desired result. I am sure Britain and France would gladly fall in line, and I have enough faith in human nature to believe that Russia would see the light and agree to the restraint and supervision which at present appear repugnant to her. Germany and later Japan can, of course, be forced to abide by the program.

Many of us are so afraid of Russsia we fairly jump when the name is mentioned. I pretend to know nothing of Russia, but surely she has learned that war is a sorry business and surely it must be possible to convince her that this must be done.

The war with Japan goes on and I have almost been accused of treason by some for proposing the stoppage of this work before Japan is brought to terms. This is not my idea. The present facilities are, I believe, capable of producing in the near future an amount of the material sufficient to serve as a demonstration. I question whether added production would be necessary to bring about the surrender of Japan. This is of course a matter of opinion wherein my opinion is admittedly not well informed. . . .

It is obvious that many other better minds than mine are earnestly considering this problem, but I am sincerely disturbed by the following considerations. From its very nature this project has been and must be wrapped in the greatest secrecy. Only a small proportion of those working on the project really know what we are making. For that reason the only people who know about it are those who are most deeply interested in it. The men of the Corps of Engineers, the OSRD [Office of Scientific Research and Development], the scientists, engineers, and manufacturers who have given their all to make this thing a success; none of us are capable of viewing the problem objectively and disinterestedly and therefore are not the proper ones to advise or decide what should be done.

Without discrediting the humanitarianism or honesty of the Army at all, surely it is not the one to decide the future course of this project. Such a weapon is the answer to all the prayers of the professional soldier. He cannot be expected to forego willingly such a potent means of bringing victory to or preparing the defense of his country.

The rest of us—the civilians in the project—are so intent on making it succeed that the suggestion that it should be stopped is rank heresy, if not treason, to most.

But these are practically the only people who know about it and therefore the only ones who can think about it. Also there is the old saw of the scientist that "you cannot stop progress." In this case I disagree, if indeed it be "progress," since the task of manufacture is so great that it can be controlled and stopped if the world as a whole can be made to agree that this must be done.

It therefore seems to me most urgent, Mr. President, that you should consult with others before it is concluded that this project should proceed full force according to the view of the great majority of those who know about it. In the name of the future of our country and of the peace of the world, I beg you, sir, not to pass this off because I happen to be an unknown, without influence or name in the public eye. I am definitely in the small minority of those now in a position to form an opinion on this matter. I respect and maintain the right of those who oppose me to their opinion just as some of them respect my opinion, but I do not believe that any of us can offer sound disinterested counsel on this question.

There surely are men in this country, however, to whom you could turn, asking them to study this problem, secure the facts, and come to a conclusion unbiased by their own deep and sincere interest in the project. Only on the judgment of such man could there be faith that full consideration had been given to all sides of this desperately grave question. I hope I do not appear presumptuous in this. I assure you that I have full faith and confidence, and that the whole country has full faith and confidence in you in fulfilling the enormous task that has befallen you and that you are going to lead us, and with us the world into an era of lasting and just peace and security, and that you are the best judge as to where and to whom you should turn in solving the multitude of problems which no man can be expected to solve unaided.

Most respectfully submitted,

OCB:R   *O. C. Brewster*

Brewster's letter arrived at the White House on or about May 29, and it is virtually certain that the readaholic Truman would not leave the examination of a secret document on this subject—routed personally by Stimson—to one of his staff. On May 31, the Interim Committee, with General Marshall in attendance, held a meeting with its scientific panel before making its recommendations to the president, and Stimson expressed the view that "atomic energy could not be considered simply in terms of military weapons, but must also be considered in terms of a new relationship of man to the universe." The committee sent its report to the president the following day. Truman committed virtually nothing to paper on the secret weapon during this period, but clues to what he was going through can be found in his diary, where he wrote on June 1 and 5 about his "very hectic days" and on June 17 that deciding which military strategy to pursue against Japan would entail his "hardest decision to date."

Truman returned the letter to Stimson on June 3 with no written comments. Stimson, meanwhile, had a high-level member of his staff, special assistant Harvey H. Bundy, contact Brewster orally to let him know that all of his letters had been delivered. Yet even this unprecedented level of assurance directly from the secretary of war still left the worried engineer in doubt that Truman had received his plea. When a written acknowledgment failed to arrive from the White House by mid-June, Brewster inquired after it.

My dear Mr. President: *June 14, 1945*

Under the date of May 24, 1945 I transmitted to you through special Army channels a communication concerning the Clinton Engineer Works in Tennessee. Since I have received no acknowledgement of this communication nor the receipt form for classified material which was attached I would greatly appreciate advice from your office as to whether this material has been received and also whether it has been brought to your attention as it is on a subject of great and immediate importance.

Most respectfully,

O. C. Brewster

OCB/s   *New York, NY*

This secret document, however, had not passed through either the common mail or classified materials channels but was hand delivered by either the secretary of war or the secretary of state for Truman's eyes only. Consequently, when Hassett asked the executive clerk, William J. Hopkins, to see what he could find on the letter, Hopkins could locate no record of its having arrived at the White House.

My dear Mr. Brewster: *July 6, 1945*

Your recent letter to the President has been received. In reply, you are advised that a careful search of our files has failed to disclose any record of the communication and form receipt to which you refer.

Very sincerely yours,
WILLIAM D. HASSETT
Secretary to the President

To Brewster, who had no way of knowing just how high-level the handling of his letter had been, the obvious—though incorrect—conclusion could only be that the copies of his letter had dead-ended at the War Department.

My dear Mr. Hassett: *July 10, 1945*

Your letter of July 6 has been received. The communication to the President concerning the Clinton Engineer Works referred to in my letter of June 14 was handed to Lt. Col. J. C. Stowers of the Corps of Engineers in New York on May 14 [24] for delivery to the President. On May 31, Mr. Harvey H. Bundy, Special Assistant to the Secretary of War, advised me that it had been delivered, along with copies to the Secretaries of State and of War.

I would suggest that an inquiry directed to Mr. Bundy might help to locate this document. I have advised Lt. Col. Stowers that apparently neither the copy to the President nor that to the Secretary of State were in fact delivered. I believe the matter to be of sufficient importance to warrant a careful investigation as to the whereabouts of this document.

Very sincerely yours,
O. C. Brewster
OCB/s   *New York, NY*

At the time Brewster wrote this last letter, the first detonation of an atomic device in the New Mexico desert was six days away, and atom bombs would be dropped on two Japanese cities in just a few weeks. Because of the personal interest Stimson took in the letter, it is likely that Brewster received some form of oral reply from his office or through other War Department channels, but there was a limit to how much more he would be able to learn of these highly secret matters. Truman was even then on his way to the Potsdam Conference with Stalin and Churchill, and the president had found, as Brewster had hoped, "men in this country to whom [he] could turn, asking them to study this problem." The Interim Committee, however, had come to conclusions that were the opposite of Brewster's, recommending not only that "the bomb should be used against Japan as soon as possible," but that "it should be used without warning."[9]

Over 400,000 Japanese civilians had already been killed or wounded in raids by American bombers, and roughly 6,000,000 had either been burnt out of their homes or evacuated from threatened areas (the numbers would eventually increase to 574,994 and 8,295,000). Truman and his advisors believed that there was a very good chance that the "tremendous shock"[10] of the atomic detonations would stampede the Japanese into an early surrender. Stimson later wrote that his committee "carefully considered such alternatives as a detailed advance warning or a demonstration in some uninhabited area. Both of these suggestions were discarded as impractical. They were not regarded as likely to be effective in compelling a surrender of Japan, and both of them involved serious risks. Even the New Mexico test would not give final proof that any given bomb was certain to explode when dropped from an airplane. . . . Nothing would have been more damaging to our effort to obtain surrender than a warning or a demonstration followed by a dud—and this was a real possibility. Furthermore, we had no bombs to waste. It was vital that a sufficient effect be quickly obtained with the few we had."[11]

Stimson related that "it was already clear in July that even before the invasion we should be able to inflict enormously severe damage on the Japanese homeland by the combined application of 'conventional' sea and air power."[12] Unfortunately, such damage had remarkably little impact on Japan's ability to inflict grievous casualties on any invasion force attempting to conquer the Home Islands, and "the Allies would be faced with the enormous task of destroying an armed force of five million men and five thousand suicide aircraft, belonging to a race which had already amply demonstrated its ability to fight literally to the death."[13]

"The critical question," said Stimson, "was whether this kind of action would induce surrender. It therefore became necessary to consider very carefully the probable state of mind of the enemy, and to assess with accuracy the line of conduct which might end his will to resist. . . ."[14]

"The committee's function was, of course, entirely advisory," he wrote. "The ultimate responsibility for the recommendation to the President rested upon me, and . . . the conclusions of the committee were similar to my own, although I reached mine independently. I felt that to extract a genuine surrender from the Emperor and his military advisers, they must be administered a tremendous shock which would carry convincing proof of our power to destroy the Empire. Such an effective shock would save many times the number of lives, both American and Japanese, that it would cost."[15]

What did Truman and his senior advisors believe that cost might be? Some historians have maintained that the huge casualty estimates later quoted by Truman were a "postwar creation" designed to justify the use of nuclear weapons, and that such numbers were never even contemplated outside of strictly military circles. Recently discovered documents at the Harry S. Truman Library tell a different story, however. Soon after Stimson circulated Brewster's letter, former president Herbert Hoover submitted his "Memorandum on Ending the Japanese War"—at Truman's request—and Truman was so struck by its estimate that the invasion could cost as many as 500,000 to 1,000,000 lives that he ordered his senior advisors to personally examine the memorandum. Truman's manpower czar, Fred M. Vinson, director of the Office of War Mobilization and Reconversion, received it first, and then former secretary of state Cordell Hull, as well as Acting Secretary of State Joseph C. Grew and Stimson, who were both instructed to prepare a written analysis before coming in for a face-to-face with the president. None of these civilian advisors batted an eye at the casualty estimate, and Truman promptly ordered a meeting with Stimson and the Joint Chiefs of Staff to discuss "the losses in killed and wounded that would result from an invasion of Japan proper."[16]

Truman authorized the use of atomic weapons against Japan while in Potsdam, and after a week of meetings, he wrote in his diary: "It is certainly a good thing for the world that Hitler's crowd or Stalin's did not discover this atomic bomb. It seems to be the most terrible thing ever discovered, but it can be made the most useful."

The first atom bomb was detonated over Hiroshima at 7:15 P.M., Washington time, on Sunday, August 5, 1945. Secret information on the blast didn't start to arrive at the White House until some four hours later, and reporters finally learned of the attack during a hastily called press conference shortly before 11:00 the following morning. Monday evening papers throughout the country carried the stunning news under banner headlines on August 6, and Americans, though glad that it was they, and not their country's enemies, who possessed the bomb, pondered what the existence of this new and terrible weapon meant for the future.

> *Sir:*   *Aug. 8, 1945*
>
> The newspapers report that <u>you are jubilant over the dropping of an "atomic bomb"</u> and the annihilation of over 100,000 people. <u>I hope that this report is incorrect</u>. Such conduct would be unworthy of a gentleman and certainly unworthy of the President.
>
> This action, taken with your consent, has abased the honor of America, and I and many others are ashamed of our country and its leaders, including yourself. The Japanese have committed many atrocities but this is the worst atrocity in the history of mankind. This country has forfeited its entire record of decency and moral leadership in one act, so low and despicable as to be unthinkable.
>
> May God have mercy on this people for so prostituting the God given power of the universe.
>
> *Faithfully yours,*
> *Edward M. Knapp*
> *Washington, DC*

Truman did his best to respond to both those who called for an even more drastic escalation in the war against Japan and those who urged restraint. It is unlikely that his answers to Senator Richard B. Russell of Georgia (who would later chair hearings investigating both Alger Hiss and the MacArthur firing) and Samuel McCrea Cavert, secretary of the Federal Council of the Churches of Christ in America, mollified either man, but they did signal that he was intent on prosecuting the war to the fullest extent while adhering to the agreements made at Potsdam.

> *Mr. President:*   *Aug. 7, 1945*
>
> Permit me to respectfully suggest that we cease our efforts to cajole Japan into surrendering in accordance with the Potsdam Declaration. Let us carry the war to them until they beg us to accept the unconditional surrender. The foul attack on Pearl Harbor brought us into war, and I am unable to see any valid reason

why we should be so much more considerate and lenient in dealing with Japan than with Germany. I earnestly insist Japan should be dealt with as harshly as Germany and that she should not be the beneficiary of a soft peace. The vast majority of the American people, including many sound thinkers who have intimate knowledge of the Orient, do not agree with Mr. Grew in his attitude that there is any thing sacrosanct about Hirohito. He should go. We have no obligation to Shintoism. The contemptuous answer of the Japs to the Potsdam Ultimatum justifies a revision of that document and sterner peace terms.

If we do not have available a sufficient number of atomic bombs with which to finish the job immediately, let us carry on with TNT and fire bombs until we can produce them.

I also hope that you will issue orders forbidding the officers in command of our Air Forces from warning Jap cities that they will be attacked. These generals do not fly over Japan and this showmanship can only result in the unnecessary loss of many fine boys in our Air Force as well as our helpless prisoners in the hands of the Japanese, including the survivors of the March of Death on Bataan who are certain to be brought into the cities that have been warned.

This was a total war as long as our enemies held all of the cards. Why should we change the rules now, after the blood, treasure and enterprise of the American people have given us the upper hand. Our people have not forgotten that the Japanese struck us the first blow in this war without the slightest warning. They believe that we should continue to strike the Japanese until they are brought groveling to their knees. We should cease our appeals to Japan to sue for peace. The next plea for peace should come from an utterly destroyed Tokyo. Welcome back home.

With assurances of esteem,
Richard B. Russell, U.S. Senator
Winder, Ga.

Dear Dick: *August 9, 1945*

I read your telegram of August seventh with a lot of interest.

I know that Japan is a terribly cruel and uncivilized nation in warfare but I can't bring myself to believe that, because they are beasts, we should ourselves act in the same manner.

For myself, I certainly regret the necessity of wiping out whole populations because of the "pigheadedness" of the leaders of a nation and, for your information, I am not going to do it unless it is absolutely necessary. It is my opinion that after the Russians enter into war the Japanese will very shortly fold up.

My object is to save as many American lives as possible but I also have a humane feeling for the women and children in Japan.

Sincerely yours,
HARRY S. TRUMAN

The Honorable Harry S. Truman: *Aug. 9, 1945*

Many Christians [are] deeply disturbed over use of atomic bombs against Japanese cities because of their necessarily indiscriminate destructive efforts and because their use sets extremely dangerous precedent for future of mankind. Bishop Oxnam, President of the Council and John Foster Dulles, Chairman of its commission on a just and durable peace, are preparing statement for probable release tomorrow urging that atomic bombs be regarded as trust for humanity and that Japanese nation be given opportunity and time to verify facts about new bomb and to accept surrender terms. Respectfully urge that ample opportunity be given Japan to reconsider ultimatum before any further devastation by atomic bomb is visited upon her people.

Federal Council of the Churches of Christ in America
Samuel McCrea Cavert, General Secretary
New York, NY

My dear Mr. Cavert: *August 11, 1945*

I appreciated very much your telegram of August ninth.

Nobody is more disturbed over the use of Atomic bombs than I am but I was greatly disturbed over the unwarranted attack by the Japanese on Pearl Harbor and their murder of our prisoners of war. The only language they seem to understand is the one we have been using to bombard them.

When you have to deal with a beast you have to treat him as a beast. It is most regrettable but nevertheless true.

Sincerely yours,
HARRY S. TRUMAN

Japan's speedy capitulation blunted much of the criticism mounting against the further use of atomic weapons, and Dulles, a deeply religious man and fervent anticommunist, believed that Truman's restrained use of the bomb would add to America's moral authority in the postwar world. Dulles was one of the authors of the United Nations' charter and was the senior advisor in the U.S. delegation at the U.N.'s opening conference in San Francisco. When it later became apparent that the United States would have to conclude a peace treaty with Japan separate from the Soviet Union, it was Dulles to whom Truman entrusted the arduous task of negotiating the treaty.

> *My dear Mr. President:*   *August 22, 1945*
>
> We express profound thankfulness, which we know is felt by millions of our fellow citizens, that the Japanese Government was brought to accept the Allied surrender terms without our continuing to the end to release the wholesale destructive force of atomic energy. As indicated by our statement of <u>August ninth</u>, it seemed to us that the way of Christian statesmanship was to use our newly discovered and awesome power as a potential for peace rather than an actuality of war. To the extent that our nation followed that way, it showed a capacity of self-restraint which greatly increases our moral authority in the world. Also, we have given a practical demonstration of the possibility of atomic energy bringing war to an end. If that precedent is constructively followed up, it may be of incalculable value to posterity.
>
> > *Respectfully yours,*
> > *G. Bromley Oxnam, President*
> > *John Foster Dulles, Chairman*
> > *Commission on a Just and Durable Peace*
> > *The Federal Council of the Churches of Christ in America*
> > *New York, NY*

Calls for scientific data on the atom bomb to be shared with the Soviet Union, or the internationalization of atomic development under the newly formed United Nations, were met with distrust by most citizens, who feared that once the "secret" was out of American hands, it was only a matter of time before the weapon was turned against the United States.

My dear Mr. President: *September 22, 1945*

In the newspapers I see that there is a discussion about turning over the secret of the <u>Atomic Bomb</u> to Russia. In view of the extreme differences between our beliefs and those of the Russians I feel that this would be a most unpatriotic thing to do.

Also from the newspapers I received the impression that Russia wishes to step far out of her present sphere into the Mediterranean and the Red Sea. In my opinion, this would be very damaging to future world relations and every effort should be made to hold them within reasonable limits. . . .

> *Very truly yours,*
> *John E. Sloane*
> *Newark, NJ*

Excellency:

As an American citizen, I feel free to write you Mr. President and am sure you'll understand. These days many distorted suggestions are being broadcast on the radio which are misleading.

Is the secret of the <u>atomic bomb</u> an American invention or propriety? If so, it belongs to Uncle Sam and *NO ONE* else, if we can; <u>let's Keep</u> it. You are the boss and I'm sure that your decision will please the American people, also those the world over.

Thank God we have a human being with American blood in his veins for President who is doing the very best for our country.

May God bless and guide you in these trying times and may He give you the Strength to carry on your good work—

> *Very truly yours,*
> *Roger Pierotti*
> *Brooklyn, NY*

Dear President: *March 27, 1946*

Regardless of what other nations think, retain the Atomic Bomb for the U.S.A. alone. It is the whip to preserve peace. And I'm not kidding as most Americans will agree.

Lots of health and good wishes.

> *Yours truly,*
> *Jos. P. Devir*
> *Philadelphia Sports Writers Association*

Honorable Sir: *June 24, 1946*
There is too much talk about the atomic secret of ours. The common sense thing is: NOT TO TALK ABOUT IT. It is our secret and it is up to us to keep it that way.

Yours truly,
Ernest Omernik
Polonia, Wis.

Other American were equally passionate in their conviction that the only route to lasting peace and security lay in the United States demonstrating its openness and goodwill by sharing all that had been learned about atomic energy.

Dear President Truman,   *November 7, 1945*
It is <u>unfortunate that, in an otherwise excellent speech</u>, you took the <u>position that we should keep the secret of the atomic bomb</u>. The trust in the good intentions of the United States, of which you spoke, is rapidly waning, due in part to our intervention in the Chinese civil war. Other nations fear our intentions concerning the bomb.
This fear is a serious threat to the success of the United Nations organization. We can insure a lasting peace only by showing the world that we are ready to co-operate in whole-hearted efforts toward that peace. Co-operation is possible only through sharing with our allies our knowledge of the most terribly marvelous discovery known to modern man.

Sincerely,
Joan Bomberg
New York, NY

And beyond the weighty matters of war and peace was the fact that the new energy source opened up a whole new range of opportunities. In the twilight of his years, an apparently successful businessman saw in it a way to cap his career while continuing to serve his country.

Dear Mr. Truman: *July 19, 1946*
<u>Please consider my services for appointment as one of the five man Atomic Fission Commission, the members of which I understand are to be of your selection.</u>

Starting my career at 18 I have acquired a rather broad industrial, engineering and manufacturing business background, all by the hard way and it seems I would be well fitted to represent commerce and industry which important factors of our economy are assumed will be represented in the Commission.

I am 57, in good health, no physical defects, height 5'11", weight 160 lbs., born in Chicago have lived most of my life in Anderson, Indiana; Protestant, English lineage, married, have grown daughter; moderate in habits, not affiliated with any group, faction, sect or organization; my record is clear and one of accomplishment.

References you might want later will include the names of bankers, manufacturers, merchants and other reputable business and professional men from Indiana cities, St. Louis, Kansas City, Memphis, New Orleans, and being in War Department service I have necessarily been approved by Civil Service after close Army investigation as is exacted by regulations for positions such as mine.

At present I am employed as a Negotiator for the Renegotiation Branch, Chemical Warfare Service of the War Department, with office at 200 W. Baltimore Street, Baltimore, Md.

Starting about 6 months before Pearl Harbor, I went with the O.P.M., later known as War Production Board, serving in technical capacities in Memphis and New Orleans and personally negotiated many millions of dollars worth of prime and sub war shipbuilding contracts between government agencies and Mississippi Valley firms; none of these transactions have ever been questioned.

Upon completion of the war shipbuilding program I accepted an offer of position as business manager and to organize a staff for the New Orleans office of a naval architectural firm under commission to the U.S. Maritime Commission to prepare plans, specifications and requisition covering a post-war shipbuilding program. This operation employed seventy odd technical people versed in ship design and construction.

Shortly following completion of the above contract I was offered and accepted my present position with the Chemical Warfare Service here in Baltimore.

I feel as to have done my part as a civilian by the use of my talents, time and experience in the war effort for which I am proud and that I did this away from my family and for compensation much lower than I would have received for similar services in private enterprise.

In no instance have I resorted to political means to attain appointment or promotion and this also applies here. I have no other means of presenting my request to you, I am not known politically or have political ambitions.

I believe that I am of an age to render mature judgment and proper action based on a long comprehensive industrial business experience gained mostly before the war by more than 25 years, continuously in doing a national and international business of my own in ferrous, non-ferrous mechanical goods and other materials where I employed from 300 to 1200 people and operated 2 plants.

I am rather well known in manufacturing circles throughout the Middle West from the Great Lakes to the Gulf and I have traveled and done business in every state in the Union besides several foreign countries and I know men engaged in many different kinds of enterprises large and small.

I make my request at arms length in all sincerity, that I am warranted consideration and capable and for no other reason that I believe that I can serve on the Atomic Fission Commission in the capacity described in a manner that will be highly satisfactory to you and all concerned with honor to myself as otherwise I would not make this request.

I would be pleased to call in person to meet with you or others you may elect for me to contact or cooperate in any other way suggested and being nearby I can readily comply on short notice.

Your kind consideration and advice will be appreciated tremendously.

> *Yours very truly,*
> *J. H. Hill*
> *Res: Lord Baltimore Hotel*
> *Baltimore, Md.*

My dear Mr. Hill: *July 23, 1946*

This will acknowledge the receipt of your letter of July nineteenth to the President, regarding your desire for appointment as a member of the Atomic Energy Commission, provided for in S. 1717. You may be sure that your application will be borne in mind.

> *Very sincerely yours,*
> *WILLIAM D. HASSETT*
> *Secretary to the President*

The businessman apparently took Hassett's Valentine for more than it was and responded with a breathless thank-you note.

Dear Mr. Hassett: *August 5, 1946*

Upon return from a Mid Western trip I find your letter of July 23, 1946, for which please accept this as an acknowledgement along with my thanks to you.

Your further advice in the matter will be awaited with considerable anxiety.

> *Very truly yours,*
> *J. H. Hill*

The rambling letter from another businessman fell solidly into the "nut mail" category.

Dear Pres. Truman: *September 21, 1945*

Since you have announced the atomic bomb, I feel it my duty to advise you of certain matters. However, since I do not wish for a repetition of mistreatment we have been accorded in the past I request that you handle this matter directly and do not refer the matter to the Bureau of Mines, the Bureau of Standards, Metal Reserve, or any other "department." I believe this matter is of sufficient importance to merit your personal attention. If you cannot do this, kindly do not read further but return my letter to me.

We have been working with uranium and other radioactive materials for many years. We have also worked with fissioning and the like. However, MANY years ago I conceived that if we could discover or create elements of larger "mass" or rather, complexity, than uranium we could derive enormous energy from their fissioning, decomposition, etc.—whatever we choose to call the rearrangements nature puts these marvelous elements through.

Several years ago I advised the Bureau of Aeronautics I could furnish 1200 airplanes which could surround this nation (distance of only ten miles apart) which would remain in the air indefinitely and be so powerful, so heavily armed with SUPERIOR "guns" that no enemy could attack us. I also know how to protect such airplanes and the nation they would protect against "atomic" bombs. I also proposed a projectile to the Bureau of Aeronautics which could be shot from this continent to Europe with deadly effect. I proposed projectile velocities up to 40,000 feet per second because those could be readily produced but advised them I knew how to develop projectiles of much higher velocities. I believe we can also produce shells from such dense metal, and of much greater tenacity, they will penetrate any barrier elements that exist in the Universe and we ought to be able to duplicate them. I believe, however, that we can get such enormous tenacity with only moderate increase in density that such metals or elements have not only enormous military value but equally important industrial value.

However, this is leading from the purpose of this letter. I note in your press release that you mention two elements and an editorial in *Chemical and Metallurgical Engineering* speculates whether your bomb uses U.235 or plutonium. This magazine states this to be Element 93 but I believe they are in error as to this. However, whether it is 93 or 94 or some element of even larger Z number, we can agree it is some heavier element, although you may also be playing with some of the thorium or actinium series.

If, however, you are using elements heavier or larger than Element 92, I believe I have come upon a source of them, contrary to the general belief that they do not exist in nature.

We have discovered Rhenium, Osmium, Iridium, Platinum, Rhodium, Ruthenium, in great quantities. However, we have noted a peculiarity. When we plate some of these metals by replacement (not by electricity) we sometimes have obtained deposits which soon disappeared, the disappearance taking place from a few seconds to hours, and, in one instance, not entirely disappearing until a day or two had elapsed.

It occurred to me that we had the "eka" series of these heavy elements, all of which lie above 92 in Z numbers. If so, we have enormous quantities of them and could have supplied our country with them at a great saving over what you have expended. I have advised the Bureau of Mines, Bureau of Aeronautics, Bureau of Standards, etc., but they merely ridiculed me.

It would be unfair for you to have government agencies begin a search for these elements or to try to discover our claims. I believe we are entitled to the fruits of this discovery. We have not been able to stake all the claims we wish to because of straitened financial condition, imposed by the war, and because most of our men have been taken from us by the war. However, we are willing to do so, and intend doing so as soon as possible. We are willing to extract the material and furnish it at reasonable prices. In fact we have the facilities for so doing and manpower should soon be available. We have received word another one expects to soon be with us. . . .

We should be able to discover or produce EkaRe, EkaOs, EkaIr, EkaPt, IkaAu, EkaHg, EkaTl, EkaPb, IkaBl, EkaPo, EkaAb, EkaRn, but especially the first four or five. We have discovered strong evidence of the eka series of Rhenium, Osmium, Iridium, Platinum, Gold and Mercury. In fact, we are certain we have them and several more. I would not hesitate to contract to supply them.

We have had explosions and flashes of radiation even when only a small amount of some of these elements were isolated, or were being processed. One bad fire may have been started in that manner.

If Element 94 is of interest to you I am sure we could supply Osmium containing it. It probably would be in a higher concentration than the material you extract from your Hanford piles.

Another extraction we have made showed a high percentage of gold by spectographic methods. Since the original material from which the extract was made showed very little gold, we have thought that EkaAu was present. The more work we do the more evidence we find of this eka series of elements of extremely large Z number. Some of these are sufficiently stable to enable their use in bombs. Our concern has mainly been to use them for power generation.

> *Very truly,*
> *Leroy A. Wilson*
> *Wilson Research, Engineering and Exploration Co.*
> *Veyo, Utah*

The development of the atom bomb and the potential of the new energy source for both good and evil was frequently discussed in schools, and a noticeable number of letters from teachers and students supported the internationalization of atomic energy.

> *Dear Mr. President:*   *April 23, 1946*
> There is a lot of talk going around about the destructive ability of atomic energy. I feel that if <u>more was said</u> about its creative <u>powers, people</u> would be much more inclined to work for a mutual goal—

that of international peace and cooperation. How can people think of peace when all they see and hear about is another war, one which will "probably wipe man off the face of the earth"?

Being a student of teaching, I feel that it is imperative that people understand what atomic energy is. I would like to be able to tell my pupils, so that they can also understand and perhaps one of them may be on the path of finding more creative powers through atomic energy.

There is nothing in this universe that can be kept a secret if one man already has it; so why not under an international committee, share the "secret" we have found? They too want to work toward a common goal and they should have a chance to do so. We Americans are not better than the rest and it is the only way cooperation and confidence of one nation for another could possibly begin to build itself up.

> *Sincerely yours,*
> *(Miss) Rebecca Haber*
> *Oneonta, NY*

His Excellency the President of the U.S.   *March 21, 1946*

I am in the seventh grade and with the rest of the class I decided it would be a good idea to really send you a letter stating our opinions about what should be done with the Atomic bomb. I think that the secrets should be given to the <u>United Nations</u> and have each nation swear to use the Atom only for peaceful purposes. If any nations should dare use it for destruction all the other nations should go against her. I may be wrong but I don't think so.

> *Yours sincerely,*
> *Miriam Boyer*
> *Prospect Junior High School*
> *Bronx, NY*

P.S. Please send me your autograph. Thank you.

It was postulated by scientists—and widely accepted by the public—that a future, all-out atomic war could well result in the extinction of mankind and even all animal life on earth. Privately, Truman shared many of the same fears as the rest of his countrymen over what the atom bomb portended for the future and worried that mankind was not ready to restrain itself from wielding a weapon that could ultimately result in its own destruction. Later this same year he would write in his diary: "The human animal and his emotions change not much from age to age. He must change now or he faces absolute and complete destruction and maybe the insect age or an atmosphereless planet will succeed him."

Truman never considered turning atomic secrets over to either the United Nations or the Soviet Union, but precisely how extensive the scientific partnership with Great Britain and Canada should remain was a subject of careful debate within his administration. Ultimately, how to proceed on this and other matters turned on the question of whether nuclear policy would be determined by military or civilian authorities. Competing legislation moving through Congress reflected this critical divergence of approach: The May-Johnson Bill essentially established a permanent Manhattan-type organization, while the McMahon Bill, backed by Truman, advocated a civilian structure with military input. According to Truman, however, "It was not easy for some members of Congress to realize just how complex a thing they were dealing with,"[17] and at least some of the public also became aware of this as the debate dragged on.

Sir,   *March 13, 1946*

We pay taxes—heavy taxes to run our Government. We suppose intelligent, honest men can be found who interest themselves primarily in the welfare of their country. Yet in a letter from Washington, D.C. written Mar. 7 '46 the following sentence raises doubts: "One competent observer of Congress said this morning that he doubted if there were more than ten or twenty Representatives who knew the points of difference betwen the May-Johnson Bill and the McMahon Bill." I hope this is a gross exaggeration.

Who am I to say what bill should be passed and when? But on every hand, those whose opinions I respect most reiterate in one form or another that from now forward the good of the world must come first. The good of a nation or a group of nations must be secondary, not just in theory but in blood-sweating, agonizing, sacrificing effort. I wish I were assured that even the majority of paid representatives of Govt. in Washington were deeply anxious for the good of the world. I wish I could be assured that a Military board, fundamentally interested in the arts of war were the best fitted to protect the world from Atomic warfare. Or, are emergency boundaries of

state and theories of government all important in God's kingdom? I
beg to remain

Your obedient servant
Mrs. Clarence E. Wolsted
Cedar Falls, Iowa

Efforts were made in March 1946 to subvert the intent of the McMahon
Bill by introducing an amendment giving the military veto power over the proposed Atomic Energy Commission. Viewing this process with disdain, some
letter writers proposed removing the whole process from Congress's hands.

Dear Mr. Truman: *March 17, 1946*
I am very concerned about the fate of the atom bomb in terms of
who or what body will control it.

I do not want the destructive results of the A-Bomb as a burden
on my conscience. If I had my way this bomb would never be used
to destroy a single human life.

I was ashamed of America's use of this bomb in the Summer of
1945. We should balance this record by seeing to it the American
people have a chance to determine how the bomb shall be used and
how it shall be controlled.

This should be by direct vote of the people. After a clarification
of the issues as to how this bomb is to be controlled and used, these
issues should be submitted to the American people in the form of a
national referendum.

I do not trust the wisdom of Congress on this issue, nor would I
place so great a responsibility on the shoulders of one man or small
group of men.

I do trust the mass wisdom of the voting population to express
themselves correctly on this crucial matter.

Will you use your good office to propose a national referendum
on the control and use of atomic energy.

Yours for one world
Pauli Murray
Washington, D.C.

Bomb tests at the Pacific atoll of Bikini prompted another flurry of letters and telegrams from individuals and organizations such as the Detroit

Council of Churches and the Bennington Vermont Chapter of the United States Student Assembly. White House logs showed that all were sent to the Navy Department "for consideration and acknowledgment." Only telegrams with multiple copies remained in the president's files.

THE PRESIDENT   JUNE 11, 1946

THE WHITE HOUSE

SEISMOLOGIST SCHNEIDEROV PREDICTS IN CURRENT SCIENCE MAGAZINE BIKINI BOMB MAY SPLIT THE EARTH STOP WHAT A RESPONSIBILITY FOR OUR PRESDIENT TO TAKE THIS NEEDLESS WASTEFUL STEP PLEASE STOP IT AND TURN ATTENTION TO WORLD UNITY

E P GERTH

SAN FRANCISCO, CA

PRESIDENT TRUMAN   MARCH 9, 1946

WASH DC

THE CITIZENS COMMITTEE FOR COMMON SENSE ANIMAL LEG-ISLATION IS DEFINITELY OPPOSED TO THE USE OF ANIMALS IN ATOMIC BOMB TESTS YOU AS REPRESENTATIVE OF A HUMANITAR-IAN AND CIVILIZED NATION MUST NOT ALLOW SUCH BARBARIC ATROCITIES TO TAKE PLACE

THE CITIZENS COMMITTEE FOR COMMON SENSE ANIMAL

LEGISLATION

LOS ANGELES, CA

The Bikini tests gave the American public its first real look at the raw power of atomic energy, and it seemed obvious to all that nuclear power could supply electricity that would be "too cheap to meter."

Dear Mr. President: *May 10, 1946*

Is not this the most propitious time to set the atomic energy into constructive use? It seems reasonable to suppose that pin point pills of this power would provide as much or more fuel than all the <u>coal mines in the world</u> could supply.

Very truly yours,
(Miss) Gertrude Moss
Cleveland, Ohio

The McMahon Bill establishing the Atomic Energy Commission (AEC) was signed into law in August 1946, but even with its passage, the fight over civilian versus military control was far from over. Numerous tactics were employed by some in Congress who worked diligently to wear Truman down and outmaneuver him in their efforts to make their views prevail. As one of the leading figures in the wartime development of the atom bomb and chairman of the AEC's General Advisory Committee, J. Robert Oppenheimer became a reluctant participant in these political battles.

On a personal level, Truman did not like the brilliant yet arrogant and somewhat high-strung physicist, and at one meeting where an agitated Oppenheimer said he had blood on his hands because of the bomb, the president glared coldly at him and shot back: "The blood is on my hands. Let me worry about that." Afterward, Truman told AEC chairman David Lilienthal that he hoped he'd never have to see the "cry baby" again.[18] On a professional level, however, the president had nothing but the greatest respect for Oppenheimer's abilities and found his views "informative and provocative."[19] Both men were frustrated by the continual political maneuvering of the opponents of the president's atomic policy, and when congressional leaders refused to allow a smooth transition of the AEC leadership—for no practical reason other than to cause Truman additional complications during his election campaign—Oppenheimer outlined his view of the situation.

My dear Mr. President: *June 19, 1948*
When, a few weeks ago we had the privilege of meeting with you to talk of the work in atomic energy, we shared your conviction that for the future of this work, it was very much to be hoped that your nominees of the Atomic Energy Commission be promptly confirmed by the Senate. In the intervening weeks, all prospects of this action appeared to have vanished. Instead, the Congress has passed legislation extending the terms of the present Commissioners for not quite two years. Under these circumstances, I fear that the options open to you are limited to letting this bill become law, or, on the other hand, making recess appointments to the Commission when the present terms expire one month from now. I am writing to you to ask in all earnestness that you let the extension of term become law, not because I believe that this was a sound and healthy procedure, but because it seems to be the preferable of the now possible alternatives.

Through close association with the work of the commission, and some acquaintance with its relation to the Joint Congressional Committee and Military Liaison Committee, I have become convinced that what the Commission most needs is a certain measure of stability and of reassurance, that without these it will have neither the authority nor the confidence to establish sound policy, to put it into execution, and to take and respond to the inevitable criticism which those responsible for an undertaking such as this must expect and will always meet. I believe that with the two year extension, there is a good chance of effective and forward looking administration. I fear that with recess appointments, and the uncertainties which these will bring with them, much of the good work that the Commission has done in the past will be lost, and many important developments and changes which must now be made will be postponed and jeopardized. I write to you in this as one who deeply shares your hopes and your concern, and who has been close enough to the work in atomic energy to have a firm opinion.

With every cordial good wish.

Respectfully yours,
J. R. Oppenheimer

Truman's influence in Congress at that time was practically nonexistent, and he could only agree.

Dear Dr. Oppenheimer: *June 23, 1948*
I appreciated very much your letter of the nineteenth in regard to the extension period which this Congress put on the terms of the Atomic Energy Commissioners.

While it was a snide thing to do, I suppose it is the best we can expect under the circumstances and we will probably have to take it.

Sincerely yours,
HARRY S. TRUMAN

Less than a month later, when it became clear that there was no immediate end in sight for the Soviet blockade of Berlin, the Defense Department formally requested that America's small stock of atom bombs be released to the Joint Chiefs of Staff. Soviet development of atomic weapons and long-range bombers would later place the question in a completely different light, but at this point, the United States still retained its nuclear monopoly. Truman again refused. He said that an atom bomb was not just another military weapon, "it is used to wipe out women and children and unarmed people," and stated flatly that "we have got to treat this differently from rifles and cannon and ordinary things like that."[20]

On September 19, 1949, U.S. scientists confirmed that the radioactive emissions being picked up over the Pacific indicated that the Soviet Union had exploded a nuclear device years ahead of when the American public had been told the communists could produce one. Rather than holding fast to the information and attempting to plug leaks to the newspapers, Truman released the information almost immediately in a straightforward press release, believing that a demonstration of "business as usual" would help dampen people's fears. On the whole, it must be said that the tactic worked, but Americans clearly perceived that overnight the world they lived in had drastically changed.

> *Dear President Truman:*   *September 24, 1949*
> Although I voted for you and was made happy by your election, there is a limit to the support one can give you.
>
> I notice every time you want Congress to appropriate money in the wild ventures of squandering the public's money on Europe and Price Support, you create an imaginary menace to force Congress to vote the money.
>
> Consequently I take your Atom Bomb scare with a dose of salt.
>
> But if you have said the truth—then it is a mighty fine time to do something to outlaw the Atom Bomb. Until now we have lived in a bravado atmosphere of superiority because we thought we were the only ones to have the bomb. Now that another nation has developed one, an armament race in Atom Bombs would be the wildest folly.
>
> Mr. President, you have a great responsibility to God, the Nation and the innocent people of this world, to do the right thing in out-lawing this ignoble weapon.
>
> Surely you have seen existing Motion Pictures of the effects of the Bomb. Already you carry a great responsibility towards God in ordering its use at Hiromshima [*sic*] and Nagasaki where over 125,000 were lost. Someday, if there is a God, you will have to defend your decision, because no man has the right to order the extermination of 125,000 souls without some kind of explanation, to the God who put them into this world.

The effects of this bomb are too barbaric for nations to use against one another.

As a citizen of this country and as an inhabitant of this world, I ask you to take immediate <u>steps to outlaw this cruel weapon for always</u>, and start development of its use for the betterment of humanity, that the innocent people everywhere living on this earth will not have to live in daily fear that anytime one of these bombs can fall over them.

Very sincerely yours,
Henry A. Pierce
Flushing, NY

Dear Mr. President: *September 25, 1949*

This letter is written to express our feelings with reference to your statement of last Friday regarding Russia's A-bomb.

With our minds and hearts ever fearful for the safety and security of our children, may we quote from a song written by an American songwriter, who believes as we do, that our future lies in the strengthening of the United Nations

> People of America, people everywhere,
> The miracles of science never cease,
> Submarines and radar, and bombers in the air,
> THIS IS OUR LAST CHANCE FOR PEACE!

> Learn a lesson from
> The atomic bomb
> That mighty nations fear,
> People I implore
> Put an end to war,
> Or our world will disappear,

> People of America, People of the world,
> From now on may our happiness increase,
> Learn in God to trust,
> Or return to dust,
> THIS IS OUR LAST CHANCE FOR PEACE!

Sincerely yours,
Mr. and Mrs. Harry Becker
Venice, Calif.

The first impulse of many letter writers was that war was now inevitable and that the United States had only one reasonable option: to strike first.

Dear Mr. President:

Now we know that the Russians have an A-Bomb, are we going to abide by the customary ethics of warfare, stand around and twiddle our thumbs until they throw another "PEARL HARBOR" on us, leveling some of our great cities to the ground and slaughtering hundreds of thousands of our people at one snap of a finger, before "WE" do something about it?

Dictators know no bounds. Let's not be silly enough to place one iota of confidence in anything they say or do. We cannot deal with a bunch of savage bandits that way. Past experience has proven that.

They have vowed to destroy us as a nation for years, soap boxed their Marxist Doctrine for the "Feeble Minded" all over the nation for the past 25 years. We know they are our arch enemies.

When they will resort to such desperate measure as to banish scientists because their findings do not fit their political schemes, not to mention many other of their equally despicable tactics, they'll stop at nothing. We can expect nothing but the most foul deal from them. Yes, they'll feign honor up until the last act. Then Honor be damned.

If this ever happened, Mr. Truman, it will be a sad, sad day for the dear old world, back to the "Dark Ages," if they should win. Delay can be fatal.

I'm for former Governor [George] Earle, who said, "BLAST THEM BEFORE THEY BLAST US," do a good job of it too. It will mean far less bloodshed in the long run.

True—This is grim—facts are sometimes very ugly things.

My prayer—Almighty God guide you aright in your every move. With my most profound respect to you. I am,

Yours truly,
Scott A. Fuller (Former Ensign USN)
Oakland, Calif.

President Truman,   *September 23, 1949*

Dear Sir: There's a possibility that the near future may bring to us Trouble and plenty bad. If we wait for our enemies to strike first we will, all of us, be dead or slaves. If we are ready and strike first, we can still be free men. But "give me liberty or give me death." I hope you are in the know. I am 83 but my eyes are good and my spirit willing. I can still see both sights in a rifle.

> *Sincerely,*
> *J. T. Allison*
> *Odessa, Texas*

Other Americans simply urged that the president stand his ground and be secure in the nation's inherent strengths.

> *Dear President Truman,*
>
> In regards to Russia having <u>the Atomic Bomb</u>, I, a supervisor of the Philadelphia Transportation Company, believe it does not mean a thing.
>
> You are listening too much to your Congressmen that are half against you. We took our Atomic Bombs to Japan and conquered them. Let Russia make all she wants, we have ours. They must bring theirs across the Atlantic, it's up to you to stop them.
>
> Nobody stopped you from taking them to Japan, and nobody will stop you from dropping them on Russia, if she insists on trouble.
>
> No wooden guns on our buildings in N.Y. like the last war, <u>we want protection</u> with American soldiers and American seamen at our seaports.
>
> I was in the service of the U.S. from 1920 to 1924. I am 45 years old and would still see service for you.
>
> I would appreciate an acknowledgement of this letter.
>
> *Very truly yours,*
> *Edward J. McCafferty*
> *P. T. C. Supervisor*
> *Philadelphia, Penn.*

Numerous writers questioned whether the Soviet feat had actually even happened.

> *President Truman:*   *September 24, 1949*
>
> Has it occurred to you that the Russian atomic explosion might have been a big bluff?
>
> In an article appearing in the weekly "Soviet Literary Gazette" it was stated that the Soviet Union stands unchanged in its belief that the atomic bomb should be outlawed; therefore, it is <u>my belief that</u>

Russia has some way or other come into the possession of one of the United States' "A" bombs and set it off as a bluff, thinking that they may be able to get the U.S. to sign a pact to outlaw this deadly and destructive weapon. Knowing that they could not win a war against us if they did not have a weapon as deadly as ours.

Keeping this in mind and adding the fact that scientists figured that it would be at least 1952 before they could make such a weapon, don't you think my theory sounds logical?

I would appreciate a letter in return with your comments on the facts contained in this letter.

> *Respectfully yours,*
> *Don Charpontier*
> *San Jose, Calif.*

"Nut mail" was to be expected, and there was no shortage of it.

> THE PRESIDENT   1949 OCT 14
> DEAR HARRY
> TAKE IT EASY. RUSSIA NEVER HAD ANY ATOMIC BOMBS AND SHE NEVER WILL HAVE ANY AS LONG AS THIS WORLD SHALL LAST. SHE SET OFF A VERY BIG BLAST THAT WAS ALL. I ASKED CHRIST TO BLOCK HER EFFORTS LONG BEFORE SHE GOT STARTED TO SEARCH FOR URANIUM. TAKE IT EASY—TAKE IT EASY.
> JOHN WILLIAM BANHOLSTER
> COQUILLE, OREGON

Publication in the *New York Times* of a nearly full-page political advertisement titled "God and the Atom" inspired many individuals to write to their president. At least a half dozen correspondents sent along a copy of the tract, written as an open letter to Truman by a New Yorker named Ferris Booth, and urged him to read it.

> *Dear Mr. Truman,*   *October 3, 1949*
> In today's *New York Times,* I noticed the enclosed advertisement entitled "God and the Atom."
> This is one of the most important pieces of printed material that has ever been published as it undoubtedly contains the solution to the Russian situation.

I have been very much interested in your international approach and therefore, may I <u>respectfully ask you to read this epic-making message and statement</u>, "God and the Atom," and tell me what you think of it.

Can you do anything personally toward implementing this highly important and timely strategic plan?

Cordially yours,
Mort N. Lansing
New York, NY

Booth's "God and the Atom" read in part:

Atomic power has always existed in the universe, and did no apparent harm, until man started minding God's business, and then came Alamogordo, Hiroshima, Nagasaki, Bikini, and Eniwetok. At present we are suffering the deserved frustration of a world which has based a preponderance of its defense upon material power. For the world has so emphasized material gains and so worshipped physical force alone, that it has forgotten who is at bat and what inning it is.

LET US OVER-SIMPLIFY THE SITUATION: Russia, obviously, is making three main assaults upon us in a triangular enveloping movement by attacking us: 1. Economically; 2. Militarily; and 3. Spiritually. The first two attacks we are presently combating in a carefully planned, organized, methodical way through the Truman Doctrine, the Marshall Plan, the ECA, the Atlantic Pact, the Military Aid Program, accommodations with Britain, etc. These efforts are, and have been in actual operation and should proceed aggressively according to their well-conceived plans.

It is Russia's third point of attack upon us, the Spiritual, that presents us with a golden opportunity of bolstering our defenses and SEIZING THE INITIATIVE, as we have against Russia's other thrusts. The issue is crystal clear:—

IT IS GOD AGAINST ATHEISM.

The rulers of Russia have adopted atheism as an instrument of government policy. We should accept that challenge and make God the top policy of the United States in governmental thought and action, as it is in the hearts and personal lives of its people. . . .

Booth called for the formation of a "World Spiritual Block under the leadership of the United States" and said that the president should be its guiding force.

The President of the United States today is deservedly the most important individual in the world. It is axiomatic that the President's leadership and world-wide prestige would not only dramatize the issue, but would be received with enthusiasm by a world hungry for hope. . . .

Might the President not consider further crystallizing the situation by addressing the people in the manner of the Russian atomic explosion announcement? Attention could be called to actual instances where spiritual force has prevented war. Among these might be mentioned:

A. Gandhi's single-handed termination of the civil violence in India by his tremendous spiritual force.

B. The enduring peace between Chile and Argentina consecrated by their erecting the Christ of the Andes 47 years ago upon their unfortified border.

Formulate steps to bolster and aggressively aid Confucianism in China as a bulwark against Communism. Confucianism, China's twenty-five-hundred-year-old ethical concept of government, is violently anti-communistic. It stresses the happiness of the individual and the subservience of the state to the people. Confucius' advice, "What you do not wish done to yourself, do not do to others," was probably the original Golden Rule. Such a concept is the antithesis of Marx, Moscow and Mao. To assist Confucianism in China where its roots have existed for 2,500 years, presents a most fertile field for combating Communism in that area.

Formulate steps to obtain the spiritual support of the world's millions of Moslems, whose great belief in Allah makes them violently opposed to atheism. Islam, of course, is a mode of life, and it is simply INCONCEIVABLE for a good Moslem to be a Communist. . . .

We must always remember that spiritual force is like gravity— although you cannot see it or touch it, it is constantly working and, in the long run, cannot be denied. Each of us must remember also that God's power is much like a radio. The power itself is always there, but the individual himself must turn it on.

No harm can be done, Mr. President, and I have super-faith that it might work wonders; at least it would give the world a lift from the jitters it has today.

It might give people definite hope that they could yet keep for themselves and their children that priceless possession which Shakespeare calls: 'The Nobleness of Life.'

Domestic and international tensions remained high with the fall of China to Mao Tse-tung's revolutionaries and accusations by Senator Joseph McCarthy that the U.S. State Department was riddled with communist infiltrators, yet letters to Truman about the bomb fell off to almost nothing. Even lengthening casualty lists from America's costly defensive battle on the Korean Peninsula provoked no appreciable mail on the subject. In hindsight, it almost seems that Americans were afraid even to broach the subject—as if even mentioning atomic weapons would somehow hasten their use. But China's sudden entry into the war in late October 1950—and a misstatement by Truman—would soon end the silence. The specter of massive Chinese armies sweeping down from Manchuria to swallow American forces whole led some to believe that only atomic weapons could right the situation.

Dear President Truman: *Nov. 16, 1950*

Atrocities by the Communists in Korea are terrible and shocking. We have asked you before to "get tough" with Stalin and his ilk, but your weak Chamberlain tactics have done practically nothing. We now demand as citizens of this wonderful United States, that as our supposed leader you "get tougher" with all those barbarian Communists and use the Atom Bomb and finish the conflict to its successful conclusion in Korea or Manchuria and elsewhere as necessary.

Sincerely yours,
Charles A. Croissant, M.D.
Worcester, Mass.

Dear Mr. President: *November 28, 1950*

Why in God's name don't you order MacArthur to use the atomic bomb? Why do you not order the destruction of Russia and all her satellites.

They are all asking for it, the United Nations is doing nothing, get the hell out of the U.N. and do something, for the love of God or we are sunk. Incidentally get rid of that powder puff Acheson. Oh dear I don't know what you are thinking of. You are driving us all crazy with your namby pamby handling of the Korean problem.

Why don't you take it into your own hands. You've got a chance to go down in history as one man who isn't afraid of the Russian Genghis Khan. Go ahead Harry, give them the old bomb. We can stand a few ourselves but we cannot stand to be slaves of the Yellow Horde.

Sincerely,
Mrs. Margaret Bayard
New York, NY

At first, only a few correspondents called for use of the atom bomb, but the day after the above letter was mailed to the White House, the president himself opened the door to the subject, and a torrent of letters swept in. Following a well-crafted statement of U.S. objectives in Korea, reporters asked if his comment that "we will take whatever steps are necessary to meet the military situation" meant that the use of the atom bomb was a possibility. Truman firmly answered that his options "include every weapon we have." But instead of cutting off further discussion along this line, he then allowed himself to be manuvered into saying that use of the nuclear weapon was under "active consideration," which it wasn't. He recognized by this point that he had allowed his saber rattling to venture too far, yet he continued to field questions, stumbling through them in an effort to soften and qualify his earlier misstatement. Things went from bad to worse, and he eventually told reporters that the decision whether to use atom bombs would be left up to "the military commander in the field," MacArthur.[21]

A hurried "clarification" released to the press did little to soften the blow, and banner headlines in newspapers from Des Moines to New Delhi warned that the bomb might be unleashed in Korea. Agitation within the British Parliament was so intense that it was only quieted by Prime Minister Clement Attlee's promise that he would personally meet with Truman to ensure that Britain's fate was not sealed by decisions made solely by Washington. Within the United States, some now saw use of the weapon not in some theoretical future but as something that could happen, and happen soon.

Dear Mr. President: *Nov. 29, 1950*
I do not believe that our boys should lose their lives fighting the Chinese Reds. Let us get out of China as fast as we can. Any military man should know that we are lost if we spend any length of time fighting in China.

I am in favor of serious business at the United Nations in order to know exactly where we stand with the Russians. <u>I am not in favor of using the Atomic Bomb at this time.</u>

I believe that General MacArthur served his usefulness in World Wars I and II, but now a new and younger man is needed in that theater of war as soon as possible.

God grant you strength to see this catastrophe ended shortly, and peace come to all Nations of the world.

Sincerely,
Marian Cohn
Chicago, Ill.

My dear Mr. Truman: *Nov. 29, 1950*

I have just learned of the serious consideration being given to use of atomic bomb in Southern Manchuria, and of our government's huge program of expansion in order to produce more atomic and hydrogen weapons.

<u>I implore you not to allow the atom bomb to be used in the</u> 'Korean' war, for its inevitable consequence would be Russia's use of her own similar weapon, and probably the proclamation of total war.

The American people suffer the immorality of our dropping the first atom bomb on Hiroshima. We have already set a precedent, but let us not continue to follow it and thence prevent Russia from using even more destructive weapons upon our provocation.

In greatest sincerity,
Betty Bredin
Wellesley, Mass.

Dear Mr. President: *Nov. 30, 1950*

I appeal to you, as our Great President, to <u>use your</u> great <u>influence towards bringing about an amicable settlement for peace</u>. We are <u>all horrified at the prospect of using the A. Bomb</u>. I pray to God and <u>appeal to your conscience</u> not to <u>permit the use of this horrible weapon</u>. We want to live and to have peace.

God Bless you for your honorable efforts to <u>obtain peace for all</u> the world.

Sincerely,
Mary S. LaPat
Forest Hills, NY

An almost equal amount of correspondence arrived from people who believed that entry of China into the conflict, as a proxy of the Soviets, justified any means necessary to protect the lives of American soldiers and win the war.

Dear Mr. President: *December 1, 1950*

All my friends say "thank God for a President with guts." <u>Your announcement regarding use of the "A" bomb is "just what the doctor ordered." Now our enemies</u> cannot say you did not tell them.

Respectfully and gratefully yours,
Dudley Hilborn
New York, NY

Your Excellency,   *11-29-50*

As a minister of the Gospel and a Bible-believing Christian, I am writing to you. I realize there are many cranks writing you and telling you what ought to be done. I am not a crank neither am I an armchair general. I am an American and proud of the fact.

There is much that has been bothering me lately. <u>This war in Korea</u>. Why is it that we fuss around at the fringe instead of getting at the heart of the matter? If we have an internal ill, we do not wash the external for its healing.

<u>You know as well as I do where this whole matter lies. That is in MOSCOW. I would rather see Moscow destroyed than to see our boys die in Korea at the hands of the Chinese Reds who shout defiance at the "so called" United Nations.</u>

<u>You can use the Atom bomb. Don't pay</u> any attention to these liberal and modernist preachers who have been so savvy with the pens until now. Why do you have to get U.N. permission for everything? Does Russia? Does China? (The Agrarian farmers, as your beloved Secretary of State likes to call them.) The very idea of bringing that rat Wu* all the way from China to let him shout defiance to all that is good and Christian!

---

*K. C. Wu had held numerous key positions in the Nationalist Chinese Government of Generalissimo Chiang Kai-shek on Formosa (Taiwan). He was not averse to openly using the "China Lobby" to press for increasing American involvement in their ongoing struggle with the Red Chinese, who had driven them off the mainland.

Mr. President, are we going to keep on fussing around until we have nothing? I am prepared to do my part.

Yours by God's Grace,
Kenneth E. Eyler, Minister
Wesleyan Methodist Church,
Lansing, Mich.

Dear Mr. President: *November 30, 1950*

While American boys are being killed by the Red Chinese invaders in Korea, it is <u>utterly absurd to delay any longer in authorizing General MacArthur</u> to bomb Chinese Communist armies and military equipment and transportation in Manchuria, and <u>also to use the atomic bomb if considered necessary</u>.

Directives to this effect should be sent to General MacArthur regardless of any delay in the United Nations. The procrastination, confusion and sabotage that have existed in both the Security Council and the General Assembly during the past five months have become an international scandal.

I am confident that you would find that the Western democracies would rally behind the leadership of the United States in case this nation possessed the moral courage to act with becoming vigor.

Finally, it seems to me that American leadership in international affairs would be greatly <u>improved by the dismissal of Mr. Acheson as Secretary</u> of State and the appointment in his place of a statesman of outstanding prestige and competence.

At the same time, Mr. President, you should act promptly to end the sniping at a truly great soldier and statesman, General Mac-Arthur, whose wisdom and versatility saved this country from a disastrous defeat in July-September of this year.

With high regards and esteem, I am

Faithfully yours,
Kenneth Colegrove,
Professor of Political Science
Northwestern University, Evanston, Ill.

To some, views like these were terribly wrong, and one woman related her family's painful experience in the last war when writing the president.

Dear Sir   *Nov. 30, 1950*

I and my whole family are <u>appalled at this talk in government</u> circles about whether or <u>not we shall use the atom bomb on our foes in Korea</u>.

We should not have used this hideous weapon in Japan, and believe me, the crime we perpetrated on helpless non-combatants there will inevitably have to be paid for by us.

My husband and I with two children were interned for three years by the Japanese in the Philippines, and we lost everything we owned, including our eldest son, who was killed with the Marine assault on Guam. We would rather go through all that again, and lose our only surviving son, than turn loose this atomic horror on anyone.

Whatsoever a man soweth that shall he also reap—and this applies to atom bombs. The only possible excuse for its use could be in retaliation if it was just used against our people. May God guide you to a sane and right decision—if and when the time comes.

> *Yours truly,*
> *Clara D. Bergamini*
> *Rowayton, Conn.*

P.S. These Senators who advocate dropping atom bombs have probably never been within hearing distance of an ordinary bomb dropping.

Another woman living just off Camp LeJeune in North Carolina thought that the nuclear weapon could be used but like many Americans, believed it could be justified only if it was first used as part of an ultimatum.

Dear Mr. President: *30 November 1950*

I am a housewife, my husband is in the U.S. Marine Corps. I have known the inconvenience of war, and from where I am it looks like war. I think it would be a good chance to avoid all out war if we give the Reds a limited amount of time to get out of Korea. If they do not, then <u>drop the Atom Bomb</u> on their capital, their supply bases. My prayers go out to you, that in your great wisdom, your decision will be one that will give us peace in our time.

> *Yours truly,*
> *Ida G. Nolen*
> *Midway Park, N.C.*

A mother of five sons in the armed services, including three currently in Korea and another missing in action since early in the fighting, pleaded with the president not to use the atom bomb. Apparently written in great anguish, her letter becomes disjointed in places, but she ultimately seems to resign herself to the possibility that the weapon may have to be used if negotiations with the communists failed. Her letter almost certainly was included in the selection of mail Hassett gave to Truman each day, and it is one of the very few answered by the president's correspondence secretary on this subject.

> *To the President of the U.S.:*   Dec. 2, 1950
>
> I am pleading with <u>you not to drop the A. Bomb</u>. I have five sons in the service. Three are in Korea. And at the moment I don't know if the other two have been sent there or not. One has been missing since July. And I know he is living somewhere over there. Deep down in my heart something tells me he is a prisoner in China.
>
> If you order the A. Bomb dropped, that will cause a civil war here because mothers and fathers won't sit back and let their sons be killed when it could have been prevented. Order the Chinese to give our prisoners up and tell them you will draw our troops out, and then let the A. Bomb drop. But first it should be dropped on Russia. Please help our boys first and dear God, send my darlings back to me. And <u>give us peace once more</u>.
>
> > *A mother with a heart full and her hands full also,*
> > *Mrs. Steve Evans*
> > *Forbus, Tenn.*

> *My dear Mrs. Evans:*   *December 14, 1950*
>
> What you say in your letter of December second regarding your loved ones has been carefully noted by the President. It is his earnest hope that you may be sustained by the well deserved pride which must be yours in the realization of your sons' devoted service at a most critical period in the history of our Nation.
>
> With the thought that you might like to have it, there is enclosed a copy of the communique of December eighth.
>
> Please accept this expression of the President's every good wish.
>
> > *Very sincerely yours,*
> > *WILLIAM D. HASSETT*
> > *Secretary to the President*

Hassett, a devout Catholic, also took the unusual step of answering a letter from a little girl in Cincinnati.

> *Dear Mr. President:*   *December 1, 1950*
> This is a just war and we must fight, but we are going to have to answer to God for the methods we use. Is the atomic bomb justified in His eyes. We need prayer and penance, these are our best weapons. Let's use them instead of the A bomb.
>
> > *Sincerely yours,*
> > *(Miss) Dorothy Borshelt*
> > *Cincinnati, OH*

> *My dear Miss Borshelt:*   *December 7, 1950*
> This will acknowledge the receipt of your letter of December first to the President. I want to assure you that your spiritual interest in writing is appreciated.
>
> > *WILLIAM D. HASSETT*
> > *Secretary to the President*

The joint communiqué released after Truman's conference with Prime Minister Attlee reviewed the situation in Korea and stated:

> For our part we are ready, as we have always been to seek an end to the hostilities by means of negotiation. The same principles of international conduct should be applied in this situation as are applied, in accordance with our obligations under the Charter of the United Nations, to any threat to world peace. Every effort must be made to achieve the purposes of the United Nations in Korea by peaceful means and to find a solution of the Korean problem on the basis of a free and independent Korea. We are confident that the great majority of the United Nations takes the same view. If the Chinese on their side display any evidence of a similar attitude, we are hopeful that the cause of peace can be upheld. If they do not, then it will be for the peoples of the world, acting through the United Nations, to decide how the principles of the Charter can best be maintained. For our part, we declare in advance our firm resolve to uphold them.[22]

A number of letters from various religious organizations against the use of the bomb were posted around the end of the first week of December, apparently as part of an organized effort, and all were duly answered with a Hassett Valentine. As soon as the public perceived that use of the weapon was not needed or likely to be used to stave off disaster in Korea, however, it was rarely mentioned in correspondence. Reference to the atom bomb again fell off to almost nothing, and even the explosion of mail following the MacArthur firing saw it mentioned hardly at all. The detonation of the hydrogen bomb near the end of his administration, on November 1, 1952, generated few letters and telegrams.

Dear Sir: *March 17, 1952*

My husband and I plan to visit Washington with our young son this Easter.

The boy has three great desires for this trip. One to attend Easter Services at the Presbyterian Church in the nation's capital. (He is a would be minister at the age of 8.) A visit to the Smithsonian Museum since he also plans to be a paleontologist when "he is not too busy as a minister." (The ambitions of the very young!!) And the more normal desire—for his age—to participate in the children's Easter Egg party usually held on the lawns at the White House.

We do not know if the letter sent is by invitation only and dislike to promise anything we cannot fulfill. Would you be kind enough to let me know whether or not this event is open to the general public.

I will greatly appreciate a reply.

Yours truly,
Ruth Catherine Sills
New York, N.Y.

My dear Mrs. Sills: *March 21, 1952*

This is in acknowledgment of your letter of March seventeenth, regarding the Easter Monday egg rolling at the White House. I am indeed very sorry to disappoint your little son, but this event was discontinued at the beginning of World War II and has not been held since. This decision was made because of the food situation and other conditions which have made impractical to plan such an occasion since then. Thank you, nevertheless, for your friendly interest in writing.

Very sincerely yours,
WILLIAM D. HASSETT
Secretary to the President

CHAPTER EIGHT

KOREA

"As you have been directly responsible for the loss of our son's life in Korea, you might just as well keep this emblem on display in your trophy room."
—from a father who sent his son's Purple Heart to Truman

The confused, vicious fighting that marked the first year of "police action" on the Korean Peninsula frequently resulted in no witnesses being available to confirm the death of a soldier or marine. To make matters worse, the North Koreans supplied no lists of prisoners in their hands. All too often, the ambiguous phrase "missing in action" was the sole information to be supplied to a parent or young wife, and even when a death was confirmed, recovery of a body at an ill-defined location now miles behind enemy lines was virtually impossible. Even when servicemen were hastily interred within U.S. lines, it was difficult to reexhume, get positive identifications, and prepare the bodies for shipment to the United States in the heat of the emergency.

Grieving families understood this very well, but some, nevertheless, turned to their president for help in bringing their boys home. The quick shipment of Gen. Walton H. Walker's body, after his death in a December 1950 jeep accident on an icy Korean road, was particularly galling to a widow of a sergeant who had been killed many months earlier in Pusan.

Dear Sir: *January 5, 1951*
To make this short and to the point, I am a sad widow of a soldier, killed in Korea on September 7, 1950.

I'd like to know if a soldier's high rank, made him better to be brought home right away for a safe burial, than for my Sgt. first class husband. If I had my way, and could get to Korea, I'd accompany my husband's body home too.

I've been very bitter about all this, and there are a lot of others who feel this way too. When I look around and see what little it matters to the big guys, that my daughters have lost a father, I can't help the bitterness. Sgt. Young was a good, faithful and true soldier for nine long years, and the Army always came before all else, including we, his family. Such faithfulness, when the family took the brunt of it, deserves better understanding, such as thousands of other soldiers.

Of course I realize the impossiblity of the shipments of bodies now, when so many more things are so very important to the war cause.

But I am waiting for the day when my husband's body can be laid to rest, from the home he bought for us, not a year ago and was so very proud of.

One more matter please.

I should like to know why the G. I. Insurance Company wants to make it so hard for a widow to get the money that is so rightfully hers, and which was also paid for by my husband. To get my insurance in a lump sum (which they don't want to do) to be paid on our home, seems very little to ask for, when a father and husband that was so very loved and adored, has been given up.

Thank you, sincerely, Mr. President, for your respectful attention.

Respectfully yours,
Mrs. Shirley Young
Salem, NJ

Like nearly all letters of this type, the original was "respectfully referred" by Hassett to the Department of Defense "for sympathetic attention and acknowledgment." In the days before photocopiers, the decision to send a copy of a letter to the Veterans Administration, in this case because of the widow's reference to problems in obtaining her husband's life insurance, necessitated that one of the office secretaries type a duplicate. Frequently a carbon copy would also be made and retained in White House files. The same procedure was followed for the next letter, posted several months later, and Hassett also wrote a response.

My dear President: March 30, 1951

I read in our local newspaper, where you found it in your heart to take some lady's only son off the fighting front. What a grand thing to do for one individual. So I am writing with the hopes you can spare a few minutes of your valuable time, to see if you could help me.

I received word on September 20, 1950 my only son was killed fighting for me and his country in Korea on Sept. 8, 1950. He went through the 2nd World War without a scratch. He saw action in France, Austria, Luxembourg, and Germany. It only took 4 or 5 weeks to get killed in Korea. It nearly drove me mad. I wrote right away to General Witsell and asked if I could please have his body sent home. I know a lady who got her son's body in 5 weeks. That was in July. My son got to Korea the last of July or the first part of August. So his body won't be away in where they are fighting now. I so desperately want his body here in our family plot.

I received word around Oct. 3, 1950 they had no record of a burial for him. I wrote again and on Dec. 11, 1950 I was told his remains had been buried in a U.N. Military grave in Korea. That made me feel better and gave me courage to wait. Then on Dec. 30, 1950 they wrote again and said, "I regret that it is not possible to assure you that the remains of your son will be returned."

Sir, I know every minute of your time is most valuable, especially now during this war, when you are straining every effort yourself for your country. If you could only sanction to the right office it may be possible for me to get my dearly beloved son's remains home and buried before I pass on.

I have an incurable ailment. I was in the hospital in June of 1948 with the intention of having gallstones removed. They found the stones were in my pancreas (lower bowel) where they cannot operate. So after 3 blood transfusions, several saline solution transfusions, I was released to be on a strict diet and pills to digest my food, but the doctor told me if I had another attack and could not fight it off, I would die. Therefore, if there is a possible way you can help me to get his body home, will you please? It may be impossible; if you think it is, I would like to know that too, so I will not keep on waiting, praying, and hoping.

If those dirty Russian dogs take South Korea from us (but they can't, you and God won't let them), they would never let anyone in there to get a body or anything else. He was in Korea the last of July or the first part of August so his body can't be so far in Korea—nowhere near where they are fighting now. If some miracle could happen, and I could get his body home and buried so when I go I could occupy the grave next to him and he wouldn't be so many, many miles away . . . it wouldn't be hard at all to go when my time comes.

Very sincerely,
Mrs. Genevieve J. Lang
Sacramento, Calif.

My dear Mrs. Lang: April 3, 1951

The President was deeply touched by your letter of March thirtieth. He realizes the burden of grief under which you wrote and asks me to assure you of his heartfelt sympathy. As the years pass he hopes that you will always be comforted by the knowledge that your son made the supreme sacrifice in defense of our country and freedom-loving everywhere.

By direction of the President, the requests you make are being referred for the consideration of the appropriate officials of the Department of Defense and the Veterans' Administration.

Very sincerely yours,
WILLIAM D. HASSETT

Unless it was to be sent to more than one government department, a letter ordinarily would not be copied by a typist before it left the White House; the only thing Hassett's office would retain would be the name and address of a correspondent, the date and ultimate destination of the letter, and a one-sentence synopsis. The practice of laboriously retyping *complete* letters about battle casualties, instead of just portions pertaining to, for example, insurance questions, may simply have been done as a safeguard in the event that a request might be brought to the attention of a constituent's representative in Congress if the writer received no satisfaction. The order to perform such labor-intensive action probably came from Hassett or Truman because of the highly charged nature of the subject. The president and most of his senior staff had experienced the ravages of war firsthand, and Truman, moreover, had written letters to the parents of soldiers who died under his command in the First World War. They all knew well what the next of kin were going through, but even knowing someone in the White House, like Press Secretary Joseph Short, was no guarantee of high-level intervention.

Dear Mr. Short: Oct. 31, 1951

Sometime ago I wrote you recalling our association in the Richmond, Va., bureau of the A.P., and mentioning that my only son had enlisted in the Marine Corps.

We received word from the Marine Corps last Tuesday, Oct. 23rd., that our son had been killed in action October 17th, in the Korean area. While I do not wish to put anyone "on the spot" I am anxious to have the body of our son returned to us as soon as possible, and with this thought in mind have been wondering if there is anything you can do, or if it does not place you in an embarrassing position, you could ask the President to do what he can to expedite the return of our son.

I know there are many other fathers and mothers who have sons buried in Korea and would like to have them returned quickly. I also believe that any of them would make the same request that I'm making if they had someone to intercede for them.

I shall always be grateful for any help or advice you may be able to offer.

Our son's address in Korea was: PFC. Leonard Vernon Todd, Jr., 151829, USMC., "A" Co., 1st tank battalion, First Marine Division.

With kindest regards I am,

Sincerely,
L. V. Todd, Sr.

Dear Todd: November 3, 1951

I am distressed to learn that your son was killed in action in Korea. You have my deepest sympathy.

I am asking the Navy to check into the possibility of bringing the body back soon. You shall hear from me further.

Sincerely yours,
JOSEPH SHORT

Truman's naval aide, Rear Adm. Robert Dennison, apparently placed some phone calls for Short and confirmed what he probably already knew—that processing the young private's body could not be easily expedited without disrupting the strained and undermanned system. It is also likely that there was an additional factor in the decision not to request special treatment for the Marine's body. If word leaked out through one of the father's news media associates of "favoritism" by the White House, a simple effort to be of assistance could well be taken as a slap in the face by families in similar circumstance who were not so well connected. As a practical matter, however, the expression of interest from a representative of the president is likely to have been felt down the chain of command and at least helped ensure that the private's body would not be further delayed in its journey home.

Dear Todd: November 6, 1951

I am enclosing a copy of a memorandum to me from Rear Admiral Robert L. Dennison, USN. I am sorry this report is not more optimistic, but I feel sure you will understand. Those have suffered the most usually are the most understanding.

Again may I express my sympathy for you and your family. You have my high personal regards.

Sincerely yours,
JOSEPH SHORT

MEMORANDUM FOR: Mr. Short, 5 November 1951

Subject: PFC Leonard Vernon TODD, Jr., USMC—father requests return of remains from Korea as soon as possible.

Mr. Todd's desire to have his son's remains returned to the United States as soon as possible is fully appreciated. I have investigated this possibility and greatly regret that it is not possible for cognizant authorities to state at this time exactly when PFC Todd's remains will be returned. The return of our dead from Korea is being carried out as expeditiously as possible. There are many factors and conditions which necessarily must govern the orderly accomplishment of this task. It would be unfair to many others in circumstances similar to Mr. Todd's to ask that this program be interrupted and possibly delayed in order to meet the wishes of any one individual. You may assure Mr. Todd, however, that just as soon as it becomes possible to determine the probable date PFC Todd's remains can be returned, he will promptly be notified by the Department of Defense.

Robert L. Dennison

Though the president's staff steered clear of granting preferential treatment that could come back to bite their boss, Truman jumped in with both feet when he learned that officials of a cemetery halted the solemn proceedings at the grave site of a soldier killed in Korea even as one of the escorting soldiers was readying his bugle to play "Taps" over the flag-draped casket. Sgt. 1st Class John R. Rice of the 1st Cavalry Division had fought in World War II and was killed in action on September 6, 1950. His body had finally reached the United States nearly a year later and was being buried at the Memorial Park Cemetery in Sioux City, Iowa, on August 28, 1951, when authorities at the "restricted" facility learned that he was an American Indian of the Winnebago tribe. Rice's wife, a white woman, had bought the plot without noticing the fine print that limited its use to "only members of the Caucasian race."

The sergeant's body was taken to a funeral home in Winnebago, Nebraska, and Army officials immediately offered to arrange transportation by military hearse and burial with full honors at any national cemetery the widow desired. Several in nearby states were discussed, and the widow chose Fort Leavenworth, Kansas, as her husband's final resting place. Meanwhile, the soldiers who had originally escorted the body to Sioux City, indignant over the treatment of Sergeant Rice and his widow, reported the incident to the press. Truman read about it the following morning and immediately offered, through his military aide, General Vaughan, to make a space available at Arlington National Cemetery if Mrs. Rice desired her husband to be interred there. The widow, Evelyn Rice, accepted Truman's offer, and her husband was buried in Arlington.

Critics of the president claimed that if the Indian had not been a soldier killed in Korea, the whole sorry affair would not have come to public attention. Others, ignoring that religion is something one chooses but that the ethnicity of an individual is no option, tried to equate segregated cemeteries with those set up and limited to various religious groups, noting that even Arlington is "restricted" to veterans. Upon reading an editorial making these points and more, a writer in Syracuse, New York, felt that the White House should respond.

> *To the Secretary to the President,*   *Sept. 1, 1951*
> Dear Sir:
> Sorry to trouble you this detail, but as a loyal Democrat and a great admirer of President Truman I could not allow it to pass.
> The enclosed editorial from a local paper is only one of many vicious ones that this editor has written. I think this one should be rebutted.
> This man [Alexander F.] Jones came up here from your city and he is such a bitter partisan that he influences many people who don't think.

He was bitterly biased in his writings on the MacArthur matter when such papers as the *Herald-Tribune* supported the dismissal. He has been caustic on all of his writings on the entire Korean situation.

I would be pleased to have you answer this terrible false editorial.

> *Very truly yours,*
> *William A. Maloney,*
> *Real Estate Broker, Auctioneer*
> *Syracuse, New York*

Dear Mr. Maloney: *Sept. 7, 1951*

Thank you for your courtesy in sending to us the article about Sergeant Rice which appeared in the *Syracuse Herald-Tribune*.

The President's action in the case of Sergeant Rice was simple and straightforward. Sergeant Rice was killed in the service of his country and when he was refused burial in a cemetery chosen by his wife, the President arranged to have him buried in Arlington. He did this as a matter of simple justice and has made no heroics about it.

This has nothing whatsoever to do with the plight of the Navajo or Hopi Indians or any other tribe. Besides, the President cannot be blamed for alleged conditions which presumably have existed for many years, nor for a lack of appropriations which are made by Congress.

Your interest is sincerely appreciated.

> *Sincerely yours,*
> *IRVING PERLMETER*
> *Assistant Secretary*

Public response as a whole was so favorable to Truman's action that there was no reason to do anything other than let the many supportive editorials and letters to the editor speak for him. Letters and telegrams to the president were laudatory and came at a time when Truman, after nearly six and a half years in office, was clearly tiring of his job and needed the words of encouragment.

Dear Mr. President: *Aug. 28, 1951*

Congratulations on your stand concerning the burial of John R. Rice (killed in action 6 Sept., 1950).

If the authorities at Memorial Park Cemetery in Sioux City, Iowa are too bigoted to receive his body, I am glad that you have decreed his final resting place to be Arlington National Cemetery.

I <u>may not agree with you in other matters but in this one I stand at your side.</u>

> *Very sincerely yours,*
> *Wallace J. Gleekman*
> *Dorchester, Mass.*

Dear Mr. Truman: *Aug. 30, 1951*

<u>Congratulations on your Christian act in offering to the family of Army Sgt. John R. Rice a place in Arlington National Cemetery for the Sgt.'s body</u>.

This act will greatly emphasize to the American people that we must all live together in peace, and this should help break down prejudices against some races.

America has become the greatest and strongest nation in the world because it has been a melting pot of many different peoples of the world, with each nationality making great contributions to our progress.

Best regards.

> *Cordially yours,*
> *Chester Bryant*
> *Knoxville, Tenn.*

Dear Mr. President: *Aug. 30, 1951*

It was with a deep sense of disgust that I read in the papers of the incident in connection with the <u>burial of Sgt. Rice in Sioux City, Iowa</u>.

As a veteran of World War II, <u>I heartily applaud your action</u> in authorizing the burial in Arlington Cemetery and providing transportation for the family. Having recently been privileged to visit the Cemetery, I know that Sgt. Rice will rest in peace among his fellow soldiers of all races, including The Unknown Soldier, "Whose identity (and race) are known but to God."

My <u>best wishes for success in your fight for what you believe to be right for the American people</u>.

> *Very truly yours,*
> *Joel L. Guthman*
> *Brooklyn, NY*

For the above correspondents and many others, Hassett prepared a form Valentine: "My dear [name]: This is to thank you for your letter of [date] in commendation of the President's action regarding the case of John R. Rice. It was most thoughtful of you to write. Very sincerely yours. . . ." But Hassett dictated a special Valentine to a little girl in Monrovia, California.

> *Dear President Trman:*   *Aug. 29, 1951*
> I just wanted to tell you what a fine thing you did for Sgt. Rice. I think an American Indian has more right to be buried in this country than anyone else. I think that place he called his home town was stinking not to let him be buried there. They thought he was good enough to fight for them in Korea and die for them. I'll bet he'll be much happier there with the other heroes. <u>I am nine years old</u> and when I get to be 21, I want to go and feed the Indians. <u>I hope you will run for president when I am 21 so I can vote for you</u>. My Mom and Pop don't always agree with you, but they sure agree with me that you have a wonderful big heart in doing this fine thing.

Beneath little Kathy's letter, which was pecked out on what was apparently a very old but still quite functional typewriter, her mother wrote an additional note.

> [Longhand] *Kathy wrote this to you after hearing the news broad-cast about Sgt. Rice. She was very indignant about the whole affair. The wording and typing is hers, with a little help from her Mom on the spelling. She also wants you to have her picture.*
>   *Mrs. Arlene Thompson*

> *My dear Kathy:*   *September 8, 1951*
> The President asks me to thank you for your letter of August twenty-ninth with which you enclosed the very nice picture of yourself. He does indeed appreciate your kind thought in writing in commendation of his action regarding the case of Sergeant John R. Rice and sends best wishes to you and your parents.
>   *Very sincerely yours,*
>   *WILLIAM D. HASSETT*

Many American Indians also wrote to Truman.

My dear Mr. President: *Aug. 29, 1951*

My friends and my family are very <u>grateful for your action in the</u> <u>case of SGT. John R. RICE</u>, who was killed in action against the enemy in the Korean War, to be buried with due honors in Arlington Cemetery.

This appropriate action substantiates the fact that this is a democratic country.

Very respectfully yours,
Sam Little
San Diego, Calif.

Dear Brother Truman: *Sept. 4, 1951*

I would if it were possible to express what is in my heart at a time like this, words are so inadequate to the task of my wishes them to perform, it seems impossible to give expressions to my true thoughts.

I am in all humility an ordinary everyday Mason and an American Indian, while it isn't possible to put my real feelings into words, I believe you know in your heart how deeply <u>I appreciate the honor</u> <u>you have bestowed upon our fellow American, the late Sgt. John R.</u> <u>Rice of the Winnebago Tribe of Indians,</u> who sacrificed his life overseas in defending the liberties we enjoy as Free Men and to the sorrowing family in their hour of need.

"Thank you" seems so inadequate, my Brother and Great White Father in Washington, but <u>I believe you know how I feel about your</u> <u>wonderful display of Loyalty, Courage, and Determination, we</u> <u>Americans hold sacred, our National Heritage to be God given and</u> <u>we shall continue to guard it zealously.</u>

Fraternally yours,
Clarence Jefferson
Shiprock, NM

Member:

Sac and Fox Tribe West of Mississippi (Tama County, Iowa).

Animas Lodge No. 15—Ancient Free and Accepted Masons of New Mexico (Farmington).

Zuni Council No. 3—Royal and Select Masters of New Mexico (Gallup).

Navajo Chapter No. 18—Royal Arch Masons of New Mexico (Gallup).

Baldwyn Commandry No. 12—Knights Templar of New Mexico (Gallup).

Dear President Truman: *Sept. 3, 1951*

The members of our Indian organization read of your act as regards Sgt. John R. Rice who died in action in Korea. We are ashamed that officials of Sioux City did the cruel thing that they did, refusing to bury an Indian in their cemetery. We were proud of you, Brother, when we read of you allowing our warrior to be buried in the Arlington Cemetery. We want you to know that we are grateful to you and appreciate it very much. May the Great Spirit bless your home for defending one of your people.

> *Cordially yours,*
> *Ray Fadden (Ra ia Tons), Sec.*
> *Akwesasne Mohawk Counselor Organization*
> *St. Regis Mohawk Reservation*
> *Hogansburg, NY*

My dear Mr. Fadden: *September 11, 1951*

This is to thank you for the letter of September third, with the enclosure, in behalf of your organization, in commendation of the President's action regarding the case of Sergeant John R. Rice. You may be assured that he appreciates your thought in writing and is grateful for your prayerful wishes.

> *Very sincerely yours,*
> *WILLIAM D. HASSETT*

Truman's offer that the Indian soldier be laid to rest in Arlington did little to soften the indignation of a woman who fired off a telegram from San Francisco.

THE PRESIDENT THE WHITE HOUSE   1951 AUG 31

IF THE INDIANS ARE GOING TO BE PUT OUT OF THE GRAVE-YARDS THEN ALL AMERICANS SHOULD SHUT UP AND LET THE RUS-SIANS COME IN.

ANN SHAHAN.

Another woman, writing from Dobbs Ferry, New York, reflected on how much impact the actions of the president can have on how Americans, as a people, view themselves.

> *Dear Mr. President:*   *Aug. 30, 1951*
>
> I want to say thank you for your <u>action in the Sgt. John R. Rice case</u>. You must have known how burned up many of us were when we heard the news. This type of truly un-American incident makes one feel ashamed and embarrassed for all Americans. It required an action like yours to bring back our feeling of self-respect.
>
> Today there must be many who share my gratitude for having you as our President.
>
> *Sincerely yours,*
> *Lenda Persiko*
> *Dobbs Ferry, NY*

Unlike the following letter from a man in Richmond, Indiana, few expressed the obvious connection between the plight of the Indians and Black Americans.

> *Dear Mr. President:*   *Sept. 6, 1951*
>
> <u>A few words to thank you for your timely words and kind action in achieving a worthy burial for Sgt. John Rice</u> and bringing comfort to not only his widow and family but to millions of Americans who ask and believe in fair treatment of their fellow Americans regardless of the color of their skin or the manner in which they worship. <u>I can only hope that in the future you will speak out with the same frank courage about the shameful way in which our Negroes in the armed forces are daily insulted, humiliated and sometimes brutally murdered by so-called officers of the law, especially in our southern states</u>, and thereby prove to the world that we practice at home what we preach abroad.
>
> *Respectfully yours,*
> *H. A. Bledsoe*
> *Richmond, Ind.*

A similar outpouring of letters did not occur over the problems experienced by the family trying to bury their son, Thomas C. Reed, a black private who was killed in action on June 3, 1951. This probably had to do with several factors. Most Americans had never really seen Indians, who tended to live far from most population centers, and could champion Rice's cause more easily than Reed's, which struck much closer to home. Coming directly on the heels of the Rice incident, the new controversy also had an "old news" quality, which worked against the likehood that it would generate as much passion. Moreover, the situation was much more ambiguous, since the Phoenix cemetery at the center of the dispute was indeed burying black soldiers in the formerly all-white veterans' plot.

As at many cemeteries around the country that carried a variety of religious or racial restrictions, the operators of the Greenwood Memorial Park feared that they could be sued by the families or lot holders who had purchased grave sites under the expectation that the cemetery was restricted. With passage of civil-rights legislation still over a decade away, cemeteries breaking the earlier contracts at that time had no legal protection from such suits yet felt a moral obligation to honor men who died fighting for their country. Greenwood's board of trustees came up with a plan that they believed would make it politically difficult for anyone filing such a suit. The family of a fallen black soldier needed to get three local veterans' organizations to file requests that he be interred in the cemetery. Then, if complaints were made by white lot holders, the cemetery could appeal to their sense of patriotism—and perhaps a fear of ostricism—if they pressed the matter.

Four black soldiers were buried at Greenwood Memorial Park under this plan, but Private Reed's family objected to the idea that these additional hurdles would have to be jumped solely because their son was not white. The wrangling went on for five weeks as Private Reed lay in a Phoenix mortuary. The situation eventually made its way into newspapers around the country on January 7, 1952, when the chairman of the cemetery board announced that he was calling the trustees together for a meeting, since the Veterans of Foreign Wars, Disabled Veterans, and American Legion had made blanket requests that black soldiers be buried in the cemetery simply on the request of the next of kin.

> *Mr. President:*   *January 8, 1952*
> I am sitting here in my humble home with a heavy heart after reading the paper about the Negro veteran who died in Korea and whose body has been in the mortuary in Phoenix, Arizona, since November 28, 1951.
> Just because he is a Negro, they won't let his body be buried in the veterans' cemetery. Now Mr. President, just think of the young

man fighting in Korea, and then being brought back to his home where they won't even give him a place to rest after fighting for his country. Or was it his country?, as he has no place to rest. Think of your son if you had one. I had one in World War II, and he hasn't been much good since he came home, but I was proud to have him come home alive.

Mr. Truman, think of Mothers who have boys fighting and the Mothers yet to give their sons. Put you and your wife in their places. I know that if you were a Negro, you would not feel right. If Negro boys are good enough to fight and die for their country, then they should be good enough to be buried any place their folks want them buried!! The town should honor them that much.

These such things that happen over here don't fit in so well with the world. If you are able to end strikes, it seems as though you could put a stop to this. We are all human, and I don't think one race is any better than the other. And I'm no Communist!! I am a full-blooded American and proud of it. Except I feel sorry for some of the Americans. My husband is a Mason, himself, and I am an Eastern Star. So you can just imagine how I feel.

I sincerely hope you and others will take heed of this letter. And I should like very much to have an answer from you immediately.

> *Sincerely,*
> *Mrs. Katherine D. Howard*
> *Long Beach, Calif.*

Unlike Rice's case, this controversy was part of the ongoing battle over civil rights, and although there were fewer letters arriving at the White House over this matter, Truman's staff prepared a formal response.

Dear Mrs. Howard: *14 January 1952*

The President has requested me to acknowledge your letter of 8 January 1952 concerning the burial of Pfc. Thomas C. Reed.

On Monday, 7 January, this matter first came to our attention and I telephoned at once to the Mayor of Phoenix, Arizona. He informed me that he would take immediate action and felt certain the distressing incident could be resolved by the local authorities.

I was very pleased to learn during the following forty-eight hours that the necessary arrangements had been made, and that Private Reed had been laid to rest in the cemetery of his family's choice.

It is most regrettable that the family of this soldier who gave his life for his country was subjected to this additional strain. Our feelings in this matter are, of course, the same as yours and the President desires me to thank you for your letter.

> Sincerely,
> HARRY H. VAUGHAN
> Major General, USAR
> Military Aide to the President

One of the first countries to aid the United Nations' effort in Korea was Turkey, which sent a full brigade of more than 5,000 combat troops to fight as part of the U.S. Eighth Army. They were also some of the very first troops to face the Chinese onslaught in the late fall of 1950 and suffered heavy casualties during the initial fighting. A young boy, whose own family had fled the communists only a few years earlier, understood very well that somewhere in Turkey there were boys about his age whose fathers had been killed fighting communism. He hoped Truman would provide the conduit for his own modest effort to help, and left no return street address.

> Valdis Vinkels,
> Andover (only),
> Conn.

Letter to the President, pm 12/24/51. (Rec'd in file room 2/11/52.)
The writer is a displaced person's son, 12 yrs. of age, who came to the United States two years ago from Latvia. He requests the President to send the enclosed five dollars, which he earned carrying newspapers, to some Turkish boy whose father has been killed in combat in Korea. Says they are very thankful to the President and the United States for bringing them to this country. Enclosed is a Five-Dollar bill ($5.00), Federal Reserve Note, Series of 1934 D, Serial No. B 69439000 C.

> *February 11, 1952*

Respectfully referred to the Department of State for appropriate handling and suitable acknowledgment.

RECEIPT REQUESTED

> WILLIAM D. HASSETT
> Secretary to the President

February 11, 1952

Received from the White House a letter to the President from Valdis Vinkels, Andover, Conn., pm 12/24/51, together with the following:

A Five-Dollar Bill ($5.00), Federal Reserve Note, Series of 1934D, Serial No. B 69439000 C.

Received by P. Knox
Department of State
Delivered by [Charles D.] McCloud
White House Messenger

Americans were greatly concerned over the fate of the many thousands of servicemen missing in Korea. During the opening months of the war, the murder of U.S. and South Korean prisoners of war was a frequent occurrence generally believed to be perpetrated by frightened or vindictive soldiers in uncontrolled small units. But as North Korea troops attempted to extricate themselves from the south after the landings at Inch'on, mass executions of POWs, landowners, police, government workers, and their families were carried out in a systematic manner by the communists.

After fighting their way back across the 38th Parallel, U.N. forces discovered many groups of murdered POWs. For example, of the 370 Americans marched north from Seoul's Sodaemun Prison on September 27, just before the city's liberation, about 300 were still alive on the night of Tuesday, October 17, when they were herded into two freight trains in Pyongyang. The rest had died of starvation, dysentery, or exposure. Many more died as the train creaked toward China, although a lucky few slipped away to freedom. On Friday, as one of the trains took refuge in a tunnel from U.N. air strikes, the train's last 89 POWs were fired on while waiting for their evening meal in a nearby field. Twenty-one survived by feigning death or escaping into the brush and were safeguarded by North Korean civilians until the 1st Cavalry Division overran the area.

China's stunning entry into the war in late 1950 had sent U.N. forces reeling almost as far south as the defensive positions they had held in the summer, and the subsequent seesaw battles of 1951 resulted in the same ground being taken, lost, and retaken as communist forces were slowly forced back above the 38th Parallel, which divided North and South Korea. Throughout the confused, brutal fighting, the number of Americans then listed as "missing in action" inextricably grew into the thousands. The many confirmed instances of atrocities being committed against American prisoners, and the communists' prolonged refusal to allow the International Red Cross to inspect POW camps—or even release the names of the prisoners they held—all added to the strain on families back home.

Dear Mr. Truman: *November 15, 1951*

As a citizen of these United States this is my first letter to a President, but I feel it is my duty to write you.

As you know the Korean War opened on June 25, 1950. On July 26, 1950 my mother received a telegram from the Defense Department saying <u>my brother Pfc. Lee B. Reed, R.A. 13165926 was missing in action since July 7, 1950. One month later, August 23, 1950, another telegram came from the Defense Department stating my brother was a prisoner of war</u> based on information through the International Red Cross. As of today we have had no further information. <u>Can you imagine our suspense and anxiety over these past fifteen months? By God's help we have survived in some way.</u>

The local Red Cross has tried to help us find out if he is still alive but to no avail. Also the Defense Department has sent us the address to write Prisoners of War and four letters to my mother's knowledge have gone out to him but still no answer.

<u>Yesterday I learned of the terrible 5,500 atrocities committed on our prisoners of war by the Reds.</u> Naturally our hearts sank, along with all the other families over the United States who had been notified of their loved ones being held prisoners. <u>We had held to a spark of hope, but now it seems we have nothing to cling to. My sympathy to each and every one.</u>

<u>Therefore, Mr. Truman, I am asking you to investigate and in some way or other find out if my brother Pfc. Lee B. Reed, R.A. 13165926, Co. K, 34th Inf. Regt., is alive and still a prisoner or was among the 5,500 boys</u> massacred. I fear so much he was in the group. I realize the fact he is just one of the missing in this war, but I feel <u>if your daughter, Margaret,</u> was in the place of my brother you would be taking the same steps.

Sincerely,
Mrs. Monnie Reed Boothe
Ronceverte, West Virginia

The information on the status of American POWs changed so frequently that Vaughan, Truman's military aide, asked Col. John R. Beishline in the Army chief of staff's office to prepare a response to Mrs. Boothe.

Dear Mrs. Boothe: *29 December 1951*

The President has asked me to reply to your letter of 15 November 1951, concerning your brother, Private First Class Lee B. Reed, who is reported to be a prisoner of war in the custody of the Communists.

The Provost Marshal General of the Army informs me that the name of your brother was not included in the list of names released by the enemy of the prisoners supposed to be held in their custody. While this information is discouraging, it is emphasized that the list was furnished by the Communists, and we all know their lack of regard for the truth. Please be assured that every effort is still being made to obtain further information about your brother and other missing persons, and that any information concerning your brother will be promptly forwarded to you by the Department of the Army.

The International Committee of the Red Cross has tried repeatedly, but without success, to obtain permission to enter the area controlled by the Communists and perform the traditional Red Cross services for prisoners of war. Unfortunately, therefore, we are unable to tell you whether your brother is receiving your letters and whether all Americans held by the Communists are being permitted to send letters back to the United States.

The information released to the press in the Hanley Report has not been accepted as official pending complete investigation of the sources upon which the information was based. In all cases where definite facts about any person have been established and verified, the person to be notified in case of emergency has been notified immediately. It is regretted that you have been caused so much added anxiety, as it is the desire of the President to avoid in every way possible the causing of additional distress to the familiies of our military personnel.

The President shares your concern for the safety of your brother, and he asks me to extend to you and to your family his heartfelt sympathy during this period of uncertainty.

Sincerely,
HARRY H. VAUGHAN

Speculation abounded on just how many men languished in the POW camps, and numerous correspondents sent in newspaper clippings with estimates climbing upward to 10,000. As in the previous letter, mention of Truman's daughter was frequently made in an effort to elicit the president's sympathy and action.

Dear Mr. President:
I have reason to believe one of the above mentioned prisoners is my son. He is as dear to me as your daughter Margaret is to you.
Let him come home to his father and me and his little year-old son soon.

> *Mrs. Thomas Peasner, Sr.*
> *Lancaster, Texas*

Representatives of the United Nations and communist armies began armistice negotiations in July 1951. With the suspension of all U.N. offensive operations in November of that year, the thrust and counterthrust at the truce table became the only discernible maneuvers in what had become a self-imposed stalemate. Originally the communists had believed that the lack of information on POWs would prompt dissension among Americans and engender a weakening of resolve to continue the war. It soon became apparent, however, that their actions were not providing the desired results. After some stalling, a list of prisoners was finally released, but the number added up to only a sixth of the Americans they earlier had claimed to have captured. Now that it suited their purposes, the communists also began to allow their captives to write letters home. The prisoners were being given a steady diet of propaganda and misinformation, which the communists believed would encourage a defeatist attitude in their letters and precipitate a drumbeat of calls to end the fighting quickly—in effect, on the communists' terms—from their families and other concerned Americans. The first in a series of letters from a POW's wife in St. Louis demonstrates that they were at least partially successful.

President Truman: *Jan. 21-52*
As I sit and write this letter I know you will never read it—much less acknowledge it. This is a letter asking you if there is a chance that the war in Korea will end in the near future. You may say "I do not know." I believe that you and Congress can end it.
July 2nd, 1950, my husband was sent to Korea—for two weeks— a police action. Sir, my husband has been a prisoner of war for the

last eighteen months, needless to say it has been more like eighteen years to his loved ones. July 11th, our group was surrounded, and a majority of our men killed. I have been very fortunate—my husband's name was on the POW list released by the Chinese and January 7th, I received my first letter. He states that his health is good *now*, but are you aware sir, that our men sitting in the prison camps know about the truce talks? Can you imagine their feelings, when day after day the word—"no progress," is released. I doubt if there is a man alive who would be willing to sit these talks out in place of a war prisoner. I fully realize that I am not the only wife hoping and waiting—many of our dearest friends were among the families whose hearts were broken when the list was released.

Perhaps I had better mention, sir, that I believe in our wonderful country—I want nothing to happen to it or our people. Now may I state how I feel about the Korean conflict.

Our delegates go to the meetings with the idea we want this and that. We do not want a military buildup in North Korea, but we establish a military school in South Korea. There are no victors in war—I was in Japan and knew a lot of those young men who lost their lives—I do not believe God means for us to fight with guns. What good has ever come from war? If these actions keep on, our country will have our young men stationed throughout the world, leaving our women and children unprotected. I have two children, one is a boy four years old. Am I raising him to send him off to a distant land? Our generation has known nothing but war.

Please sir, end this horrible war. Are our men going to be left sitting if our attention is called elsewhere? My husband is alive now and I want him back soon, very soon. We, the little people did not send our boys to Korea—it is time the men responsible bring them back. Several of our men were ransomed recently after a few days in prison. Let's not forget the other men who are waiting.

May God grant you the wisdom and the foresight to do the proper thing.

I and the other thousands of people are waiting—

Sincerely,
Mrs. Jane Culbertson
St. Louis, Mo.

My dear Mrs. Culbertson: *February 2, 1952*

Your letter of January twenty-first to the President has been received. With reference to the Korean situation, please let me assure you that everything possible is being done to bring a peaceful conclusion to negotiations in Korea, but we must understand, too, that such an involved program is necessarily slow. It is the President's firm belief that this conflict will be over when the Communists realize that the free nations of the world, including the United States, will not submit to their plan of conquest. He does not know how soon that will be, but all of us are praying, with God's help, it will be soon.

The President is very glad that you felt free to express your thoughts to him, as no one is more sympathetic than he with you and the loved ones of all our servicemen who have been called upon to share the demands made upon us in these unsettled times when it is necessary to use our armed forces, and those of our allies, for the protection of our heritage of freedom. As the President constantly strives to find the right answers to all these problems, it helps him immeasurably to know that you are remembering him in your prayers for Divine guidance.

Very sincerely yours,
WILLIAM D. HASSETT

Meanwhile, the Red Chinese were also becoming more adept at psychological warfare directed against troops in the field. The widespread and well-documented murders of U.S. and South Korean prisoners by North Korean communists in 1950 had received worldwide attention. The Chinese believed that this "bad press" severely damaged their cause by undermining the communists' relations with both neutral and combatant nations; put their representatives and proxies at a disadvantage in various international forums, including the U.N.; and stiffened the will of U.N. forces to fight long and hard on the battlefield. Consequently, the major focus of the Chinese propaganda effort along the portions of the front held by U.S. and British Commonwealth troops was directed at convincing them that it was now safe to surrender.

During the fluid warfare of early 1951, several small groups of prisoners who were having trouble keeping up with retreating communists were left behind instead of being shot, and these releases were often referred to in Chinese surrender leaflets. Simple, well-written "safe conduct passes" to the "safety" of the communist front lines were also common but usually had any potential effectiveness negated by loony Rise-Up-Against-the-Imperialist-Oppressors messages on the reverse that were produced by propagandists who assumed that U.S. soldiers held the same world view as the communists. More sophisticated efforts were produced near the end of the hostilities, some of which included actual text from mainstream American newspapers.

One such effort included a letter to Truman from an angry Marine lieutenant commanding a heavy weapons platoon in the Thebaic Mountain foothills. It had been sent to the editor of the lieutenant's hometown newspaper, the *Fort Wayne News-Sentinel*, with the expectation that it would be forwarded to his commander in chief. The paper's editors, however, had a better idea. The *News-Sentinel* had long been highly critical of Truman and decided to feature both the lieutenant's letter and cover letter at the top of the March 26, 1951, edition's front page. Its appearance was soon noticed by one of the foreign embassies friendly to the communist Chinese, and the message started its long journey back to the front lines, where it surfaced in the form of a propaganda leaflet.

To the Editor of the News-Sentinel: *Tuesday, March 13, 1951*
Dear Sir:

Will you please relay the following questions to Harry S. Truman?

How many YEARS are you going to let the American manpower, materials, and money drain into this Korean sewer? How many more of my men must die on account of your stubborn refusal to pull out of Korea?

The undersigned dares you to take the following issue to the people.

Shall we pull out of Korea?

Some day you will answer for this sellout of American manpower and materials. Unfortunately, on account of you and your Administration, most of the boys over here won't be alive to register their righteous wrath against this sellout.

Again the question Mr. Truman, how long must we stay here in the God-forsaken hole of Korea?

Signed,
Gale C. Buuck
Lt. USMC

Note to the Editor:

I believe that you stand a better chance of getting this message to H.S.T. than I do. Do what you will with it but I had to sound off.

I could write 20 pages on the utter uselessness of this war in Korea. All my men hope for two Purple Hearts, or a wound severe enough which will make them eligible to return home.

Two days ago, I lost over 50 percent of my men taking one hill—and for what? None of us know why we are here and none of us can understand why we stay.

Never have American men fought in a more useless war. (At least that's the way they feel about it.)

Surely, someone back home ought to wake up Congress or somebody and get us out of here.

Thank you for your kind attention.

Lt. Gale C. Buuck
"E" Co. 2nd Bn. 7th Mar.
1st Marine Division

Under the headline "Bravo, Lieutenant," several days later, a *News-Sentinel* editorial by Clifford Ward seconded the Marine's opinion and closed with a less-than-cheerful guess at his future in the Corps: "Maybe the President will enlighten you on some of these points, Lieutenant, but we doubt it. And should you be signing your next letter 'Sergeant' or 'Private,' we'll understand."[1] The lieutenant, however, emerged from the incident with only a bruised wrist from the reprimand that came down through the chain of command. He entered the Marine Corps Reserves when his hitch was up and remained a member until 1961.

The difficult negotiations between the antagonists ground slowly forward, yet most of the agenda items discussed by the communist and U.N. representatives were actually cleared up early on in the process. The issue of what to do with each other's prisoners stalled any additional progress, however, when it was discovered in the spring of 1952 that less than half of the 132,000 North Korean and Chinese prisoners wished to be returned to the communists.

The central dilemma for Truman during the prolonged negotiations was whether prime consideration should be given to the American, South Korean, and U.N. troops in the front lines who were held by the communists, or to the thousands of Chinese and Korean soldiers who saw their chance to escape communism. In effect, the roughly 375,000 casualties suffered by both sides between April 1952 and the end of the war (including more than 15,000 American dead and wounded) were the result of the United States' and the United Nations' refusal, under the president's leadership, to force these prisoners to return to a life under communist domination. The price of freedom is not cheap, and Truman spoke plainly when he announced: "We will not buy an armistice by turning over human beings for slaughter or slavery." Several years later, he wrote, "As far as I was concerned, this was not a point for bargaining."[2]

Understandably, this did little to console or calm the fears of Americans who worried over the fate of the soldiers, and Mrs. Culbertson, who had written to Truman in January, wrote twice more in the following months. After receiving the original response from Hassett in February, there were no more answers from the White House, and her letters were "respectfully referred" along with all the others to the War Department for acknowledgment. Hassett's assistants kept only a brief synopsis for the files and noted that she had been in contact before.

> *Mrs. Jane Culbertson, St. Louis, Mo.*
> *Letter addressed to the President, dated 3/22/52.*
> Husband held as Korean POW for 21 mos. Comments on exchange of prisoners; seems we are holding prisoners who do not want to be returned to Communists. Asks if lives of the prisoners we are protecting means more than lives of UN forces held as prisoners by Communists. Urges every effort be exerted to free the UN prisoners held by the Communists.

> *Mrs. R. E. Culbertson (Jane Culbertson), St. Louis, Mo.*
> *Letter addressed to the President, dated 5/4/52.*
> Writer's husband has been a prisoner of war for past 22 months—comments on deadlock of truce talks because of the exchange of prisoner issue—Writer is rather bitter—adverse comments; has written before on same subject. Urges immediate action on release of American prisoners held by the Communists. Requests ack'mt.

The White House could answer comparatively few letters, yet it was impossible to stay aloof from the steady stream of angushed pleas. Attached to a synopsis of one of the letters forwarded to the War Department is a typed note to Hassett's chief assistant, Nancy G. McCleary, from a staffer whose last name is today lost.

> *Ltr. to the Pres., dtd. 3/10/52*
> *From: Mr. A. F. Clayton*
> *1318 Swissvale Avenue,*
> *Wilkinsburg, Pennsylvania.*
> Suggests that we should take delegation of Chinese and North Koreans to our prison camps and let them help screen the prisoners and see what we have been talking about for six months re prisoner exchanges.
> NGM: This is apparently the 3rd ltr written in by Mr. Clayton. His son a prisoner-of-war—do you think this wd be acknowledge-able this time, mentioning the son, so it won't look the office was heartless????
>
> *mona*

Hassett acceded to the request and wrote Mr. Clayton: "The President is pushing forward every possible effort to bring about a peaceful conclusion to the negotiations in Korea, which includes the exchange of Prisoners of War, but such an involved program does require patience and time. When citizens of our country write the President as you do in a spirit of devotion to our Nation's welfare, he is always glad to have the benefit of their views. Therefore, the suggestion you offer is being brought to the attention of the appropriate officials of the Government."

For many Americans, the thought of forcibly returning the POWs who did not want to live under communism was repugnant, and a correspondent from Brooklyn, New York, echoed some of Truman's own heated diary comments from the period.

> *Mr. President,*   *April 5, 1952*
> I heard today on the radio that the Chinese Communists proposed in the Panmunjom Armistice talks that they offer immunity to the anticommunists and other prisoners that surrendered voluntarily. I believe that if such promise of the Communists is accepted by the United Nations armistice commission and <u>if such prisoners are returned</u>, it <u>would be one of the biggest injustices against</u>

humanity, moral laws and against the free world, committed exactly by the same international body, the U.N., whose existence is for the purpose of avoiding such things. Because we all know of what value Communist promises are. We all know what fate awaits any individual in the commmunist country when he only dares to *express a single word* that is against their interests. Such fate of such an individual is *liquidation*. Can the responsible leaders, that take a decision to return anticommunists and other voluntarily surrendered prisoners, be sure that such prisoners will not be put to death after they will be paraded in front of the communist armed forces and every town and city in order to set an example of what happens to any communist soldier which will be done in the future who surrenders to the U.N. forces. And what shock can be greater to the morale of the free world, especially in Southwest Asia, where the blame of the death of tens of thousands of surrendered prisoners will be put on the United States, by the usual communist propaganda.

If anti-communist and voluntary prisoners are returned to the Communists, and if such prisoners are put to death or in concentration camps to a slow death, it will be one of the greatest defeats for the free world because:

1) Most of the prisoners surrendered *after* the U.N. forces *lured them, by throwing leaflets*, with promises for freedom and better future. By surrendering, these prisoners besides making easier the task of the U.N. forces on the battlefield, but also saved a good many casualties among the American troops. Is it moral to surrender to the Communists such prisoners that they may be put to death or be deported for the rest of their lives to concentration camps to be put slowly to death?

2) Unless the free world would want to surrender voluntarily to the Communists, sooner or later a war must come. There is no compromise between the free world and Communists as there is no compromise between cancer and a human body. In case of war, one of the main hopes of the free world is to convince masses of communist soldiers to surrender to the free world's forces. But by sending back now anti-Communists and voluntarily surrendered prisoners, and the Communists setting an example in China and North Korea by killing and deportations to concentration camps and hard labor and slow death, there would be *no more surrenders in a future war* with the Communists.* And this alone will be one of the main

causes of defeat of the free world, taking in consideration of the enormous manpower reserve of the Communist world.

Of course we would like to have back our prisoners of war. But I wonder if any American prisoners would be asked in advance if he would like that his return should be conditioned by the sending back of 25 anticommunist prisoners so that they may be shot, or slowly tortured in a concentration camp? What would his reply be?

Very respectfully yours,
A. S. Rigg

[Longhand] *And this is the main objective of the communists by asking that all prisoners of war should be forcibly returned.*

Naturally, there were others who believed that there was one, and only one, thing that mattered in the negotiations: getting the U.S. prisoners back. Noticing the name of the following writer and the Missouri town she was from, one of Hassett's markers underlined her name, perhaps thinking that she might be a descendant of the Younger brothers who rode in the notorious James Gang during their flurry of bank and train robberies after the Civil War.

Mr. President: *May 8, 1952*

Do you really think it would be more *uncivilized* or *unChristian* to turn over the Korean and Chinese prisoners to "slaughter and slavery" than have hundreds of our United Nation and American boys slaughtered and wounded and made slaves.

Have we asked our boys whether they wanted to go to Korea or not? No. Fathers, young ones, who went through the last war are being taken. Why ask the prisoners when our own soldiers have no choice? What must our men who are prisoners of the Communists think when you say you won't "buy an armistice" by turning human beings over for slaughter and slavery. If you had to turn over 100 Communists for each American prisoner, it would be a fair trade.

Our POW's must feel good to think that after all they have and are going through that the U.N. and Congress and the President considers the wishes and welfare of the Communist prisoners above their release much less the thousands of others.

Every one I talk with feels the same and are all getting to feel there is no point in trying. All would like something done. Of course the other matters are really important, but the P.O.W. business, all feel is unjust and ridiculous. Why are their (POW's) wishes considered when none of the soldiers or their families' are?

Please answer.

Sincerely,
Mrs. Huey E. Younger
Marshall, Mo.

P.S. Also, what will become of the U.S. when all our best young men are killed, enslaved or crippled? Why are we so easily taken in? I know hundreds who would write but feel their wishes aren't considered. Nothing will be done. Please answer.

The POW question, always a hot political issue, became even more politicized during the run-up to the 1952 elections. Letters that previously would have been forwarded to the Defense Department were now being answered personally—and in some detail—even though Truman was not running for reelection.

Dear Mr. President,   *May 14, 1952*
Our son Cpl. James R. Ellison, R. A. 16291237, has been a Prisoner of War in North Korea as of May 18, 1951. This next Sunday will be the beginning of another year for James and many other boys. Our last letter from him was dated Feb. 2, 1952. Up to that time he had never received one letter from home. We understand mail is supposed to be going thru to the boys. How wonderful for their morale to be able to receive mail from home.

How about the peace talks in Korea? Let the Communists have all their Prisoners back. Why should we begin to feed all those that don't want to return? If we have peace, there will be no more fighting so why should we be afraid to give them all back. Before we know it, we won't be able to get our own boys home. We certainly want our son home very soon and we're sure other parents and wives feel the same way. Don't you think we can give a little more on the Prisoner situation than we have?

We have two other sons in the Air Force, so we try to be as patriotic as we know how. But this mess in Korea is very trying, so please Mr. President, why not have peace in Korea as I'm sure the whole world would be more settled. We thank you for taking your time to read this letter.

> *Very sincerely,*
> *Mr. and Mrs. George Ellison*
> *Kenosha, Wis.*

My dear Mr. and Mrs. Ellison: June 6, 1952

Your letter to the President has been received,and I want to asure you in all earnestness that he is not unmindful of what it means to you to have your son in Korea. In fact, there is no one outside of the parents of our servicemen who is more concerned than the President, especially when that loved one is a prisoner of war, and he asks me to tell you that he shares the anxiety you express for your boy.

All of us, in one way or another, are making a contribution toward the safety of our Nation, and we are also sharing together, through sympathy and understanding, whatever trials we are called upon to bear. We hope you know that it is the President's constant effort to bring peace to the world. Until that goal is attained it is necessary to use our armed forces, together with those of our allies, for the protection of our freedoms wherever communism is the aggressor, and I am sure you realize that it was the Communists who started the hostilities in Korea in defiance of the peaceful nations who are pledged together in the United Nations to prevent war. I cannot emphasize too strongly that the labors of our representatives in the Far East toward ending this conflict with the exchange of Prisoners of War, are unceasing. The President urges that you pray long with him that the All Wise Providence will guide them in their work so that your son may be returned home to you.

> *Very sincerely yours,*
> *WILLIAM D. HASSETT*

The large number of soldiers missing in action (which the communists had originally claimed to have captured, then denied they were holding) gnawed at many Americans. Moreover, the president's unwillingness to let himself and American foreign policy be held captive to the machinations of

Beijing and Moscow on the prisoner issue seemed heartless to a great many voters.

> *Mr. Truman:*   *[Received] June 22, 1952*
> With the rest of the United States, I am shocked and horrified to learn that only 3198 prisoners of war are accounted for. Where are the other 9600 boys?
> I never thought to see the day when I would thank God that the second oldest of my three sons who fought in World War II—a fighter pilot who lies buried in Italy—at least I know where he is.
> For 31 years with my first vote I have been a loyal Democrat. Now at long last, I've had enough—
> *Ruth M. Higgins*
> *Newport Beach, Calif.*

Dwight D. Eisenhower soundly beat the man Truman supported in the November elections, Adlai Stevenson. In his 1952 campaign, Eisenhower repeatedly pledged, "I will go to Korea," and the president-elect fulfilled his promise with an uneventful four-day tour of the battlefield in early December. As a practical matter, there was little he could do that had not already been done by the Truman administration. The break in the deadlock came when the Chinese suddenly accepted a renewed U.S. proposal that sick and wounded prisoners be exchanged.

The great demands of the war were draining China's weak economy and hindering its much-publicized five-year industrialization plan. At a September 1952 meeting in Moscow, the Chinese foreign minister, Chou En-lai, tried unsuccessfully to persuade premier Joseph Stalin to further increase Soviet military and economic aid. After Stalin's death on March 5, 1953, communist leaders apparently reviewed his confrontational policies, and the new Soviet premier, Georgy Malenkov, spoke in favor of "peaceful coexistence" between the communist and capitalist worlds.

Not only was the proposal to exchange the sick and wounded now accepted after numerous earlier rejections, but the larger question of a general POW exchange appeared to be on its way to a settlement.

Even as negotiators finalized the wording on the armistice agreement, the communists initiated a series of offensive operations in a last-ditch effort to gain positional advantage along the cease-fire line and leave the impression that they had forced America and the U.N. into ending the war. At

10:00 A.M. on Monday, July 27, 1953, representatives from both sides affixed their signatures to nine maroon-colored copies of the settlement for the communist delegation and an equal number of blue-bound copies for the United Nations. Twelve hours later, the cease-fire went into effect. The war in Korea was over.

During one of the war's final bloody spasms, George C. Banning, a young soldier from Connecticut, died in the North Korean hills above the 38th Parallel. When his family received the Purple Heart medal, which is presented not only to the wounded, but also to the next of kin of a soldier killed in action, his father immediately sent it to the now-retired president in Independence, Missouri.

> *Mr. Truman*
> As you have been directly responsible for the loss of our son's life in Korea, you might just as well keep this emblem on display in your trophy room, as a memory of one of your historic deeds.
> Our major regret at this time is that your daughter was not there to receive the same treatment our son received in Korea.
> *Signed*
> *William Banning*
> *New Canaan, Conn.*

Truman had been sent five similar letters when he was still in office, and in each case, the Army notified the families that the awards would be held in case they reconsidered. This time, however, the letter and medal were kept by Truman and were found in his desk after he died in 1972. Ironically, the father's angry wish that it be placed "on display in your trophy room" was fulfilled nearly forty years later when the Harry S. Truman Library created an exhibit to mark the anniversary of the war.

Dear Mr. President,   *April 2, 1952*

I am Elizabeth Rowland of Winthrop Road, Union, N.J.————
I, with my father and mother, sister and brother, am going to Washington for Easter week. I would like to go to the White House and go on the egg hunt. I would like to go rolling eggs too. But best of all, I would like too [*sic*] shake your hand. I <u>am in grade 3</u>, St. Michael's School in Union. I would like to show you my idea of the White House.

> *Very truly yours,*
> *Elizabeth Rowland*

My dear Elizabeth: *April 11, 1952*

This is in acknowledgment of your letter of April second to the President. I am very sorry to disappoint you but the Easter Egg Rolling on the White House grounds was discontinued at the beginning of the war and has never been held since. It is not expected that it will be held this year either. I regret, too, that it will not be possible to arrange for you to shake hands with the President. If time would permit, it would give him pleasure to meet all of his friends when they visit Washington. Unhappily, this is not the case and, of course, he cannot discriminate by making an exception in order to comply with a particular request.

Your friendliness in writing and letting us see your drawing is appreciated.

> *Very sincerely yours,*
> *MATTHEW J. CONNELLY*
> *Secretary to the President*

CHAPTER NINE

JOE MCCARTHY • MARINE CORPS' "PROPAGANDA MACHINE" •
ASSASSINATION ATTEMPT • THE HUME AFFAIR

Reno Nev   *[Telegram: Saturday] Feb 11 [1950] 1139A*
The President,

In a Lincoln Day speech at Wheeling Thursday night, I stated that the State Department harbors a nest of communists and communist sympathizers who are helping to shape our foreign policy. I further stated that I have in my possession the names of 57 communists who are in the state department at present. A State Department spokesman promptly denied this and claimed that there is not a single communist in the department. You can convince yourself of the falsity of the State Department claim very easily. You will recall that you personally appointed a board to screen state department employees for the purpose of weeding out fellow travelers. Your board did a painstaking job and named hundreds which it listed as "dangerous to the security of the nation" because of communistic connections.

While the records are not available to me, I know absolutely that of one group of approximately 300 certified to the secretary for discharge, he actually discharged only approximately 80. I understand that this was done after lengthy consultation with Alger Hiss. I would suggest therefore, Mr. President, that you simply pick up your phone and ask Mr. Acheson how many of those whom your board has labeled as dangerous he failed to discharge. The day the House Un-American Activities Committee exposed Alger Hiss as an important link in an international communist spy ring, you signed an order forbidding the State Department's giving to the Congress any information in regard to the disloyalty or the communistic connections of anyone in that department despite this State Department blackout, we have been able to compile a list of 57 communists in the State

Department. This list is available to you, but you can get a much longer list by ordering Secretary Acheson to give you a list of these whom your own board listed as being disloyal, and who are still working in the State Department. I believe the following is the minimum which can be expected of you in this case.

1. That you demand that Acheson give you and the proper Congressional committee the names and a complete report on all of those who were placed in the department by Alger Hiss, and all of those still working in the State Department who were listed by your board as bad security risks because of the communistic connections.

2. That under no circumstances could a congressional committee obtain any information or help from the Executive Department in exposing communists.

Failure on your part will label the Democratic Party of being the bedfellow of international communism. Certainly this label is not deserved by the hundreds of thousands of loyal American Democrats throughout the nation, and by the sizable number of able loyal Democrats in both the Senate and the House.

Joe McCarthy

Senator McCarthy's telegram arrived at the White House at 7:31 that evening, but Truman was already well aware of its contents. The senator's series of speeches in Wheeling, Reno, and Salt Lake City had caused a sensation, and accounts of his charges were splashed across newspapers throughout the country. The president kept the message in his desk for more than two years before finally turning it over to his secretary, Rose Conway, who filed it with the rest of his papers after adding the notation "No acknowledgment to this wire in file, 5/21/52." In the intervening years, countless innocent people had been falsely accused of "subversive" activity. Lives had been ruined, and the "witch hunt" would continue for years to come, but warning bells had actually sounded long before the senator from Wisconsin discovered that labeling people as communists would be his surest path to political stardom.

The discovery of an extensive spy ring directed at obtaining atom bomb secrets came at the same time as Stalin's call to prepare for war and Churchill's "Iron Curtain" speech, and not only inflamed the fears of those who were already opposed to communism, but also alerted the broad mass of Americans that the growing threat wasn't limited to Europe; it included the possibility of subversion at home as well. Truman's own administration contained a senior member he considered "a pacifist 100 percent," who courted the support of American communists, but Henry Wallace was the last cabinet-level link to the far left of the Democratic Party and was retained until his antics made it impossible for him to be kept on any longer. Shortly before he was fired, Truman wrote in his diary that Secretary Wallace "wasn't as sound intellectually as I'd thought," and added:

> He wants us to disband our armed forces, give Russia our atomic secrets and trust a bunch of adventurers in the Kremlin Politbureau. I do not understand a "dreamer" like that. The German-American Bund under Fritz Kuhn was not half so dangerous. The Reds, phonies, and "parlor pinks" seem to be banded together and are becoming a national danger. I am afraid they are a sabotage front for Uncle Joe Stalin. They can see no wrong in Russia's four and one-half million armed force, in Russia's loot of Poland, Austria, Hungary, Romania, Manchuria. They can see no wrong in Russia's living off the occupied countries to support the military occupation. But when we help our friends in China who fought on our side it is terrible. When Russia loots the industrial plant of those same friends it is all right. When Russia occupies Persia for oil that is heavenly although Persia was Russia's ally in the terrible German War.

But although Truman was anxious to ditch Wallace as soon as it was politically possible, he was willing to fight tooth and nail to keep another former New Dealer from being jettisoned by a hypersensitive Congress. In the midst of congressional debate over aid to Greece and Turkey, the Senate was asked to confirm Truman's reappointment of David Lilienthal as the head of the fledgling Atomic Energy Commission. The Harvard Law School graduate had been picked to run the Tennessee Valley Authority by Roosevelt and was considerably more liberal than most Democrats. Moreover, because he insisted on hiring project workers based on merit instead of patronage, Lilienthal had also alienated a key member of the party, Chairman of the Senate Appropriations Committee Kenneth McKellar of Tennessee, and could expect few to defend him on the Senate floor against Republican charges that he was "soft on communism." Truman did eventually win Senate approval for his nominee, after a bruising confrontation, but it was clear that the loyalty question was one he was going to have to get out ahead of if he was to have any chance of retaining the presidency in 1948.

Republicans had swept the midterm elections, and it was immediately apparent that they would use their dominance in Congress to squeeze further political advantage from the developing anticommunist hysteria. Of particular concern was the House Un-American Activities Committee, now under Republican chairmanship. To head off charges that the administration itself was willing to allow communists in the U.S. government at the exact time that he was pressing for a hard-line response to communism overseas, Truman issued two executive orders establishing a loyalty and security program for federal employees.

Truman personally believed that "the Communist bugaboo" was "a lot of baloney." It was hoped that an elaborate system of review procedures would prevent misuse of confidential information held by the Civil Service Commission and gathered during background checks conducted by the Federal Bureau of Investigation—information that would invariably contain "items based on suspicion, rumor, prejudice, and malice" which could "do great harm to the reputation and careers of many innocent people."[1] Truman believed that the program would satisfy calls that the government be guarded against disloyal employees, yet protect its workers from unfounded accusations he was certain would have been trumpeted by the Un-American Activities Committee and Republicans seeking to regain control of the presidency. Organizations promoting patriotism and "Americanism" were overjoyed at Truman's move.

The President   *Nov. 27, 1946*
Camp 236 Patriotic Order Sons of America, Stroudsburg, Penn., heartily commends you for appointment of committee to consider removal from federal offices of employees owing allegiance to foreign countries.

C. W. Counterman,
Secy., East Stroudsburg, Penn.

My dear Mr. Counterman: *December 5, 1946*
Your telegram of November twenty-seventh to the President on behalf of your organization has been received. Please be assured that he is appreciative of the expression of approval which it conveys.

Very sincerely yours,
WILLIAM D. HASSETT

Dear Mr. President: *December 2, 1946*

It was most gratifying to read in the press that you had <u>appointed a commission to pass upon the loyalty of the two million employees of the Federal Government</u>.

Last September I presented to, and our Board at its October meeting approved a three-point program:

1. To improve the morale of our people (which in my own opinion, based largely upon my legislative and judicial experience) is at its lowest ebb;

2. To revive respect for law and order; reverence for the Constitution of the United States, the Flag of our Republic and the institutions which it represents;

3. To suppress and ultimately eradicate all un-American activities, especially in our public offices, which are undermining the foundations of our Government.

Your action accentuates Point 3. I am very happy to inform you that Senator Tom Connally, <u>with whom I served in the House of Representatives</u>, is a member and former President of our Society in Texas; former Senator Arthur H. Vandenberg is a member of our Society in Michigan; former Senator Warren R. Austin is a member of our Society in Vermont; Hon. Bernard M. Baruch is a member of this Society and my own Chapter, and former Chief Justice Charles Evans Hughes is one of our oldest members. We recently elected Col. Henry L. Stimson and Generals Eisenhower, MacArthur and Wainwright are members of this Society.

The above facts I mention that you may appreciate the genuineness of our program.

> *Respectfully yours,*
> *Hon. Murray Hulbert, President*
> *Empire State Society,*
> *Sons of the American Revolution*
> *New York, N.Y.*

My dear Mr. Hulbert: *December 9, 1946*

The President has asked me to thank you for your letter of December second. He appreciates your thoughtfulness in letting him see the program adopted recently by the members of your Society.

> *Very sincerely yours,*
> *WILLIAM D. HASSETT*

Republican strategists had planned to use this new version of the "Red scare" as a vehicle to ride back into the White House, but Truman's loyalty program succeeded just long enough in deflecting criticism of his administration that he was able to barely make it through the 1948 election. Interestingly, he also had the unwitting help of both the Republican and Progressive Party candidates. Republican Thomas Dewey, taking the high road, avoided Red-baiting and called for voters to support his program of progress and national unity, whereas Wallace seemed to eagerly embrace the role of lightning rod for the ardent anticommunists. It wasn't until Truman's second term that China fell to the communists and Joe McCarthy exploded onto the scene. And as luck would have it, another event that was to have a far-reaching impact did not come to a head until after the election.

On August 3, 1948, Whittaker Chambers, a senior editor at *Time* magazine and confessed ex-communist, came before the Un-American Activities Committee with a seemingly bizarre charge. Chambers maintained that Alger Hiss, the man John Foster Dulles had recently appointed as president of the Carnegie Endowment for International Peace, was in fact a communist sympathizer. In a series of escalating charges and countercharges, possibly orchestrated in such a way as to encourage Hiss to lie to the initial—and seemingly minor—accusations, the former State Department official perjured himself before the House committee. He was indicted on two counts of perjury and would also have been charged with espionage if the statute of limitations had not run out on his passage of classified documents to the Soviet Union.

The sensational trials that followed resulted first in a hung jury and then in a conviction that sent Hiss to prison and inflamed public opinion on both sides of the issue. Shortly after Chambers's initial accusations, Truman, who up to this point had successfully distanced himself from the fracas, made one of the numerous press conference gaffes that cost his presidency dearly. Attempting to solicit an answer that would generate a headline, a reporter asked, "Do you think the Capitol Hill spy scare is a 'red herring' to divert public attention from inflation?" Truman answered, "Yes I do," and added that Congress was "slandering a lot of people that don't deserve it."[2] Incensed at Truman's statement, a retired congressman who had chaired a precursor to the House Un-American Activities Committee asked Truman a number of questions that were on the minds of a good many Americans.

> *Dear Mr. President:*   *December 23, 1948*
> You have persisted in attacking the Un-American Activities Committee, duly appointed by the House of Representatives, and

denouncing its recent startling exposures of spies and traitors in our midst as "red herrings." I sincerely respect you, Mr. President, because you were a tough combat officer in World War I, and on account of your Missouri mulishness, but there is such a thing as carrying stubbornness too far. You must know by this time that you were wrong in raising the "red herring" issue.

Who appointed <u>Alger Hiss</u> to the State Department?

Who appointed him as adviser to F.D.R. at the Yalta Conference?

Who appointed him as Executive Secretary of the Dumbarton Oaks Conference in 1946?

Who appointed him as Secretary-General of the San Francisco Conference for the organization of the United Nations in 1945?

In order that I may not be considered raising a partisan issue, I agree that the public is entitled to know from <u>John Foster Dulles</u>, a Republican, if he had anything to do with various key appointments of Mr. Alger Hiss in the State Department and as President of the Carnegie Endowment for International Peace.

We already had too much secret diplomacy at Yalta, Teheran and Potsdam which we are now paying for in China and Berlin, and not enough faith in the American people.

Why should any public offical or loyal American want to protect Communist spies and traitors? Every individual implicated in the stealing of secret documents from the State, War or Navy Departments should be publicly exposed and punished.

Mr. President, who is the State Department trying to cover up?

Mr. President, who were and who are the agents of the Communist Party in the State Department and other Departments of the Government?

Mr. President, the American people are entitled to know how Alger Hiss and other Communist sympathizers and Red stooges infiltrated into important Government positions.

Mr. President, how long will Communist spies and traitors be permitted to infest the Federal service and abuse the patience of the American people? It is time that the various Departments of the Government realized that they are the servants and not the masters of the people!

The diabolical espionage plot with its stolen documents and microfilm must be openly exposed, and every one connected with it punished. LET NO GUILTY MAN OR WOMAN ESCAPE, NO

MATTER HOW IMPORTANT OR POWERFUL, DEAD OR ALIVE.

The <u>Un-American Activities Committee</u> has rendered an important public service. It should be commended, not condemned, and its activities continued by the incoming Congress.

There can be no appeasement of Communist spies and traitors or those aiding and abetting them. There can be no compromise with Treason under any guise.

I am writing this as an American and not as a partisan Republican.

> *Hamilton Fish*
> *Chairman of the House Committee*
> *to Investigate Communist Propaganda*
> *and Activities in 1930–31*
> *New York, N.Y.*

My dear Mr. Fish: *January 6, 1949*

I read your letter of December twenty-third with a lot of interest and sometime or other I shall explain just exactly the situation to which you refer.

You naturally are looking at the programs, which you claim are wrong, with a partisan prejudiced eye for which I can't blame you.

> *Sincerely yours,*
> *HARRY S. TRUMAN*

Dear Mr. President: *July 15, 1949*

On January 6, 1949, you wrote to me that you had read my "letter of December twenty third with a lot of interest and sometime or other I shall explain just exactly the situation to which you refer."

That was six months ago. Since then the first trial of <u>Alger Hiss</u> has been concluded, and by a vote of 8 to 4, according to the Press, the jurors believed him guilty of perjury in relation to certain documents stolen from the State Department and given to Communist spies.

Mr. President, do you still consider the Hiss case a "red herring?" Is the Judy Coplon case also a "red herring?"

And what about <u>Henry Julian Wadleigh</u> of the State Department who declared in open Court that he had stolen secret State Department documents for the Communists? Is he to get off without trial of any kind?

Who appointed Alger Hiss to the State Department?

Who appointed him as advisor to F.D.R. at the Yalta Conference?

Who appointed him as Executive Secretary of the Dumbarton Oaks Conference in 1944?

Who appointed him as Secretary General of the San Francisco Conference for the organization of the United Nations in 1945?

These questions, Mr. President, are still unanswered. Who is the State Department trying to cover up?

Mr. President, the American people are entitled to know how Alger Hiss and numerous Communist sympathizers, fellow travelers and Red "stooges" infiltrated into important key positions in various Departments of our Government.

Treason is not a partisan issue! There can be no compromise or appeasement with treason against the United States by officials sworn to uphold and defend the Constitution and our Country against its enemies within and without.

This applies to the Legislative, Executive and Judicial Departments!

Mr. President, you had a fine combat record in World War I, and even your Republican opponents know of your loyalty and Americanism.

Is it not time to withdraw the "red herring" charge, and to cooperate with the Un-American Activities Committee in helping drive every last Communist and fellow-traveler out of the State Department and other positions within the Federal Government?

With kind regards,

> *Respectfully yours,*
> *Hamilton Fish*

Others saw the charges as politics in its most base form.

Dear Mr. President,   *1/31/50*

I write you as one who has never been in sympathy with communism and who hates fascism.

Alger Hiss is, in my opinion, the victim of vengeful, ignorant malice; the malice of those who for the most part have very little capacity for disinterested moral indignation. The malignancy of those who, frustrated in their efforts for some twenty years to deceive the American people to put them into power, now turn to this contemptible method of casting aspersions on the fully elected representatives of the people.

<u>I hope this man will in the end be cleared. If not, I hope that you will feel able to use your power of pardon in this case.</u>
With sincere best wishes to you,

Elmer Wilcox Trolander, Chicago, Ill.

Nearly all of the mail relating to the Hiss trial (most of it critical) was forwarded to the State Department, but some material was retained in White House files, particularly telegrams, which arrived in multiple copies.

June 27, 1949
Respectfully referred to the Department of Justice.
WILLIAM D. HASSETT

DEAR MR. TRUMAN.   6/16/49
ALGER HISS NEVER DID ANYTHING WRONG IN HIS LIFE. PLEASE SEE THAT HE IS NOT TAKEN FOR A RIDE.
ELIZABETH G. NANCE
BALTIMORE, MARYLAND

As things began to heat up, Congress passed the Internal Security Act of 1950, which would have required all communist organizations to register with the attorney general plus furnish lists of their members. Truman promptly vetoed the bill, believing it would only drive their members underground, making the groups harder to monitor, and said that though the idea seemed "simple and attractive . . . it is about as practical as requiring thieves to register with the sheriff."[3] There were, of course, legitimate security concerns that had to be addressed at precisely the same time that Truman was under assault from those who believed that he was not taking a hard enough stand against the communists. The question of how far the government could go in withholding information from the public—information potentially damaging to national defense—had always been a vexing problem. Even Truman's former secretary of state, Jimmy Byrnes, had complained bitterly about "the desire of many officials to 'overclassify' documents." Byrnes noted that although he had issued specific instructions to "liberalize the classification of all messages," he was "afraid that [he] did not make much progress" against the entrenched bureaucracy.[4] Consequently, when additional security measures had to be imposed, they were enacted with a degree of trepidation, and Truman immediately heard from citizens who felt that he had gone too far.

Dear Harry: *Sept. 24, 1951*

I have just <u>read about your edict regarding the release of information by the various bureaus of the government regarding security</u>. I agree with the several commentators and editorialists—<u>we're coming to a pretty picture when we suppress news from the taxpayers</u>.

How do you think the people back in Missouri will like this? Possibly the professional Truman haters, etc., will do plenty of screaming—I'm not one of them. However, the waste and stupidity in the government is staggering—and I don't pretend to blame you for it either. It's the result of 20 years of handouts.

I just work for a living—but as one Mason to another, you can bet that I am going to do plenty of talking about this. <u>This is the first step down the road of big government socialistic suppression of liberties—and I am not quoting from the N.A.M. [National Association of Manufacturers] when I say this.</u>

Why don't you wise up—we are getting tired of paying thru the nose for waste and corruption. <u>I pay out 25% of my income to the government of which probably one-half is thrown down the rat hole.</u>

<u>I can assure you that there are plenty of other voters like myself</u> that have never done anything except sit on our fannies politically, <u>that are now going to start boiling.</u>

Let's cut out the waste and handouts—<u>the more news that gets out about government other than military and state is for the best</u>—why make jobs for more swell-headed bums.

> *Fraternally yours,*
> *Marshall Jones*
> *West Trenton, N.J.*

Dear President Truman: *Sept. 27, 1951*

As one of the many many little people who support you, regardless of party, <u>I am writing to protest against your recent executive order extending security classifications to all government bureaus</u>.

Secrecy is bad enough, though probably necessary, in the State and Defense Departments. When extended to other civil departments, it not only invites abuse, in spite of your warning, but it is a severe curtailment of the freedom for which we are all fighting. This and the lack of confidence inevitably bred by secrecy can do more damage than any possible knowledge the Russians might glean.

As a practical politician, too, you surely know how much we rank and file voters value our freedom to know and criticize what is going on in Washington. It is a safety valve as well as a privilege of democracy. So for this freedom of everyday citizens to know as well as for "freedom of the press" <u>I urge you to repeal this executive order</u>.

> *Respectfully yours,*
> *Gladys E. Grant*
> *Scotch Plains, N.J.*

The White House response to people writing on this sensitive issue was a form letter that was both uncharacteristically detailed and comprehensive. This was done, in part, to make it clear to the administration's supporters that real security concerns prompted the executive order and that Truman had not simply been goaded into announcing it by Republicans extremists. All letters were individually addressed and typed from scratch in spite of their great length.

Dear Mrs. Grant: *October 11, 1951*

The President has asked me to reply to your recent letter concerning his Executive Order on security information.

I respectfully suggest that you have been misinformed as to what the order provides and why it is necessary. I am enclosing a copy of the President's own statement on this subject.

From the President's own words and from the text of the order itself—a copy of which will also be sent to you if you desire—you will see that the order specifically prohibits the withholding of any information on security grounds unless the disclosure of the information would injure the security of the United States.

Apparently the cause of much confusion about his order is the failure of various writers and commentators to explain that a great many military and diplomatic secrets must be known to and handled by a large number of government agencies outside of the Defense and State Departments. The President's order merely instructed these agencies to protect such military secrets as carefully as have the armed forces over a period of ten years. The order does not permit any agency to classify and withhold non-security information.

It is only natural that citizens should be on guard against censorship. The President, most of all, agrees with this principle and, furthermore, has taken firm action to enforce it. I call your attention to the prompt and vigorous action he took in immediately revoking a recent bulletin of the Office of Price Administration which violated his express instruction that no non-security information should be withheld under his Executive order.

The President does not believe in sacrificing either the safety of the United States or our constitutional freedoms. With the help of his fellow Americans, he will fight to protect both.

Very sincerely yours,
JOSEPH SHORT
Secretary to the President

The president, like most Democratic leaders, initially viewed McCarthy's explosive emergence onto the national scene as little more than the proverbial flash in the pan, and Truman believed that he was "a ballyhoo artist who has to cover up his shortcomings by [making] wild charges."[5] Democratic lawmakers believed that the senator's accusations would melt under the strong light of public scrutiny and immediately called for a complete investigation of the charges, forming a special subcommittee of the Foreign Relations Committee for the task. McCarthy, far from being cowed, deftly outmaneuvered his colleagues. "You are not fooling me," he haughtily claimed. "This committee [is] not seeking to get the names of security risks, but . . . to find out the names of my informants so they can be kicked out of the State Department tomorrow."[6] Six weeks after he went public with his Wheeling speech, McCarthy still had not named a single communist and was casting out even more charges.

It was apparent that the cagey senator was going to be able to keep himself before the public eye, and Truman felt that he had to try to put what was happening into perspective for the American people. He believed that McCarthy was doing a great disservice to the anticommunist cause and issued the carefully considered statement that "the greatest asset that the Kremlin has is Senator McCarthy."[7] Republican leaders howled that Truman had libeled McCarthy, and when the president was queried about this at another press conference, he feigned surprise: "Do you think that's possible?"[8] McCarthy supporters were not amused, and Truman let no question on the veracity of his charges go unanswered.

Mr. Truman: *April 14, 1950*
We are all fed up ad nauseam with your inane cowardly attitude toward the Honorable Senator of Wisconsin, Honorable McCarthy.

When will sanity ever return to our capital in Washington?

> *Yours in disgust,*
> *John Vanderbeek*
> *Holland, Mich.*

Dear Mr. President: *August 26, 1951*

In a recent speech, Senator Joseph R. McCarthy publicly issued a challenge to you and to the State Department to specify which of his statements or accusations is or has been untrue.

I among others <u>wish to cut through all the double talk</u> and confu-<u>sion so as to determine who it is that is telling the truth and who is lying. May I request, therefore, that you or the State Department point out specifically and publicly wherein Senator McCarthy has lied, for that is what you have implicitly accused him of</u> doing.

A copy of this letter is being forwarded to Senator <u>McCarthy</u>.

> *Very sincerely yours,*
> *Charles M. West*
> *Pittston, Penn.*

McCarthy was being publicly urged by the Republican leadership to "keep talking and if one case didn't work out, to bring up another."[9] It's not likely that he needed much encouragement. As one individual after another in the Truman administration was added to his hit list, members of the White House staff became increasingly apprehensive at who might be next. For example, when White House aide David Lloyd learned that his name had been mentioned by McCarthy's attorney during a civil libel suit, he immediately asked George Elsey for any information he could gather on the testimony and received the following reply: "I am attaching a copy of a page from the deposition of General Walter B. Smith, taken on September 29, 1952, in connection with the Benton-McCarthy libel suit. There was no other reference to you than the extract appearing on the attached page, and nothing in the text would give any indication as to why McCarthy's lawyer asked the question relating to you. The totality of the transcript mentioning Lloyd consisted of one question and answer: Q. Did you meet [Governor Adlai] Stevenson's assistant, David D. Lloyd, while you were over there, while they were over on this strategic bombing mission? A. I may have but I don't recall if I did. I am sure I met Governor Stevenson at the time, although when I met him the other day I didn't remember it."[10]

If White House staffers seem to have been overly concerned with the senator from Wisconsin, it is important to remember Henry Kissinger's old adage "Even paranoids have real enemies,"[11] as well as the number of individuals in or close to the administration whose careers were threatened with ruin by McCarthy, a man who had less concern for gaining criminal convictions than for the charges themselves.

TARGET: ACHESON

Tall, trim, impeccably dressed and sporting a mustache, Secretary of State Dean Acheson spoke with a Connecticut accent that some found a little too "British" and unbearably effete. To all outward appearances, he was the perfect embodiment of the typical State Department bureaucrat Truman held in such contempt, yet even in his most private writings, Truman never gave even the slightest hint that he thought of Acheson as one of the "striped pants boys." Long before the emergence of McCarthy, the president was receiving a steady amount of criticism regarding Acheson, and the drumbeat of treason charges from the senator pushed the quantity and tone of hate mail to such proportions that it was thought prudent to station guards at his residence twenty-four hours a day. When Alger Hiss was finally convicted of perjury, Acheson stated publicly that he wouldn't "turn his back" on his friend of many years. Characteristiclly, McCarthy interrupted proceedings in the Senate to announce the secretary's "most fantastic statement" and posed the rhetorical question: Would Acheson "not turn his back on any other Communists in the State Department?"[12]

> *My dear Sir:*   *September 7, 1948?**
> Again I am asking you, in the interest of the United States and of other people in the world, to get rid of your present Secretary of State and to appoint someone with more vision and a better understanding of the dangers facing us.
> How can you be anything but appalled as so many thoughtful citizens are, at the tragic state of affairs in Korea brought about by a sadly mistaken policy for the East by Mr. Acheson and those to whom he listens. He has been of no help to you in the past; why expect any in the future? I protest that you should be so lacking in

---

*This letter was received in 1950. One of Hassett's markers underlined "1948" twice and added a question mark as well. Apparently the letter writer had still not gotten over Truman's upset victory in the 1948 election.

courage and wisdom as to continue to keep him. A president of a great nation should put the interests of his country first and of his political career last.

Although a Democrat all my life, and a member of a Democratic family for generations, I cannot support you and your policies, especially your stubborn retention of a man who has shown himself so incapable and so untrustworthy.

Very truly yours,
Marie Virginia Heaphy
Baltimore, Md.

TARGET: JESSUP

The American public knew little about Ambassador-at-Large Philip Jessup before McCarthy focused his crosshairs on the career diplomat. Jessup had been the deputy chief of the U.S. Mission at the United Nations, which had conducted key negotiations that resulted in the lifting of the Soviet blockade of Berlin. He had been involved in many of the seemingly unending crises of the Truman administration and had even escorted the president to his fateful meeting with Gen. Douglas MacArthur before China's entry into the Korean War. As with virtually all of the individuals McCarthy went after, the ambassador was the focus of a brief but intense assault. If, as in Jessup's case, the senator's effort did not quickly display promise of an easy victory, it was invariably dropped, as McCarthy went on to search for new prey—and more headlines.

My dear President Truman: *August 23, 1951*

Last night I listened to a speech by Senator Joseph McCarthy. Senator McCarthy gave proof that our Ambassador-at-Large, Philip Jessup, has communistic tendencies. Surely the senator would not make such a statement unless he had absolute proof that it is the truth.

In view of this fact, he is certainly the wrong type of man to represent the United States and is dangerous. Please do everything you can to have him removed from his office and replaced by someone who is truly loyal to the United States, and not one who loves Soviet Russia.

Mr. McCarthy also stated that Jessup suggested that we dump all our atomic material in the ocean. To me that sounds like the suggestion of a communist to have us totally unprepared for war so that then Russia could walk right in and take over this country.

Mr. Truman, <u>regardless of what your feelings are toward Mr. McCarthy, you must admit the man is trying to weed out the communists in our government, and you should give him credit</u> as he knows what he is talking about.

Sincerely yours,
Mrs. G. C. Hemphill
Long Island City, N.Y.

TARGET: LATTIMORE

Owen J. Lattimore had spent his childhood and much of his adult life in China and was currently the director of the Page School of International Relations at Johns Hopkins University. The professor, whose time with the U.S. State Department consisted of a grand total of four months in late 1945 and 1946 as a consultant on the American War Reparations Mission in Japan, suddenly discovered that he was the "top Russian espionage agent" in the United States and "onetime" boss of Alger Hiss. As with all of McCarthy's outlandish charges, this one was delivered with complete certitude and virtually no proof. It was up to the Senate to provide the proof, and McCarthy worked to have it do his bidding by issuing a combination of veiled threats and enticements to glory. "If you crack this case," he told members of the Foreign Relations Committee, "it will be the biggest espionage case in the history of this country."[13] Truman, however, had a somewhat different opinion of the newest "revelations" and at a hastily arranged news conference publicly dismissed McCarthy's charge that the professor was a spy as "silly."[14] Lattimore's sister was touched and gratified by Truman's words of support.

> *Dear Mr. President:*   *April 12, 1950*
>
> My husband, Bob Andrews, had the honor of meeting you six years ago in New Orleans, and since that time our family has felt a close personal interest in you that has grown with your splendid years of service in the White House.
>
> Your sense of honor and justice, and above all your kindliness, make me count on you as a friend and I put my confidence in you. I am sure that you will stand firmly on the side of right in this case of Senator McCarthy against Owen Lattimore, my brother.

It is cruel for an innocent man to be made the victim of lies told for political purposes; it is against all the principles for which our country stands. We all know this—that people of good will—and Bob and I are deeply grateful that you, Mr. President, are a man of good will. We have complete faith in you.

> *Sincerely yours,*
> *Eleanor Lattimore Andrews*
> *Edisto Island, S.C.*

Dear Mrs. Andrews: *April 17, 1950*

I appreciated very much your good letter of the twelfth. I think our friend "McCarthy" will eventually get all that is coming to him. He has no sense of decency or honor and I've referred to him lately as the greatest asset the Kremlin has.

You can understand now, I imagine, what the President has to stand—every day in the week he is under a constant barrage of people who have no respect for the truth and whose objective is to belittle and discredit him. While they are not successful in these attacks they are never pleasant, so I know just how you feel about the attack on your brother. The best thing to do is to face it and the truth will come out.

> *Sincerely yours,*
> *HARRY S. TRUMAN*

Dear Mr. President: *April 21, 1950*

I am deeply <u>grateful for your letter</u>, and appreciate so much your taking the time to write to me. The President's task, I'm fully aware, is the most difficult of anyone's. So your spirit of confidence is the more heartening—and contagious.

With thanks and with my warmest wishes,

> *Sincerely yours,*
> *Eleanor Lattimore Andrews*

TARGET: NASH

Philleo Nash had made more than a few enemies among both conservative elements of the Republican Party and the far left because of his liaison work with—and, indeed, advocacy of—pro-Jewish, civil-rights, and labor positions within the Truman administration. It was only a matter of time before usable innuendoes were fed to McCarthy. But unlike most of the senator's targets, Nash had inadvertently developed a constituency that was more than willing to weigh in on his defense.

> *Dear Mr. President:*   *February 4, 1952*
> Please be advised that we greatly deplore the attack recently made on your Mr. Philleo Nash by Senator McCarthy and wish to express to you our confident belief that the charges made were unjustified and untrue.
> Although we do not underestimate the confusion created in the public mind by such scare tactics, the groups we represent and the public at large will find no impairment of Mr. Nash's usefulness for being subjected to a McCarthy smear.
> > *Respectfully yours,*
> > *Elmer W. Henderson*
> > *Director, American Council on Human Rights*

> *Dear Mr. Henderson:*   *February 26, 1952*
> It was thoughtful of you to write the President as you did on February fourth, expressing your confidence in Mr. Philleo Nash. I want to thank you, in his behalf, for your letter and to assure you of his appreciation of your interest.
> > *Very sincerely yours,*
> > *WILLIAM D. HASSETT*
> > *Secretary to the President*

THE PRESIDENT: CHICAGO, ILL. FEB. 4, 1952

HAVE JUST READ REPETITION OF DISGUSTING MCCARTHY SMEAR OF PHILLEO NASH. NASH IS CERTAINLY NO COMMUNIST NOR IS HE A PARTY LINE SYMPATHIZER. I KNEW HIM INTIMATELY IN WASHINGTON DURING THE WAR. HIS RECORD IN GOVERNMENT COMPLETELY REFUTES THE BASELESS CHARGES NOW LEVELLED AGAINST HIM. YOUR STAND GRATIFYING TO ALL OF NASH'S FRIENDS AS WELL AS TO ALL BELIEVERS IN JUSTICE.

TRUMAN K. GIBSON, JR.

Dear Mr. Gibson: *February 26, 1952*

It was thoughtful of you to wire the President as you did on February fourth, expressing your confidence in Mr. Philleo Nash. I want to thank you, in his behalf, for your message and to assure you of his appreciation of your interest.

> *Very sincerely yours,*
> *WILLIAM D. HASSETT*
> *Secretary to the President*

Letters supporting McCarthy arrived on virtually a daily basis throughout the latter years of Truman's presidency. Patriotism, fear of communist subversion, and suspicion of conspiracy at high places dominated the texts.

Dear Mr. President: *August 23, 1951*

Senator McCarthy spoke here yesterday, and last night he answered you on the radio.

This morning I went to five newsstands to buy the morning paper, and all stands were sold out.

The evidence submitted by Senator McCarthy was very convincing as to the red activities in our government and it would seem that you are the one who is "over the barrel."

We think it is about time that you get busy and do something to oust these fellows from the Federal payroll and also close the doors to those not on the payroll who are exercising too much bad influence in the affairs of our government.

The people as a whole are fed up with publicity agents trying to save these fellows—it's too late for this—they have to go. McCarthy and MacArthur have the ideas to save AMERICA.

> *Cordially,*
> *L. M. Greany*
> *L. M. Greany & Co. Securities*
> *Cleveland, Ohio*

Others feared what this meant for the country and wanted to let their president know he had their support.

Dear Mr. Truman,   *2/7/52*

May I express my heartfelt support of your remarks in re Senator Joseph McCarthy.

He and his ilk are a major threat to a free society. They must be openly opposed by all persons of courage and intelligence, regardless of political party.

> *Yours very truly,*
> *John G. Norris*
> *Princeton, N.J.*

Suggestions on how to counter McCarthyism were plentiful, although frequently more than a little looney.

> *Sir:*   *August 15, 1951*
> Put McCarthy on Ice:
> In view of the monstrous things <u>McCarthy</u> done to the Bill of Rights, I hereby nominate him for
>   Presidump of the Hundred Pissant ~~Americans.~~ Amurricans.
> I am sending this letter to ten friends with the suggestion that such of them as wish to second this nomination—and so help to bury under an avalanche of ridicule this man and the evil he has fostered—send copies to ten friends, with the request that each recipient send it to ten friends, etc.
> Let's start the snow-ball rolling!
>> *Respectfully,*
>> *J. Y. Rudderman*
>> *Indianapolis, Ind.*
>
> [Longhand] *You're doing a fair-to-middling job on the toughest job in the world and I wish you well. —JYR*

> *Dear Mr. President,*   *Feb. 7, 1952*
> Your <u>vigorous and forthright opposition to Senator Joseph McCarthy deserves the support of every American citizen who cares anything at all for our liberties</u>. I am wondering, however, if this opposition could not be supplemented to great advantage by another form, namely, that of ridicule. Men of this type are likely to be pretty thick-skinned under ordinary forms of attack, although, of course, some of the shafts do get through. But they are usually ultra-sensitive to ridicule.
> Would <u>it not be possible to start a campaign of this kind against this malignant individual</u>? A verse or jingle that would be catchy,

cartoons in paper and magazines that have a large circulation, jibes in speeches, perhaps a take-off on television suggest some of the avenues along which such an approach might be made.

I am not suggesting this as a substitute for the kind of blows you and others have been dealing Senator McCarthy. Those are needed. But I do think that laughter of this nature can have a very deflating effect.

> *Yours sincerely,*
> *Edwin E. Aiken*
> *Baldwinville, Mass.*

As for the individuals who became the focus of McCarthy's wrath, once charged, they found that it could take years of diligent effort to get their personal and professional situations straightened out, and even after they believed their lives had returned to a degree of normalcy, repercussions from the original charges would unexpectedly pop up to haunt them, as when Owen Lattimore was denied a passport for overseas travel until Truman intervened.

> *Dear Mr. President:*   *June 29, 1952*
> Eleanor and I want to thank you personally for the action of the <u>State Department</u> in apologizing to <u>Owen Lattimore</u> for the recent incident.
>
> This action is a blow to <u>Joe McCarthy</u> and all his followers and helps to immunize people against the sort of infection they spread.
>
> With warmest personal regards,
> *Faithfully,*
> *Bob Andrews*
> *Edisto Island, S.C.*

Two years had elapsed since Lattimore had been denounced by McCarthy, and many others caught in the witch hunt likewise found that the wheels of justice frequently dragged too slowly for the situation to be rectified. It was later pointed out that "only" a few thousand federal employees had resigned under pressure and 212 were actually dismissed. Although these numbers indeed represent only a minuscule percentage of the more than 3 million loyalty investigations carried out by the Civil Service Commission and the FBI, that was of little consolation for those who happened to be one of the "few."

July 28, 1952 Memorandum for The President from
Charles S. Murphy [Special Council to the President]

Attached is a long letter you have received from Mrs. Esther C. Brunauer, who has been discharged from the Department of State as a security risk. In this letter, Mrs. Brunauer raises some serious questions concerning the manner in which her case was handled. I believe there is enough substance to the questions raised by Mrs. Brunauer so that they ought not to be disregarded. Accordingly, I recommend that you refer her letter to the Secretary of State, asking him to look into the matter personally. A draft of letter for your signature is attached, if you wish to do this.

My dear Mr. President   *July 9, 1952*

I write you for the purpose of calling your attention to what seems to me to be a very serious question affecting the integrity of the Loyalty Program and the civil rights of employees of the Federal Government. The question is briefly this: May an agency of the Government, in a "security risk" proceeding or other personnel action against one of its employees, decide that another Federal employee, employed in another Federal agency, who has been affirmatively cleared as to loyalty under the Loyalty Program, and as to whom no further charges under the Loyalty Program have been made, is, notwithstanding such clearance, an individual as to whose loyalty a reasonable doubt exists? If you agree with me that determinations under the Loyalty Program may not be thus be disregarded, I respectfully request that you, or some one in the Executive Office of the President designated by you, look into my own and my husband's case and advise the Secretary of State to that effect.

Almost a quarter of a century ago, shortly after my husband, Stephen Brunauer, came to this country from Hungary, he was a member, for three and one-half years, of the Hungarian Section of the Young Workers League (the forerunner of the Young Communist League). He left this organization in 1927, and since that time has never been a member of, or associated in any way, with any organization charged with being subversive. He is one of our country's outstanding scientists, intensely loyal to the United States, extremely grateful for the opportunities which he has had here, and is widely known in scientific circles and elsewhere as bitterly opposed to Communism in all of its manifestations. From 1942 to 1946 he served on active duty with the United States Navy as a Naval Reserve Officer and made numerous significant contributions to the might of both the Army and the Navy. For his service in the Navy he was awarded a commendation ribbon by the Secretary of the Navy, and was also decorated by the British Government with the Order of the British Empire.

After his release from active duty in 1946, he decided to stay with the Navy as a civilian employee in the Bureau of Ordnance, and from 1946 to 1951 headed up the Bureau of Ordnance Explosives Research and Development program.

After the Loyalty Program was initiated by you in 1947, my husband was, by reason of his membership from 1924 to 1927 in a Communist organization, the subject of a loyalty proceeding under that Program in the Navy Department. That proceeding resulted in a loyalty clearance on July 1, 1948, and presumably such clearance was approved by the Civil Service Loyalty Review Board upon post-audit.

I myself was cleared by the Department of State on both loyalty and security grounds in 1948, and in that proceeding my husband appeared and testified at length concerning his brief membership in the Young Workers League. Because of the Navy Department and the State Department proceedings, the former concerning my husband and the latter myself, both my husband and myself were abusively and falsely attacked by Senator McCarthy before the Tydings Subcommittee in the spring of 1950. I appeared before that subcommittee and testified under oath; my husband submitted a written statement under oath. My testimony was supported by some thirty-seven letters from prominent and responsible Americans of unquestioned integrity; my husband's testimony was supported by one hundred and one letters from high-ranking Naval officers, eminent scientists and other outstanding persons. The Tydings Subcommittee cleared us both.

As you know, the Navy Department since 1942 has had authority to discharge employees on security grounds. In the nine years my husband was in the Department, during all of which he handled SECRET work, the Department never raised any question concerning his security status until April 10, 1951. On the morning of that day, my husband was suddenly suspended by the Department of the

Navy under Public Law 733, 81st Congress, charged with being a
"security risk." At the same moment I was suspended by the Department of State, where I was employed, without charges of any kind
being preferred against me. The Department of State, without con-
sulting me, issued a press release announcing to the world that my
husband had just been suspended by the Navy Department charged
as a "security risk" and that because of the Navy Department's action
against him, my suspension by the Department of State was "taken
automatically."

I shall not go into the Navy Department action against my husband except to say it did not originate "in channels," but was taken
by your former Secretary of the Navy, Mr. Francis Mathews, personally, without even informing the Chief of the Bureau of Ordnance, and that it was actuated by considerations having nothing to
do with national security. My husband was not and is not a security
risk and no number of allegations that he is will make him one. He
answered the Navy Department charges in detail under oath and
offered to appear before the Secretary, or any board designated by
the Secretary, for questioning as to any matter he might have left in
doubt or not covered in his answer. At the same time he stated that
while he desired reinstatement, he desired it only if the Secretary
felt that such reinstatement would not embarrass the Department
and that my husband could continue to make valuable contributions to the Navy in future; and he advised the Secretary that
because of this he was putting his resignation at the Department's
disposal. The resignation was accepted forthwith—the same day
the answer was filed.

Some six weeks after my suspension by the Department of State,
the Department served me with charges under Public Law 733 and
the Departmental Regulations issued pursuant thereto (as well as
charges under the new loyalty standard promulgated by you on April
28, 1951), and a hearing was held on those charges from July 10 to
July 12, 1952. It soon became evident that the only charge of any
importance was that I was in close and habitual association with my
husband.

Nine months of official silence followed the conclusion of the hearing, despite the fact that the Regulations emphasize the necessity for
prompt action on the part of the officials who must make the decisions. During this nine months I received no official communication

whatever about the status of my case, although on several occasions I was unofficially given the impression by high officials of the Department that I would be cleared. On several other occasions, in answer to my inquiries, I was promised that action would be taken "soon." On April 15, 1952, more than a year after my suspension, I received an official communication informing me that the Loyalty-Security Board of the Department of State had determined (1) that no doubt existed concerning my loyalty, but (2) that I constituted a security risk under the Departmental Regulations. I immediately exercised my right of appeal to the Secretary of State from so much of the Board's decision as held me to be a security risk, and on May 19, I had a hearing before a special board of three officers of the Department of State. In a letter dated June 16, 1952, I was informed that the appeal board had affirmed the decision of the Loyalty-Security Board, and that I was therefore dismissed as a security risk.

My own conscience is clear and I know that I am not a security risk. And I also know that the decision holding me to be a security risk was reached by a line of reasoning that violates the Department's own Regulations.

Section 393.2 of the Regulations and Procedures of the Department of State provides in part as follows (the remainder of the Section does not apply to my case):

"393.2 *Categories Constituting Security Risks*

Reasonable grounds shall be deemed to exist for belief that the removal of an officer or employee is necessary or advisable in the interest of national security when he falls into one or more of the following categories:

"a. A person who engages in, supports, or advocates treason, subversion, or sedition, or who is a member of, affiliated with, or in sympathetic association with the Communist, Nazi or Fascist parties, or of any foreign or domestic party or movement which seeks to alter the form of government of the United States by means or whose policy is to advocate or approve the commission of acts of force or violence to deny other persons their rights under the Constitution of the United States; or a person who consistently believes in or supports the ideologies and policies of such a party or movement.

"b. A person who is engaged in espionage or who is acting directly or indirectly under the instructions of any foreign government; or who deliberately performs his duties, or otherwise acts to serve the interests of another government in preference to the interest of the United States. . . ."

"d. A person who has habitual or close association with persons known or believed to be in *categories a or b* to an extent which would justify the conclusion that he might, through such association, voluntarily or otherwise divulge classified information without authority." (Emphasis supplied)

I was found to be a "security risk" by the Department of State solely because I have close and habitual association with my husband, Stephen Brunauer. I learned this officially from the Department's original press release announcing my suspension, I learned it by inference from the course of my hearing, I learned it again officially when I was informed by the appeal board as to the matter to which I should particularly address myself upon my appeal, and I have learned it unofficially since. Now it is very apparent that under the Department's Regulations I can be a security risk by reason of close and habitual association with my husband only if my husband is a person described in category "a" or category "b" of Section 393.2, quoted above. And it is also apparent that the standards set forth in these two categories are loyalty standards. In other words, under the Departmental Regulations, I can be found to be a security risk by reason of close and habitual association with a person only if that person is a disloyal person.

As I previously stated, my husband was cleared on loyalty grounds by the Navy Department in 1949, and that clearance has never been disturbed. Indeed when he was suspended by that Department under Public Law 733 on April 10, 1951, he was not charged on any ground related to loyalty. Moveover when on April 28, 1951, the loyalty standard was changed by you from the "reasonable grounds for belief" test to the "reasonable doubt" test, the Navy Department made no loyalty charges against my husband under the new test, although my husband had the status of a Navy Department employee, albeit under suspension, for more than six weeks after the new test became effective. The Department's failure to make such charges is extremely significant because Paragraph 1(b) of the "uniform Criteria for Administration of Loyalty and Security Policies and Procedures for Civilian Personnel in the Department of Defense," promulgated by the Secretary of Defense on January 19, 1951, directs that—

"cases in which the available evidence indicates that the employee can be charged with being disloyal to the Government of the United States under the standards and criteria developed pursuant to Executive Order 9835 will be processed simultaneously under both Executive Order 9835 and Public Law 733 [Emphasis supplied].*"*

The failure of the Navy Department, while my husband was under suspension on security charges under Public Law 733, to charge him on loyalty grounds under the new standard in the face of a directive ordering that he is so charged if the available evidence indicated such charges could be made, proves, objectively what both my husband and myself in our hearts know subjectively—that there was no evidence upon which charges of disloyalty could be made. So the 1949 loyalty clearance of my husband still stands.

What the State Department has done in finding me to be a security risk by reason of close and habitual association with my husband is either to create, for the purpose of my case, a new category of "security risk" in disregard of its own Regulations or to overrule the Navy Department's determination under the Loyalty Program as to my husband's loyalty. I cannot believe, when a determination as to an employee's loyalty has been made under the Loyalty Program by one department, that such determination may be overruled by another department under the security program in a proceeding involving a different employee. Yet that is the effect of what the State Department has done in my case if the decision was based on any category set forth in the Regulations.

I believe once a determination has been made under the Loyalty Program that an individual is loyal to the Government of the United States, that such determination is conclusive upon every agency of the Government until it has been reversed under the Loyalty Program in a proceeding in which that individual is the respondent and in which he or she has the procedural protections, meager though they may be, and the appeal rights that are provided for in that program. If this were not so, the integrity of the Loyalty Program would be completely destroyed and any agency of the Government would have the right in a proceeding against an employee of that agency under the security program to determine that an employee of another agency who is not a party to the proceeding, and has no means of defending himself in that proceeding, is disloyal to the United States.

If I have correctly stated the legal effect of determinations under the Loyalty Program concerning an employee's loyalty, the Department of State had no authority under the Departmental Regulations to discharge me as a "security risk" by reason of close and habitual association with my husband, for he was cleared under the Loyalty Program, and that clearance is still in effect today. If the Department of State did not, perchance, decide on this ground then it violated its Regulations by inventing a hitherto non-existent category of security risk for my special benefit. I again respectfully request that you, or some one in the Executive Office of the President designated by you, look into my case, and instruct the Secretary of State that in a proceeding under the security program against one of his employees, he may not disregard a determination of another agency of the Government under the Loyalty Program concerning the loyalty of another employee.

On several occasions you have expressed your determination to protect the civil rights of employees of the Federal Government, and undoubtedly you feel that the laws, orders, and regulations which constitute the Loyalty Program and the Security Program are designed so that this end is accomplished. As one who has seen from the other side the application of these laws, orders, and regulations, I must tell you that, unfortunately, the civilian employees of the Federal Government have become second-class citizens, deprived of the benefits of due process of law with respect to their livelihood and personal reputations. . . .

I am sure that while this Loyalty-Service Security system has been growing up and has been fastening itself piecemeal into the Federal bureaucracy, you have not realized fully what inroads were being made on the rights of Americans under the Constitution. Do you realize that in this system a person is presumed guilty until he can prove his innocence, and that he goes on being accused over and over again no matter how many times he proves his innocence? As a matter of fact, the technique now is to keep loading new and less consequential charges upon old, disproved ones. When does a Board say to the individual, and to the world "This allegation is false; this one, though true, does not have the significance imputed to it"?

Do you realize the nature of the charges and the "evidence" used in loyalty and security proceedings? The charges are usually vague, or, if they are definite they are likely to be inconsequential, so that the accused is left feeling that there must be some sinister bit of "framed" evidence somewhere in the background that he never has a chance to refute because he is never told what it is.

Do you realize that charges are made and hearings conducted on the basis of "information" supplied by anonymous informants who cannot be held accountable for what they say, and that the rules of evidence that prevail in a courtroom are nonexistent in a loyalty or security proceeding?

It is true that the members of Boards are advised to take this into account in coming to a decision. But in my own experience, two Boards, whose members knew nothing whatever about me except in connection with the proceedings, gave more weight to the prejudiced, often vague information supplied by anonymous informants, most of whom had obviously met me or my husband only briefly, than to the testimony of people who knew us well—people who had worked side by side with my husband or me for years—including my Chief in the Department of State, a Senator, a former Senator, the Librarian of Congress, a Judge of the United States Tax Court, a member of the Subversive Activities Control Board and the director of one of the most important scientific laboratories working with the Armed Forces; and, from the 1948 hearings, the testimony of a distinguished retired Admiral who had served as Chief of Naval Operations, Acting Secretary of the Navy, and Ambassador to the Soviet Union.

This situation is partly due to the violation in recent years of the principle of separation of powers embedded in the Constitution. The Executive and Legislative Branches have usurped the powers of the Judiciary to an alarming extent. What makes this especially serious is that in the exercise of judicial powers the Executive and Legislative Branches use anything but judicial principles and techniques in exercising those powers. . . .

Do you not believe that the problems which the Loyalty-Security system purports to solve might be dealt with infinitely better by rigorous adherence to the genius of the American Constitution?

> *Respectfully,*
> *Esther C. Brunauer*

My dear Mr. Secretary: *Kansas City, Missouri, July 30, 1952*

I am referring to you a letter, dated July 9, 1952, which I have received from Mrs. Esther C. Brunauer, who has been discharged from the Department of State as a security risk.

Some of Mrs. Brunauer's comments on the handling of her loyalty-security case would give me considerable concern if what she says is accurate. I am very much interested in these matters, as you know, and I would appreciate your personal views regarding Mrs. Brunauer's dismissal and the remarks contained in her letter.

Very sincerely yours,
HARRY S. TRUMAN

Presidential interest came too late for Mrs. Brunauer, a political appointee not covered by civil service protections, since a Republican administration under Eisenhower would soon come to power and sweep the Democratic appointments of two decades from office.

Many people, outraged over injustices against fellow Americans, believed that continually responding to McCarthy's charges kept the administration locked in a perpetual defensive mode and encouraged Truman to put McCarthy on the defensive.

Dear Mr. President: *July 27, 1950*

Please permit me to urge your influence be exerted to <u>remove Senator Joseph R. McCarthy from his post in the Senate of the United States</u>. We have been most interested in his charges; if true, they should indeed have been prosecuted. But it is clear by now that Mr. McCarthy was using his high post dishonestly. We cannot now respect the man; we do not trust his further efforts in behalf of the people of the United States. He has most seriously denigrated our Senate, undermined our respect for the institution itself, cheapened his colleagues. Therefore I hope two-thirds of the Senate will at least be given the opportunity of expressing their disapproval of his dastardly tactics.

Most respectfully,
Manning Moore
Santos Ojeda, New York, N.Y.

The President   *May 27, 1950*

Whereas the Wisconsin State Council of Machinists representing 80,000 workers throughout the state have investigated the records and activities of Senator Joseph McCarthy and whereas we have found his charges, smears and innuendoes and unAmerican activities wholly unbecoming a United States Senator. And whereas said senator does not fairly nor conscientiously represent the people of the state of Wisconsin, and his actions are at variance with the liberal principles of this great state now; therefore, be it resolved that the President of the United States use his good office to request the United States Senate to institute impeachment proceedings against Senator Joseph McCarthy at once.

> *Wisconsin State Council of International*
> *Association of Machinists*
> *Henry J. Winkel, Secretary and Treasurer*

At this point in time, there was not the slightest chance that Republican leaders in the Senate would do anything to slow down the momentum of McCarthy during the run-up to the midterm elections when, with the help of McCarthy's drumbeat, they expected to further increase their majorities in both houses of Congress. Still, it would be useful for senators to hear complaints from their constituents, and the White House encouraged correspondents like Manning Moore of New York to contact them directly (which also had the potential double benefit of generating additional mail against the Wisconsin senator). Of course, it would be useless for Winkel to complain to McCarthy's own office, so he was encouraged to send his suggestion to someone who might be able to put it to good use.

> *Dear Mr. Winkel:*   *June 14, 1950*
> The President has asked me to reply to your telegram suggesting that he request the United States Senate to institute impeachment proceedings against Senator Joseph McCarthy.
> While your interest in this matter is appreciated, the President feels that this is a matter peculiarly within the jurisdiction of the Senate itself. The Constitution provides that the Senate may, by a two-thirds vote, expel a member. Consequently, it would seem appropriate for any views you wish to express on this matter to be addressed to the Vice President of the United States, in his capacity as the Senate's presiding officer.
> With all good wishes,
>
> > *Sincerely yours,*
> > *CHARLES S. MURPHY*
> > *Special Counsel to the President*

The resolution to oust McCarthy from his Senate seat, put forward by Connecticut's freshman senator, William Benton, was well before its time; its stated purpose doomed to failure. Nevertheless, as an effort to both put McCarthy on the defensive and "buck up the troops," it served admirably.

Dear President Truman: *August 17, 1951*

Congratulations on your implied support of the Benton resolution for the removal of McCarthy from the U. S. Senate.

This resolution was long overdue and the country is in dire need of such action to bring it closer to the normal democratic approach to problems from which it has strayed because of McCarthyism.

The courage shown in your forthright stand is indeed admirable.

Very truly yours,
Americans for Democratic Action
Far Rockaway, N.Y.

My dear Mr. President: *October 15, 1951*

Please let me congratulate you on your uncompromising stand against McCarthyism. You will recall the words of Jefferson, "I have sworn upon the altar of God eternal hostility against every form of tyranny over the mind of man." McCarthyism has become such a tyranny without parallel in the history of our country. To that tyranny I devoutly hope you, like Jefferson, have sworn "eternal hostility."

A distinguished German scholar who was a refugee from Nazi tyranny assures me that there is no difference in kind between Hitlerism and McCarthyism, both being the same form of bacteriological warfare against the minds and souls of men.

McCarthyism is the most dangerous menace to our cherished freedoms of thought and speech, worse than Communism itself.

In Senator Benton you have an able and valuable ally. I hope you may find it possible to lend active support to his resolution by whatever method you may deem most effective and appropriate.

Sincerely and respectfully,
A. Barr Comstock
Washington, D.C.

Dear Mr. Comstock: *October 18, 1951*

Ever so many thanks for your kind letter of October fifteenth. I am glad to read again Jefferson's famous declaration of eternal hostility against every form of tyranny over the mind of man. That is a sentiment that is deeply engraved on my heart.

I like also the observation of your German friend that there is no difference between Hitlerism and McCarthyism, both being the same form of bacteriological warfare against the minds and souls of men.

Cordially and sincerely,
HARRY S. TRUMAN

Dear Mr. President: *October 22, 1951*

It was with considerable interest that we followed <u>your recent speeches with reference to Senator McCarthy of Wisconsin.</u>

We wish to state at this time that <u>we are in hearty agreement with your opposition to his slanderous methods and smear tactics</u>. The greatest threat to our democracy and civil liberties lies in the fear that he creates in the hearts of the American people. It has come to the point where people are afraid to speak their minds freely and openly and where honest men in and out of the government are being intimidated.

Your outspoken opposition to the kinds of things that McCarthy represents brings a strong ray of hope that these methods will be stopped. We trust that you will continue to safeguard our Constitutional rights in a spirit of fair play.

In addition, we hope that you will support such current efforts as: Senator Benton's resolution to rebuke and remove Senator McCarthy and efforts to safeguard the right of government employees accused of being "security risks" or "subversives" to have a fair public trial.

We pledge our continued support of your policies along these lines and hope they will be vigorously implemented by action.

Respectfully yours,
Lenard Spector
Chairman, West Bronx Compass Club
Bronx, N.Y.

My dear Mr. Spector: *Key West, Florida, November 29, 1951*

Your recent letter, on behalf of your Club, has been received. You can be sure that the President appreciates your interest in writing and submitting your views, and that the confidence in his leadership which you express means very much to him.

> Very sincerely yours,
> WILLIAM D. HASSETT
> Secretary to the President

McCarthy's answer to the Benton Resolution was to slap his colleague with a libel suit. Benton was unfazed. He had only recently left his job as assistant secretary of state in charge of the "Voice of America," and after many years in the advertising industry (the freshman senator was also the chairman of the Muzak Corporation and the longtime chairman and publisher of the *Encyclopedia Britannica*), he was more than happy to see the case go to court. Benton had the resources and disposition not only to string it out, but to continue on the offensive. Even as Harry and Bess prepared to move from 1600 Pennsylvania Avenue to make way for the Eisenhowers, Truman received a message from the feisty senator, who was still doing his best to encourage IRS and FBI investigations into McCarthy.

The President,   *January 17, 1953*

I congratulate you on your eloquent and most moving broadcast of Thursday evening. It was a great valedictory to your eight years as the leading citizen of the free world.

I hope that before you begin you role as our country's most distinguished private citizen, you can provide guidance on an issue which can have high moral significance for the future of our democracy.

My attorney has called my attention to certain facts brought out by the Senate subcommittee which investigated the finances of Senator McCarthy. The subcommittee report notes at page 37 that of $172,623.18 deposited by Senator McCarthy from January 1, 1948, to November 12, 1952, a total of $59,592.52 has not been identified as to source, including approximately $19,000 in currency deposited. Of $96,921.26 deposited by his administrative assistant, Ray Kiermas, in the same period, a total of $44,908.43 has not been traced to its source, including $29,230 deposited in currency.

Report also notes at page 33 that during 1946 McCarthy reduced his bank loans $28,401.06 from funds which could not be traced to any known bank or brokerage account, and at page 34 notes that total paid off on loan from untraced funds was

$39,900.89. Since subcommittee had both federal and state income tax returns, of both McCarthy and Kiermas, it appears possible that as much as $144,401.84 was not reported for income tax purposes.

I hope that in these closing hours of your administration, you may see fit publicly to direct these facts to the attention of the Bureau of Internal Revenue and of the Department of Justice.

William Benton

During the run-up to the 1952 elections, one correspondent anticipated that Truman's attacks on McCarthy would virtually guarantee the senator's reelection and hoped that Truman's relative unpopularity would also help propel a like-minded colleague of McCarthy into the vice presidency.

Dear Mr. President,   *Sept. 11, 1952*
I want to congratulate you on your success in helping to elect Senator Joseph McCarthy of Wisconsin by being against him.

Please do not fail to say a few words about Senator Nixon on your whistle stop tour of this year. You remember Senator Nixon was instrumental in placing your 1948 whistle stop friend (Red Herring) Alger Hiss behind prison bars.

Very respectfully,
S. M. Nabors
Corinth, Miss.

Having lost the White House for the first time in twenty years, Democrats were anxious to have Truman make one last effort to bring down the man whom many saw as a threat to democracy and largely responsible for their misfortune. Hassett, who had originally wanted to retire in 1945, had finally returned to Vermont the previous summer, and his successor, Beth Short, as well as much of the staff, were already looking for new jobs. Consequently, few of the letters that in the past would have generated answers from the White House received any form of acknowledgment.

Dear Mr. President,   *January 5, 1953*
Before your term of office officially expires, I want to register my disgust with the complete lack of courage displayed by the members of Congress with regard to the subcommittee report on the financial chicanery of Senator McCarthy, and urge you to personally use your voice and influence to expose this vicious demagogue.

Although a staunch Democrat by political conviction, and a liberal by moral and social necessity, I have frequently found many minor irritations with your administration, such as the sanctuary provided by you for former Mayor Wm. O'Dwyer of New York City. But on the whole <u>I am in fervent harmony with the broad political philosophy which has motivated you during the past years</u>, especially with regard to our fading civil liberties. However, these ever adamantine protections to the individual do not seem to concern the forthcoming administration, and continue to be harassed and impinged by men using the genuine threat of communism to further their own ambitions and solvency.

It seems, sadly, that when one man can so terrify a nation, as Senator McCarthy has done, and can perpetrate such flagrant derelictions of the public trust with such arrogant impunity and with the underlying threat of a reprisal in the grand McCarthy manner, then our democracy is in dire peril. When free men no longer stand to declare the truth as they see it, America is shaking at its foundations, and fascism is on the way.

I therefore urge you as president to make some sort of public broadcast with the intent of publicizing the outright mendacity of this senator by outlining the data contained in the editorial from the *New York Post* which accompanies this missive. By doing this you can overcome the reluctance of the Republican press to print what might be contradictory to the fabric of lies with which they stupored the people and won the election.

If this might violate some Washington rule of etiquette, it would also reveal the new type of primitive which has evolved in our Congress reaping their own harvests during national distress.

I have always admired your frankness in the face of contemporary demi-gods and hope you will not forego the opportunity to strike a parting blow for your country. Best wishes to you on your coming retirement, and may you and your kind continue to thrive in the environment of democracy.

Yours truly,
Howard Bloom
Brooklyn, N.Y.

Honorable President Truman,   *Dec. 31, 1952*

I do not often write to public officials, but reading in last night's paper that McCarthy, that unspeakable character from Wisconsin, was presented six medals for meritorious (?) service to his country, I've boiled over. I think <u>we ought to demand these medals be recalled</u>. What real hero can be proud to wear the Distinguished Flying Cross, knowing it was also presented to <u>McCarthy</u> for such vague reasons.

I remember his speech to save storm troopers who had wantonly murdered American prisoners of war. I hope you will request the resignation of Secty. of Navy Kimball, who approved the presenting of these medals. I hope—oh well, what's the use. I'm just blowing off stream, talking to the wastebasket, as that is where this will go, unread.

Yours very sincerely,
Mrs. Helen Deering
Portland, Ore.

Truman's running fight with McCarthy is well known, but the senator's influence on presidential decision making was often much more subtle—and destructive—than is commonly recognized. For example, the desision to snub the Marine Corps League based on its tenuous connection to McCarthy was indicative not only of Truman's belief that the Marines were somewhat over-rated, but also that they would go to any length to strengthen their position within the armed services.

Dear Mr. President: *July 11, 1950*

The work of the Marine Corps League is such I believe as to warrant its continued existence. This is contingent upon the amount of funds we are able to raise in the 1950 campaign.

Though we are a marine organization, we are accredited to the Veterans' Administration as the service organization for all veterans. More than 50% of our cases are veterans of the other branches of the service. Our case load, of some 10,000 per year, is definitely on the increase. In order to cope with it, we must have the support of the community leadership.

Our sponsors for the 1950 campaign include, of course, the Governor of the State of New York, the Mayor of the City of New York and various other state, city, and federal officials.

Through the years of our existence, and though we are offically accredited to the Department of Welfare, we are proud of the fact that we have only had to refer two cases for home relief. We are dedicated to the inherent self-respect of the individual and we try to find him a job, a place to live if need be, settling his financial affairs and lending him a bit of money to get a start. Neither we nor the veterans want to see these cases handled by the Welfare Department.

As President of the United States, we ask that you join us as Honorary Chairman. Please accept my personal assurance that you will not be called upon for any active assistance whatsoever as I am well aware of your busy schedule especially in these trying times.

May I on behalf of the League and myself assure you of our confidence in your actions under these recent complications. Hoping that your reply will be affirmative, I remain

Respectfully,
Gene Tunney
League Chairman, New York Detachment
Marine Corps League
Captain, U.S.N.R., Inactive

This former naval officer and marine was more than just a public figure; he was a genuine celebrity. Captain Tunney had headed the U.S. Navy's fitness program throughout World War II. A former heavyweight boxing champion who had twice defeated Jack Dempsey, he was also a combat veteran of World War I and had, in fact, gotten his start in the sport when he won an American Expeditionary Force championship in Paris. Hassett forwarded the request and pointedly noted that the Marine Corps League earlier that spring had presented its 1950 Americanism Award to none other than Joseph McCarthy. Instead of taking any action on the request of what might normally be considered a routine matter, it was temporarily tabled. By the end of the month, the decision to delay an answer looked fortuitous, since the timing of Tunney's letter now looked highly suspicious. Eben Ayers picks up the story in his diary:

August 1, Tuesday: When we went in for our staff meeting this morning, the President said an "alarming" thing had just happened. He went on to tell us that Rep. Carl Vinson and Rep. Dewey Short, the former chairman and the latter ranking Republican member of the House armed services committee, were trying to get Admiral [Forrest] Sherman, chief of naval operations, to the Hill and were going to provide for a third division of the U.S. Marine Corps. The President said he was trying to get Senator [Millard] Tydings on the telephone. He said he was "hot under the collar" at these two trying to tell the armed forces men what they should have and upsetting the whole program. [Truman's naval aide] Admiral [Robert] Dennison asked the President if he knew what Sherman told them when they called him, and the President nodded. I asked Dennison and he said that Sherman said he would recommend what was proper.

It may never be known whether Tunney's proposal was part of a coordinated effort to advance wider objectives of Marine Corps boosters by publicly tying Truman to a semiofficial—but very public—initiative immediately before the "three-divisions" proposal was announced in Congress. Immediately after the meeting, Hassett forwarded a for-the-record memo to appointments secretary Connelly.

MEMORANDUM FOR SECRETARY CONNELLY
Dear Matt:
In determining any obligation the President has to the Marine Corps League, the fact should not be overlooked that on April eighth last, at Passaic, N.J., the Marine Corps League presented its Americanism Award to Sen. McCarthy.

Please read clipping from the *New York Times* which I placed in the Marine Corps League file.

You will note also that Sen. McCarthy, speaking without the cloak of legislative immunity, refused to repeat his charge that Prof. Lattimore is a communist and the "top Soviet spy" in the United States.
W. D. H.

No reply of any kind was sent to Tunney. Considering both his position and his celebrity status, it was highly unusual that he never received even a Valentine from someone on the White House staff. Several weeks later, Truman received yet another request involving the Marines, this time from a Los Angeles congressman. It was not about the three-divisions proposal or the Marine Corps League but was a plea for his support that the corps be granted equal representation on the Joint Chiefs of Staff.

My dear Mr. President: *August 21, 1950*

The United States Marine Corps has again on the battlefields of Korea demonstrated that it is an effective hard-hitting mobile force which can be depended upon to produce results on the battlefield.

Over the past 180 years, the Marine Corps time and again have proved that they are invaluable to the defense of America and fight the aggressors which threaten American security.

In my opinion, the United States Marine Corps is entitled to full recognition as a major branch of the Armed Services of the U.S., and should have its own representative on the Joint Chiefs of Staff in the Department of Defense. I, therefore, sincerely urge that as Commander-in-Chief of the Armed Forces you will grant the Marine Corps representation on the Joint Chiefs of Staff.

Very truly yours,
Gordon L. McDonough, M. C.
15th District, California

To Truman, the old Army colonel, it must have looked as if the Marines certainly knew how to conduct simultaneous attacks on multiple axes. The president answered this letter personally, and in a manner that would have set off all kinds of warning lights within his staff—if he had showed it to them before it was posted.

My dear Congressman McDonough: August 29, 1950

I read with a lot of interest your letter in regard to the Marine Corps. For your information the Marine Corps is the Navy's police force and as long as I am President that is what it will remain. They have a propaganda machine that is almost equal to Stalin's.

Nobody desires to belittle the efforts of the Marine Corps but when the Marine Corps goes into the army, it works with and for the army and that is the way it should be.

I am more than happy to have your expression of interest in this naval military organization. The Chief of Naval Operations is the Chief of Staff of the Navy of which the Marines are a part.

Sincerely yours,
HARRY S. TRUMAN

The commander in chief's comment that the corps was the "Navy's police force" was a reference to their activities in the Caribbean and China during the first third of the century and neglected to take into account that, by congressional act, its primary mission was the seizing and securing of naval bases. Truman's statement that "it works with and for the army" had to do with two things: First, strategic assumptions after the Second World War held that independent operations like the island hopping in the Pacific were aberrations dictated by circumstances and were not likely to happen again. And second, that when the Marines did take part in large-scale ground combat, as in both world wars and the current fighting in Korea, their units were incorporated into larger Army organizations. Although both contentions were arguably true—within specific contexts—they did not reflect the political realities created by marine valor in the Pacific or the current fighting in Korea, where they were, in fact, getting ready to spearhead an invasion at Inch'on, an operation that post World War II strategists had confidently maintained would never again be necessary. Topping things off was the ill-conceived comparison to Stalin. Truman's comments were dynamite, and his congressional opponents were happy to light the fuse. The ensuing explosion was duly recorded in Ayers's diary.

> September 6, Wednesday: This was a hectic day at the office. . . . Our troubles arose from a letter the president had written August 29 to Rep. Gordon L. McDonough of California in reply to one from the congressman. Representative McDonough placed it in the Congressional Record of September 1. . . . It did not become public, however, until Senator [Bourke] Hickenlooper picked it up and sounded off, although as we were later told, John O'Donnell of the *New York News* picked it up. The result, in any event, was a storm of protests and criticisms which were reflected in telegrams that poured in here during the night—about 125 of them—with more during the day. They came from people all over the country—Marines, former Marines, mothers, fathers, and others.
>
> Charlie Ross brought it up at the staff meeting. There was some brief discussion and the conference went on then through the usual routine. Ross then brought it up again, making plain that he felt something must be done to meet the situation. The Marine Corps League is meeting in convention and the delegates there sounded off. Ross proposed that the president go to the meeting and address the crowd. This was backed up by George Elsey and Donald Dawson but met a half-hearted response from some and was opposed by Matt Connelly. The suggestion was also made by Admiral Dennison

that the president address a letter to someone. It was left to be settled later.

Afterward Dennison and Elsey went to work on a letter. Dennison got in touch with the commandant of the marine corps, General
[Clifton] Cates. . . . In the late afternoon the letter was completed.
General Cates was called to the White House at 5:00 p.m. and the
letter, addressed to him, was given to him, with a copy of a letter to
Commandant [Clay] Nixon of the Marine Corps League. The letter
to Nixon was sent by a White House messenger together with a
copy of the letter to General Cates and was delivered to Nixon at the
Statler Hotel between 5:00 and 5:30 and [the Cates letter] read by
him to the meeting.

It was greeted by some catcalls and boos, but there were shouts to
read it again and the commandant did that. The general reaction
was good.

NEWS RELEASE   *SEPTEMBER 6, 1950*
The President has today sent the following letter to Commandant
Clay Nixon, Marine Corps League:

My dear Mr. Nixon:
I am concerned over the situation which has arisen because of the
publishing of my letter of August 29th to Representative McDonough.

I have this date addressed a letter to the Commandant of the
Marine Corps, a copy of which I am enclosing.

I should be happy to have you read my letter to the members of
your organization.

> *Sincerely yours,*
> *HARRY S. TRUMAN*

Truman simultaneously sent a letter to General Cates, which was also
released to the press.

Dear General Cates:
I sincerely regret the unfortunate choice of language which I used
in my letter of August 29 to Congressman McDonough concerning
the Marine Corps.

What I had in mind at the time this letter was written was the specific question raised by Mr. McDonough, namely the representation of the Marine Corps on the Joint Chiefs of Staff. I have been disturbed by the number of communications which have been brought to my attention proposing that the Marine Corps have such representation. I feel that, in as much as the Marine Corps is by law an integral part of the Department of the Navy, it is already represented on the Joint Chiefs of Staff by the Chief of Naval Operations. That the Congress concurs in this point of view is evidenced by the fact that, in passing the National Security Act of 1947, and again in amending the Act in 1949, the Congress considered the question of Marine Corps representation on the Joint Chiefs of Staff and did not provide for it. It is my feeling that many of the renewed pleas for such representation are the result of propaganda inspired by individuals who may not be aware of* the best interests of our Defense Establishment as a whole, and it was this feeling which I was expressing to Mr. McDonough. I am certain that the Marine Corps itself does not indulge in such propaganda.

I am profoundly aware of the magnificent history of the United States Marine Corps, and of the many heroic deeds of the Marines since the Corps was established in 1775. I personally learned of the splendid combat spirit of the Marines when the Fourth Marine Brigade of the Second Infantry Division fought in France in 1918.

On numerous occasions since I assumed office, I have stated my conviction that the Marine Corps has a vital role in our organization for national security and I will continue to support and maintain its identity.

I regard the Marine Corps as a force available for use in any emergency, whatever or whenever necessary. When I spoke of the Marines as the 'Navy's police force,' I had in mind its immediate readiness, and the provision of the National Security Act which states that 'The Marine Corps shall be organized, trained, and equipped to provide fleet marine forces of combined arms, together with supporting air components, for services with the fleet in the seizure or defense of advanced naval bases and for the conduct of such land operations as may be essential to the prosecution of a naval campaign.'

---

*The words "be aware of" replaced the original draft's much more pointed "have in mind."

The Corps' ability to carry out whatever task may be assigned to it has been splendidly demonstrated many times in our history. It has again been shown by the immediate response of the Marine Corps to a call for duty in Korea. Since Marine ground and air forces have arrived in Korea I have received a daily report of their actions. The country may feel sure that the record of the Marines there will add new laurels to the already illustrious record of the Marine Corps.

Sincerely yours,
HARRY S. TRUMAN

The original opening sentence in the letter to Commandant Nixon read: "I sincerely regret that, for reasons I have already expressed to you, I can not attend the Marine Corps League banquet which is to be held this Friday." It was dropped when Truman decided that making a personal appearance would be useful. The next day, he told his staff that he had changed his mind, but Admiral Cates, who arrived at the Oval Office early in the morning, and Ross were able to persuade him to appear. Truman gave a brief speech, which, according to Ayers, received "a fine reception." What Ayers did not mention, and very likely did not know, was that immediately before Truman's arrival at the convention, Commandant Nixon delivered an order to the assembled delegates: "No wisecracks will be tolerated. . . . You will behave like Marines."[15]

This highly unusual presidential apology and the Marines' gracious acceptance should have been the end of the story, but the letters and telegrams continued to pour into both the White House and McDonough's office. The senator saw that there was still considerable political mileage to be gained from the incident. The letter to Truman from Marine Corps League National Commandant Maurice Fagan describes what happened next.

Dear Mr. President:					*September 28, 1950*
My attention has been called to press clippings publicizing Congressman McDonough's proposal to auction your letter to him and contribute the money to the Marine Corps League.

Let me assure you, Mr. President, that this proposal comes to me both as a surprise and a shock.

Believe me, Mr. President, I am certain that I bespeak the sentiments of all my associates and the rank and file of the membership of the league, when I say that we must disavow participation in any such scheme and must refuse to accept any monies that may be obtained in this manner.

Obviously we cannot permit the honorable record of the Marine Corps League to become tainted by involvement in partisan politics.

May I take this occasion to reaffirm our loyalty to the Commander-in-Chief of the Army, the Navy, the Air Force and the Marines.

Assuring you that we sincerely regret this unfortunate incident, I am

> *Sincerely yours,*
> *Maurice J. Fagan, National Commandant*
> *Marine Corps League*
> *Philadelphia, Penn.*

Along with the letter to Truman was a carbon copy of a message Fagan sent to Congressman McDonough.

> *Dear Congressman:*   *September 28, 1950*
>
> Your proposal to sell the controversial letter to you from President Truman and your offer to contribute the funds to the Marine Corps League places the league in an embarrassing position.
>
> As national commandant of the league I am compelled to call your attention to the fact that there is grave danger that the league may find itself used for political purposes.
>
> There has been a sincere apology, which has been accepted, therefore, the league considers the letter incident closed. We cannot in good grace, ethics, or conscience do otherwise.
>
> I am certain that upon sober reflection you will agree with me that the Marine Corps League should have had the courtesy of being consulted before it was committed to be a party to any proposal involving it.
>
> In the absence of contrary action by the league, I must disclaim any participation in the scheme and must decline to accept money raised under such circumstances.
>
> *Sincerely yours,*
> *Maurice J. Fagan*
> *National Commandant*

Truman was extremely pleased by Fagan's quick action and dictated a thank you during a brief break from work aboard the presidential yacht.

U.S.S. WILLIAMSBURG

Dear Mr. Fagan: *Chesapeake Bay Area, 4 October 1950*

I am grateful for the expression of loyalty contained in your letter to me of September 28th, and I am sincerely appreciative of the honorable and forthright position taken by you and your associates of the Marine Corps League in refusing to participate, in any way, in the scheme to raise money by the auction of my letter to Congressman McDonough.

Sincerely yours,
HARRY S. TRUMAN

But while the support of upper-level Marines was appreciated, Truman and his staff knew that the public at large was, at best, only dimly aware of this and that much damage had been done. The following is sampling of the messages received before the incident had blown over.

THE PRESIDENT   1950 SEP 7
DEAR SIR: OUR SON WAS SHOT DOWN IN YUGASOKA, JAPAN. WHO ARE YOU TO DISCREDIT THE UNITED STATES MARINE CORPS?
T. J. CARSON
BROOKLYN, N.Y.

MR. PRESIDENT: 1950 SEP 6
AS A MOTHER OF A MARINE WOUNDED IN IWO JIMA, YOU OWE THE MARINES IN THIS COUNTRY A PUBLIC APOLOGY. YOU MUST ANSWER TO THE MOTHERS WHOSE SONS FOUGHT AND DIED IN THE MARINE CORPS FOR THE DEMOCRACY OF THIS COUNTRY. AREN'T THE MARINES GUARDING YOU IN THE WHITE HOUSE?
MRS. MARY G. FLANIGAN
HARTFORD, CONN.

THE PRESIDENT: 1950 SEP 5
THE PRIDE OF A FORMER MARINE IS OUTRAGED BY YOUR REMARKS CONCERNING THE CORPS. THE BLOOD OF THOUSANDS OF DEAD MARINES SPOIL AT THE REMARK OF THEIR COMMANDER-IN-CHIEF. MARINES, WHOSE PRINCIPLE PROPAGANDA MACHINE IS THE EYE WITNESS REPORTING OF BATTLE-WISE CORRESPONDENTS, ASK YOU, SIR, TO REMEMBER THE RECORD OF THE CORPS.

AND, SIR, MAY GENERAL MACARTHUR BE DIRECTED TO EMPLOY
MARINES TO THE FULLEST EXTENT OF THEIR FIGHTING CAPABILI-
TIES. MAY I ASK, IN THE NAME OF HARD FIGHTING BUT POORLY
SPOKEN MEN, THAT A MARINE OFFICER REPLACE GENERAL
MACARTHUR TO ASSURE A SPEEDY END TO THE POLICE ACTION IN
KOREA.

    JOHN FROGGE, FORMER PVT. USMC
    GARDEN CITY, N.Y.

Dear Honorable President: *1950 SEP 5*

Just a suggestion please: When the 38th parallel is reached in
Korea, why not let the U.S. Marines (Your policemen of the Navy)
be the judge as to when and where to stop.

                     Very respectfully,
                     Branch C. Cullens
                     Waycross, Ga.

    HON HARRY S TRUMAN   1950 SEP 5

    IF THE MARINES ARE POLICEMEN, THEY SHOULD HAVE BEEN
ACTIVE IN KANSAS CITY WHEN TOM PENDERGAST WAS SELECTING
YOU FOR SENATOR.

    J. T. CONNERS
    TDCL BAY VILLAGE, OHIO

Messages of support were few (very few) and far between, yet tended to
be longer and more reasoned.

My dear Mr. President: *Sep. 6, 1950*

Thank God! You had the courage to write Gordon L. McDonough exactly the kind of answer to his letter that you did.

Sorry for Hickenlooper's statement in which he misrepresents
your statement so badly. He said you insulted the Marine Corps by
calling their shedding of blood on every battlefield since 1775 propaganda. Any man with a brain cell knows that you never intended
to infer that the military acts of the Corps were propaganda. What
you did mean, and what every man in the armed services who came
near the Marines knows, that they are first-rate propagandists.

Consider the Marine Hymn: "First to fight for right and freedom,
etc." Isn't this first class propaganda? And they have caused many to

believe this. Many of them even believe it. As a matter of fact, most wars have been like the present police action, other branches have fought first. How long was the army there before the Marines arrived in Korea? Then the Marines popped off: "Send the army home, the Marines are here."

I may not be of much help, but I am going to do my bit. I am writing both McDonough and Hickenlooper, and I have already written Fulton Lewis, Jr., also his sponsor.

I am loyally and politically your admiring friend. I was born within sight of the house where you were born. I saw you at Ft. Riley, Kansas, 1908, when I was a member of Co. B. Second Mo. National Guard.

I was with the Marines in the recent war while my son was a Captain in the Air Corps. (Chief pilot of a superfortress, atom bomb crew). At present I am in the Navy Reserve, expecting a call any day. I would like to plug the "red helpers" all I can before I leave.

H. L. Allen
Los Angeles, Calif.

[Longhand] *N. B. Mr. Secretary. It's not necessary to call this to the President's attention, neither a reply. Just had to "get it off my chest."*

Truman was completely responsible for this controversy and the resultant deluge of criticism. The next wave of letters and telegrams were almost universally sympathetic, but these were generated by an event that was not at all of his making. On October 29, 1950, fighting broke out in San Juan, Puerto Rico, as the island's ineffectual nationalists, called *Indepentistas,* attemped to seize control of the government through armed insurrection. The action was quickly suppressed. Two days later, a pair of fanatical Puerto Ricans arrived in Washington from New York on a self-appointed mission to kill the president.

Truman had done more to promote self-determination for the island's population than any of his predecessors. He had appointed the first native-born governor, extended Social Security to the island, and pushed Congress to pass laws permitting Puerto Ricans to elect the governor and other officials. Truman also had not ruled out independence from the United States as one of the options available to the Puerto Rican people, along with commonwealth status and complete statehood. But as the surviving terrorist later maintained, it wasn't *Truman* they were after; he was "just a symbol of the system," and "you don't attack the man, you attack the system."[16]

On the afternoon of November 1, 1950, a gunfight erupted on Pennsylvania Avenue outside the Trumans' temporary Blair House residence. The Secret Service had always looked upon the site, located right up on the street, as an overly inviting target and security nightmare. (Unknown to evening passersby strolling down the street, Truman's study was but a few yards away, just inside the front entrance of the connecting Lee House next door.) Now a White House policeman lay dead, and two others were gravely wounded. One attacker had been killed, and the other lay bleeding on the sidewalk from a gunshot wound to the chest, just ten stairsteps from an open entranceway barred only by the flimsy latch of a screen door. Truman always insisted that he had never been in any real danger (the door was immediately covered on the inside by at least two Secret Service agents armed with Thompson submachine guns), but he was deeply disturbed by the sacrifices made by young men he knew very well.

More than 7,000 letters and telegrams arrived at the White House expressing relief and gratitude that the president had not been injured. They were written by Americans from every walk of life and social stature, and Truman insisted that all be properly acknowledged. He personally signed each response. Hassett produced a half dozen formula openings to be used as the basis for the replies, nearly all of which would be individually tailored to the concerns of the correspondents in subsequent sentences. Salutations to male correspondents were usually made out to their first name in an effort to provide a personal touch. Every few days, Truman would be funneled a fresh stack of letters and prepared answers, which he usually signed as he conducted routine business with his staff.

THE PRESIDENT: 1950 NOV 1
DEEPLY ALARMED FROM REPORT OF YOUR ATTEMPTED ASSASSI-
NATION. REJOICE WITH ALL MY FELLOW AMERICANS THAT
THROUGH THE GRACE OF OUR HEAVENLY FATHER YOUR LIFE WAS
SPARED FOR FURTHER WORLD SERVICE.
SAMUEL SOLINS
WELCH, W.V.

Dear Sam: *November 3, 1950*
Thank you for your telegram of November first expressing

thoughtful regard for my personal safety. This has indeed been a great tragedy and I am grateful for your kindness in wiring me.

Very sincerely yours,
HARRY S. TRUMAN

THE PRESIDENT: 1950 NOV 1
I REJOICE WITH THE PEOPLE OF OUR NATION AND STATE THAT
YOUR LIFE HAS BEEN SPARED. WE ARE THANKFUL TO GOD AND JOIN
IN A PRAYER OF THANKSGIVING FOR YOUR HEROIC DEFENDERS.
PAUL E. FITZPATRICK
NEW YORK, N.Y.

Dear Paul: *November 3, 1950*
It certainly was kind and thoughtful of you to wire as you did. I am grateful for your solicitous expressions, and, at the same time, I am truly saddened because our valiant guards sacrificed so much in my defense.

Very sincerely yours,
HARRY S. TRUMAN

My dear Mr. President: *November 2, 1950*
My feelings concerning the incident occurred yesterday are expressed in the opening statements I made to the Military Order of Foreign Wars of the United States:

"I am sure that I echo the satisfaction of everyone here that the President escaped the attempt on his life today. The President of the United States is the symbol of our nation and assassination is not a part of the American way of life."

Yours faithfully,
Herbert Hoover
New York, N.Y.

Dear Mr. President: *November 3, 1950*
It is impossible to tell you how much your letter of November second means to me. Please know that I am truly grateful for these expressions, especially because they came from you.

Very sincerely yours,
HARRY S. TRUMAN

Dear Harry and Bess: *Nov. 2*

It was such a shock to us to hear of yesterday's tragedies. Please be more careful than ever. There never was a time where our nation needed your mettle, your experience and knowledge as a leader of the world. Let's keep America and our flag our forefathers fought for regardless.

I tried to call you yesterday evening but could not get through. Much love—and just know I am always standing by.

> *Mrs. Lenora A. Boxley*
> *New York, N.Y.*

Dear Mrs. Boxley: *November 7, 1950*

Bess and I wanted to thank you for your kind letter of the second. It was good of you and so many others to be concerned over our safety in connection with the terrible incident at Blair House and we both deeply appreciate the kind things you say. I am sorry that you could not get your call through, but, as you may imagine, our switchboard was flooded with messages.

We join in all good wishes to you.

> *Very sincerely yours,*
> *HARRY S. TRUMAN*

Dear Mr. President: *Nov. 2, 1950*

That was a "*good* miss" you had yesterday. I feel deeply sorry over what happened to your guards but thank the Lord the assassination attempt was so poorly planned that you suffered no harm. Please give Mrs. Truman my very best as I know she will be on pins and needles for a while.

It was very kind of you to express concern over my long tour in the hospital but now it's my turn to express concern and say for God's sake be careful. I do not believe that the U.S. is overrun with wild-eyed fanatics or that there are anymore than these who would try to shoot you but the present world situation is so tense, you cannot take too many chances. When Capt. H. S. Truman bravely chanced getting shot was a long time ago, and it would not do for President Truman to unduly endanger himself. My personal concern is: I don't want to see *Mr.* Harry Truman shot.

I know this *fussing* is unbecoming of a naval officer, but "take it easy."

> *Very sincerely,*
> *Jim Suddath*
> *Washington, D.C.*

Dear Jim: *November 7, 1950*

It certainly was kind of you to write me as you did after that tragic occurrence here last week. I highly appreciate your solicitude for my safety and have already told Mrs. Truman that you sent her your best regards. As you can understand, we are both deeply distressed over the great sacrifices made by our valued guards.

My best wishes for your continued good health.

> *Very sincerely yours,*
> *HARRY S. TRUMAN*

My dear Mr. President: *November 4, 1950*

The membership of the First Magyar Presbyterian Church, 233 East 116th Street, New York 29, N. Y., the oldest Hungarian church in this country, was deeply shocked by the recent event aimed at the head of the nation at a time when the whole world is looking to it for salvation.

We pray for a strengthening of the spirit for the continuation of leadership in this perplexed time.

> *Faithfully yours,*
> *(Rev.) Ladislaus Haransyi*
> *Pastor*

Dear Reverend Harsanyi: *November 7, 1950*

Thank you for your kindness in sending me that letter. You and the members of your congregation may be sure that I am grateful for your thoughtfulness as well as for your prayers.

> *Very sincerely yours,*
> *HARRY S. TRUMAN*

A great many Puerto Ricans, mortified at the actions of the would-be assassins, hastened to separate themselves from those ostensibly acting in their name. One San Juan businessman dashed off a telegram to his president in Spanish the morning after the incident. Apparently worried that sending it in his native tongue would delay its arrival, he drafted another in English that was transmitted late in the afternoon. His suspicion was justified. Although there were undoubtedly several people within the White House who could translate the initial message, the staff followed standard procedures and forwarded it to the State Department, which had delegated personnel fluent enough to guarantee that no mistakes in interpretation would be made. Meanwhile, a sharp-eyed individual on Hassett's staff noticed that the second telegram had arrived from the same person. A presidential response covering both messages was held up until the "official" translation came back from the State Department.

> LT HON HARRY S TRUMAN: 1950 NOV 2
> ME UNO A MI PUEBLO EN EL SENTIMIENTO POR EL ATENTADO CONTRA SU VIDA POR UN GRUPO DE FANATICOS QUE A NADIE REPRESENTAN EN NUESTRO PAIS DIOSGUARDE SU VIDA.
> SANTIAGO JIMENEZ SOLIS
> PRESIDENTE FEDERACION DEL COMERCIO DE PUERTO RICO

> [TRANSLATION]
> HIS EXCELLENCY HARRY S. TRUMAN   NOV 2 1950
> I JOIN MY PEOPLE IN SORROW AT THE ATTEMPT ON YOUR LIFE BY A GROUP OF FANATICS WHO REPRESENT NO ONE IN OUR COUNTRY. MAY GOD PRESERVE YOUR LIFE.
> SANTIAGO JIMENEZ SOLIS
> PRESIDENT OF THE FEDERATION OF COMMERCE OF PUERTO RICO

> 1950 NOV 2
> HON HARRY S TRUMAN PRESIDENT OF UNITED STATES
> THE FEDERATION OF COMMERCE OF PUERTO RICO HEARTILY AND WARMLY CELEBRATES THAT YOUR MOST PRECIOUS LIFE SHOULD HAVE BEEN SPARED IN THESE MOMENTS IN WHICH YOU ARE SO OPENLY FIGHTING TO MAKE THIS WORLD SAFE FOR DEMOCRACY. WE MOST STRONGLY CONDEMN ATTEMPT ON YOUR LIFE AND THANK GOD FOR HAVING SAVED YOUR LIFE FOR THE BENEFIT OF THE WORLD AND OF PUERTO RICO IN WHICH YOU'RE

SO HIGHLY ESTEEMED.

SANTIAGO JIMENEZ SOLIS, PRESIDENT

FEDERATION OF COMMERCE OF PUERTO RICO

Dear Mr. Jimenez: *November 14, 1950*

This is to express my thanks to you and your associates of the Federation of Commerce for your thoughtfulness in sending me that message. These expressions of regard for my safety are deeply appreciated.

Very sincerely yours,

HARRY S. TRUMAN

November 28, 1950, was a black day for the president. At the normally breezy morning staff meeting, Truman looked slowly around the table at the faces of his immediate lieutenants, Matt Connelly, George Elsey, William Hopkins, Charlie Murphy, William Hassett, Harry Vaughan, Eban Ayers, and Charlie Ross, before informing them that the chairman of the Joint Chiefs of Staff, Omar Bradley, had relayed "a terrible message" earlier that morning.[17] General MacArthur reported that the heady victory march up the Korean peninsula after the remarkable landing at Inch'on had come to an abrupt halt near the Chinese border, as several hundred thousand Red Chinese soldiers fell upon the U.N. forces. Their intent was not to form a buffer along their border but to annihilate his army. MacArthur's message warned that his men were up against an "overwhelming force" and that "consequently, we face an entirely new war."[18]

Author John Hersey, writing a profile of Truman for *The New Yorker*, was also present and recorded how the president solemnly told the assembled staff: "This is the worst situation we have had yet. We'll just have to meet it as we've met all the rest."[19] Truman outlined the latest development and alternatives for the grim-faced men, then ticked off the steps that would have to be taken immediately with the Cabinet and Congress. He also mentioned that the Soviet government newspaper, *Pravda*, had recently run an article claiming that "the American government is divided, and how our people are divided in hatred."[20] It was obvious to Truman that the communists had severely misjudged American resolve, and Ayers recorded what he told the staff: "This situation . . . was brought about as a result of the vile, vicious campaign of lies that has been carried on by some people—such, he meant, as Senator McCarthy and others—who have been talking and attacking Secretary of State Acheson and the administration." Throughout the session, Truman scratched his name on a stack of letters brought in by Hopkins. The bulk of them were some of the last responses to go out on the assassination attempt.

> *Dear Mr. President:*   *November 10, 1950*
>
> As a citizen of the United States of America and brother in the B.P.O.E. [Benevolent and Protective Order of Elks], permit me to convey to you my regrets over the disgraceful attempt made recently on your life.
>
> The people of Puerto Rico are, in their immense majority, a community of peaceful, law abiding, loyal American citizens and as such have condemned the unjustified acts of violence that took place recently. May I join the majority of this people in the satisfaction that the criminal attempt perpetrated upon you was frustrated.
>
> With best personal wishes believe me,
>
>   *Fraternally yours,*
>   *F. I. Lugo, Certified Public Accountant*
>   *Member of San Juan Lodge No. 972*

> *Dear Mr. Lugo:*   *November 28, 1950*
>
> It is kind of you to join with other citizens of Puerto Rico in expressing indignation over the recent occurrence here. My thanks for your fine assurances and your good wishes.
>
>   *Very sincerely yours,*
>   *HARRY S. TRUMAN*

Almost anything one could say about the pressure Truman was under during this period would be an understatement. The sturdy Missourian had taken more than his fair share of lumps during an extremely dangerous and complex time in history, but the last week had seen the apparent triumph in Korea degenerate into a ghastly retreat. Moreover, a needless misstatement about his willingness to use atomic weapons to stem the communists' advance had led to an international incident so severe that it genuinely endangered America's alliance with its most valuable ally, Great Britain. On December 5, Truman entered into direct consultations with the British prime minister, Clement Attlee, who had flown to Washington for the emergency meeting. Now, in the midst of a delicate damage-control effort, the president's dear friend and press secretary suddenly died after completing an evening press briefing. Charlie Ross, who had just been playfully chided by his secretary to not mumble, joked, "You know I always speak *very* distinctly," and fell out of his chair sideways.[21] The NBC television crew at first thought he was clowning around, but Ross had suffered a coronary occlusion and was dead by the time Dr. Graham dashed upstairs to his side.

Within hours, Truman's daughter, Margaret, a budding opera singer, was scheduled to perform at Constitution Hall. In spite his grief over Ross's death, Truman felt that he must attend her recital, particularly since his guests were the British ambassador and prime minister. The president did his best to put on a bright face at all the appropriate times, but it did not escape the notice of some, who, like Margaret, were unaware of what had happened, that he looked unusually downcast that night. The following morning, he awoke to find a *Washington Post* review of his daughter's performance that was so scathing that, according to Secretary of Defense Marshall, the only thing not criticized "was the varnish on the piano."[22] Truman had been under tremendous strain, and this was the last straw. As White House usher J. B. West later explained, "He could take anything himself, but just let sombeody say a word against his womenfolk."[23] Before breakfast, and without waiting to go to the Oval Office, he immediately penned a letter on a White House memo pad.

> *Mr. Hume:*
>
> I've just read your lousy review of Margaret's concert. I've come to the conclusion that you are an "eight ulcer man on four ulcer pay."
>
> It seems to me that you are a frustrated old man [Hume was thirty-four] who wishes he could have been successful. When you write such poppy-cock as was in the back section of the paper you work for it shows conclusively that you're off the beam and at least four of your ulcers are at work.
>
> Some day I hope to meet you. When that happens you'll need a new nose, a lot of beefsteak for black eyes, and perhaps a supporter below!
>
> [Westbrook] Pegler, a gutter snipe, is a gentleman alongside you. I hope you'll accept that statement as a worse insult than a reflection on your ancestry.
>
> *HARRY S. TRUMAN*

Truman found an envelope, addressed it, affixed a 3-cent stamp, and innocently asked an elderly servant to drop it in a mailbox. He kept the secret of his letter bomb to himself, making no mention of it to anyone on the staff, and certainly not to Bess or Margaret. The explosion came several days later. The *Washington Post* declined to print the angry letter because they were fully aware of the tragic circumstances surrounding its writing, but copies were soon circulating, and it found its way to the front page of another D.C. paper, the *Daily News*. The Truman women were mortified. Bess was convinced that her husband had ended her daughter's career, but Margaret believed that it would only increase the ticket sales of upcoming concerts. In the short run, Margaret turned out to be more right than her mother, but it did little to soften the blow from another round of press criticism. Truman was very pleased to inform them, however, that the office mail was running solidly in his favor.

"Dad discussed the letter with his aides," recalled Margaret, "and was annoyed to find that they all thought it was a mistake. They felt that it damaged his image as President and would only add to his political difficulties. 'Wait till the mail comes in,' Dad said, 'I'll make you a bet that eighty percent of it is on my side of the argument.'

"A week later, after a staff meeting, Dad ordered everybody to follow him, and they marched to the mail room. The clerks had stacked the thousands of 'Hume' letters received in piles and made up a chart showing the percentages for and against the President. Slightly over 80 percent favored Dad's defense of me. Most of the letter writers were mothers who said they understood exactly how Dad felt and would have expected their husbands to defend their daughters the same way. 'The trouble with you guys is,' Dad said to the staff as he strode back to work, 'you just don't understand human nature.'"[24]

This is a wonderful parable, elegant in its simplicity. It is also a fabrication. What seems likely is that Truman was simply trying to place the incident in the best possible light for his family, and the White House staff similarly put out the word to the press that the public was showing great support. What the official mail logs for the period show is that, far from "thousands," the total amount of mail classified by Hassett's markers as pertaining primarily to the subject (correspondents frequently touched on several topics in the course of their letters) was only 877 items by the time the controversy died out in early January. Well over half of them criticized Truman. Moreover, of those who identified themselves as mothers, fewer applauded the president's defense of his daughter's honor than commented that they wished Truman had the same concern for the boys in Korea as he did for Margaret's singing career. There was a great resurgence in the number of letters referring either directly or indirectly to the Hume fiasco in the avalanche of mail that arrived in the wake of the MacArthur firing several months later, but they arrived well after the event, are not the letters' main subject, and are uniformly critical of Truman's behavior.

Dear Mr. President: *December 10, 1950*

Did it ever occur to you, when taking time from your rather important duties to write a letter to a critic of your child, how fathers of boys being killed and maimed in Korea feel about your foreign policies that got us into this mess?

Very sincerely,
William A. Hazlett

Mr. H. S. T.   *12/12/50*

Well Mr. H. S. T., whoever you are, this editorial from our best Pasadena paper will show you what we think of you.

That RAT JOE, in Moscow has been making a monkey out of you from the start, now Hume has done a good job of it also, and you finished it up when your tail let go of that high up limb in Washington, and you fell into the gutter by writing that nasty letter to a little guy, supposed to be a music critic.

Could you not see that he trapped you into it for his own purpose of getting publicity for himself?

No one would have heard about him had it not been for your poor judgment.

Now every one in the nation knows about him and you are the GOAT, TOO BAD.

You should have been too busy with world affairs to give him the satisfaction of any notice on your part, DON'T YOU SEE?

We all like your daughter, and we feel that the only mistake she has made, outside of the fact that she chose you for a Dad, was when she let herself be roped in on that CHEAP advertising radio program with TOOLA BLANKHEAD [*sic*], the other Sunday.

Just see what [opera singer] Mary Garden has to say about it. Should you not be as wise as Mary?

Shame on you H. S. T. We need a man not a mouse in the White House, so please get some real good advisors around you and NEVER do a thing until you have asked them if you should or not.

Sympathetically,
N. J. Harrison
Pasadena, Calif.

Mr. Harry Truman,
Your daughter is *flat* part of the time. *You* are flat all the time.
Lela Hubbard

Hi Champ,   *Dec. 12, 1950*
I was going to put "chump" but I don't want a broken nose. I
think that was the most ignorant thing you could have done. After
all your daughter Margaret is in a field where she must except [*sic*]
criticism as well as praise. I heard about it over the radio last Saturday night and I almost flipped. After all, a man in your position
should know better than to act like a child over something as trivial
as that. Why do we have freedom of the press if a man can't say what
he thinks by the means of print without getting threatened or receiving insults like that "ulcer" routine.*
Well that's all I have to say. When do I receive my broken nose.
Yours Worriedly,
Jack Devlin
Detroit, Mich.

Like this man from Detroit, many correspondents thought the president's actions extremely childish. Numerous parents referred to comments
their own children made about his outburst, and some kids took it upon
themselves to scold the president.

Dear Sir: *Dec. 12, 1950*
When the article concerning your letter to Mr. Paul Hume, music
critic, appeared in our local paper, our sixteen-year-old daughter
read your letter, turned to me and said, "Mama, that sounds just like
something a little kid would write."
I'm quite sure that her comment expresses the reaction of the
whole nation. It's too bad that you weren't a big enough man to
uphold the dignity and prestige your office requires.
Yours very truly,
Mrs. Park L. Henry
Washington, Penn.

---

*Author David McCullough noted that Truman picked up the phrase from F.D.R.'s
press secretary, Steve Early.

Dear Mr. Truman,   *Dec. 10, 1950*

Since when has the people of the United States of America not the right to criticize darling, dearest little Margaret's singing without being "punched in the nose" so to speak.

> *Yours truly,*
> *Miss Bry Ann Jones*
> *(Age 11)*
> *San Antonio, Texas*

P.S. You should hear what my mother and dad say about you.

Hassett's staff divided the Hume letters into several categories, primarily "pro" and "con." As the following "pro" items demonstrate, they had a rather liberal intrepretation of what constituted a letter of support.

Mr. President Truman:

I see in the news where you got fighting mad when someone didn't think your daughter's singing wasn't so good.

How do you think the parents of the teenage boy in Korea feel when all the odds are against them? Please get the boys out of there and give them a chance for a career too. I am not just pleading for my son but for all the boys that are left there and am praying that my son will be among them.

> *A Mother,*
> *Mae Allman*
> *Indianapolis, Ind.*

Mr. President: *Dec. 10, 1950*

Please hurry and do something for those boys being pushed back into Korea, you just went through one experience of how it feels when one so close to you is hurt. We love our boy just as much. I have a son-in-law in Hamhung fighting for survival for his daughter and wife. My other son-in-law is in Kentucky with a cracked lining in his skull from the last war. My only son is in Fort Dix. Being prepared for war, we all love our sons the same as you do your daughter. Please hurry and do something.

> *Resp.*
> *Mrs. Jos. Armington*
> *Providence, R.I.*

One would get the impression, from reading Margaret's secondhand account of the public response, that letters of support were much like the one from this housewife from Louisville, Kentucky, who sent her message on festive Christmas stationery emblazoned with the words "Season's Greetings."

My dear Mr. President: *Christmas 1950*
I have a daughter 25 years old, whom I dare say I love as much as you do Margaret. You have been accused of being plain "low-brow" for giving vent to feelings. I personally admire you greater for being unable to conceal behind a Presidential mantle.

I have no patience with, nor sympathy for the sobs [sob sisters], either, and I must say that I admire you the more for your so-called "outburst."

It is most refreshing to feel that we have a President who loves his daughter enough to fling presidential expediences to the wind for the very sake of something that enemies within and without seem to place so little value on.

I assure you that there are thousands who think about the matter like I do, the very Happiness of whose Christmases depend on yours.
         Respectfully,
         Altha Baugh
         Louisville, Ky.

But in reality, it was the menfolk who made up Truman's cheering section.

Dear President,   *Dec. 11, 1950*
I want to congratulate you for having the guts to speak up in defending your daughter. I have a daughter 21 years old and married. I have faith in you in defending my daughter and myself and all other good Americans.

May God Bless you.
         Mr. Fred Archambo
         Munisking, Mich.

Dear Harry: *December 8, 1950*
I happen to be a small merchant in a small town and I'm not in the habit of writing letters for fun, but I have just finished reading the article in regard to a letter written by you to one Paul Hume, where you said in part, "You would like to punch him in the nose."

I like that and in fact I'd like to do the job for you and at the same time there are four or five others that a good punch in the nose would do a lot of good.

It's too bad that a person in your position can't make a personal statement without having some ape make a national issue out of it.

More power to you.

> *Sincerely,*
> *Ed Mullally*
> *The Pierre Bootery*
> *Pierre, S.D.*

Dear Mr. President: *12-10-50*

Sorry to hear you let a critic get under your skin and wanted to tell you that you have my sympathy!

Believe me, you have my A-Men when you mention Pegler as a S.O.B. together with Winchell, Luella Parsons, etc., they represent about the lowest form of animal life.

> *Regards,*
> *Warren W. Andrews*
> *Chicago, Ill.*

Some men found Truman's fighting words reminiscent of past presidents who also had a reputation for direct action, and if Truman actually saw these letters, he certainly would have approved of the comparisons.

Dear Mr. President: *December 9, 1950*

You have my hearty support in your designs upon the music critic. I have heard Margaret sing and she has a fine voice. Not only that, but she is an exceptionally fine girl and everybody loves her. The only difference between you and Andrew Jackson is, instead of wanting to punch his nose, he would have invited him to a duel.

With good luck in everything, I am,

> *Your friend,*
> *Von Mayes*
> *Attorney*
> *Caruthersville, Mo.*

Dear Harry: *December 9, 1950*

As one Field Artillery man to another, I got a big kick out of the enclosed news item published in today's *Philadelphia Inquirer.* I would punch that bastard in the nose too.

After your positive stand for no appeasement to the Reds during your conferences with the pussy-footing British during the past week, hot Goddamn, I believe we have a bigger and better Teddy Roosevelt as our leader at the top.

Give them hell Harry, use every weapon we have and don't pull any punches.

Final results are the only things that count in history. We all back you 100 percent. I speak for five servicemen in this house.

Remember, the communists respect only force, not words. Get our National Guard into federal service as quickly as possible because before long you will have to throw the book at Stalin and you will need a big one.

> *Sincerely yours,*
> *Robert G. MacKendrick*
> *Norwood, Penn.*

P.S. Please don't take up the valuable time of your office answering this letter. It's just like a pat on the back. I hope that you don't take offense because I address you as "Harry." I am employed at Scott Paper Company, Chester, Pa., where we all address our beloved President Thomas B. McCabe, "TOM."

More concerned with the expanding war than with the Hume fracas was a former vaudevillian who had worked his way into radio in the 1930s and, more recently, into the infant medium of television. His telegram displayed a light touch that was all too rare in the missives of both Truman's supporters and detractors.

THE PRESIDENT,   1950 DEC 11

DO SOMETHING. LET'S GET INDUSTRY ON A WAR FOOTING. MERRY XMAS. I LIKE MARGARET'S SINGING.

MOREY AMSTERDAM

And a whimsical WAVE from Los Angeles did not consider Margaret very good at her chosen profession but could sympathize with her troubles.

Dear Sir: *10 Dec 1950*

The enclosed article was in the *Los Angeles Times*. After reading it I see Margaret and I have a great deal in common. According to the critics, she can't sing and I don't have the aptitude to make 3/c Dental Tech, according to one Naval officer.

My story goes like this: I was on active duty during WW II, from 23 June 1943 to 6 Nov. 1945, Inactive Reserves, 6 Sept. 1946 to 1 Oct. 1949, Organized Reserve, 1 Oct. to the present date. Located at Los Alamitos Naval Air Base, Long Beach, California.

The Navy sent me through Hospital Corps School, at the National Naval Medical Center, Bethesda, Maryland. Through Dental School, at Corona Naval Hospital, Corona, California. I will receive my Associated Arts Degree from Los Angeles City College on 30 January 1951.

—but Miss Margaret can't sing and I don't have brains enough to be anything but a seaman (Dentalman) for SEVEN years.

Very truly yours,
Velma Arnold Cascarelli
WAVE USNR
Los Angeles, Calif.

NEW YORK, N.Y.   MAR 21, 1952
JOSEPH SHORT
COULD YOU PLEASE WIRE ME COLLECT WHETHER THERE WILL
BE EGG ROLLING ON THE WHITE HOUSE LAWN ON EASTER MON-
DAY. THANK YOU.
    LOUIS FORSTER
    THE NEW YORKER

    TO LOUS FORSTER
    THE NEW YORKER MAGAZINE
    WHITE HOUSE EGG ROLLING DISCONTINUED THIRTEEN YEARS
AGO. NO PLANS TO RESUME.
    IRVING PERLMETER

CHAPTER TEN

THREATS • FRIENDS • ATOM BOMB • LEAVING OFFICE

Until the attempt on his life at Blair House, Truman had thought little of his personal safety. "A President has to expect those things,"[1] he said, and "[if] someone wants to shoot you, they'll probably do it. . . . It just goes with the job."[2] But the death of one young guard and the wounding of two others brought home to him as nothing else could that lax security only invited trouble and that there were others besides himself to consider. "After the assault on the Blair House I learned that the men who want to keep me alive are the ones who get hurt and not the President. I'd always thought that I might be able to take care of an assassin as old Andy Jackson did but I found that the guards get hurt and not the President. So now I conform to the rules without protest."[3]

Truman went on a highly publicized morning walk the day after the attack—under greatly increased protection—as much for his own need to feel free of his presidential "prison" as to display a sense of normalcy to the nation. Bess, however, "was visibly upset for days,"[4] according to White House usher J. B. West, and both she and Margaret wanted him to stop the practice altogether. Several days later, in St. Louis, he took their advice when the Secret Service warned him of possible trouble from what Truman described as "more crackpots." For a time, the president was driven to different parts of Washington for his walks, but his daily regimen soon centered back in the area around the White House. The commute later in the mornings from Blair House to the Executive Offices, which actually presented more of a security problem than the much longer walks, was done only by car after the attack.

Numerous events Truman would have liked to attend, such as various family gatherings and the 1951 reunion of his old 35th Division comrades, had to be missed because of threats against him or the sheer disruption that his presence would entail. But some events he refused to skip no matter what the situation.

By tradition, the president *always* attends the annual Army-Navy football game in Philadelphia, sitting on the Army side of the field during one half and the Navy during the other. A reasonably credible tip had been received that someone was going to try to shoot Truman with a high-powered rifle as he walked across the gridiron at halftime. Threat or no, Truman was determined to maintain the tradition. He never told his family anything about the warning, and it was only much later that Margaret found out that the Secret Service "had men stationed at every conceivable point throughout the stadium where a rifleman might position himself."[5] When the time came, Truman strolled across the field grinning and waving to the cheering crowd, then took his seat without incident.

The Secret Service routinely recorded anywhere from 150 to 200 threats per month against Truman. Implied or direct, oral or written, all had to receive at least some degree of investigation. Even though this number might sound high, the Truman administration actually represented somewhat of a breather for agents, since Roosevelt had received three to four times as many. Almost 98 percent came from "mentally unbalanced" individuals, a few of whom either received jail terms or were committed to asylums. Correspondents who rhetorically asked if Truman "wanted to take a swing" at them, too, during the Hume episode were ignored in spite of their implied willingness to engage in fisticuffs with the commander in chief.

The Secret Service did not read letters as they came into the White House but depended on Hassett's markers to do the initial screening after they were briefed on what to watch for. The only time the quantity of letters sent to the Secret Service reached FDR proportions was during the MacArthur controversy, when roughly 1,500 were turned over between April 19 and May 3, 1951. Letters like one from 1949 that included the line "the day will come when I will have your heart out and give it to the ants as food" was certainly a candidate for closer scrutiny, but others were less obvious. The staff was instructed to route messages to the agents if they were in doubt, so many of the forwarded letters were highly ambiguous. A synopsis was sometimes retained in the files.

Miss Anne E. Quinn
Veteran of World War I
Bedford Hills, N.Y.
Registered letter to the President, dated 4/16/51
The writer severely criticizes the President for the dismissal of General MacArthur. Says it is illegal that the President's title as

Commander-in-Chief is only honorary. Concludes her letter by saying "A time-worn maxim seems to hold true in your case, 'Whom
the Gods destroy, they first make mad.' How about it Captain?"

Sent to Secret Service, 4/30/51.

Some people sent letters over a period of years. They also would be seemingly ignored for years unless they crossed over the line. A White House special assistant to Dr. Steelman on the Scientific Research Board finally became
alarmed when one gentleman's correspondence took an ominous turn.

MEMORANDUM FOR HANK Re: 23469—
Glare Research Institute, Chicago
From: David H. Stowe

While this appears to be another of a series of "crank letters"
because of the implications that his so-called discovery is now available to a foreign country and because of his inclusion of a purported
story of a military intelligence officer, it is felt advisable to send the
entire file to the Secret Service for clarification.

A few months later, another letter arrived.

Hank [Henrietta Parker]:   *2/25/48*

If this is the same guy whose letter was referred to the Secret Service before, this letter should be sent up there, too. I don't know
whether or not we will get a report back from the Secret Service on
this, but if we do, I would like to know for future reference.

D. STOWE
The White House

Barely a month had passed before yet another message was received.

Hon. John R. Steelman, Scientific Research Board
March 30, 1948
Honorable Sir:

Your one and only reply to me of October 16, 1947, informed
me that the National Bureau of Standards, Commerce Department,
is responsible for undertaking research in discoveries. The recent
difficulties of Dr. Edward U. Condon, director of the Bureau of

Standards, seem to show that the Bureau of Standards is a poor place for undertaking such work.

This same letter also mentions that the President's Scientific Research Board is not equipped to consider or evaluate scientific and technological inventions and discoveries. The Scientific Research Board has, however, considered and evaluated various of the "noted" scientists for government positions, such as the above mentioned Dr. Condon. Several other scientists are in the category and would be better off removed from their positions.

Rumors of the past week have been that we are again on the verge of another war. In all probability, some of the old World War II projects will be dusted off and started going again. Some of those are listed as follows: Dr. Mathew Luckiesh of the Cleveland or Toledo General Electric Lamp Division and his Purkinje theory of blackout lighting. During the course of the recent war, this theory moved from red lights to orange to yellow, then to white and finally to complete blackouts. Dr. Luckiesh, opposed to any form of blue lighting, tried every type of light but blue light in his experiments, and if he had tried blue lights, he would have solved the blackout problem. However, unfortunately for him, we solved this problem before he did.

Another marvel of the recent war was Dr. O. E. Hulbert of the Naval Research Laboratory and his "Propogation [*sic*] in a Scattering and Absorbing Medium," which was published in the 1943 *Journal of the Optical Society*. The trouble with the Hulbert theory was that the "scattering and absorbing medium" did not know how to propagate mathematically according to Dr. Hulbert's formula. Having ideas of its own, nature managed to do the opposite of what the noted Dr. Hulbert figured it would do.

Across the Atlantic Ocean in Germany, Dr. Carl von Weiszacker, a German scientist who managed to get a copy of the *Journal of the Optical Society*, knew what to do. He copied the Hulbert mathematical formula and devised the Japanese balloon bomb, which unfortunately for the inaccuracy of the Hulbert formula, did not do the damage they were expected to do.

After the close of the war, Dr. Astopowich found that the Hulbert-Weiszacker formula would be a nice basis for his attempt in claiming the "counterglow" discovery right. This left this Institute holding the bag on the discovery claim for the contra blue rays.

The latest innovation of the "noted" scientists is the cloud icing experiments to induce rainfall. Included in this should be the atomic cloud ventures. A few weeks ago, under the name of the Simpson Bill H. R. 4582, a "public" hearing was held by the Committee on Interstate and Foreign Commerce, for the purpose of authorizing the expenditure of a half-million dollars for the Chief of the Weather Bureau to conduct experiments in this regard. Any high school boy knows that you cannot get anything out of something that does not contain what you want. Nothing from any figure still leaves nothing, and even Einstein will not dispute this. However, the Chief of the Weather Bureau will receive his half-million dollars to conduct this experiment at Wilmington, Ohio, this summer providing that the citizens of Wilmington, Ohio, do not get an injunction against the Weather Bureau to stay out of their area.

The dispute between this Institute and the General Electric Company led to the discovery rights of the contra blue rays going to foreign protection. This fact alone should have prompted the House Committee on Interstate and Foreign Commerce to investigate General Electric's reason for starting this dispute. The attached copy of an excerpt from a recent magazine is an excellent topic upon some of the "storybook" types of research accomplishments that our government should avoid.

In the prospects of another war, your scientific research board has two courses to follow: one is to dust off some of the above mentioned scientific endeavors and use them again. The Purkinje theory will last until one of our cities is hit by some kind of a bomb. The other course, the safer one, is to scan the lists of the National Roster of Scientific and Specialized Personnel, together with other noncommercial scientists, and begin all over again, protecting the endeavors of these specialized scientists with the proper legislation to protect their work which should be done under the first article of the Constitution of the United States.

Respectfully yours,
G. Francis Nauheimer, Director
Glare Research Institute
Chicago, Ill.

This newest offering from Nauheimer combined prodigious amounts of pseudo-scienctific jargon with a generous sprinkling of name dropping. Could the fellow from Chicago actually know what he was talking about? Steelman's assistant got in touch with another Chicagoan, the noted educator Robert Maynard Hutchins, chancellor of the University of Chicago, to find out. He passed the results on to his boss: "Hutchinson [*sic*] says this man is crazy. The University of Chicago wrote the head of the Weather Bureau that Nauheimer had no laboratory and he was a paranoid to be taken very seriously."

Of far greater concern than nut mail from the "director" of the bogus institute in Chicago was the possibility that advances in explosives technology could lead to a tragedy in the mailroom or one of the numerous White House offices. Even before World War II, extremely efficient high explosive compounds, such as gelignite, had been developed that were far more suitable for use in "package bombs" than the comparatively heavy TNT. The end of the war left prodigious quantities of gelignite and the slightly more stable "plastic explosive" C-3 in the hands of irregular forces in Europe and Asia. Security agencies both here and abroad were painfully aware that such material could either be used by their former guerrilla allies, many of whom were now members of revolutionary groups, or simply sold to persons unknown in the burgeoning black markets of Europe.

Luckily, the relative instability and bulkiness of the compounds available in the late 1940s presented security agencies with opportunities for early detection. Even the 1950s generation of plastic explosives, represented by C-4, was not yet a concern while Truman was in office. Unlike C-4, which can be cut into thin sheets with a knife like so many slices of Spam, C-3 is not terribly pliable, and depending on the type used, it breaks up or flakes off when cut. This means that the *minimum* size package it can be mailed in—with a resonable expectation that it will actually work—is a large, nine-by-twelve-inch envelope. Gelignite is less powerful than C-3 but is still potentially lethal, since someone opening a package would be immediately adjacent to the explosion. A dangerous amount can be placed in a smaller, lighter package than C-3 requires, but it still has to be mailed in something considerably larger than a standard envelope.

The nature of these two Truman-era explosives greatly simplified the job of White House clerks and security personnel on the lookout for suspicious mail. If the item was both larger and substantially thicker than a common envelope and was tightly wrapped with abundant amounts of tape, which minimized the possibility of a premature explosion or disconnection of components, it sent the warning lights flashing.

In June 1947, the Stern Gang in Palestine sent at least eight letter bombs to the current and former British foreign secretaries, in addition to other key

officials. All were intercepted. Subsequent tests by British authorities demonstrated that such a bomb would have maimed, or possibly killed, anyone
unlucky enough to ignite the hidden detonator. Washington was immediately warned of the incident, and none too soon, according to Margaret Truman: "A number of cream-colored envelopes, about eight by six inches,
arrived in the White House, addressed to the President and various members
of the staff." Margaret stated that "Inside them was a smaller envelope
marked 'Private and Confidential.' Inside that second envelope was pow-
dered gelignite, a pencil battery and a detonator rigged to explode the gelignite when the envelope was opened. Fortunately the White House mail room
was alert to the possibility that such letters might arrive. The mail room
turned the letters over to the Secret Service and they were defused by their
bomb experts."[6]

Apparently the only letter bombs passing through the White House
doors during Truman's last years in office were of the paper and ink variety,
and these were frequently written by the president himself. In spite of the
drubbing he took in the press over his angry note to Paul Hume, Truman
was unrepentant over what he viewed as a righteous defense of his family. An
avid concertgoer and serious student of classical music, Truman held himself
in check when coming across reviews he disagreed with (which, not surprisingly, were frequently authored by Hume), but he finally succumbed after
reading "a disgraceful piece of poppycock" in the *Washington Post*.

On February 3, 1952, the president and Mrs. Truman attended an afternoon piano recital by the Greek virtuosa Gina Bachauer at Lisner Auditorium. Truman thought the performance first rate; Hume conceded that
Bachauer's showmanship was "sensational" but that "if you want musical values, they were less evident." Truman, pen in hand, underlined passages and
scribbled notes directly on the newspaper whenever he came upon a particularly galling piece of text. You can almost feel his blood pressure rising.

She can pound out Liszt in rock-busting style. In this case it is the Spanish
Rhapsody, musically worthless, but pianistically full of innovation.
    How does he know?
    She depends on the soft pedal more than custom and Hayden require.
Bach's C Major Toccata, Adagio and Fugue in C Major were brilliant without
being noble.
    Bunk!
    They showed an immediate command of the piano, but little knowledge of
Bach. The Adagio should remain quiet throughout, and the fugue entrances do
not permit such freedom of tempo as they were given.

How does he know[?] Bach is dead!

Brahms variations have much more true music in them than the razzle-dazzle treatment yesterday shows. Not only the slow waltzes, which were badly misshapen, but much of the wizard writing should have greater depth.

More lousy bunk!

Finally, Truman could take it no more, and he penned a scathing letter to Hume's boss, Philip Graham, editor in chief of the *Washington Post*.

> *Dear Phil:*   *February 4, 1952*
>
> Why don't you retire this frustrated old fuddy duddy and hire a reviewer of musical people who appear here, who knows what it is all about? At least you should send somebody with him to a piano recital who knows the score.
>
> This review of his on yesterday's recital is a disgraceful piece of poppycock. You should be ashamed of your paper for having printed it. You are not, of course, because the publicity sheets are never wrong!
>
> *Sincerely,*
> *H. S. T.*
>
> Read Dr. Gunn's piece!*

As with Truman's original Hume letter, Graham also refrained from printing this message. There already was enough fire on substantive policy matters in the *Washington Post*, and publishing "Hume II" would have shown extremely poor judgment in the overheated climate of the day. Fifty years later, a similar letter from a president might be printed without a second thought.

Truman obviously couldn't take shots at everyone who criticized or misrepresented him, his policies, and his family, but he would occasionally pen a few comments on newspaper clippings or letters like the one from a painfully self-important writer who billed his article "Truman Story" in *The Catholic World* as "the FDR-HST chronicle as I have known it" revealing "things never before told."

> *Dear Mr. President:*   *March 23, 1951*
>
> When in 1944 I gathered personalia one item given me by a Missourian was that as a boy you "chauffered" an Emerson. Although the

---

*Glenn Dillard Gunn's "Capacity Crowd Cheers Gina Bachauer's Recital" in the February 4, 1952, *Washington Times-Herald*.

editor deleted the name, I checked and found that in 1877, a B. K. Emerson patented a moldboard plow, and the reference appears in dusty tomes perhaps not consulted for many years.

That backward glance—about the time I was fresh from Rome and President Cleveland himself showed me the Executive Mansion—warranted a more graphic treatment but space limitations made that impossible.

As to President Roosevelt's feelings when the press quoted you about Mrs. Truman's approval in whatever you wrote or said officially, I sent you the confidential information on July 28, 1944, but whether you saw it or not I do not know because no reply came, but that is understandable, since it was the beginning of the campaign.

My next article in this "presidential" series will be my interpretation and impressions of Mr. Hoover.

And may I, as one who heard both Mabel McKinley and Margaret Wilson sing, bespeak my enjoyment of Miss Truman's new release, American Songs, with her perfect portrayal of a revolutionary days modulation. I could almost visualize such a scene and chorus in all the simple panoply of those times.

Sincerely yours,
H. R. Pinci
New York, N.Y.

At the bottom, Truman wrote, "It is rotten, a slanted, non-factual piece, based on misinformation. I hope you'll have more facts and more sense in the other articles." Having gotten this off his chest, the letter—and its author—were promptly forgotten.

After years in public office when the bad press frequently outnumbered the good, Truman was unimpressed when individuals who had attacked everything from his associates to his choice of hats suddenly found a few good words to say.

Dear Harry: *February 22, 1951*

It seems to me that our *Kansas City Star* features prominently articles in criticism of your administration. Maybe this is news:

Yesterday I attended a luncheon of the Chamber of Commerce where there was an overflow audience of about 500. The speaker was Roy Roberts. He reviewed conditions as per his impressions from his recent visit to Washington and his interviews with many individuals of prominence. He held his audience completely for over 45 minutes, longer than usual.

What surprised me was there was no criticism and virtually his approval of both the foreign and domestic policy of your administration. I thought this would interest you and please you.

Let me wish you continued success and with best personal regards, I am

> *Sincerely yours,*
> *Walter H. Negbaur*
> *The Business League of Kansas City, Mo.*

Dear Walter: *February 27, 1951*

I appreciated most highly your letter of the twenty-second, regarding the speech by Roy Roberts. Editors are peculiar animals— they throw mud and bricks at you the whole year-round—then they make one favorable statement which happens to agree with facts and they think they should be hugged and kissed for it.

It was certainly kind and thoughtful of you to tell me about Roy's speech.

> *Sincerely yours,*
> HARRY S. TRUMAN

Not all publications were held in as low esteem by Truman as the "lying" *Kansas City Star,* and the editor of *The New Yorker,* a magazine Truman particularly enjoyed, was extremely embarrassed by one bit of news from the White House.

My dear Mr. President: *October 24, 1950*

Charles Ross advises me that you have remarked to him that you are not receiving copies of *The New Yorker.* In the face of your wanting to see the magazine, it is humiliating that it isn't being delivered to you, for we thought in the editorial department that it was being sent. That it isn't is the fault of the business office, which operates rather bureaucratically. We've put you down as an honorary subscriber (the first and only such) and will try to get the copies to you on that basis. We are flattered by your interest, I assure you.

> *Yours respectfully,*
> *Harold W. Ross*
> *The New Yorker*

Dear Mr. Ross: <u>Personal</u>   *October 31, 1950*

I appreciate most highly yours of the twenty-fourth. I get a great deal of pleasure out of *The New Yorker* and I can't tell you how highly I appreciate being your only honorary subscriber. If your business office had sent me a bill for the subscription, I probably would have sent you a check. I sent General [Robert] Eichelberger a check for his book [*Our Jungle Road to Tokyo,* New York: Viking Press, 1950]. He sent me the book and kept the check, so you see I am ahead in both instances.

It was very kind and thoughtful of you to do me the honor of sending me your good magazine. I enjoy reading it very much.

Sincerely yours,

HARRY S. TRUMAN

In spite of Truman's reputation for almost uniformly bad relations with the news media, he actually maintained many warm friendships with members of the press corps, such as William Mox, whom he had known since at least his Senate days.

Dear Mr. President:

At long last the *Trib* has finally got off the necks of you and Harry Vaughan. It has been sickening the way they carried on in their editorials and their cartoon on the front page. Russ, Jack and I took a daily beating from one of our execs that voted wrong. He always waited for an audience in our "Tab Room" before bringing up the subject.

By the way, the Vice President appeared to enjoy himself in our lunch room. He is almost as nice a guy as you.

Willie Wrothing will be with me for a couple days. Russ and I are planning to make his short visit as pleasant as possible.

Had a letter from Bill O'Connor and he tells me that he has been recommended for U.S. Dist. Attorney. He will make a good one if he gets the appointment.

I'm glad that you stuck to H. V. through all the hullaballoo. The G.O.P. doesn't like it and will try to capitalize on it from now on. You've been through it before and came out with flying colors, so I look to see a repetition of your past performances and will make them like it eventually. It burns the R—— out of me and makes me feels so helpless.

My best wishes for your health and happiness. It is my sincere hope that the abuse you are getting rolls off you like water off a duck. Remember me to Margaret and Mrs. Truman.

Sincerely,

Bill

Chicago Sun Times

Dear Bill: <u>Personal</u>   *September 29, 1949*

I certainly appreciated your good letter of the fourteenth and don't let that terrible *Tribune* worry you into hysterics—they have been going on like that ever since I can remember and, as far as I know, they never have yet won a victory with the same kind of attacks they make on public officials.

Some day I think justice will overtake Bertie ["Colonel" Robert R. McCormick, publisher of the *Chicago Tribune*]. As you know, his rival in character assassination, William Randolph Hearst, is reaping his reward right now and I have an idea that Bertie will wind up in about the same shape.

I am entirely familiar with the gentleman who is sympathetic with Bertie's attack—the man in your crowd, I mean. He wrote an editorial not long ago for the *Sun Times,* a copy of which I have on my desk. I wish I could write an editorial for national distribution on some things I know about him.

Tell Russ [Stewart] hello. Don't let these things get you down.

Sincerely yours,

HARRY S. TRUMAN

Exchanges like the above were not at all unusual. In spite of a killing schedule, Truman kept up a valiant—and largely successful—effort to maintain correspondence with his friends and family. Understandably, many of the letters written during his presidency were much shorter than those he wrote to the same individuals after he returned to Independence, but he always made it a point to give enough of a reply that people would know he had read their letters.

Edward Meisburger, one of Truman's most trusted sergeants during World War I, was with the U.S. Army Corps of Engineers at the time of the devastating Kansas City flood of 1951. He was so concerned with the ongoing situation along the area's river systems that for a time it was the main topic of his letters.

Dear Mr. President: *May 7, 1952*

I appreciated very much your thoughtfulness and your contribution of world-demanding time in making reply from Key West March 22 to my letter of comment regarding flood problems and the Corps of Engineers program for attaining flood control. It also was very reassuring to me to have your reaffirmation of the trust you place in General [Lewis A.] Pick's knowledge and leadership. I can venture no opinion regarding administrative aspects of the Federal civil works program, but I am more convinced daily as a result of close association with these trained and experienced engineers that control of flood waters which you saw in July, 1951, and only recently on the upper Missouri can come only from an adequate system of larger reservoirs employed to reduce the downstream flow so that it will be contained within the banks or within local protection works such as thus far provided at Omaha and at the Kansas Citys.

This treatment of flood waters has been agreed upon by the engineers of both the Corps and the Soil Conservation Service of the Department of Agriculture, although some "curbstone" engineers persist upon reading into the picture a wide difference of opinion between the Corps and the USDA. A pertinent example of the Soil Conservation Service appraisal of the Corps' downstream works is the current Department of Agriculture plan for the Big Blue River Basin where the Corps Tuttle Creek Dam would very substantially reduce the crests on the Kansas River and also contribute to lessening damages on the lower Missouri River. It was no revelation to competent engineers in both the Corps and the Department of Agriculture that the latter, as it has done, would label its Big Blue Basin plan as supplemental to Tuttle Creek Reservoir and in no wise a substitute for the control the reservoir would exert on the Kansas River. And it certainly takes no profound engineer to see that reservoir control was the only practicable solution during the recent snow-melt when the great mass of water, formed above a thick ice crust, had almost instantaneous runoff into the streams. All the terraces, ponds, etc., they could build would not have halted or held those waters. A similar situation prevailed last summer in the Kansas River Basin, only in that instance, there was no ice crust but there did prevail a soil saturated to the extent that the July deluge ran off like rain down a window pane.

Despite all these physical aspects which appear simple of understanding, confusion is placed in the minds of many of the people by some "authorities" who have no property or any tangible interests whatever in the basins which are concerned with flood problems. Much of this confusion appears in magazines and newspaper articles and some, it is regrettable to say, comes under the heading of what is supposed to be newspaper reporting. In that connection I am reminded of a statement credited to you in Mr. Josephus Daniels' book to the effect that you would like to spend the rest of your life working for more factual writing in some columns of the press. We have some who try to get the facts and abide by them, but many others who disregard the facts and fit their stories and editorials together to meet their own ends. You know well the type, and through reading most of the clippings from the papers in this area, I find that those who use their cleverness in making light of the Corps of Engineers and their work are the same ones who most often are critical of everything the Government or the administration does or attempts to do.

As you have so often stated, the whole structure of the Government and the loyalty and efficiency of its workers, are placed under a cloud by such ill-informed and biased attacks.

Everywhere I seem to sense the feeling, even from sources known to be antagonistic to the administration, that something vital and hard to replace, was removed from the American picture when you removed yourself from further service as President.

Sincerely and respectfully,
Eddie Meisburger,
Army Corps of Engineers
Kansas City, Mo.

Dear Eddie:　　　　　　　　　*May 16, 1952*

I appreciated most highly your letter of the seventh regarding the flood control situation and the Corps of Engineers.

I've been working on that subject for a long long time. I think that General Pick and I understand each other and that eventually the whole situation will work out.

I received a wedding invitation from your boy in Germany. We are sending him a little memento which I hope will be useful to him.

Sincerely yours,
HARRY S. TRUMAN

Truman had been a partner in an unsuccessful business venture with oil man David Morgan before America entered World War I, and they remained lifelong friends.

Dear Harry: *January 23, 1952*

Now that you have disposed of the all-important Messages to Congress, you can relax a bit, and add up the score, including the article in Section C of the *Sunday Star* (Washington, D.C.) which I presume you have read. It all makes interesting material. What do you think?

We have been doing very well so far in weather, a very mild January so far; December was bad and drilling was at a standstill. I have rotary tools moving down to Elk County to make some tests on leases I have owned for years, sub-leased them and reserved an overriding royalty, hope this development works out, I could use it.

Eleanor has been on the job there in Washington for two weeks now, has not been assigned to any foreign post as yet, will probably be in Washington for another 2 months. She would very much like to be assigned to some foreign post that would present the most possibilities for advancement, as well as desirable living and social conditions. She is working, waiting, and wishing. Could you suggest something that would be fitting or perhaps make some recommendation? I am sure she would merit it. Her present address is

1300 17th Street, N.W.

I will appreciate hearing from you and anything you can do will be greatly appreciated.

My clipping service seems to grow constantly.

Lots of GOOD LUCK,

> *Sincerely,*
> *David H. Morgan*
> *Oil and Gas Production*
> *Eureka, Kans.*

[Longhand] *I doubt if Eleanor would approve my suggestion that you make any recommendations. She is a bit independent, so if you do, just keep it betwixt you and I! Thanks—Dave*

Dear Dave: *January 28, 1952*

I appreciated very much your letter of the twenty-third. I am glad you liked the Congressional Messages and the article in the *Washington Star* of last Sunday.

I hope your project works out all right.

I wish you, yourself, would tell Eleanor the best way in the world for her to progress in this situation, in which she is now placed, is to attend strictly to business and be very careful not to bring outside influences to bear until she has been there long enough to know what it is all about.

The State Department is a peculiar organization, made up principally of extremely bright people who made tremendous college marks but who have had very little association with actual people down to the ground. They are clannish and snooty and sometimes I feel like firing the whole bunch but it requires a tremendous amount of education to accomplish the purposes for which the State Department is set up. In a great many key places I have men of common sense and we are improving the situation right along.

The present Secretary of State is one of the best that has ever been in the office, but on lower levels we still have the career men who have been taken out of the colleges without any experience with the common people. I'll give you one particular instance to show you just how the situation works.

Alben Barkley, when he was United States Senator, was in Egypt with a bunch of Congressmen and Senators on a parliamentary union meeting. The Charge d'affaires in Cairo escorted them. He wore a checked suit, carried a cane, wore a cap and talked with an Oxford accent. Barkley kept looking at him and wondering if the gentleman could have been reared in Egypt. Finally he asked him what his antecedents were. The man said he was a native of Topeka, Kansas.

Of course, if he dared go back to Topeka wearing this checked suit, the cap and carrying a cane, he would have lasted about ten minutes in the Kansas Hotel lobby.

So you tell Eleanor to attend strictly to her job and let the situation take its course for the time being.

Sincerely yours,
HARRY S. TRUMAN

In a letter five months later, Morgan commented on numerous matters, and wrote, "You don't suppose MacArthur will spill the soup now that he is the 'Key-noter'" at the Republican convention. He also added a handwritten postscript, "Eleanor writes she is most pleased with her Rome assg't at the

Am. Embassy," to which Truman playfully replied, "From what I hear, that is a very good place to be."

Bob Messall had been a loyal and completely dedicated right-hand man to Truman during his first term in Washington and always began letters to his old boss "Dear Senator." Unfortunately for Messall, his working association with the future president extended only briefly into the second Senate term because some of his unsavory financial dealings came to Truman's attention. Nearly a decade later, Messall—now a Washington "public relations counsel"—was still at it, and he tried to use Truman's great interest in history as a hook to involve him in a bank's promotional campaign.

My dear Senator: *June 5, 1948*

Several months ago I was talking to a personal friend of mine, Mr. Roland T. Carr, Assistant Vice President of the Riggs National Bank, regarding some business matters. After our conversation, Mr. Carr asked me if I would be kind enough to speak to you about the fact that the Riggs National Bank would like very much for your name, or any member of your family's name, listed as a depositor of this institution, since they have had quite a list of very famous people dating back to 1876. Of course, they are very proud of this record and Roland sincerely asked me if I would request you to give consideration to opening any kind of an account, even if it was a "kitchen account," so they could very proudly include the name of TRUMAN in their list of great and historical people. I am enclosing a copy of Mr. Carr's letter to me of March 25th, and also a complete set of their historical ads.

Senator, Mr. Carr is an ambitious and hard-working young man and since this responsibility is entirely all his, you would do Mr. Carr a personal favor if you would give this matter serious consideration.

Sincerely,
Victor R. Messall
Public Relations Counsel

P.S. In checking a few days ago, I find that article mentioned for the *Saturday Evening Post* by the Riggs National Bank, has been delayed for four or five weeks in addition to the time mentioned in Mr. Carr's letter of March 25th. This would give them ample time to include your name in the *Saturday Evening Post* article, providing of course you can make a decision very shortly, preferably within the next week or ten days. (enclosures 20)

Schemes like this are what prompted Truman to keep Messall at arm's length, but a second letter from Messall written the same day, concerning an old friend from 12th Street in Kansas City, where Truman had once owned a small men's clothing store, was of much more interest to the president.

> *My dear Senator:*   *June 5, 1948*
>
> I wrote you several months ago advertising that I had sent you some maps, under separate cover, of some very old and valuable historical maps from your good friend Frank Glenn of Kansas City. You very gratefully acknowledged receipt of the maps and I think at the time I mentioned to you that Mr. Glenn had several more of these maps he wanted to send to you. I have since received these other maps and I am sending them to you under separate cover, and I am sure you will enjoy them.
>
> I am sorry to tell you that Frank Glenn was evicted from his book store headquarters in the Muelebach lobby and had to obtain some other space. It seems that Barney Ellis was anxious to reinstall the Western Union office in the space occupied by Mr. Glenn.
>
> With kindest personal regards, I remain
>
> > *Sincerely,*
> > *Victor R. Messall*

> *Dear Vic:*   *June 21, 1948*
>
> I appreciated very much your letter of the fifth and as soon as the maps arrive from Frank Glenn I'll certainly be glad to acknowledge them personally.
>
> I don't see how it is possible for me now to open a new account. I've been doing business with the Hamilton National Bank since I came to Washington and they have always been just as decent to me as any bank could possibly be to a customer.
>
> I appreciate having the posters from the Riggs National Bank— they are certainly interesting.
>
> I was glad to see you in Kansas City—sorry I didn't have a chance to talk with you.
>
> > *Sincerely yours,*
> > *HARRY S. TRUMAN*

A manufacturer in New York sent Truman an item he would keep near at hand for the rest of his life. It was found with other personal items twenty-one years after his death in the locked drawer of a credenza behind his desk. A search of the Truman Library's records revealed how it came into his possession.

My dear Mr. President: *July 14, 1949*

We are label distributors to the tie manufacturers, and still have in our possession a brass die which we made for you in July 1919 and are enclosing an impression.

We thought you might like having the die as a memento. If you would, we would be very pleased to send it to you.

> *Respectfully,*
> *B. Wolff*
> *Henry A. Jacobs & Co., Inc.*
> *New York, N.Y.*

Dear Mr. Wolff: *July 18, 1949*

I certainly appreciated your note on the fourteenth of July very much and I would be highly pleased if you sent me the die referred to in your letter.

> *Sincerely yours,*
> *HARRY S. TRUMAN*

My Dear Mr. President: *July 22, 1949*

We are enclosing the TRUMAN-JACOBSEN die about which we wrote previously and you advised you would like to have the die in your possession.

> *Respectfully,*
> *B. Wolff*
> *Henry A. Jacobs & Co., Inc.*
> *New York, N.Y.*

Truman's fellow Missourians were anxious to honor his accomplishments, and as this letter to William Southern, Jr., demonstrates, he worked diligently to dampen one aspect of their enthusiasm. Southern was the publisher-editor of the *Independence Examiner* and also Bess Truman's uncle-in-law.

Dear Mr. Southern: *February 25, 1946*

Bess called my attention to an article in the *Independence Examiner* Saturday, February sixteenth edition, in which a proposal is made to change the name of Van Horn Road to Truman Road.

If you will remember I was Presiding Judge of the County Court, people wanted to name every road in the County for me and I wouldn't allow it. The only place my name appears is on the new Courthouse in Kansas City and the remodeled one in Independence, along with other members of the Court and the Architects, in very inconspicuous places. I have no desire to have roads, bridges or buildings named after me.

Old man Van Horn was a good old Republican who helped the "red legs"* rob Jackson County and served two or three terms in Congress. I certainly don't think they ought to take his name off the road where he built that fine house. It doesn't hurt us to honor an old newspaper man with one road name.

I hope Mrs. Southern is well and that I'll have an opportunity sometime in the not too far distant future to pay another visit to my hometown. I hope this time without too much pomp and circumstance.

Sincerely,
HARRY S. TRUMAN

In spite of Truman's behind-the-scenes effort to kill the initiative, and the grumblings of some local residents, the east-west street running by his house was renamed Truman Road. After he emerged victorious in the 1948 election, an old friend in the area east of Truman's native Jackson County proposed that the name change be made official there as well. Although Truman was still not happy about the situation, he graciously accepted the honor in the spirit in which it was given.

---

*There are several shades of meaning to the term "red legs" as used by Truman here, all of which would have been understood by Mr. Southern, who shared a common heritage and understanding of the area's history and politics with Truman. First, "red legs," longtime army slang for artillerymen, was also the nickname of a group of uniformed, pro-Northern border thugs during the Civil War who were granted semiofficial status by Union forces. After the war, the term was used locally in rural areas to describe anyone or anything pertaining to militias supporting the Union. Van Horn, who came to Kansas City before the Civil War as a Democrat, broke ranks with the secessionists in the hinterland of Jackson County and ended the war an ardent Republican in charge of a Union militia unit. As Kansas City developed into a rail and trade center in the "Northern" model under the leadership of Van Horn and others, the rest of the agrarian—and still pro-Southern—county was largely left to fend for itself and even helped pay for improvements that benefited the burgeoning metropolis but not its own economy. Truman's first daunting task when elected to county office, almost sixty years after the war, was to put the county's dilapidated and incomplete rural road system in order.

Dear Mr. President: *January 12, 1949*

I have received your very nice response to my telegram sent to you when we were sure of your re-election.

I prepared and presented to the County Court of Lafayette County a resolution, copy of which I am enclosing herein, to name the road to Lafayette County that connects with the Old Spring Branch Road "Truman Road." The County Court unanimously adopted the resolution, so "Truman Road" actually runs west from a point four miles south of Wellington, Missouri, to Baltimore Avenue in Kansas City.

I was very much interested in doing this because I was responsible for the Road District and W.P.A., widening and rocking the road a long time ago. I have a 320-acre farm just one-half mile south of the road, and our mutual friend, Mr. Bundschu, has a farm on the road here in Lafayette County.

All of your friends who know of the great amount of work that you have put into good roads are very happy that our County Court gladly adopted the resolution that I presented.

I am leaving with the Jackson County folks who are coming to your inauguration. I am going to bring Ike, Jr., with me. I am sure that sometime during our brief stay that both of us will have an opportunity to see you.* Ike, Jr., will never cease being appreciative of the nice letter that you sent to him when he was first stricken with polio in 1946.

With kindest regards and every good wish, I am,

> *Sincerely,*
> *Ike Skelton, Attorney-at-Law*
> *Lexington, Mo.*

Dear Ike: *January 24, 1949*

Thanks very much for yours of the twelfth, enclosing me a Resolution passed by the County Court of Lafayette County, Missouri naming a road for me. I appreciate it very much.

---

*"Ike, Jr.," really Ike Skelton IV, did not meet Truman until years after the trip to Washington with his father, but he was seated near the president during the inauguration banquet when Truman gleefully lampooned columnist H. V. Kaltenborn over his election-night coverage. Ike Skelton was elected to Congress in 1976 and rose to become the minority leader on several key defense committees.

I hope you had a good time at the Inauguration.

Sincerely yours,
HARRY S. TRUMAN

The president also sent a note of thanks to the members of the County Court who approved Skelton's resolution.

Dear Mr. Kuhlman: *January 24, 1949*

Please express my appreciation to the County Court of Lafayette County for their kindness in extending the Truman Road through Lafayette County. I appreciate it very much.

While I was on the County Court of Jackson County, I was very careful to prevent any roads being named for me. Now I seem to have one running from Kansas City through Lafayette County named for me.

I hope the time will never come when you will want to take the signs down.

Sincerely yours,
HARRY S. TRUMAN

Elated supporters back in Missouri also came up with other ways to honor Truman for his accomplishments.

Dear President Truman: *March 14, 1949*

While in Washington the week before last, I asked Tom Evans to convey to you the message that a large number of people had talked to me about starting a foundation to purchase the Truman Farm and to restore it to the condition as it existed at the time you and your mother lived there and to construct and maintain a building to house the various articles of interest and value in connection with the lives and history of you and your family. I also mentioned to Tom that in the event it was decided to form this Foundation, I wanted to give $1,000.00 as a contribution to the project and that I wanted to offer my services in setting up the Foundation and in raising money for the construction and maintenance of the various buildings.

The movement to set up this Foundation has been gaining momentum for the past few months, but I have hesitated bringing this to your attention, knowing how you feel about memorials to living persons and not knowing just how you would feel about conveying away title to the Truman Farm, but I feel that this Foundation, if formed, would be a living memorial to your way of living and what you stand for. We have Mount Vernon and Hyde Park, but here would be a Foundation perpetually dedicated to the fact that all individuals in the United States, regardless of their position in life, have an opportunity of becoming President of the United States.

I know that you will give this matter long and serious thought, and I sincerely hope that you will consent to this Foundation being set up, and that I might take part in establishing the same.

Sincerely yours,
Enos A. Axtell, Attorney at Law
Kansas City, Mo.

Dear Enos: *March 21, 1949*

I certainly appreciated your good letter of the fourteenth and I am, of course, highly complimented at what you propose to do but I am not being consulted about the matter about which you wrote.

I don't expect to sell the farm, which I now own myself, as I expect to make some improvements on it and hope to live there when I get through being President.

Sincerely yours,
HARRY S. TRUMAN

Bess's brother, Frank Wallace, lived on Truman Road, but like many in Independence, he made it a point to still use the name Van Horn Road in his address. Upon receiving a letter from a business associate that floated the idea of erecting a statue of Truman in the Missouri capital, he immediately forwarded it to the president, who responded after the inauguration.

Dear Frank: *December 28, 1948*

In reading an article in the *Kansas City Star* Sunday paper last night regarding your good family and the Truman family, the thought struck me that since Mr. Truman is our first President of Missouri, that we should erect a nice statue of some kind here in Jefferson City, in order to show our appreciation. He is of course our first President of Missouri, and as written you before, he is going down in history as one of our greatest Presidents.

I, of course, feel that the citizens of Independence as well as Kansas City would be a little jealous, in the event we erect this project at Jefferson City; nevertheless, I feel that this is the place, right in the Missouri Capitol Grounds.

I am also writing Bryce Smith in Kansas City in order to get an expression from him.

Best wishes always.

> *Yours very truly,*
> *Henry Dulle*
> *G. H. Dulle Milling Company*
> *Jefferson City, Mo.*

[Longhand] *Don't think we would have any trouble in raising funds.*

Dear Frank: *January 25, 1949*

I am returning to you the letter from Henry J. Dulle and I wish you would tell him how much I appreciate his thoughtfulness in making the suggestion about a statue in Jefferson City but, I think, it would be better to wait until sometime in the future to do that because you can never tell what will happen to a man while he is alive. I may do something later on that will cause him to want to pull the statue down. However, I appreciate what he wants to do very much.

> *Sincerely yours,*
> *Harry*

[Longhand]—*Hope you arrived home without an incident. My best to Natalie.*

Truman carried on an extensive correspondence with his family and thus kept close tabs on what was happening back in Jackson County. He would also use them for a little intelligence gathering on a variety of matters, including the myriad individuals from the area who claimed to know him, as in this letter to his brother John Vivian Truman.

Dear Vivian: *April 8, 1948*

I am enclosing you a letter from a "bird" down at Montrose, Missouri. I don't think I ever heard of him and I am sure if I ever met him it was by accident and not intentional.

You might try to worm out of him what is on his mind. I think he is trying to get to Washington paid for by me.

> *Sincerely,*
> Harry

[Enclosed]

Dear Friend Harry: *April 1, 1948*

Pardon my seeming forwardness in addressing you thus, but I feel that I do know you as a friend. And to acquaint you with my identity, perhaps you will remember that I worked on the Lula Long [Longview] farm shortly after World War I as a bus driver and while thus engaged, had occasion to transport a number of folks to your place for an evening entertainment. I well remember the $5.00 tip you gave me on that occasion.

The purpose of my letter is to acquaint you with the possibility that I might have some information of vital importance to the welfare of the nation. This was obtained by chance and has never been told to any person. It cannot be sent by mail and should you be in Kansas City in the near future, I would like an appointment to talk with you in person. Or I could make the trip there if transportation could be provided.

I sincerely believe that this information should be at least placed in proper hands for whatever it might be worth.

May I hear from you?

With kindest personal regards, I remain

> *Yours sincerely,*
> *[name]*
> *Montrose, Mo.*

Dear Harry: *April 16, 1948*

Upon receipt of your letter of the eighth, I had an investigation made of [name] at Montrose, Missouri, and I doubt very much if you have ever met the man. I am returning his letter and have made some notations on the bottom which I think covers the case thoroughly. I will make no further comment on him.

We are having our township meeting tonight to send some delegates to Independence who will, of course, pick our delegates to the state convention.

I had a meeting with Garrett Smalley [publisher of the *Kansas*

City News Press] and think I put him straight on the matter that was discussed yesterday, provided he doesn't do it his way. I told him to write no story that had anyone's name at all in it.

I was glad to see yesterday morning's paper in which you stated that you intended to stay in the White House another four years. I think the reaction from that, at least here, is very favorable and I am hearing some more favorable reports from the South. I think these fellows will come home by the time they are needed.

The farmers in our community are just now finishing up with sowing their oats—a few are not through yet. This, of course, is caused by wet weather. The boys are going to put in 300 acres of corn this year and they find now that a good deal of the ground is still too wet to disk with any satisfaction. They have plenty of equipment, however, and whenever conditions are right, they can put the corn in in short order.

I hope if you find time to come to Bolivar that you will take enough time off to pay us a visit and go over things here.

Yours truly,
J. Vivian Truman
Grandview, Mo.

[Longhand from John Vivian] *Mary just came in. She says hello and all is ok.*

[Longhand from the president's sister, Mary Jane, running across the bottom, then up the side of the paper] *Vivian is making fun of my new red shoes. What would you say? Ha Ha—They are to be worn with a new grey evening dress, and I like them. Mary Jane.*

John Vivian and Mary Jane Truman also added notes to the bottom of "the bird's" letter.

[John Vivian:] *This man has been in jail & has been in trouble for stealing. Generally known as a screwball.* [Mary Jane:] *& petty thief.* [John Vivian:] *Lives on a 40 A[cre] farm near Montrose.*

Dear Vivian: *April 20, 1948*
I appreciated your letter of the sixteenth. I was sure I didn't know the fellow down at Montrose so I'll pay no attention to the letter.

Glad you had a talk with Garrett Smalley but you want to be very careful with him because he has had the typical newspaper complex ever since I have known him and you can't trust him too far.

I hope the boys have good luck in getting that big corn crop in and that the weather will be right for a good crop.

I am glad Mary is all right, and I hope everything continues to go right with you and the boys.

Sincerely,
Harry

Throughout it all, however, Truman and his staff dealt with a wide range of correspondence on priority matters, like national health insurance, which remained unsettled after nearly eight years in office.

Dear President Truman: *16 January 1946*

For three years, two of which were spent overseas, I have been in the Army of the United States, in the Army Nurse Corps, taking care of the soldiers who were fighting for the liberty of the American people. Now that I have returned, to what I thought was a democratic United States, I find that the people at home have spent valuable time concocting a bill for socialized medicine—or, in other words, "The Public Health Bill."

I have read, reread and studied this bill (which I find hard to believe was prepared by a group of Americans) and <u>as a veteran of World War II and a member of the Medical Profession, I wish to register my objection to the Public Health Bill</u>. If ever I am in need of a doctor I certainly want to have the privilege of choosing my physician.

Is it possible that while our boys were at the front giving their legs, arms or life for freedom and liberty, the people we left in charge of affairs in Washington have lost faith and the land of opportunity and freedom has taken steps toward a totalitarian state—please don't let us down—or could it be that we have fought this war in vain?

Yours truly,
Mildred Bearss, Captain, N-744695
West Palm Beach, Fla.

Dear President,   *Feb. 6, 1946*

I sincerely hope you have success in getting your Health Bill passed by the Senate. Because a nation is as healthy as its people while we have done wonders in the past. Suppose we had government health insurance, free examinations once a year and hospitalization for the sick, we could in a matter of years eliminate the 50 percent of people who can't stand physical requirements for army or navy service.

As stated before, a nation is as healthy as its people; therefore, this is a government (national) responsibility not local.

Hope you have success in getting this Bill passed.

> *I am yours truly,*
> *W. Nicholas*
> *Sierra Madre, Calif.*

My dear Mr. Nicholas: *February 13, 1946*

The President has asked me to thank you for your letter of February sixth. He wants you to know that he appreciates your letting him have this expression of your views.

> *Very sincerely yours,*
> *WILLIAM D. HASSETT*
> *Secretary to the President*

Dear President Truman: *September 13, 1948*

It is with a great deal of sadness that I see you approve on compulsory health insurance which is the beginning of communism and socialism in America. I personally do not see who would vote for you only those who approve of the Russian type of living. Communists and Socialists certainly love to read what you have in the papers today.

> *Regretfully yours,*
> *Karl John Karnaky, M.D.*

P.S. The patients will have a right to choose their own doctor, and the patient and the doctor could refuse to join in the process. That is the way Germany started and it soon became completely totalitarian.

> *K. J. K.*

My dear Mr. President: *September 1, 1949*

I want you to know how much I appreciate your letter in response to my communication from Windemere, England.

We were away from Kansas City two and one-half months, staying longer in England than on the Continent. We were constantly warned every place we went, and especially in England: "Not to let THIS happen in the United States."

I know the Harry Truman, so much admired by Bryce Smith, Tom Evans and thousands of other substantial Kansas City citizens, would not do anything, knowingly or willingly, to create a welfare state. You plow too straight a furrow!

Also you know that where welfare states have existed; where they guarantee everything from birth to the grave, incentive is destroyed. You are aware from your confidential reports that England has more guarantees of security and less actual than any other country in the world. Since the Government has promised everything, they have no will to work and no desire to save.

Every industry that has been nationalized, except coal, has a deficit. Coal is now a monopoly and the price has raised tremendously. The average Briton has more leisure now and less of everything else. They have been on a four year holiday from financial responsibility and there is not the slightest doubt, but that the results are disquieting, to say the least.

They must have increased production per man hour of goods at a price we and other nations can afford to pay. An increase in taxation would not help, for they already are taxed approximately 8 shillings out of each pound, which means forty percent.

In addition they have a 20 percent to 100 percent sales tax—they call it purchase tax. I know what a cry would go up if you were to advocate even a 10 percent federal sales tax to reduce our huge national debt.

Mr. Bevan is known as the "Synthetic Evangelist." He creates such an emotional appeal, without logical background, that quite a number of the former Labor members of Parliament have moved their seats to the other side of the House.

Mr. Clement Attlee told Parliament in 1946: "When it comes to economic planning we agree with Soviet Russia." That is certainly not the American Way.

Instead of being honest with their people about conditions in 1940 they blamed you for their troubles because you cut off lend lease. They will blame you again this year and each year you do not let them raid the United States Treasury. So many fine British people said, "Stop sending money—let us have our crisis and then we will work out our own destiny as we always have."

All of the serious troubles which delay production and distribution are in the industries which have already been nationalized. Peace reigns in private industry, including steel, where excellent labor management relations have been unbroken for practically 20 years. Steel has the best record of all for its efficiency.

Under political management last year England's Civil Air loss was 100 million dollars; railroads had an estimated loss of another 100 million, etc. Also they have had a loss of pride, dignity and freedom.

I know that any health program you might advocate would not in any way resemble that of England, which has been such a costly, dismal failure, that even its own advocates are willing to drop it unless we send the money necessary to keep it going.

A few of the headlines regarding the health plan are:

"Fifty Thousand Hospital Beds Closed—Too Few Nurses"

"Doctors Asked to Prescribe Toothpaste"

"Glasses Prescribed for Headaches That Aspirin Would Have Cured"

"T.B. Patients Wait Eight Months for a Bed"

"Toothache Cases Get Ten Weeks on Sick Benefits"

"The Health Plan Costs Tens of Millions above the Estimate; More Than Any Scheme Could Stand"

"Northwest Hospitals Cost 1,265,000 Pounds More Than the Estimate Notwithstanding Economies of 532,000 Pounds"

"The Health Scheme Has Increased Absenteeism throughout the Nation"

The "give me more" and the unthinking people of England like the Health Plan because they are deceived into thinking it is free. It is probably the most costly of any medical service in the world when all expenses are totaled. There are now 31 thousand on the payrolls classed as "administrators." All of these persons are promised pensions. Three hundred employees are required to approve or disapprove the dentists' recommendations. They tell the dentist what he may do. Six hundred are required to check druggists' bills, not knowing whether the patient took the medicine or exchanged it for toothpaste or other merchandise. Four thousand are employed in 138 groups to supervise the medical men and write checks for the physicians' services.

The medical service rendered the average Briton does not in any way compare with the service rendered our people, even in the lower income groups.

The best physicians and surgeons make up the attending Staff of Kansas City General and Mercy Hospitals. They give their services absolutely free without any thought of remuneration.

With the present Blue Cross and Blue Shield there are very few employed families who could not afford to pay the $1.00 per week.

The general physician in England admits he can only examine one patient out of ten in his "surgeries." (office)

I did not go to England as a political or economic observer, neither am I posing as one now. I did go at the invitation to lecture before the International Congress of Otolaryngology, which met in London, on the subject of "Cancer of the Larynx."

I know the enormous pressure under which you work and I know that you must trust certain people as your advisors. Also I know that you cannot assume all of your advisors are as unselfish or as honest as you are yourself.

You made certain promises during the heat of a political campaign, which you are trying so hard to keep in every detail. No other President, to my knowledge, has kept all of his campaign promises to the letter.

The Nation is so grateful to you and Secretary Louis Johnson for the first big economy move. My congratulations to you both! I know that now that you have started on your economy program you will carry it through. I do hope you will get your Reorganization Bill through Congress, so real efficiency and economy can be practiced everywhere. This would permit a reduction in the rate of taxation (which in the 1920s increased the Federal Income) and the economic giant, known as the USA, would then go into full swing. The Laborer, the Boss and everyone would be prosperous. The "pork-barrel minded" members of Congress will scream, but that will do their lungs good. I know you will stand pat on the economy program you have started.

Heavy taxation and "let the Government take care of you" is not working in England and, in my humble opinion, it would not work here.

Mr. President, this letter is being written in the utmost sincerity and with no thought of being presumptuous or disrespectful. After viewing first-hand conditions prevailing in England, I feel I would be lacking in patriotism if I did not express my personal conviction—"Don't let THIS happen to us."

Very truly,
Dr. Sam E. Roberts
Kansas City, Mo.

Dear Sam: *September 8, 1949*

I read your letter of September first with a lot of interest. You evidently got an immense amount of political information in the two and one-half months you were in Britain and it is most interesting. I have many reports on the situation in Great Britain and I have come to the conclusion that the British have always handled their internal affairs to their own satisfaction and I propose to let them continue to do it. We have never been in complete agreement with them on anything. That disagreement started in 1776. If you remember fundamentally, however, our basic ideas are not far apart—they gave us our fundamental and basic law and have been our allies in nearly every war we have fought since 1860. You must remember they have been through two of the most terrible experiences in the history of the world—experiences which cost them the young men of two generations. Had our losses been in proportion we would have lost between twelve and fifteen million of our young men. Try to contemplate what that would mean to this country.

I note carefully what you say about Mercy Hospital and the General Hospital. I am not worried about that end of the population, nor am I worried about those who make $25,000 a year and over. The health of the people between those two extremes is what is most important to the country and when we find 34 percent of our young men and women unfit for military service because of physical and mental defects, there is something wrong with the health of the country and I am trying to find a remedy for it. When it comes to the point where a man getting $2400 a year has to pay $500 for prenatal care and then an additional hospital bill on top of that there is something wrong with the system. Before I get out of this office, I am going to find out what is wrong and I am going to try and remedy it. I'd suggest you doctors had better be hunting for a remedy yourselves unless you want a drastic one.

Sincerely yours,
HARRY S. TRUMAN

My dear Mr. President: *August 7, 1952*

I know of your very deep concern with the economic effects upon most of our citizens of the mounting costs of medical, hospital, and other health services. I share this concern and I also share your views on the necessity for appropriate steps being taken both to reduce the hazard of ill health and to prevent the cost of medical and hospital services causing excessive and disruptive inroads into the economic means of most of our citizens.

I am sure therefore that you will be interested in factual information which strongly indicates that the present cost of medical and hospital expenses in many cases places an extreme and oppressive strain upon the economic position of those in the lower income brackets, such as skilled and semi-skilled workers and those holding minor clerical positions.

To comply with the requirements of the Securities Act, the three largest "small loan" companies, in connection with the sales of their securities to the public, are required to file registration statements and prospectuses with this Commission. As you know, these companies are engaged in the business of making loans, usually limited by state law to not more than $300 to any one individual, at rates of interest which vary from state to state but usually are within the range of approximately $2^{1}/2$% to 3% per month on the unpaid monthly balances of outstanding loans. In most cases the effective rates of interest required to be paid on these loans on an annual basis range from 30 to 36%.

I am attaching to this letter a table which indicates the number of loan applications filed with these three, the largest of such companies, which are made for the purpose of medical, dental and hospital expenses; the percentage of such loan applications to all applications; and, the range of annual income of the majority of such borrowers. I also enclose copies of the latest prospectuses of each of these companies. You will note that approximately 14% to 17% of all loans made by these companies are for the purpose, and at the extremely high interest rates, which I have described. You will note also that the annual income of the majority of such borrowers does not in most cases exceed $3600 per annum.

I believe that these statistics are very persuasive evidence of the need for health insurance which you have so earnestly and persistently advocated. I hope they will be of service in achieving that objective.

> *Respectfully yours,*
> *Donald C. Cook, Chairman*
> *Securities and Exchange Commission*

Dear Don: *August 14, 1952*

I can't tell you how very much I appreciated your letter of the seventh. You certainly have gotten right to the meat of the situation with which we are faced.

My objective in a health insurance proposition is to meet the very difficult situation with which people in the two thousand to six thousand group are placed when it comes to health services. These "skin flint" loan companies, who charge the people from twenty-seven to fifty percent interest on small loans, I think are the worst vultures we have to contend with—they and the American Medical Association are the very reason there has been such a howl about health insurance. One of their sources of ill-gotten income would be dried up. I can see very well why these loan companies wouldn't want health insurance but for the life of me I can't get the doctors' point of view because the objective is to help these people have a nest egg so the doctors and hospitals can be paid.

Thanks a lot for sending me this information. It will be exceedingly useful to me in the coming campaign.

> *Sincerely yours,*
> *HARRY S. TRUMAN*

Another bit of unfinished business involved our former adversaries, Germany and Japan, with whom the United States remained in a technical state of war since peace treaties had not been concluded with either country. A final peace treaty would not be concluded with Germany until long after Truman's death, when the fall of the Soviet Union finally allowed Western and Soviet "occupation" troops to vacate the formerly divided city of Berlin. Some Americans clearly felt that the United States was being far too lenient with Germany in the aftermath of the Soviets' 1948–49 blockade of Berlin; others were appalled at what they viewed as their country's heavy-handed approach with the German people.

Dear Mr. President,   *February 21, 1952*

In the summer of 1945, I was among the hundreds of GI's in Antwerp, Belgium, who cheered as you drove through the city on your way to Potsdam. Surrounded, as we were, by the ruins of once beautiful European metropolis, seeing the hardships and suffering of the Belgian people, all of us felt certain that your arrival in Europe, to meet with Churchill and Stalin would, once and for all, end the curse of militarism and death that has for so long been a hallmark of the German government.

It was with something of a shock, therefore, that while doing some work in the library, I <u>had occasion to reread the Potsdam agreement, to which your signature as President of the United States, is affixed</u>. A shock, sir, because on reading carefully through that treaty—on which so much hope for peace rested—I find that <u>it has been broken and violated—not by Stalin—but by you—our own President</u>.

The things we—our country, yours and mine—are permitting and sponsoring in Gemany today is a <u>kick to the belly to every living GI of World War II</u> (of which I am proud to have been a part), and a desecration of the graves of the brave men who died in Europe to defeat the Nazis.

It would seem to me, <u>Mr. President, in all due respect, that in the future, before you publicly make charges about the value of other nations' signatures on treaties, that it would do you and America well to examine your own record in this connection</u>. Our country can only develop worldwide disrepute if you continue these policies in Germany, and the responsibility, I believe, <u>must rest squarely on your shoulders</u>.

Respectfully yours,
David Golden
New York, N.Y.

My dear Mr. President: *February 1, 1951*

A West Virginian who is now in Germany recently sent to me the enclosure. I can readily understand why there is so much feeling about the situation discussed in this article, and I am communicating with you in the hope that some means may be developed whereby Americans working in Germany will not be placed in this difficult position. I am sure that such circumstances give the Americans concerned an extra problem in their living among our erstwhile enemies.

With kindest regards, I am

Most sincerely yours,
Harley M. Kilgore, U.S. Senator
West Virginia

Augsburg, December 1950

To the American inhabitants of our houses and dwellings

More than 5 years ago you came to us in order to release us from terror and to bring us freedom and right. Already at that time we had to vacate our houses, our dwellings within a few hours and could not take wtih us but the most necessary things. We then had to abandon what we had acquired by long years working and saving.

Since that time, a great deal of us have been living in the most humble conditions.

Old and sick people are bitterly afflicted at the homesickness for their house and garden, the last joy of their evening of life.

Our children for whom we built the house are dwelling with us in overcrowded rooms or nasty toprooms, in many cases even in huts or summer houses whilst at a small distance stands the house their parents assigned them and which is now closed for them like a lost paradise.

Did you not warrant us the right to honestly and well acquired property?

Why are you still placing our home outside the law stamping us to second class citizens?

You, who brought us the principles of right and freedom, have in first line the duty to live according to these principles in order to set a good example to us! If you tell our children at school about the sympathy American people have for the Germans underlining your words with some candies, our children will not believe that you withhold them the fruit and the berries of our gardens.

The political situation is too a serious one to keep up such a large class of people deprived of their civic rights and consequently discontent ones.

As long as there are in Germany hundreds of thousands of people for whom the presence of the Forces of Occupation does not mean anything else than expulsion from house and home, no real approach between Americans and decent Germans will be possible.

Eliminate this source of bitterness and hate!

For five long years you are living in our houses! How long are you willing to do so?

Have your own dwellings built, then you may rely on our faithfulness and support when things become serious.

Apply to your authorities and take care that dwellings will be built for you immediately.

Truman, of course, realized the importance of developing better relations with the Germans, but he also knew that the American and other Allied soldiers in the country were the only thing standing in the way of a communist takeover. Until more infrastructure could be built for the long-term stationing of NATO forces, Germans would just have to live with the current system, which actually involved only a tiny portion of the U.S. troop commitment.

Dear Harley: *February 3, 1951*

I appreciated your letter of the first, enclosing me a wail from the Germans whose houses are being occupied by our people in the Occupation of Germany. Of course, there is no doubt but that this is the way they feel, but I don't suppose you would have our people who are governing our part of Germany live in tents would you?

Sincerely yours,
HARRY S. TRUMAN

Lack of Soviet involvement in the occupation of Japan enabled a semblance of normalcy to be established with that nation in a comparatively short period of time.

Dear Mr. President: *September 2, 1951*

We, the members of the Goodwill men's Bible class of the Calvary Baptist Church, Kansas City, Missouri, wish to take this means of expressing to you our deep interest in the San Francisco Conference to secure a peace treaty with Japan. We have each one convenanted to pause for prayer at the opening hour of the conference, and to continue our prayers daily that a just and durable peace may be arrived at, not only with Japan but with all other nations of the world. We sincerely feel that our greatness as a nation is due to the blessings of Almighty God, and we further believe that only as He is honored and revered by all nations will peace truly come to the world. We believe that simple sincere prayer offered to God will do more to insure the success of the peace conference than all the political manipulations that will take place within or without the conference. We earnestly plead that you use your influence as the Chief Executive of our great nation to cause prayer to be made upon every possible occasion to the end that God's blessings may continue to abide upon us as a nation and as a world.

Respectfully yours,
The Goodwill Class
Calvary Baptist Church
Kansas City, Mo.

My dear Mr. Edwards: *September 11, 1951*

The President has received the letter of September second, from yourself and Mr. Davidson, and has noted with interest the spiritual undertakings of your Bible class. It is this spirit of faith that has been our bulwark throughout the ages and, as the President has expressed in public addresses and proclamations, we need to unite in universal prayer now more than ever. On April second at the laying of the cornerstone of the New York Avenue Presbyterian Church in Washington, D.C., he pointed out that by a living allegiance to our religious faith this country can carry through the trials which are ahead. You can be sure, therefore, that your thoughtfulness in writing as you did is appreciated.

Very sincerely yours,
WILLIAM D. HASSETT
Secretary to the President

The peace conference also presented admirers of Douglas MacArthur another opportunity to sing the general's praises while taking a shot or two at Truman and Acheson.

Dear Harry,   *August 27, 1951*

Listen Harry, you stubborn Missouri mule, why can't you give old General <u>MacArthur</u> a place on the Japanese peace conference. He, more than anyone else, is responsible for the affair. Harry, appoint him and we will love you. Harry, leave him out of it and November 1952 will be to—ugh.

> *Sincerely yours,*
> *Robert G. MacKendrick*
> *1918 Combat Field Artilleryman*
> *Norwood, Penn.*

Dear Mr. President: *August 23, 1951*

Acheson has once again given you some more stupid advice. I have reference, of course, to your not having made it your business to make sure <u>General of the Army Douglas MacArthur</u> was either a delegate or received a formal invitation from the conference to attend the Japanese conference next month. If there is one man living who should be at that conference, it is General MacArthur. On this I think you will agree with me and the ever so many Americans who feel the same way.

Acheson just hasn't got what it takes and neither have a great many of his assistants. Why do you, Mr. President, tolerate him and his State Department crowd? Surely not because of their record. I find it increasingly difficult to remain a good Democrat as you continue to insist on keeping Acheson and his gang around.

It will be a great mistake if you do not make sure General MacArthur attends that conference.

> *Yours truly,*
> *W. E. Smiddy, Jr.*
> *Jackson Heights, N.Y.*

A surprisingly deep strain of anti-British feeling was also still evident in the country, and news of an impending visit by Churchill, who had been returned to 10 Downing Street by British voters, prompted a flurry of ugly letters.

Dear President Truman: *November 11, 1951*

The British are coming—again and I am instructing my congressman and senator now that if you promise them another dime you <u>should be impeached</u> immediately and tried for treason!

I am getting damned tired of working for a bunch of sops in Washington and an endless variety of bankrupt nations abroad.

> *Sincerely yours,*
> *Walter M. Kollmorgen*
> *Lawrence, Kans.*

Dear Mr. Truman: *Dec. 31, 1951*

Why don't you put the worthless British in their place? Just tell them to get to work! What right did you have to let the parasites wrap their rottenness around our necks in the first place? Sec. Acheson is a brainless echo of the diseased, knife in the back, so-called "friends!"

The island has plenty of coal but strip the d—— fool Americans they have not any sense. And you prove it every day.

You will tell them more of our secrets so they can sell it to Russia and China.

How can any man or group of men be such fools?

> *Sam Kahn*
> *New York, N.Y.*

Dear Sir: *Nov. 26, 1951*

So <u>Churchill</u> is going to pay you a visit. Hope he doesn't take you for a ride like he did Roosevelt and the American people. Remember? "You make the tools, we'll do the job." That was later changed to "Now that you have made the tools, bring them over." That was later changed to "Now that you have made the tools and brought them over, come over and use them."

At the time of the Normandy invasion, Churchill said that the manpower would be a so-so deal but as soon as the invasion was over this country would have to furnish all the men because this country was larger than England, sure 143 million to their 47 million. When the war was over he said this country should pay for the war because this country was the larger, sure 143 million to their 47 million. But when the San Francisco Charter was formed, we got one vote to their six. We were no longer compared to England but pitted against the whole British Empire. Don't be a sucker and be fooled by this glib talker. How many billion will he want this time? December 31, 76 million will be due this country as interest in the $3^3/4$ billion loan of 1946. Is he going to bring that interest money with him or is he going to welsh?

> *Yours respectfully,*
> *R. F. Hecker*
> *Cleveland, Ohio*

During his last visit with Truman as president, Churchill was showing all of his seventy-seven years. Joe Short related to his young assistant, Roger Tubby, that at one point during a cruise on the Presidential yacht *Williamsburg*, he appeared to have fallen asleep in his deck chair. Truman sat across from him grinning at the picture Churchill presented. With a whiskey and soda at his elbow and a long, thick, unlit cigar cradled in the famous V of his fingers, the old warrior was apparently dozing with his chin resting solidly against his chest. The prime minister slowly raised his eyelids and seemed to study the face of the grinning Missourian across from him. Finally the silence was broken, as he spoke slowly in his deep, nasal voice. "The last time you and I sat across the conference table was at Potsdam, Mr. President."

Truman nodded.

"I must confess, sir, I held you in very low regard then. I loathed your taking the place of Franklin Roosevelt."

Truman was momentarily dumbfounded, his grin completely gone.

After a pause that seemed to last forever, Churchill continued. "I misjudged you badly. Since that time, you, more than any other man, have saved Western Civilization.

"When Britain could no longer hold out in Greece, you, and you alone, sir, made the decision that saved that ancient land from the Communists.

"You acted in similar regard to Azerbaijan when the Soviets tried to take over Iran. Then there was your resolute stand on Trieste, and your Marshall Plan which rescued Western Europe wallowing in the shallows and indeed easy prey to Joseph Stalin's malevolent intentions. Then you established the North Atlantic Treaty Alliance and collective security for those nations against the military machinations of the Soviet Union. Then there was your audacious Berlin Airlift. And, of course, there was Korea."[7]

Truman's wide grin had returned.

As Truman prepared to leave office, he received a request from Air Force historian James L. Cate at the University of Chicago for information on the timing of certain decisions and orders pertaining to dropping of the atom bomb in 1945. George Elsey, who had been at Potsdam with Truman and was intimately familiar with the decision to use the bomb, was then attending a NATO conference in Paris. Consequently, the president's response was staffed through Kenneth W. Hechler and David Lloyd, who suggested modifications to its contents. Some forty years later, one of those changes was heavily debated by academicians concerned with the question of why Truman had thought it was necesssary to use the weapon against the Japanese.

Sir: *December 6, 1952*

For several years it has been my privilege to serve as one of the editors and authors of *The Army Air Forces in World War II,* a history published on a non-profit basis under the joint sponsorship of the U.S. Air Force and the University of Chicago. One of my tasks for the fifth volume, now in press, was to write an account of the atomic bomb attacks against Hiroshima and Nagasaki. In respect to the decision to use the bomb I have been faced with an apparent discrepancy in the evidence which I have been unable to resolve, and, in spite of a reluctance to intrude upon the time of the President, I am turning to you for information for which you are the best and perhaps the sole authority.

I have read with great interest your own statements—that released on 6 August 1945 and that contained in your letter to Dr. Karl T. Compton, dated 16 December 1946 and published in the *Atlantic Monthly* of February 1947. I have read also the late Mr. Stimson's more detailed account in *Harper's Magazine* of February 1947 which is in perfect accord with yours—the gist being that the dread decision for which you courageously assumed responsibility was made at Potsdam "in the face of" Premier Suzuki's rejection of the warning contained in the Potsdam Declaration of 26 July, and that the motive was to avoid the great loss of life that would have attended the invasion of Kyushu scheduled for November.

More recently I have seen a photostatic copy of the directive of Gen. Carl Spaatz ordering him to deliver the first atomic bomb against one of four designated targets; the document has been declassified and I am enclosing a true copy. The letter is dated at Washington on 25 July 1945 and bears the signature of Gen. Thomas T. Handy, Acting Chief of Staff during General Marshall's absence at Potsdam. According to General Arnold's statement elsewhere [H. H. Arnold *Global Mission,* New York: 1949, p. 589], this directive was based on a memorandum dispatched by courier to Washington after a conference on 22 July between himself, Secretary Stimson, and General Marshall.

The directive contains an unqualified order to launch the attack "as soon as weather will permit visual bombing about 3 August 1945." There is no reference to the Potsdam Declaration which was to be issued on the next day and no statement as to what should be done in the event of a Japanese offer to surrender before 3 August. It is possible that the written directive was qualified by oral instructions, or that it was intended that it be countermanded by a radio message if the Japanese did accept the Potsdam terms, or that the directive was an erroneous representation of Secretary Stimson's real intentions. Nevertheless, as it stands the directive seems to indicate that the decision to use the bomb had been made at least one day before the promulgation of the Potsdam Declaration and two days before Suzuki's rejection thereof on 28 July, Tokyo time. Such an interpretation is in flat contradiction to the explanation implicit in the published statements, that the final decision was made only after the Japanese refusal of the ultimatum.

Because of the extraordinary importance of this problem, I am appealing to you for more complete information as to the time and the circumstances under which you arrived at the final decision, and for permission to quote your reply in the volume of which I have spoken. Your well-known interest in history has encouraged me to seek my information at the source, as the historian should, without apology other than for having intruded on your crowded schedule with a letter made overly long by my desire to state the problem accurately.

> *Very truly yours,*
> *James L. Cate*
> *Professor of Medieval History*
> *University of Chicago*

Enclosure

Having come at a time when the White House staff was packing its bags to make way for the Eisenhower administration, it was first offered to the Air Force, which declined becoming the lead agency on the project.

December 23, 1952
MEMORANDUM TO GENERAL LANDRY:
Attached is a letter from Professor Cate of the University of Chicago asking clarification of the precise circumstances under which the first atomic bomb was dropped on Hiroshima.

If this letter is to be answered, it may take some research in official files and discussion with the President. Since this is an Air Force project, perhaps it would be more appropriate if you checked into this thing.

If, when the information is available, you wish us to write a reply, we will be glad to do so.

IRVING PERLMETER
The White House

30 December 1952
MEMORANDUM FOR THE PRESIDENT
Mr. President, it would be very desirable, if you could do it, to let this historian have such information as could be used in the history that he is writing concerning the circumstances under which the first atomic bombs were dropped.

R. B. LANDRY
Major General, USAF

After consultations with Defense Department historian Dr. Rudolph Winnacker and several others, David Lloyd summed up the findings in a memo for Truman.

January 6, 1953
MEMORANDUM FOR THE PRESIDENT:
At your request I have reviewed your draft letter to Professor Cate and I have made a few slight revisions after checking the details.

In your draft, you state that General Marshall told you that a landing in Japan would cost a quarter of a million casualties to the United States, and an equal number of the enemy. Mr. Stimson, in his book written by McGeorge Bundy says that Marshall's estimate was over a million casualties. Your recollection seems more reasonable than Stimson's, but in order to avoid a conflict, I have changed the wording to read that General Marshall expected a minimum of a quarter of a million casualties and possibly a much greater number—as much as a million.*

Secretary Forrestal does not appear to have been at the Potsdam meetings until July 28, and your conferences about the atom bomb appear to have taken place early in the meeting, on July 22, 23 and 24. Accordingly, I have deleted the Secretary of the Navy from the list of those with whom you conferred.

---

*Truman had already used the words "minimum of" in the original draft.

I have also inserted a paragraph explaining why the orders to General Spaatz were dated July 25 rather than after the ultimatum. This has been checked with the historian of the Department of Defense.

Russian entry into the war was less than a week before the surrender.

I have deleted the last sentence of your draft, since I think that it might be unfairly used by the propagandists of the political opposition. It states a fundamental truth, but in a very restrained way, and it seemed to me that it might raise more problems than it would help.

I attach various memoranda to me on this subject from Kenneth Hechler who did the research.

DAVID D. LLOYD

Truman gave his approval to the changes, which included removal of his original ending sentence: "Russia in Asia has been a great liability since."

My dear Professor Cate: *January 12, 1953*
Your letter of December 6, 1952 has just now been delivered to me.

When the message came to Potsdam that a successful atomic explosion had taken place in New Mexico, there was much excitement and conversation about the effect on the war then in progress with Japan.

The next day I told the Prime Minister of Great Britain and Generalissimo Stalin that the explosion had been a success. The British Prime Minister understood and appreciated what I'd told him. Premier Stalin smiled and thanked me for reporting the explosion to him, but I'm sure he did not understand its significance.

I called a meeting of the Secretary of State, Mr. Byrnes, the Secretary of War, Mr. Stimson, Admiral Leahy, General Marshall, General Eisenhower, Admiral King, and some others, to discuss what should be done with the awful weapon.

I asked General Marshall what it would cost in lives to land on the Tokio plain and other places in Japan. It was his opinion that such an invasion would cost at a minimum one quarter of a million casualties, and might cost as much as a million, on the American side alone, with an equal number of the enemy. The other military and naval men present agreed.

I asked Secretary Stimson which cities in Japan were devoted exclusively to war production. He promptly named Hiroshima and Nagasaki, among others.

We sent an ultimatum to Japan. It was rejected.

I ordered atomic bombs dropped on the two cities named on the way back from Potsdam, when we were in the middle of the Atlantic Ocean.

In your letter, you raise the fact that the directive to General Spaatz to prepare for delivering the bomb is dated July twenty-fifth. It was, of course, necessary to set the military wheels in motion, as these orders did, but the final decision was in my hands, and was not made until we were returning from Potsdam.

Dropping the bomb ended the war, saved lives, and gave the free nations a chance to face the facts.

When it looked as if Japan would quit, Russia hurried into the fray less than a week before the surrender, so as to be in at the settlement. No military contribution was made by the Russians toward victory over Japan. Prisoners were surrendered and Manchuria occupied by the Soviets, as was Korea, north of the 38th parallel.

> *Sincerely yours,*
> *HARRY S. TRUMAN*

The controversy surrounding this letter during the *Enola Gay* debate of 1995 focused on two questions: Did such a meeting between Truman and his senior advisors actually take place, and did Marshall inform him that casualties could reach as high as a million men?

Truman's recollection of the casualty estimates has been the focus of much debate by historians, even though it is somewhat beside the point, since what Marshall is reputed to have said was completely in line with current Army thinking as well as the long-implemented manpower policy of 1945, a policy that included a steep jump in Selective Service call-ups in the spring and summer of 1945 and a huge expansion of the Army's training base, which peaked months *after* the last shots were fired in Europe.[8] The documents associated with Truman at the Potsdam Conference, however, do not pass the muster of some scholars today, and the lack of specificity in the conference log and notes from the less-formal meetings are often used to buttress the contention that expectations by military and civilian leaders of huge losses during the invasions were a "postwar creation."[9] Truman's own shorthand manner of recounting events certainly adds to the confusion, and consequently, when he said that Marshall's comments were made during a meeting with his senior advisors—specifically, Stimson, Leahy, Marshall, Eisenhower, King, and the new secretary of state, Jimmy Byrnes—Truman is quite possibly referring to a meeting that might or might not have happened exactly the way he stated.

In the conglomeration of notes making up Truman's "diary" and the great volume of letters he wrote to his wife, family, and friends from the 1930s through the 1950s, Truman repeatedly simplifies events in a way that anyone making a close comparison of the material with ongoing events might find somewhat confusing. Unlike the virtual day-by-day accounts of Presidents Eisenhower and Carter, things that occurred are frequently not commented on until days or even weeks later, and when they do make their appearance in Truman's hastily written notes, they are often phrased in a way that gives the appearance that they just happened. Consultations with a variety of individuals, which White House logs clearly demonstrate took place over the space of weeks and even months, can show up as occurring in one session, and events of seemingly great importance many years later are given little or no mention. To further complicate matters, such items are interspersed among commentaries of events that follow accurate timelines and have varying levels of detail. In short, Harry Truman wrote about whatever was important to him at the time of the writing. This highly personal material was written for himself and his family, and it is clear that he frequently used his diary to play with ideas for later use in speeches or to simply get things off his chest. Although such material provides valuable insights into Truman's views and makes fascinating reading,[10] it also opens the door to misinterpretations, misunderstandings, and misuse.

For example, it has been suggested that it is "unlikely" that a "formal" meeting between Truman and his advisors took place on casualties and the atom bomb, based on the undeniable fact that "none of the available diaries for Potsdam, including those by Leahy, Arnold and Truman, as well as those by Stimson and McCloy, mentions such a meeting."[11] Virtually none of the diaries in question, however, are in any way comprehensive, and they are frequently quite sketchy. Moreover, there are two very important points to remember.

First, the proposition that American casualties for the invasion of Japan could parallel those suffered in the struggle against Germany was not new. It had been discussed at some length for nearly a year and with particular intensity in May and June. Although this subject is of great interest to some scholars today, it was, in many ways, "old news" to Truman and his principal advisors by Potsdam in the sense that it was already accepted that casualties would be extremely heavy (see page 292).

Second, the successful test of the first nuclear device was an event of immense proportions, but not only are there no direct references to atomic weapons during Potsdam in these individuals' diaries, there are none at any time before Hiroshima either, except the occasional cryptic reference to the code name for the weapon, "S-1," and Truman's own notes from July 25, 1945.[12] The matter was, after all, top secret. Although it is sometimes hard for today's researchers to understand, the classification "top secret" was—and still is—taken very seriously by individuals responsible for the lives of Americans going into harm's way, and diary references from Truman's advisors don't start pouring out until *after* the August 6 public release of information on the August 5 (Washington time) destruction of Hiroshima.

An examination of documents from the Potsdam Conference and the *Log of the President's Trip to the Berlin Conference* shows that there were numerous formal and informal occasions in which Truman met with Stimson, Leahy, Marshall, Eisenhower, King, and the new secretary of state, Jimmy Byrnes, singly and in groups, with Eisenhower the most frequent odd man out because of other duties. In his letter to Professor Cate, Truman said he called all of these gentlemen together for "a meeting" to discuss the atom bomb.[13] But though the *Log* is mum on the specifics of the meeting, and even who was in attendance, the date and time are easily recognized.

Truman was first made aware of the successful test of an atomic device in the New Mexico desert on the evening of July 16, but no mention can be found in the *Log* of Stimson's delivery of the message at approximately 7:30 P.M. There was also no time before the morning of July 18, after additional details of the explosion's size and scope had become available on the 17th, that a meeting with his advisors could have taken place in a discreet manner. And though there are many portions of Truman's time that are essentially undocumented in the *Log,* the morning of July 18 is particularly vague and very extended. The document states only that he had breakfast (customarily at 8:00 A.M. or a little earlier), then gives no other timed listing until a reference for 1:15 in the afternoon, when he left for a luncheon appointment with Prime Minister Churchill. Likewise, Truman's diary entry for the 18th says only that he had breakfast, then had lunch with Churchill at 1:30 P.M. There is, however, an important *Log* entry between breakfast and lunch. It reads: "The President conferred with the Secretary of State and a number of his advisors during the forenoon."[14] Moreover, it was from this meeting that, according to Churchill, Truman brought "the telegrams about the recent experiment" which were discussed during a lengthy, private session along with other bomb-related matters.[15]

At this point, it is useful to remember that the earlier delivery of news on the successful and highly secret nuclear test was not noted in the *Log* at all. Applying the same logic that has been used to dismiss Marshall's million-casualties statement during what the *Log* refers to as a meeting between "the President [and] his advisors" to the absence of virtually any *Log* reference to Truman's learning of the New Mexico test from Stimson would lead to the obvious—and erroneous—conclusion that the president had never been informed of this momentous event.

Further evidence that the meeting was not concocted for the benefit of Professor Cate in 1952 also comes from a Truman diary entry on December 2, 1950. In the midst of China's entry into the Korean War and the grim conflict with MacArthur over the direction military strategy and foreign policy should take, the president wrote: "Now [MacArthur's] in serious trouble. We must get him out of it if we can. The conference [with Dean Acheson and Omar Bradley] was the most solemn one I've had since the Atomic Bomb conference in Berlin. We continue it in the morning. It looks very bad."

But if one wishes to discard the *Log* account for July 18, 1945, there is also another entry in Truman's diary that is of interest. On the morning after the July 24 plenary session with Marshall and other senior U.S. and British leaders, Truman again met with Marshall when the general joined a meeting, already in progress, with the British commander in chief in Southeast Asia, Lord Louis Mountbatten. In Truman's notes covering July 25, the president said he "had Gen. Marshall come in and discuss with me the tactical and political situation," adding, "he is a levelheaded man." In a second set of notes covering the 25th, he referred to the meeting as "a most important session" and wrote extensively on the recent successful atomic test, which he indicates that he, Marshall, and Mountbatten discussed at some length.

Truman had convened a June 18 meeting of his senior advisors at the White House to discuss the casualties question, yet he had never really gotten an answer to the question of precisely how many men the invasion might cost. At some point in his discussions with the general one month later in Potsdam, it may have simply come down to the point where the commander in chief of America's armed forces asked the same question any president would ask his senior military advisor: "Well, general, what do you really think?" Though it is unfortunate that Truman's diary entries are not more specific, when the president states that he and Marshall discussed the "tactical situation," it's useful to remember that there was only one tactical operation in the offing during the summer of 1945, and that was the invasion of Japan.

The question of specifically what was discussed at the July 18 meeting— and whether it actually did take place—did not come up until long after the death of the participants. One historian has ventured the opinion that Truman's letter to Professor Cate, in which he recounts Marshall's educated guess that casualties could have reached a million men, is not a "reliable source" because the figure was not in the president's first draft; it was added at the suggestion of a White House staffer and was made "long after" the war in 1952. On the other hand, McGeorge Bundy's vague 1988 statement that "defenders of the use of the bomb, Stimson among them, were not always careful about numbers of casualties expected" is characterized by the same historian as authoritative and is presented as proof of Stimson's and Truman's duplicity.[16]

Although the image that many carry of Truman is that of a chief executive who frequently shot from the hip in his oral and written statements, it was not an unusual occurrence for him to have his staff read over his hastily penned drafts and offer their suggestions. Some were taken; others were not. In the original draft of the Cate letter, Truman recounted only the "minimum" number of expected casualties that Marshall gave him as part of a strategic analysis—which happened to be a quarter of a million men—and made no reference to any maximum. Of course, if there was a minimum figure, there must have been a maximum. His former Secretary of War Stimson had publicly recounted that maximum figure, stating that he (Stimson) had been advised that the casualty figure "might" exceed a million men.[17]

Presidential assistants Ken Hechler and David Lloyd felt that running a maximum figure along with the minimum was important, and a memo was forwarded to Truman that, among other things, reminded him of Stimson's statement. That Truman received this reminder by young staffers, who had not sat in on any meetings between him and Marshall, is not, as has been proposed, something that can be used to either prove or disprove what Truman and Marshall discussed in a private meeting. Neither does it alter the fact that Truman personally approved the addition to his letter, which credited Marshall as the source, and used the number and attribution in his memoirs as well, albeit in a more exaggerated and rhetorical fashion.

It is also important to note that Marshall never refuted Truman's statement, even in an oblique way. What he did say was that conquering Japan by invasion would have been "terribly bitter and frightfully expensive in lives and treasure." He said that claims that the war would have ended soon, even without the use of atomic weapons, "were rather silly" and maintained that "it was quite necessary to drop the bomb to shorten the war," adding, "I think it was very wise to use it."[18]

As the time neared for Truman to make his long journey into retirement, Americans who had cheered him and those who had criticized him took stock of the Truman presidency.

> *Dear Mister President:*   *May 8, 1952*
>
> I am just a common housewife, but this being America, I dare to write to my Commander-In-Chief.
>
> Just thought you might like to know <u>we believe in you</u> and think you have <u>made a fine president</u>. Everytime your picture comes on a newsreel in a theater, my husband and I always give you a big hand, sometimes we are the only ones that do, but that does not stop us.
>
> You must be a very big man to take over the job of President in these critical times and we are <u>sincerely sorry you are not going to enter this coming election</u>. I have listened over the radio and television about the stalemate in the <u>Prisoners of War exchange</u>.
>
> A simple solution occurred to me, so I'll send it along for what it may be worth to you:
>
> Wouldn't it be a simple thing to <u>screen the prisoners of war (on both sides) through a board committee consisting of two Russian military or political men and two of our own men??</u>
>
> <u>Let the prisoners decide for themselves</u> before this board which would give <u>equal protection to the men of both sides??</u>
>
> Maybe it's worth a try.
>
> *Sincerely your great admirer,*
> *Mrs. Vera Dowell Sierra*
> *Santa Barbara, Calif.*

P.S. My father Richard J. H. Dowell, was a member of the Democratic Central Committee at Sacramento for many years prior to his death.

Dear President Truman,   *May 29, 1952*

Will you accept my <u>congratulations upon being able to always have a smile</u>.

Recently a Post Office Inspector called at my post office and as always entered without a sign of a smile and immediately found 40-11 things I had been doing wrong and by the time he left I felt lower than a worm.

Actually between the inspectors and the public sometimes I feel I am awfully abused, but as I was thinking over the situation, I wondered how you must feel with everyone criticizing, complaining and even condemning the things you are doing and trying to do.

Do you feel that everything you do is wrong? Are you terrified or frightened when Congress criticizes you or the press writes unfavorable reports? You look so cheerful—but do you really feel that way?

If you ever get time and do answer this letter, please tell me your recipe for your smile.

         Sincerely,
         Naomi Garritt
         Cragsmoor, N.Y.

Dear Miss Garritt: *June 12, 1952*

Your letter of May twenty-ninth to the President was a very human one. All of us get sad and discouraged at time, but I agree with you that few people show it less than the President.

He gave his recipe for this last February twenth-first while addressing a Masonic Breakfast in Washington. He said "When a man has to work 17 hours a day, there isn't much chance of his getting into devilment, and for that reason you all wonder why I can be gay and healthy after all the bricks and stones and mud and things that are thrown my way. It is because I work all the time, and because I think I am doing something to help the people of this nation to live better than they otherwise would live, and also because the efforts that are now being put forth are in the hope that eventually we will have a peaceful world."

         Sincerely yours,
         JOSEPH SHORT
         Secretary to the President

Individuals and organizations were also quick to offer their services.

Dear Mr. President: *June 23, 1952*

We have noticed in the newspapers that after your term of office is completed in November, you would like to visit Israel. It will indeed be a happy occasion when you who were the first head of a state to recognize the new nation, visit the land in person.

We would feel greatly honored if you would allow us to help you plan your itinerary abroad, whether or not you fly with us. Perhaps, after your many years of official duties, you might enjoy travelling incognito.

We are looking forward to hearing from you.

> *Very sincerely yours,*
> *El Al Israel Airlines Ltd.*
> *Isobel Aronin*
> *New York, N.Y.*

Dear Mr. Aronin: *June 30, 1952*

The President appreciated very much your thoughtful offer to be of service in arranging an itinerary for him should he plan to travel abroad after his term of office is completed.

Although no plans are being made at this time for such a trip, you may be assured that your kindness will be remembered and your offer borne in mind.

With all good wishes,

> *Sincerely yours,*
> *MATTHEW J. CONNELLY*
> *Secretary to the President*

A surprising number of such letters were even answered by Truman himself.

Dear Mr. President,   *17 Nov. 1952*

We are former members of the Marine Honor Guard that was maintained at Key West, Florida, during your many visits there. On several occasions we had the honor of meeting and speaking directly to you. Needless to say, those moments maintain an elevated position in our memories.

We have speculated at length concerning your proposed world-wide trip and the security that will be provided for you. As former members of your supplementary bodyguard, we would like to volunteer our services "free gratis" as personal bodyguards or aides in any manner that would assist you.

Although we are both entered in college and law school respectively, we feel the association with you would benefit us far more than any institution of higher learning in preparing ourselves to become worthwhile citizens in this great democracy. The honor and distinction of serving a great and worthy American like yourself, would be more than adequate compensation.

The fact that you were able to take over the helm of our ship of state in those perilous days following World War II, and keep this vessel on an even keel has been proof to us of your supremeness in position.

Both Mr. Brown, who incidently is President of the Young Democratic Club of Washington, D.C., and myself consider it a privilege to have served you in the past and an honor we both would like to accept in the future.

> *Sincerely,*
> *William A. Wehr, Jr.*
> *Beaver, Penn.*
> *James V. Brown*
> *Washington, D.C.*

Dear Mr. Wehr: *December 15, 1952*

It was wonderful of you and Mr. James V. Brown to offer your help in case I go traveling after I leave the White House.

My gratitude is not lessened one bit by the fact that I do not think I will need bodyguards after I am no longer President. The greatest treasure I will take with me from the White House will be the kind thoughts of my fellow citizens.

> *Very sincerely yours,*
> *HARRY S. TRUMAN*

An extremely large number of letters arrived from friends. In traditional fashion, Truman answered each and every one of them.

My dear Mr. President: *Jan. 12*

Just noted in Drew Pearson's column that you are planning to write your memoirs.

I hope it is so. It will give the stupid people of this nation an idea of what transpired in the White House during the past 8 years.

There are many that compare you with our great Presidents and rightfully so. Lincoln was a great man but his tenure in office wasn't beset by the many important decisions that confronted you.

As this great nation matures, each generation will appreciate what a wonderful job was done by you to keep our nation strong and progressive, with the goal to keep people free of communism.

Enjoyed your note and hope the tie really pleased you. Also had a nice note from Margaret and Mrs. Truman.

Flew out here from Chicago to do a special job for my firm and will leave here in the morning.

Willie Worthing is coming in from a convention in Miami and will spend a day or two with me in Chicago.

I am very happy in my new position and the work is very interesting. The guy I work for can't be beat.

Wishing you and the family continued success, health and happiness, I remain

> *Sincerely,*
> *Bill [Mox]*
> *Chicago, Ill.*

Dear Bill: *January 16, 1953*

I certainly did appreciate your letter of the twelfth from Sioux City. I've only got two or three more days now and then I'll be a free man and can take you on equal terms.

> *Sincerely yours,*
> *HARRY S. TRUMAN*

[Longhand] *Don't use Willie too roughly*

Dear Mr. President: *December 25, 1952*

This bountiful Christmas has been TOPPED by a splendid photograph of you in a beautiful frame.

Your great phrase "To My Good Friend" is a high and priceless honor for which I am humbly grateful. My descendants will see this treasure overhanging the desk in our farm home. They will look upon it with respect similar to that we of our generation pay to the historical builders of America.

Our family and business associates never experienced such a wonderful Christmas. I congratulate you for the achievements at the base of this unparalleled prosperity.

Respectfully and gratefully yours,
Fred P. Murphy
Stamford, N.Y.

Dear Fred: *December 30, 1952*

Thanks a lot for that good letter of yours dated Christmas Day.

I hope the time will come when I will have a chance to take a look at that farm of yours and see whether or not you really know anything about agriculture. I have grave doubts about your knowledge of the operation of a farm. I also have doubts about my own ability to operate one these days.

My two nephews run the 600 acre farm at home by themselves, whereas my father and I used to hire five or six men to operate it during the busy season. These kids make money and we didn't— that is the difference.

If you need a few instructions I will have one of the boys come back and give you a little help—they are both experts in the matter of the operation of a farm.

I hope you have a Happy and Prosperous 1953.

Sincerely yours,
HARRY S. TRUMAN

On January 20, 1953, Bess's prayers were answered and her husband became a free man. Returning to Independence, Missouri, he looked forward to writing his memoirs, overseeing the eventual construction of his beloved presidential library, and finally being able to just relax and travel around the country with Bess at his own pace. There was, however, one small project he and his devoted staff had to tackle first: wading through the 72,000 letters at the local post office addressed to private citizen Harry S. Truman.

Dear Mr. Eisenhower,   *March 8, 1953*

I just learned on a radio broadcast that you and Mrs. Eisenhower are arranging an Easter egg hunt. This seems a charming thing to do and very much like "Ike and Mamie."

The radio voice also mentioned that your predecessor had considered the custom a waste of food. School teacher that I am, an idea instantly flashed into my head. Do Easter eggs *have* to be food? Why not a wooden or composition egg of some kind. Such an egg could be beautifully decorated and could constitute a very nice souvenir for the child who rolled it at the White House. With the price of hen eggs, it is quite possible that an artificial—or better, *artistic*—egg could be less expensive. . . .

Our devoted love to you and to Mrs. Eisenhower—

Sincerely,
Mildred Madsen
Santa Rosa, Calif.

Dear Mrs. Madsen: *March 18, 1953*

The President asked me to to thank you for your friendly thought in sending the President that letter of March eighth submitting your suggestion.

May I assure you also that the President appreciates your good wishes.

Sincerely,
Sherman Adams

NOTES

CHAPTER 1

1. Margaret Truman, *Bess W. Truman* (New York: MacMillan Publishing Co., 1986), 230.
2. Margaret Truman, *Harry S. Truman* (New York: William Morrow and Co., 1973), 209.
3. Harry S. Truman, *Memoirs*, vol. 1, *Years of Decision* (New York: Doubleday and Co., 1955), 67.
4. Francis H. Heller, ed., *The Truman White House: The Administration of the Presidency, 1945–1953* (Lawrence, KS: The Regents Press of Kansas, 1980), 9.
5. Truman, *Memoirs*, vol. 1, 228.
6. Ibid., 227–28.
7. Charles Robbins, *Last of His Kind: An Informal Portrait of Harry S. Truman* (New York: William Morrow and Co., 1979), 117–18.
8. Robert H. Ferrell, ed., *Off the Record: The Private Papers of Harry. S. Truman* (New York: Harper & Row, 1980), 5.
9. David McCullough, *Truman* (New York: Simon and Schuster, 1992), 623.
10. Samuel Elliot Morison, *The Oxford History of the American People* (New York: Oxford University Press, 1965), 945.
11. Ibid., 946.
12. Ibid., 948.
13. Ibid., 949.
14. Louis McHenry Howe, "The President's Mail Bag," *The American Magazine*, June 1934, 22.
15. Heller, ed., *The Truman White House*, 153.
16. Ferrell, ed., *Off the Record*, 241.
17. Heller, ed., *The Truman White House*, 110.

18. J. B. West, *Upstairs at the White House: My Life with the First Ladies* (New York: Warner Books, 1973), 71.

19. Ibid., 74.

20. Truman, *Memoirs,* vol. 1, 351.

21. Truman, *Memoirs,* vol. 2, *Years of Trial and Hope* (New York: Doubleday and Co., 1956), 361.

22. Margaret Truman, *Harry S. Truman,* 355–56.

23. Merle Miller, *Plain Speaking: An Oral Biography of Harry S. Truman* (New York: Berkley Publishing Corp., 1973, 1974), 52.

24. Margaret Truman, *Harry S. Truman,* 351.

25. Ferrell, ed., *Off the Record,* 214–15.

26. Margaret Truman, *Harry S. Truman,* 331.

27. McCullough, *Truman,* 858.

28. Margaret Truman, *Harry S. Truman,* 451.

29. Howe, "The President's Mail Bag," 23.

30. Margaret Truman, *Harry S. Truman,* 450.

31. Heller, ed., *The Truman White House,* 45.

32. Ibid., 158–59.

33. Ibid., 65.

CHAPTER 2

1. Heller, ed., *The Truman White House,* 55.

2. Ibid., 63.

3. Ibid., 82.

4. Margaret Truman, *Bess W. Truman,* 278.

5. Ibid.

6. Ibid., 279.

7. Ferrell, ed., *Off the Record,* 70.

8. Heller, ed., *The Truman White House,* 52–53.

9. Harry S. Truman, *Memoirs,* vol. 1, 484–85.

10. Harry S. Truman, *Memoirs,* vol. 2, 180.

11. Alfred Steinberg, *The Man from Missouri: The Life and Times of Harry S. Truman* (New York: G. P. Putnam's Sons), 315.

12. Truman, *Memoirs,* vol. 2, 184.

13. West, *Upstairs at the White House,* 70.

14. Robert H. Ferrell, ed., *Dear Bess: The Letters from Harry to Bess Truman, 1910–1959* (New York: W. W. Norton, 1983), 33.

15. Jonathan Daniels, *The Man of Independence* (Philadelphia: J. B. Lippincott, 1950), 121.

16. Miller, *Plain Speaking,* 123.

17. Harry Vaughan: Oral History, Harry S. Truman Library (HSTL).

18. Daniels, *The Man of Independence,* 126–27.

19. Edgar Hinde: Oral History, HSTL.

20. Miller, *Plain Speaking,* 128.

21. Margaret Truman, *Harry S. Truman,* 68.

22. Miller, *Plain Speaking,* 28.

23. Ibid.

24. Truman, *Memoirs,* vol. 2, 182.

25. Margaret Truman, *Harry S. Truman,* 127–29; text of speech from HSTL.

26. Ibid., 155–56.

27. Heller, ed., *The Truman White House,* 77.

28. Mary Jane Truman, from an Interview conducted by Jonathan Daniels in preparation of *The Man of Independence,* HSTL.

29. Margaret Truman, *Harry S. Truman,* 392.

30. Miller, *Plain Speaking,* 259.

31. Ibid., 419–20.

32. Ibid., 259.

33. Truman, *Memoirs,* vol. 2, 183.

34. McCullough, *Truman,* 592.

35. Margaret Truman, *Bess W. Truman,* 305.

36. Truman, *Memoirs,* vol. 2, 183.

37. Heller, ed., *The Truman White House,* 88.

38. Miller, *Plain Speaking,* 38.

CHAPTER 3

1. Eleanor Roosevelt, *This I Remember,* memoirs, vol. 2, (New York: Harper & Brothers Publishers, 1949), 95.

2. McCullough, *Truman,* 594.

3. Margaret Truman, *Bess W. Truman,* 314.

4. McCullough, *Truman,* 594.

5. Margaret Truman, *Bess W. Truman,* 314.

6. Miller, *Plain Speaking,* 136.

7. Margaret Truman, *Bess W. Truman,* 315.

CHAPTER 4

1. Charles E. Bohlen, *Witness to History, 1929–1969* (New York: W. W. Norton & Co., 1973), 240.

2. Charles E. Bohlen, *The Transformation of American Foreign Policy* (New York: W. W. Norton & Co., 1969), 86.

3. Steinberg, *The Man from Missouri,* 308.

4. Ibid., 303.

5. Ferrell, ed., *Off the Record,* 109.

6. Robert H. Ferrell, ed., *Truman in the White House: The Diary of Eben A. Ayers* (Columbia, MO: University of Missouri Press, 1991), 266.

CHAPTER 5

1. Jack Wilson, "What Kind of Pianist Is Truman?" *Look.*

2. *Public Papers of the Presidents of the United States: Harry S. Truman,* 1947 (Washington, DC: United States Government Printing Office, 1963), 330.

CHAPTER 6

1. D. Clayton James, *The Years of MacArthur,* vol. 1, *1880–1941* (Boston: Houghton Mifflin Co., 1970), 403–4.

2. Truman, *Memoirs,* vol. 1, 520–21.

3. Roy E. Appleman, *South to the Naktong, North to the Yalu (June–November 1950)* in the series *United States Army in the Korean War* (Washington, DC: Department of the Army, 1961), 495.

4. D. Clayton James, *The Years of MacArthur,* vol. 3, *Triumph and Disaster, 1945–1964* (Boston: Houghton Mifflin Co., 1985), 366.

5. Ibid., 536.

6. Ibid., 553.

7. Truman, *Memoirs,* vol. 2, 435.

8. Matthew B. Ridgway, *Soldier: The Memoirs of Matthew B. Ridgway* (New York: Harper, 1956), 201.

9. J. Lawton Collins, *War in Peacetime: The History and Lessons of Korea* (Boston: Houghton Mifflin Co., 1969), 237.

10. Morison, *Oxford History of the American People,* 1072.

11. James, *Triumph and Disaster,* 457.

12. Ridgway, discussion with faculty and staff of the U.S. Army Command and General Staff College, Fort Leavenworth, Kansas, May 9, 1984.

13. Heller, ed., *The Truman White House,* 148.

CHAPTER 7

1. Miller, *Plain Speaking,* 165.

2. Truman, *Memoirs,* vol. 1, 173.

3. Papers of Henry L. Stimson, Yale University Library (YUL).

4. Truman, *Memoirs,* vol. 1, 10.

5. Henry L. Stimson, "The Decision to Use the Atomic Bomb," *Harpers Magazine,* February 1947, 99. See also Robert P. Newman, "Hiroshima and the Trashing of Henry Stimson," *New England Quarterly,* March 1998, 5–32.

6. Ibid., 99–100.

7. Ibid., 100.

8. Stimson memo to Marshall, May 30, 1945, Records of the Manhattan Engineer District, 1942–1948, National Archives and Records Service, Alexandria, Virginia.

9. Stimson, "The Decision to Use the Atomic Bomb," 100.

10. Ibid., 101. Also see Forrest C. Pogue, *George C. Marshall: Statesman, 1945–1949* (New York: Viking Penguin, 1987), 19, 23; and Truman, *Memoirs,* vol. 1, 418.

11. Stimson, "The Decision to Use the Atomic Bomb," 100.

12. Ibid., 102.

13. Ibid.

14. Ibid.

15. Ibid., 101.

16. The Hoover memorandum and Truman's subsequent memorandums to Stimson, Grew, Hull, and Vinson are under State Dept., WWII in the White House Official File, Confidential File, HSTL.

17. Truman, *Memoirs,* vol. 2, 297.

18. David E. Lilienthal, *The Journals of David E. Lilienthal, 1945–1950,* vol. 2 (New York: Harper & Row Publishers, 1964), 118.

19. Truman, *Memoirs,* vol. 2, 301.

20. Lilienthal, *Journals,* 388.

21. *Public Papers of Harry S. Truman,* 1950, 724–28.

22. Truman, *Memoirs,* vol. 2, 411.

CHAPTER 8

1. "Bravo, Lieutenant," Fort Wayne, Indiana, *News-Sentinel* March 29, 1951.

2. Truman, *Memoirs,* vol. 2, 460.

CHAPTER 9

1. Truman, *Memoirs,* vol. 2, 281.

2. *Public Papers of Harry S. Truman,* 1948, 433.

3. *Here's Harry* (Kansas City, MO: Hallmark Cards, 1976), n.p.

4. James F. Byrnes, *Speaking Frankly* (New York: Harper & Brothers Publishers, 1947), 254.

5. Robert J. Donovan, *The Presidency of Harry S. Truman, 1949–1953,* vol. 2, *Tumultuous Years* (New York: W. W. Norton & Co., 1982), 166.

6. McCullough, *Truman,* 766. Also see Thomas C. Reeves, *The Life and Times of Joe McCarthy: A Biography* (New York: Stein and Day, 1982), 252.

7. *Public Papers of Harry S. Truman,* 1950, 232–38.

8. McCullough, *Truman,* 769.

9. Reeves, *Life and Times of Joe McCarthy,* 263.

10. Lloyd Papers, Box 9, McCarthy Folder, HSTL.

11. John Lehman, "The Navy's Enemies," *Wall Street Journal,* May 21, 1996.

12. McCullough, *Truman,* 760.

13. Reeves, *Life and Times of Joe McCarthy,* 261–62.

14. *Public Papers of Harry S. Truman,* 1950, 232–38.

15. "The Presidency: 'When I Make a Mistake'," *Time,* September 18, 1950, 25.

16. McCullough, *Truman,* 812.

17. John Hersey, "Profiles: Mr. President," no. 2, "Ten O'Clock Meeting," *The New Yorker,* April 14, 1951, 52.

18. James, *Triumph and Disaster,* 536.

19. Hersey, "Ten O'Clock Meeting," 53.

20. Ibid., 54.

21. McCullough, *Truman,* 826.

22. Margaret Truman, *Harry S. Truman,* 502.

23. West, *Upstaris at the White House,* 118.

24. Margaret Truman, *Harry S. Truman,* 503.

CHAPTER 10

1. West, *Upstairs at the White House,* 117.

2. Miller, *Plain Speaking,* 366.

3. Ferrell, ed., 240.

4. West, *Upstairs at the White House,* 117.

5. Margaret Truman, *Harry S. Truman,* 489.

6. Ibid.

7. McCullough, *Truman,* 874–75; Steinberg, *The Man from Missouri,* 11–12.

8. Barton J. Bernstein, "A Postwar Myth: 500,000 Lives Saved," *Bulletin of the Atomic Scientists,* June–July 1986, 38–40; Gar Alperovitz, "Why the United States Dropped the Bomb," *Technology Review,* August 1990,

22–34; Kai Bird, "The Curators Cave In," *New York Times,* October 9, 1994.

9. Ferrell, *Dear Bess*; Ferrell, *Off the Record*; and Robert H. Ferrell, *The Autobiography of Harry S. Truman* (Boulder, CO: Colorado Associated University Press, 1980). See also the Truman diary, HSTL.

10. Barton J. Bernstein, letter: "To Be Among Those Numbers," *Joint Force Quarterly,* spring 1996, 6–7.

11. Henry L. Stimson diary, June 19, 1945, and others, YUL.

12. Lt. William M. Rigdon, USN, *Log of the President's Trip to the Berlin Conference, July 6, 1945 to August 7, 1945* (Washington, DC: Office of the President, 1945), 16–37. Extracts from the *Log* are printed in U.S. Department of State, *Foreign Relations of the United States, Diplomatic Papers: The Conference of Berlin (The Potsdam Conference),* 1945, 2 vols. (Washington, DC: GPO, 1960), 2: 4–28, See also Naval Aide Files, HSTL.

13. Rigdon, *Log,* 23.

14. Ibid.

15. Martin Gilbert, *Winston S. Churchill,* vol. 8, *"Never Despair,"* 1945–1965 (Boston: Houghton Mifflin Co., 1988), 66.

16. Bernstein letter to *Joint Force Quarterly.* The quote is from McGeorge Bundy in *Danger and Survival: Choices about the Bomb in the First Years* (New York: Random House, 1988), 647.

17. Stimson, "The Decision to Use the Atomic Bomb," 102.

18. Pogue, *George C. Marshall,* 23.

CORRESPONDENCE INDEX

Abbreviations:

MJC	Matthew J. Connelly
WDH	William D. Hassett
CGR	Charles G. Ross
HST	Harry S. Truman

Adams, Bonnie, Kennesaw, GA, 132–33 (reply WDH)
Adams, Rodden W., Laconia, NH, 37–38
Adler, Rose, Brooklyn, NY, 272
Aiken, Edwin E., Baldwinville, MA, 380–81
Alderman, James S., Dallas, TX, 149–50
Allan, Caroline L., Philadelphia, 255–56
Allen, George, Camp Chafee, AR, 251
Allen, H. L., Los Angeles, 407–8
Alleyne, Robert C., Brooklyn, NY, 272
Allgood, (Mrs.) George, Birmingham, AL, 176 (reply WDH)
Allman, Mac, Indianapolis, IN, 420
Alsup, Charles, St. Louis, MO, 253–54
Amacker, W. K., Shreveport, LA, 256
Americans for Democratic Action, Far Rockaway, NY, 392
Amsterdam, Morey, 423
Anderson, Everett B., 12 (reply Wallace H. Graham)
Anderson, Jackie, Waycross, GA, 26 (reply Eben A. Ayers; memo, Rose Conway)
Andrews, Bob, Edisto Island, SC, 381
Andrews. Eleanor L., Edisto Island, SC, 376–77 (reply HST)
Andrews, Warren W., Chicago, 422
Archambo, Fred, Munisking, MI, 421
anthony, Henry L., Chicago, 56–57
Arman, Harold, Hastings, MI, 207 (reply Joseph Short)
Armington, (Mrs.) Joseph, Providence, RI, 420

Armstrong, John J., New York, 246
Arnett, Marjorie, Detroit, 272–73
Arnold, R. T., Jacksonville, FL, 34
Aronin, Isabel, New York, 478 (reply MJC)
Ashman, Richard, New Orleans, 167–68
Axtell, Enos A., Kansas City, MO, 447–48 (reply HST)

Baer, Arthur B., St. Louis, 164 (reply WDH)
Banholster, John W., Coquille, OR, 314
Banning, William, New Canaan, CT, 358
Barton, Roy A., Caribou, ME, 121 (reply WDH)
Baugh, Altha, Louisville, KY, 421
Bayard, Margaret, New York, 317–18
Bearss, Mildred, West Palm Beach, 452
Becker, (Mr. and Mrs.) Harry, Venice, CA, 311
Benedict, Claude A., Johnstown, OH, 212–13
Benton, William, Washington, DC, 394–95
Bergamini, Clara D., Rowayton, CT, 322
Berle, Adolph A., Jr., New York, 67–69 (reply Clark M. Clifford)
Bisley, Helen C., Oak Park, IL, 117
Blake, Glenn R., Portland, OR, 36
Bledsoe, H. A., Richmond, IN, 339
Bloom, Howard, Brooklyn, NY, 395–96
Boland, Frank A., Columbus, OH, 247
Bolomey, Alfred A. and Henry D. Lauson, New York, 95
Bomberg, Joan, New York, 298
Boothe, (Mrs.) Monnie Reed, Ronceverte, WV, 344–45 (reply Harry H.
    Vaughan)
Borkey, A. V., Wrightstown, NJ, 96
Borshelt, Dorothy, Cincinnati, OH, 324 (reply WDH)
Botner, W. B., Winter Haven, FL, 261
Bott, (Mrs.) Douglass, Riverside, NJ, 190 (reply WDH)
Bouton, E. F., Brooklyn, NY, 99
Boxley, Lenora A., New York, 411 (reply HST)
Bowie, Harold A., Brooklyn, NY, 259
Boyd, Howard M., Syracuse, NY, 54–55
Boyer, Miriam, Bronx, NY, 304
Boyles, (Mrs.) Harry V., Sanford, FL, 58–59
Branstetter, W. T., Pasco, WA, 213
Bredin, Betty, Wellesley, MA, 319
Brewster, O. C., New York, 283–89 (reply Harvey H. Bundy); 289–90
    (reply WDH); 290

Bridges, Sandra K., Tulsa, OK, 262

Briggs, Schuler, et al., Frostbury, MD, 261–62

Brinkley, Carol, Lexington, NC, 31 (reply MJC)

Brock, William J., Buffalo, NY, 90–91 (reply WDH)

Brooks, Charles W., Washington, DC, 208–8 (reply WDH)

Brown, C. H., Derby, CT, 242–43

Brown, Willie F., Fort Campbell, KY, 17–18 (memos Harry Vaughan and HST)

Bruce, Christine M., Tilton, NH, 38–39

Brunauer, Esther C., Washington, DC, 382–90 (memos Charles S. Murphy and HST)

Bryant, Chester, Knoxville, TN, 335

Bryant School, Sherman, TX, 218

Bryson, C. H., Columbus, OH, 83 (reply HST)

Budd, Lloyd E., New York, 243

Bull, Irving, Longmont, CO, 260–61

Butler, Mary J., New York, 35

Butz, Francis E., Fond du Lac, WI, 252

Buuck, Gale C., Central Korea, 349–50

Callen, (Mrs.) Edward, Hollywood, CA, 99

Calvary Baptist Church, Kansas City, MO, 462–63 (reply WDH)

Campbell, Ronald C., North Plainfield, NJ, 114

Canady, Ward, Toledo, OH, 219 (reply HST)

Carson, T. J., Brooklyn, NY, 406

Cascarelli, Velma A., Los Angeles, 424

Cate, James L., Chicago, 467–71 (reply HST; memos Irving Perlmeter, R. B. Landry, David D. Lloyd)

Cavert, Samuel M., New York, 295 (reply HST)

Chalker, Annette, Kennesaw, GA, 133–34

Charpontier, Don, San Jose, CA, 313–14

Churchill Winston S., Miami Beach, FL, 156–57 (reply HST); Great Britain, 153–56 (reply HST; memo Dean Acheson); Chartwell, Westerham, Kent, 159–61 (reply HST)

Citizens Committee for Common Sense Animal Legislation, Los Angeles, 307

Clark, Gilmore D., Washington, DC, 110–12 (reply HST)

Clayton, A. F., Williamsburg, PA, 352 (reply WDH)

Climons, Hezekia, 64–65

Coers, Morris H., Covington, KY, 226 (replies HST and unsolicited letter to Sherman Minton)

Cohn, Marian, Chicago, 318–19

Colegrove, Kenneth, Evanston, IL, 321
Collett, Jim C., Kansas City, MO, 192–94 (reply HST; memo James H. Foskett)
Comstock, A. Barr, Washington, DC, 392–93 (reply HST)
Conners, J. T., Toch Bay Village, OH, 407
Connolly, Harold W., New Bedford, MA, 152–53
Cook, Donald C., 458–59 (reply HST)
Cooney, Patricia A., Detroit, 200
Cottlow, Augusta, 181–82 (reply HST)
Counterman, C. W., East Stroudsburg, PA, 363 (reply WDH)
Croisssant, Charles A., Worcester, MA, 317
Culbertson, Jane, St. Louis, MO, 346–48 (reply WDH); 351
Cullens, Branch C., Waycross, GA, 407

Dandridge, Dave, Memphis, TN, 55–56 (reply David K. Niles)
Dawson, Leonard E., Denver, CO, 113
Deering, Helen, Portland, OR, 397
Denman, Harry, Nashville, 225–26 (reply WDH)
Devir, Joseph P., Philadelphia, 297
Devlin, Jack, Detroit, 419
DiJusta, Connie, 248
Dixon, Amelia A., Walton, KY, 66
Doggett, Charles H., 46–47
Don, Isadore, Brooklyn, NY, 103
Driscoll, Jerry E., Russell, KS, 168–69 (reply HST)
Dudeck, Darrin, Eugene, OR, 183–84
Duncan, (Mrs.) M. K., Dayton, OH, 125–26
Dunlap, Earl, Robbins, NC, 212

Eddleman, H. Leo, Louisville, KY, 147–49
Edenfield, John and Viola I. A. Michaels, Cannes, France, 190
Eisen, Esther, Bronx, NY, 35
Ellison, (Mr. and Mrs.) George, Kenosho, WI, 355–56 (reply WDH)
Ellman, Sadelle S., Yonkers Chapter of Hadassa, Yonkers, NY, 145
Elzy, Gussie, Toledo, OH, 277–78 (reply WDH)
Evans, Andrew S., Washington, DC, 74
Evans, (Mrs.) Steve, Forbus, TN, 323 (reply WDH)
Eyler, Kenneth E., Lansing, MI, 320–21

Fadden, Ray, Hogansberg, NY, 338 (reply WDH)
Fagan, Maurice J., Philadelphia, 404–6 (reply HST)
Farrar, (Mrs.) Billie, Dallas, 254–55

Faustine, (Mrs.) W. G. and (Mrs.) J. H. Gehrfein, Erie, PA, 117–18

Fay, Herbert W., Springfield, IL, 178–79 (reply CGR)

Ferguson, Donald R., LaGrange, IN, 253

Fick, Mildred, Pomona, CA, 260

Findlater, William B., Grand Rapids, MI, 48

Fish, Hamilton, New York, 365–67 (reply HST); 367–68

Fisher, Charles W., Oakland, CA, 249–50

Fitzgerald, Dutch, Tulsa, OK, 262

Fitzpatrick, Paul E., New York, 410 (reply HST)

Flanigan, Paul E., New York, 410 (reply HST)

Fohne, William R., Los Angeles, 252–53

Foley, Rose, 257–59

Fonmals, Russell J., New York, 243

Ford, Richard, New York, 186

Forster, Louis J., Jr., New York, 230 (reply Joseph Short); 425 (reply Irving
    Perlmeter)

Forster, Marionne J., Jefferson City, MO, 223

Foster, C. L., Columbus, GA, 47

Fox, Caroline, New York, 109

Franks, Anna, 100

Freight Cargo Agency, New York, 190–91

Frese, Hazel W., Baltimore, MD, 209–10 (reply CGR)

Frogge, John, Garden City, NY, 406–7

Fuller, Scott A., Oakland, CA, 312

Gabriel, Charles C., Cleveland, OH, 88 (reply WDH)

Garritt, Naomi, Cragsmoor, NY, 477 (reply Joseph Short)

Gerard, James W., New York, 81–82 (reply HST)

Gerson, Paul, Hollywood, CA, 186–87

Gerth, E. P., San Francisco, CA, 307

Gibson, Truman K., Jr., Chicago, 378–79 (reply WDH)

Gildersleeve, Virginia C., New York, 134–36 (reply HST)

Gleekman, Wallace J., Dorchester, MA, 334–35 (reply WDH)

Golden, David, New York, 460

Golden, Stanley H., 13–14 (reply WDH)

Goldwater, Barry, Phoenix, AZ, 243

Goodman, (Mrs.) E. B., 218–19 (reply HST)

Grady, Francis B., Scranton, PA, 203

Grant, Gladys E., Scotch Plains, NJ, 370–72 (reply Joseph Short)

Greany, L. M., Cleveland, OH, 379

Greenough, (Mrs.) Carroll), Georgetown, VA, 110

Greller, Allen E., Bronx, NY, 201–2 (reply WDH)

Grimsel, Robert A., Cliffside Park, NJ, 20 (reply MJC)
Guthman, Joel L., Brooklyn, NY, 335

Haber, Rebecca, Oneonta, NY, 303–4
Haransyl, Ladislaus, New York, 412 (reply HST)
Harris, (Mrs.) C. M., Port Angeles, WA, 105
Harrison, C. J., Pasadena, CA, 418
Harrison, (Mrs.) W. G., Toledo, OH, 56
Hart, Kerry and Lisa Howe, Baltimore, MD, 188–89 (reply MJC)
Hart, Robert B., Marseilles, IL, 172–73 (reply Eben A. Ayers)
Hascall, Betty, Independence, OH, 176–77 (reply Eben A. Ayers)
Hawkes, J. W., Washington, DC, 91–93 (reply HST; memo Samuel Rosen-
    man)
Hayashi, James A., Madison, WI, 273–74
Haywood, Maroy B., Washington, DC, 19–20 (reply MJC)
Hazlett, William A., 418
Heaphy, Mary V., Baltimore, MD, 374–75
Hecker, R. F., Cleveland, OH, 465
Hemphill, (Mrs.) G. C., Long Island City, NY, 375–76
Henderson, Elmer W., 378 (reply WDH)
Henry, (Mrs.) Park L., Washington, PA, 419
Heusinger, William A., San Antonio, TX, 171
Higgins, Ruth M., Newport Beach, CA, 357
Higly, Morris, Childress, TX, letters not available (reply HST, 10–11)
Hilborn, Dudley, New York, 320
Hill, J. H., Baltimore, MD, 298–300 (reply WDH); 301
Hinz, Otto F., Chicago, 205 (reply CGR)
Hirschfield, (Mrs.) Edwin C., Louisville, KY, 215–16 (reply Roger Tubby)
Hogenmiller, Linus, Farmington, MO, 224–25
Hoover, Herbert, New York, 410 (reply HST)
Howard, Katherine D., Long Beach, CA, 340–42 (reply Harry H. Vaughan)
Hubbard, Lela, 419
Hubbart, Dwight L., Austin, TX, 72
Hugel, Elizabeth, Heidelberg, Germany, 191–92
Huges, (Mrs.) I., San Jose, CA, 50–54
Hulbert, Murray, New York, 364 (reply WDH)

Irvine, E. Eastman, New York, 221–22

Jefferson, Clarence, Shiprock, NM, 337
Jessen, A. C., Houston, TX, 89–90
Johnson, DeWayne, Los Angeles, 184–85 (reply CGR)

Johnson, Marion, Chicago, 227
Johnson, T. Elmer, Ashland, OH, 97–99
Johnston, Phillip, Los Angeles, 163–64
Jones, Bry A., San Antonio, TX, 420
Jones, Marshall, West Trenton, NJ, 370

Kahn, Sam, New York, 465
Karalekas, William C., Newton Highlands, MA, 214 (reply Harry H. Vaughan)
Karnaky, Karl J., 453
Kenny, Joseph F., New York, 189
Kilgore, Harley M., Washington, DC, 460–62 (reply HST)
Kimball, Fiske, Philadelphia, 120 (reply HST)
Kirkland, Lawton, Atlanta, GA, 191
Klausner, Samuel Z., New York, 150–51 (reply WDH)
Klejna, Walter J., Bronx, NY, 244–46
Kline, Neva W., Buffalo, NY, 250–51
Knapp, Edward M., Washington, DC, 293
Knez, Angela, Vallejo, CA, 200 (reply MJC)
Knopoik, Robert W., 248
Kohner, Alfred J., Brooklyn, NY, 257
Kollmorgen, Walter M., Lawrence, KS, 464
Kummel, Anna, Trenton, NJ, 121–22 (reply CGR)

La Fon, William I., Jr., Southampton, NY, 87
Lang, Genevieve J., Sacramento, CA, 328–30 (reply WDH)
Langman, Otto, New York, 119
LaPat, Mary S., Forest Hills, NY, 319
Layne, (Mrs.) B. A., Eldon, MO, 223–24 (reply Marione J. Foerster)
Lebow, Abraham, Jersey City, NJ, 145
Lewis, Joseph C., Fort Wayne, IN, 165 (reply WDH)
Lichy, Lenna G., Fallbrook, CA, 194–96 (reply Joseph Short)
Little, Sam, San Diego, CA, 337
Locke, Clara M., Memphis, TN, 108
Longstreet, Helen D., Washington, DC, 216
Lugo, E. L., San Juan, Puerto Rico, 415 (reply HST)
Lynch, John, Muskogee, OK, 198 (reply HST)

MacKendrick, Robert G., Norwood, PA, 423; 463–64
MacNicoll, Alex, San Francisco, 225
Madsden, Mildred, Santa Rosa, CA, 482 (reply Sherman Adams)
Maloney, William A., Syracuse, NY, 333–34 (reply Irving Perlmeter)
Mansing, Mort N., New York, 314–17

Marcus, Heather, et al., Sugar Grove, PA, 196

Mathieson, Walter, Chicago, 104

Matthews, E., Washington, DC, 118

Mayerberg, Samuel S., Kansas City, MO, 275–76 (reply HST)

Mayes, Von, Caruthersville, MO, 422

McCafferty, Edward J., Philadelphia, 313

McCarthy, Joe, Washington, DC, 360–61

McDonough, Gordon L., Washington, DC, 400 (reply HST)

McFarland, Fred R., Augusta, ME, 200–201 (reply CGR)

Meisburger, Eddie, Kansas City, MO, 438–39 (reply HST)

Messall, Victor R., Washington, DC, 442; 443 (reply HST)

Meyer, Helen, Spencer, NY, 118

Middletown Citizens Committee, Middletown, OH, 463

Miller, (Mrs.) Carl E., Lorrin, OH, 116

Miller, Grace B., Hartford, CT, 115–16

Mills, Marie J., Minneapolis, 202–3

Moore, Manning, Santos Ojeda, NY, 390

Morgan, David H., Eureka, KS, 440–41 (reply HST)

Morris, L. E., Philadelphia, 170

Moss, Gertrude, Cleveland, OH, 307

Mox, William, Chicago, 436–37 (reply HST)

Mullally, Ed, Pierre, SD, 422

Murphy, Fred P., Stamford, NY, 480–81 (reply HST)

Murray, Pauli, Washington, DC, 306

Nabors, S. M., Corinth, MS, 395

Nance, Elizabeth G., Baltimore, MD, 369

Nauheimer, G. Francis, Chicago, 428 (memo David Stowe); 428–30

Neyham, Walter H., Kansas City, MO, 434–35 (reply HST)

Neustaedter, John A., Fargo, ND, 203–4 (reply CGR)

Nicholas, George, et al., Camp Beale, CA, 85

Nicholas, W., Sierre Madre, CA, 453 (reply WDH)

Nichols, Clyde, Kansas City, MO, 83–84 (reply HST)

Nolen, Ida G., Midway Park, NC, 322

Norris, John G., Princeton, NJ, 379–80

O'Brien, Martin R., Aurora, IL, letter not available (reply MJC, 101; memo WDH)

O'Brien, Patrick H., Philadelphia, 170

O'Donnell, F. H., Holyoke, MA, 182–83 (reply Eben A. Ayers); 183

Omernik, Ernest, Polonia, WI, 298

O'Neill, Richard W., 235–37 (reply HST; memos CGR and Louis H. Renfrow)

Oppenheimer, J. R., 308–9 (reply HST)
Otman, Roy T., Los Angeles, 82
Owens, Shirley, Poplar Bluff, MO, 127–28 (reply MJC)
Oxnam, G. Bromley and John F. Dulles, New York, 296

Packard, (first name unknown), New York, 79 (reply Eben A. Ayers)
Page, (Mrs.) M. V., Anderson, SC, 48
Parsons, H. Grace, St. Petersburg, FL, 62–63
Pauley, Susan, Beverly Hills, CA, 263–64 (reply HST)
Peasner, (Mrs.) Thomas, Sr., Lancaster, TX, 346
Peixotto, Bridget C., Queens, NY, 188
Pender, Robert B., Utica, NY, 89 (reply Mrs. Joseph Short)
Persiko, Lenda, Dobbs Ferry, NY, 339
Peschel, Delores and Emily Truedell, Norfolk, NE, 175 (reply CGR)
Peterson, C. Stewart, Baltimore, MD, 126 (reply Harry H. Vaughan)
Piazza, (Mrs.) C. E., Waco, TX, 206 (reply WDH)
Pierce, Henry A., Flushing, NY, 310–11
Pierotti, Roger, Brooklyn, NY, 297
Pinchot, Cornelia B., 274 (reply HST)
Pinci, H. R., New York, 433–34
Ponath, A. W., Appleton, WI, 123–25 (reply CGR)
Porter, (Mrs.) C. L. Edgemere, ID, 49–50
Powell, Josephine, Hollywood, FL, 107

Quinn, Anne E., Bedford Hills, NY, 427–28

Rigg, A. S., Brooklyn, NY, 352–54
Roberts, Dan R., Boiling Springs, NC, 207–8 (reply WDH)
Roberts, Ernest W., Kansas City, MO, 59–61 (reply HST)
Roberts, Sam E., Kansas City, MO, 453–57 (reply HST)
Robinson, R. A., Fremont, NE, 80–81
Rogers, A. P., New York, 175 (reply WDH)
Rogers, (Mrs.) Mazie, Chicago, 196–97 (reply CGR)
Roosevelt, Eleanor, Geneva, Switzerland, 267–68 (reply HST)
Ross, Harold W., New York, 435–36 (reply HST)
Rowland, Elizabeth, Union, NJ, 358–59 (reply MJC)
Rudderman, J. Y., Indianapolis, IN, 380
Russell, Richard B., Winder, GA, 293–95 (reply HST)

Schauffer, Edward, Kansas City, MO, 27–28 (reply CGR)
Schlesinger, Joel L., Newark, NJ, 83 (reply HST)
Schmiat, E., 131
Schneider, Richard, 64

Schubert, Marcella, New York, 131–32

Sereno, Renzo, Peru, IL, 28–30 (replys WDH and HST; memos)

Shadlowsky, William F., et al., USS. *Albemarle*, 86

Shahan, Ann, San Francisco, 338

Shepperd, Pearl, Columbus, GA, 174 (reply WDH)

Shotwell, James T., New York, 265 (reply HST)

Siegel, Elizabeth L., New York, 151–52

Sierra, Vera D., Santa Barbara, CA, 476

Sills, Ruth C., New York, 325–26 (reply WDH)

Simpson, Henry W., St. Louis, MO, 102 (reply WDH)

Sinclair, Upton, Monrovia, CA, 264–65 (reply HST)

Skelton, Ike, Lexington, MO, 268–69 (reply HST); 446–47 (reply HST)

Skerry, Leslie M., Bedford, NH, 269–72 (reply HST)

Slayback, Martha E., 23–24 (reply CGR; memo Henrietta Nesbitt)

Sloane, John F., Newark, NJ, 297

Smiddy, W. E., Jr., Jackson Heights, NY, 464

Smith, Rex E., Corvallis, OR, 15 (reply WDH)

Solins, Samuel, Welch, WV, 409–10 (reply HST)

Solis, Jimenez, Santiago, Puerto Rico, 413–14 (reply HST)

Soon, Mary S., Pasadena, CA, 97 (reply MJC)

Spanel, A. N., New York, 145–46 (reply HST)

Spears, Mildred, Lookout Mountain, TN, 108

Spector, Leonard, Bronx, NY, 393–94 (reply WDH)

Stephens, John, Scotia, NY, 192

Stewart, Elwood H., New Haven, CT, 87

Stone, Carol, Sebring, FL, 276–77

Street, Stewart A., Washington, DC, 71

Stuart, Miriam, New York, 94–95 (reply WDH)

Suddath, Jim, Washington, DC, 411–12 (reply HST)

Swing, Betty, New York, 265–66 (reply HST); 266–67

Tenzer, Herbert, Brooklyn, NY, 129 (reply CGR)

Thomas, Erma J., San Diego, CA, 114–15

Thomas, Norman, New York, 165–67 (reply HST)

Thompson, Kathy, Monrovia, CA, 336 (reply WDH)

Thompson, MayBel, New York, 125

Thomsen, C. W., St. Joseph, MO, 25 (reply CGR; memo Rose A. Conway)

Todd, L. V., Sr., Richmond, VA, 331–32 (reply Joseph Short; memo Robert
    L. Dennison)

Trainer, Joseph J., Newton, PA, 146

Treichel, James E., Milwaukee, WI, 217

Trevor, Caroline, New York, 119

Trolander, Elmer, W., Chicago, 368–69 (reply WDH)

Truman, F., Rogerstone Mon., England, 221
Tunney, Gene, New York, 397–99 (memo WDH)
Tunningley, Fred, Linden, NE, 112–13

Utermahlen, G. Carroll, Fullerton, MD, 179–80

Vanderbeck, John, Holland, MI, 372–73

Wacker, Verna, Detroit, MI, 70 (reply WDH)
Washington Post, 171–72 (reply HST)
Wayhand, Frank R., Colchester, IL, 228
Wehr, William A., Jr. and James V. Brown, Beaver, PA, 478–79 (reply HST)
Weizmann, Chaim, New York, 137–38 (reply HST); 138–44 (reply HST)
West, Charles M., Pittston, PA, 373
Westheimer, Ollie, St. Louis, MO, 73–74; 74
Whittier, K. A., Fokosuka, Japan, 228 (reply WDH)
Wigglesworth, Russell H., Durango, CO, 210–11 (reply CGR)
Wilkins, Roy, New York, 76–78 (reply HST)
Williamson, Arlene, Greensboro, NC, 74–75
Winkel, Henry J., 390–91 (reply Charles S. Murphy)
Wolsted, (Mrs.) Clarence E., Cedar Falls, IA, 305–6
Woodley, Helen, Washington, DC, 197–98 (reply MJC)
Wooten, (Mrs.) M. Rutledge, Asheville, NC, 211 (reply CGR)

Yager, Rosemary, et al., 147
Young, Shirley, Salem, NJ, 327–28 (reply WDH)
Younger, (Mrs.) Huey E., Marshall, MO, 354–55

Zelvis, Leon, Phillipines, 234
Ziegler, Adrian, M., Brookline, MA, 21–22 (replies Reathel Odum and WDH); 22
Zinkhoff, Dave, Philadelphia, 218

Individuals receiving unsolicited letters from HST:

Cates, Clifton, 402
Graham, Phil, 433
Hume, Paul, 416
Nixon, Clay, 402
Southern, William, 444–45
Truman, Vivian, 449–52

INDEX

Abyssinian Baptist Church, New York, 33

Acheson, Dean, 142, 154–55, 158, 160, 241, 246–48, 250–52, 255, 259, 317, 321, 360–61, 374, 382, 414, 441, 463–65, 474

Adams, Sherman, 482

Air Force, U.S., 100, 122, 237, 239, 249, 294, 355, 405, 408, 466, 468, 471

Albermarle, 86

Algeria, 81

Alien and Sedition Laws, 81

American Council on Human Rights, 378

American Legion, 86–87, 340

American Medical Association (AMA), 459

American Pioneer Guild, 178

American Veterans of Israel, 150–51

American War Mothers, 202

American War Reparations Mission, 376

Americans for Democratic Action, 73, 274, 392

Amersterdam, Morey, xii, 423

Anderson, Clifton P., 99

Anderson, Marian, 33, 36

Antonini, Luigi, 166

Arab League, 136–37

Ararat Shrine, 11

Arlington National Cemetery, 333–35, 338

Army, U.S., 66, 84, 100–101, 127, 259, 280, 288, 328, 345, 383, 400, 405, 408, 452–53, 460, 471; American Expeditionary Force, 398, Nurse Corps, 452; Chemical Warfare Service, 299; Corps of Engineers, 238–39, 287, 290; Eighth Army, 237, 240; 11th Airborne Division, 17–18; 1st Cavalry Division, 333, 343; National Guard, 73, 161, 231–32, 408, 423; Organized Reserve, 271; 108th Combat Engineer Battalion, 233–34; 129th Field Artillery, 42–43, 59; 2nd Infantry Division, 403; 35th Infantry Division, 426

Arnold, Hap H., 467, 472

Associated Press, 331

Atlantic Monthly, 467

Atlee, Clement, 136, 318, 324, 415–16, 454

atom bomb, xi, xiii, 155, 317, 325; Interim Committee on S-1, 282, 289; Korea, 247–48, 321–22, 415, 474; Manhattan Project, 280–84; postwar development of, 296–309, 361; Russian development of, 311–14, 316, 319; tests, 290–91, 306–7, 315, 470, 473; use against Japan, 291–96, 310, 313, 319, 466–76

Atomic Energy Commission, 298–300, 306, 308–9, 362

Austin, Warren R., 364

Australia, 234, 237
Austria, 329, 362
Axtell, Enos A., 447–48
Ayers, Eben A., 23–24, 79, 141–43, 171, 173, 177, 183, 234, 398, 401–2, 404, 414

Bachauer, Gina, 423–33
Baer, Arthur B., 164
Balkans, 133–34
Baltimore Evening Sun, 179
Bankhead, Tallulah, 418
Bard, Ralph, 282
Barkley, Alben, 242, 254–55, 391, 436, 441
Baruch, Bernard M., 364
Beishline, John R., 345
Belgian Congo, 286
Belium, 93, 159, 254, 460
Bell, David, 30
Benton, William, 373, 392–94
Berle, Adlof, 67, 68, 69
Berlin, 366, 459; blockade and airlift, xiii, 88, 162–66, 309, 366, 459, 466
Best, George Graham, 195
Bethesda Naval Medical Center, 424
Bevan, Ernest, 454
Bible, 21, 49, 53, 56, 59, 139, 147, 462–63
Bikini Island. *See* atom bomb, tests
black markets, 95–99, 431
Blair House, 1–3, 409, 411, 426
B'nai B'rith, 11
Bohlen, Charles E., 130–31
Bonus Marchers, 232
Booth, Ferris, 314–17
Bradley, Omar, 9–10, 227, 233, 241, 414, 474
Breskin, Barnee, 177
Brewster, Oswald C., 282–90
Bristol, 85
Brown, Tillie, 27–28
Brunot, James, 91
Buchenwald, 95
Bundy, Harvey H., 289–90

Bundy, McGeorge, 469
Burke, Edmund, 28
Bush, Vannevar, 282
Bute, John Stuart, 28
Buuck, Gale C., xiv, 349–51
Byrnes, James, 72, 157, 281–83, 369, 470, 472–73

Calvary Baptist Church, Kansas City, MO, 463–64
Camp LeJeune, NC, 322
Canada, 286, 305
Cannes International Film Festival, 190
Carnegie Institution, 282, 365, 366
Carter, James Earl, 472
Cate, James L., 466–71, 474
Cates, Clifton, 402
Catholic World, 433
Cavert, Samuel McCrea, 293, 295–96
Chalker, Annette, 132–34
Chamberlain, Neville, 317
Chambers, Whittaker, 365
Chapman, Oscar, 107
Chiang Kai-shek, 270, 320
Chicago Sun-Times, 437
Chicago Tribune, 38, 171, 436–37
Chicago, University of, 467–68
China, 80, 316, 366, 400; civil war in, 298, 365; Communist army, 239–40, 248–50, 258, 267, 276, 342, 347–49, 414; Communist government, 238–41, 244–46, 249, 252, 258, 260, 267–68, 270, 273, 317–24, 349–50, 352–54, 366, 375–76, 414, 465, 474; Nationalist government, 241, 254, 270, 320, 362
Chou En-lai, 357
Churchill, Winston, xxii–xiii, 153–57, 178, 361, 460, 464–65, 466; Iron Curtain speech, 130, 156–58, 361; at Potsdam, 156, 291, 466, 470, 473–74; on Truman, 466
civil rights, xi, 32–78, 149, 373; "black cabinet," 32; civil rights commission, 33, 41; and Cold War, 63–65; execu-

tive order on, 41, 66, 68–69, 70–71; and Korean War, 70–71, 333–42; legislation, 55, 57. *See also* Adam Clayton Powell, Hazel Scott, Ku Klux Klan, and National Association for the Advancement of Colored People (NAACP)
civil service, 66, 299
Civil Service Commission, 299, 363, 381, 390; loyalty program of, 363–65, 381–89; loyalty review board, 383
Civil War, 35, 51, 354
Clay, Lucius B., 95
Clayton, William, 282
Cleveland, Grover, 434
Cleveland Plain Dealer, 116
Clifford, Clark M., 67–69
Clinton Engineer Works, 283, 289–90
Cockerell, Francis Marion, 195
Coers, Morris H., 226–27
Collet, Jim Caskie, 193
Collins, J. Lawton, 238–240
Colonial Dames, 11, 119
Commission of Fine Arts, 110–12, 119
Communist Party (U.S.), 64–66, 385; espionage of, 360, 366–76, 399. *See also* Young Communist League
Compton, Arthur H., 282
Compton, Karl T., 282, 467
Conant, James B., 282
Congress, U.S., 6, 35, 40–42, 55, 65, 86, 103, 112, 131, 135, 161–62, 232, 234, 242, 246, 259, 263, 267, 270, 272, 275, 308–10, 313, 322, 330, 334, 360–62, 364–65, 367, 372, 376, 390–91, 403, 414, 436, 440, 445, 456, 460–62, 477; joint session of, 276; special session of, 171
Connally, Tom, 255, 364
Connelly, Matthew J., 18–20, 27, 30–31, 96–97, 107, 189, 198, 200, 212, 399, 401, 414, 478
Conway, Rose, 10, 14, 25, 361
Cook, Donald C., 458–59

Coolidge, Calvin, ix, 202
Coplon, Judy, 367
Cottlow, August, 181–82
Coward, William H., 195
Crim, Howell, 106, 110–11
Crockett, Davy, 271
Crowley, Leo, 4
Czechoslovakia, 159, 162, 240, 286

Daniel, Price Marion, 99
Daniels, Josephus, 439
Dardanelles, 133, 150
Daughters of the American Revolution (DAR), 11, 33–39
Dawson, Donald, 401
Decontrol Acts, 99, 126
Defense Department, 241, 309, 328, 330, 332, 344, 355, 370–72, 400, 469–70. *See also* War Department
deGaulle, Charles, 81
Delano, William Adams, 110–12, 120
Democratic Party, 36, 39, 45–46, 57, 59, 65–67, 69, 73, 143–44, 161, 167, 237, 248, 263, 265, 270, 333, 357, 361, 362, 373, 375, 396, 479; Democratic National Committee, 167–68, 172, 192, 266, 476, convention of, 169–71. *See also* elections
Denebold, 85
Dempsey, Jack, 398
Dennison, Robert L., 331–32, 399, 401–2
Detroit Council of Churches, 306–7
Detroit Free Press, 200
Dewey, Thomas, ix, 57, 69, 165, 171
Disabled Veterans of America, 340
Dixiecrats, 41, 57, 61, 66–67, 69, 72, 165. *See also* Democratic Party
Donnelly, Phil M., 192–94
Dred Scott, 64
Driscoll, Jerry E., 169
Dulles, John Foster, 295–96

Eagles, Fraternal Order of, 11
Earle George, 312

Early, Stephen T., 7, 419
Eastern Star, Order of the, 56, 341
Eccles, Marriner, 168
Egypt, 138, 441
Eichelberger, Robert, 436
Eisenhower, Dwight D., 72–74, 227, 231, 233–34, 255–56, 271, 357, 364, 394, 468, 470, 472–73, 482
elections: county, 42–44; congressional, 44–46, 391; presidential, ix, xiii, 2, 6, 9, 57–70, 73, 138, 149, 165–71, 265, 276, 365, 390, 441; and civil rights, 47, 59, 66–70, 72–73; special sessions of Congress, 171. *See also* Democratic Party and Republican Party
Eliot, George, 27
Elks, Fraternal Order of, 11, 415
Ellis, Barney, 443
Elsey, George M., 30, 67, 373, 401–2, 414, 466
Enola Gay, 471
European Recover Program. *See* Marshall Plan
Evans, Tom, 447, 454
Ewing, Oscar Ross, 73
Export-Import Bank, 144

Fagan, Maurice J., 404–6
"Fair Deal," 40–41
Fair Employment Practices Committee (FEPC), 33, 40–41, 47–48
Farley, James A., 235
Fay, Herbert Wells, 178–79
Federal Bureau of Investigation (FBI), 65, 363, 381, 394
Federal Council of Churches of Christ in America, 293, 295
Feeney, Joseph, 18, 30
Fermi, Enrico, 282
Ferrell, Robert H, 171
Fields, Alonzo, 1
Fifer, Joseph, 178
First Magyar Presbyterian Church, 412
flying saucers, 184–85

Fort Campbell, KY, 17
Fort Dix, NJ, 420
Fort Leavenworth, KS, 333
Fort Riley, KS, 232, 408
Fort Wayne News Sentinel, 349–50
Forrestal, James V., 158, 168, 469
Foskett, James H., 193–94
France, 81–82, 93, 95, 152, 159, 254, 256, 285, 287, 329
Fugitive Slave Law, 64

Gandhi, Mahatma, 316
Garden, Mary, 418
German-American Bund, 362
George, Todd, 43
Georgetown Garden Club, 109–10
Germany, 4, 9, 159–60, 165, 241, 392, 439, 453, 460; Nazis, 45, 80, 90–91, 93, 95, 284–85, 294, 329, 472; occupation of, 82, 90–96, 106, 158, 162–65, 263, 287, 459; plight of Jews in, 45, 54, 95, 134–35; western, 159–60, 162. *See also* Berlin and Nazis
G.I. Bill, 53
Gildersleeve, Virginia C., 134–36
Glenn, Frank, 443
Goldwater, Barry, xii, 231, 243
Grady Henry F., 154
Graham, Walter H., 12–13, 416, 433
Great Britain, 80, 95, 130–31, 133, 140, 153–55, 158, 241, 242, 245–47, 250, 254, 256, 258–60, 267–68, 285, 287, 305, 315, 318, 415, 423, 453–57, 464–65, 466
Great Depression, 6
Greece, xiii, 93, 131–33, 153–56, 362, 466
Greek-Turkish Aid Bill, 131–32
Grew, Joseph C., 4, 294
Groves, Leslie R., 281
Gunn, Glenn Dillard, 433

Hall, Mrs. Timothy C., 53
Handy, Thomas T., 467

Hanley Report, 345
Hannegan, Bob, 167
Harding, Warren G., 168
Harlem Globetrotters, 218
Harper's Magazine, 467
Harriman, Averell, 3–4, 158, 168, 241, 259
Harrison, George L., 282
Harvard University, 282, 362
Hassett, William D., xv, 1–2, 7–8, 11, 13–17, 21–22, 46, 50, 84, 86, 91, 95, 100–101, 104, 119, 121, 136, 141–43, 151, 174–76, 190, 197, 202, 206, 208–9, 224, 226, 229, 241, 278, 290, 323–24, 326, 330, 338, 342, 348, 351–52, 354, 356, 363–64, 369, 378–79, 395, 399, 409, 414, 417, 420, 427, 453, 463; "Department of National Headaches," 46; "Valentines," 13–14, 21, 69, 150, 197, 234, 275, 301, 325, 336, 399
Hawkes, Albert Wahl, 91–94
Hayes, Rutherford B., 105
Hearst, William Randolph, 437
Hechler, Kenneth W., 30, 466, 470, 475
Henderson, Elmer W., 378
Hersey, John, 414
Herzog, Isaac Halevi, 151
Hickenlooper, Bourke, 401, 407–8
Hill, D. H., 169
Hinde, Edgar, 42–44
Hirohito, 292, 294
Hiroshima. *See* atom bomb
Hiss, Alger, 246, 254, 293, 360–61, 365, 366–69, 374
Hitler, Adolf, 90–91, 393
Hoban, James, 111–12
Hoover, Herbert, ix, 6, 187, 292, 410, 434
Hopkins, Harry, 156–57
Hopkins, William J., 2, 17, 20, 30, 142, 290, 414
Hornet, 208
House Committee to Investigate Com-
munist Propaganda and Activities, 367
House Un-American Activities Committee, 360, 363, 365, 367–68
Howard University, 71
Howe, Louis McHenry, 7, 16
Hughes, Charles Evans, 364
Hughes, Edward J., 179
Hull, Cordell, 292
Human Rights Commission. *See* United Nations
Hume, Paul, xii, xiii, 182–253, 416–21, 427, 432–33
Humphrey, Hubert, 72–73
Hungary, 362, 382
hydrogen bomb, 319, 325

Ickes, Harold L., 168
Immanuel Baptist Church, Covington, KY, 226–27
Independence Examiner, 444
Independence, MO, xi, 9, 23, 27, 40, 76, 171, 199, 358, 444, 449–50, 481
Independent Democrats, 43–44. *See also* Ku Klux Klan
India, 256, 258, 267
Indian (American), 150, 333–39
Interim Committee on S-1. *See* atom bomb
Interior, Department of, 106–7
Internal Revenue Service (IRS), 394–95
Internal Security Act, 369
Iran, 130–31, 362, 466
Iraq, 138
Israel, 137–38, 141–48, 150–52, 377
Italy, 91, 152–53, 357

Jackson, Andrew, 61, 264, 422, 426
Jackson County, MO, 42, 445–47, 449
Jacobsen, Eddie, 42–44, 211, 444
James Gang, 354
Japan, 165, 260, 287, 347, 376, 406, 459, 462; Korean War and, 237–40; peace treaty of, 20, 462–64; in World War II, 80–81, 232, 263,

294, 322, 376, 466, 467–68, 470–73, 475–76. *See also* atom bomb, Japan; and Truman, Harry S., decision to bomb Japan
Japanese-Americans, 62
Jefferson, Thomas, 5, 109–10, 119–20, 131, 264, 392–93
Jenner, William, 242
Jerusalem, 136, 146–47. *See also* Israel
Jessup, Phillip, 251, 254, 267, 375–76
Jewish Welfare Society, 11
Jobs for Veterans Campaign, 102–3
Johnson, Louis A., 238, 456
Joint Chiefs of Staff (JCS), 238–41, 251, 292, 309, 399, 400, 403
Jones, Alexander F., 333
Johns Hopkins University, 376
Junior Scholastic, 218
Justice Department, 65, 395

Kansas City, MO, 26, 27, 44, 181, 407, 437–38, 443, 445, 447, 449–50, 456–57, 462
Kansas City News Press, 450–52
Kansas City Star, 43, 434–35, 448
Kansas City Times, 168
Kelley, Edward J., 233
Kennan, George F., 158
Kiermas, Ray, 394
Kilgore, Harley M., 460–62
Kimball, Dan, 397
Kimball, Fiske, 120
King, Ernest J., 470, 472–73
Knights of Columbus, 11
Korean War, xi–xiii, 104, 158, 237–42, 276, 317–25, 343–44, 346, 348, 350–51, 357–58, 374–75, 400–401, 404, 408, 415, 417–18, 420, 466; Australian forces, 237; British forces, 161, 254, 348; POWs, 343–48, 350–57, 476; Turkish forces, 342; UN forces, 39–40, 276, 342, 348, 350–51, 414; casualties, 21, 245, 249, 276. *See also* China and MacArthur, Douglas

Ku Klux Klan, 43–45, 61, 212
Kuhn, Fritz, 362

labor unions and organizations, 36, 84, 377; Building Service Employees Union, 36; International Ladies' Garmet Workers' Union, 166; Ohio Federation of Telephone Workers, 88; Wisconsin State Council of Machinists, 390–91
Ladies Home Journal, 53
Lafayette County, MO, 446–47
Lamar, MO, 175, 196
Landry, Robert B., 468–69
Latta, Maurice, 2, 14, 136, 142
Lattimore, Owen, 251, 254, 376–77, 381, 399
Latvia, 342
Lawrence, Ernest O., 282
Leahy, William D., 157–58, 470, 472–73
Lebanon, 138
Lee, Robert E., 216, 231
Lee's Summit, MO, 42–44
Lend-Lease, 4, 89
Lewis, Fulton, 251, 408
Lilenthal, David, 362
Lincoln, Abraham, 41, 58, 109, 178, 228, 480
Lincoln Memorial, 36
"Little White House," 9, 14, 104, 119, 120, 393, 478
Lloyd, David D., 30, 373, 466, 469–70, 475
London Times, 267–68
Lone Jack, MO, 194–95
Longstreet, Helen Dortch, 216
Longstreet, James, 216
Look, 53, 177, 260
Los Alamitos Naval Air Base, CA, 424
Los Angeles Times, 164
Loyalty Program. *See* Civil Service Commission
Lucas, Scott W., 100–101
Luxembourg, 159, 329

MacArthur, Douglas, ix, xiii, 5, 28–30, 165, 205, 364, 375, 379, 441, 463–64; in Korea, 237–42, 317–19, 321, 406, 414; firing of, 242–46, 247–67, 268–77, 293, 418, 427–28

McCabe, Thomas B., 423

McCarthy, Joseph, xi, 242, 270, 317, 360–61, 365, 373–81, 390–98, 414

McCarthyism, 61, 64, 380, 392–93

McCloy, John J., 472

McCormick, Robert R., 437

McCormick Press, 167

McCullough, David, 5

McDonough, Gordon L., 401–6, 408

McGrath, Howard, 167–68

McIntyre, Marvin H., 7

McKellar, Kenneth, 362

McKinley, Mabel, 434

McKinley, William, 5

McMahon, Bill, 305–6, 308

Madison, Dolley, 105

Malenkov, Georgy, 357

Manchuria, 239, 317, 319, 321, 362

Manhattan Project. *See* atom bomb

Mao Tse-tung, 316–17

Marine Corps, U.S., ix, 47, 84, 100, 322, 331–32, 397, 399, 400–403, 406–8; band, 86, honor guard, 478; 1st Marine Division, 331, 350, 4th Marine Brigade, 403; Marine Corps Reserve, 350

Marine Corps League, 397–99, 401–6

Maritime Commission, 299

Marlin, Raymond B., 100–101

Marshall, George C., 231–33, 251–52, 255, 259, 283, 289–90, 416, 467, 469, 471–76

Marshall Plan, ix, xiii, 113–14, 152, 161–62, 315, 466

Martin, Joseph, 242

Marx, Karl, 316

Masons, Fraternal Order of, 337–38, 341, 477

Massachusetts Institute of Technology, 282

Mathews, Francis, 384

May-Johnson Bill, 305

Mayerberg, Samuel S. 275–76

medals: Bronze Star, 85; Distinguished Flying Cross, 397; Distinguished Service Medal, fn.271; Medal of Honor, 271; Order of the British Empire, 384; Purple Heart, 85, 327, 350, 358; Soldier's Medal, 85

Mediterranean Sea, 133–34

Meisburger, Edward, 437–39

Mellon, Andrew W., 6

Messall, Victor R., 442–43

Mesta, Perle, 266

Military Order of the Foreign Wars of the United States, 410

Miller, Guffey, 266

Miller, Merle, 61

Milligen Maurice, 168–69

Milwaukee Journal, 217

Minton, Sherman, 226–27

Missouri, 192–94

Missouri Waltz, 168, 177

Monnet, Jean, 267

Montgomery, Bernard Law, 271

"moon hoax," 185

Morgan, David H., 440–41

Morison, Samuel Eliot, 241

Mountbatten, Louis, 474

Mox, William, 436–37, 480

Murphy, Charles S., 8, 17, 30, 382, 391, 414

Murphy, Fred P., 480–81

Murray, Arthur (Lord Elibank), 267–68

Nacy, Richard R., 192–93

Nagasaki. *See* atom bomb

Nash, Phillco, 28–30, 32–33, 46, 70, 377–79

National Association for the Advancement of Colored People (NAACP), 41, 58, 64, 72. *See also* civil rights

National Association of Manufacturers, 370

National Broadcasting Corporation (NBC), 416
National Capitol Park and Planning Commission, 110
National Defense Research Committee, 282
National Security Acts, 401, 403
National Women's Party, 266
Navy, U.S., 70, 84, 85–86, 100, 232, 241, 263, 331, 383–84, 387, 400, 403, 405, 423–24
Nazis, 39, 45, 95, 284, 385, 392, 460. *See also* Germany, Nazis
Nesbitt, Henrietta, 23–24
Netherlands, 93
Neustadt, Richard E., 30
New Deal, ix, 40, 73, 167–68, 232, 237
New Guinea, 100
New York Avenue Presbyterian Church, Washington, DC, 463
New York Herald-Tribune, 182
New York News, 401
New York Post, 396
New York Sun, 185
New York Times, 122–23, 134–36, 181, 314, 399
New Yorker, 79, 230, 414, 425, 435–36
Niles, David K., 32, 55–56, 67, 141–44, 151
Nimitz, Chester, 271
Nixon, Clay, 402
Nixon, Richard M. 242
Noland, Ethel, 222
North Atlantic Treaty Organization (NATO), ix, 159–60, 255, 462, 466
Norway, 93
"nut mail," ix, 11–12, 182, 261, 280, 314

O'Brien, Martin R., 101
O'Connor, Bill, 436
O'Donnell, John, 401
Odum, Reathel, 21
O'Dwyer, William, 396

Office of Price Administration (OPA), 37, 108, 372
Office of Scientific Research and Development (OSRD), 282, 287
Office of War Mobilization and Reconversion, 292
O'Neill, Richard W., 234–37
Oppenheimer, J. Robert, xii, 282, 308–9
Oxnam, G. Bromley, 295–96

Pace, Frank, 241–42
Paderewski, Ignace Jan, 177
Palestine, 134–41, 147, 149–50, 431; British Mandate, 134–37
Palmer, J. Michael, 61
Parsons, Luella, 422
Patriotic Order Sons of America, 363
Patterson, Robert, 161
Patton, George S., Jr., 231
Paul I, 131–32
Pauley, Edwin, 168, 263
Pearl Harbor, 89, 293, 295, 312
Pearson, Drew, 480
Pegler, Westbrook, 143, 416, 422
Pendergast, Jim, 42–43
Pendergast, Mike, 42–43
Pendergast, Tom, v, 42–43, 45, 168–69, 250, 407
Pepper, Claude, 58
Perlmeter, Irving, 334, 425, 469
Pershing, John J., 231
Philadelphia (cruiser), 207
Philadelphia Inquirer, 423
Philadelphia Museum of Art, 119, 120
Pick, Lewis A., 438–39
Philippines, 80, 150, 232–34, 322
Phoenix, AZ, 340–41
Pinchot, Cornella Bryce, 274
Poland, 93, 130, 244, 362
Polk, James K., 220
Pope Pius XII, 203
Port Arthur, China, 239
Potsdam Conference, 4, 9, 81–83, 130, 156, 163, 243, 291–92, 460, 466–75

Potsdam Declaration, 293–94, 366, 467–68

Powell, Adam Clayton, 33–34, 40, 42

Pravda, 414

Price Control Board, 98

Progressive Citizens of America, 46, 66–67

Progressive Party, 274

Pruden, Edward, 149

Pryor Times Democrat (OK), 199

Public Health Bill, 452

Puerto Rico, xiii, 408–9, 412–15

rationing, 96–99

Rayburn, Sam, 253

Red Cross, 344–45

Red Legs, 445

Reed, James A., 169, 194

Reed, Thomas C., 339, 340–42

Renfrow, Louis H., 236

Republican Party, 39, 43–44, 57, 59, 61, 65, 76, 99, 121, 132, 161, 165, 170–71, 175, 242, 252, 263, 265, 270, 362–63, 371–73, 390, 396, 398, 436, 445; conventions, 234, 276, 441. *See also* elections

Rice, John R., 333–40

Ridgway, Matthew B., 238, 240, 242, 276

Roberts, Roy, 434–35

Robeson, Paul, 64

Rockefeller, John D., 6

Rogers, Will, 6–7

Romania, 362

Roosevelt, Eleanor, 3, 33–34, 53, 105, 267–68

Roosevelt, Franklin D., ix, xiii, 1–8, 13, 15–16, 33, 39–40, 45, 58, 89, 103, 114, 122, 126, 132, 158, 231–32, 260, 263, 281, 366, 368, 427, 433, 465–66

Roosevelt, Theodore, 249, 274, 423

Rosenman, Samuel, 92–93

Ross, Charles G., 17, 23, 25, 123, 125, 129, 141–42, 175, 179, 182–83, 185, 197, 199, 201, 205, 210–11, 235, 236, 401, 404, 414–16, 435

Runte, Clarence A., 104

Russell, Richard B., 293–94

Russia. *See* Soviet Union

"Sacred Cow," 122–27

San Diego Tribune, 204

Saturday Evening Post, 442

Schauffler, Edward, 27–28

Schwellenback, Lewis, 280

Schumann, Maurice, 267

Scott, Hazel, 33–34, 36

Scripps-Howard, 13

Secret Service, 18, 201, 409, 426–28, 431–32

Securities and Exchange Commission (SEC), 459

Selective Service, 471

Sherman, Forrest P., 238, 399, 400

Sherman, Raymond, 100–101

Short, Beth Campbell, 9, 17, 395

Short, Dewey, 398

Short, Joseph, 196, 207, 230, 330–32, 372, 425, 466, 477

Shotwell, James T., 265

Sinclair, Upton, xii, 264–65

Sioux City, IA, 333, 335, 338

Skelton, Ike (III), 268–69, 445–47

Skelton, Ike (IV), xiv, 446

Smalley, Garrett, 450–51

Smith, Al, 43

Smith, Bryce, 454

Smith, Ira, 5–7

Smith, Merriman, 142

Smith, Walter B, 373

Smithsonian Institution, 325

Snyder, John W., 168

Socialist Party, 165–66, 260

Social Security, 73, 408

Society for the Prevention of World War III, 94

Sons of the American Revolution (SAR), 11, 364

southern politics, 37–38, 41, 47–48,

58–63, 66–67, 73–74. *See also* Dix-iecrats
Southern, William Jr., 444–45
Soviet Literary Gazette, 313
Soviet Union, 3, 73, 82, 95, 130–31, 133, 137, 148, 150, 157–64, 234, 241, 245–47, 249, 254–55, 260, 285, 287, 295–96, 305, 309–16, 318–20, 323, 329, 362, 365, 370, 372, 375, 377, 399, 414, 418, 453–54, 459–60, 465–66, 470–71, 476
Spaatz, Carl, 467, 470–71
Spanish-American War, 35
Spearman, Alec, 153–55
Stalin, Joseph, 4, 80, 162–63, 165–66, 178, 243, 252, 254, 291, 317, 357, 361–62, 400–401, 418, 460, 466, 470
Stassen, Harold E., 168
State Department, U.S., 136–37, 166, 241, 246–48, 317, 343, 360–61, 366, 370–74, 381–82, 383–89, 413, 441, 464
Steelman, John R., 8, 428, 431
Stern Gang, 431–32
Stevenson, Adlai, 357, 373
Stewart, Russ, 436–37
Stimson, Henry, 161, 280–83, 289–92, 364, 467–75; on Truman, 281
Stowe, David H., 428
Stowe, Harriet Beacher, 38
Stowers, J. C., 290
Suez Canal, 150
Sullivan, James R., 169
Supreme Court, 33, 64, 73
Suzuki, Kantaro, 467–68
Swing, Betty Gram, 265–66
Syracuse Herald-Tribune, 334
Syria, 81, 138

Taft-Hartley Act, 167
Taft, Robert A., 73, 242
Taft, William H., 181
Tarawa, 190
Taylor, Henry J., 184
Taylor, Myron, 150

television, 267–68, 416, 423
Tennessee, 225
Tennessee Valley Authority (TVA), 362
Tennyson, Afred, Lord, 188
Thomas, Norman, 165–67
Thurmond, Strom, 41, 66, 69, 165; on Truman, 41
Time, 365
Tokyo, 208, 238, 240–41, 273, 294, 468, 470
Transjordan, 138
Treasury Department, 161, 454
Trieste, 466
Truman, Archibald W., 221
Truman, Anderson Shippe, 174, 211
Truman, Bess, 2–3, 9–10, 23–24, 33–38, 41–42, 60, 181, 215–16, 260, 394, 411–12, 417, 426, 432, 444, 448, 480–81
Truman Committee, 37, 219–81
Truman Doctrine, ix, 131, 315
Truman, Harry S., ix, 10, 40, 170–71, 183, 185, 212–15, 358, 426, 441; on Dean Acheson, 441; on AMA, 459; assassination attempt and threats, 44, 253–54, 408–15, 426–28, 430–32; atom bomb, 280–81, 294–95, 304–5, 308, 318; decision to bomb Japan, 291–92, 466–76; birth certificate of, 223–24; favorite books, 26–28; business ventures of, 42–43, 440, 444; civil rights record of, 33–34, 40–42, 44–46, 57, 60–63, 70, 73; on Constitution Hall, 33–40, 42; domestic life, 3, 9, 23–24, 41, 416–17, 426, 481; political career, 42–46, 279–81, 445; on Easter egg rolling, 31, 79, 105–7, 106–7, 129, 173, 229, 278, 326, 358, 424, 482; on Dwight Eisenhower, 73; family history, 211, 221–22; on Germany, 93, 462; health of, 2–4, 9, 13–14; on health insurance, 457, 459; on Hubert Humphry, 73; Hume letter, 253–54, 416–24; on Israel, 134–52; on Korea, 351, 414–

15; on Douglas MacArthur, 231, 237, 241, 271–72, 275–76; MacArthur firing, 242–77; on the Marine Corps, 400, 402–4; on Joseph McCarthy and McCarthyism, 363, 372, 376–77, 389–90, 393, 414; military service of, 25, 42, 59, 198, 231–32, 280, 426; U.S.S. *Missouri*, 192–94; on music, 175–77, 181–82, 432–33; practical jokes of, 13, 226–27; "Sacred Cow," 122–26; "S" as middle initial, 25, 174; Truman farm, 447–48, 451–52, 481; on Jonathan Wainwright, 231–32, 234; on Henry Wallace, 362; White House renovation, 107–12, 120–26; work habits of, ix, xi, 1–5, 8–10, 15–17, 437; youth of, 41, 194–96

Truman, Harry S., letters of, 10–11, 16, 30, 60–61, 78, 82–84, 93, 111–12, 120, 136, 138, 143–44, 146, 155–56, 157, 160–61, 166–67, 169, 172, 198, 219–20, 222, 227, 237, 268, 274–76, 294–95, 309, 367, 377, 389–90, 393, 400, 402–4, 406, 409–12, 415–16, 433, 435–37, 439–41, 443–52, 457, 459, 462, 470–71, 479–81; memos of, 18, 93

Truman, J. Vivian, 195, 449–52

Truman, Margaret, ix–xii, 2, 5, 9–11, 13, 23, 33, 112, 122, 181, 192, 223, 246, 253, 260, 344, 346, 416–17, 418–24, 426–27, 432, 480

Truman, Martha Ellen, 12–13, 40, 41, 57–58, 127

Truman, Mary Jane, 40, 57–58, 195, 451–52

Tubby, Roger, 215–16, 242, 466

Tunney, Gene, xii, 397–98

Turkey, xiii, 130–32, 342, 362

Tydings, Millard, 383, 399

United Nations, 94, 131, 135, 136, 139, 41, 144–45, 147–48, 150, 164, 166, 266, 273, 276, 296, 298, 311, 317, 319–21, 324, 368; Dumbarton Oaks Conference, 366, 368; Human Rights Commission, 267, Korean War, 237–42, 244, 249, 254, 342, 346, 348, 352–54, 355–58, 368, 375; United Nations Relief and Rehabilitation Administration (UNRRA), 92–93; San Francisco Conference, 296, 368, 465

University of Missouri, 198

University of Virginia, 110, 120

Ural Mountains, 286

U.S. Student Assembly, 307

U.S. News and World Report, 184

Vandenberg, Arthur H., 161, 364

Vandenberg, Hoyt S., 240

Vanfleet, James A., 132, 154

VanHorn, Robert, 445, 448

Vaughan, Harry H., 17–18, 126, 214–15, 217, 269, 271, 333, 342, 345, 414, 436

Veterans Administration, 103–4, 127, 232, 328, 330, 397

Veterans of Foreign Wars (VFW), 241, 340

Vinson, Carl, 398

Vinson, Fred M., 292

Vladivostok, 239

Voice of America, 394

Wadleigh, Henry Julian, 367

Wagner Labor Relations Act, 132

Wainwright, Jonathan, 231–32, 234, 364

Wake Island, 238

Walker, Walton H., 237, 240

Wallace, Carrie, 28

Wallace, Frank, 448–49

Wallace, Henry, 46–47, 57, 66–67, 69, 131, 165–68, 263, 274, 362, 365

Walter Reed Hospital, 11–12, 70

War Department, 84, 100, 282, 290–91, 366. *See also* Defense Department

Ward, Clifford, 350

Ward, Mrs. William B., 104

War Plan Orange, 232
War Production Board, 299
War Relief Control Board, 91
Washington, DC, 34, 39, 105
Washington, George, 28, 109, 131,
    178, 250, 260
Washington Daily News, 417
Washington Post, 171, 182, 253, 416–
    17, 432–33; Crow Banquet, 171–72
Washington Star, 440
Washington Times-Herald, 433
Wasp, 208
Weizmann, Chaim, xii, 137–38, 140–
    44
West, J. B., 1, 9, 41, 416, 426
West Virginia, 193
Wherry, Kenneth Spencer, 270
White House, 2, 5–7, 10, 13, 23–24,
    32, 41, 181, 216, 426; attendance
    logs, 472; balcony addition, xii,
    110–22; Easter egg rolling, 31, 79,
    105–7, 129, 173, 229, 278, 326,
    358, 424, 482; letter bombs, 431–
    32; mail, 242, 274–75, 409, 427,
    431–32; meals, 10, 23–24; renova-
    tion, 107–10.
Wilkins, Roy, 76–78
Williamsburg, 9, 13, 406, 466
Wilson, Earl, 13
Wilson, Margaret, 434
Wilson, Woodrow, 6

Winchell, Walter, 422
Winegar, Alice, 70
Winnacker, Rudolph, 469
World Almanac, 221–22
World War I, 25, 40, 42, 59, 62, 87,
    89, 134, 175–76, 218, 231, 259,
    279, 319, 330, 366, 368, 398, 427,
    440, 450
World War II, ix, xiii, 66, 80–81, 86–
    89, 134, 232, 257, 263, 272, 279,
    319, 325, 329, 333, 335, 398, 401,
    406, 424, 431, 460, 465, 471–76,
    479; casualties, 100–101, 291–92,
    310, 457, 467, 469, 470–76; demo-
    bilization, 84–85; veterans, 101–5
"World War III," 66, 94, 158–59, 258,
    264, 272, 304
Worthing, Willie, 436, 480
Wright Brothers, 125
Wu, K. C., 320

Yalta Conference, 3, 130, 366, 368
Yalu River, 239, 269, 73
Yorktown, 208
Young Communist League, 325, 382–
    83
Young Men's Christian Association, 96
Young, Solomon, 211
Younger brothers, 354

Zinkhoff, Dave, 218